SPYCRAFT™

*"In my humble opinion, in the nuclear world,
the real enemy is war itself."*

*— Lt. Commander Ron Hunter,
Crimson Tide*

CREATED BY
LEAD WRITER · MECHANICS LEAD

Patrick Kapera • Kevin Wilson

LINE DEVELOPER

Patrick Kapera

SYSTEM DEVELOPMENT AND EDITING

Scott Gearin

ADDITIONAL WRITING

Shawn Carman, Steve Crow, Sean Michael Fish, B.D. Flory,
Scott Gearin, Brendon Goodyear, Iain McAllister,
John R. Phythyon, Jr., Les Simpson, Jim Wardrip

ADDITIONAL ASSISTANCE

Robert Dake, Bill LaBarge, Joe Unger

ART DIRECTOR

jim pinto

COVER ART

Veronica V. Jones

INTERIOR ART

Storn Cook, Jonathan Hunt, A. Bleys Ingram, Garry McKee,
Richard Pollard, Mike Sellers, Ethan Slayton, Dan Smith,
Paul H. Way, and Jeff Wright

EDITORS

D.J. Trindle, B.D. Flory, Les Simpson

INDEXER

Janice Sellers

CREATIVE DIRECTOR

Mark Jelfo

GRAPHIC DESIGNER

Steve Hough

CHIEF EXECUTIVE OFFICER

John Zinser

CHIEF OF OPERATIONS

Maureen Yates

PRODUCTION MANAGER

Mary Valles

IN MEMORY OF JOHN ZINSER, SR. 1938 – 2001

THE SPYCRAFT/SHADOWFORCE ARCHER STORY TEAM IS...

Chad Brunner, Shawn Carman, Steve Crow,
B.D. Flory, Paul Nelson, Les Simpson, Steve Wallace

THE SPYCRAFT/SHADOWFORCE ARCHER DESIGN TEAM IS...

Sean Michael Fish, B.D. Flory,
Scott Gearin, Jim Wardrip

SPECIAL THANKS TO...

Steve Bailey, Jon Bancroft, Steve Barr, beyond-adventure.com, Matt Birdsall, Kevin P. Boerwinkle, Amber Buchheit,
Simon Campcy, Ryan Carman, Ken Carpenter, Tracy Carpenter, Rich Carter, deathseeker.com, Steve Emmott,
Kat Figueroa, Marcelo Figueroa, Neal Fischer, Joe Fulgham, Games Unplugged, gamingoutpost.com, Jerry Ham,
Leticia Hayler, Steve Hewitt, Nabil Homsi, Danny Landers, Ray Lau, Tony Lee, Dave Lepore, Stepheni Lewis-Carman,
Matt McGowan, Kevin Millard, David Molinar, Jose H. Molinar, Jessica Ocker, Sam Ortiz, Hector Rodriguez,
David Salisbury, Crystal Simpson, Aaron Smith, Mandy Smith, Marshall and Sonya Smith, Ree Soesbee, John Stapeley,
Betsy and Bill Stuck, Omar Topete, David Trask, everyone at Traveling Man (visit them in Leeds), Jackie Unger, Mary Valles,
Rob Vaux, Derron Whitaker, Dave Williams, Eric Yaple, Maureen Yates, Mike Zaret, John Zinser, and Mary Zinser

A very special thanks also to Peter Adkison, Monte Cook, Ryan Dancey,
Johnathan Tweet, Anthony Valterra, Skip Williams, and our friends at Wizards of the Coast

PLAYTEST TEAM XYZZY IS...

John Cater, Jason Dyer, David Dyte, Gunther Schmidl, Dan Schmidt, Dan Shiovitz, and Emily Short

PLAYTESTERS

Dale Adams, William Adley, Ed Alexanian, Brian Anderson, Heath Anthony, Chaz Aris, Steve Bailey, Kevin Ballew, John Ballew, Jon Bancroft, Steve Barr, Jeff Bates, Matt Birdsall, Scott Boding, Cody Branzovsky, Scott Brotherton, William Buckley, Richard Buckner III, Ryan Buesing, Brian and Cynthia Bullock, Michael Burch, Simon Campey, Ryan Carman, Shawn Carman, Cheryl Carmody, Ken Carpenter, Tracy Carpenter, Brian Carroll, Jim Carroll, Aaron Cartels, Rich Carter, Richard Cattle, Chris Celestino, Melissa Childs-Wiley, Neil Christy, Brian Clark, Ryan Clark, Tom Clayton, Casey Cole, Mark Craddock, Joshua Cremosnik, Steve Crow, Gerry Crowe, Scott Cullen, Christine D'Allaird, Tim D'Allaird, Robert Dake, Chris Dauer, Lance Day, John Dees, Julie Dees, Mark Denny, Dana DeVries, Lisa DeVries, Jay Dunkleburger, Rochelle Dvorak, Suzanne Dvorak, Jake Eddington, Richard Eldridge, Tim Elkins, Steve Emmott, Lance Engle, Tim Fletcher, Chris Foley, Joshua Ford, Doug Foster, Mike Franklin, Andrew Franks, Mike Friedl, Mara Valentine Fritts, Thomas Fritts, Ron Gephart, Mark Granquist, Michael Grove, Greg Gruschow, Rob Hall, Jerry Ham, Paula Hershman, Phil Herthel, Steve Heubusch, Marshall Hitch, Mick Hitch, Matthew Hoeveler, Stephen P. Holleran, Nabil Homsi, Nathan Hood, Carl Hotchkiss, Jason Isaac, Sy Hughes, John Henry Jackson, Mike Jackson, Maureen Jackson, Ryan Jensen, Garner Johnson, JD Jorgenson, Sara Jorgenson, Elana Kahana, Kalai Kahana, Brian Kamen, Jeremy Kilburn, Erick King, Paul Kleiman, Bill LaBarge, Karen LaBarge, Nick Lalone, Justin Lewis, Shannon R Lewis, Josh Light, Morgan Littleton, Dave Lockman, Jason Loughmiller, Mark Lowry, Eric Machen, Brian Martinez, M. Leigh Martin, Ray Matthews, George Matzen, Chris McCardle, Matt McGowan, James Hunter McLamb, James McPherson, Mark Means, Shane Meeks, Clint Menezes, Kevin Millard, Ken Mills, David C. Misner, Bill Mize, David Molinar, Jose H. Molinar, J. David Moody, Joshua O'Connor-Rose, Ben O'Leary, Jessica Ocker, Matt Oliver, Sam Ortiz, Glenn Owens, Trey Palmer, Steve Partridge, Miguel A. Perez, Jr., Kent Peet, Bear Peters, Felicia Peters, Michael Petrovich, Stephan Pfuetze, Pat Phillips, John Piziali, Janel Price, Matt Raddings, Tom Reed, Ben Reid, Micah Reid, Dan Reilly, Allen Riley, Lara Rivero, Rolando Rivero, Ken Roberts, Hector Rodriguez, Joseph Rutledge, Steven Rutledge, Patrick Rykwalder, David Salisbury, Mike Sander, Jason Sato, Nancy Sauer, Heath D. Scheiman, Matthew Schenck, Jason Schnell, Bill Schwartz, Craig Scudgington, Kristopher Scudgington, Richard Shaffstall, Crystal Simpson, Les Simpson, Aaron Smalley, Aaron Smith, Abagail Smith, Jeff Smith, Jessica Smith, Mandy Smith, Marshall and Sonya Smith, Gary Sondergaard, John Stapeley, Cynthia Stewart, Simon Stroud, Karl Michael Surber, Taoman, Steve Temple, Adam Thomas, Omar Topete, Heather Townsend, David Trask, Shawn Trevor, Jackie Unger, Joseph Unger, Matt Van Kirk, Randy Vaughn, Isabella Villiani, Frank L. Voros, Garland Walker, James Walker, Sharon Walker, Todd Wallace, Wayne West, Stephen Wilcoxon, Shannon Wiley, Todd Wilkinson, David Williams, Melissa C. Williams, Wayne Williams, Benji Wilson, Sean Winchell, Shaun Witney, Erik Yaple, Mike Zaret, Jay Zicht, John Zinser, Brandon Zuern

ATTRIBUTIONS

Opening quote, page 1 – from *Crimson Tide*, written by Michael Schiffer and Richard P. Henrick

Chapter 1 quote, page 9 – from *Mission: Impossible 2*, written by Brannon Braga, Ronald D. Moore, and Robert Towne (based on the TV show by Bruce Geller)

Chapter 2 quote, page 35 – from *Sneakers*, written by Lawrence Lasker, and Walter F. Parkes, and Phil Alden Robinson

Chapter 3 quote, page 67 – from *The Matrix*, written by Andy and Larry Wachowski (the Wachowski Brothers)

Chapter 4 quote, page 95 – from *Tomorrow Never Dies*, written by Bruce Feirstein (based on characters by Ian Fleming)

Chapter 5 quote, page 103 – from *Goldeneye*, written by Jeffrey Caine, Bruce Feirstein, and Michael France (based on characters by Ian Fleming)

Chapter 6 quote, page 155 – from *The Last Boy Scout*, written by Shane Black and Greg Hicks II

Chapter 7 quote, page 183 – from *Top Gun*, written by Jim Cash and Jack Epps, Jr.

Chapter 8 quote – from *The Adventure of Abbey Grange*, written by Sir Arthur Conan Doyle

Chapter 9 quote – from the *X-Files: Tunguska*, written by Chris Carter and Frank Spotnitz

SPYCRAFT

TABLE OF CONTENTS

Honor Among Spies

"Espionage is a game. A deadly game to be sure, but a game nonetheless. And all games have rules."

Decades of Cold War espionage have given rise to a strange code of honor among intelligence operatives. These individuals are the elite warriors of society, fighting a private shadow war to determine the fate of the world. Like samurai or gentleman duelists of a bygone age, they recognize one another as kindred spirits, treating even the most despised enemy with the measure of respect due an equal. Though this unspoken code of conduct has never been committed to paper, there are certain widely recognized rules by which modern superspies live... and die.

DEFEAT IS A MATTER OF DEGREES.

Espionage is akin to a global game of chess. Agents, civilian specialists, governments, and even countries fall like pawns before the shadowy kings and queens of the intelligence community. But the spy handlers of the world must always be wary of sacrificing too many of their tools, lest their power base collapse and leave their sensitive information centers vulnerable to enemy attack. This delicate game of cloak and dagger — defeating the enemy while simultaneously protecting one's own interests — demands discretion, and the understanding that no war can be won all at once.

SUBTLETY IS YOUR GREATEST WEAPON.

The gun, the blade, and the fist are clumsy tools at best. The truly gifted do not need them, and can achieve victory with words alone. Seduction, deception, obfuscation — these are the weapons of the elite spy. A victory won with words alone is the ultimate display of skill and style, and a major feather in the cap of any intelligence agent.

BUSINESS IS BUSINESS.

Grudges between spies are inevitable, but taking a grievance into the private sector benefits no one. Oaths of vengeance and personal vendettas lead to distraction and dereliction of duty. Were this allowed to occur, the espionage world would quickly slip into chaos as operatives abandoned their roles to fulfill perceived debts of honor against hated enemies. No intelligence agency condones or permits private acts of retribution against enemy agents under any circumstances. Spying is a business, and there is no room for petty or vindictive squabbling among employees.

NEVER REVEAL YOUR OPPONENT TO ANYONE OUTSIDE THE GAME.

This is the most intractable tenet of the secret agent's code. Revealing your enemies' existence to the authorities, media, or other parties certainly restricts and complicates their missions — but it affects yours as well. By removing outside influences, the Great Game of espionage becomes a contest of skill and daring that only the boldest and most cunning can survive.

Those who violate this precept of the code rarely last long. They are often preemptively eliminated by their enemies to prevent exposure, and even allies place little stock in those who do not respect the covert nature of espionage operations.

Introduction

When you play *Spycraft*, you take on the role of a superspy working for a top-secret espionage organization, striving to thwart the efforts of those who would destroy or dominate the world. This superspy is imaginary, and exists solely in your mind and the minds of your friends. One person among you — the **Game Control** (abbreviated "GC") — takes the role of everyone you meet in this imaginary world and scripts the challenges you face, including your enemies. Though the GC speaks for the villains, everyone plays this game together as friends.

There are many things you can expect during a game of *Spycraft*:

- You, the agents, work for a large, multinational organization (the "Agency"), which operates outside the law, but which also strives to protect the world from global threats. In your game, the Agency may be a branch of government, such as the CIA or MI6, but doesn't have to be.

- You have access to the Agency's network and high-tech gadgets, many of which are not possible in our world.

- You are given missions to accomplish by **Control** *(your in-game superior — see pages 206 and 266)*, which you are expected to complete for the most part on your own. You are allowed much latitude when completing these missions.

- You don't have to deal with the mundane details of daily life, such as earning a salary, buying clothes or food, getting sick (unless there's a deadly virus involved), paying taxes, and the like.

- You are generally luckier, faster, and tougher to kill than ordinary people.

- You can easily adapt to strange and exotic locales.

- You can regularly pull off bold stunts and wild acts that ordinary people would consider impossible.

- Your enemies are usually either multinational organizations comparable to your own, criminal masterminds with vast wealth, resources, and personnel, or both.

- Your enemies fall into three categories — **minions** (who are easy to defeat), **henchmen** (who are difficult to defeat), and **masterminds** (who are your equal, or better, and whose diabolical schemes are usually the focus of your mission).

- Your enemies often, but not always, include dangerously attractive exotic seducers (called **foils**), whose motives are rarely known when they are encountered.

- Your enemies generally outnumber you and are at least as well-equipped. The odds against you are always high.

GETTING STARTED

Players should skim through at least the first four chapters before play, and should come up with an agent as well. Conferring with the other players is a good idea, so that you create agents who work well together, and whose abilities complement one another.

The GC should read through at least Chapters 1-4, 6, and 9 of this book before play, and decide on a starting mission. Details about designing missions (called **serials**) are located in Chapter 9: Control.

While the GC has more to do than the other players, everyone can help. There are many ways to do this *(see Chapters 8 and 9)*, but the simplest one is for the other players to acquire everything needed to play:

- A nice, quiet place to play (preferably where the group won't be disturbed for a few hours).

- Pencils, paper and agent sheets *(see page 287-288)*.

- Dice: at least one four-sided die (d4), four six-sided dice (d6), one eight-sided die (d8), two differently-colored ten-sided dice (d10), and one twenty-sided die (d20).

- (If desired) A wet-erase mat or graph paper, to illustrate the agents' locations and track their movement.

Once you have everything, set aside some time and show up for your first mission briefing!

DICE

This book uses a number of die roll abbreviations that you should familiarize yourself with. These abbreviations are noted as "XdY+Z." "X" is the amount of dice rolled, "Y" is the type of die rolled (d6, d10, etc.), and "Z," if listed, is added or subtracted from the total rolled. For instance, "2d4+2" means that you should roll two four-sided dice and add two to the result, while "20d6–10" means that you should roll twenty six-sided dice and subtract ten from the result.

Percentile dice (d%) generate a number from 1 to 100. To roll percentile dice, roll two different-colored ten-sided dice. One of these (chosen before you roll) generates the tens digit, while the other generates the ones digit. If, for example, you roll a 9 and a 4, your total roll is 94. Rolls of 0 and 2, respectively, total 2. If two 0s are rolled, the total of the roll is 100.

ROUNDING

When any *Spycraft* rule asks for division and doesn't specify whether you should round up or down (or keep the fraction), always round down.

SHADOWFORCE ARCHER

The first espionage setting for *Spycraft* (and AEG's official espionage world) is presented in the *Shadowforce Archer Worldbook*. A hyper-kinetic reflection of the classic superspy model, this setting features powerful new organizations, dangerous new threats, psion and mystic powers, hulking chemical monsters, an original hundred-year conspiracy-history, new base and prestige classes, and many new feats, all in one book.

The *Shadowforce Archer* setting will evolve over coming months through sourcebook releases and a serialized, multimedia campaign the players have direct control over. If you're looking for an ongoing, fully interactive storyline that you're in charge of, this is the world for you. Check out **www.shadowforcearcher.com** and the AEG website for additional information about this project.

WHAT THIS BOOK CONTAINS

This book is broken into 9 chapters. All of the chapters may be read by anyone, though Chapter 9 has much more to do with running games than playing them, and is therefore most useful to the Game Control.

Agent Creation (Chapter 1) offers many d20 options for creating an espionage agent, including departments and base classes for the most prevalent archetypes of the genre.

Skills (Chapter 2) includes all the base skills featured in the *Spycraft* game, as well as the rules for using skills in play.

Feats (Chapter 3) presents over 150 new and revised feats for your agent, as well as the basic rules for feat use.

Finishing Touches (Chapter 4) completes the agent creation process, and includes rules for backgrounds, action dice, and aging.

Gear (Chapter 5) shows the process of equipping your agent, including gear, gadgets, and vehicles.

Combat (Chapter 6) presents the *Spycraft* rules system, with examples of play.

Vehicles and Chases (Chapter 7) allows you to play through the exciting chases seen in movies — on foot, on the ground, in the air, or on the sea.

Tradecraft (Chapter 8) is geared toward helping players acclimate to the spy genre, from playing a secret agent to investigating criminal activities. Additional rules for players are also found in this chapter, along with information about traveling and movement.

Control (Chapter 9) is the GC's part of the book, though players may find it helpful as well. This section details the Mastermind system (see the next column), and a number of rules not commonly needed by the players (e.g. poisons, security systems, and the like). Finally, this chapter includes guidelines for creating missions and using NPCs (non-player characters).

WHAT'S DIFFERENT

Spycraft shares most characteristics with other d20 games. A few of its mechanics are different or unique, however, and might be of interest to experienced d20 players.

Multi-classing. There are no experience penalties for mixing class levels in *Spycraft*. Agents are highly skilled, and have maximum flexibility to pursue training to assist their activities in the field.

No attacks of opportunity. *Spycraft* uses a combat system tuned more for gunfights than swordplay, and the action system has been greatly simplified to keep things fast and furious.

Vitality and wounds. Firearms present a small but real risk of severe injury or death at all times in this cinematic RPG, which uses elements of damage first seen in the d20 *Star Wars™* system. Even the greatest super-spies should think twice before they leap into the fray.

Armor. Accurate representation of modern protective gear has prompted a different approach to armor. In *Spycraft*, armor rarely increases your Defense — instead, it offers substantial damage reduction and even protection against critical hits.

Action Dice. *Spycraft* agents are regularly able to beat the odds. This is represented with a new mechanic — action dice. You can use action dice to increase rolls, activate NPC critical failures and special abilities, heal damage, and for many other effects.

Error Ranges. In addition to the standard threat range used for critical hits and successes, *Spycraft* employs a similar (inverse) critical failure system. Shoddy equipment or lack of skill increases the odds of a dangerous fumble with every roll.

Budget and Gadget Points. The fictional Agency of *Spycraft* games assigns gear to agents based on their need and "pull" with the organization. This is represented in the game with budget and gadget points, which balance game utility against the agent's level.

Chase System. *Spycraft* features an all-new system for running movie-style vehicle and foot chases, pitting the players against the GC in a battle of wits, skill, and daring. Each driver constantly vies to manipulate conditions in his favor, choosing from a list of predator or prey maneuvers and attack options that interact with one another every round.

Mastermind System. The Mastermind System takes the standard OGL adventure and challenge creation system and turns it into a plot device. The GC designs his very own character – the season's criminal mastermind – with an organization, henchmen, minions, and foils, all balanced point-for-point against the agents.

TERMS YOU NEED TO KNOW

The Agency: This is the group that your in-game persona works for. It is broken into departments *(see page 17)*, to which your in-game persona is assigned.

Agent: This is what we call a player character, the in-game personality you play as part of this game. By taking on a role in *Spycraft,* you are playing an agent. Designing an agent is your first assignment as a player; rules for doing so begin on page 9.

Control: This is the in-game character that your agents refer to, and usually the key or head figure in your agency. More details about Controls can be found on pages 206 and 266.

Game Control (GC): This is what we call a Dungeon Master (DM). The Game Control is responsible for designing the adventures your agents go on, roleplaying the NPCs they meet, and determining what happens by interpreting the rules.

Serial: This is what we call an adventure. A more complete description of serials and how they are designed can be found on page 261.

Season: This is what we call a campaign. Seasons are composed of several serials.

Threats: These are the villain organizations that your agents go up against. They are composed of masterminds (generally more powerful than the agents), henchmen (generally of the same power as the agents), and minions (generally weaker and more numerous).

*"Good morning, Mr. Hunt. Your mission,
should you choose to accept it..."*
*– Mission Commander Swanbeck,
Mission: Impossible 2*

AGENT CREATION 1

INTRODUCTION

The purpose of this chapter is to create and play superspies whose task it is to thwart criminal masterminds and their vast world-threatening organizations. The rules for playing these agents are located throughout Chapters 6, 8, and 9. Here, we help you conceive and design an agent to your liking — the agent you were born to play!

WHAT AGENTS DO.

The role of the secret agent is broad and varied, and takes up large portions of this book. To get started, though, you can skim the following sections for ideas:

- Agent Departments: page 17.

- Agent Classes: page 20.

- Espionage: page 200.

- Missions: page 201.

- Investigation: page 210.

Alternately, you might just want to choose a favorite spy from the movies, books, or TV as a model for your own agent. Make whatever changes you need to ensure he's fun to play, and dive into the specifics of agent creation.

WHERE TO START?

Assuming you want to design your own unique agent from the ground up, here's a list of questions geared to help you visualize him. There are two things to remember when answering these questions. First, try to 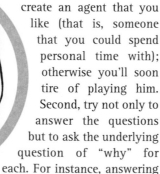 create an agent that you like (that is, someone that you could spend personal time with); otherwise you'll soon tire of playing him. Second, try not only to answer the questions but to ask the underlying question of "why" for each. For instance, answering the question "What is the most important event in your agent's life?" may be as simple as "His graduation from college." Asking why, however, might reveal that he values knowledge, recognition, or even life experience (making the event important because it 'freed' him).

Name three traits you would like to see in your agent. Sometimes, it is easiest to start with broad strokes. Choose a few descriptive words as the founding theme of your agent. Some examples of such traits are "virtuous," "cunning," and "witty."

Name three traits your agent doesn't like in someone else. By the same token, knowing some basic opinions your agent has can help determine his personality and motivations, which we'll get to in a moment.

Where was your agent born, and when? One of the first things you should consider is your agent's place of birth, and age. Another question to ask — was your agent born in the nation he currently works for?

What is your ideal agent's specialty? Is he an expert marksman? A world-renowned hunter? A flawless disguise artist? A master manipulator? Sometimes, answering this question is as easy as knowing your agent's favorite subject in high school or college, and extrapolating from there.

What does your agent look like? Physically describe your agent, focusing on the defining characteristics that make him unique. One or two is usually enough. Also, determine your agent's build, height, and weight.

Does your agent have any quirks? Does your agent use a catch phrase, mannerism, signature move or piece of equipment that he is remembered for?

What does your agent love most? Does he love work most? He might be a workaholic. A person? He might be a hopeless romantic. Himself? He might be incapable of seeing beyond his own needs and desires.

What are your agent's favorite things? What is your agent's favorite book? Movie? TV show? Color? Magazine? Possession? Work of art? Genre of fiction or period of history? Kind of music? Band? Leisure-time activity? Food? Drink? Section of a bookstore? Car model? Weapon? Clothing type? Each of these decisions adds a little more depth to your agent without predetermining his course in the game. It is by no means necessary to know all these things about your agent, or even most of them. Just answer as many as you can at the moment and leave the rest for later.

What was the most important event in your agent's life? Consider his perspective. The most important event in someone's life is usually linked to his strongest opinions or memories. For instance, if your agent is self-reliant, the most important event in his life might be the death of his parents. Alternately, if the most important event in your agent's life was the first time he took a life, he might now be remorseful and pacifistic.

What does your agent think of espionage? Just because it's his career doesn't mean that he has to like it. Your agent might be trying to get out (what's stopping him?) or trying to wage the war against evil on his own terms. On the other hand, he might relish the superspy lifestyle, living it to the hilt.

Why does the agent live a life of lies? What brought your agent into the Game, and what keeps him here? Refer to the previous question for potential help in answering this one.

What is your agent's motivation? Finally, why does your agent work for the common good? Is he inherently altruistic, patriotic, or guided by an obligation of some kind? Does he feel responsible for the world?

QUESTIONS FOR PROS:

Here are a few more questions for those of you who have done this a few times...

What is your agent's family like? Are his parents alive? Are there any siblings? Where do each of them live? How does your agent feel about them? When creating your agent's family, be sure to let the GC know how you feel about them being used in serials — especially if you're opposed to them being used as bait or leverage. (This particular trap has turned more than one game sour.)

What are your agent's personal views? How does your agent feel about religion? Does he practice a particular faith? How does he view politics? Does he support a specific political party?

What are your agent's values? Rating the following from 1 to 20 (1 being most treasured) can help you determine his personality, as well as his actions during play: beauty, career success, fame, family, friends, happiness, integrity, justice, knowledge, love, money, personal perfection, political values, possessions, power, religious values, reputation, self-respect, sex, and winning.

What is your agent's greatest fear? Your agent's fears can guide him or undermine him, but they should never master him. Roleplaying an agent whose fears are insurmountable is rarely fun, but allowing a fear to guide your actions can add unexpected drama to a mission.

How does your agent feel about his nation? Take a hard look at each ideal and practice of your agent's employers and contrast them with his own. Decide whether he believes in them or not. Developing an agent whose opinions clash with those of his superiors can add a layer of tension otherwise unavailable during play.

What about himself would your agent change? Naming one thing that your agent is uncomfortable or unhappy with offers him something to strive for during play.

PERSONALITY TESTS

Available online and in most large bookstores, personality tests offer insights about people based on their responses to a number of seemingly unconnected questions. Taking one in character (answering the questions as your agent would) can bring incredible realizations about your agent, or help to define the differences between your original concept and the 'working model.'

TEAM DYNAMICS

Advanced players may wish their agents to mesh with those of the other players right from the start. This requires more than merely choosing complementary classes (though that's a good start). The agents must be able to get along with one another as people, and must be able to coordinate during a crisis.

One of the easiest ways to make this happen is to pass each player's answers to the questions in this section around to the others before ability scores are rolled. If anything sticks out as a potential problem, perhaps another answer is called for — or an understanding of how it will affect team relations.

Also, having each of the other players ask one additional question about your agent can also help define whether he can work as part of the team.

SPYCRAFT

WHAT'S ALL THIS?

This page tells you where to find information about each portion of the agent sheet found at the back of this book.

See page 15 for ability score modifiers and their effects.

Your agent level is equal to the sum of your class levels. See page 17 for department options.

See page 99 for action dice. See page 159 for base speed. See page 217 for inspiration and education checks.

See pages 125-131 for your gear options. Remember that personal gear remains with you from mission to mission, while all other gear must be returned at the end of each mission.

See page 20 for class options. You have room for three classes on this sheet, but you can choose more.

See page 10 for questions about your agent that might help here.

See page 14 to find your vitality and wound points. See page 158 for Defense. See page 159 for initiative.

Field expenses are assigned at the start of each mission. Experience points (XP) are awarded at the end of each mission.

The sheet provides a list of all the basic combat actions in the game, and how long each action takes to use.

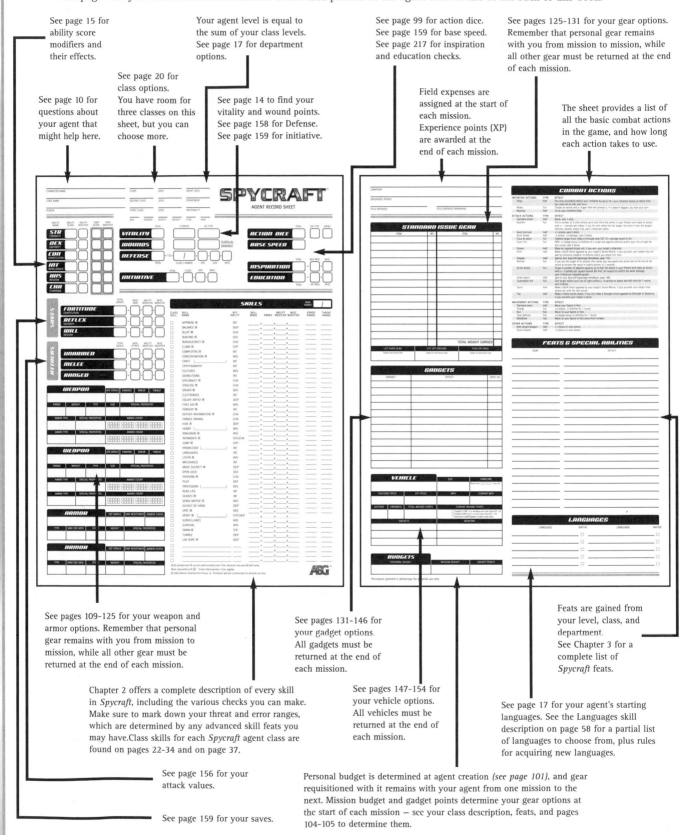

See pages 109-125 for your weapon and armor options. Remember that personal gear remains with you from mission to mission, while all other gear must be returned at the end of each mission.

Chapter 2 offers a complete description of every skill in *Spycraft*, including the various checks you can make. Make sure to mark down your threat and error ranges, which are determined by any advanced skill feats you may have. Class skills for each *Spycraft* agent class are found on pages 22-34 and on page 37.

See page 156 for your attack values.

See page 159 for your saves.

See pages 131-146 for your gadget options. All gadgets must be returned at the end of each mission.

See pages 147-154 for your vehicle options. All vehicles must be returned at the end of each mission.

Feats are gained from your level, class, and department. See Chapter 3 for a complete list of *Spycraft* feats.

See page 17 for your agent's starting languages. See the Languages skill description on page 58 for a partial list of languages to choose from, plus rules for acquiring new languages.

Personal budget is determined at agent creation *(see page 101)*, and gear requisitioned with it remains with your agent from one mission to the next. Mission budget and gadget points determine your gear options at the start of each mission — see your class description, feats, and pages 104-105 to determine them.

D20 AGENT OPTIONS

The *Player's Handbook™* describes most aspects of agent design, and players should refer to that volume when creating their agents. Adjustments to agent design specific to *Spycraft* agents are found in the next section. Where the rules in this book are different from the rules in the *Player's Handbook™*, use the *Spycraft* rules.

RACE/DEPARTMENT

There is only one race in *Spycraft* – human. None of the racial benefits for being human described in the *Player's Handbook™* apply to *Spycraft* agents, however. Instead, each agent comes from a department (chosen the same way as a race – see the *Player's Handbook™*). *Spycraft* departments are described on page 17.

The Agency's standard departments include:

- Department 0: The Home Office
- Department 1: The Power Brokerage
- Department 2: Military Operations
- Department 3: Computer Espionage
- Department 4: Urban Assault
- Department 5: Black Ops
- Department 6: Wetworks
- "The Basement"

SPIES VS. SUPERSPIES

This game is about playing larger than life heroes facing off against powerful, world-spanning threats. The action is always extreme and the stakes are always high. As such, players may instantly assume that they can do everything they've seen in the movies and read about in books the first time they sit down to play. However, this game is also about growth, and experience, both of which are only gained by tackling a few missions.

Players should not expect to play James Bond at 1st level. Commander Bond – and his espionage and action genre peers – are high-level agents with years, if not decades, of field experience. You don't need to commit years to your agent to bring him to the same level of expertise (in fact, you don't have to wait at all if you play high-level games from the start), but when you create a 1st-level agent, think of what James Bond must have been like when he was just starting out as a spy.

CLASS

None of the classes described in the *Player's Handbook™* are available to *Spycraft* agents. Instead, we have provided six all-new base classes in this book. The Agency's standard classes include:

- Faceman
- Fixer
- Pointman
- Snoop
- Soldier
- Wheelman

For more information about Spycraft classes, see page 20.

SKILLS

The class and cross-class skills you may choose from in *Spycraft* are listed under Skills (*see page 35*), as well as in your class description.

FEATS

The feats you may choose from in *Spycraft* are listed under Feats (*see page 67*), as well as in your class description.

D20 DERIVED VALUES

Your department, class, ability modifiers, and feats determine the following information, as described in the *Player's Handbook*:

- Saving throws
- Melee attack bonus
- Ranged attack bonus
- Skill modifiers

SPYCRAFT AGENT OPTIONS

Spycraft features several new agent options, described here.

ACTION DICE

Each agent begins with 3 or more action dice at the start of every game session. You can spend these dice to turn the odds in your favor. *For more information on action dice, see page 99.*

BACKGROUNDS

Backgrounds are subplots you can build into your agent's history, which crop up during missions. When one of your backgrounds comes up during a mission, you gain additional experience. You have the option of spending some of your skill points at 1st or higher levels to purchase a background. *For more information about backgrounds, see page 96.*

FAVOR CHECKS

Your agent may call upon the Agency's resources to support his actions in the field by circumventing customs, providing civilian, military, and criminal specialists, and providing a wide variety of other services. This is referred to as a **favor check,** and your agent's bonus for it is equal to his level, plus an additional modifier depending on his class. *For more information about favor checks, see page 217.*

INSPIRATION AND EDUCATION CHECKS

Your agent has two ways to get information from your GC – inspiration and education. Inspiration is used to get hints from the GC when you're stumped – your agent's inspiration bonus is equal to his level plus his Wisdom modifier. Education represents your agent's training, information that might help out in a given situation. Your agent's education bonus is equal to his level plus his Intelligence modifier. *For more information on inspiration and education rolls, see page 219.*

VITALITY AND WOUND POINTS

Every agent has vitality points that represent his luck, endurance, and training, and wound points that represent his toughness and ability to take physical punishment. Combined, vitality and wounds determine the chances of your agent staying alive.

Soldiers and Wheelmen receive the most vitality points (1d12 + Con modifier per level). Pointmen and facemen receive an average number of vitality points (1d10 + Con modifier per level). Fixers and snoops receive the fewest vitality points (1d8 + Con modifier per level).

At 1st level, each agent receives the normal maximum vitality points for his class and level (e.g. a soldier with a +2 Constitution modifier receives 14 vitality points). When an agent gains a level, the player rolls the appropriate die, adding the Con modifier to the roll to see how many vitality points the agent receives. The agent may not gain less than 1 vitality point when gaining a level, regardless of the agent's Con modifier.

All agents receive wound points equal to their Constitution score. Certain abilities may award an agent more wound points, but normally they do not increase as the agent goes up in level.

SPYCRAFT DERIVED VALUES

In addition to the options listed above, your agent's department, class, ability modifiers, and feats, determine the following information:

- Base Defense (page 158)
- Initiative modifier (page 159)
- Gadget points (page 105)

REQUISITIONING GEAR

At first level, multiply your Charisma modifier by 5, and add 40 + your class bonus to the result. The total is your personal budget, which is used to purchase equipment your agent carries with him from one mission to the next. These points may *only* be spent on standard-issue gear, as described on pages 104-106. Any personal budget not spent is lost. Write all your personal gear on your agent sheet.

FLESHING OUT YOUR AGENT

Pick a name for your agent, as well as a codename. The latter could be pulled from mythology, such as Orpheus, or an ordinary household word, like Domino. Answer any remaining questions from pages 10-11, or leave them to be determined during play.

WHAT ABOUT GADGETS?

Some of you may be wondering where gadgets come into play during agent creation. The simple answer is that they don't. Being a game of classic spy action, gadgets in *Spycraft* are handled by R&D, and handed out on a mission-by-mission basis. Consequently, they are chosen during the Gearing Up phase of each mission.

During agent creation, two values are calculated that aren't immediately used — budget points (BP) and gadget points (GP). The first value is used to purchase standard-issue gear that you need for each mission. The second is used for mission items which are normally outside the range of your standard budget — gadgets and vehicles. *For more information about these two values, see pages 104-105.*

ABILITY SCORES

Each of the following abilities ranges from 3 to 18 and describes some of your agent's strengths and weaknesses. When you are creating your agent you should assign your highest scores to those abilities that represent your agent's strengths, and your lowest scores to those abilities that represent your agent's weaknesses. Keep in mind that certain abilities are more important than others for certain classes, and remember that, when you choose a department, one or more of your agent's abilities receives a bonus or penalty *(see Table 1.2: Department Training)*.

Your agent's department adjusts some of your ability scores. Use these adjusted scores to determine your ability modifiers on the following table:

TABLE 1.1: ABILITY MODIFIERS

Score	Modifier
1	–5
2–3	–4
4–5	–3
6–7	–2
8–9	–1
10–11	0
12–13	+1
14–15	+2
16–17	+3
18–19	+4
20–21	+5
22–23	+6
24–25	+7
26–27	+8
etc...	etc...

STRENGTH (STR)

Strength measures your agent's physical power and musculature. It is especially valuable to agents who want to be skilled in hand-to-hand combat.

You apply your agent's Strength modifier to:

- Melee attack rolls.

- Damage rolls when using your bare hands, a melee weapon, a hurled weapon, a bow, or a sling. (Exceptions: Off-hand attacks receive only half the Strength modifier, while two-handed attacks receive one and a half times the Strength modifier. The damage from explosives, such as grenades, is never modified by your Strength modifier, whether thrown or not.)

- Climb, Jump, and Swim checks, and any other skill checks using Strength as the key ability.

- Strength checks (for breaking down doors, breaking handcuff chains, and the like).

DEXTERITY (DEX)

Dexterity measures your agent's hand-eye coordination, reflexes, agility, and balance. It is especially valuable to agents who want to be good drivers or skilled in the use of firearms.

You apply your agent's Dexterity modifier to:

- Ranged attack rolls, including firearms, bows, slings, and hurled weapons.

- Base Defense, provided that the agent can react to the attack. (Your Dexterity modifier to Defense might be reduced if you are wearing armor — *see Maximum Dexterity Bonus, page 109.*)

- Reflex saving throws, for avoiding grenades, expected explosions, and similar attacks.

- Driver, Move Silently, and Open Lock checks, and any other skill checks using Dexterity as the key ability.

- Dexterity checks (for grabbing a falling teammate, initiative, and the like).

CONSTITUTION (CON)

Constitution determines your agent's health and toughness. An agent's wound points are equal to his Constitution, so it's important for everyone, but it's especially valuable to agents who want to be able to take a great deal of physical abuse before they go down.

You apply your agent's Constitution modifier to:

- Each die roll for gaining additional vitality points. (Exceptions: A Constitution penalty can never reduce a vitality point roll below 1. Agents always gain at least 1 vitality point every time they gain a level.) If an agent's Constitution changes, his subsequent wound and vitality point increases change accordingly; his current vitality and wound points are unaffected.

- Fortitude saving throws, for resisting poison, gas, and similar threats.

- Any skill checks using Constitution as the key ability.

- Constitution checks (staying awake a long time, ignoring pain while carrying out a complicated task, etc.)

INTELLIGENCE (INT)

Intelligence represents your agent's ability to learn and reason. This ability is especially valuable to agents who want a wide variety of skills.

You apply your agent's Intelligence modifier to:

- The number of languages your agent automatically knows at agent creation.

- Education checks to remember something your agent might know.

- The number of skill points your agent gains when he achieves each level. (Exception: An Intelligence penalty can never reduce the number of skill points gained each level below 1. Agents always gain at least 1 skill point every time they gain a level.) If an agent's Intelligence changes, his existing skill points do not increase or decrease.

- Search, Knowledge, and Cryptography checks, and any other skill checks using Intelligence as the key ability.

- Intelligence checks (discovering patterns in a string of numbers, finding a break in a tile pattern, etc.)

WISDOM (WIS)

Wisdom measures your agent's willpower, common sense, intuition, perception, and experience in the real world. It is especially valuable to agents who want to have a handle on the world around them.

You apply your agent's Wisdom modifier to:

- Will saving throws (for resisting torture, brainwashing, and certain social checks).

- Inspiration checks to receive hints from the GC.

- Heal, Listen, and Profession checks, and any other skill checks using Wisdom as the key ability.

- Wisdom checks (for noticing people who are out of place at a party, randomly guessing the correct wire to stop a bomb, etc.)

CHARISMA (CHA)

Charisma determines your agent's strength of personality, persuasiveness, and physical attractiveness. It is especially valuable to agents who want to be able to lead, swindle, or seduce other people.

You apply your agent's Charisma modifier to:

- The roll you make for your agent's mission budget *(see page 104)* at the start of each assignment.

- Bluff, Intimidate, and Perform checks, and any other skill checks using Charisma as the key ability, as well as checks representing an attempt to influence others.

- Charisma checks (for making a first impression on someone, fascinating someone across the room, etc.)

CHANGING ABILITY SCORES

Certain events can increase or decrease your ability scores during the course of play. When an ability score changes, all statistics associated with it change accordingly. Ability scores may change in the following ways:

- An agent's ability scores can change through gaining levels and aging, as per the *Player's Handbook™*.

- Poisons, chemical boosters, diseases, critical wounds, special attacks, and other effects can temporarily increase or decrease your agent's abilities. Ability points lost to damage return naturally, usually at a rate of 1 point per day per ability. Bonus ability points usually wear off much faster than that (per the rules for the effect that boosted them).

Department

Your agent has been trained by a department of the foremost intelligence Agency in the world, put through an intense training program that makes boot camp look like a day at the beach. Not only are secret agents expected to be in peak physical shape, they must also memorize endless facts, false identities, and foreign languages. They go through grueling sessions designed to build up their resistance to brainwashing and torture. Perhaps most challenging of all, agents are taught the inner workings of the human mind, and how to manipulate that information to their own ends.

Not all departments train their operatives the same way. Department 2 (Military Operations), for instance, allows its agents to choose the abilities they enhance and slight, while other departments make these decisions for them, or offer no ability training at all. When you choose a department for your agent to work for, you are in fact defining part of your agent's personality and history.

DEPARTMENT TRAINING

Department effects remain with you for the life of your agent. Should you ever leave your department, you retain all the abilities of your original department, without modification. Even if you join a new department later in your career, you do not gain its special abilities.

native Languages

Agents know how to speak a great number of languages. It is essential to their survival in many cases. However, most agents can speak only a few languages perfectly, without even the slightest hint of an accent. These are known as native languages. All agents receive English as one of their native languages, as well as the language of their homeland. Your agent also receives a number of extra native languages of your choice equal to his Intelligence modifier plus one. A partial list of languages to choose from may be found on page 58, under the Languages skill.

In addition, your agent learns a new language (or improves one he already knows) each time he improves his Languages skill, and may make a Languages skill check to 'get by' in areas where he doesn't know the language *(see page 58 for details about using the Languages skill in this way)*.

All agents can read and write every language they speak. Illiterate agents don't last very long.

DEPARTMENT LISTING

This section briefly describes the basic departments you can choose from when creating an agent. Departments are designated as "D-#," according to department number. In game, agents often refer to their department this way: "Are you from D-2?", for example, or "D-6 has sent a specialist to help us." The Basement – being "invisible" to the rest of the Agency – is an exception to this standard, and has no department designation. It is simply referred to as "the Basement."

D-0: THE HOME OFFICE

Agents from the home office are the prototypical superspies of the modern era. Trained to deal with a broad range of threats, they tend to be confident and suave, and are known for pulling off the impossible thanks both to their well-honed skills and to the uncanny luck that follows them wherever they go.

SPECIAL TALENTS

- +1 department bonus to any action die rolls you make (if an ability lets you roll two dice for the price of one, you receive a +1 bonus to each). Home office agents receive an additional +1 department bonus to action die rolls at 4th level, and every four levels thereafter. Do not count this bonus when checking to see if an action die explodes *(see Spending Action Dice on page 99)*.

- You may select 2 cross-class skills to become class skills. Home office agents choose an additional cross-class skill to become a class skill at 4th level, and every four levels thereafter. These skills remain class skills even if you multiclass *(see page 34)*.

- Bonus feat: Any covert or chase feat. You must still meet all prerequisites for the feat, including ability score and base attack bonus minimums.

D-1: THE POWER BROKERAGE

Operatives of the infamous "Power Brokerage" are the political elite of the Agency. With global economies and wide-ranging networks of moles, doubles, specialists, and traitors as their weapons of choice, operatives of the Power Brokerage are the undisputed masters of manipulation. Power Brokerage training emphasizes guile and wits rather than the blunt use of physical prowess.

SPECIAL TALENTS

- +2 Charisma, –2 Strength.

- +5 budget points as part of their personal budget *(see page 104)*. Department 1 agents also receive a bonus of +2 budget points to each mission budget, plus an additional +1 budget point bonus at 2nd level, and every two levels thereafter (i.e. +3 at 2nd level, +4 at 4th level, etc.). Finally, they receive a bonus of +1 gadget point (beyond their standard allotment) at the start of each mission, plus another additional gadget point per mission at 4th level, and every four levels thereafter.

- +1 department bonus to Diplomacy and Intimidate checks. Department 1 agents receive an additional +1 department bonus to these checks at 4th level, and every four levels thereafter.

- Bonus feat: Any style feat. You must still meet all prerequisites for the feat, including ability score and base attack bonus minimums.

D-2: MILITARY OPERATIONS

Department 2 agents are broadly trained, but their focus is the use of military hardware and tactics. They are the Agency's front line, called in when brute force without discretion is required.

SPECIAL TALENTS

- +2 to any one ability of your choice, –2 to any one ability of your choice. You may apply both the bonus and the penalty to the same ability, if you so desire.

- +1 department bonus to Fortitude saving throws. Military Ops agents receive an additional +1 department bonus to Fortitude saving throws at 4th level, and every four levels thereafter.

- +1 department bonus to skill checks for one class skill of your choice, chosen at agent creation. Military Ops agents receive an additional +1 department bonus to skill checks for their chosen skill at 4th level, and every four levels thereafter.

- Bonus feat: Any basic combat feat. You must still meet all prerequisites for the feat, including ability score and base attack bonus minimums.

D-3: COMPUTER ESPIONAGE

Department 3 agents are cocky young rebels of the Information Age. These masters of the electronic arts can hack into practically any system and explore its secrets, or turn it against itself. They are calm, calculating, and brutally efficient, though their intense state of mind often prevents them from noticing little details other agents look for. Department 3 agents tend to be the youngest operatives at the Agency.

SPECIAL TALENTS

- +2 Intelligence, –2 Wisdom.

- Department 3 agents receive a free laptop computer with a +1 power rating *(see page 44 for more information about using computers in play)*. The computer is upgraded in power automatically by +1 at 4th level and every four levels thereafter.

- +1 department bonus to Computers and Electronics checks. Department 3 agents receive an additional +1 department bonus to these checks at 4th level, and every four levels thereafter.

- Bonus Feat: Any gear feat. You must still meet all prerequisites for the feat, including ability score and base attack bonus minimums.

D-4: URBAN ASSAULT

Agents of Department 4 are efficient, disciplined military operatives who focus on urban and close-quarters combat. Department 4 is called in when military operations take place in crowded areas, and when maximum stealth combined with precision combat is required.

SPECIAL TALENTS

- +2 Dexterity, –2 Intelligence.

- +1 department bonus to Spot and Hide checks. Urban Assault agents get an additional +1 department bonus to these checks at 4th level, and every four levels thereafter.

- +1 to attack rolls when attacking during a Ready action *(see Ready, page 162)*. This bonus increases by +1 at 4th level, and every four levels thereafter.

- Bonus Feat: Any ranged combat feat. You must still meet all prerequisites for the feat, including ability score and base attack bonus minimums.

D-5: BLACK OPS

Black Ops agents are tough and grizzled — they have to be, in order to survive the increasingly corrupt underbelly of the intelligence community where they work. Many lament their surroundings and are working hard to clean them up, while others bury themselves in their tasks and try to ignore the dirty deals going on around them.

SPECIAL TALENTS

- +2 Constitution, −2 Dexterity.

- 4 extra vitality points at 1st level and 1 extra vitality point at each additional level.

- 1 extra wound point at 1st level. Black Ops agents also receive 1 extra wound point at 4th level, and every four levels thereafter.

- Bonus Feat: Any melee combat feat. You must still meet all prerequisites for the feat, including ability score and base attack bonus minimums.

D-6: WETWORKS

Department 6 agents focus in the use of unarmed combat training to eliminate targets. Their assignments are often extremely long-term, requiring them to slip into a target's home or organization and lie in wait for weeks or months before fulfilling their deadly objective. The intense training of this department ensures that its agents can go without much of the extraordinary gear that operatives of other departments rely upon, but it also makes them ill-suited for the chaos of open firefights, where luck and brash courage are often as important as skill.

SPECIAL TALENTS

- +2 Strength, −2 Constitution.

- +1 department bonus to Initiative checks. Wetworks agents receive an additional +1 department bonus to Initiative at 4th level, and every four levels thereafter.

- +1 department bonus to Reflex saving throws. Wetworks agents receive an additional +1 department bonus to Reflex saving throws at 4th level, and every four levels thereafter.

- Bonus Feat: Any unarmed combat feat. You must still meet all prerequisites for the feat, including ability score and base attack bonus minimums.

"THE BASEMENT"

Deep in the bowels of the Agency is a near-forgotten office called "the Basement," where a motley crew of rejected and disenfranchised operatives wage a private war against cults, serial killers, and other fringe opponents. Basement agents are ill-respected by their peers, but they are the only ones with the special knowledge and experience to take on their private brand of enemy.

SPECIAL TALENTS

- +2 Wisdom, −2 Charisma.

- 4 extra skill points at 1st level and 1 extra skill point at each additional level. (The 4 extra skill points at 1st level are added as a bonus after you have calculated your starting skill points, not multiplied in. *See the Player's Handbook™ for more information.*)

- +1 department bonus to Will saving throws. Basement agents receive an additional +1 department bonus to Will saving throws at 4th level, and every four levels thereafter.

- Bonus Feat: Any basic skill feat (most Basement agents gravitate toward the Scholarly feat). You must still meet all prerequisites for the feat, including ability score and base attack bonus minimums.

TABLE 1.2: DEPARTMENT TRAINING		
Department	**Ability Adjustments**	**Bonus Feat**
0: The Home Office	None	Any covert or chase feat
1: The Power Brokerage	+2 Charisma, −2 Strength	Any style feat
2: Military Operations	+2 to your choice, −2 to your choice	Any basic combat feat
3: Computer Espionage	+2 Intelligence, −2 Wisdom	Any gear feat
4: Urban Assault	+2 Dexterity, −2 Intelligence	Any ranged combat feat
5: Black Ops	+2 Constitution, −2 Dexterity	Any melee combat feat
6: Wetworks	+2 Strength, −2 Constitution	Any unarmed combat feat
"The Basement"	+2 Wisdom, −2 Charisma	Any basic skill feat

CLASS

Your agent's class determines what role he plays on the team. It represents the type of training he has received, and provides a number of special abilities that aid him and the team during missions. Class is one of the first choices you should make when creating an agent, since it helps you place your ability scores and suggests which department may be best for the agent.

THE CLASSES

There are six main classes, or team positions, that you can choose from. They are:

Faceman: As the team's confidence man and master of disguise, the faceman is often sent in to gather intelligence before a mission.

Fixer: The team member who has what the team needs when the team needs it, the fixer doubles as a burglar and early warning system.

Pointman: The pointman helps out the other members of the team by enhancing their talents, but is also the most versatile team member in his own right.

Snoop: Armed only with a laptop and a few trusty tools, the snoop is half hacker and half electronic bloodhound.

Soldier: The muscle of the team, the soldier is trained to do one thing only: eliminate anything or anyone who gets in the team's way.

Wheelman: Aside from knowing how to drive anything with or without wheels, the wheelman is good in a fight and serves as the team mechanic.

Class Name Abbreviations: Class names are abbreviated as follows: Fac, Faceman; Fix, Fixer; Ptm, Pointman; Snp, Snoop; Sol, Soldier; Whl, Wheelman.

THE MULTICLASS AGENT

As your agent advances in level, he may add new classes to his repertoire. This gives him a broader range of abilities at the expense of progression in his first class. A snoop might add a level in soldier, for example, in order to increase his fighting skills, but as a result his snoop class wouldn't be as powerful as it otherwise could be. *There are no experience point penalties for multi-classing in Spycraft.*

LEVEL-DEPENDENT BENEFITS

As your agent gains experience by going on missions, he grows more capable. When an agent's level increases, he gains feats and ability increases as per the *Player's Handbook™* as well as all benefits listed under the *Spycraft* class description.

In addition, at the start of each game session, each agent receives a number of action dice, as defined below. The number of action dice that an agent starts each play session with, and the type of die used are determined by the agent's level:

TABLE 1.3: ACTION DICE	
Level	Action Dice
1-5	3 (d4)
6-10	4 (d6)
11-15	5 (d8)
16-20	6 (d10)

The first number on the table is the number of action dice the agent starts with. The die type your agent rolls when he uses his action dice is listed in parentheses.

All unspent action dice are lost at the session's end. The agent then starts over with a fresh pool of action dice at the start of the next session of play.

For more information about action dice, see page 99.

CLASS DESCRIPTIONS

The rest of this section contains descriptions of each base class, in alphabetical order. Each description first offers a general summary of the class's function, both on its own and as part of an agent team. The descriptions offered on these pages are broad — individual agents are likely to vary from these stereotypes, based on the specifics of their backgrounds and the setting and stories the Game Control presents.

GAME RULE INFORMATION

After the general summary of each class are several pieces of game rule information.

Abilities: This entry gives some advice on which abilities are most important for a member of this class to possess. It isn't necessary to follow this advice, but beginners may want to put their highest ability scores in the abilities listed here.

Vitality: This entry states how many vitality points an agent of this class receives upon gaining a level. Typically, an agent gains 1d8, 1d10 or 1d12 vitality points per level, modified by his Constitution modifier (to a minimum of 1 per level). At 1st level, the agent receives the maximum possible vitality points, rather than rolling. An agent also receives wound points equal to his Constitution. *For more information on vitality and wound points, see page 14.*

Class Skills: This section lists the class skills for the class in question. Skills not listed in this section are considered cross-class skills. It also lists the skill points gained at each level. *For more information about using these skill points, see the Player's Handbook™.*

Class Features: These are special abilities or restrictions that members of the class automatically receive. Class features may include some or all of the following:

Weapon and Armor Proficiency: This section describes which weapons and armor the agent is familiar with. Agents can become familiar with additional types of weapons and armor by acquiring the various Armor or Weapon Proficiency feats *(see pages 68 and 71)* outside their class benefits.

Other Features: Each class has certain unique abilities. Occasionally, an agent gets to choose between several different abilities upon reaching a particular level.

A Note on Core Abilities: Some special abilities listed under the classes are described as "core abilities". These abilities can only be obtained as a 1st-level agent unless another ability specifically states otherwise. Agents who multiclass into the class do not receive these abilities. For instance, the faceman gains the Adaptable core ability at 1st level. However, a 3rd-level wheelman who multiclasses to gain a level in faceman could never gain the Adaptable ability without a special rule permitting him to.

There is one exception to this rule — prestige classes *(see the box on page 34 for more).*

Class Table: This table describes how a member of the class grows in power as he gains levels. Each class table includes the following:

Level: The agent's level in the class (his "class level").

Base Att Bon: The agent's base attack bonus.

Fort Save: The agent's base save bonus for Fortitude saving throws. The agent's Constitution modifier is also added to Fortitude saving throws.

Ref Save: The agent's base save bonus for Reflex saving throws. The agent's Dexterity modifier is also added to Reflex saving throws.

Will Save: The agent's base save bonus for Will saving throws. The agent's Wisdom modifier is also added to Will saving throws.

Def Bon: The agent's bonus to his Defense. If armor is worn, the armor's bonus replaces this bonus — the two modifiers do not stack.

Init Bon: The agent's base initiative bonus.

Gadg Pts: The bonus number of gadget points an agent receives for each mission *(see Gear, page 104).* This number is added to a base of 2, 4, or 6 and may be modified by other rules and agent options.

Budg Pts: The bonus number of budget points an agent receives for each mission *(see Gear, page 105).* This bonus is added to a base determined by the agent's Cha modifier and a random roll *(again, see the Gear section),* and may be modified by other rules and agent options.

Special: This section lists level-dependent class abilities, each of which is explained in the "Class Features" section for the class *(see above).*

LEVEL VS. AGENT STATUS

The class system exists to provide a simple scale for balancing an agent's strength against challenges that the Game Control throws at the team. Without this system, game balance is far more difficult to gauge and missions far more difficult for the GC to prepare.

However, the class system should not be considered a judge of the in-game status of an agent. For example, a 1st-level soldier with a military background should not automatically be considered to be of the lowest rank, nor should it be assumed that a 20th-level fixer is known by every contact on his home continent.

As in life, agents should be judged not solely by their level but also by their actions. That 1st-level soldier may have saved the British Prime Minister during his very first mission, resulting in a national commendation and immediate recognition throughout the European intelligence community. Likewise, that 20th-level fixer might operate through so many proxies that his face and name never become known, or he might simply prefer to keep to himself, never gaining a reputation outside his restricted client pool.

The lesson to be learned here is that you should not allow your level to limit your imagination. *Spycraft* agents are rigorous examples of the truest heroes of the modern age, even though their accolades are rarely sung.

If you want to design a legendary snoop whose exploits are renowned throughout Cold War Russia, don't let your 1st-level status get in the way. Talk with your GC — he might let you design the agent (and his background) for the cost of coming up with a number of NPCs named in your bio, or might propose a compromise by which your ex-KGB officer fled his homeland and is starting over in the United States. The possibilities, as usual in an RPG, are endless.

Likewise, if a wheelman famous through the racecar circuit is more your speed, you could probably simulate the proper abilities with extremely high Charisma (and a little Dexterity to back it up), plus a well-chosen feat or two. The GC may be willing to offer you a few in-story perks for your aspiring 1st-level agent (a pit crew of specialists, for example, or free travel expenses), in exchange for some details about your public career — or just the thrill of running a game involving a celebrity.

It's not necessary for an agent to be high level for him to be impressive in play. Conversely, it's often a great challenge to design a high level agent who is restricted by his conditions in play. Play the story you want, and leave the mechanics to balance the game.

Open Lock	Dex
Perform	Cha
Profession	Wis
Read Lips	Int
Search	Int
Sense Motive	Wis
Sleight of Hand	Dex
Spot	Wis

Skill Points at 1st level: (6 + Int modifier) × 4.
Skill Points at Each Additional Level: 6 + Int modifier.

CLASS FEATURES

The following are class features of the faceman.

Starting Feats: The faceman begins play with the following feats.
Armor Proficiency (Light)
Armor Proficiency (Medium)
Weapon Group Proficiency (Hurled)
Weapon Group Proficiency (Melee)
Weapon Group Proficiency (Handgun)
Weapon Group Proficiency (Rifle)

Adaptable: Whenever the faceman spends an action die to add to a Charisma- or Wisdom-based skill check, two dice are added instead of one (e.g. a 1st-level faceman's bonus of 1d4 becomes 2d4). This is the faceman's core ability.

Linguist: The faceman selects two extra foreign languages to learn at 1st level, and gains an additional foreign language at 4th level and every 4 levels after that. Also, when speaking a foreign language, he is always considered to be a native speaker and his accent is indistinguishable from that of a person raised to speak the language. The effects of this ability stack with starting agent languages and any languages learned in the field *(see the Languages skill, page 58)*.

Cold Read: Starting at 2nd level, once per game session as a free action, the faceman may ask the GC three personal questions about an NPC he has just met, such as "What does the man in the suit do for a living?" or "What is the lady's favorite author?" The GC may refuse to answer by spending an action die for each question ignored. At 11th and 19th level, the faceman may ask three additional questions each game session. These new questions may be about the same NPC, or a new NPC the faceman has encountered.

Quick Change: Starting at 3rd level, once per game session as a half action, the faceman can change his mannerisms and clothes just enough to appear to be someone else. Essentially, he can use the Disguise skill without the usual time or disguise kit requirements. The faceman cannot use this ability while he is being observed, unless he is able to momentarily step out of sight (e.g. behind a column at a bus station).

FACEMAN

Facemen are masters of disguise and talented confidence men, trained for infiltration and sting operations. Without them, a team may have difficulty with face to face deception, not to mention infiltrating the enemy and discerning their master plan.

Abilities: Many of the faceman's class skills are based on Charisma and Wisdom, so those two top his most useful abilities list, with Charisma being the more important of the two. A faceman's winning smile and charming personality are his two greatest weapons.

Vitality: 1d10 plus Con modifier per level.

CLASS SKILLS

The faceman's class skills and key abilities are listed below *(see page 40 for skill descriptions):*

Class Skill	Key Ability
Bluff	Cha
Craft	Int
Cultures	Wis
Diplomacy	Cha
Disguise	Cha
Driver	Dex
Forgery	Int
Gather Information	Cha
Hobby	Wis
Innuendo	Wis
Knowledge	Int
Languages	Wis

Lvl	Base Att Bon	Fort Save	Ref Save	Will Save	Def Bon	Init Bon	Budg Pts	Gadg Pts	Special
1	+0	+1	+0	+1	+1	+1	3	0	Starting feats, *adaptable*, linguist +2
2	+1	+2	+0	+2	+1	+2	6	1	Cold read 1/session
3	+2	+2	+1	+2	+2	+3	9	1	Quick change 1/session
4	+3	+2	+1	+2	+2	+3	12	2	Backup 1/session, linguist +3
5	+3	+3	+1	+3	+3	+4	15	2	Quick change 2/session
6	+4	+3	+2	+3	+4	+5	18	3	Fake it 1/session
7	+5	+4	+2	+4	+4	+6	21	3	Quick change 3/session
8	+6	+4	+2	+4	+5	+6	24	4	Backup 2/session, linguist +4
9	+6	+4	+3	+4	+5	+7	27	4	Fake it 2/session, quick change 4/session
10	+7	+5	+3	+5	+6	+8	30	5	1,000 faces 1/session
11	+8	+5	+3	+5	+7	+9	33	5	Cold read 2/session, quick change 5/session
12	+9	+6	+4	+6	+7	+10	36	6	Backup 3/session, fake it 3/session, linguist +5
13	+9	+6	+4	+6	+8	+10	39	6	Quick change 6/session
14	+10	+6	+4	+6	+8	+11	42	7	Bald-faced lie 1/session
15	+11	+6	+5	+6	+9	+12	45	7	Fake it 4/session, quick change 7/session
16	+12	+7	+5	+7	+10	+13	48	8	Backup 4/session, linguist +6
17	+12	+7	+5	+7	+10	+14	51	8	Quick change 8/session
18	+13	+8	+6	+8	+11	+14	54	9	Fake it 5/session
19	+14	+8	+6	+8	+11	+15	57	9	Cold read 3/session, quick change 9/session
20	+15	+9	+6	+9	+12	+16	60	10	1,000 faces 2/session, backup 5/session, linguist +7

TABLE 1.4: THE FACEMAN

The disguise stands up normally under casual scrutiny, but any careful inspection receives a +5 circumstance bonus to penetrate the disguise. For every 2 levels after 3rd, the faceman may use this ability an additional time per game session.

Backup: Starting at 4th level, once per game session, the faceman may call upon an acquaintance who remembers him fondly. This friend is considered helpful when using the disposition system *(see page 269)*. The friend shows up within 1d6 hours and helps out one time to the best of his ability, as long as doing so doesn't put him or his loved ones in danger. The friend has one specific skill or object (such as a boat or plane) at his disposal, chosen by the faceman. If the faceman is calling upon the friend for a skill, the skill is equal to this faceman's class level. If calling upon the friend for the use of an object, it cannot cost more than this faceman's class level in either budget points or gadget points, and must be returned to the friend after use. For every 4 levels after 4th, the faceman may use this ability an additional time per game session.

Fake It: Starting at 6th level, once per game session, the faceman may credibly pretend to have a skill that he doesn't actually possess. This does not actually allow him to use the skill; it merely allows him to act like he can. Thus, he could stand next to an operating surgeon and pretend he knows what's going on, but he couldn't perform the surgery himself. When required to make a Bluff check to fake having the skill, the faceman gains a +20 bonus. For every 3 levels after 6th, the faceman may use this ability an additional time per game session.

1,000 Faces: Starting at 10th level, once per game session, the faceman may perfectly imitate the appearance, speech, and mannerisms of any one person. After studying the target a number of days equal to the target's level, the faceman may add his class level to any Disguise or Perform checks made when imitating the target. This ability imparts no special knowledge of the target. At 20th level, the faceman may use this ability twice per game session.

Bald-Faced Lie: Starting at 14th level, once per game session, the faceman may tell one lie to an NPC. If the NPC isn't positive that the faceman is lying (as would be the case if the faceman tried to tell him, "The sky is green.") then the lie is believed. This ability is only used up if the lie is believed.

FIXER

The fixer is the team's "acquisitions expert". He gets them what they need, when they need it, through whatever means necessary. He is an expert at breaking and entering, as well as adapting to unexpected situations. Without a fixer, the team might not be able to react in time if a mission takes a turn for the worse.

Abilities: Many of the fixer's class skills are based on Dexterity, making that his most vital ability. Intelligence is also quite important to the fixer, since it gives him additional skill points every level. He must be fast and smart to survive.

Vitality: 1d8 plus Con modifier per level.

CLASS SKILLS

The fixer's class skills and key abilities are listed below *(see page 40 for skill descriptions):*

Class Skill	Key Ability
Appraise	Int
Balance	Dex
Bluff	Cha
Boating	Dex
Climb	Str
Craft	Int
Demolitions	Int
Driver	Dex
Electronics	Int
Escape Artist	Dex

Forgery	Int
Hide	Dex
Hobby	Wis
Innuendo	Wis
Jump	Str
Knowledge	Int
Languages	Wis
Listen	Wis
Move Silently	Dex
Open Lock	Dex
Profession	Wis
Search	Int
Sleight of Hand	Dex
Spot	Wis
Tumble	Dex

Skill Points at 1st level: (8 + Int modifier) × 4.
Skill Points at Each Additional Level: 8 + Int modifier.

CLASS FEATURES

All of the following are class features of the fixer.

Starting Feats: The fixer begins play with the following feats.
Armor Proficiency (Light)
Weapon Group Proficiency (Hurled)
Weapon Group Proficiency (Melee)
Weapon Group Proficiency (Handgun)
Weapon Group Proficiency (Rifle)

Dexterous: Whenever the fixer spends an action die to add to a Dexterity-based skill check, two dice are added instead of one (e.g. a 1st-level fixer's bonus of 1d4 becomes 2d4). This is the fixer's core ability.

Procure: The fixer may requisition items and gadgets anywhere in the field at normal cost, just as if he were back at headquarters. If there is a nearby city and the fixer can communicate and meet with a representative of the Agency, then this ability takes 20 minutes per 4 budget points or 1 gadget point spent; otherwise it requires 1 hour per 4 budget points or 1 gadget point spent, while he scrounges the area to find the required items. The fixer must either be able to contact his HQ or a personal contact, or scout his surroundings, to use this ability.

Evasion: Starting at 2nd level, the fixer gains evasion. Whenever he has the opportunity to make a Reflex save in order to suffer half damage from an effect (such as a grenade), he instead suffers no damage with a successful save. Starting at 11th level, the fixer suffers only half damage with a failed save, and starting at 19th level, he suffers only one-quarter damage with a failed save.

Sneak Attack: Starting at 3rd level, the fixer deals extra damage when either flanking a target *(see Flanking, page 171)* or attacking a target that is

Lvl	Base Att Bon	Fort Save	Ref Save	Will Save	Def Bon	Init Bon	Budg Pts	Gadg Pts	Special
				TABLE 1.5: THE FIXER					
1	+0	+1	+2	+0	+1	+0	1	1	Starting feats, *dexterous*, procure
2	+1	+2	+3	+0	+2	+1	2	2	Evasion (no damage on save)
3	+2	+2	+3	+1	+3	+1	3	3	Sneak attack +1d6
4	+3	+2	+4	+1	+3	+2	4	4	Uncanny dodge (Dex bonus to Defense)
5	+3	+3	+4	+1	+4	+2	5	5	Sneak attack +2d6
6	+4	+3	+5	+2	+5	+2	6	6	Special ability
7	+5	+4	+5	+2	+6	+3	7	7	Sneak attack +3d6
8	+6	+4	+6	+2	+6	+3	8	8	Uncanny dodge (can't be flanked)
9	+6	+4	+6	+3	+7	+4	9	9	Sneak attack +4d6, special ability
10	+7	+5	+7	+3	+8	+4	10	10	Defensive roll 1/session
11	+8	+5	+7	+3	+9	+4	11	11	Evasion (fail saves for 1/2), sneak attack +5d6
12	+9	+6	+8	+4	+10	+5	12	12	Special ability, uncanny dodge (+1 vs. traps)
13	+9	+6	+8	+4	+10	+5	13	13	Sneak attack +6d6
14	+10	+6	+9	+4	+11	+6	14	14	Wildcard gadget
15	+11	+7	+9	+5	+12	+6	15	15	Sneak attack +7d6, special ability
16	+12	+7	+10	+5	+13	+6	16	16	Uncanny dodge (+2 against traps)
17	+12	+8	+10	+5	+14	+7	17	17	Sneak attack +8d6
18	+13	+8	+11	+6	+14	+7	18	18	Special ability
19	+14	+8	+11	+6	+15	+8	19	19	Evasion (fail saves for 1/4), sneak attack +9d6
20	+15	+9	+12	+6	+16	+8	20	20	Defensive roll 2/session, uncanny dodge (+3 vs. traps)

currently denied its Dexterity bonus to Defense (such as flat-footed or immobilized opponents). The extra damage is +1d6 at 3rd level, and an additional 1d6 every 2 levels thereafter.

Ranged attacks normally gain this bonus only if the target is within one range increment. Beyond that, the accuracy needed to hit the target's vitals is difficult to achieve. Also, the fixer may not take the autofire or strafe actions when using sneak attack.

The fixer may make a sneak attack with any weapon (or unarmed attack), even one that deals subdual damage. However, the fixer cannot use a weapon that deals normal damage to inflict subdual damage during a sneak attack, even with the –4 penalty usually applied, and he cannot use strafing fire when sneak attacking.

Finally, the fixer cannot sneak attack targets who are immune to critical hits, who have total concealment, or whose vitals are out of reach.

Uncanny Dodge: Starting at 4th level, the fixer gains the ability to instinctively react to danger. He always retains his Dexterity bonus to Defense, even if caught flat-footed (the bonus is still lost if the fixer is immobilized, though), making it much more difficult to sneak attack him.

At 8th level, opponents must be 4 levels higher than the fixer in order to flank him. Remember that an agent cannot use the sneak attack ability unless flanking the target of the attack.

At 12th level, the fixer receives a +1 bonus to all Reflex saves made to avoid security systems and traps and a +1 bonus to Defense against attacks by security systems and traps. At 16th level, these bonuses increase to +2, and at 20th level, the bonuses increase to +3.

Special Ability: At 6th level, and every 3 levels thereafter, the fixer receives one of the following abilities of his choice.

Fast Movement: The fixer's speed increases by +10 ft. when not wearing heavy armor and not carrying a heavy load (see Carrying Capacity, page 106).

Feat: The fixer gains a bonus covert or gear feat. He must still meet all of its prerequisites, including ability score and base attack bonus minimums.

Improvisation: Once per game session as a full action, the fixer can improvise any simple object needed out of whatever's lying around. Even if stripped naked and thrown into a cell, he could fashion a lockpick out of some hair stiffened with a bit of dried blood. The item's actual cost (see page 108) cannot be more than $25, and is subject to GC approval. This ability may be gained multiple times, allowing an extra use of the ability per game session each time.

Master Thief: Once per game session, the fixer automatically succeeds at a non-combat Dexterity-based skill check. This ability may be gained multiple times, allowing an extra use of the ability per game session each time.

Skill Mastery: The fixer selects a number of skills equal to 3 + his Intelligence modifier. He may always take 10 when using these skills, even if stress and distraction would normally interfere. The fixer may gain this ability multiple times, but he must select different skills each time.

Stash It: As a full action, the fixer may conceal one object weighing 1 lb. or less on his person. Searches automatically fail to find this object unless the GC pays 3 action dice before rolling.

Defensive Roll: Starting at 10th level, once per game session as a free action, the fixer may roll with a potentially lethal blow to avoid some of the damage from it. When he would suffer wound point damage in combat (from a weapon or other physical attack) the fixer can attempt to roll with the damage. He makes a Reflex saving throw (DC = damage dealt) and, if he's successful, he takes only half damage from the blow. If the fixer is denied his Dexterity bonus to Defense, he can't use the defensive roll. The evasion ability cannot be used in conjunction with this ability. At 20th level, the fixer may use this ability twice per game session.

Wildcard Gadget: Starting at 14th level, once per game session as a free action, the fixer gains the use of a wildcard gadget. This allows him to call up a single-function gadget he needs, whenever he needs it (the gadget is considered to have been hidden on his person until the fixer announces its use). This 'wildcard gadget' cannot be found in a search until its function has been decided upon, and it only functions once before becoming useless until the next game session.

Some sample functions are:

Zip Gun: Deals damage as a 9mm handgun.

Explosive: Uses standard explosive rules; damage value of 6d6.

Rebreather: Allows the fixer to breathe underwater for up to one hour.

Mini-chute: Serves as a parachute.

Trap: Inflicts damage as a grenade to the target and everyone in a 5-ft. radius when activated.

Other: The wildcard gadget can do anything within reason, as long as the Game Control approves.

POINTMAN

Pointmen train in many skills, and often enhance or assist the other members of the team. They are also the most flexible team members available. A team that lacks a pointman will have trouble becoming more than the sum of its parts.

Abilities: No single ability is most important for pointmen, but Charisma and Wisdom come close. These abilities form the basis of most of his pre-set class skills, and are most often used when interacting with other people — something a good pointman does a lot.

Vitality: 1d10 plus Con modifier per level.

CLASS SKILLS

The pointman's class skills and key abilities are listed below *(see page 40 for skill descriptions):*

Class Skill*	Key Ability
Bluff	Cha
Bureaucracy	Cha
Craft	Int
Diplomacy	Cha
Driver	Dex
First Aid	Wis
Knowledge	Int
Profession	Wis
Sense Motive	Wis
Sport	Str or Dex

Skill Points at 1st level: (6 + Int modifier) × 4.
Skill Points at Each Additional Level: 6 + Int modifier.

TABLE 1.6: THE POINTMAN

Lvl	Base Att Bon	Fort Save	Ref Save	Will Save	Def Bon	Init Bon	Budg Pts	Gadg Pts	Special
1	+0	+1	+1	+2	+0	+0	3	0	Starting feats, *generous*, versatility (6 skills)
2	+1	+2	+2	+3	+1	+1	6	1	Assistance (1/2 time)
3	+2	+2	+2	+3	+1	+1	9	2	Lead 1/session, versatility (7 skills)
4	+3	+2	+2	+4	+2	+2	12	3	Tactics 1/session
5	+3	+3	+3	+4	+2	+2	15	3	Lead 2/session
6	+4	+3	+3	+5	+2	+2	18	4	Cross-class ability, versatility (8 skills)
7	+5	+4	+4	+5	+3	+3	21	5	Lead 3/session
8	+6	+4	+4	+6	+3	+3	24	6	Tactics 2/session (+2 bonus)
9	+6	+4	+4	+6	+4	+4	27	6	Cross-class ability, lead 4/session, versatility (9 skills)
10	+7	+5	+5	+7	+4	+4	30	7	Serendipity 1/session
11	+8	+5	+5	+7	+4	+4	33	8	Assistance (1/4 time), lead 5/session
12	+9	+6	+6	+8	+5	+5	36	9	Cross-class ability, tactics 3/session, versatility (10 skills)
13	+9	+6	+6	+8	+5	+5	39	9	Lead 6/session
14	+10	+6	+6	+9	+6	+6	42	10	Strategy 1/session
15	+11	+7	+7	+9	+6	+6	45	11	Cross-class ability, lead 7/session, versatility (11 skills)
16	+12	+7	+7	+10	+6	+6	48	12	Tactics 4/session (+3 bonus)
17	+12	+8	+8	+10	+7	+7	51	12	Lead 8/session
18	+13	+8	+8	+11	+7	+7	54	13	Cross-class ability, versatility (12 skills)
19	+14	+8	+8	+11	+8	+8	57	14	Assistance (1/10 time), lead 9/session
20	+15	+9	+9	+12	+8	+8	60	15	Serendipity 2/session, tactics 5/session

CLASS FEATURES

The following are pointman class features.

Starting Feats: The pointman begins play with the following feats.

Armor Proficiency (Light)
Armor Proficiency (Medium)
Weapon Group Proficiency (Melee)
Weapon Group Proficiency (Handgun)
Weapon Group Proficiency (Rifle)

Generous: A pointman may spend action dice to add to the rolls of his allies just as if adding to his own rolls, so long as he is within line of sight or can speak directly to them (including over the radio) throughout their action. The pointman's action die modifiers supersede those of the target when this ability is used. This is the pointman's core ability.

Versatility: At 1st level, a pointman may select 6 cross-class skills to become class skills. In addition, he may select another cross-class skill to become a class skill at 3rd level and every three levels thereafter. When multiclassing, the pointman's versatility skills are considered cross-class skills unless his new class also features them as class skills.

Assistance: Starting at 2nd level, a pointman may reduce the amount of time it takes one of his teammates to use one of their class abilities or skills by assisting them. This assistance can only affect activities that would otherwise take 1 hour or longer. At 2nd level, the pointman's assistance divides the time required in half (rounded up). At 11th level, his assistance divides the time required by 4 (rounded up). Finally, at 19th level, the pointman's assistance divides the time required by 10 (rounded up).

Lead: Starting at 3rd level, once per game session, the pointman's entire team may use his result from a skill roll for one action they are performing as a group, such as climbing, sneaking, or setting explosives. For example, if a team is sneaking past some sleepy guards, and the team's pointman uses this ability, then only he needs to make a Move Silently roll, using his skill for the roll. If the pointman succeeds, then the entire team succeeds, but if he fails, the entire team fails. For every 2 levels after 3rd, the pointman may use this ability an additional time per game session.

Tactics: At 4th level, once per game session as a free action, the pointman may issue an order to a number of allies equal to his Charisma modifier. This order must be specific, such as "cover Molly while she gets the door open!" as opposed to "help Molly!" While the allies are carrying out this order, they receive a +1 to all rolls related to carrying out the order (at the GC's discretion). At 8th level, this bonus is increased to +2, and at 16th level, this bonus is increased to +3. Finally, for every 4 levels the pointman gains after 4th level (at 8th, 12th, etc.), he may issue an additional order per session.

Cross-class Ability: At 6th level, the pointman gains one ability from a class listed below. An ability followed by text such as "1/session, 2/session" may be taken multiple times, gaining the improvements listed after each 'upgrade'.

Faceman: Linguist; cold read 1/session; quick change 1/session, 2/session; backup 1/session.

Fixer: Procure; evasion (no damage on save); sneak attack +1d6, +2d6; uncanny dodge (Dex bonus to Def).

Snoop: Flawless search; intuition 1/session; back door ×1; Jury-rig +2, +3.

Soldier: Bonus feat ×1, ×2; damage reduction 1/–; armor use +1.

Wheelman: Daredevil; kick start 1/session; familiarity +1, +2.

Serendipity: At 10th level, once per session, an item, person, lucky break, or bout of inspiration comes to the team's rescue, just when they need it most. During times of crisis, the GC may, without a prompt from the pointman, introduce an element to help the team.

Some examples are a contact (with information equal to a successful favor check of 20 or less), a hint (as if the pointman had succeeded with an inspiration check at DC 20), a piece of gear (BP cost equal to the pointman's level), a gadget or vehicle (GP cost equal to half the pointman's level), or critical success with a skill check (even if the pointman didn't make one). Regardless of the effect, this ability implies sudden and unexpected fortune, and the GC should strive to keep his serendipitous assistance fresh and inventive.

The pointman may ask for his lucky break at any time, though the GC may refuse by offering the pointman two action dice instead. This ability is considered to be used if the pointman accepts the dice, and the pointman does not earn experience for gaining these action dice.

At 20th level, the GC may introduce up to two lucky breaks per session.

Strategy: Beginning at 14th level, once per game session as a free action, the pointman may activate this ability at the start of a combat round. All allies within line of sight who can hear the pointman's voice (including the pointman himself) gain one extra half action this round. An individual may only benefit from this ability once per round.

Snoop

The snoop is the master of gathering and analyzing data. He is trained in computer hacking, cryptography, and electronic counter-measures. Without a snoop on the team, vital pieces of information arc almost certain to be overlooked.

Abilities: Snoops emphasize Intelligence. With so many skills to buy as they gain levels, they need all the skill points they can get. Also, many of their skills are based on Wisdom, making it important as well.

Vitality: 1d8 plus Con modifier per level.

CLASS SKILLS

The snoop's class skills and key abilities are listed below *(see page 40 for skill descriptions):*

TABLE 1.7: THE SNOOP

Lvl	Base Att Bon	Fort Save	Ref Save	Will Save	Def Bon	Init Bon	Budg Pts	Gadg Pts	Special
1	+0	+0	+1	+1	+1	+1	2	1	Starting feats, *astute*, flawless search
2	+1	+0	+2	+2	+2	+1	4	2	Intuition 1/session
3	+1	+1	+2	+2	+3	+2	6	3	Jury-rig +2
4	+2	+1	+2	+2	+3	+2	8	4	Back door
5	+2	+1	+3	+3	+4	+3	10	5	Jury-rig +3
6	+3	+2	+3	+3	+5	+4	12	6	Special ability
7	+3	+2	+4	+4	+6	+4	14	7	Jury-rig +4
8	+4	+2	+4	+4	+6	+5	16	8	Back door
9	+4	+3	+4	+4	+7	+5	18	9	Jury-rig +5, special ability
10	+5	+3	+5	+5	+8	+6	20	10	Master cracker 1/session
11	+5	+3	+5	+5	+9	+7	22	11	Intuition 2/session, jury-rig +6
12	+6	+4	+6	+6	+10	+7	24	12	Back door, special ability
13	+6	+4	+6	+6	+10	+8	26	13	Jury-rig +7
14	+7	+4	+6	+6	+11	+8	28	14	Global search
15	+7	+5	+7	+7	+12	+9	30	15	Jury-rig +8, special ability
16	+8	+5	+7	+7	+13	+10	32	16	Back door
17	+8	+5	+8	+8	+14	+10	34	17	Jury-rig +9
18	+9	+6	+8	+8	+14	+11	36	18	Special ability
19	+9	+6	+8	+8	+15	+11	38	19	Intuition 3/session, Jury-rig +10
20	+10	+6	+9	+9	+16	+12	40	20	Back door, master cracker 2/session

Class Skill	Key Ability
Appraise	Int
Bureaucracy	Cha
Computers	Int
Concentration	Wis
Craft	Int
Cryptography	Int
Cultures	Wis
Diplomacy	Cha
Driver	Dex
Electronics	Int
First Aid	Wis
Gather Information	Cha
Hide	Dex
Hobby	Wis
Knowledge	Int
Languages	Wis
Listen	Wis
Mechanics	Int
Move Silently	Dex
Profession	Wis
Read Lips	Int
Search	Int
Sense Motive	Wis
Spot	Wis
Surveillance	Wis

Skill Points at 1st level: (8 + Int modifier) × 4.
Skill Points at Each Additional Level: 8 + Int modifier.

CLASS FEATURES

All of the following are class features of the snoop.

Starting Feats: The snoop begins play with the following feats.
Armor Proficiency (Light)
Weapon Group Proficiency (Melee)
Weapon Group Proficiency (Handgun)

Astute: Whenever the snoop spends an action die to add to an Intelligence-based skill check, two dice are added instead of one (e.g. a 1st-level snoop's bonus of 1d4 becomes 2d4). This is the snoop's core ability.

Flawless Search: When rolling a Search or Spot check to find clues or other important information, the snoop may never completely fail unless he rolls an error (*see page 39*). Even when an error is rolled, the GC must spend two action dice to activate a critical failure. The snoop normally finds at least one clue, or a vague piece of information – if either exists to be found.

Intuition: Starting at 2nd level, once per game session as a free action, the snoop can have the GC give him a hint about how to use a clue or piece of information the team has discovered (e.g. "the text appears to be written in an old Babylonian religious script"). At 11th and 19th level, the snoop can use this ability one additional time per game session.

Jury-rig: Starting at 3rd level, the snoop gains a +2 competence bonus with Computers or Electronics checks made to attempt temporary or jury-rigged repairs. (*See the Computers and Electronics skill descriptions for more information on temporary repairs.*) This bonus increases by +1 every 2 levels after 3rd.

Back Door: Upon reaching 4th level, the snoop may select one computer system on which he has previously hacked the root account *(see the Computers skill, page 44)*. He has managed to install a back door in this computer system, allowing him unlimited access to it without requiring further Computer checks. For every 4 levels after 4th, the snoop gains one additional back door. He may save his back doors, leaving them unassigned, as long as he wants. Additionally, the snoop may move any of his back door slots to a different system at any time, as long as he has hacked the new system's root account. However, once he has removed a back door from a system, the snoop must hack that system's root account again before he can re-install a back door in it.

Special Ability: At 6th level, and every 3 levels thereafter, the snoop receives one of the following abilities of his choice.

Comb the Streets: Once per game session, the snoop may locate someone within the local city using either a physical description or a current ID. This takes one day for each level of the target. This ability may be gained multiple times, allowing an extra use of the ability per game session for each time it has been purchased.

Intercept Communication: Once per game session, the snoop may intercept a telephone call, email, or other communication originating from a specific person or location, and clandestinely listen in without making a Surveillance skill check. This ability may be gained multiple times, allowing an extra use of the ability per game session for each time it has been purchased.

Intelligence Analysis: The snoop may quickly sift through large amounts of electronic data in order to find information relevant to a particular topic. This takes approximately 10 minutes for each CD-ROM (containing roughly as much data as an encyclopedia set) he wants to sift through. Search and Spot checks must still be made to notice important information while using this ability, unless it is obvious, in which case the GC may rule that it is found automatically once the time is taken to sift through the material.

Electronics Familiarity: The snoop is familiar with all types of electronic devices, even control consoles found deep within enemy lairs. (See the Electronics skill description for the effects of familiarity with a device.)

Feat: The snoop gains a bonus gear or skill feat. He must still meet all of the feat's prerequisites, including ability score and base attack bonus minimums.

Skill Mastery: The snoop selects a number of skills equal to 3 + his Intelligence modifier. He may always take 10 when using these skills, even if stress and distraction would normally interfere. This ability may be gained multiple times, but the snoop must select different skills each time.

Master Cracker: Starting at 10th level, once per game session, the snoop may automatically figure out one password, PIN, or similar piece of information. This ability requires at least a full action to use, and the GC may require the team to perform a task, such as breaking into a certain building, in order to acquire the information. At 20th level, the snoop may use this ability twice per game session.

Global Search: Starting at 14th level, once per game session, the snoop may find out what city anyone is in, anywhere in the world. This requires either a physical description or current ID of the target, and takes two days for every level of the target. Finally, the GC may require the team to perform a task, such as getting in touch with a known snitch, to acquire the information.

SOLDIER

During firefights, the soldier is the group's backbone. No other member of the team is as heavily trained in combat techniques and strategies, though how that training manifests differs from soldier to soldier. Some are intense martial artists, while others are master marksmen. Without at least one soldier around, the team is likely to find itself outgunned in a fight.

Abilities: The physical abilities – Strength, Constitution, and Dexterity – are the most important for the soldier. They enable superiority in combat, and for a soldier, nothing is more vital.

Vitality: 1d12 plus Con modifier per level.

CLASS SKILLS

The soldier's class skills, and the key ability for each, are listed below *(see page 40 for skill descriptions):*

Class Skill	Key Ability
Balance	Dex
Climb	Str
Craft	Int
Demolitions	Int
Driver	Dex
First Aid	Wis
Intimidate	Str or Cha
Jump	Str

	Base Att Bon	Fort Save	Ref Save	Will Save	Def Bon	Init Bon	Budg Pts	Gadg Pts	
Lvl									**Special**
1	+1	+2	+1	+0	+0	+1	2	0	Starting feats, *accurate*, bonus feat
2	+2	+3	+2	+0	+1	+2	4	1	Damage reduction 1/–
3	+3	+3	+2	+1	+1	+3	6	1	Bonus feat
4	+4	+4	+2	+1	+2	+3	8	2	Armor use +1
5	+5	+4	+3	+1	+2	+4	10	2	Bonus feat
6	+6	+5	+3	+2	+2	+5	12	3	Weapon specialization
7	+7	+5	+4	+2	+3	+6	14	3	Bonus feat
8	+8	+6	+4	+2	+3	+6	16	4	Armor use +2
9	+9	+6	+4	+3	+4	+7	18	4	Bonus feat, weapon specialization
10	+10	+7	+5	+3	+4	+8	20	5	Portable cover (¼ cover)
11	+11	+7	+5	+3	+4	+9	22	5	Bonus feat, damage reduction 2/–
12	+12	+8	+6	+4	+5	+10	24	6	Armor use +3, weapon specialization
13	+13	+8	+6	+4	+5	+10	26	6	Bonus feat
14	+14	+9	+6	+4	+6	+11	28	7	One in a million
15	+15	+9	+7	+5	+6	+12	30	7	Bonus feat, weapon specialization
16	+16	+10	+7	+5	+6	+13	32	8	Armor use +4
17	+17	+10	+8	+5	+7	+14	34	8	Bonus feat
18	+18	+11	+8	+6	+7	+14	36	9	Weapon specialization
19	+19	+11	+8	+6	+8	+15	38	9	Bonus feat, damage reduction 3/–
20	+20	+12	+9	+6	+8	+16	40	10	Armor use +5 portable cover (½ cover)

Table 1.8: The Soldier

Profession	Wis
Sport	Str or Dex
Spot	Wis
Survival	Wis
Swim	Str
Tumble	Dex
Use Rope	Dex

Skill Points at 1st level: (4 + Int modifier) × 4.
Skill Points at Each Additional Level: 4 + Int modifier.

CLASS FEATURES

All of the following are class features of the soldier.

Starting Feats: The soldier begins play with the following feats.

Armor Proficiency (Light)
Armor Proficiency (Medium)
Armor Proficiency (Heavy)
Weapon Group Proficiency (Hurled)
Weapon Group Proficiency (Melee)
Weapon Group Proficiency (Handgun)
Weapon Group Proficiency (Rifle)
Weapon Group Proficiency (Tactical)

Accurate: Whenever the soldier spends an action die to add to an attack roll, or a Strength- or Constitution-based skill check, two dice are added instead of one (e.g. a 1st-level soldier's bonus of 1d4 becomes 2d4). This is the soldier's core ability.

Bonus Feat: At 1st level, the soldier receives a bonus feat from any combat tree (basic, melee, ranged, or unarmed). He must still meet all prerequisites for the feat, including ability score and base attack bonus minimums. For every 2 levels after 1st level, the soldier receives an additional bonus combat feat. These feats are in addition to the feats that agents normally receive every 3 levels.

Damage Reduction: Starting at 2nd level, the soldier is capable of shrugging off damage from each blow he suffers. Subtract 1 from the damage the soldier takes each time he is dealt damage. At 11th level, subtract 2 each time he is dealt damage, and at 19th level, begin subtracting 3 when the soldier is damaged. This ability cannot reduce the amount of damage suffered below 0, but it does stack with the damage reduction provided by any armor or other equipment the soldier is wearing. *For more information about damage reduction, see page 178.*

Armor Use: Starting at 4th level, the soldier's total Defense bonus when wearing armor is increased by +1 and the total armor check penalty he suffers from wearing armor is reduced by 1. Every 4 levels thereafter, the Defense bonus increases by +1 and the armor check penalty decreases by 1. This ability cannot reduce the soldier's armor check penalty below 0.

Weapon Specialization: At 6th level, the soldier chooses one weapon that he is proficient with (such as barehanded, dagger, grapple, or shotgun) to specialize in. He inflicts +2 damage when wielding that weapon. If his choice is a ranged weapon, the damage bonus only applies if the soldier is within one range increment. Every 3 levels after 6th, the soldier selects another weapon to specialize in.

Portable Cover: Starting at 10th level, whenever the soldier takes a standard attack action, he is considered to have one-quarter cover until his next action, even if standing out in the open. At 20th level, this increases to one-half cover. As usual with cover, use only the highest modifier when stacking cover bonuses (e.g. a 10th-level soldier in three-quarters cover does not receive additional benefit from this ability).

One in a Million: Starting at 14th level, once per game session, the soldier automatically rolls a natural 20 when performing a physical activity such as an attack roll, a Fortitude or Reflex save, or a Strength-, Constitution-, or Dexterity-based skill check. This roll may be turned into a critical success as usual. The use of this ability must be declared before the roll is made.

WHEELMAN

The wheelman thrives on high-speed chases and the rush of deadly battles. He is both the team's vehicle specialist and a trained combatant second only to the soldier class. Without a wheelman, the team might find itself unable to cope when a mission requires breakneck speed and nerves of steel, or a quick getaway.

Abilities: Dexterity is by far the most important ability for a wheelman, since it is the basis for all vehicle skills, as well as ranged attack rolls. Intelligence is his secondary ability, as a source of extra skill points, many of which are devoted to combat skills.

Vitality: 1d12 plus Con modifier per level.

CLASS SKILLS

The wheelman's class skills, and the key ability for each, are listed below *(see page 40 for skill descriptions):*

Class Skill	Key Ability
Balance	Dex
Boating	Dex
Craft	Int
Demolitions	Int
Disguise	Cha
Driver	Dex
Escape Artist	Dex
Handle Animal	Cha
Intimidate	Str or Cha
Jump	Str

Lvl	Base Att Bon	Fort Save	Ref Save	Will Save	Def Bon	Init Bon	Budg Pts	Gadg Pts	Special
1	+1	+0	+2	+0	+1	+1	2	0 (4)	Starting feats, *custom ride (4 GP)*, daredevil, *lucky*
2	+2	+0	+3	+0	+1	+1	4	1 (4)	Kick start 1/session
3	+3	+1	+3	+1	+2	+2	6	2 (4)	Bonus feat
4	+4	+1	+4	+1	+2	+2	8	3 (5)	Custom ride (5 GP), familiarity +1
5	+5	+1	+4	+1	+3	+3	10	3 (5)	Bonus feat
6	+6	+2	+5	+2	+4	+4	12	4 (5)	Elbow grease +2
7	+7	+2	+5	+2	+4	+4	14	5 (5)	Bonus feat
8	+8	+2	+6	+2	+5	+5	16	6 (6)	Custom ride (6 GP), familiarity +2
9	+9	+3	+6	+3	+5	+5	18	6 (6)	Bonus feat, elbow grease +4
10	+10	+3	+7	+3	+6	+6	20	7 (6)	Soup her up (25%)
11	+11	+3	+7	+3	+7	+7	22	8 (6)	Bonus feat, kick start 2/session
12	+12	+4	+8	+4	+7	+7	24	9 (7)	Custom ride (7 GP), elbow grease +6, familiarity +3
13	+13	+4	+8	+4	+8	+8	26	9 (7)	Bonus feat
14	+14	+4	+9	+4	+8	+8	28	10 (7)	"That's Impossible!"
15	+15	+5	+9	+5	+9	+9	30	11 (7)	Bonus feat, elbow grease +8
16	+16	+5	+10	+5	+10	+10	32	12 (8)	Custom ride (8 GP), familiarity +4
17	+17	+5	+10	+5	+10	+10	34	12 (8)	Bonus feat
18	+18	+6	+11	+6	+11	+11	36	13 (8)	Elbow grease +10
19	+19	+6	+11	+6	+11	+11	38	14 (8)	Bonus feat, kick start 3/session
20	+20	+6	+12	+6	+12	+12	40	15 (9)	Custom ride (9 GP), familiarity +5, soup her up (50%)

TABLE 1.9: THE WHEELMAN

Mechanics	Int
Open Lock	Dex
Perform	Cha
Pilot	Dex
Profession	Wis
Sport	Str or Dex
Spot	Wis
Surveillance	Wis
Survival	Wis
Swim	Str

Skill Points at 1st level: (6 + Int modifier) × 4.

Skill Points at Each Additional Level: 6 + Int modifier.

CLASS FEATURES

All of the following are class features of the wheelman.

Starting Feats: The wheelman begins play with the following feats.

Armor Proficiency (Light)

Armor Proficiency (Medium)

Weapon Group Proficiency (Melee)

Weapon Group Proficiency (Handgun)

Weapon Group Proficiency (Rifle)

Weapon Group Proficiency (Tactical)

Lucky: Whenever the wheelman spends an action die to add to a vehicle-related skill check (such as Mechanics or Driver), two dice are added instead of one (e.g. a 1st-level wheelman's bonus of 1d4 becomes 2d4). In addition, the Game Control must spend an extra action die to cause the wheelman to suffer a critical failure with a vehicle-related skill check. This is one of the wheelman's two core abilities.

Custom Ride: At the start of each mission, the wheelman receives 4 gadget points with which he can purchase a team vehicle, vehicles, or vehicular gadgets. This bonus is increased by 1 gadget point at 4th level, and every four levels thereafter. The wheelman may spend these gadget points independently or together with his regular allotment, and they may be pooled with those of the other team members. These bonus gadget points may only be used for vehicles and vehicular gadgets, including those for a signature vehicle. When multiclassing, these gadget points are only received if the agent is gaining a level in his wheelman class. This is one of the wheelman's two core abilities.

Daredevil: During chases, the wheelman may use daredevil-only Maneuvers and augment certain other maneuvers *(see Chapter 7: Chases for more).*

Kick Start: Starting at 2nd level, once per game session, the wheelman can change a failed Mechanics skill check to a success by giving the target device a whack in frustration. At 11th and 19th level, the wheelman can use this ability one additional time per game session.

Bonus Feat: At 3rd level, the wheelman receives the Speed Demon feat or a bonus chase feat. He must still meet all of the feat's prerequisites, including ability score and base attack bonus minimums. For every two levels after 3rd, the wheelman receives another bonus chase feat or an Advanced Skill feat with Speed Demon as a prerequisite.

Familiarity: Starting at 4th level, the wheelman gains a +1 bonus to Mechanics and Driver, Pilot, Boating, and maneuver checks when used with a specific vehicle he designates as familiar. This same bonus is applied to the wheelman's attack roll whenever firing the vehicle's weapons. To designate a vehicle as familiar, the wheelman must have operated it for at least 20 days, minus a number of days equal to his Wisdom modifier. The wheelman's custom ride *(see above)* may be designated as familiar, as can a signature vehicle *(see page 87).* A wheelman may only be familiar with one vehicle at a time. This bonus increases by +1 at 8th level, and by an additional +1 every 4 levels thereafter.

Elbow Grease: Starting at 6th level, the wheelman gains a +2 competence bonus to Mechanics checks made to attempt temporary or jury-rigged repairs *(as per the Mechanics skill, see page 59).* This bonus increases by +2 for every 3 levels gained after 6th.

Soup Her Up: Starting at 10th level, any vehicle that the wheelman is familiar with (as per the familiarity ability, above) and works on regularly (at least once a week) increases all of its traits by 25%. (For example, a vehicle's speed of 100 would increase to 125.) At 20th level, this bonus rises to a 50% increase to all the vehicle's traits.

"That's Impossible!": Starting at 14th level, once per game session when driving a vehicle, the wheelman can force it to utterly defy physics for one maneuver. The wheelman can cause a car to jump a gap without a ramp, leap a motorcycle over a train just as a flatcar goes past, balance an 18-wheeler on half its wheels, vertically loop a helicopter with a two-bladed rotor, etc. *For more information about using this ability during a chase, see pages 189-190.* Outside of chases, the Game Control determines the effects of this ability, based on requests made by the wheelman.

MULTI-CLASSED AGENTS

An agent may add new classes as he advances in level. The class abilities from the agent's various classes add together to determine his overall abilities.

CLASS AND LEVEL FEATURES

A multiclass agent's abilities are the sum of the abilities of each of his classes, as follows.

Level, base attack bonus, feats, class features, ability increases, saving throws and skills improve and adjust for a multiclassing agent as per the multiclassing rules in the *Player's Handbook™.*

Agent level: This is the agent's total level. It is derived from his overall XP, and determines when generic level-dependent benefits are gained, as per the Player's Handbook™. "Class level" is the agent's level in a particular class, as per the individual class tables.

Vitality, defense bonus, initiative bonus, gadget points, and budget points: Each of these statistics is found by adding together the bonuses given by each of the agent's class levels.

Starting Action Dice: The agent receives action dice according to his agent level, regardless of individual class levels.

ACQUIRING A NEW CLASS

The *Player's Handbook™* explains a number of benefits that your agent does not gain when he acquires a new class. In addition, the agent does not gain the following 1st level benefits:

- Maximum vitality points from 1st level
- Quadruple the normal skill points per level
- Personal budget
- Core abilities

PRESTIGE CLASSES

Future sourcebooks for *Spycraft*, including the upcoming *Shadowforce Archer Worldbook,* will feature a new kind of class — the prestige class. Prestige classes are advanced agent options. They are themed and have a number of prerequisites that your agent must meet. Their abilities are focused, and somewhat more powerful than the base classes presented here. In most ways, prestige classes operate the same as base classes — with one exception. You gain only the core ability of your first prestige class in addition to the core ability of your base class, no matter how many times you multi-class.

"There is a war out there, old friend. A World War. And it's not about who's got the most bullets. It's about who controls the information. What we see and hear, how we work, what we think. It's all about the information."

– Cosmo,
Sneakers

SKILLS

SKILLS

This section contains rules that apply to all skills. The following section provides rules for using individual skills. Rules for acquiring and increasing skill ranks can be found in the *Player's Handbook™*.

NORMAL SKILL CHECKS

Skill checks are made against a set difficulty unless you are opposing or competing against someone else. Normally, before you make a skill check, your Game Control rates the task you're attempting and assigns it a **Difficulty Class** (DC). DCs usually fall between 5 and 30. Then you roll 1d20 and add your skill bonus *(see the next column)*. If the total of your roll equals or exceeds the DC of the task you were attempting, you succeed. Otherwise, you fail. GCs should note that a DC of 10 + the agent's skill bonus results in success approximately 50% of the time, while 5 + the agent's skill bonus results in success approximately 75% of the time.

Example 1: Donovan is trying to pick a lock. His GC decides that the lock has a fairly difficult DC of 20 to open. The result of Donovan's Open Lock check must be 20 or higher for him to pick the lock.

Example 2: Donovan's GC instead decides that the lock is almost impossible to open (DC 35). Donovan's Open Lock check must be 35 or more to open it.

OPPOSED SKILL CHECKS

If you're opposing or competing against someone else when you use a skill, then each person involved in the opposed check rolls 1d20 and adds the appropriate skill bonuses. The highest total wins the competition. Equal totals are considered a tie unless this provides no clear result, in which case they are rerolled. Everybody involved in the check uses his most relevant skill.

A critical success *(see page 39)* with an opposed skill check may only be beaten by a critical success with a higher check total.

Example 1: Donovan and 5 others are racing. Each makes a Driver check, and the person with the highest result wins the race, with the second-highest result coming in second place, etc. If two or more rolls are tied, the players cross the finish line together.

Example 2: Donovan is trying to sneak past a guard whose back is to him. He makes a Move Silently check and the guard makes a Listen check. If Donovan's result is higher than the guard's,

he sneaks by. Otherwise the guard hears him. In this case, since a tie provides an unclear result, an equal result requires Donovan and the guard to reroll.

SKILL BONUS

Your skill bonus with a particular skill is:

Skill rank + ability modifier + miscellaneous modifiers

Skill	Ability	Untrained	Fac	Fix	Ptm	Snp	Sol	Whl
TABLE 2.1: SKILLS								
Appraise	Int	Yes	•	✔	•	✔	•	•
Balance	Dex	Yes	•	✔	•	•	✔	✔
Bluff	Cha	Yes	✔	✔	✔	•	•	•
Boating	Dex	Yes	•	✔	•	•	•	✔
Bureaucracy	Cha	Yes	•	•	✔	✔	•	•
Climb	Str	Yes	•	✔	•	•	✔	•
Computers	Int	Yes	•	•	•	✔	•	•
Concentration	Wis	Yes	•	•	•	✔	•	•
Craft	Int	No	✔	✔	✔	✔	✔	✔
Cryptography	Int	No	•	•	•	✔	•	•
Cultures	Wis	No	✔	•	•	✔	•	•
Demolitions	Int	No	•	✔	•	•	✔	✔
Diplomacy	Cha	Yes	✔	•	•	✔	•	•
Disguise	Cha	Yes	✔	•	•	•	•	✔
Driver	Dex	Yes	✔	✔	✔	✔	✔	✔
Electronics	Int	No	•	✔	•	✔	•	•
Escape Artist	Dex	Yes	•	✔	•	•	•	✔
First Aid	Wis	Yes	•	•	✔	✔	✔	•
Forgery	Int	Yes	✔	✔	•	•	•	•
Gather Information	Cha	Yes	✔	•	•	✔	•	•
Handle Animal	Cha	No	•	•	•	•	•	✔
Hide	Dex	Yes	•	✔	•	✔	•	•
Hobby	Wis	Yes	✔	✔	•	✔	•	•
Innuendo	Wis	Yes	✔	✔	•	•	•	•
Intimidate	Str or Cha	Yes	•	•	•	•	✔	✔
Jump	Str	Yes	•	✔	•	•	✔	✔
Knowledge	Int	No	✔	✔	✔	✔	•	•
Languages	Wis	Yes	✔	✔	•	✔	•	•
Listen	Wis	Yes	•	✔	•	✔	•	•
Mechanics	Int	No	•	•	•	✔	•	✔
Move Silently	Dex	Yes	•	✔	•	✔	•	•
Open Lock	Dex	No	✔	✔	•	•	•	✔
Perform	Cha	Yes	✔	•	•	•	•	✔
Pilot	Dex	No	•	•	•	•	•	✔
Profession	Wis	No	✔	✔	✔	✔	✔	✔
Read Lips	Int	No	✔	•	•	✔	•	•
Search	Int	Yes	✔	✔	•	✔	•	•
Sense Motive	Wis	Yes	✔	•	✔	✔	•	•
Sleight of Hand	Dex	No	✔	✔	•	•	•	•
Sport	Str or Dex	Yes	•	•	✔	•	✔	✔
Spot	Wis	Yes	✔	✔	•	✔	✔	✔
Surveillance	Wis	No	•	•	•	✔	•	✔
Survival	Wis	No	•	•	•	•	✔	✔
Swim	Str	Yes	•	•	•	•	✔	✔
Tumble	Dex	No	•	✔	•	•	✔	•
Use Rope	Dex	Yes	•	•	•	•	✔	•

✔ = Class Skill   • = Cross-Class Skill

SKILL RANK

You add your rank in a skill to any skill checks made using it. If you have ½ a rank in a skill, ignore it for this purpose.

ABILITY MODIFIER

Each skill is most closely related to one of your abilities, as shown on Table 2.1: Skills. You add that ability's modifier to any skill checks made using the skill. For instance, Climb is most heavily dependent upon an agent's Strength, so you add your Strength modifier to all Climb checks.

Example: If your Strength is 17, you add +3 to all your Climb checks.

MISCELLANEOUS MODIFIERS

Equipment, the situation a skill is used in, and armor check penalties are all common skill check modifiers.

RETRIES

Usually you can retry failed skill checks indefinitely. Sometimes, however, a skill has consequences for failure that must be taken into account. Some skills only

STACKING BONUSES

There are a lot of bonuses in *Spycraft,* but all of them fall into one of two categories — named and unnamed. When you benefit from more than one named bonus of the same type (armor, synergy, etc.), only the best bonus applies. For instance, if you receive a +1 armor bonus from a feat, and then gain a +2 armor bonus from a piece of gear, then only the bonus gained from the gear is added to your Defense.

Further, bonuses gained from the same source (such as two or more armor bonuses gained from wearing protective gear) don't stack with one another. Like-named bonuses from the same source do not stack.

If two like-named or same-source bonuses with time limits affect you at the same time, one may take over for the other when the duration of the first ends. For instance, if you are being attacked by ranged fire in moderate darkness (+1 concealment bonus) inside a dense fog bank (+6 concealment bonus), you only benefit from the +6 bonus. If, later in the scene, the fog bank rolls out, you are still left with the +1 bonus from the lighting.

Unnamed bonuses stack with all other bonuses all the time, unless otherwise stated in their description.

Dodge bonuses always stack, unless otherwise noted.

give you one chance at a particular task, and it's commonly useless to repeat a check once you've succeeded at it.

If a skill check carries no penalties for failure, then you can take 20 on it *(see next page)*.

The amount of time required for each skill check, and whether the skill can be retried after failure, are listed in the skill's entry.

UNTRAINED CHECKS

If Table 2.1: Skills says that you can use a skill untrained, you can make checks even if you have no ranks in that skill. You simply make the skill check as though you had a skill rank of 0. However, your error range increases by 1 (e.g. from 1 to 1-2 or 1-2 to 1-3).

In order to use a skill that cannot be used untrained, you must have at least one full rank with it. Half ranks don't allow the use of a skill that requires training.

ABILITY CHECKS

Sometimes you do things that no listed skill covers, such as trying to break down a door. There's no Break Door skill, and none of the other skills are even close. In this case, the GC chooses one of your abilities to apply to the check (for this example, Strength), and you make an ability check. An ability check works just like an untrained skill check — you are considered to have a skill rank of 0.

Breaking doors and other items is the most common ability check, and is covered in more detail in Chapters 6 and 9, on pages 168 and 234.

CONDITIONAL MODIFIERS

Generally speaking, your Game Control can apply a +2 bonus to a skill check for each favorable condition in effect that would make it easier for you to succeed. Your Game Control could also apply a –2 penalty to a skill check for each unfavorable condition in effect that would make it harder for you to succeed.

Example: If you were climbing a cliff in a stiff wind, your GC might apply a –2 penalty to your Climb check.

TIME AND SKILLS CHECKS

A skill's description tells you how long it takes to use that skill for various tasks.

AUTOMATIC SUCCESS/FAILURE

A natural 1 (an actual roll of 1 on a d20) is always a failure, while a natural 20 (an actual roll of 20 on a d20) is always a success. A natural 20 might also be a critical success *(see Critical Successes, opposite),* while a natural 1 might be a critical failure *(see Critical Failures, opposite).*

CRITICAL SUCCESSES

Whenever you roll a natural 20 (the d20 is actually showing a 20) for a skill check, you automatically succeed, and you've scored a **threat** – a potential critical success. In order to turn a threat into a critical success, you must spend one action die. If you choose not to do so, then your skill check is just a normal success.

In addition, you can sometimes score a threat with a roll lower than 20 (usually because of a feat or special ability). Any roll lower than a 20 is not an automatic success, and if the skill check fails, it doesn't count as a threat.

The effects of a critical success vary from skill to skill, and are subject to the GC's discretion, but suggestions are listed in each skill's description.

CRITICAL FAILURES

Whenever you roll a natural 1 (the d20 is actually showing a 1) for a skill check, you automatically fail and you've scored an **error** – a potential critical failure. In order to turn an error into a critical failure, your GC must spend one action die. If your GC chooses not to do so, then your skill check is just a normal failure.

In addition, you can sometimes score an error with a roll higher than 1 (usually because you're using experimental or shoddy equipment). Any roll higher than a 1 is not an automatic failure, and if the skill check succeeds, it doesn't count as an error.

The effects of a critical failure vary from skill to skill, and are subject to the GC's discretion, but suggestions are listed in each skill's description.

TAKING 10

If you aren't in a hurry (i.e. you have ten times the amount of time required for a skill check) and aren't being distracted, you may choose to take 10. Instead of rolling 1d20 for your skill check, calculate it as though you had rolled a 10. (Thus, if your skill bonus is +5 and you take 10, your result is 15.) For many simple tasks, taking 10 makes it impossible to fail, but you cannot take 10 if you are being distracted or threatened.

TAKING 20

If you have plenty of time (20 times the amount of time you would normally spend for a skill check), and the skill you are attempting carries no penalty for failure, then you may choose to take 20. Instead of rolling 1d20 for your skill check, calculate it as though you had rolled a 20. (Thus, if your skill bonus is +5 and you take 20, your result is 25.) Taking 20 takes twenty times as long as making a normal skill check (e.g. a skill that normally takes 1 minute to use takes 20 minutes if you take 20). You cannot take 20 if failing the skill check carries any penalty, and you may not score a threat when taking 20.

COOPERATION

If multiple agents are working together to perform a single task, one agent must be chosen as the leader of the attempt. The other agents who are helping each make a skill check against a DC of 10 (they cannot take 10 or take 20 with this check). For every assistant who succeeds with this check, the leader gets a +2 bonus to the main skill check, which determines whether the overall effort succeeds or not. Often, the GC may limit the number of assistants who can help with a skill check, since after a certain point they just get in each other's way. (For example, only three or four people might attempt to break down a single door).

SKILL SYNERGY

If you have two skills that work well together, such as Jump and Tumble, they may help each other out. In general, having 5 or more ranks in one such skill gives you a +2 synergy bonus to skill checks with the other, as noted in the skill description.

ACTION DICE AND SKILL USE

Action dice can be spent to affect your skill checks in the following ways.

ADDING TO SKILL CHECKS

You may spend an action die after any skill check you make. You then roll an additional die (type determined by your level, as shown below) and add it to the result of your skill check. You may continue spending action dice to add to the skill check as long as you have any left.

When rolling an action die, if you roll the highest number possible on the die (such as a 6 on a d6), it "explodes," meaning that you re-roll the die, adding the number you roll to the previous total. So, if you roll a 6 on a d6, and then re-roll it, getting a 4, the total value for that action die is 10. An action die can keep exploding as long as you keep rolling its maximum value.

Level	Die Type
1st-5th	d4
6th-10th	d6
11th-15th	d8
16th-20th	d10

Example 1: A 1st-level pointman rolls a 17 for a Driver check, just shy of the 20 he needs. He decides to spend an action die and, rolling a d4, gets a 3. Adding 3 to his previous total of 17, he now has a total of 20, enough to succeed.

Example 2: A 6th-level soldier rolls a 12 for a Stealth check and needs a 20. Spending an action die, he rolls a d6 and gets a 6. The die explodes, so he re-rolls it, this time getting a 3. When added to the previous 6, this gives a total of 9, which is enough to increase the original roll of 12 to 21, a success.

ACTIVATING CRITICAL SUCCESSES

When you roll a threat, you may spend an action die to score a critical success. The effects of critical successes vary with the skill used and the current circumstances. Because of this, your GC must ultimately decide upon the effects of each critical success, but there are suggestions listed under each skill to give you an idea of what you can expect when you score a critical success with it. In some cases, your GC may decide that a critical success has no effect. In that case, you get your action die back, if you spent one.

KEY TO SKILL DESCRIPTIONS

All skill descriptions follow this format.

SKILL NAME ([KEY ABILITY]; ARMOR CHECK PENALTY; TRAINED ONLY)

The skill name line includes the following information.

Key Ability: The ability whose modifier is applied to checks with this skill.

Armor Check Penalty: If this tag is listed, then you apply the armor check penalty of any armor you're wearing to all checks made with this skill.

Trained Only: If this tag is listed, then you cannot attempt untrained checks with this skill.

In addition, skill descriptions include the following sections:

Check (Time): What you can do with a successful check, how much time it takes, and what the DC of the check is.

Retry: The conditions under which you may retry the skill.

Special: Other important notes about the skill.

Critical Success: Some of the possible effects of a critical success made while using the skill.

Critical Failure: Some of the possible effects of a critical failure made while using the skill.

THE SKILLS

The following is a list of every skill in *Spycraft*.

APPRAISE (INT)

Appraise is used to estimate the value of an object.

Check (1 minute): You can estimate the value of a common or well-known item within 10% of its value (DC 12). Failure with the skill check indicates that you estimate the value from 50% to 150% of the actual value (the GC rolls 2d6+3, multiplies by 10%, multiplies that by the actual value, and provides the resulting value as the estimate).

Rare objects require a skill check with DC 15, 20, or higher. If successful, the estimate is 70% to 130% of the item's actual value (the Game Control rolls 2d4+5, multiplies by 10%, multiplies that by the actual value, and provides the resulting value as the estimate). Failure indicates that you cannot estimate the value of the item. Totally alien objects and common items that are not easily recognized for what they are add +5 to the DC.

Retry: Not allowed for the same item, regardless of previous result.

Special: When an untrained agent attempts to use the skill, failure with a common item results in no estimate and success with a rare item results in an estimate that is 50% to 150% of the item's actual value (2d6+3, multiplied by 10%).

Critical Success: The estimate is perfect.

Critical Failure: The estimate is wildly inaccurate. A worthless bottle could be mistaken for a valuable antique, or the worth of a Ming vase could be overlooked.

BALANCE (DEX; ARMOR CHECK PENALTY)

This skill is used to keep your balance on a tightrope, narrow beam, uneven floor, or other unstable surface.

Check (Full Action): A successful check allows you to move up to half your speed across a precarious surface. A failed check means you are off-balance and spend the round regaining your balance. Failure by 5 or more means you fall and take appropriate damage *(see Falling, page 236)*. The DC of your skill check depends on the surface you are standing on.

Surface	DC
Uneven floor	10
7-12 inches wide	10
2-6 inches wide	15
Less than 2 inches wide	20
Angled surface	+10*
Slippery surface	+10*
Moving at full speed	+5*
Moving at double speed	+10†

* Cumulative penalties; use all that apply.

† Two checks with all penalties must be made to move at double speed. Failing either means you fall down.

Being Attacked While Off-Balance: If someone attacks you while you are off-balance, they receive a +2 bonus to their attack roll. In addition, if you don't have at least 5 ranks in Balance, you lose your Dexterity bonus to Defense, if any. If you take any damage, you must immediately make another Balance check, adding 5 to your DC.

Special: If you have 5 or more ranks in Tumble, you get a +2 synergy bonus to Balance checks.

Critical Success: You move at twice the speed you were trying to move at, up to double speed.

Critical Failure: You fall. Alternately, you freeze up where you are, forcing someone else to come help you.

BLUFF (CHA)

You are very convincing and can make unlikely claims seem reasonable. This skill requires a mixture of talents: acting, cunning, misdirection, propagandizing, and the use of body language. A bluff usually has short-term effects as it takes little scrutiny for the subject to see flaws in the bluff and reconsider his position.

Bluff is best suited for sowing the seeds of confusion in a security force, causing someone to look in a certain direction for a moment, or seducing someone.

Check (10 minutes): You can attempt to seduce someone. For more about this use of the Bluff skill, *see the disposition system on page 269.*

Check (Full Action — 1 minute): You can attempt to bluff someone. Make a Bluff check opposed by your target's Sense Motive check. Circumstances factor into the check as favorable (added to your modifiers) or unfavorable (added to the target's modifiers).

A bluff requires interaction of some sort between the target and the bluffing character, and takes at least one round. The more complicated the bluff, the more time required.

The GC should resolve the outcome of the bluff, applying greater modifiers for unbelievable bluffs or favorable modifiers for totally reasonable bluffs. Huge modifiers (10 or greater) can be applied to bluffs that require the target to go against their nature, self-interest, orders or personality.

Circumstances	Modifier
Target wants to believe the bluff	–5
Bluff believable/target unaffected	+0
Bluff pushing it/target at minor risk	+5
Bluff hard to believe/target at large risk	+10
Bluff ludicrous/target at great risk	+20

If the target succeeds by 10 or less, they don't see through the bluff so much as refuse to go along with it. If they succeed by more than 10, they see through the bluff.

A successful bluff results in the target buying into the bluff and going along with it, within reason, at least for a short period of time.

Check (Half Action): You can use the Bluff skill to feint at an opponent so that he can't dodge your next attack. A feint is opposed by the target's Sense Motive skill. If you succeed with your check, your target may not add his Dexterity bonus to Defense against your next attack. This effect lasts until you attack the target or the end of your next action, whichever comes first. *For more information about feints, see page 167.*

Alternately, a successful Bluff check to create a diversion can provide you or your team time to hide, run or take cover.

Check (Full Action — 10 minutes): You can attempt to shadow someone (i.e. follow them without them realizing what you are doing), masking your movements as part of a surrounding crowd. (If there is no crowd to blend into, you must use the Hide skill to shadow someone – *see page 55.)*

Make a Bluff check opposed by the target's Sense Motive. Success indicates that your target has not noticed what you are doing. The GC may make this roll in secret so that you don't know whether the target has made you (i.e. spotted you) or not. This roll must be made again each ten minutes you are shadowing someone.

Retry: A failed Bluff check does not normally allow for another attempt, but feints and diversions can be used repeatedly during combat. A failed shadowing attempt may not be retried – the target already knows you're following him.

Special: Five or more ranks in Bluff offer you a +2 synergy bonus when used in conjunction with Intimidate or Sleight of Hand. They also offer a +2 synergy bonus to Disguise checks when you are being observed and attempting to stay in character.

Use of the Bluff skill can be affected by the disposition system – *see page 269.*

Critical Success: If seducing someone, they have become infatuated with you, and may possibly fall in love with you. If bluffing or creating a diversion, your opponents are absolutely fooled. If using feint against an opponent, he becomes flat-footed. If shadowing someone, you don't need to make another check for half an hour.

Critical Failure: Your target isn't fooled for a second, and instantly realizes your intent. If you were attempting to seduce someone, he or she may refuse to have anything else to do with you. If shadowing someone, you are immediately spotted but believe that you have not been. For the duration of the scene, any further Bluff, Sense Motive, or Spot checks made on you by your target receive a +2 bonus.

BOATING (DEX)

Boating is used to steer all watercraft of all shapes and sizes.

Check (Half Action): No skill checks are required to perform standard boating functions, but complex tasks, such as those that arise during combat or other threatening circumstances, require a roll. *See also Chases, page 183.*

Task	DC
Shallow turn/avoid obstacle	5
Average maneuver/navigate shallows	10
Tight turn/dangerous area	15
High stress check/very dangerous area	20
Heroic or complex set of maneuvers	25+
Unfamiliar type of vehicle	+5

Vehicles are rated for handling *(see page 184).* This rating may help or hinder the vehicle's pilot.

Retry: Yes, but there is a lapse of time between tries – GC's discretion, based on current conditions. If you absolutely have to turn immediately to avoid a reef, but fail the check, a second attempt is impossible.

Special: This skill covers the physical act of boating; knowledge of boating and making money with it as a sport are covered by the knowledge and sport skills, respectively. If you have 5 or more ranks in Boating, you get a +2 synergy bonus to any Knowledge and Mechanics checks concerning water craft, as well as a +2 synergy bonus to any Sport checks to professionally compete with them.

Critical Success: When not in a chase, you manage to avoid mishap even when it is seemingly impossible to do so. Your vehicle is not only unscathed by whatever pitfall you avoided, but you sail past it without a single chip in your paint. During a chase, your maneuver is successful unless an opposing driver scores a critical success with a higher total. Also, you receive a +4 bonus to your next maneuver or crash check.

Critical Failure: The boat hits an obstacle, turns over, or runs out of gas. The GC may rule that this is equivalent to failing a crash check *(see page 193).*

BUREAUCRACY (CHA)

You can cut through red tape and navigate the treacherous halls of a bureaucracy.

Check (5 minutes): You can attempt to bypass normal office procedures, favorably impress bureaucrats, or tell if an individual would be receptive to bribes.

Task	DC
Bypass bureaucrat or secretary (move up one layer of management)	10*
Rush paperwork through immediately	15
Know if person would be offended by bribe	15
Tactfully offer someone a bribe	15
Convince person to ignore policy	20
Convince person to break policy	25
Individual believes you are important (i.e. visiting dignitary, rich investor, law enforcement officer, etc.)	–2
Individual believes you are poor/unimportant	+2
Individual believes you could threaten his job	–5
Individual has been successfully bribed	–5†

* Add +2 to this DC for every layer of management past the first that you are dealing with.

† Each time the standard bribe ($100 times management layer) is doubled, an additional −2 is added to this modifier.

A bureaucracy is made up of "layers" of management. Each layer represents a bureaucrat in charge of the people working "under" him. A small company typically has only 1 or 2 layers, but a multinational corporation might have as many as 12.

The first third of the management layers at a company represents its lower management. These bureaucrats are directly in charge of the company's employees. Lower management is useful if you want to look at personnel files, get into the mail room, get hired, look at company e-mail logs, or get permission to tour a company facility.

The second third of the management layers at a company represents its middle management. Their purpose is largely to keep the riffraff (i.e. you) away from the upper management. Middle management is usually only useful if you want something that the lower management don't want to give you. By going over their heads to middle management, you can have their decisions overruled. Working with middle management is also important if you want to become involved in the company's policies and classified projects.

The final third of the management layers at a company represents its upper management. These are the bureaucrats who set company policy, manage its classified projects, and oversee its various departments. Upper management is where you need to go to change company policies, talk about classified projects, or overrule the decisions of middle management.

Bribes: It is possible to bribe bureaucrats in order to receive special consideration. Not all bureaucrats are susceptible to this, but for those who are, $100 times their management layer is enough to reduce the DCs for all future dealings with them by 5. Every time this amount is doubled, future DCs are reduced by an 2 more. Typically, highly moral or wealthy bureaucrats are immune to being bribed, and may take offense at such an offer (increasing the DCs for further dealings with them by 5).

Critical Success: Not only do you successfully complete your task, but all DCs for further dealings with this bureaucrat are reduced by 2.

Critical Failure: Not only do you fail to complete your task, but all DCs for further dealings with this bureaucrat are increased by 2.

CLIMB (STR; ARMOR CHECK PENALTY)

This skill may be used to climb a wall, scale a cliff, or get by tall obstacles that require quick scaling ability.

Check (Half Action): You can move up, down, or across a wall, slope or other precarious surface, at half speed. A wall is any surface with an incline of greater than 60°, while any surface with an incline of 60° or less is considered a slope.

A failed Climb check indicates that you have made no progress. A check that fails by 5 or more indicates that you've fallen from whatever height you were at.

The Difficulty Class (DC) of the skill check depends upon the surface and any other conditions for the climb.

Example Surface	DC
Slope too steep to walk up or knotted rope with wall to brace against	0
Rope with wall to brace against or knotted rope	5
Surface with ledges to climb between (e.g. very rough wall)	10
Surface with adequate hand- and footholds (e.g. rough natural rock or a tree); an unknotted rope	15
Uneven surface with slight handholds and footholds	20
Rough surface (e.g. a natural rock wall or a brick wall)	25
Overhang or ceiling with handholds but no footholds	25
Smooth, flat, vertical surface that cannot be climbed	—
Surface slippery or wet*	+5
Moving at full speed*	+5
Moving at double speed.†	+5
Climbing a corner where the agent can brace between two perpendicular surfaces*	−10
Climbing inside a narrow confinement where the agent can brace between two parallel surfaces*	−10

* Cumulative penalties; use all that apply.

† Two checks with all penalties must be made to move at double speed. Failing either means you fall down.

Being Attacked while Climbing: If someone attacks you while you are climbing, they receive a +2 bonus to their attack roll. In addition, you lose your Dexterity bonus to Defense, if any. If you take any damage, you must immediately make another Climb check, adding 5 to your DC. Failure means that you fall and take appropriate damage *(see Falling, page 236)*.

Making Your Own Handholds and Footholds: By inserting pitons into a wall, the agent creates his own handholds and footholds. Each piton so inserted — usually pounded into the wall with a hammer or driven in with a climber's power tool — takes one minute. One piton is required every yard. An agent with an ice axe or similar tool can cut hand- and footholds in an ice wall. An agent with a climber's power tool can spike pitons into concrete. A surface with handholds and footholds has a DC of 15.

Catching Yourself when Falling: It's impossible to catch yourself while falling alongside a vertical wall, but a broken wall, with occasional ledges or plants, allows you to catch yourself by making a Climbing check (DC = surface's DC + 20). It's easier for you to catch yourself on a slope (DC = surface's DC + 10).

Special: Using a rope, you can raise or lower another person using sheer strength, with a weight limit equal to double your maximum load *(see Carrying Capacity, page 106)*. You can raise or lower the person a distance equal to one-quarter of your speed per round. If the person held by the rope is helping (making use of any handholds that are available), the distance raised/lowered is increased to one-half your speed.

Critical Success: You move at twice the speed you were trying to move at, up to double speed.

Critical Failure: You fall. Alternately, you freeze up where you are, forcing someone else to come help you.

COMPUTERS (INT)

You can access and operate computer systems, write or modify computer programs, repair and set up computers, and operate most complex systems that serve as computer peripherals, such as scanners, digital cameras, scientific instruments, and many modern computer-controlled security systems. Using a computer to gather information requires the Gather Information skill and is described under that entry.

Check (Varies): Mundane, everyday tasks do not require a Computers check. Performing mundane tasks within a rigid time-frame, or more complex or invasive tasks, requires a skill check. Computer use is at least a full action, but it may take you hours or days to write a particularly complicated program or break into a well-secured system (per the GC).

Task	DC
Modify an existing program	15
Create a new program	15-30
Break into a secured system	20+
Review system for recent breach	15
Unfamiliar system or program	+5 or more
Break into the root account of a secured system	+5 to +10

Computers are rated for power. A computer's power rating is applied as a modifier (positive or negative) to all skill checks made with it.

Modify Existing Program (Varies): It is relatively easy to make minor changes to an existing program — changing the purpose of the software, altering its use of data, or even causing the equipment to shut down. If the program to be modified is protected with its own security, you must first bypass that security *(see below)*.

Create New Program (Varies): More complex than modifying an existing program, a new program can completely change the purpose of the equipment using the program.

Viruses: These often destructive programs make it very difficult to use infected systems, applying a modifier of +5 to as much as +20 to the DC of Computers checks made with them, or even render them useless. Viruses usually require a Computers check of 10 more than their DC modifier to create, and can be programmed to have any number of specific effects (e.g. locking up a network of hundreds of computers, sending information from targeted computers back to a system across the Internet, waiting until a file with particular code is opened and then deleting vital chunks of the operating system, etc.), as allowed by the GC.

Break into a Secured System (10+ minutes): You can break through the security measures protecting a computer system. The DC of this task is determined by the quality of the system's security. Once you've broken into a system, you can view, copy, delete, or run programs and files within, unless access to them has been restricted. Typically, secret organizations do not hook their computer systems up to the Internet — you must access them on site.

In some cases, such as when a computer specialist is online and attempting to keep you out, an opposed Computers check may be required to break into a system. If the specialist wins the check, he notices your attempt and can kick you out of the system automatically, or make another contested Computers check to try and trace your location.

Review System (1+ minutes): Once you have accessed a system, you may make a Computers skill check to perform a 'quick-sweep' of recent logs, temporary files, and other data to determine whether the system has been irregularly accessed by other users (i.e. hackers). If the system has been breached, your roll becomes an opposed check against the Computers skill check of the person who tampered with it. Success discovers and reveals the nature of the breach.

If you are performing this review on a system you are familiar with (e.g. one that you own), you receive a +5 modifier to your Computers skill check.

Likewise, succeeding with a review system check using an unfamiliar computer provides a +2 bonus to future Computers checks to search or modify the system. A successful system review also reveals any other users logged into the system, though it does not identify them *(see also Trace User, below)*.

Trace User (5+ minutes): Once you have accessed a system, you can attempt to isolate the electronic ID of any other user logged onto it (provided you are aware of their presence, by virtue of a system review or other method). This requires an opposed Computers skill check between you and the user you are trying to identify. Success with this check reveals the target user's electronic ID, from which other important data (such as their Internet service provider, personal information, and even their physical location) can be gleaned.

Root Accounts: A systems administrator ("sysadmin") performs maintenance on the system using what is known as the "root" account. If you gain access to this account, you can do anything you want to the system, including accessing restricted files, creating user accounts for future use, or even destroying valuable data. Skill checks are not required while you are logged into a computer's root account. Spooks using a back door are considered to be working with the system's root account unless the Game Control determines otherwise.

Repair Computer (Varies): You can repair a damaged computer. This can take a few rounds, an hour or two, or even days to complete, depending on the magnitude of the repair, availability of parts and proper equipment, and the situation (e.g. whether you are attempting the repair during your spare time or in the middle of a raging firefight).

Task	DC
Replace/install peripheral	10
Simple repair	15
Troubleshoot and/or complex repair	20
Major repairs on multiple peripherals	25+
Quick/temporary fix*	–5
High stress situation	+5
Unfamiliar parts/system	+5
Tools and/or parts unavailable	+15

* 10% chance of failure (non-cumulative) each time the equipment is used.

Retry: If writing or modifying a program or virus, yes, once you've tested the program and you know it's buggy. If repairing a computer, yes, but you must begin the task again. The parts are not consumed. The check can be made again after the required repair time has elapsed. If breaking into a secured system, yes, but you are traced if you fail three successive tries. If reviewing a system, yes, though you must commit the maximum

time required for the check (which may be more than was required for the original check). If tracing a user, no (the user has already proven that he can best you).

Special: If you have 5 or more ranks in Cryptography, you receive a +2 synergy bonus when breaking into computer systems.

Critical Success: The program you were writing or modifying works particularly well, or your repairs are very stable (no chance of failure if it was a temporary fix). If creating a virus, it is more effective than you expected (adding a +5 to the modifier it applies to DCs using an infected system). If you are breaking into a computer system, your presence and signs of your tampering can only be noticed by the system's other users if they score a critical success. If reviewing a system, you discover all information you were looking for and your bonus with future Computers checks using the system is increased to +4. If tracing a user, you gain all the information available about them through their ISP, including their physical location or the router hub closest to them, if available.

Critical Failure: The program you were writing or modifying is buggy and works erratically (viruses may invade the computer you were using to write them), or your repairs are shoddy and utterly destroy the equipment the next time it's used. If you are breaking into a computer system, your presence is immediately noticed and your location is traced. If reviewing a system, you are locked out after its users review your system, gaining a +4 bonus against it. If tracing a user, you leave yourself open to the target, who may trace your electronic ID to gain information about you.

CONCENTRATION (WIS)

You can focus on completing a task even when badly injured or otherwise distracted.

Check (Free Action): You can attempt to continue working on a task you are performing in spite of distractions, such as being shot at, or being trapped in a room while the ceiling is descending to crush you. The table below summarizes some possible distractions and the DC needed to ignore them. Most distractions require you to make a Concentration check at the start of every round.

Distraction	DC
Dealt an injury	10 + damage dealt
Suffering continuous damage (e.g. suffocation)	10 + half of cont. damage last dealt
Life or death situation	10
Shouting/other loud noises	10
Vigorous motion (e.g. a bumpy car ride)	10
Violent motion (e.g. a small boat in rapids)	15
Driven rain or sleet	10
Driven hail, dust, or debris	15
Extremely violent weather (e.g. gale winds)	20
Entangled (e.g. in a net)	15
Grappling or pinned	20

If the Concentration check succeeds, then you may continue your skill use as normal if the situation allows it (e.g. you could not continue to use a computer if grappled, but you could continue a Bluff check).

If the Concentration check fails, you make no progress with your skill use this round. If it fails by 5 or more, any previous work with the skill is undone.

Retry: You may always retry Concentration checks, but a failure by 5 or more forces you to start your task over, assuming that the skill allows retries.

Critical Success: No further Concentration checks are required. If you are capable of completing the task, you do.

Critical Failure: Your concentration is ruined. You cannot attempt the task again until at least one of the current distractions is removed.

CRAFT (INT; TRAINED ONLY)

You have been trained in a craft or trade, such as carpentry, painting, welding, or any other pursuit that could prove useful and isn't covered by another skill.

You can take this skill multiple times, each time applying it to a separate craft. For example, you could have Craft (Carpentry) at rank 4 and Craft (Welding) at rank 3. Your ranks in one Craft don't affect your skill checks with another.

The purpose of a craft is to create something; if it does not, it is a Hobby *(see page 55)*, a Profession *(see page 61)*, or a Sport *(see page 64)*. Each craft requires its own special tools.

Check: You may make use of your Craft to earn an income, earning your skill check result times $25 per full week of work. This roll must be made again each week that an income is desired (assuming the time and effort to earn the income is also put forth).

Alternately, you can use your Craft to create items. The DC of the task is determined by the complexity and desired quality of the item to be created. When constructing an item, use the following steps to determine cost and time required:

1. Find the item's price, or have the GC set the value of the item if it is not listed. Multiply the value by 10 to find the task value of the item.

2. Find the DC *(see the Item Complexity table to the right)* or have the GC set a DC.

3. Pay the raw materials cost (one-third the item's finished value).

4. Make one or more skill checks, each check representing one week's work.

If the Craft check succeeds, multiply the check result by the DC. If that result is equal to the task value of the item, it has been completed. If the result is double or triple the task value, then it has been completed in one-half or one-third of that week, respectively. If the result did not equal or exceed the task value of the item, the result equals the amount of task value completed for the week – the remaining task value of the item is reduced by the result and work continues on the item for another week. Each week the task value is reduced until the item is completed.

Laborers affect Craft checks per the rules for Cooperation *(see page 39)*.

If the check fails, no progress is made for that week. If the check fails by 5 or more, some of the raw materials are ruined – pay one-half of the original material cost to replace them.

Item Complexity	DC
Low (simple tool or utensil)	5
Medium (simple weapon)	10
High (weapon)	15
Extreme (vehicle)	20
Incredible (high-tech device)	30+

Retry: Yes. However, each time that the check fails by 5 or more, you must pay one-half of the raw material costs. When earning an income, only one attempt can be made per week.

Special: Unskilled laborers can earn an average of $200 a week assisting a craftsman.

Critical Success: Double the progress made on the item this week.

Critical Failure: The item is totally ruined and the agent must begin the project again from scratch.

CRYPTOGRAPHY (INT; TRAINED ONLY)

Cryptography is used for cracking and creating encryption codes.

Check (1 day): You can create or crack encryption codes. Like most modern cryptographers, you require a computer to do your best work, but you can still create primitive codes without one. You need not be able to read and write the language a message is written in to encrypt or decrypt it, but you get +2 to your Cryptography checks if you do.

To create a code, you make a Cryptography check, adding the power rating of any computer you use in the attempt. Your Game Control makes this roll in secret and notes the result next to the code for future reference.

In order to crack a code, you must make a Cryptography check against the result of the skill check that was originally made to create it. Again, if you are using a computer to aid your work, add its power rating to the attempt. Once you've cracked a code, you can read any message using that cipher without making additional checks (assuming you understand the language, of course).

Retry: Yes. You may retry any Cryptography check once per day.

Critical Success: If you are creating a code, you stumble across an 'unbreakable' code that can only be cracked with a critical success.

Critical Failure: If creating a code, it is flawed, and anyone who attempts to decode it automatically succeeds. If trying to crack a code, you cannot make any further attempts to crack this code; someone else must do so.

CULTURES (WIS; TRAINED ONLY)

You can blend into foreign cultures and have an encyclopedic knowledge of foreign customs.

Check (Free Action): You can determine the proper action dictated by local customs.

Situation	DC
Common situation (table manners)	10
Uncommon situation (annual event)	15
Rare situation (once in a lifetime event)	20
You are very familiar with local customs	−5
You were raised to follow the local customs	−10
You are somewhat familiar with local customs	+0
You are unfamiliar with local customs	+5

If the check succeeds, you know what to do in a given cultural situation.

If the check fails, you don't know what to do in the situation at hand. If the check fails by 5 or more, you remember an incorrect response for the situation instead.

Retry: No. Once you've had time to think about a given situation, you either know the correct response or you don't. Should the same question come up at a later date (assuming opportunity for additional study on the subject) then another check may be appropriate (at Game Control's discretion).

Special: If you have 8 or more ranks in Cultures you gain a +2 bonus with most disposition checks *(see page 269)*.

Critical Success: Your response to the situation is not only correct, it shows a great understanding of the culture and impresses members of the culture who witness it.

Critical Failure: Your response to the situation is not only incorrect, it is insultingly so. Any member of the culture who witnesses it is deeply offended.

DEMOLITIONS (INT; TRAINED ONLY)

Demolitions can be used to create, set and disarm explosives, and covers all the various types of explosives used by spies, police, and the military.

Check (Varies): Using explosives is always risky. The table below provides standard DCs for Demolitions checks.

Task	DC
Set explosive device	10
Disarm standard device	15
Build device from kit	10
Build device from scratch	25
Disarm scratch-built device	See below
Agent is rushed	+2
Improper tools/materials	+2
Good tools/materials	−2

Set Explosive Device (5 minutes–several hours): While setting an explosive device is simple, setting it to cause the most damage requires some training. A failed Demolitions check when setting an explosive allows all targets a +4 bonus to their Reflex saving throws to avoid damage and reduces the amount of structural damage caused by the explosion to 75% (a 25% loss from the explosive's normal damage). It takes no less than 5 minutes to set an explosive but may take up multiple hours, depending on the complexity and purpose of the device.

You may also use this action to create shaped charges from C4. The base damage of a shaped charge is determined by the amount of C4 used to build it (4d6 per ¼-lb. block). For every 5 by which you beat the DC of 10, the damage of the shaped charge is increased by +1d6 per ¼ lb. block used (to a maximum of 10d6 per ¼-lb. block). This damage only affects a 45-degree angle in one direction, and the blast increment *(see page 172)* is only applied to targets within this area of effect. The blast increment of a shaped charge is 15 ft.

Disarm Standard Explosive Device (1 minute per 10 budget points of device's cost): This assumes that the explosive was manufactured as opposed to custom or scratch-built. With manufactured explosives, the construction and color coding of wires is fairly standardized. If you have schematics, you gain a +5 modifier to this skill check. Failing the check means that you cannot figure out the device. Failing by 5 or more results in the device's immediate detonation. Disarming a standard device takes no less than 1 minute but may take considerably longer based on the complexity of the device. Complexity is based on cost, with the device taking one minute of disarming time for every 10 budget points (or fraction thereof) it cost to build.

Example 1: Donovan is disarming a device that cost 50 budget points to build. His skill check takes 5 minutes.

Example 2: Donovan is disarming a device that cost 5 BP to build. His skill check takes 1 minute (the minimum for a disarming skill check for a standard device).

Build Explosive from Kit (5 minutes per 10 budget points of device's cost): Building an explosive from a kit is a simple procedure and the explosives are usually inert until the last few steps. If the skill check fails, the explosive does not function. If the check fails by 5 or more, the explosive detonates during construction. This takes 5 minutes for every 10 budget points (or fraction thereof) the device cost. *For more about demolitions kits, see page 126.*

Build Explosive Device from Scratch (30 minutes per damage die): Constructing a scratch-built explosive is very dangerous, and therefore rarely undertaken by people with a strong will to live. However, such devices are also the most difficult to disarm. If the skill check fails, the explosive does not function and all materials are wasted. If the check fails by 5 or more, the explosive detonates during construction. For every 1d6 of damage done by the explosive, materials cost 4 budget points or $200 and the time required to build the device is 30 minutes.

Example: A device that with a damage value of 8d6 costs 32 budget points and requires 4 hours to build.

Disarm Scratch-Built Explosive Device (2 minutes per 10 budget points of device's cost): Of all the high-risk tasks that a demolitions expert can undertake, disarming a scratch-built explosive is always the most dangerous. This skill check is opposed — compare the result of the disarming agent's Demolitions check against the result of the explosive builder's Demolitions check to construct the device. If the Demolitions check of the disarming agent exceeds the builder's check, the device is disarmed; otherwise it detonates in one minute (just enough time for the agents to toss it out a window and run like the wind).

Retry: No.

Special: If you have 5 or more ranks in Computers you gain a +2 synergy bonus with Demolitions checks that involve a device with computerized components. If you have 5 or more ranks in Electronics you gain a +2 synergy bonus with Demolitions checks that involve a device with electronic components. If you have 5 or more ranks in Mechanics you gain a +2 synergy bonus with Demolitions checks that involve a device with mechanical components.

Critical Success: If setting or building an explosive device, the device is set or built in half the normal time (rounded up). If disarming a device, the device is disarmed in half the normal time (rounded up), or 1 second before it detonates — whichever comes first.

Critical Failure: The device detonates immediately.

DIPLOMACY (CHA)

You are capable of negotiating calmly with educated opponents, persuading warring factions to consider a treaty, or talking the price down on international passage at a contested border. This skill involves tact, persuasion, influence, social grace and subtlety. You know what to say, how to say it, and when and where it needs to be said.

Check (varies): When using Diplomacy to haggle with someone, you each make a skill check. For every 5 points by which you beat your opponent, the sale price of an item can be adjusted upward or downward by 5% of the market price (your choice). If you lose the check, your opponent may alter the price in the same way.

Check (varies): When used to argue with one or more other characters before an unbiased party, all arguing participants make Diplomacy checks. The character with the highest Diplomacy total is successful in persuading the unbiased party to see his position over that of the others.

Retry: No. Once an agent makes up his mind, continuing to harass him with an alternate point of view doesn't do any good.

Special: If you have 5 or more ranks in Bluff or Sense Motive, you gain a cumulative +2 synergy bonus with all Diplomacy checks. Also, a Cultures Rank of 5 or higher gives you a +2 synergy bonus with Diplomacy checks.

Use of the Diplomacy skill can be affected by the disposition system — *see page 269.*

Critical Success: If haggling, you can alter the price upward or downward by 50% in addition to the amount determined by success (to a minimum of 10% of the market price if haggling down, or a maximum of 190% of the market price if haggling up). If trying to convince someone of your position, your opponent is completely converted to your viewpoint.

Critical Failure: If haggling, your opponent can alter the price upward or downward by 50% (to a minimum of 10% of the market price if you were haggling up, or a maximum of 90% of the market price if you were haggling down). If trying to convince someone of your position, you make a fool out of yourself and lose the argument.

Disguise (Cha)

You can use Disguise to change a person's appearance, adjusting features, adding or covering distinguishing marks, altering basic body shape, and the like.

Check (Varies): Disguise may be used on others or yourself with no penalty.

Creating a disguise requires a disguise kit for 1d6+10 minutes, as well as any necessary props. Complicated disguises may take up to 3d6+10 minutes to create, at the GC's discretion.

There is no DC for a Disguise check – the result of the check becomes the DC when another character makes a Spot check to see through the Disguise. When you make or adopt a disguise, the GC makes a secret Disguise check for you, applying the following modifiers to his roll.

Disguise	Spot Check Modifier
Minor details (close resemblance)	–5
Different height (+/– up to 5%)*	+2
Different weight (+/– up to 5%)*	+2
Different sex	+4
Different skin color	+4
Different class	+2
Different age	+2†

* or as allowed by your GC.
† per age category *(see page 102)*

In general, if you don't do anything to draw attention to yourself while disguised, then others are not allowed to make Spot checks to see through your disguise. People who are paid to observe, but who are not particularly watchful (including most paid guards) make Spot checks with a –5 modifier. Suspicious characters and those who are on the look-out for someone in disguise make Spot checks without a modifier.

When impersonating a specific character, anyone familiar with the character impersonated receives the following modifiers to their Spot check:

Familiarity	Bonus
Recognize by sight	+4
Friend or associate	+6
Close friend	+8
Intimate friend or family member	+10

When allowed, the Spot check is made immediately and once each hour thereafter while the disguised agent is in the presence of the person making the test. If the disguised character is in the presence of many people making a Spot check, the GC may assume a skill bonus of +1 for the entire group (or more if the group is particularly observant) and make a single roll for all of them.

Retry: Yes, though any Disguise check result replaces all previous results, even if lower than the previous result.

Special: If the disguised character has 5 or more ranks in Bluff, the DC of Spot checks to see through the disguise is increased by +2.

Critical Success: The disguise is perfect. Only a critical success with a Spot check can see through it.

Critical Failure: The disguise looks perfect, but something goes wrong with it at a critical moment (latex skin comes loose, padding slips into the wrong places, etc.).

Driver (Dex)

Driver is used to steer ground vehicles, from cars to motorcycles to tanks. Riding animals uses the Handle Animal skill *(see page 54 for more)*.

Check (Half Action): No skill checks are required to perform standard driving moves, but complex driving tasks, such as during combat or other threatening circumstances, require a roll. *See also Chases, page 183.*

Task	DC
Shallow turn/avoid obstacle	5
Average maneuver/multiple turns	10
Tight turn/drive over uneven surface	15
High stress maneuver/make jump	20
Heroic or complex set of maneuvers	25+
Unfamiliar type of vehicle	+5

Vehicles are rated for handling (see page 184). This rating may help or hinder the vehicle's driver.

Retry: Yes, but there is a lapse of time between the tries. If you absolutely have to turn immediately to avoid an oncoming semi, but fail the check, a second attempt is usually impossible (per the GC's discretion coupled with current circumstances).

Special: This skill covers the physical act of driving; knowledge of driving and making money with it as a sport are covered by the knowledge and sport skills, respectively. If you have 5 or more ranks in Driver, you get a +2 synergy bonus to any Knowledge or Mechanics checks concerning cars, as well as a +2 synergy bonus to any Sport checks to professionally compete with them. If you have 5 or more ranks in Knowledge with an area or city, you receive a +2 synergy bonus to Driver checks made therein. If you have 5 or more ranks in Balance, you receive a +2 synergy bonus to skill checks when riding a personal (balance-based) vehicle, such as a motorcycle (see page 147).

Critical Success: When not in a chase, you manage to avoid mishap even when it is seemingly impossible to do so. Your vehicle is not only unscathed by whatever pitfall you avoided, but you sail past it without a single chip in your paint. During a chase, your maneuver is successful unless an opposing driver scores a critical success with a higher total. Also, you receive a +4 bonus to your next maneuver or crash check.

Critical Failure: The vehicle hits an obstacle, skids out of control, or stalls. The GC may rule that this is equivalent to failing a crash check (see page 193).

ELECTRONICS (INT; TRAINED ONLY)

Electronics is used to repair electronic devices or disarm traps that primarily use electronic components, such as electronic eyes. (The Hide skill is used to avoid/bypass electronic surveillance devices without disabling them.) No skill is required to operate simple electronic devices or devices the user is familiar with.

Check (Varies): Mundane, everyday tasks do not require an Electronics check, but attempting mundane tasks with a time limit or performing more complex or invasive tasks does.

Task	DC
Operate unfamiliar electronic device	15+
Disarm or bypass electronic device	20+

Operate Unfamiliar Electronic Device (Full Action): A successful check allows you to operate the device in question. The DC for your check depends on the complexity of the device, and is set by the GC. After you've figured out how to operate a device once, you needn't do so again.

Disarm/Disable Electronic Device: Your Game Control should make this skill check in secret, so you don't know the magnitude of your success or failure. The time required for the check depends upon the device.

Device	Time	DC
Simple (pressure pad, crude electric eye)	1 round	10
Tricky (door keypad, video camera)	1d4 rounds	15
Difficult (motion sensor, heat sensor)	2d4 rounds	20
Obnoxious (retina scan, voiceprint analyzer)	3d4 rounds	25-40
Leave no sign of work	—	+5
Delayed breakdown* (1d4 minute delay)	—	+5
Unfamiliar device	—	+5

* The device is sabotaged and left to break down at a later time determined by the agent.

If the check succeeds, the sabotage is successful and the device ceases to operate or malfunctions in the manner desired.

If the check fails, you have failed to disable the device. If you fail by 5 or more, the device goes off, an alarm is tripped, or you think that you've sabotaged the device, but it continues working normally.

Repair Electronic Device (Varies): You can repair a damaged electronic device. Such a task can take a few rounds, an hour or two, or even days to complete, depending on the magnitude of the repair, availability of parts and proper equipment, and the situation (e.g. whether you're conducting the repairs during your spare time or in the middle of a raging firefight). The Game Control is the final arbiter of how long an attempted repair takes.

Task	DC
Replace part	10
Simple repair	15
Troubleshoot and/or complex repair	20
Major repairs involving multiple parts	25+
Quick/temporary fix*	−5
High stress situation	+5
Unfamiliar parts/device	+5
Tools and/or parts unavailable	+15

* 10% chance of failure (non-cumulative) each time the equipment is used.

Retry: If operating an unfamiliar device, yes. If repairing a device, yes, but you must begin the task again. Parts are not consumed by a repair attempt. The check can be made again after the required repair time has elapsed.

If bypassing or disarming a device, yes, but only if you know that your previous attempt was a failure.

Special: If the specific schematics of the device are available, you gain a +5 bonus to your skill check.

Critical Success: You instantly figure out how to use the device, or your repairs are very stable (there is no chance of failure if it was a temporary fix). If you are bypassing or disarming a device, the device is bypassed or disarmed in half the normal time (rounded up), or 1 second before it triggers — whichever comes first.

Critical Failure: You are unable to figure out how to use the device, or your repairs are shoddy and utterly destroy the equipment the next time it's used. If you are bypassing or disarming a device, it immediately goes off, or you believe your sabotage to be successful, when in fact the device continues to work perfectly (at the GC's discretion).

ESCAPE ARTIST (DEX; ARMOR CHECK PENALTY)

You may use Escape Artist to slide your limbs out of manacles, slip out of an enemy's grapple hold, or squeeze through a small window.

Check (Varies): Under most circumstances, an Escape Artist check is not opposed—most restraints have an associated DC. Breaking free of a grapple or the bonds of a rope, though, requires an opposed check: in the first instance against the binder's grapple check, and in the second, against the binder's Use Rope check + 10 (it's easier to tie someone up than it is to escape).

Restraint	Time	DC
Ropes	1+ minutes	Binder's Use Rope check +10
Net	Full action	20
Handcuffs	1+ minutes	30
Manacles	1+ minutes	35
Tight space	1+ minutes	30
Grappler	Half action	Binder's grapple check

Escaping from a net requires a full round (two rounds for a hook-lined net). Slipping out of manacles or rope requires at least one minute. Sliding through a tight space requires at least one minute but may take considerably longer if the agent has to move along the space for any distance.

Retry: Yes, additional tests are allowed, but your GC may place a limit on how often an attempt can be made. This is especially important if you are involved in an ongoing activity, such as getting out of multiple bonds or slipping through a tight space, particularly if (for instance) the air supply is dwindling. If the situation permits, however (i.e. you aren't being opposed), you can take 20.

Special: If you are being observed while bound, or are trying to escape bonds without being noticed, your Escape Artist check is opposed by the observer's Spot skill as well. Compare the same skill roll you make to escape your bonds to your observer's Spot skill check. The results depend on which checks you succeed with, if any.

If you win both checks, the observers don't notice your attempt until you're free. If you lose both checks, you remain bound and your observers know you are trying to escape — they can then make another Use Rope check to tighten your bonds. Success adds +2 to their Use Rope total, while a critical success adds +5. Failure has no effect on their Use Rope total. If you win the check to free yourself but lose the check to avoid being spotted, your observers are aware of your escape and may intervene using the standard combat rules.

If you lose the check to escape your bonds but win the check to avoid being spotted, nothing happens and you may retry your escape attempt in the normal time.

Critical Success: You escape your bonds in half the normal time. If you are in a tight space, you don't need to make any further Escape Artist checks to escape. If attempting to escape under scrutiny, you receive one surprise round to act before your observers may do anything.

Critical Failure: You are trapped. You cannot make any further Escape Artist checks to escape — someone else must free you.

FIRST AID (WIS)

First Aid allows you to administer emergency aid to someone who has been poisoned or suffered damage that reduced him below 0 wounds. In addition, you can care for someone suffering from long-term wounds or diseases.

Check (Half Action): You may attempt to render aid to a person who has been injured or poisoned by making a First Aid check. If trying to stabilize a dying person, a successful check results in the person being restored to 0 wound points. If treating poison, a successful First Aid check means that the victim suffers no additional effects from the poison this round. You can make a check every round you're administering aid to the injured party, but only for up to 10 rounds. Beyond that, the poison victim must either ride out the remaining effects of the poison, or be given an antidote.

Task	DC
Stabilize dying person	15
Treat poison	Poison's DC

Check (1 Day): You may attempt to provide long-term care to an injured or diseased person. If caring for

an injured person, a successful check means that their natural healing is doubled for the day. If treating a disease, a successful check means that the disease's progress is halted for one day, but only for up to 10 days. Beyond that, the victim must either ride out the effects of the disease, or be treated in a hospital.

Task	DC
Long-term care	15
Treat disease	Disease's DC

Retry: If you fail a check, you may try again the following round, keeping track of the total First Aid allowed (10 rounds or days only for a particular injury, poison, or disease).

Special: If you have 5 or more ranks in Profession (Doctor), you receive a +2 synergy bonus to First Aid checks.

Critical Success: If stabilizing a dying person, they are restored to 1 wound point rather than 0. If treating a poison victim, the poison is completely neutralized. If providing long-term care to a person, their healing rate is tripled for the day. Finally, if treating a disease, the victim gets to make a saving throw against the disease's DC. If successful, the disease goes into remission and is cured in the following weeks.

Critical Failure: If stabilizing a dying person, the person goes into shock and immediately dies. If providing long-term care, the patient receives no natural healing for the day. Finally, if treating a poison or disease, you cannot make any further First Aid checks to control it.

FORGERY (INT)

You may use Forgery to write a document in someone else's handwriting or create counterfeit documents. If successful, the forged document can pass an inspection, causing the reader to think that it is genuine. This skill is also useful for detecting forgeries.

Check (Varies): Use of this skill requires access to writing implements, materials, or printing devices appropriate to the document or object being forged. If a specific person's handwriting is being forged, a sample of that handwriting is required – the longer the forged document, the longer the sample needs to be.

Forgery requires at least 10 minutes, but may require days, depending on the complexity of the item/document being forged and the availability of any required materials. There should be a cost for uncommon materials. Both of these variables are determined by your GC.

The Forgery check is made secretly by the GC.

Forging	Modifier
Document handwriting not specific to a person	+8
Only forging a signature (and a sample is available)	+4
Document/object well-known	+5
Document/object unfamiliar	–5
Document designed to resist forgery (holograms, watermarks)	–8
Sample handwriting not available	N/A *

* Not applicable: this task is impossible.

When the forged document is submitted for inspection, the reader is allowed to make a Forgery check opposed by the document's original Forgery check when created. The following modifiers apply to the check:

Modifier Conditions	Modifier
Document type unknown to reader	–2
Document type somewhat known	+0
Document type well-known to reader	+2
Casual inspection	–2
Intensive inspection	+2
Document/object put through validation test	+5*

* Depending upon the type of test, the GC may decide that the forgery is automatically discovered.

Retry: If the initial Forgery check fails, but the item/document is discovered before being shown to anyone else, the forgery can be destroyed and the process tried again. This requires that someone able to expose the document as a forgery inspect it and tell the forger what's wrong with it.

Special: If the forger has Computer at rank 5 or above, he gains a +2 synergy bonus to Forgery checks made for objects that must carry data. Also, the forger receives a +2 synergy bonus if he has other related skills at rank 5 or higher (such as if the object to be forged is a surveillance photo and the forger has Surveillance at rank 5 or higher). Finally, to create documents and detect forgeries, the forger must be able to read and write the language in question.

Critical Success: The forgery is perfect. It can only be detected with a critical success.

Critical Failure: The forgery appears to be perfect, and passes any test the forger puts it through, but is automatically noticed when presented for inspection in a crucial situation (the ink runs, the glue fails, etc.).

GATHER INFORMATION (CHA)

You are able to foster important contacts, solicit rumors, spread misinformation and pick valuable information out of seemingly trivial conversation.

Check (4 hours): By coaxing conversation, buying drinks, seeking knowledgeable sources, listening to rumors, etc., you may make a Gather Information check to answer important questions.

Type of Information	DC
Generic information ("See anything unusual lately?")	10
Fairly specific ("Have you seen this man?")	15
Very specific ("What name was he using?")	20
Dangerous ("Where can I find Tony the Shark?")	30

Retry: Yes, but it takes at least another 4 hours of coaxing to make another skill check.

Special: When searching for information on a computer system, you use your Computer skill, but gain a+2 synergy bonus if you have 5 or more ranks in Gather Information. Also, a Cultures Rank of 5 or higher gives you a +2 synergy bonus with appropriate Gather Information checks.

Use of the Gather Information skill can be affected by the disposition system – *see page 269.*

Critical Success: You not only find the answer to your question, you also receive any related information.

Critical Failure: You receive faulty information, or the person you're asking about gets wind of your intention.

HANDLE ANIMAL (CHA; TRAINED ONLY)

This skill is used to train and ride animals. You might use it to teach a guard dog to attack on command, or to break in a horse for riding or train one for a race.

Check (Half Action): You don't need to make a Handle Animal check when riding normally and your mount is calm. However, when attempting to maintain control of a beast that is scared or edgy, or trying to convince the mount to go beyond its comfort zone (like jumping a ravine), a test is required. Most checks to ride an animal have a DC of 15, with the following modifiers:

Situation	Modifier
Pass near flames	+2
Pass through flames	+5
Mount has no saddle	+2
Mount in terror	+5
Mount is injured (or unhealthy)	+5

Check: The time and DC required for other uses of this skill vary depending on what you want to accomplish:

Task	Time	DC
Handle domestic animal	Varies	10
'Push' domestic animal	Varies	15
Teach animal tasks	2 months	15
Teach animal unusual tasks	2 months	20
Domesticate wild animal	1 year	15 + vitality dice

When training or raising an animal, your skill check is made halfway through the task's completion. That way, if you fail the check, you haven't wasted the entire time. Each animal you're working with requires 3 hours of your time every day. You can only train and/or raise up to 3 animals at a time.

Handle a Domestic Animal: You can command a trained animal, drive beasts of labor, and tend to tired animals.

'Push' a Domestic Animal: You can urge extra effort out of a trained animal, such as riding a horse past its normal endurance, or working with a frustrated bomb sniffing dog.

Teach an Animal Tasks: You can teach a domestic animal to perform a specific job, such as guarding, attacking, carrying someone, hunting and tracking, etc. An animal can only be trained for one general purpose.

Teach an Animal Unusual Tasks: You can teach an animal to do things unusual for its breed, such as convincing a horse to sit. You can also teach it specialized or complex jobs, such as a horse coming when it's whistled for, opening an unlocked door (and simply breaking it down if it's closed), or counting with its hoof.

Domesticate a Wild Animal: You can raise a wild animal from infancy, making it domestic. Once you've domesticated an animal, you can train it. Some animals – notably large carnivores – always remain unpredictable, even after being domesticated.

Retry: When riding an animal, yes, but there is a lapse of time between the tries. If you absolutely have to turn immediately to avoid oncoming traffic or an unstable bridge, but fail the check, a second attempt is usually impossible (per the GC's discretion based on current conditions). For handling or pushing domestic animals, yes. For raising or training an animal, no.

Special: Knowledge of riding and making money with it as a sport are covered by the Knowledge and Sport skills, respectively. If you have 5 or more ranks in Handle Animal, you receive a +2 synergy bonus to any Knowledge or First Aid checks concerning animals, as well as a +2 synergy bonus to any Sport checks to professionally compete with them.

Also, you may make untrained checks to handle and push animals.

Critical Success: When not in a chase, you manage to avoid mishap even when it is seemingly impossible to do so. Your vehicle is not only unscathed by whatever pitfall you avoided, but you sail past it without disturbing your mount's winning appearance. During a chase, your maneuver is successful unless an opposing rider scores a critical success with a higher total. Also, you receive a +4 bonus to your next maneuver or crash check. If training an animal, the task takes half the time it normally would and/or the animal learns its tasks especially well. The animal might also form a strong bond of friendship with you. If handling or pushing an animal, you get very good results from the animal.

Critical Failure: If riding an animal, you fall off and the animal bolts. The GC may apply falling damage, as appropriate *(see page 236)*. If training or raising an animal, it is ruined for future training, and develops a strong dislike for you. You can never use the Handle Animal skill on the animal again, and all Handle Animal checks made by other trainers receive a –5 penalty with the animal. If handling or pushing an animal, it panics, and you must bring it back under control (with a Handle Animal check, DC 20 + all applicable modifiers) to do anything with it.

HIDE (DEX; ARMOR CHECK PENALTY)

When unobserved for a few seconds, you are able to use the Hide skill in order to slip away into the shadows. You can then move unseen while there are shadows to hide within or objects to hide behind.

Check (Half Action): You can attempt to hide yourself from sight, even from visual security systems (such as cameras - laser senses are not fooled by use of the Hide skill). Make a Hide check opposed by the Spot check of anyone who might notice you. While hiding, you can move up to half speed with no penalty. When moving more than half speed, up to normal speed, there is a –5 penalty to your Hide check. Hiding is extremely difficult when moving faster than normal speed, so you suffer a –20 penalty.

The skill check is modified by your size.

Size	Modifier
Fine	+16
Diminutive	+12
Tiny	+8
Small	+4
Medium	+0
Large	–4
Huge	–8
Gargantuan	–12
Colossal	–16

You may not attempt to hide while being observed, even casually (such as when you are in a conversation with several people at an embassy party). If observers are distracted for a moment, however, (perhaps by using the Bluff skill to create a diversion) you may attempt to find a place to hide in the interval (your Game Control may opt to assign a penalty of up to –10, based on the length of the interval).

Check (Full Action—10 minutes): You can attempt to shadow someone (i.e. follow them without them realizing what you are doing), hiding in shadows and slipping from alley to alley. (If there is a crowd to blend into, you may use the Bluff skill to shadow someone — *see page 41.)*

Make a Hide skill check opposed by the target's Spot skill. Success indicates that your target has not noticed what you are doing. The GC may make this roll in secret so that you don't know whether the target has made you (i.e. spotted you) or not. This roll must be made again each ten minutes you are shadowing someone.

Retry: No. The target has already seen you or knows that you're following him.

Special: A Surveillance Rank of 5 or higher gives you a +2 synergy bonus with Hide checks when attempting to bypass video security equipment. Also, a Tumble Rank of 5 or higher gives you a +2 synergy bonus with Hide checks when attempting to bypass fixed security sensors (such as electric eyes). Finally, if you understand the specific schematics of a security system or the timetable of guards' movements, you gain a +5 bonus to the Hide check when trying to evade them.

This skill merely masks the agent from sight — remaining quiet requires the Move Silently skill. The Hide and Move Silently skills are mutually exclusive and grant no synergy bonuses to each other. Optionally, the GC may allow you to make a single roll for both using a skill bonus equal to the average of the two skill ranks, rounded down. You must have at least one rank in each skill to use this option.

Critical Success: You find a perfect hiding place. Attempts to Spot you automatically fail until you leave it. If shadowing someone, you don't need to make another check for half an hour.

Critical Failure: Everyone within line of sight automatically sees you trying to hide. If shadowing someone, you are immediately spotted but believe that you have not been. For the duration of the scene, any further Bluff, Sense Motive, or Spot checks made on you by your target receive a +2 bonus.

HOBBY (WIS)

You are skilled at a particular hobby, such as clubbing, creative writing, gambling, gaming, gardening, Internet surfing, jogging, puzzle solving, reading, shopping, socializing, tinkering, traveling, or working on cars.

You can take this skill multiple times, each time applying it to a separate Hobby. For example, you could have Hobby (Reading) at rank 4 and Hobby (Gaming) at rank 3. Your ranks in one Hobby don't affect your skill checks in another.

A Hobby is unlike a Craft (see page 47), a Profession (see page 61), or Sport (see page 64), in that you do it just for fun. Although a few rare individuals make money at their hobbies, this is the exception rather than the rule.

Check: You have a great deal of knowledge about your hobby and the tools that are needed to practice it. In addition, you are capable of performing your hobby. Your Game Control sets DCs for specific tasks.

Retry: Specific tasks can usually be retried, unless failure results in injury or the destruction of your tools.

Special: If you have 5 or more ranks in a Hobby, you get a +2 synergy bonus to any Knowledge checks that have anything to do with that Hobby.

Critical Success: You perform your Hobby particularly skillfully, create something remarkable, or have the time of your life.

Critical Failure: You perform your Hobby poorly, possibly resulting in an injury if it is a physical hobby or destroying materials if they are used.

INNUENDO (WIS)

Using a combination of body language, hand signals, and your own personal code, you can communicate and understand secret messages while appearing to talk about something entirely different. Alternately, you can intercept and understand such messages if you hear them.

Check (1 minute): You may communicate or intercept a secret message while disguising the conversation as something else. You can only use Innuendo to communicate a message to another person with this skill. Your Game Control makes this check in secret for you.

Task	DC
Communicate a simple message ("Meet me at midnight.")	10
Communicate a harder message ("Meet me at the safe house on Bramble Avenue tomorrow night at six.")	15
Communicate a complex message ("Meet me at 453 West Oak Drive next Tuesday at 10:45 PM. I'll be disguised as a priest.")	20
Intercept and understand a message you just overheard.	*

* Message's Innuendo check

Check (10 minutes): You can attempt to seduce someone. For more about this use of the Innuendo skill, see the disposition system on *page 269*.

Retry: You may retry when communicating, but not when receiving or intercepting.

Special: If you have 5 or more ranks in Bluff, you receive a +2 synergy bonus to communicate messages. If you have 5 or more ranks in Sense Motive, you receive a +2 synergy bonus to receive or intercept messages.

Critical Success: You automatically communicate, receive, or intercept the message. If communicating a message, it was so cleverly disguised that it can only be intercepted on a critical success.

Critical Failure: You communicate, receive, or intercept the message completely incorrectly. For instance, you might mistake a description of your next contact for a description of a dangerous enemy agent.

INTIMIDATE (VARIOUS)

Using Intimidate, you can cause an aggressor to back down or a stubborn bartender to provide information. It is the skill to inspire fear and insecurity in someone, and draws upon several different abilities, depending on the sort of intimidation being used. If you are a thickly muscled brute, or you're using harsh physical threats and growls, you apply your Strength modifier. If you're a clever agent, or casually discussing what your squad may be forced to do to the target of your intimidation, you'd use your Charisma modifier.

Check (Full Action): You can encourage someone to be much more cooperative with you in one of many ways (determined by the Game Control). The target of the intimidation may provide information, perform a demanded action, or perhaps just stop yelling, if that's the goal for the check. The DC for an Intimidate check is 10 plus the target's level. If the target has any bonuses against fear, increase the DC for the intimidating agent by the bonus.

Retry: Not usually. If the check fails, the agent is not impressed by the intimidation. Retrying after a success is also folly, as intimidation usually garners the best result possible with a single success, and targets are rarely willing to do anything that would get them killed or go against their nature through intimidation.

Special: If you have 5 or more ranks in Bluff, you gain a +2 synergy bonus on Intimidate checks.

Use of the Intimidate skill can be affected by the disposition system – *see page 269*.

Critical Success: You completely cow your target and plant a permanent kernel of fear in his heart where you are concerned. Just the thought of you makes him nervous. The DCs for your Intimidate checks against him are dropped by 5 in the future (to a minimum of 5).

Critical Failure: You not only fail to intimidate your target, you make him angry and uncooperative. The DCs for your Intimidate checks against him are raised by 5 in the future. There is no maximum that your DC to Intimidate someone can be raised to.

JUMP (STR; ARMOR CHECK PENALTY)

Jump allows you to attempt horizontal or vertical leaps with confidence. Jumps can be made from a standing or running start.

Check (Half Action): You jump a minimum distance plus an additional distance depending on the magnitude of the Jump check's success. If jumping between two moving vehicles, apply a penalty of –4 to the check. The maximum distance an agent can jump is related to his height.

Type of Jump	Min. Distance	Leap Interval	Max. Distance
Running*	5 ft.	1 point	Height × 6
Standing	3 ft.	2 points	Height × 2
Running high*	2 ft.	4 points	Height × 1.5
Standing high	2 ft.	8 points	Height
Jump back	1 ft.	8 points	Height

* You must move 20 ft. before a running jump. An agent can't take a running jump in heavy armor.

The DC for a jump is always 10. When an agent succeeds with a Jump check, he divides the difference between his Jump total and the DC by the leap interval shown on the table for the type of jump he is performing (rounding down). The result is added to the minimum jump distance listed above to determine the actual distance jumped. If this number is above the maximum jump distance listed above, the agent jumps the maximum distance.

Example: Donovan is leaping from a balcony to grab hold of a helicopter's landing strut (a 20-foot jump). He has a running start of 25 ft., enough to qualify for the running jump option, and therefore covers a base distance of 5 ft. with a leap interval of 1 point. He scores a Jump check total of 27, which translates to an additional 17 ft. (17 over his DC / a leap interval of 1 = 17). Added to his base distance of 5 ft., we find that Donovan has jumped 22 ft., just enough to reach the helicopter's strut as guards burst from the building and open fire...

The distances listed on the table above are for agents with a speed of 30 ft. per round. If feats, abilities, or other conditions cause you to move faster or slower than that, your jumping distances should be modified proportionally (always rounding down).

Example: Donovan later gains the Increased Speed feat, which increases his base Speed to 40 ft. per round. He makes a running jump that clears a total distance of 10 ft. As his speed is one-third higher than average now, he adds one-third to the Jump result, or 3 feet (10/3, rounded down). His total Jump result, factoring in his 40-foot Speed, is 13 feet.

Distance jumped is counted against your movement for the round. For instance, In the first example above, Donovan moved 22 ft. If he were in a position to move after grabbing hold of the helicopter's landing gear, he could still move 8 additional feet as part of the same movement action. In the second example above, Donovan leapt 13 feet of his increased standard movement of 40 feet. He can still move 27 feet as part of the same movement action.

Retry: You are allowed one check each time you attempt a jump.

Special: If you have 5 or more ranks in Tumble, you gain a +2 synergy bonus with Jump checks.

Leaping to safety (e.g. out of a vehicle that is about to crash or away from an explosion) is a function of the Reflex saving throw. *See page 159 for more.*

Critical Success: You jump your maximum distance.

Critical Failure: You fall into any gap you were attempting to jump across. This may inflict damage, per the conditions of the Jump and the GC's discretion.

KNOWLEDGE (INT; TRAINED ONLY)

Like the Craft skill, the Knowledge skill includes many possible areas of expertise. When taking a Knowledge skill, you must select a specific area of study to which the skill relates. In order to have knowledge in more areas, you must take the skill multiple times, once for each area of knowledge. Ranks in one area of knowledge apply to that knowledge only. Some possible Knowledge options include conspiracy theory, criminal behavior, forensics, munitions (your GC may require you to further specify this Knowledge skill, perhaps by nation of origin), occult science, political science, vehicles, and a wide variety of professions (law, military, politics, etc.) and sports (baseball, football, rugby, stock car racing, statistics, etc.).

Check (Half Action): Difficulties for Knowledge checks depend on the complexity of the information desired.

Question Type	DC
Simple (What's the melting point of ice?)	10*
Basic (What nation does this gun come from?)	15*
Involved (How do you make nitroglycerin?)	20
Complex (What's that rare type of clay on the minion's boots?)	25

* These types of questions are free actions to remember and must not be rolled for again after success.

Retry: No. Once you've had time to think a complex question over, you either know the answer or you don't. Should the same question come up at a later date (assuming opportunity for additional study on the subject) then another check may be appropriate (at your Game Control's discretion).

Special: Untrained checks may be made if the question is fairly common knowledge (DC 15 or less).

Specialized questions, and questions about the intelligence community, spy organizations, and the like, may require an Education roll *(see page 219),* per the GC's discretion. Each Knowledge skill you have which is peripheral to such a question grants you a +2 synergy bonus to the Education check.

Critical Success: You know the information as well as any closely related knowledge.

Critical Failure: You remember incorrect information.

LANGUAGES (WIS)

You have wide experience with many languages.

Check: You know one foreign language of your choice for every rank you have in this skill. You gain an additional language when you gain a rank in this skill. Some possible languages include Afrikaans, American Sign Language (ASL), Apache, Arabic (Egyptian), Arabic (Modern), Armenian, Assyrian, Azerbaijani, Bantu, Bosnian, Cherokee, Cheyenne, Chinese, Croatian, Czech, Danish, Dutch, Farsi, Finnish, French, Georgian, German, Greek (Ancient), Greek (Modern), Haitian, Hebrew, Hungarian, Icelandic, Indonesian, Italian, Japanese, Khmer, Kiwi, Korean, Latin, Latvian, Lithuanian, Malay, Navajo, Norwegian, Polish, Portuguese, Romanian, Russian, Sanskrit, Serbian, Slovak, Slovenian, Spanish, Swahili, Swedish, Tagalog, Thai, Turkish, Ukrainian, and Vietnamese.

All agents know how to speak, read, and write English as a native language unless they arrange with the GC to trade it for another language.

Check (Free Action): Whenever you come across a foreign language that you don't already know and haven't encountered in the course of play before, make a Languages check to see if you know it.

Language Type	DC
Common (English, Spanish, etc.)	15
Uncommon (Croatian, Swahili, etc.)	20
Rare (Bantu, Navajo, etc.)	25
Ancient/Specialized (Ancient Greek, etc.)	30

If the check succeeds, write the language down on your agent sheet. You know how to speak, read, and write it. The language is not new to you — it is simply assumed that you learned it over the course of your education or career as a superspy. It just hasn't come up in the course of the game before now.

If the check fails, you are unfamiliar with the language. The only way you can learn it is by selecting it when you gain a rank in this skill *(see above).*

Normally, when you speak a foreign language, you speak it with an identifiable accent. You can rid yourself of your accent with a foreign language by selecting it a second time instead of gaining a new foreign language when you gain a rank in this skill.

Special: You automatically know one or more languages at agent creation, according to your department. These are your native languages — you don't have an accent when speaking them. Once again, all agents start with English as a native language unless they arrange otherwise with the GC.

Critical Success: Not only do you know the language, but you can speak it without an accent.

Critical Failure: You are completely unfamiliar with the language. In fact, you must select it twice when gaining new languages just to acquire it (with an accent).

LISTEN (WIS)

You may attempt to hear distant gun shots, listen at a door, hear the distant footsteps of approaching enemies, eavesdrop on a conversation, or detect someone sneaking up from behind.

Check (Varies): You make a Listen check against the appropriate DC, or an opposed check against an opponent's Move Silently check. The GC may make the check in secret, so that the results are not known to you. (Not hearing anything after rolling a success would be a clue that there is nothing there.) A Listen check can either require a round ("I'm listening at the door"), or be a reaction (GC to player after a secret roll: "You hear movement behind you").

Sound	DC
People talking normally	0
Person walking in medium armor, trying not to make noise	5
Distant gun shots	5
Unarmored person walking, trying not to make noise	10
People whispering	10
For each 10 ft. between listener and noise	+1
Through a door	+5
Through a normal wall	+15
Through a blast door or reinforced wall	Not possible

Retry: Yes.

Critical Success: You know exactly what you've heard.

Critical Failure: You mishear something, possibly with comical or disastrous effects.

MECHANICS (INT; TRAINED ONLY)

Mechanics is used to repair mechanical devices or to disarm traps that use primarily mechanical components (e.g. a scything blade). No skill is required to operate simple mechanical devices or devices the user is familiar with.

Check (Varies): No skill checks are required for everyday mechanical tasks, but operating unfamiliar devices and working within a rigid time frame or under difficult circumstances (such as combat) requires a roll.

Task	DC
Operate unfamiliar mechanical device	15+
Disarm or bypass mechanical device	20+

Operate Unfamiliar Mechanical Device (Full Action): A successful check allows you to operate the device. The DC for your check depends on the device's complexity, and is set by your Game Control. Once you've figured out how to operate a device once, you don't need to do so again.

Disarm/Bypass Mechanical Device: Your GC should make this skill check in secret, so you don't know the magnitude of your success or failure. The time required for the check depends upon the device.

Device	Time	DC
Simple (mechanical switch)	1 round	10
Tricky (gear-driven device)	1d4 rounds	15
Difficult (clockwork device)	2d4 rounds	20
Obnoxious (engine, automaton)	3d4 rounds	25-40
Leave no sign of work	—	+5
Delayed breakdown * (1d4 minute delay)	—	+5
Unfamiliar device	—	+5

* The device is sabotaged and left to break down at a later time determined by the agent.

If the check succeeds, the sabotage is successful and the device ceases to operate or malfunctions in the manner you desired.

If the check fails, you have failed to disable the device. If you fail by 5 or more, the device goes off, an alarm is tripped, or you think that you've sabotaged the device, but it continues working normally.

Repair Mechanical Device (Varies): You can repair a damaged mechanical device. Such a task can require a few rounds, an hour or two, or even days to complete, depending on the magnitude of the repair, availability of parts and proper equipment, and the situation (i.e. whether during your spare time or in the middle of a raging firefight).

Task	DC
Replace part	10
Simple repair	15
Troubleshoot and/or complex repair	20
Major repairs involving multiple parts	25+
Quick/temporary fix*	−5
High stress situation	+5
Unfamiliar parts/device	+5
Tools and/or parts unavailable	+15

* 10% chance of failure (non-cumulative) each time the equipment is used.

Retry: If operating an unfamiliar device, yes. If repairing a device, yes, but you must begin the task again. Parts are not consumed by an unsuccessful repair check. The check can be made again after the required repair time has elapsed. If bypassing or disarming a device, yes, but only if you know that your previous attempt was a failure.

Critical Success: You instantly figure out how to use the device, or your repairs are very stable (no chance of failure if it was a temporary fix). If you are bypassing or disarming a device, the device is bypassed or disarmed in half the normal time (rounded up), or 1 second before it triggers — whichever comes first.

Critical Failure: You are unable to figure out how to use the device, or your repairs are shoddy and utterly destroy the equipment the next time it's used. If you are bypassing or disarming a device, it immediately goes off, or you believe your sabotage to be successful when in fact the device continues to work perfectly (at the GC's discretion).

MOVE SILENTLY (DEX; ARMOR CHECK PENALTY)

This perennial spy favorite allows you to move while making nearly no sound.

Check (Half Action): The Move Silently check is opposed by the Listen check of anyone who might hear the agent. While moving silently, the agent can move up to full speed with no penalty. When moving more than full speed, up to twice speed, there is a –5 penalty to the Move Silently check.

Special: A Balance skill of 5 or more ranks grants a +2 synergy bonus to Move Silently checks made when balance is a factor (such as when moving across precarious rafters or catwalks above an enemy). A Climb skill of 5 or more ranks grants a +2 synergy bonus to Move Silently checks made when scaling a wall or slope. A Use Rope skill of 5 or more ranks grants a +2 synergy bonus to Move Silently checks made when rappelling or climbing with proper gear (in this last case, the bonus is cumulative with the +2 from a Climbing skill of 5 or more ranks).

This skill merely masks the sound an agent makes as he moves – staying out of sight requires the Hide skill. The Hide and Move Silently skills are mutually exclusive and grant no synergy bonuses to each other.

Optionally, the GC may allow you to make a single roll for both using a skill bonus equal to the average of the two skill ranks, rounded down. You must have at least one rank in each skill to use this option.

Critical Success: You don't make a sound. There's nothing for anyone to hear.

Critical Failure: You stumble and make a loud noise, alerting everyone in the area to your presence.

OPEN LOCK (DEX; TRAINED ONLY)

Open Lock is used to pick padlocks (with tools), open combination locks (by listening to the tumblers), and perform similar tasks.

To open an electronic lock, use the Electronics skill.

Check (Full Action): You may attempt to open a lock.

Lock Quality	DC
Very simple lock	20
Average lock	25
Good lock	30
Amazing lock	40
Working without a simple tool (pick, pry bar, wire, etc.)	N/A*
Working without a locksmith kit (i.e. using a simple tool)	+2
Using a high-quality locksmith kit	–2

* Not applicable: this task is impossible.

Special: Although this skill cannot be used untrained, you might be able to break a lock open instead *(see Strike an Object, page 168)*.

Critical Success: You pick the lock in half the usual time and leave no signs of forced entry.

Critical Failure: You accidentally jam the lock. It must now be taken apart to be opened (requiring another skill check with a +10 DC modifier), or forced (according to the rules for breaking things — *see page 168).*

PERFORM (CHA)

This skill is used to perform in public. Performance types include acting, dancing, modeling, public speaking, singing, etc. You are capable of one form of performance per rank you have in this skill, and can make money with your talent.

Check (1 day): You may attempt to entertain an audience with your performance.

Roll	Quality of Performance
4 or less	Terrible. Your next performance for this audience suffers a –5 penalty. You earn $1d4 if performing in public.
5-9	Poor. Your next performance for this audience suffers a –2 penalty. You earn $2d4 if performing in public.
10-14	Routine. You earn $2d10 if performing in public.
15-19	Enjoyable. You earn $2d20 if performing in public.
20-24	Great. You earn $3d20 if performing in public. You may be invited to join a professional performing group or develop a reputation over time.
25-29	Memorable. You earn $4d20 if performing in public. You may come to the attention of a talent scout or develop a national reputation over time. Your next performance for this audience gains a +2 bonus.
30+	Extraordinary. You earn $6d20 if performing in public. You may come to the attention of a major entertainment company or develop an international reputation over time. Your next performance for this audience gains a +5 bonus.

Retry: You can use this skill once a day to earn money. Individual performances cannot be retried. Either you were good, or you weren't.

Critical Success: You double your earnings and/or immediately come to the attention of someone who can make you a star. Your next performance for this audience gets a +10 bonus.

Critical Failure: You are booed off the stage. Your next performance for this audience suffers a –10 penalty.

PILOT (DEX; TRAINED ONLY)

Pilot is used to maneuver all aircraft.

Check (Half Action): No skill checks are required to perform standard piloting functions, but complex tasks, such as those that arise during combat or other threatening circumstances, require a roll. *See also Chases, see page 183.*

Task	DC
Low risk turn/roll	5
Average maneuver	10
Tight turn/roll	15
High stress maneuver	20
Heroic or complex set of maneuvers	25+
Unfamiliar type of vehicle	+5

Vehicles are rated for handling *(see page 184).* This rating may help or hinder the vehicle's pilot.

Retry: Yes, but there is a lapse of time between the tries. If you absolutely have to turn immediately to avoid a mountain, but fail the check, a second attempt is usually impossible (per the GC's discretion based on current conditions).

Special: This skill covers the physical act of piloting; knowledge of piloting and making money with it as a sport are covered by the knowledge and sport skills, respectively. If you have 5 or more ranks in Pilot, you get a +2 synergy bonus to any Knowledge or Mechanics checks concerning aircraft, as well as a +2 synergy bonus to any Sport checks to professionally compete with them.

Critical Success: When not in a chase, you manage to avoid mishap even when it is seemingly impossible to do so. Your vehicle is not only unscathed by whatever pitfall you avoided, but you sail past it without a single chip in your paint. During a chase, your maneuver is successful unless an opposing driver scores a critical success with a higher total. Also, you receive a +4 bonus to your next maneuver or crash check.

Critical Failure: The aircraft stalls out or an engine catches on fire. The GC may rule that this is equivalent to failing a crash check *(see page 193).*

PROFESSION (WIS; TRAINED ONLY)

You are trained to perform a certain job or professional role, such as computer technician, diplomat, hunter, mechanic, military officer, spy, teacher, terrorist, or web programmer.

You can purchase this skill multiple times, each time applying it to a separate profession. For example, you could have Profession (Lawyer) at rank 4 and Profession (Doctor) at rank 3. Your ranks in one Profession don't affect your skill checks in another.

A Profession is unlike a Craft *(see page 47)* in that nothing is created. Service industry jobs are mostly Professions; manufacturing jobs are mostly Crafts. If an activity is typically done for fun rather than profit, such as gaming or stamp collecting, it's a Hobby *(see page 55)*. Finally, if an activity is an organized physical activity, it's likely a Sport *(see page 64)*.

Check: You may make use of your trade to earn an income (your skill check result × $35 per full week of work).

In addition, you know how to use the tools of your trade, and can perform tasks common to your profession. You are also capable of supervising any unskilled laborers that normally assist members of your profession, and can solve problems that crop up in the day-to-day completion of your tasks. For instance, a dentist can fill cavities, supervise dental assistants, fill out insurance forms, take tooth x-rays, and soothe a patient in pain, among other things. Your Game Control sets DCs for specific tasks.

Retry: When earning an income, only one attempt per week may be made. Specific tasks can usually be retried.

Special: Unskilled laborers earn an average of $300 a week.

Critical Success: You earn double your normal income, or perform the task you were attempting particularly well.

Critical Failure: You earn no money that week, or perform the task you were attempting particularly poorly.

READ LIPS (INT; TRAINED ONLY)

Read Lips allows you to watch someone else's lips and understand what they're saying.

Check (1 minute): You may attempt to understand what someone in your line of sight is saying by watching their lips. You must be able to understand the language they are speaking, and you cannot do anything else other than move half your speed while you are using this skill. The Game Control makes this check in secret for you.

Modifier Conditions	DC
Read lips of one person up to 10 ft. away	10
Every 10 additional ft. away (up to 30 ft. total)	+5
Each additional person to be read (up to 4 total)	+5
Complicated speech	+5
Inarticulate speaker	+5

If the check succeeds, then you understand most of what was said during that minute, but you miss certain details. If the check fails, you don't understand what was said. If the check fails by 5 or more, you misunderstand what was said.

Retry: You can use Read Lips once per minute.

Critical Success: You understand exactly what was said during the minute.

Critical Failure: You disastrously misunderstand what was said during the minute (e.g. you might mistake the word "contact" for the word "target").

SEARCH (INT)

Search can be used to perform a detailed search – rifling a desk for secret compartments, feeling a wall for a secret doorway, finding traps, frisking a suspect, or looking for anything else that is not visible. This is an active skill. You must be able to closely examine the object of the search; you cannot perform this skill from across the room.

Check (Full Action): You can search a 5-ft. by 5-ft. area, a single person, or a pile of items 5 ft. on a side.

Task	DC
Toss an area looking for a specific, familiar item	10
Ransack a room looking for one or more unfamiliar items	15
Discover a secret door, obvious clue, simple trap, or hidden compartment	20
Discover a more complex trap, well-hidden clue, or secret door	21+

Frisking Someone (Varies): Frisking someone is automatically successful unless they attempt to conceal one or more items from you, in which case you make an opposed Search check against their Hide check for each item they try to conceal. Your opponent's Hide check is modified by the size of the item he is trying to conceal (Diminutive +8, Tiny +4, Small +0, Medium –4, and Large –8. You cannot conceal items bigger than Large). If you succeed, you find the item; otherwise your target has successfully concealed it from you. Your GC may apply up to a +/–5 modifier to your Search check, depending upon the thoroughness of your search and other conditions.

Critical Success: You find everything in the square you're searching, as well as anything in all adjacent squares, or you find all items the person is attempting to hide from you.

Critical Failure: If the square you are searching contains a trap, you trigger it. If it contains a clue, the clue is kicked into a harder to find spot or destroyed. In any event, nothing convinces you that the square or person you searched is hiding anything of interest.

SENSE MOTIVE (WIS)

You are particularly alert to changes of mannerism, body language, and other symptoms of insincerity, and can use them to roughly gauge someone's intentions. This skill requires patience and careful observation, but it is one of a spy's best friends.

Check (Free Action): The Game Control should always make Sense Motive checks in secret, telling you what feelings or indications you get. Sense Motive is particularly useful when another person is attempting to Bluff or Intimidate you. If you fail a Sense Motive check by 10 or more, you are misled by your finely honed senses and glean incorrect information.

Task	DC
Sense sincerity	20 + target's Cha modifier
Hunch	25 + target's Cha modifier
Sense control	30

Sense Sincerity: Success with this check reveals whether a target is being insincere or dishonest. Note that someone can be honest without being entirely truthful. For instance, someone can convince you that performing some task would benefit you without disclosing that it would also benefit him.

Hunch: When making this check, you get a sense of what may be behind someone else's behavior. A successful hunch may help you notice if the person you're talking to is an imposter, under duress, or setting you up.

Sense Control: A successful check can detect if someone is being controlled with a drug or hypnosis, or has been brainwashed.

Check (10 minutes): You can attempt to deflect a seduction attempt. *For more about this use of the Sense Motive skill, see the disposition system on page 269.*

Retry: With the exception of refusing a seduction attempt, which cannot be retried, a Sense Motive check can be retried exactly once.

Special: A Cultures Rank of 5 or higher grants you a +2 synergy bonus to Sense Motive checks.

Use of the Sense Motive skill can be affected by the disposition system – *see page 269.*

Critical Success: You receive extremely accurate information from your senses (e.g. he's holding something back, or he's been drugged).

Critical Failure: You are totally misled by your senses (e.g. it looks like your team leader is lying to you about your mission when he's not).

SLEIGHT OF HAND (DEX; ARMOR CHECK PENALTY; TRAINED ONLY)

You can perform simple card tricks, palm small objects, and slip objects into or out of someone's pocket (yours or someone else's) without being observed, even under scrutiny. Items larger than a small book or video-cassette impose penalties or are impossible to conceal with Sleight of Hand.

Check (Half Action): When performing Sleight of Hand while under scrutiny, your check is opposed by the viewer's Spot check. The viewer's check does not affect the success/failure of your check, but may allow him to see what you do with the object.

Task	DC
Palm coin-sized object	10
Minor legerdemain (deal from bottom of deck)	15
Pick pocket	20
Task is under close observation	+5

When you attempt to remove an item from someone else's possession (or plant something on him), that person is automatically allowed to make a Spot check as if they were scrutinizing you.

Retry: Additional Sleight of Hand checks observed by the same target are made at +10 to the original DC.

Special: If you have 5 or more ranks in Bluff, you gain a +2 synergy bonus to Sleight of Hand checks.

Critical Success: Your Sleight of Hand was perfect. It can only be noticed with a critical success.

Critical Failure: Your Sleight of Hand attempt is automatically noticed by anyone observing you (or having their pockets picked by you).

SPORT (STR OR DEX; ARMOR CHECK PENALTY)

This skill is used to perform a sport, such as baseball, basketball, football, hockey (field or ice), jai-alai, racing (boat, drag, horse, plane, or stock car), rugby, soccer, swimming, tennis, or track and field.

You can take this skill multiple times, each time applying it to a separate sport. For example, you could have Sport (Skiing) at rank 4 and Sport (Scuba Diving) at rank 3. Your ranks in one Sport don't affect your skill checks in another.

A Sport is unlike a Craft *(see page 47)*, Hobby *(see page 55)*, or Profession *(see page 61)* in that it is an organized physical activity. Although a few rare individuals make money at sports, this is the exception rather than the rule.

Check: You are capable of playing a sport. Your Game Control sets DCs for specific tasks.

Retry: Specific tasks can usually be retried, unless failure results in injury.

Special: If you have 5 or more ranks in a sport, you get a +2 synergy bonus to any Knowledge checks that have anything to do with that Sport.

Critical Success: You play your sport with great skill, break records, or have the time of your life.

Critical Failure: You play your sport poorly, likely resulting in injury, humiliation, or both.

SPOT (WIS)

Spot can be used to notice that the man next to you at the airport is watching you, to catch a glimpse of movement in a dark corner and know that someone is hiding there, or to see a faint trail of blood leading away from a murder scene.

Check (Free Action): You can notice anything that is not obvious to the casual observer. This is useful in catching a pickpocket, seeing someone who is hiding, or penetrating a disguise.

Spot is often an opposed check, so the DC is one higher than the check it is opposing. For instance, if an enemy is hiding in the shadows and his Hide check result was 23, you would need a Spot check result of 24 or higher to notice him.

Condition	Modifier
Every 10 ft. between you and the target	–1
You are distracted	–5

Retry: Each time you have an opportunity to notice something, you automatically make a Spot check as a free action. You may also spend a full action to make another Spot check to notice something that you missed with a free action check. A full action Spot check is only

possible with things that are still there to be found. For instance, a full action Spot check might help after you have failed to notice a peculiar scar on the back of a victim's neck (something that is still there), but would be of no help to notice a pickpocket stealing your partner's passport (which has already happened).

Critical Success: You automatically win an opposed check (e.g. piercing a disguise even if its creator rolled a critical success as well) or notice all possible information or evidence in the area.

Critical Failure: You mistakenly believe that you saw something (a pickpocketing attempt, etc.) that didn't really happen, or completely miss all information or evidence in the area. You cannot find any of this information or evidence without a critical success.

SURVEILLANCE (WIS; TRAINED ONLY)

Surveillance is used to analyze and enhance intelligence photographs and video. You can also use it to notice important events during a long stakeout or spot signs of someone watching you.

Check: The time taken and DC vary depending on what you want to accomplish.

Task	Time	DC
Analyze photograph or frame of video	1 hour	20+
Enhance photograph or frame of video	5 minutes	10*
Notice important event during stakeout	Free action	10†
Notice signs of surveillance	Full action	Opposed
Hide/find bug	5 minutes	Opposed

* Add 5 to this DC for each previous enhancement.
† Add 2 to this DC for each day spent on stakeout.

Analyze Photograph or Video: You can carefully examine an image to get a clear picture of an individual shown in it, read any visible text, or otherwise extract information from it. Your Game Control sets the DC based on the quality of the recording equipment and the conditions when the image was taken. Any appropriate concealment bonuses that would apply when the image was taken (such as light fog or darkness) are also added to the DC.

Condition	DC
Black and white security camera	25-30
Infrared camera	25*
Color security camera	20-25
Camcorder	20-25
Professional film footage or photo	15-20

* Ignores concealment bonuses from darkness, but doesn't allow identification of individuals.

Enhance Photograph or Video: You must have a computer to enhance an image. Add the computer's power rating to this check. If successful, reduce the image's DC for purposes of analysis by 2.

Stakeouts and Surveillance: When something happens while you're on a stakeout, your Game Control makes this check secretly to see if you notice the event. Alternately, you can actively watch your surroundings and try to spot signs that you are under surveillance. Your Game Control makes a secret opposed Surveillance check against the Surveillance check of anyone spying on you. If the total of your check beats their result, you notice them.

Hide/Find Bugs: You can find listening devices by making an opposed Surveillance check against the person who hid the bug in the first place. If using a bug detector, you receive +5 to this check.

Retry: When noticing events during a stakeout, no. When analyzing an image, yes, but only after enhancing the image again. You cannot retry enhancement checks — once you fail one, the image is as clear as you can make it. When looking for bugs, yes. When hiding bugs, yes, as long as the bug hasn't been found yet.

Critical Success: You gain the information you are seeking from the photograph, or you reduce the image's DC by 4 if enhancing it. If hiding a bug or trying not to be spotted while spying on someone, then only a critical success finds the bug or spots you.

Critical Failure: You can gain no information from the image you are studying. If you were enhancing it, you introduced false information into the image. If hiding a bug or trying not to be spotted while spying on someone, you or the bug are automatically found.

SURVEILLANCE (WIS; TRAINED ONLY)

Survival is used to find shelter and edible plants in the wilderness, hunt game, and spot natural dangers such as quicksand or pitfalls. For agents who venture into hostile (read: non-urban) terrain frequently, this skill is invaluable.

Check (1 day): A successful check allows you to keep yourself and others alive and fed in the wilderness.

Task	DC
Move ½ your normal overland speed while hunting and foraging	10
For each additional person you feed/shelter	+2
Gain +2 to Fort saves against severe weather while moving ½ your normal overland speed, or +4 while staying in shelter	+1
For each additional person who is benefiting from the Fort save bonus	+1
Spot a natural danger	15
Know position and direction	15*

* +5 to the DC if you are currently lost, +10 to the DC if you are hopelessly lost.

Retry: Yes. You retry your Survival check each day you are traveling through the wilderness. The result of that check lasts until the next day. You cannot retry checks to spot a natural danger that you have encountered.

Special: Survival is used in conjunction with the Track skill feat *(see page 90)* to search for others in the wilderness.

Critical Success: You don't need to make another Survival check for one full week and all food, shelter, and modifiers for all people you are helping are in effect through that time as well.

Critical Failure: You become hopelessly lost. You could run into a natural hazard or a dangerous animal as well, per the Game Control's discretion.

SWIM (STR)

You are able to dive (freestyle or scuba), navigate underwater obstacles, and swim at a reasonable speed.

Check (Varies): A successful check allows you to swim at $1/4$ your speed as a half action or $1/2$ your speed as a full action. The Swim check DC depends on the type of water.

Water	DC
Calm water	10
Rough water	15
Stormy water	20
Whitewater rapids	25
Attempting to help another swimmer	+5
For each cumulative round you've spent underwater	–1
For every 5 lbs. of equipment carried	–1

Each hour that you spend swimming, you must make a Swim check against DC 20 or suffer 1d4 points of subdual damage as a result of fatigue. This subdual damage can only heal from rest once you have left the water.

Retry: When swimming, you must retry your Swim check every round. A failure indicates that you made no progress this round, while failing by 5 or more indicates that you have begun to drown *(see page 231)*.

Special: This skill covers the physical act of swimming; knowledge of swimming and making money with it as a sport are covered by the knowledge and sport skills, respectively.

Critical Success: You move twice your normal swimming speed this round.

Critical Failure: You become tangled up in some obstruction and begin to drown *(see page 231)*. Someone else must save you from drowning.

TUMBLE (DEX; ARMOR CHECK PENALTY; TRAINED ONLY)

Tumble allows you to land more softly than others when falling and to tumble away from opponents adjacent to you.

Check (Free Action): While moving, you can tumble 20 feet with a successful Tumble check. While tumbling, you do not have to stop if you move into a square that is adjacent to an opponent, and you can pass through occupied squares (but you cannot end your tumble in an occupied square). If you fail your Tumble check when passing by opponents or through an occupied square, you stop in an adjacent square and lose your Dexterity bonus to Defense, if any, until your next action.

Task	DC
Treat a fall as though it were 10 ft. shorter	10
Tumble 20 ft.	15
Tumble 20 ft., moving through occupied squares	25

Retry: You may attempt to reduce falling distance once per fall. You may attempt to tumble as movement once per action.

Special: If you have 5 or more ranks in Tumble, you gain an additional +1 dodge Defense bonus when fighting defensively in combat and an additional +2 dodge Defense bonus when using the total defense action in combat.

If you have 5 or more ranks in Jump, you get a +2 synergy bonus with Tumble checks.

Critical Success: You may tumble your entire move this action.

Critical Failure: You trip and fall prone at a spot during your move chosen by your GC.

USE ROPE (DEX; ARMOR CHECK PENALTY)

Use Rope allows you to tie and untie knots, and bind prisoners with rope.

Check (Half Action): You can attempt several tasks involving a rope.

Task	DC
Tie a good knot	10
Tie a knot that slips, slides slowly, or unties itself with a tug of the rope	15
Tie a rope around yourself one-handed	15
Splice two ropes together (5 minutes)	15

If you tie someone up with a rope, any Escape Artist check he makes is opposed by your Use Rope check. You receive a +10 bonus to this check since it's easier to tie someone up than it is to escape from such bonds. You only need to make the Use Rope check if and when the bound person tries to escape.

Special: If you have 5 or more ranks in Escape Artist, you get a +2 synergy bonus to Use Rope checks made to tie someone up.

Critical Success: The knot won't come undone even under extreme circumstances, or the bound person needs a critical success with his Escape Artist check to escape.

Critical Failure: The knot comes undone at a critical moment, or the bound person easily escapes his bindings.

"What are you trying to tell me? That I can dodge bullets?"

"No, Neo. I'm telling you that when you're ready, you won't have to."

– Neo and Morpheus, The Matrix

FEATS

Feats are special abilities or enhancements to existing abilities that you may choose to customize your agent. Feats have no ranks; agents either have a feat or they don't.

Rules for acquiring feats can be found in the *Player's Handbook™*.

FEAT TREES

Spycraft breaks feats into several categories, or "trees," for purposes of organization and agent development. These trees are combat feats (further broken down into basic combat feats, melee combat feats, ranged combat feats, and unarmed combat feats), chase feats, covert feats, gear feats, skill feats, and style feats.

COMBAT FEATS

These feats focus on various methods of fighting. Usually, you may choose from any of the following trees, though bonus feats may limit you to only one or two of them.

Basic Combat Feats *(pages 68-71):* These feats concern combat fundamentals, and are often prerequisites for feats in other categories.

Melee Combat Feats *(pages 72-75):* These feats focus on combat using knives, axes, and other hand-held weapons.

Ranged Combat Feats *(pages 75-78):* These feats focus on the use of firearms.

Unarmed Combat Feats *(pages 78-81):* These feats enhance your prowess without weapons, and — in the core release — focus on Hong Kong "wire fu"-style martial arts.

CHASE FEATS (PAGES 81-84)

This feat tree focuses on driving and piloting.

COVERT FEATS (PAGES 84-86)

This tree involves stealth, evasion, and subterfuge.

GEAR FEATS (PAGES 86-87)

These feats offer you new equipment options.

SKILL FEATS (PAGES 87-91)

All of these feats improve your skills.

STYLE FEATS (PAGES 91-94)

This group focuses on savoir faire and personal wealth.

FEAT DESCRIPTIONS

This is the format for feat descriptions. Not all feats have every entry.

feat name

Description: A description of what the feat actually does or represents.

Prerequisites: A list of requirements that must be met in order to take the feat.

Benefit: In game terms, what the feat lets you to do.

Normal: A list of things that an agent without this feat is limited in or prevented from doing.

Special: Other important information about this feat.

BASIC COMBAT FEATS

These feats typically have very few prerequisites, and are themselves prerequisites for many other feats.

AMBIDEXTERITY

You can use both hands with equal coordination. You are neither right-handed nor left-handed.

Prerequisites: Dexterity 15+.

Benefit: Both of your hands are considered your primary hand when calculating penalties.

Normal: Agents without the Ambidexterity feat who use their off-hand suffer a –4 penalty to all attack rolls, ability checks, and skill checks. *For more information, see Attacking With Two Weapons, page 165.*

Special: The Two-Weapon Fighting feat reduces the penalty for fighting with two weapons by –2 for each. This effect stacks with the Ambidexterity feat.

ARMOR GROUP PROFICIENCY

When wearing an armor type with which you are proficient, apply its armor check penalty only to Balance, Climb, Escape Artist, Hide, Jump, Move Silently, Sleight of Hand and Tumble checks, and apply the armor's base speed penalty. If this reduces your speed to 0 or less, you may only make one standard 5-ft. bonus step *(see page 160)* per round while wearing this type of armor.

Normal: Agents wearing armor with which they are not proficient suffer the armor check penalty on all attack rolls and on all skill rolls that require any movement (including the Handle Animal skill when riding). Also, they suffer two times the armor's speed penalty

Again, if this reduces your speed to 0 or less, you may only make one standard 5-ft. bonus step (*see page 160*) per round while wearing this armor.

Armor Proficiency (Light): This agent is proficient with light armor.

Armor Proficiency (Medium): This agent is proficient with medium armor. Prerequisites: Armor Proficiency (light).

Armor Proficiency (Heavy): This agent is proficient with heavy armor. Prerequisites: Armor Proficiency (light) and (medium).

To see the effects of the various types of armor, see Standard-Issue Gear, pages 125-131.

CAREER OPERATIVE

Your experiences as a superspy make you very hard to kill.

Prerequisites: Agent level 6+.

Benefit: You gain a +1 bonus to your Fortitude, Reflex, and Will saves.

COMBAT INSTINCTS

You react instinctively when an opportunity presents itself in melee combat.

Benefit: If you are not flat-footed when an adjacent opponent's melee attack roll misses you by more than 5, you may immediately make a single attack (*see page 160*) as a free action against that opponent. You may use this feat a number of times per round equal to your Dexterity modifier.

CONFIDENT CHARGE

You can charge around corners.

Prerequisites: Dex 13+, Wis 13+.

Benefit: When you take a charge action in combat, you can make a number of turns equal to your Dexterity modifier. None of these turns can exceed 90 degrees.

ENDURANCE

You have incredible stamina.

Benefit: When making a check to perform a physical action over a period of time (such as swimming, holding your breath, running, etc.) you gain a +4 bonus to the skill or ability check. Further, you only suffer a –1 penalty to Strength and Dexterity while fatigued (reduced to 0 vitality points).

EXPERTISE

You are trained in using your combat skills for defensive purposes as well as offensive.

Prerequisites: Int 13+.

Benefit: When using the standard attack action, you may take a penalty of up to –5 on your attack and add the same number (up to +5) to your Defense as a dodge bonus. The penalty/bonus amount may not exceed your base attack bonus, and lasts until your next action.

Normal: Without this feat, you can fight defensively when using a standard attack action, taking a –4 penalty to attacks and gaining a +2 dodge bonus to Defense until your next action.

GREAT FORTITUDE

You are much tougher than usual.

Benefit: +2 bonus on Fortitude saves.

IMPROVED DISARM

Skilled at disarming opponents in melee combat.

Prerequisites: Int 13+, Expertise.

Benefit: When attempting to disarm an opponent, you receive a +1 bonus to the attempt, and if you fail, there is no chance for the opponent to disarm you in return.

IMPROVED INITIATIVE

You react faster than normal during a fight.

Benefit: +4 bonus on all initiative checks.

IMPROVED TWO-WEAPON FIGHTING

Expert in fighting while using two weapons.

Prerequisites: Ambidexterity, Two-Weapon Fighting, base attack +9 or higher.

Benefit: Instead of gaining a single extra attack action during the round with an off-hand weapon (*see Attacking with Two Weapons, page 165*), you have two extra attacks with your off-hand weapon, though the second extra attack suffers a –5 penalty (*see page 165*).

Normal: Without this feat, you only get one extra attack per round with a second weapon.

INCREASED SPEED

You move significantly faster than normal.

Prerequisites: Run.

Benefit: Your base speed is increased by 10 ft. per round (*see Moving, page 174*).

IRON WILL

You have extremely strong willpower.

Benefit: +2 bonus on all Will saves.

LIGHTNING REFLEXES

You have faster than normal reflexes.

Benefit: +2 bonus on all Reflex saves.

BASIC COMBAT FEATS

AMBIDEXTERITY Dex 15+	**GREAT FORTITUDE**	**SURGE OF SPEED**
ARMOR PROF. LIGHT	**IMPROVED INITIATIVE**	**TOUGHNESS**
ARMOR PROF. MEDIUM	**IRON WILL**	**TWO-WEAPON FIGHTING**
ARMOR PROF. HEAVY	**LIGHTNING REFLEXES**	**IMP. TWO-WEAPON FIGHTING** Ambidexterity, BAB +9 or higher
CAREER OPERATIVE Agent Level 6+	**MOBILITY** Dex 13+	**WEAPON GROUP PROF.**
COMBAT INSTINCTS	**QUICK DRAW** Dex 13+, BAB +1 or higher	**WEAPON FOCUS** BAB +1 or higher
CONFIDENT CHARGE Dex 13+, Wis 13+	**QUICK HEALER** Con 13+	**ZEN FOCUS** Wis 13+
ENDURANCE	**RUN**	**ZEN SHOT** BAB +4 or higher
EXPERTISE Int 13+	**INCREASED SPEED**	**ZEN MASTERY** BAB +9 or higher
IMPROVED DISARM	**SIDESTEP** Dex 13+	

MOBILITY

Adept at moving past opponents and dodging blows.

Prerequisites: Dex 13+.

Benefit: You may move away from adjacent opponents in the middle of combat. In addition, you may move up to twice your speed when taking the total defense action.

Normal: Without this feat, you are limited to your 5-ft. bonus step *(see page 160)* when adjacent to an opponent, unless you are taking a withdraw action, or your opponent is prone.

QUICK DRAW

You can bring a weapon into action with inhuman speed.

Prerequisites: Dex 13+, base attack bonus +1 or higher.

Benefit: You may draw and ready a weapon that you have equipped as a free action rather than a half action. Quick draw does not allow you to reload a weapon in this same time frame, but you may disable a safety or activate a power source. You may draw up to two weapons, or draw and holster a single weapon, as free actions each round.

QUICK HEALER

Your wounds heal faster than normal.

Prerequisites: Con 13+.

Benefit: When you recover vitality or wound points as a result of natural healing (but not surgical or other types of healing), you recover twice the normal number of points.

RUN

You are able to run faster than normal.

Benefit: When running, you are able to move five times your normal speed instead of four times that speed *(see Moving, page 174)*. When making a running jump *(see the Jump skill description, page 57)*, the distance or height of the jump is increased by 1/4 (multiply by 1.25) but not beyond the maximum.

SIDESTEP

You are good at evading attacks.

Prerequisites: Dex 13+.

Benefit: During your action, you may select an opponent and receive a +2 dodge bonus to your Defense against attacks made by that opponent. Alternately, you may designate all opponents attacking you. In this case,

you gain a +1 dodge bonus to your Defense against attacks made by any and all of the designated opponents. This effect lasts until your next action.

SURGE OF SPEED

You may perform an additional action each round.

Benefit: You may take an extra half action during your turn. This action may not be an attack. This feat may be used once per game session, plus another time for every 4 agent levels you have attained, but never more than once in any single round.

TOUGHNESS

You are tougher than normal.

Benefit: Gain either +2 wound points or +4 vitality points, your choice.

Special: This feat may be taken multiple times.

TWO-WEAPON FIGHTING

You are able to fight with a weapon in each hand, making one extra attack each round for the off-hand weapon.

Benefit: Your penalties for fighting with two weapons are reduced by 2 (for each weapon).

Normal: *See Attacking With Two Weapons, page 165.*

Special: The Ambidexterity feat reduces the attack penalty for using a second weapon by 4. This ability can stack with the Two-Weapon Fighting feat.

WEAPON FOCUS

Choose a specific weapon with which you have spent a lot of time training. You may choose unarmed strike or grapple as the weapon.

Prerequisites: Proficient with weapon, base attack bonus +1 or higher.

Benefit: +1 bonus to all attack rolls when using the selected weapon.

Special: This feat may be taken multiple times, each time applying it to a different weapon.

WEAPON GROUP PROFICIENCY

Choose a group of weapons from the following list with which you are proficient.

Hurled: This weapon class includes all non-firearm missile weapons, including throwing knives, shuriken, bows, crossbows, slings, and grenades. Melee weapons fall into this category when thrown.

Handgun: This weapon class includes all ranged weapons that are held in one hand, from revolvers to pistols to dartguns and mace.

Melee: This weapon class includes all melee weapons, including swords, knives, blackjacks, and even improvised weapons such as chairs or bottles.

Rifle: This weapon class includes most ranged weapons that are held in two hands, including short stock assault weapons, percussion, and energy weapons.

Tactical: Extremely powerful rifles (such as fully automatic machine guns or high-powered sniper rifles) and other extremely deadly weapons such as flame throwers, rocket launchers, and mortars, fall into this weapon class.

Exotic: This includes bizarre weapons that aren't often used, like hand crossbows, harpoons, or nets. This weapon group proficiency must be taken once for each group of exotic weapons with which you wish to become proficient. There are two exotic weapon groups in the *Spycraft* core release—archaic and martial arts. Exotic weapons are listed by group on pages 121-123.

You understand how to use, reload, and care for all weapons you are proficient with.

Benefit: You make attack rolls with the weapon normally.

Normal: If you use a handgun with which you are not proficient, you suffer a –6 penalty to your attack rolls. If you use any other weapon with which you are not proficient, you suffer a –4 penalty to your attack rolls.

Special: This feat may be taken multiple times, each time applying it to a different weapon group.

ZEN FOCUS

You can sense the approximate location of foes without being able to see them.

Prerequisites: Wis 13+

Benefit: When attacking an opponent with a ranged attack, reduce concealment bonuses to your target's Defense by half (rounding down).

ZEN SHOT

You have the uncanny ability to precisely track your enemies when firing at them.

Prerequisites: Zen Focus, base attack bonus +4.

Benefit: When attacking an opponent with a ranged attack, ignore concealment bonuses to your target's Defense.

ZEN MASTERY

You may use your inner clarity to guide an attack more accurately to its target.

Prerequisites: Zen Shot, base attack bonus +9.

Benefit: You may add your Wisdom modifier to your attack bonus when attacking with any hurled weapon. This bonus is in addition to any other modifiers to the roll, including any other ability modifiers.

MELEE COMBAT FEATS

These combat feats come into play when you are wielding a melee weapon. Typically, melee combat feats allow you to perform special moves or enhance your combat capabilities in other ways.

ASSASSIN

You are trained to target your opponent's vital areas.

Prerequisites: Darting Weapon, base attack bonus +6 or higher.

Benefit: Your threat range is increased by 1 when using a melee weapon.

BLIND-FIGHT

While in melee, you can sense the approximate location of foes without being able to see them.

Benefit: When attacking an opponent with an unarmed or melee attack, reduce concealment bonuses to your target's Defense by half (rounding down).

BLINDSIGHT 5-FT. RADIUS

You can sense nearby opponents even in total darkness.

Prerequisites: Wis 13+, Blind-Fight, base attack bonus +4 or higher.

Benefit: When attacking an opponent with an unarmed or melee attack, ignore concealment bonuses to your target's Defense.

CLEAVE

Your strength allows you to effectively follow through with a melee attack.

Prerequisites: Power Attack.

Benefit: If one of your melee attacks reduces an opponent's wound points to 0 or below, dropping the opponent, you may immediately make a melee attack against another adjacent opponent (though you may not move before making this extra attack). The extra attack is made using the same weapon, with the same bonuses, as the attack that dropped the previous opponent. This feat may only be used once per round.

MELEÉ COMBAT FEATS

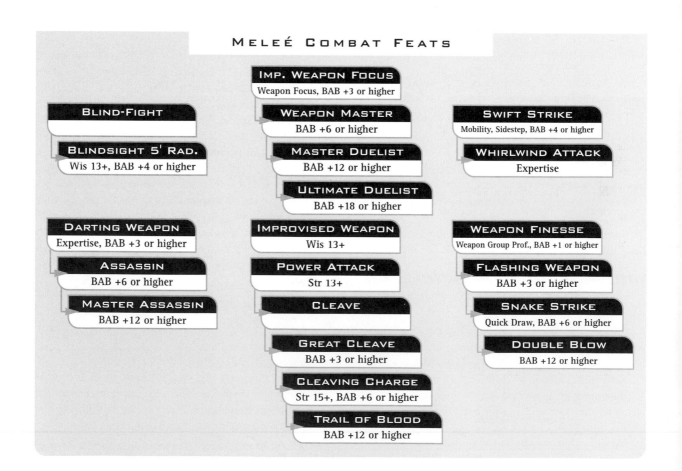

IMP. WEAPON FOCUS — Weapon Focus, BAB +3 or higher

BLIND-FIGHT

WEAPON MASTER — BAB +6 or higher

SWIFT STRIKE — Mobility, Sidestep, BAB +4 or higher

BLINDSIGHT 5' RAD. — Wis 13+, BAB +4 or higher

MASTER DUELIST — BAB +12 or higher

WHIRLWIND ATTACK — Expertise

ULTIMATE DUELIST — BAB +18 or higher

DARTING WEAPON — Expertise, BAB +3 or higher

IMPROVISED WEAPON — Wis 13+

WEAPON FINESSE — Weapon Group Prof., BAB +1 or higher

ASSASSIN — BAB +6 or higher

POWER ATTACK — Str 13+

FLASHING WEAPON — BAB +3 or higher

MASTER ASSASSIN — BAB +12 or higher

CLEAVE

SNAKE STRIKE — Quick Draw, BAB +6 or higher

GREAT CLEAVE — BAB +3 or higher

DOUBLE BLOW — BAB +12 or higher

CLEAVING CHARGE — Str 15+, BAB +6 or higher

TRAIL OF BLOOD — BAB +12 or higher

CLEAVING CHARGE

You can wade through your opponents.

Prerequisites: Str 15+, Great Cleave, base attack bonus +6 or higher.

Benefit: As Great Cleave, except that you may move one 5-ft. square before each extra attack. You may not exceed half your speed during the action.

DARTING WEAPON

Your melee attacks are incredibly fast.

Prerequisites: Expertise, base attack bonus +3 or higher.

Benefit: At the start of the round, you may subtract a number from all melee attack rolls and add the same number to your initiative check. This number may not exceed your base attack bonus, and the effects last until the start of the next round. You may not make ranged attacks this round.

DOUBLE BLOW

You attack quicker than most when using a melee weapon.

Prerequisites: Snake Strike, base attack bonus +12 or higher.

Benefit: Each time you spend a half action to make a melee attack you may choose to make two melee attacks. If you do so, every attack roll you make this round (including each melee attack) suffers a –5 penalty. This effect does not stack with the benefits of Flashing Weapon (you may only benefit from one or the other in any single round), but you may use Double Blow with all of your melee attacks in a single round (allowing up to twice as many melee attacks as you have half actions that round).

FLASHING WEAPON

You are able to wield a melee weapon with increased speed, but decreased accuracy.

Prerequisites: Weapon Finesse, base attack bonus +3 or higher.

Benefit: During your first attack of the round, you may make one extra melee attack that normally takes a half action. Every attack you make this round (including those during your first attack action) suffers a –2 penalty. This effect does not stack with the benefits of Double Blow (you may only benefit from one or the other in any single round).

GREAT CLEAVE

You are able to wield a melee weapon with great force, allowing you to strike multiple times when dropping opponents.

Prerequisites: Cleave, base attack bonus +3 or higher.

Benefit: As Cleave, except that it can be used any number of times per round.

IMPROVED WEAPON FOCUS

You have greatly improved upon your training with a certain type of melee weapon.

Prerequisites: Weapon Focus for selected melee weapon, base attack bonus +3 or higher.

Benefit: +2 bonus to all damage rolls when using the selected melee weapon.

Special: This feat may be taken multiple times, each time applying it to a different melee weapon. It may be not be taken more than once for any single weapon.

IMPROVISED WEAPON

You are able to turn ordinary items in your vicinity into brutally efficient combat tools.

Prerequisites: Wis 13+

Benefit: As a half action, you may find an object nearby that you can use as an improvised melee weapon (e.g. a ladder, a fire extinguisher, a pool cue, etc.). The GC chooses the object you find, which may be Small, Medium, or Large in size (objects less than Small size or greater than Large size may not be used as improvised weapons). This weapon adds a +2 modifier to both damage rolls and Defense for a number of rounds equal to your Wisdom modifier. The object is considered a melee weapon and is therefore subject to disarm rules. The object may also be broken *(see page 168)*. Unarmed combat feats and abilities cannot be applied to an improvised weapon. You may only benefit from one improvised weapon at any time. This feat may only be used in areas where objects are available to be found (e.g. it doesn't work in a clean room or barren cell). This feat may be used a number of times each session equal to your total initiative bonus.

MASTER ASSASSIN

You are an expert at striking at your opponents' weak spots with a weapon.

Prerequisites: Assassin, base attack bonus +12 or higher.

Benefit: Your threat range is increased by 2 when using a melee weapon (in addition to the benefit of the Assassin feat). In addition, you no longer have to spend an action die to turn a threat into a critical hit when using a melee weapon.

MASTER DUELIST

You are an expert with a certain type of weapon.

Prerequisites: Weapon Master with selected weapon, base attack bonus +12 or higher.

Benefit: Your bonuses from Weapon Master are increased to +3 to attack rolls and +6 to damage rolls

when using the selected weapon. Finally, once per game session, you may choose to re-roll a failed attack roll when using the selected weapon. You may not re-roll a critical failure.

Special: This feat may be taken multiple times, each time applying it to a different weapon.

POWER ATTACK

Your melee attacks are incredibly powerful.

Prerequisites: Str 13+.

Benefit: At the start of your first action during the round, before taking any attack rolls, you may subtract a number from all of your melee attack rolls and add the same number to all of your melee damage rolls. This number may not exceed your base attack bonus, and lasts until your first action during the next round.

SNAKE STRIKE

You are so fast at drawing your weapon that you consistently take your opponents by surprise.

Prerequisites: Flashing Weapon, Quick Draw, base attack bonus +6 or higher.

Benefit: When you draw a melee weapon to attack an opponent that you are not currently engaged in combat with, you may first make a feint attempt against that opponent as a free action.

SWIFT STRIKE

You may move while making a melee attack.

Prerequisites: Mobility, Sidestep, base attack bonus +4 or higher.

Benefit: When you take the standard attack action while making a melee attack, you can move up to half your speed. You may move part of this distance before your attack and part after your attack, as long as you don't exceed half your speed during the action.

TRAIL OF BLOOD

You can mow down your enemies, leaving a swath of death behind you.

Prerequisites: Cleaving Charge, base attack bonus +12 or higher.

Benefit: As Cleaving Charge, except that you may move up to three 5-ft. squares before each extra attack. You may not exceed your speed during the action.

ULTIMATE DUELIST

You have mastered a certain type of weapon.

Prerequisites: Master Duelist with selected weapon, base attack bonus +18 or higher.

Benefit: Your bonuses from Master Duelist are increased to +4 to attack rolls and +10 to damage rolls when using the selected weapon. In addition, three times per game session, you may choose to re-roll a failed attack roll when using the selected weapon. You may not re-roll a critical failure.

Special: This feat may be taken multiple times, each time applying it to a different weapon.

WEAPON FINESSE

By relying more on your dexterity than your strength, you have mastered one weapon.

Prerequisites: Proficient with weapon, base attack bonus +1 or higher.

Benefit: Choose one light melee weapon. When using that weapon, you use your Dexterity modifier instead of your Strength modifier for attack rolls.

Special: This feat may be taken multiple times, each time applying it to a different weapon.

WEAPON MASTER

You are skilled with a certain type of weapon.

Prerequisites: Improved Weapon Focus with selected weapon, base attack bonus +6 or higher.

Benefit: Your bonuses from Improved Weapon Focus are increased to +2 to attack rolls and +4 to damage rolls bonus when using the selected weapon.

Special: This feat may be taken multiple times, each time applying it to a different weapon.

Whirlwind Attack

You can enter a controlled state of frenzy, during which you can attack all opponents within your reach with one melee attack.

Prerequisites: Expertise, Swift Strike.

Benefit: As a full action, instead of making your normal attacks, you may make one attack with your full base attack bonus against each adjacent opponent.

Ranged Combat Feats

These combat feats require the use of a ranged weapon. Typically, ranged combat feats allow you to perform special moves or enhance your combat capabilities in other ways.

Bullseye

You can take flamboyant shots that are especially lethal.

Prerequisites: Precise Shot, base attack bonus of +3 or higher.

Benefit: When you are about to make a ranged attack that uses a single shot or missile (no bursts, autofire, or strafing) on a target within two range increments, before you roll, you may subtract a number from your attack roll and add the same number to your damage roll for this attack only. This number cannot exceed your base attack bonus.

Controlled Burst

You are skilled at firing controlled bursts, able to hit the right marks for maximum effect upon your targets.

Prerequisites: Rapid Shot.

Benefit: When making either a wide or narrow burst attack *(see page 166)*, you receive a +1 bonus to both your attack and damage rolls in addition to the regular burst modifiers, bringing your narrow bursts to –2 to attack and +3 to damage, and your wide bursts to +2 to attack and +1 to damage.

Controlled Strafe

You are skilled at making controlled strafe attacks.

Prerequisites: Controlled Burst, base attack bonus +6 or higher.

Benefit: When making a strafe attack *(see page 167)*, you receive only a –1 penalty to your attack roll for each targeted square beyond the first. When making an autofire attack *(see page 165),* you do not count the first volley when determining the attack penalty.

Coordinate Fire

You are most effective when working in concert with your teammates.

Prerequisites: Lay Down Fire, base attack bonus +6 or higher.

Benefit: When firing a ranged weapon at an opponent, you gain a +1 bonus to your attack roll for each of your allies who has fired upon that same opponent earlier in this round.

Diving Shot

You may take evasive actions while attacking.

Prerequisites: Shot on the Run, base attack bonus +6 or higher.

Benefit: When you take any half action ranged attack (including bursts), you may move a number of feet up to your speed. You may move part of this distance before your shot and part after your shot, as long as you don't exceed your speed during the action. In addition, if you move at least one 5-ft. square during your action, you receive a +2 bonus to your Defense until the start of your next action.

Extreme Range

You're so skilled with ranged weapons that your shots are effective over great distances.

Prerequisites: Far Shot, base attack bonus +3 or higher.

Benefit: When you use a ranged weapon such as a pistol or bow, its range increment is doubled (multiply by 2). When you use a hurled weapon such as a dagger or grenade, its range increment is tripled (multiply by 3).

Far Shot

You have practiced firing at increased range.

Benefit: When you use a ranged weapon, its range increment rises by one-half (multiply by 1.5). When you use a hurled weapon, its range increment is doubled (multiply by 2).

Hail of Bullets

You can fire more than one burst per attack.

Prerequisites: Controlled Strafe, base attack bonus +12 or higher.

Benefit: Each time you spend a half action to make a burst attack you may choose to make two burst attacks. If you do so, every attack roll you make this round (including each burst attack) suffers a –5 penalty. This effect does not stack with the benefits of Rapid Shot (you may only benefit from one or the other in any single round), but you may use Hail of Bullets with all of your ranged attacks in a single round (allowing up to twice as many ranged attacks as you have half actions that round).

INCREASED PRECISION

You may make precision shots at range.

Prerequisites: Extreme Range, base attack bonus +6 or higher.

Benefit: The range at which you can make sneak attacks *(see page 24)* and use your Point Blank Shot feat is increased by one range increment.

Special: You can take this feat three times.

LAY DOWN FIRE

You are extremely effective at laying down cover or suppressive fire.

Prerequisites: Point Blank Shot, base attack bonus +3 or higher.

Benefit: You give allies a +6 bonus to Defense instead of a +4 when you provide them with cover fire. In addition, the penalty you inflict on enemies when you lay down suppressive fire on them is increased to −6.

LIGHTNING DRAW

You often catch your opponents by surprise.

Prerequisites: Quick Draw, Snap Shot, base attack bonus +6 or higher.

Benefit: When you draw a ranged weapon to attack an opponent that you are not currently engaged in combat with, you may first make a feint attempt against that opponent as a free action.

MARKSMAN

When you have time to aim your shots, you can shoot a ranged weapon with deadly effectiveness.

Prerequisites: Precise Shot, base attack bonus +3 or higher.

Benefit: You gain a +2 bonus to your attack roll when aiming a weapon instead of a +1. Also, you gain a +3 bonus to your attack roll when bracing a weapon instead of a +2.

MASTER SNIPER

You are an expert at making killing shots with ranged weapons at long range.

Prerequisites: Sniper, base attack bonus +18 or higher.

Benefit: When you receive a bonus to your attack roll due to aiming or bracing your weapon, your threat range is increased by the amount of the bonus. Thus, if your threat range is 19-20 and you have a +2 bonus to your attack roll due to aiming, your threat range is increased to 17-20.

POINT BLANK SHOT

You have been trained to shoot accurately at close range.

Prerequisites: Dex 13+.

Benefit: +1 bonus on attack and damage rolls with ranged weapons against opponents within one range increment.

PRECISE SHOT

You are especially skilled at firing into melee combat or past intervening obstacles.

Prerequisites: Point Blank Shot.

Benefit: You can use ranged weapons, whether fired or hurled, to attack an opponent engaged in melee without suffering the standard −4 penalty *(see Shooting or Throwing into a Melee, page 171)*.

QUICK RELOAD

You can reload a weapon with incredible speed.

Prerequisites: Dex 13+, Speed Trigger, base attack bonus +3 or higher.

Benefit: You can take the reload weapon action as a free action rather than a half action. This feat may be used only once per round.

RAPID SHOT

You are able to fire ranged weapons at an increased rate, but you suffer a loss of accuracy.

Prerequisites: Dex 13+, Speed Trigger, base attack bonus +3 or higher.

Benefit: During your first attack of the round, you may make one extra ranged attack that normally takes a half action. Every attack you make this round (including those during your first attack action) suffers a –2 penalty. This effect does not stack with the benefits of Hail of Bullets (you may only benefit from one or the other in any single round).

SHARP-SHOOTING

You may fire ranged weapons accurately through cover.

Prerequisites: Precise Shot, base attack bonus +3 or higher.

Benefit: You gain a +2 bonus to your attack roll when making a ranged attack against an opponent benefiting from partial (i.e. some, but not total) cover.

SHOT ON THE RUN

You may move while making a ranged attack.

Prerequisites: Mobility, Point Blank Shot, Sidestep.

Benefit: When you take any half action ranged attack (including a burst), you may move up to a number of feet equal to your speed. You may move part of this distance before your shot and part after, as long as you don't exceed half your speed during the action.

SNAP SHOT

You are able to get a shot off faster than most.

Prerequisites: Rapid Shot.

Benefit: At the start of the round, you may subtract a number from all ranged attack rolls and add the same number to your initiative check. This number may not exceed your base attack bonus, and the effects last until the start of the next round. You may not make melee attacks this round.

SNIPER

You have been trained to make killing shots with ranged weapons at long range.

Prerequisites: Increased Precision, Marksman, Sharp-Shooting, base attack bonus +9 or higher.

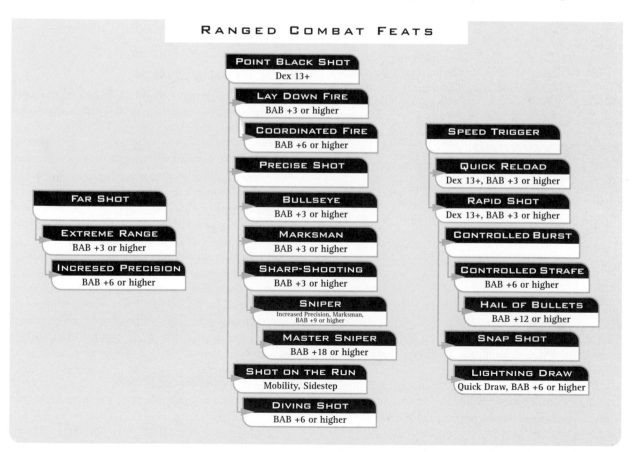

RANGED COMBAT FEATS

POINT BLACK SHOT — Dex 13+

LAY DOWN FIRE — BAB +3 or higher

COORDINATED FIRE — BAB +6 or higher

PRECISE SHOT

BULLSEYE — BAB +3 or higher

MARKSMAN — BAB +3 or higher

SHARP-SHOOTING — BAB +3 or higher

SNIPER — Increased Precision, Marksman, BAB +9 or higher

MASTER SNIPER — BAB +18 or higher

SHOT ON THE RUN — Mobility, Sidestep

DIVING SHOT — BAB +6 or higher

FAR SHOT

EXTREME RANGE — BAB +3 or higher

INCRESED PRECISION — BAB +6 or higher

SPEED TRIGGER

QUICK RELOAD — Dex 13+, BAB +3 or higher

RAPID SHOT — Dex 13+, BAB +3 or higher

CONTROLLED BURST

CONTROLLED STRAFE — BAB +6 or higher

HAIL OF BULLETS — BAB +12 or higher

SNAP SHOT

LIGHTNING DRAW — Quick Draw, BAB +6 or higher

UNARMED COMBAT FEATS

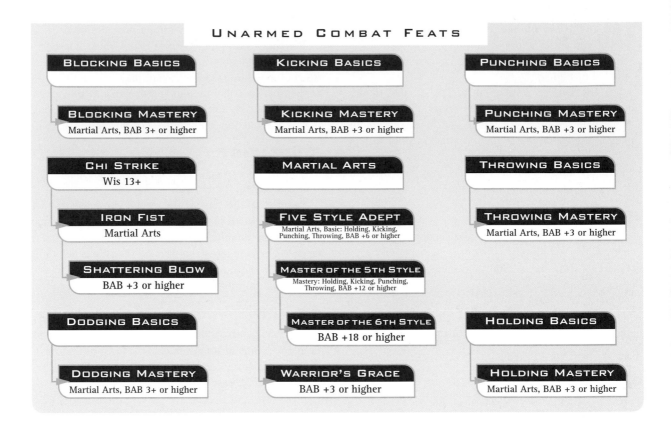

BLOCKING BASICS

BLOCKING MASTERY
Martial Arts, BAB 3+ or higher

CHI STRIKE
Wis 13+

IRON FIST
Martial Arts

SHATTERING BLOW
BAB +3 or higher

DODGING BASICS

DODGING MASTERY
Martial Arts, BAB 3+ or higher

KICKING BASICS

KICKING MASTERY
Martial Arts, BAB +3 or higher

MARTIAL ARTS

FIVE STYLE ADEPT
Martial Arts, Basic: Holding, Kicking, Punching, Throwing, BAB +6 or higher

MASTER OF THE 5TH STYLE
Mastery: Holding, Kicking, Punching, Throwing, BAB +12 or higher

MASTER OF THE 6TH STYLE
BAB +18 or higher

WARRIOR'S GRACE
BAB +3 or higher

PUNCHING BASICS

PUNCHING MASTERY
Martial Arts, BAB +3 or higher

THROWING BASICS

THROWING MASTERY
Martial Arts, BAB +3 or higher

HOLDING BASICS

HOLDING MASTERY
Martial Arts, BAB +3 or higher

Benefit: Your threat range is increased by 1 when firing a ranged weapon, and if you score a threat with a ranged weapon, you do not have to spend an action die to turn the threat into a critical hit.

SPEED TRIGGER

You are skilled with extremely rapid gunfire, even with single-shot firearms.

Benefit: You may make burst attacks even with firearms that do not normally allow burst fire (so long as the weapon has at least three shots remaining).

UNARMED COMBAT FEATS

These combat feats are used when you find yourself without a weapon. Typically, unarmed combat feats allow you to use martial arts moves.

Unarmed Abilities: When making an unarmed attack, you may only use one "named" ability, such as "Palm Strike," at a time. Thus, if you had the Punching Basics feat *(see below)*, you could use either Palm Strike or Knuckle Punch, but not both on the same attack.

BLOCKING BASICS

You have trained in the fundamentals of blocking and redirecting opponents' melee and unarmed attacks.

Benefit: This feat grants you the following abilities.

Break Weapon: When you are attacked with a weapon by an opponent within 5 ft., you may automatically make a Strength check to break his weapon. The weapon's Break DC is increased by 2 when you use this ability. This ability may only be used when you are fighting defensively or using the total defense movement option *(see page 176)*.

Shifting Throw: When you are unsuccessfully attacked by an opponent, you may move him to any adjacent square that doesn't place him in immediate jeopardy (such as flipping him into a woodchipper or over a cliff). All your allies within one range increment gain a +2 bonus to attack your opponent during their next action.

BLOCKING MASTERY

You are a flurry of movement few opponents can touch.

Prerequisites: Martial Arts, Blocking Basics, melee attack bonus +3 or higher.

Benefit: This feat grants you the following abilities.

Adrenaline Burst: When you spend an action die to increase your attack with a melee or unarmed weapon, your Defense is increased by the same value until your next action.

Redirection: When you are unsuccessfully attacked by an opponent, you may, as a free action, make a Reflex save with a DC equal to the Defense of any other opponent within 5 ft. Success indicates that you have shifted the second opponent into the path of the first one's attack, and that he suffers the full damage value of the attack. This ability may only be used when you are fighting defensively or using the total defense movement option *(see page 176)*.

CHI STRIKE

Your unarmed attacks are incredibly powerful.

Prerequisites: Wis 13+.

Benefit: At the start of your first action during the round, before taking any attack rolls, you may subtract a number from all of your unarmed attack rolls and add the same number to all of your unarmed damage rolls. This number may not exceed your base attack bonus, and lasts until your first action during the next round.

DODGING BASICS

You have trained in the fundamentals of avoiding attacks.

Benefit: This feat grants you the following abilities.

Deflect Arrows: If you have at least one hand free, then once per round when you'd normally be hit with a hurled weapon, or a thrown melee or exotic weapon, you may make a Reflex save (DC 15 + attacker's base attack bonus) as a free action. If you succeed, you deflect the attack. You must be aware of the attack and not flat-footed. Your Game Control may rule that certain unusual ranged attacks cannot be deflected.

Flying Back Flip: Once per round, when an opponent misses you with a melee attack, you may move one 5-ft. square as a free action. If this takes you out of his reach, he must move closer to attack you with further melee attacks.

DODGING MASTERY

You have mastered several styles of martial arts that emphasize avoidance.

Prerequisites: Martial Arts, Dodging Basics, base attack bonus +3 or higher.

Benefit: This feat grants you the following abilities.

Dodge Bullets: This ability works just like deflect arrows, under Dodging Basics, except that it also allows you to avoid firearm ranged attacks. You may only use either deflect arrows or dodge bullets once per round.

Iron Man: Once per combat, when you are struck with an attack that inflicts at least 1 point of damage,

you can tense your body to reduce the damage being dealt to you by your base attack bonus. Thus, if your base attack bonus is +6 and you are suffering an 8 point attack, the damage is reduced to 2 points.

FIVE STYLE ADEPT

You have blended four primary attack styles of the world into a new technique of your own creation.

Prerequisites: Martial Arts, Holding Basics, Kicking Basics, Punching Basics, Throwing Basics, base attack bonus +6 or higher.

Benefit: Your Unarmed attacks inflict 1d8 damage. In addition, a natural 19 or 20 on the attack roll indicates a threat and potential critical hit *(see Critical Hits, page 164)*.

HOLDING BASICS

You have trained in the fundamentals of holds and locks, making it both easier for you to grapple someone and harder for them to escape once you have been successful.

Benefit: This feat grants you the following abilities.

Joint Lock: Opponents receive a –4 penalty to all attempts to escape your pins.

One-handed Choke: You can grapple or pin an opponent using only one hand, leaving the other free for other tasks, such as attacking or deflecting arrows.

HOLDING MASTERY

You have mastered several styles of martial arts that emphasize holds and locks.

Prerequisites: Martial Arts, Holding Basics, base attack bonus +3 or higher.

Benefit: This feat grants you the following abilities.

Bone Grind: When damaging your opponent during a grapple, in addition to your normal damage, you deal 1 point of either temporary Strength damage or temporary Dexterity damage to your opponent. *See Changing Ability Scores, page 16, for more information about this type of damage.*

Nerve Lock: Opponents receive a –8 penalty to all attempts to escape your pins, and a –4 penalty to all attempts to escape your grapples.

IRON FIST

You have practiced a variety of breaking and smashing techniques, and can easily shatter items with your attacks.

Prerequisites: Martial Arts, Chi Strike.

Benefit: When you attempt to break an object using brute force, the object's Break DC is reduced by 4. Also, while making a Strike an Object action, you make attacks as if you are using a melee weapon even if making an unarmed attack, and you double your

Strength modifier for damaging objects (including armor and weapons). You are not considered to be using a melee weapon for any other purpose, including the use of melee combat feats and attack options.

KICKING BASICS

You have trained in the fundamentals of kicks.

Benefit: This feat grants you the following abilities.

Jump Kick: You may move one 5-ft. square before you make an unarmed attack. This does not prevent you from taking a bonus step during the round as described on page 160.

Roundhouse Kick: You may attack two opponents that are adjacent both to you and to each other with a single unarmed attack. Make one attack roll and compare it to each targeted opponent's Defense value. If you hit either or both of them, make a single damage roll and deal that damage to each opponent you hit.

KICKING MASTERY

You have mastered several styles of martial arts that emphasize kicks, and can mesh them together as one fluid fighting style, as well as focus them into powerful attacks.

Prerequisites: Martial Arts, Kicking Basics, base attack bonus +3 or higher.

Benefit: This feat grants you the following abilities.

Drop Kick: Once per round, you may take a –6 penalty to your attack roll before making an unarmed attack. If you hit, that attack deals double damage (thus, 1d6+3 becomes 2d6+6).

Flying Jump Kick: You may move up to two 5-ft. squares before you make an unarmed attack. This does not prevent you from taking a bonus step during the round as described on page 160.

MARTIAL ARTS

You have received focused training in unarmed combat and are able to deal greater damage or even critical hits when using unarmed attacks.

Benefit: Your unarmed attacks deal 1d6 damage. You do not suffer a –4 attack penalty in order to inflict normal damage instead of subdual damage *(see page 173)*. In addition, a natural 20 on the attack roll is a threat *(see Critical Hits, page 164)*.

MASTER OF THE FIFTH STYLE

Your personal style has gained international recognition.

Prerequisites: Five Style Adept, Holding Mastery, Kicking Mastery, Punching Mastery, Throwing Mastery, base attack bonus +12 or higher.

Benefit: Your unarmed attacks deal 1d10 damage. In addition, a natural 18, 19, or 20 on the attack roll is a threat *(see Critical Hits, page 164)*, and you no longer need to spend an action die to turn a threat caused by an unarmed attack into a critical hit.

Finally, you may make two unarmed attacks when you take the standard attack action, but if you do so, every attack you make this round suffers a –5 penalty. This effect does not stack with the benefits of Warrior's Grace (you may only benefit from one or the other in any single round), but you may use Master of the Fifth Style with all of your unarmed attacks in a single round (allowing up to twice as many unarmed attacks as you have half actions that round).

MASTER OF THE SIXTH STYLE

People compete professionally with your personal martial arts style.

Prerequisites: Master of the Fifth Style, base attack bonus +18 or higher.

Benefit: Your unarmed attacks deal 1d12 damage. In addition, a natural 17, 18, 19 or 20 on the attack roll is a threat *(see Critical Hits, page 164)*. Finally, you may make two unarmed attacks when you take the standard attack action without suffering the penalty listed under Master of the Fifth Style.

PUNCHING BASICS

You are trained in the fundamentals of punches.

Benefit: This feat grants you the following abilities.

Knuckle Punch: If you make a successful unarmed attack, you deal normal damage, plus your Strength modifier multiplied by 1.5 (rounded up).

Palm Strike: When you strike an opponent with a successful unarmed attack, the force of your blow moves him one 5-ft. square directly away from you. If the target square is occupied, your opponent remains where he is and suffers 1 point of subdual damage in addition to any damage from your successful attack.

PUNCHING MASTERY

You have mastered several styles of martial arts that emphasize punches and nerve touches.

Prerequisites: Martial Arts, Punching Basics, base attack bonus +3 or higher.

Benefit: This feat grants you the following abilities.

Flying Palm: When you strike an opponent with a successful unarmed attack, the force of your blow moves him up to three 5-ft. squares directly away from you. If the target square is occupied, your opponent remains where he is and suffers 1d4 subdual damage in addition to any damage from your successful attack.

Pain Touch: Once per combat, when you strike an opponent with a successful unarmed attack, you stun the opponent for one round in addition to dealing your normal damage. A stunned agent can't act, he loses his Dexterity bonus to Defense, and attackers get a +2 to hit him. This ability doesn't affect opponents that are immune to critical hits.

SHATTERING BLOW

You have mastered a variety of breaking and shattering techniques, allowing you to destroy inanimate objects with alarming ease.

Prerequisites: Iron Fist, base attack bonus +3 or higher.

Benefit: All of your unarmed attacks do at least 1d8 damage (if not higher due to other feats, class features, and abilities). Also, you quadruple (4x) your Strength modifier when damaging an object.

When you attempt to break an object using brute force, the object's Break DC is reduced by 8 instead of 4.

THROWING BASICS

You have trained in the fundamentals of throws and sweeps.

Benefit: This feat grants you the following abilities.

Flying Tackle: You may move one 5-ft. square before you make a trip attempt. This does not prevent you from taking a bonus step as described on page 160.

Foot Sweep: If you successfully trip an opponent in melee combat, you immediately receive, as a free action, a single attack against that opponent.

THROWING MASTERY

You have mastered several styles of martial arts that emphasize throws and sweeps.

Prerequisites: Martial Arts, Throwing Basics, base attack bonus +3 or higher.

Benefit: This feat grants you the following abilities.

Flying Throw: If you successfully trip an opponent in melee combat, you may move that opponent up to three 5-ft. squares directly away from you. If the target square is occupied, your opponent remains where he is and suffers 1d4 subdual damage.

Take Down: Once per combat, when you successfully trip an opponent, you stun him for one round. A stunned agent can't act, loses his Dex bonus to Defense, and attackers receive a +2 bonus to hit him. This ability doesn't affect opponents that are immune to critical hits.

WARRIOR'S GRACE

You are able to deliver a rapid string of martial arts attacks, at the price of accuracy.

Prerequisites: Martial Arts, base attack +3 or higher.

Benefit: During your first attack of the round, you may make one extra unarmed attack that normally takes a half action. Every attack you make this round (including those during your first attack action) suffers a –2 penalty. This effect does not stack with the benefits of Master of the Fifth Style or Master of the Sixth Style (you may only benefit from one of the three in any single round).

CHASE FEATS

Transportation and chases are an integral part of the spy genre. Expert drivers become more adept at pursuit and escape, fighting from a vehicle, and even crashing (when they want to, of course)!

...A GUN IN THE OTHER

You are a master of kicking butt from the driver seat.

Prerequisites: Drive By, One Hand on the Wheel..., base attack bonus +6 or higher.

Benefit: You suffer no penalty when shooting from a vehicle as the driver.

Normal: Making an attack while driving normally results in a –6 modifier to the attack roll.

BABY IT

You can coax a damaged vehicle to continue to perform.

Benefit: You may ignore any penalties caused by the first critical suffered by a vehicle you are operating.

CHASE SKILL FEATS

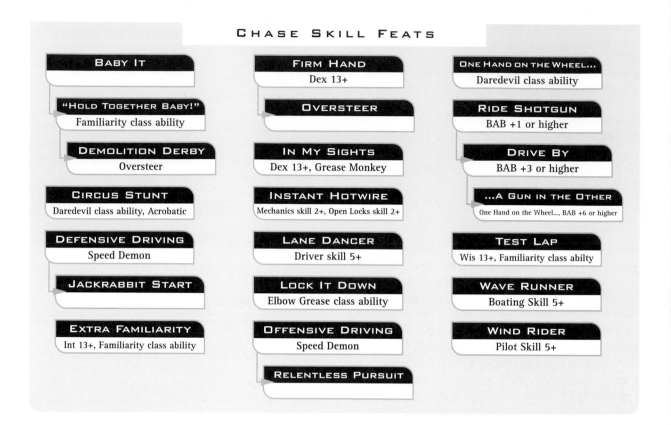

BABY IT

"HOLD TOGETHER BABY!"
Familiarity class ability

DEMOLITION DERBY
Oversteer

CIRCUS STUNT
Daredevil class ability, Acrobatic

DEFENSIVE DRIVING
Speed Demon

JACKRABBIT START

EXTRA FAMILIARITY
Int 13+, Familiarity class ability

FIRM HAND
Dex 13+

OVERSTEER

IN MY SIGHTS
Dex 13+, Grease Monkey

INSTANT HOTWIRE
Mechanics skill 2+, Open Locks skill 2+

LANE DANCER
Driver skill 5+

LOCK IT DOWN
Elbow Grease class ability

OFFENSIVE DRIVING
Speed Demon

RELENTLESS PURSUIT

ONE HAND ON THE WHEEL...
Daredevil class ability

RIDE SHOTGUN
BAB +1 or higher

DRIVE BY
BAB +3 or higher

...A GUN IN THE OTHER
One Hand on the Wheel..., BAB +6 or higher

TEST LAP
Wis 13+, Familiarity class abilty

WAVE RUNNER
Boating Skill 5+

WIND RIDER
Pilot Skill 5+

CIRCUS STUNT

You have more than a little practice with leaping from one vehicle to another. Just don't look down.

Prerequisites: Daredevil class ability, Acrobatic.

Benefit: You may add half your Boating, Driver, or Pilot skill (as appropriate, rounded down) to any attempt to jump from one moving vehicle to another. Further, you may reduce the damage you take from deliberately leaping out of a moving vehicle by 1 point per die (to a minimum of 1 point per die).

DEFENSIVE DRIVING

You are an expert at eluding pursuit.

Prerequisites: Speed Demon.

Benefit: Anytime you receive a penalty from the maneuver table *(see page 188)* while performing a prey maneuver, that penalty is halved (rounded down, minimum 1). Further, your critical threat range is increased by 1 while making prey maneuvers.

DEMOLITION DERBY

You are an expert at using the using the crumple zones and structure of your vehicle to soak up damage without losing performance.

Prerequisites: "Hold Together Baby!", Oversteer.

Benefit: You vehicle gains +2 hardness against combat damage and all crash or impact damage is reduced by 1 point per die (to a minimum of 1 point per die).

DRIVE BY

You are an expert at hitting targets as you race past them.

Prerequisites: Ride Shotgun, base attack bonus +3 or higher.

Benefit: You may ignore up to the first –2 in penalties for the speed of your vehicle when making an attack from a vehicle.

Normal: Drivers and passengers suffer a –2 penalty to their attack rolls for every 50 MPH their vehicle is traveling (rounded down).

EXTRA FAMILIARITY

You are well versed in the technical and performance details of a wide variety of vehicles.

Prerequisites: Int 13+, Familiarity class ability.

Benefit: You retain half your familiarity bonus (rounded down) with a number of vehicles you have previously acquired the familiarity bonus with, up to a maximum number of vehicles equal to your Intelligence Bonus. Each time you become familiar with a new vehicle, the previous one moves into this category and one of your other familiarities (of your choice) is dropped.

Example: Jackson, a wheelman, chooses to replace his first familiarity (a sports car he's named "Vasha") with a new vehicle, a streamlined motorcycle he calls "Scarlet." Vasha now moves into Jackson's extra familiarity feat family, and he gains half his familiarity bonus with her. He gains his full familiarity bonus with Scarlet.

FIRM HAND

You are good at maintaining control of a damaged vehicle.

Prerequisites: Dex 13+.

Benefit: You can ignore up to the first –4 in handling penalties for vehicle damage or terrain.

"HOLD TOGETHER BABY!"

You can continue to limp a vehicle along that other drivers would consider wrecked.

Prerequisites: Familiarity class ability, Baby It.

Benefit: When a vehicle you are driving is first reduced to 0 or fewer wounds it continues to operate as if the vehicle were crippled *(see Vehicle Damage page 193)*. Each time the vehicle is damaged after that, make a crash check with a +5 cumulative modifier (+5 to the first roll, +10 to the second, +15 to the third, and so on). Failure with any of these rolls reduces the vehicle to disabled status and results in a crash. Apply damage to the vehicle and all occupants as described on page 193.

"IN MY SIGHTS"

You know where to shoot vehicles for maximum effect.

Prerequisites: Int 13+, Grease Monkey.

Benefit: Your critical threat range is increased by 1 when targeting a vehicle with an attack. If you score a critical hit against a vehicle you may choose the location of the critical.

INSTANT HOTWIRE

You are a master at circumventing vehicle security.

Prerequisites: Mechanics skill 2+, Open Locks skill 2+.

Benefit: You receive a +2 bonus to all attempts to foil a vehicle's security systems. Further, attempting to open a locked vehicle or start one without the keys is a free action for you.

JACKRABBIT START

When it's time to start running, you're already long gone.

Prerequisites: Defensive Driving.

Benefit: At the start of any chase you may roll an additional d6 for the Initial Lead roll and keep the two dice you prefer.

Normal: A fixed 2d6 roll normally determines the Initial Lead for a chase.

Special: This feat may be taken a second time, allowing the agent to roll four dice to choose from.

LANE DANCER

You are highly skilled at weaving in and out of traffic and other obstacles at high speed.

Prerequisites: Driver skill 5+.

Benefit: You may treat tight terrain as close, or close terrain as open, while operating a ground vehicle. Further, you gain a +2 to all rolls to avoid collisions with non-moving obstacles while operating any vehicle.

LOCK IT DOWN

You can patch a vehicle back together with duct tape and bubblegum... while it is moving.

Prerequisites: Elbow Grease class ability.

Benefit: By spending four half-actions you can attempt to jury-rig repairs to compensate for the damage from a vehicular critical. The DC is equal to eight times the number of criticals the vehicle has received.

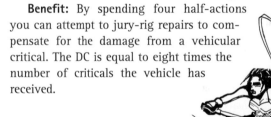

OFFENSIVE DRIVING

You are an expert at pursuit.

Prerequisites: Speed Demon.

Benefit: Any time you receive a penalty from the maneuver table *(see page 188)* while performing a predator maneuver, that penalty is halved (rounded down, minimum 1). Further, your critical threat range is increased by 1 while making predator maneuvers.

ONE HAND ON THE WHEEL...

You can still manage a few small tasks while driving like a madman.

Prerequisites: Daredevil class ability.

Benefit: If you are the driver of a vehicle this round, you only suffer a –2 penalty to maneuver checks if you take a half action. You still may not take any full actions as the driver of a vehicle.

Normal: Drivers normally face a –4 penalty to their maneuver checks if they take a half action that round *(see Step 6: Other Actions on page 186)*.

OVERSTEER

You are good at avoiding and mitigating crashes.

Prerequisites: Firm Hand.

Benefit: You receive a +3 modifier to all crash checks. You also reduce crash damage by 1d6. In addition, you receive +20% to your roll to see if your vehicle is upright after a crash.

RELENTLESS PURSUIT

Once you're on the trail, you never give up the hunt.

Prerequisites: Offensive Driving.

Benefit: The minimum lead the prey needs to make any finishing maneuver while you remain a predator in the chase is increased by +5 lengths. Once per chase you may convert a predator threat into a critical success without spending an action die.

RIDE SHOTGUN

You are experienced with compensating for the bumps and turns of high-speed chases.

Prerequisites: Base attack bonus +1 or higher.

Benefit: You do not suffer the –2 attack penalty for being a passenger in a moving vehicle, and suffer only a –4 attack penalty as the driver of a moving vehicle.

Normal: Swerving cars and jerking helicopters make terrible firing platforms. Penalties start at –2 and can go significantly higher when shooting from a moving vehicle as a passenger. Drivers normally face a –6 penalty when shooting while driving.

TEST LAP

You can break in a new vehicle in no time flat.

Prerequisites: Wis 13+, Familiarity class ability.

Benefit: When you begin work to acquire a familiarity bonus with a new vehicle, you may spend two uninterrupted hours examining and operating the vehicle. After the two hours you receive half your normal familiarity bonus (rounded up). The remainder of the bonus becomes available after the usual period *(see below)*.

Normal: Wheelmen must normally practice with a vehicle for a number of days equal to 20 minus their Wisdom modifier before they gain any familiarity bonus.

WAVE RUNNER

You are completely undaunted by high seas, narrow channels, or even churning rapids.

Prerequisites: Boating skill 5+.

Benefit: You may treat tight terrain as close, or close terrain as open, while operating a water vehicle. You also receive a +2 to all rolls to avoid capsizing.

WIND RIDER

You are adept at riding out turbulence and guessing which way to turn so as not to fight with sudden gusts.

Prerequisites: Pilot skill 5+.

Benefit: You may treat tight terrain as close, or close terrain as open, while operating an aircraft. You also gain a +2 to saving throws vs. explosives while in a moving aircraft.

COVERT FEATS

These feats focus on getting around quietly and quickly, and are therefore quite useful for all spies.

BREAK FALL

You have learned how to cushion the impact of a fall.

Prerequisites: Dex 13+, Climb skill 4+, Tumble skill 4+.

Benefit: You ignore damage suffered from the first 10 ft. of any fall (e.g. when you fall 20 ft., you only suffer damage for 10). Further, you may also voluntarily raise the DC of a Tumble check to further mitigate damage from a fall. For each +5 modifier you add to the Tumble DC, damage is taken as if the fall were 10 feet shorter (e.g. by adding a +10 modifier to the DC, you could ignore up to 40 feet of falling damage). You must still succeed with your Tumble check or suffer the damage from the full distance fallen, minus the first 10 ft.

COVERT FEATS

BREAK FALL
Dex 13+, Climb and Tumble skills 4+

JUMP UP
Dex 13+

IMP. EQUILIBRIUM
Dex 13+, Balance and Climb skills 4+

MOVING TARGET
Dex 13+, Tumble skill 8+

HIDDEN RUN
Hide and Move Silently skills 8+

NIMBLE FINGERS
Escape Artist, Open Lock,
and Sleight of Hand skills 4+

SPIDER WALK
Balance and Climb skills 8+

TRACELESS
Int 13+

HIDDEN RUN

You are a fleeting shadow, nearly invisible even as you rush past opponents.

Prerequisites: Improved Equilibrium, Hide skill 8+, Move Silently skill 8+.

Benefit: You may move up to your normal speed with no penalty to your Hide or Move Silently skill checks. You may move faster than your normal speed (e.g. you can run) with a +4 modifier to your Hide and Move Silently DCs.

IMPROVED EQUILIBRIUM

You are able to perform acrobatic maneuvers on high rooftops, sloping ledges, and other precarious surfaces with remarkable ease.

Prerequisites: Dex 13+, Balance skill 4+, Climb skill 4+.

Benefit: You may move up to your normal speed over precarious surfaces or while climbing with no penalty to your Balance or Climb skill checks.

JUMP UP

You are able to quickly jump back up after a fall.

Prerequisites: Dex 13+.

Benefit: You can stand up from a prone position as a free action rather than a half action.

MOVING TARGET

By tumbling and springing in unexpected directions, you can make yourself difficult to hit.

Prerequisites: Dex 13+, Tumble skill 8+.

Benefit: Your dodge bonus for fighting defensively *(see page 171)* is increased by +2. This stacks with the dodge bonus you receive when fighting defensively for having more than 5 ranks in the Tumble skill, but may not be combined with the effects of Expertise.

Further, your penalty to attack rolls when fighting defensively is reduced by half (from –4 to –2). This feat does not stack with other abilities and feats which reduce your penalty for fighting defensively.

NIMBLE FINGERS

Your natural skills as a thief have been finely honed by years of experience and training.

Prerequisites: Escape Artist skill 4+, Open Lock skill 4+, Sleight of Hand skill 4+.

Benefit: You may use each of the following abilities once per session, plus an additional time per session for every four agent levels you have attained (once more at 4th level, twice more at 8th level, etc.).

Fast Slip: With a successful Escape Artist check, you shrug off your bonds in half the usual time. With a critical success, you do so in a single round.

Fast Pick: With a successful Open Lock check, you pick the lock in half the usual time. With a critical success, you do so in a single round.

Fast Swipe: You may make a Sleight of Hand skill check as a free action.

Special: If you have the Quick Use feat for any of these skills, its effects are applied *after* the effects of this feat.

SPIDER WALK

You are so practiced at climbing, you have no trouble negotiating wet or slippery surfaces.

Prerequisites: Improved Equilibrium, Balance skill 8+, Climb skill 8+.

Benefit: You may add your Dexterity modifier to your skill check when climbing. This bonus is in addition to any other modifiers to the roll, including any other ability modifiers. Additionally, when making a Balance or Climb check, any modifier to your DC from slippery, wet, or angled surfaces is reduced by half (rounding down, minimum 1). Finally, your opponents receive no bonus to attack you when you're climbing.

TRACELESS

You have developed the habit of removing signs of your presence.

Prerequisites: Int 13+.

Benefit: The DC for any attempt to notice your presence or passage (i.e. whether you're in the same room as them now or have been before) is increased by a number equal to your Intelligence modifier. If you are no longer present and this adjusts the DC to spot you to 10 or more, the Track feat *(see page 90)* is required to trace your steps. Further, no one may take 10 or 20 when making a skill check to notice your presence or passage. This ability works whether the pursuer is making an opposed skill check or not.

GEAR FEATS

These feats offer more equipment, gadgets, and even vehicles to agents with the right connections.

EXTRA BUDGET

You have a friend in the equipment dispensary who can provide you with extra equipment.

Benefit: You gain an additional 5 budget points during the Gearing Up phase of each mission.

Special: This feat may be taken up to four times, each time granting an additional 5 budget points budget per mission.

EXTRA R&D SUPPORT

You have a friend in the Research & Development department who can provide you with extra gadgets.

Benefit: You gain 2 additional gadget points during the Gearing Up phase of each mission.

Special: This feat may be taken up to four times, each time granting 2 additional gadget points per mission.

SIGNATURE GEAR

You carry a signature piece of gear. Agents frequently include personal flourishes on signature gear, or use it in particular noticeable ways.

Benefit: You may select one piece of gear (valued at up to 8 budget points) as permanent personal gear. These budget points are spent independently of your standard allotment, and may not be shared with the budget points of other agents, or with budget points gained from any other source (such as other feats). These budget points may be spent on a single piece of non-gadget gear and its upgrades. Your signature gear may be a weapon. Any budget points not spent on your signature gear are lost.

This feat may be taken up to four times (by using applicable feat slots as they are earned), granting 8 additional budget points to be spent on your signature gear each time you take it (for a total of 16 BP if the feat is taken twice, 24 BP if it is taken three times, and 32 BP if it is taken four times). These additional budget points may be used to upgrade or exchange your signature gear (e.g. add sights, braces, and a bipod to a sniper rifle). When upgrading, you may spend up to 8 budget points for each time you have taken this feat, even if you didn't spend all the budget points when you first gained the signature gear or during previous upgrades. This is the only time when you may upgrade or exchange your signature gear. Any budget points not immediately spent when the feat is taken an additional time are lost.

During agent creation, you may spend personal budget to purchase additional options for your signature gear, which are then considered part of your permanent gear. Likewise, you may spend part of a mission's budget to purchase such options, but they must then be returned at the end of the mission (unless they are listed as permanent in the gear description).

Whenever you make an attack or skill check using your signature gear, you receive a bonus of +1 to the roll. Further, any action dice spent to increase rolls using your signature gear receive a +1 bonus (this does not affect the die exploding).

Special: If your signature gear is lost, you gain a Stolen Object background *(see page 98)* at no cost. If your signature gear is destroyed, you gain a permanent mission budget bonus of +2 for each feat invested in the signature gear. This bonus budget may be shared with other agents as normal. You may then spend one or more feat slots to acquire another piece of signature gear at a later time, beginning with a fresh item and upgrading as described above.

SIGNATURE GADGET OR VEHICLE

You own and use a signature gadget or vehicle. Agents frequently include personal flourishes on signature items, or use them in particular ways.

Benefit: You may select one gadget (up to 3 gadget points) as permanent personal gear. These gadget points are spent independently of your standard allotment, and may not be shared with the gadget points of other agents, or with gadget points gained from any other source (such as other feats). These picks may be spent on a single gadget or vehicle and its upgrades. Any of these gadget points not spent on your signature gadget or vehicle are lost.

This feat may be taken up to three times (by using applicable feat slots as they are earned), granting 3 additional gadget points to be used on your signature gadget or vehicle each time you take it (for a total of 6 GP if the feat is taken twice, and 9 GP if it is taken three times). These additional gadget points may be used to upgrade or exchange your signature gadget or vehicle (e.g. add options to an attache case or exchange a motorcycle for an SUV). When upgrading, you may spend up to 3 gadget points for each time you have taken this feat, even if you didn't spend all the gadget points when you first gained the signature item or during previous upgrades. This is the only time when you may upgrade or exchange your signature gadget or vehicle. Any of the additional gadget points not immediately spent when the feat is taken a second or third time are lost.

You may always spend gadget points from your standard mission allotment (or the team's) to purchase additional options for a signature gadget or vehicle, but they must then be returned at the end of the mission (unless they are listed as permanent in the gadget or vehicle description).

Whenever you make an attack, maneuver, or skill check using your signature gadget or vehicle, you receive a bonus of +1 to the roll. Further, any action dice spent to increase rolls using your signature gadget or vehicle receive a +1 bonus (this does not affect the die exploding).

Special: If your signature gadget or vehicle is lost, you gain a Stolen Object background *(see page 98)* at no cost. If your signature gadget or vehicle is destroyed, you gain a permanent bonus of +2 gadget

points at the start of each mission for each feat invested in the signature gadget or vehicle. These gadget points may be shared with other agents as normal. You may then spend one or more feat slots to acquire another signature gadget or vehicle at a later time, beginning with a fresh item and upgrading as described above.

BASIC SKILL FEATS

Every skill in the *Spycraft* game may be enhanced by a feat in this category.

ACROBATIC

You are very agile.

Prerequisites: Balance skill 1+, Jump skill 1+, Tumble skill 1+.

Benefit: +2 bonus to all Balance, Jump, and Tumble checks. In addition, your threat range with these skills increases to 19-20.

ALERTNESS

You are extremely observant and have a heightened sense of awareness.

Prerequisites: Listen skill 1+, Search skill 1+, Spot skill 1+.

Benefit: +2 bonus to all Listen, Search, and Spot checks. In addition, your threat range with these skills increases to 19-20.

ATHLETIC

A natural athlete, you perform simple athletic feats with ease.

Prerequisites: Climb skill 1+, Sport skill 1+, Swim skill 1+.

Benefit: +2 bonus to all Climb, Sport, and Swim checks. In addition, your threat range with these skills increases to 19-20.

FIELD OPERATIVE

Your hands-on experience has taught you how to gather and pass on information right under the nose of the enemy.

Prerequisites: Innuendo skill 1+, Read Lips skill 1+, Sense Motive skill 1+.

Benefit: +2 bonus to all Innuendo, Read Lips, and Sense Motive checks. In addition, your threat range with these skills increases to 19-20.

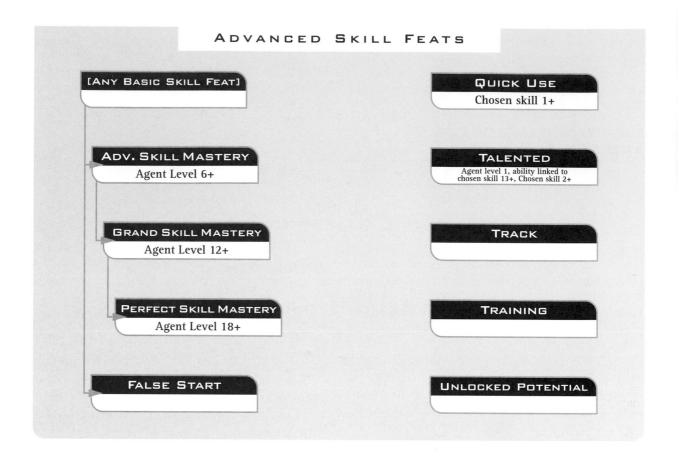

ADVANCED SKILL FEATS

[ANY BASIC SKILL FEAT]

ADV. SKILL MASTERY
Agent Level 6+

GRAND SKILL MASTERY
Agent Level 12+

PERFECT SKILL MASTERY
Agent Level 18+

FALSE START

QUICK USE
Chosen skill 1+

TALENTED
Agent level 1, ability linked to
chosen skill 13+, Chosen skill 2+

TRACK

TRAINING

UNLOCKED POTENTIAL

GREASE MONKEY

You're gifted with machines and electronics.

Prerequisites: Electronics skill 1+, Mechanics skill 1+.

Benefit: +2 bonus to all Electronics, and Mechanics checks. In addition, your threat range with these skills increases to 19-20.

MAGICIAN

You are skilled in the arts of prestidigitation.

Prerequisites: Escape Artist skill 1+, Open Lock skill 1+, Sleight of Hand skill 1+.

Benefit: +2 bonus to all Escape Artist, Open Lock, and Sleight of Hand checks. In addition, your threat range with these skills increases to 19-20.

MASTER FENCE

You can make and spot great forgeries.

Prerequisites: Appraise skill 1+, Forgery skill 1+, Gather Information skill 1+.

Benefit: +2 bonus to all Appraise, Forgery, and Gather Information checks. In addition, your threat range with these skills increases to 19-20.

MATHEMATICAL GENIUS

You have an innate understanding of mathematics that greatly aids your understanding of computers and cryptography.

Prerequisites: Computers skill 1+, Cryptography skill 1+.

Benefit: +2 bonus to all Computers and Cryptography checks. In addition, your threat range with these skills increases to 19-20.

MIMIC

You're a natural at impersonating others.

Prerequisites: Disguise skill 1+, Perform skill 1+.

Benefit: +2 bonus to all Disguise and Perform checks. In addition, your threat range with these skills increases to 19-20.

ORDINARY PAST

You used to lead an ordinary 9 to 5 lifestyle.

Prerequisites: Craft skill 1+, Hobby skill 1+, Profession skill 1+.

Benefit: +2 bonus to all Craft, Hobby, and Profession checks. In addition, your threat range with these skills increases to 19-20.

OUTDOORSMAN

You have spent a lot of time in the wilderness.

Prerequisites: Handle Animal skill 1+, Survival skill 1+, Use Rope skill 1+.

Benefit: +2 bonus to all Handle Animal, Survival, and Use Rope checks. In addition, your threat range with these skills increases to 19-20.

PERSUASIVE

You have tremendous powers of persuasion.

Prerequisites: Bluff skill 1+, Diplomacy skill 1+, Intimidate skill 1+.

Benefit: +2 bonus to all Bluff, Diplomacy, and Intimidate checks. In addition, your threat range with these skills increases to 19-20.

POLICE TRAINING

You are especially familiar with police techniques, including bomb squad practices.

Prerequisites: Bureaucracy skill 1+, Demolitions skill 1+, Surveillance skill 1+.

Benefit: +2 bonus to all Bureaucracy, Demolitions, and Surveillance skill checks. In addition, your threat range with these skills increases to 19-20.

SCHOLARLY

You have delved into a number of esoteric subjects in your spare time.

Prerequisites: Concentration skill 1+, Knowledge skill 1+.

Benefit: +2 bonus to all Concentration and Knowledge checks. In addition, your threat range with these skills increases to 19-20.

SPEED DEMON

You love fast vehicles of all shapes and sizes.

Prerequisites: Boating skill 1+, Driver skill 1+, Pilot skill 1+.

Benefit: +2 to all Boating, Driver and Pilot checks. In addition, your threat range with these skills increases to 19-20.

STEALTHY

You rarely leave a strong impression.

Prerequisites: Hide skill 1+, Move Silently skill 1+.

Benefit: +2 to all Hide and Move Silently skill checks. In addition, your threat range with these skills increases to 19-20.

WORLD TRAVELER

You were a member of the Peace Corp or similar organization, and received training required to provide basic medical support in other countries.

Prerequisites: Cultures skill 1+, First Aid skill 1+, Languages skill 1+.

Benefit: +2 bonus to all Cultures, First Aid, and Languages skill checks. In addition, your threat range with these skills increases to 19-20.

ADVANCED SKILL FEATS

These feats either build upon the basic skill feats or affect your skills in an unusual way.

ADVANCED SKILL MASTERY

You have worked diligently to improve one of your basic skill feats.

Prerequisites: Chosen basic skill feat, agent level 6+.

Benefit: Choose one of your basic skill feats. The bonus to skill checks provided by that feat is increased from +2 to +3 and the threat range with skills affected by it is increased to 18-20. (For example, if you chose the Stealthy feat, the skills affected would be Hide and Move Silently.) In addition, your Game Control must pay an extra action die to activate a critical failure when you are using one of those skills.

Special: You can take this feat multiple times. Each time you take the feat, it applies to a new basic skill feat.

FALSE START

You have become so accustomed to using your skills that you automatically know when your use of them is flawed.

Prerequisites: Chosen basic skill feat.

Benefit: If you fail a check with a skill that would take longer than a round to complete, you may begin again (starting the attempt over) as follows.

Standard Time Required	You may start again...
More than 1 round	Next round
More than 1 minute	Next minute
More than 10 minutes	Next 10 minutes
More than 1 hour	Next hour
More than 1 day	Next day
More than 1 week	Next week
etc.	etc.

If the skill check requires materials, half the materials are used up and must be replaced before you can begin again.

Special: You may take 20 using only 15 times the normal amount of time. The effects of this feat only apply to the basic skill feat it is chosen for.

GRAND SKILL MASTERY

You excel with one particular skill.

Prerequisites: Agent level 12+, Advanced Skill Mastery for the chosen basic skill feat.

Benefit: Choose one of your basic skill feats. The bonus to skill checks provided by that feat is increased from +3 to +4 and the threat range for skills affected by it is increased to 17-20. In addition, you no longer need to spend an action die to turn a threat into a critical success when using one of those skills. Finally, once per game session, you may choose to re-roll a failed skill check using one of those skills. You may not re-roll a critical failure.

Special: You can take this feat multiple times. Each time you take the feat, it applies to a new basic skill feat.

PERFECT SKILL MASTERY

You have become one of the world's greatest experts in a particular field.

Prerequisites: Agent level 18+, Grand Skill Mastery for the chosen basic skill feat.

Benefit: Choose one of your basic skill feats. The bonus to skill checks provided by that feat is increased from +4 to +5, and the threat range for skills affected by it is increased to 16-20. In addition, your GC must pay an extra action die (added to the one from Advanced Skill Mastery) to activate a critical failure when you are using one of those skills. Finally, you may now use the re-roll ability granted by Grand Skill Mastery up to three times per game session, though you cannot re-roll the same skill check more than once and you still may not reroll critical failures.

Special: You can take this feat multiple times. Each time you take the feat, it applies to a new basic skill feat.

QUICK USE

You are very quick and efficient with a particular skill.

Prerequisites: Chosen skill 1+.

Benefit: Choose one of your skills. If that skill normally takes more than 1 round to use (up to one minute), each action with it now takes half the standard time. If that skill normally takes a full action to use, it now takes you only a half action to use. If that skill normally takes a half action to use, it is now a free action for you. You may use only one skill as a free action per round by virtue of this feat.

Special: You can take this feat multiple times. Each time you take the feat, the effects apply to a new skill.

TALENTED

You are extraordinarily gifted in the use of a single skill.

Prerequisites: Agent level exactly 1, ability linked to chosen skill 13+, chosen skill 2+.

Benefit: You gain one rank in the chosen skill, the maximum rank you may have the skill at is increased by one, and the chosen skill is always considered a class skill regardless of class.

Special: This feat may only be taken once.

TRACK

You can follow the trail of prey — human and animal — across nearly any type of terrain.

Benefit: When tracking a subject outside of buildings or structures, you must make a successful Survival test to find tracks or follow them every mile. When tracking a subject inside a building or ship, a successful Spot check is required to find tracks or follow them every 300 feet. Another skill check is required each time the tracks become more difficult to follow, such as when other tracks cross them or when tracks backtrack and diverge.

When tracking, the agent must move at half normal speed (or at his normal speed with a −5 penalty to the skill check). The DC of the check depends upon the tracking surface and other conditions:

Surface	DC
Very Soft	5
Soft	10
Firm	15
Hard	25

Very soft ground: A surface that holds deep impressions of footprints such as sand, mud, or snow.

Soft ground: Any surface soft enough to yield to pressure, but firmer than wet mud or fresh snow. This includes loose dirt, very wet grass, and gravel. The quarry may leave frequent but shallow prints.

Firm ground: Includes normal outdoor surfaces, such as lawns, fields, packed earth, woods, etc. Also includes soft or dirty indoor surfaces such as thick rugs and dusty floors. The quarry may leave traces, such as broken twigs, scuffs, and occasional partial footprints.

Hard ground: Any surface that won't hold footprints, such as rock, concrete, and tile floors. Streambeds fall into this category, with any footprints being washed away or obscured. The quarry likely leaves few marks—limited to an occasional scuff, overturned rocks, or the like.

Conditions	Modifier
Every 3 people in the target group	−1
Size of targets:*	
Fine	+8
Diminutive	+4
Tiny	+2
Small	+1
Medium	0
Large	−1
Huge	−2
Gargantuan	−4
Colossal	−8
Each 24 hours since tracks were left	+1
Each hour of rain since tracks were left	+1
Fresh snow since tracks were left	+10
Poor Visibility:†	
Overcast or moonless night	+6
Moonlight	+3
Fog or precipitation	+3
Quarry hiding trail‡	+5

* For group of mixed sizes, apply modifiers only for largest size category.

† Apply only one modifier, the largest, for this category.

‡ While moving at half speed.

If this agent fails a tracking check (a Spot or Survival skill check), he can retry after one hour (when outdoors) or 10 minutes (when indoors) of searching for the trail.

Normal: Agents without this feat can use the Search skill to find tracks, but can only follow tracks with a DC of 10 or less.

TRAINING

You have devoted a great deal of your spare time to improving your skills.

Benefit: You gain 4 skill points.

Special: This feat may be taken multiple times, offering you four additional skill points each time.

UNLOCKED POTENTIAL

You have incredible potential for improvement with one of your skills.

Benefit: Choose one of your class skills. The rank limit for that skill is increased by 3. (Thus, the first time you apply this feat to a skill, its rank limit becomes your agent level + 6.)

Special: You may take this feat multiple times, and you may apply it to the same skill more than once.

STYLE FEATS

These feats deal with matters of espionage lifestyle and methods, enhancing your basic ability as a spy.

CARD SHARK

You dabbled with competitive gambling for many years.

Benefit: You receive a +3 to your roll for any competitive casino game *(see page 241),* and are considered to be fully versed in the intricacies of all major competitive casino games. You roll two dice when spending an action die to win such games.

CHARMER

You have a way of bringing people around.

Benefit: Your threat range when establishing the disposition of NPCs who start at neutral, friendly, or helpful is increased to 18-20. Further, you get a +1 to all Charisma-based skills targeting such agents.

FILTHY RICH

You don't just live the high life — you were born to it. You've usually got enough money to buy or bribe your way through problems that other agents must resolve with... training.

Benefit: You have a considerable fortune of your own outside of agency pay, all of it generating interest. You gain a bonus of +$1,000 to your field expenses at the start of each mission. Additionally, when reducing your next experience reward to gain emergency expenses *(per the rules on page 105),* your gain $100 for every XP you commit, and may commit a maximum of 1000 XP times your level. This feat does not increase your personal or mission budgets.

FIVE STAR SERVICE

You are known around the world as a connoisseur of the high life.

Prerequisites: Filthy Rich.

Benefit: You have a standing account with the world's foremost hotels, casinos, airlines, and other travel accommodations. You are never refused at the door of these establishments, and may use their services without spending any budget or personal cash.

When gambling or shopping, your credit is equal to $50,000, plus or minus $5,000 times your Charisma modifier. You may attempt to increase this credit limit by making an opposed Bluff check against the establishment's financial director (a casino's floor manager, a hotel's general manager, etc.). Every point your roll beats the director's roll by increases your credit limit by $5,000. A critical success increases it by $50,000 more.

STYLE FEATS

CARD SHARK	**FORTUNATE**	**POLITICAL FAVORS** Agent Level 3+
CHARMER	**HARD CORE**	**PRIVATE IDENTITY**
FILTHY RICH	**THE LOOK** Cha 13+	**SAFE HOUSE**
FIVE STAR SERVICE	**MARK** Wis 13+	**SILVER TONGUE**
PERSONAL STAFF	**OLD DEBTS** Backup class ability	**UNDERMINE** Cha 13+, Innuendo and Sense Motive skills 2+
FLAWLESS IDENTITY	**PLAY THE ODDS**	**HANDLER**

Be careful, however — a critical failure cuts your standard credit limit in half. You are still responsible for repaying any money you spend on credit — this feat merely establishes your practical ceiling at each establishment.

Also, should you visit areas where five-star accommodations are unavailable, your deportment grants you an opposed Bluff or Intimidate check (depending on the approach you prefer) against the person in charge of the finest rooms, clubs, and travel arrangements available to convince them to allow you to stay, fly, or gamble with their services as described above. Credit limits at lesser establishments begin at $5,000 per star, plus $500 times your Charisma modifier (e.g. success with your Bluff or Intimidate check at a two-star casino would earn you a starting credit limit of $11,000 if you have a Charisma modifier of +2). Credit increases are gained in $500 increments, and critical success increases your limit by $2,000 per star.

FLAWLESS IDENTITY

You have a perfect cover identity, complete with history, eyewitnesses, and documentation. In addition, you have compartmentalized your mind so that when you assume the cover identity, you truly believe that you are that person.

Benefit: You have one or more cover identities that are perfect in every way. Examination of your documentation, talking to your 'friends and family,' and even hypnosis all fail to pierce the facade. It takes a half action to mentally 'switch over' to a cover identity. While you are using this ability, your true personality is submerged, but secretly in control of your actions. You can switch back to your true identity at any time as a free action. You have one flawless identity for every 5 agent levels you have (rounded up).

FORTUNATE

You are unusually lucky, even for a trained agent.

Benefit: You begin each game session with an extra d4 action die. This bonus action die is a d4 regardless of the type you normally roll.

Special: You may take this feat up to three times, gaining an extra d4 action die for each additional feat.

HANDLER

You are experienced in recruiting and cultivating moles within enemy organizations.

Prerequisites: Undermine.

Benefit: At the start of each session you may "invest" two action dice into developing a "mole," a member of an enemy organization whom you have turned through bribery or blackmail. The maximum number of dice that you may invest in any mole is equal to your agent level. These dice remain invested in this mole until he betrays you or dies. The total action dice

you have invested in a mole determines his level in the enemy organization, and what help he can provide to you *(see below)*. You may have a number of moles equal to your Charisma modifier at any time.

Dice Invested	Type of Mole
1	Specialist
4	Minion
10	Operative/Foil
15	Henchman
20	Control*

* In this case, Control docs not refer to the Mastermind (the ultimate villain of a season), but to one of his close advisors or right-hand men.

Once per session, you may contact your mole. You may spend an additional action die to contact him in one hour; otherwise, it takes 24 hours to get in touch with him. If you are able to meet the mole where he lives or works, you may contact him immediately.

Once in contact with your mole, you can request his help. Describe a specific piece of information the mole can provide or a specific task he can perform. The information or task must be something that he can acquire or accomplish (e.g. you cannot ask a minion for the keys to his Control's private vault—unless, of course, he guards it). You may ask a mole for help that he or any lesser mole can provide (e.g. you may ask a hench-man to relieve the minions guarding a safehouse, then let you in, if you like). Make an opposed Diplomacy skill check against the mole, applying any modifiers that follow.

Condition	Modifier
Mole dislikes his superiors	+5 to your roll
Mole is ambivalent about superiors	+0
Mole likes his superiors	+5 to mole's roll
Mole believes in your cause	+5 to your roll
Mole stands to gain from request	+10 to your roll
Request places mole at no risk	+0
Request places mole at small risk	+5 to mole's roll
Request places mole at large risk	+10 to mole's roll
Request places mole in great risk	+20 to mole's roll

Additional modifiers may apply based on how the mole feels about you. *Check the disposition system on page 269 for more information.*

With success, the mole agrees and either immediately provides you with the information you want or promises to perform the task you asked for as soon as possible, as appropriate. A critical success with this roll either results in the mole's defection to the Agency after he fulfills your request or an automatic success with your next request (you must still roll to check for criticals when you make the next request). With a critical failure, all action dice you have invested

in the mole are lost, and he dissolves your relationship, refusing to meet with you again.

You may have moles in any number of organizations at any given time, but the number of dice invested in each organization is tracked independently from the others.

HARD CORE

There is a core of fierce professionalism in you that makes even your worst enemies treat you with respect.

Benefit: Your threat range when establishing the disposition of NPCs who start at unfriendly, hostile, or adversary is increased to 18-20. Further, you get a +1 to all Charisma-based skills targeting such agents.

THE LOOK

Whether it's devilishly handsome good looks, a laugh that melts hearts, all the right curves, or a smile that makes people weak in the knees, you've got what it takes to make members of the opposite sex stop and give you the eye.

Prerequisites: Cha 13+.

Benefit: You gain a +1 bonus to all Charisma-based skills when dealing with the opposite sex.

Normal: Most agents manage to look like they belong on a movie set. You look like someone paid a few million bucks for the privilege of having you there.

MARK

You can size someone up with a glance.

Prerequisites: Wis 13+.

Benefit: As a free action, you may target an NPC with this feat, 'sizing him up.' Name three skills. The GC must tell you which of those skills the target has the highest bonus with (i.e. which of those skills the target has the highest combined skill rank and ability modifier with), and which of the skills the target has the lowest bonus with. For example, if you named the Bluff, Sense Motive, and Intimidate skills and the target had those skills at 4, 6, and 0 ranks, respectively, the GC would answer, "The target's best at Sense Motive, followed by Bluff, then Intimidate." This feat does not confer the target's actual skill ranks or ability bonuses – only their relative strength to each other. You may use this ability a number of times equal to your Wisdom modifier (though you may only use it once per round), and you may use it on the same person more than once.

OLD DEBTS

Friends help you move. Real friends help you move bodies...

Prerequisites: Backup class ability.

Benefit: Once per session, you may pressure a contact you are calling upon with your faceman's backup ability. The backup NPC supports you as if he is an ally *(see the disposition system on page 269)*.

Normal: Agents called in with the backup ability are normally considered to be helpful.

PERSONAL STAFF

You have a small network of servants, assistants, and aides you may call upon in non-combat situations.

Prerequisites: Filthy Rich.

Benefit: You gain a number of non-combatant minions (butlers, secretaries, cooks, drivers, etc) equal to your Charisma modifier +2. You may fire and replace them, and they are considered to be helpful to their employer.

PLAY THE ODDS

You are a cold and calculating gambler, able to study the odds and formulate strategies for victory that make bookies shudder.

Benefit: You receive a +3 to your roll for any house game *(see page 241)*. If the game is completely new to you, you need only play a single round to get the feel of it (play without penalties). Additionally, you roll two dice when spending an action die to influence the outcome of house games.

POLITICAL FAVORS

You have put critical information in front of powerful individuals in the past. Now they owe you a little *quid pro quo.*

Prerequisites: Agent level 3+.

Benefit: You receive a +1 bonus to all Charisma-based skill rolls targeting politicians and all attempts to gain government intervention *(see favor checks, page 217)*. Once per serial you may make a phone call and either completely shrug off a non-capital criminal charge against you or gain legitimate access to a secure (but not secret) government facility.

PRIVATE IDENTITY

It's an agent's worst nightmare: being burned by the agency. But if that day comes, at least you'll have a few resources set aside to start fresh or clear your name.

Benefit: You have a hidden identity, including a full set of papers, birth certificates, passports, and common licenses for the country of your choice, and $1000 stashed away. A cursory computer search supports this other persona and its fake history, though there are no witnesses to support it. Should your cover identity ever become compromised, this feat confers the underworld contacts and resources required to rebuild it. To reestablish your secret identity, you must reduce your next experience reward by 2,500. XP rewards may be reduced to 0 with this option. Any deficit remaining

carries on to your next XP reward, and so on, until you have paid to reestablish your secret identity. The secret ID is not ready to be used again until the entire XP deficit has been paid off.

Normal: The Agency regularly provides its agents with fully accredited false identities. This is one the agent maintains on his own, in secret.

Special: This feat may be taken any number of times, each time creating an additional identity, also kept in secret.

SAFE HOUSE

Whether it's an old family estate or just a rented flat, there's always a roof over your head—usually one not far from the action.

Benefit: Once per session while you are in a major city, you may make use of a private safe house you own. At a bare minimum there are enough beds and couches for you and the rest of the team to sleep on, a garage, plenty of food for a couple of nights, a TV, phone service, and really thick curtains. Safe houses contain nothing else unless additional budget or gadget points, or field expenses, are spent to purchase the contents desired.

Special: You only need to purchase this feat once and you are considered to have a place to crash in every major city in the world. You may make up the locations and details of these safe houses as the game progresses, though the GC may overrule you at any time, describing a safe house as he wishes.

SILVER TONGUE

You have a knack for making even the unthinkable sound not only possible, but very, very appealing.

Benefit: You receive a +2 to all seduction rolls *(see page 271)*. Further, your threat range for such attempts in increased by 2 (e.g. a 19-20 becomes a 17-20).

UNDERMINE

You excel at playing with people's insecurities.

Prerequisites: Cha 13+, Innuendo skill 2+, Sense Motive skill 2+.

Benefit: You may use cunning suggestions to undermine another character's resolve. After speaking to him for a full round you may make an Innuendo check opposed by the target's Sense Motive. If you succeed, a seed of doubt has been planted in the target and he suffers a –1 penalty to his skill checks and a –4 penalty to his initiative for a number of rounds equal to twice your Charisma modifier.

Special: You must be able to understand and be understood by the target before you can undermine them. Any single character can only be undermined once per session.

"So tell me James, do you still sleep with a gun under your pillow?"

– Paris Carver,
Tomorrow Never Dies

FINISHING TOUCHES

BACKGROUNDS

The lives of secret agents are filled with dangerous twists and an endless array of enemies, allies, governments, and criminal organizations entering their lives with dizzying frequency. Much of this 'personal baggage' is simulated in the *Spycraft* system with backgrounds.

WHAT ARE BACKGROUNDS?

Put simply, backgrounds are subplots revolving around your agent. The big distinction with backgrounds, however, is that you can determine which subplots you take. Unlike mission subplots which the GC springs on you during play, backgrounds are voluntary agent options that allow you to tailor your spy's history, enemies, and challenges to your liking, and receive some extra experience in the process.

BUYING BACKGROUNDS

Backgrounds are purchased when you create your agent, or any time your agent gains a level. Purchasing one or two backgrounds at the start allows your spy to come into the game with a little history, but you might also want to leave a little room to flag as a nemesis a villain you find intriguing or to invest a little more heavily in a promise made to a romantic interest during one of your missions.

Regardless of when you purchase a background, the cost is from 1 to 5 skill points. After you've added a background, you may choose to add more points to it later, as long as it doesn't exceed a total of 5 points. You may only have a maximum of 5 skill points' worth of backgrounds, or two backgrounds, at any time.

The more skill points you invest, the more dangerous the background is. For example, a 1-point Hunted background might mean that your agent is only one of many targets the hunters are looking for, or that the hunters are not very powerful. A 3-point Hunted background, however, might indicate a competent team of trackers who search for your agent regularly. A 5-point Hunted background invariably prompts a life-or-death duel of wits and cunning, and may mean that the hunters are extremely skilled (perhaps even more so than your agent), well-equipped (perhaps with gadgets or other high-end weapons), or funded by a prominent criminal organization or small world power. The approximate effects of investing in each background are described within each option.

You should discuss any background you are considering with the GC to determine its nature and cost.

EARNING THEIR KEEP

By now you're asking yourself what backgrounds do for you. The answer is simple: they build character, literally. Whenever a background plays into a mission your agent is currently assigned to, he gains experience points according to Table 4.1. Simply look up the number of skill points you invested in the background, multiply by your agent's current level and — at the conclusion of the mission — add the listed experience bonus to your mission reward.

Table 4.1 lists two experience bonuses for each pairing. The number to the left is the amount gained if the background plays only a minor role in the mission, while the number to the right is awarded if the background was the mission's focus, or a central element. The Game Control is the ultimate arbiter of how much a background is involved in each mission (after all, he knows what's happening behind the scenes).

TABLE 4.1: BACKGROUND INVESTMENTS/RETURNS	
Background Cost	Award (Minor Role/Focus)*
1	25/50
2	50/100
3	75/150
4	100/200
5	150/300

Example: After encountering the criminal mastermind Kholera for the second time (and defeating him both times), Donovan invests four of the skill points he gains at third level in a Nemesis background. Two missions later, Donovan encounters Kholera again, though only as part of a secondary plotline. At the end of that mission, he gains 300 experience points. Kholera's brief encounter with Donovan prompts him to launch a mission of his own — to capture the agent — which plays out as Donovan's next serial. Since this serial features Kholera as a central element, Donovan (who is still third level) gains 600 experience points at its conclusion.

If your GC ignores a background you have purchased for three missions, you may "cash" it in for ten times the experience reward listed on the right of Table 4.1.

Example: You purchase a 3-point background and the Game Control ignores it for three missions. You then have the option of cashing it in for 1500 (10 × 150) experience points.

After you have cashed in a background, you may not select the same background again until at least three more missions have passed, unless the GC decides otherwise.

There are two more things to remember about backgrounds. First, all backgrounds involve conflict; if a background you choose for your agent doesn't involve conflict – be it physical, mental, or spiritual – and supporting challenges that crop up during the game, then it isn't a background and can't be purchased. If a background's involvement during a mission does not involve conflict, your agent gains no bonus experience for it. Second, no agent may have more than 5 skill points' worth of backgrounds, or two backgrounds, at any time.

Finally, backgrounds remain with you through the end of a season and into a new one, though your GC has the option of "cashing" them in for you at that time – for ten times the experience reward listed on the right of Table 4.1.

BACKGROUND FREQUENCY

Each background should show up at least once per season. Of course, if you select a background without consulting with your GC, he probably won't work it into his story, which means that it will show up less often – consequently granting you fewer experience points.

FULFILLING BACKGROUNDS

All good subplots come to an end. Backgrounds should also end eventually, either because of something your agent does (e.g. killing his nemesis) or something the Game Control works into the plot. The Game Control may end a background at any time, for any reason. He must inform you when he does so, though he may withhold the reason for purposes of the backstory.

Double the normal experience award is gained when a background ends, and the GC may award additional experience or action dice for dramatic or cooperative roleplay.

BACKGROUND OPTIONS

The following is an incomplete list of backgrounds, including only the most common examples.

AMNESIA

The Amnesia background has no impact on your ability scores, skills, or other statistics. It simply means that you can't remember anything before a point determined by the Game Control. It also means that a group is trying to kill or capture you, the numbers and strength of which are determined by the points you invest in the background.

Amnesia options in *Spycraft* might include failed programming or erasure.

DEBT

The amount of money owed and the power of the collectors is determined by the points invested in the background, as is their diligence in reclaiming their money. Even at a single point, the debt should be large enough that the agent cannot simply use field or emergency expenses to clear the debt (possibly gaining XP in the process of clearing the background).

DEFEATED

You might have been defeated by an enemy, by a rival, or due to lack of skill or a twist of fate. Regardless, this background means that you are determined to return the favor, no matter the cost. The points invested determine the hazards of your goal (e.g. the power of your enemy, or the difficulty of your task).

FEAR

The Fear background is common among spies, whose frantic, paranoid lifestyles nurture all manner of mental ailments. The number of points invested in a Fear background determines the strength and rarity of your fear. There are hundreds of phobias, but common ones in *Spycraft* include fear of shadows, crowds, cameras, and intimacy.

GAME CONTROL FIAT

By choosing this background, you're letting the GC know that you want a subplot, and the approximate danger level you'd like, but you're also telling him that you'd like to be surprised. Sometime when you least expect it, he'll spring it on you. Until then, you'll have to wonder... is it something on this list, or something entirely new?

HUNTED

You are wanted – by the enemy, by the law, or perhaps even by your own peers. The number of skill points invested determines your pursuers' strength, their network of contacts, and the resources they have at their disposal.

HUNTING

You're searching for something you've lost, or something you've been ordered to recover. The points invested determine the value or importance of the item you're after, how much danger is involved in getting it back, and whether a timetable is involved and how short that timetable is.

LONG-TERM MISSION

You have a secondary mission which often overlaps other assignments you receive. The points invested determine how often you are activated for the mission (i.e. how often the mission comes up), and how difficult and dangerous the mission is.

LOST (OR FORBIDDEN) LOVE

Maybe you're in a relationship you shouldn't be having, or that could be damaging if discovered, such as a dalliance with an enemy agent. The number of points invested determines the injury you could sustain if your lover is revealed.

On the other hand, your lover might have been taken from you. The number of points invested indicates the power of the persons who split you up or those who hold your lover hostage.

MISTAKEN IDENTITY

Someone wants something from you, or is convinced that you're someone you're not. All you know is that you need to find out what's happening soon. Points invested determine how much personal danger the confusion places you in, the power and resources of the people threatening you, and the difficulty of solving the situation.

NEMESIS

You have an enemy who is dedicated to disrupting your life, or maybe even injuring or killing you. The number of points invested in a Nemesis determines how often he comes after you, the complexity and danger of his plots, and the resources at his disposal.

OBLIGATION

You owe someone – maybe for something specific, or a lingering debt of thanks. The points invested determine how difficult the request is to complete, and the power and influence of the recipient. Failing to fulfill this obligation might result in a Nemesis if you're not careful...

ROMANCE

Points invested determine how often your romantic interest comes into play, how much attention or help they require, and how many rivals you have for their affections.

STOLEN OBJECT

You have lost something: an object important to you, a close ally, a friend, or your superiors. Now you've dedicated yourself to getting it back—no matter the cost.

Points invested in this background determine how powerful the person or organization who stole the object is, as well as how badly you, your friends, or your superiors need the object back.

TRUE IDENTITY

You have assumed your current identity to achieve some goal or run from your former life. Points invested determine how important or well known your former identity was, and how lethal the forces trying to reveal you are. A classic espionage-specific True Identity is the "deep cover" mission, in which you live a false life to infiltrate a hostile region or enemy organization to gather information, allies, or perform a long-term mission.

VENDETTA

You have an enemy that you long to destroy. Points invested determine your target's power and influence, and how prepared he is for you.

VOW

In a wilderness of lies, you have made a promise that you intend to keep. Points invested determine the difficulty of doing so.

Action Dice

Action dice represent the lucky breaks so commonly enjoyed by action movie heroes. The enemies' guns jam, their shots miss, and the hero pulls off incredible feats by the skin of his teeth. Use your action dice sparingly – you don't have many to start with.

STARTING ACTION DICE

A 1st-level agent receives 3 action dice at the start of each game session, as shown on Table 1.3: Action Dice, on page 20. All action dice left at the end of a gaming session are lost.

SPENDING YOUR ACTION DICE

You may spend your action dice in the following ways. In addition, there are several special ways you can spend action dice when making skill checks or during combat – these are mentioned within specific abilities and rule descriptions.

Unless otherwise stated, an agent may not spend action dice to increase the roll of another, add to another's Defense, activate another's critical successes, heal another, or request an inspiration check for another. They may only spend action dice to gain these benefits for themselves. Anyone within line of sight to a GC character who scores an error may spend action dice to activate the critical failure, and any member of the team may spend action dice to request a favor check.

1. ADD TO A DIE ROLL

You may add the total roll of an action die to any die roll you make, with a few exceptions – rolls for ability score increases of any kind, rolls for vitality points at each new level, and rolls for personal budget and mission expenses. All other rolls may be increased unless the ability, feat, or rule prompting the roll says otherwise.

You may declare to add the roll of one or more action dice to a roll at any time, *even after the roll.* However, you may not use action dice after the GC has described the outcome of an action or roll.

When spending an action die to increase a roll, you roll one of your action dice and add the result to your attack roll, damage roll, skill check, saving throw, etc. You may keep spending action dice to increase a die roll as long as you have action dice left to spend, up to the point when the GC describes the outcome.

When rolling an action die, if you roll the highest number possible on the die (such as a natural 6 on a d6), it "explodes," meaning that you re-roll the die, adding the number you roll to the previous total. So, if you roll a 6 on a d6, and then re-roll it, getting a 4, the total value of the action die is 10. An action die can keep exploding as long as you keep rolling its maximum value.

Example 1: A 1st-level leader rolls a 17 for Driver check, just shy of the 20 he needs. He decides to spend an action die, then rolls a d4, getting a 3. Adding that to his previous total of 17, he now has a total of 20, enough to succeed.

Example 2: A 6th-level soldier rolls a 12 for an attack roll and needs a 20. Spending an action die, he rolls a d6 and gets a 6. The die explodes, so he re-rolls it, this time getting a 3. When added to the previous 6, this gives a total of 9, which is enough to increase the 12 to a 21, a hit.

2. ADD TO YOUR DEFENSE.

Once per round as a free action, you may spend a single action die to increase your Defense by the total you roll. This luck bonus stays in effect until the end of the round.

Example: Donovan, close to unconsciousness, needs to avoid being hit this round. He spends a d4 action die, rolling a 4 and then a 3 (for a total of 7). His Defense is increased by 7 until the end of the round.

3. ACTIVATE THREATS AND GC ERRORS

As described in the skills section, rolling a natural 20 (i.e. the 20 is showing on the die) usually means that you've scored a threat. When you've rolled a threat, you may spend one action die to activate a critical success, gaining the benefits listed under the ability, feat, or skill description, or as determined by the Game Control (if there is no benefit for a critical success, you get your action die back if you spent one). In combat, scoring a critical success with an attack roll results in the damage being applied directly to the target's wounds.

Example 1: Donovan rolls a natural 20 when using his Jump skill. He spends an action die to turn the threat into a critical success, which indicates that he has leapt the maximum distance possible *(see page 57)*.

Example 2: Donovan fires upon one of Kholera's minions, rolling a natural 20. He spends an action die to activate the critical. The damage applies directly to the minion's wounds, ignoring his vitality.

Further, when the GC rolls a natural 1 (i.e. a 1 is showing on the die), he has scored an error. You may spend one or more action dice to activate a GC error, gaining the effects listed on Table 9.3: Sample Critical Miss Effects *(see page 228)* or an effect determined by the GC.

Example: When rolling to see if a minion hits Donovan with a rifle, the GC rolls a 1. Steve spends two action dice and the minion's weapon jams. Steve could have spent an additional action die to cause the minion's weapon to misfire, or two more to cause the minion's weapon to explode.

4. HEAL YOURSELF

When not engaged in combat, you may spend any number of action dice to regain some vitality or wound points. For each action die you spend, you either roll an action die and regain that many vitality points, or regain 2 wound points.

Example: After the combat with Kholera's minions, Donovan spends an action die to heal. He rolls a d4, getting a 4. He rolls it again, getting a 3. He heals 7 vitality points. He could have chosen to heal two wound points instead.

5. ASK FOR AN INSPIRATION CHECK.

When you're stumped about what to do next (for example, you're caught in the villain's deathtrap with no apparent escape route), you can ask the GC for an inspiration check. If he agrees, you spend an action die and roll 1d20, adding your agent level, against a DC set by the Game Control. With success, you are provided a hint about what to do (the more you beat the DC by, the better the hint).

Example: Several weeks later, Donovan is hunting one of Kholera's henchmen through Singapore. He knows the trail is present, but can't make anything of the clues. He asks the GC for an inspiration check. The GC accepts, and sets a DC of 10. Donovan rolls a 9, which is increased to 14 by his level (5). He succeeds, and receives a hint about what to do next.

6. ASK FOR A FAVOR CHECK.

When you need help beyond that of your teammates, you can request aid from the Agency's home office. This requires a favor check. There are many types of help the Agency can provide, including specialists (NPCs with skills and knowledge you need in the field), bypassing customs, and interfering with local authorities. The Agency isn't always in a position to fill your request, however, and sometimes simply chooses not to. Favor checks work like inspiration checks — roll 1d20 and add your agent level against a DC set by the Game Control.

Example: Now aware that Kholera's henchman has been captured by local authorities in Singapore, and not wanting to lay siege upon the police to get him out, Donovan contacts the Agency and requests that the henchman be released. He spends an action die and the GC sets a DC of 10. Donovan rolls a 4, which is increased to 9 by his level (5). The Agency is unable to obtain the henchman's release.

Action dice spent on Inspiration and favor checks are lost even if the roll fails. *For more information about inspiration and favor checks, see pages 217-219.*

GAINING ACTION DICE

Your Game Control awards you one or more action dice when he feels that you have roleplayed your agent exceptionally, exhibited leadership or problem-solving ability, or otherwise entertained the group. These dice are added to your pool and may be spent immediately.

In addition, when you are awarded an action die in this manner, you also receive 25 XP times your overall agent level. Thus, a 5th level Faceman/4th level soldier receives 225 XP when awarded an action die by his GC. Be sure to spend all of your action dice, since they vanish at the end of the game session. Spending action dice does not affect the amount of experience points you gain.

PERSONAL GEAR

You receive a number of budget points equal to your Charisma modifier ×5, plus your class budget bonus, plus 40. Consult the rules on page 104 to purchase your personal gear.

DESCRIPTION

Now you should flesh your agent out a bit — give him a name, decide what he looks and acts like, and give him a purpose in life.

name

Pick a name appropriate to your agent's country of origin and culture. A good name helps you form a mental image of your agent—is he named after someone famous? Someone infamous? If you're having trouble thinking of a name, just check a phonebook for the proper area, or pick up a good book of baby names.

codename

Your agent's codename is more personal and more often used during missions than his real name. It should usually reflect the agent's personality in some fashion. You might pull it from mythology or some other classical source, such as Perseus or Porthos, or you might base it on some aspect of the agent's skills, such as Wheels or Scope. A good codename should be short, easy to pronounce, and catchy.

AGE

At creation, your agent is most likely between 23 and 28 (22 + 1d6) years old. This makes him old enough to finish the Agency's extensive training courses, yet young enough for a long and exciting career. You may want to make him older or younger, but make sure it's okay with your Game Control — some GCs place restrictions on the ages of the team's agents.

Over time, your agent's physical abilities decrease while his mental abilities increase. *See Table 4.2: Aging Effects for details.* Aging modifiers can't reduce an ability below 1.

GENDER

Your agent can either be male or female, depending on the concept you've developed.

HEIGHT AND WEIGHT

You can either choose your agent's height and weight (get your GC's permission if you want a particularly unusual-looking agent) or you can randomly select his height and weight by rolling on Table 4.3: Random Height and Weight.

The result of the die roll listed under Height Modifier is added to the listed Base Height in order to determine the agent's height. Then, that same number is multiplied by the result of the die roll listed under Weight Modifier and added to the listed Base Weight to determine the agent's weight.

Example: While rolling the height for Donovan, Steve gets an 8 (which is in inches). Adding this to the base height of 4 ft. 10 in., he finds that Donovan is 5ft. 6 in. Then, he rolls a 5 for Donovan's weight modifier. Multiplying this by the 8 he rolled earlier, he finds that Donovan weighs 120 + 40, or 160 lbs.

APPEARANCE

Using your agent's ability scores as a general guide, decide what he looks like. An agent with a high Strength score might be heavily muscled, while an agent with a low Charisma score could be ugly, or have a nasty scar on his face. Decide what color the agent's eyes and hair are, and the style in which he wears his hair. What kind of clothes does your agent wear? Answering these sorts of questions can help you visualize your agent more clearly.

PERSONALITY

Decide how your agent acts and thinks. Is he stubborn? Does he bite his fingernails or fidget when forced to sit still? Is he right- or left-handed? Small mannerisms can help make your agent more realistic and easier to roleplay.

MORALS

You may want your agent to be religious, or to follow a certain code of honor. Or you might want him to be a ruthless assassin, doing whatever it takes to get the job done. Just remember that your agent's actions have consequences. Many players don't like to play with untrustworthy or vicious agents on their team, since that means they have to watch that agent as well as the enemy.

BACKGROUND

Decide your agent's past. Who raised him? How did he join the Agency? What were the two most important events of his life? Start simple and build from there. Pick one or two pivotal events that shaped your agent and explore them. As you become more familiar with your agent, you'll find new ways to expand his background.

GOALS

A goal or a driving motivation can help determine how your agent reacts to a given situation. Is he a patriot? Then it's unlikely he would betray his country except under extreme circumstances. Is he driven by revenge? Then he might drop everything to seek vengeance on someone who has wronged him in the past. As always, start small and build up. Change your agent's goals, background, and personality as you become more comfortable and familiar with him.

TABLE 4.2: AGING EFFECTS		
Age	Age Category	Ability Modifiers
1–11	Child	–3 to Str and Con, –1 Dex, Int, Wis, and Cha
12–15	Young adult	–1 to Str, Dex, Int, Wis, Con, and Cha
16–40	Adult	No modifiers
41–59	Middle age	–1 to Str, Dex, and Con, +1 to Int, Wis, and Cha
60–79	Old	–2 to Str, Dex, and Con, +1 to Int, Wis, and Cha
80+	Venerable	–3 to Str, Dex, and Con, +1 to Int, Wis, and Cha

TABLE 4.3: RANDOM HEIGHT AND WEIGHT				
Gender	Base Height	Height Modifier	Base Weight	Weight Modifier
Male	4′ 10≤	+2d12≤	120 lbs.	× 2d4 lbs.
Female	4′ 5≤	+2d12≤	85 lbs.	× 2d4 lbs.

*"Walther PPK, 7.65mm. Only three men
I know use such a gun. I believe
I've killed two of them."*

*— Valentin Zukhovsky,
Goldeneye*

GEAR

5

Gear Basics

This section focuses on standard issue gear — everything but gadgets and vehicles, both of which are covered later in this chapter. Described here are the mechanics for acquiring your permanent gear when your agent is created, as well as how to requisition gear during each mission. Also included are rules for how much you can carry and light sources and vision modifiers, followed by several sections detailing all the standard issue gear in the *Spycraft* game.

EQUIPMENT BASICS

There are three types of gear in *Spycraft*: gadgets, vehicles, and everything else (this last category is referred to as **standard-issue gear**).

The Agency does not deal in cash, but instead assigns each agent various budgets to spend on gear, broken up by gear type and whether the budget applies while at the home office or in the field. *Spycraft* breaks these budgets into the following categories.

Budget Points (BP): Budget points are used to requisition standard-issue gear from the Agency. Unless otherwise stated, they can only be spent to requisition standard-issue gear. Budget points have no dollar value, and cannot be "cashed in" or converted to gadget points or field expenses.

Gadget Points (GP): Gadget points are used to requisition experimental super-science items and vehicles from the Agency. Gadgets and vehicles may not be requisitioned with budget points or field expenses. Gadget points have no dollar value, and cannot be "cashed in" or converted to budget points or field expenses.

Field Expenses (FE): Field Expenses are funds spent as cash in the field, usually to buy things from non-Agency vendors (such as information, black market items, and paying off casino tabs). Field expenses are money, and can be spent as such at any time. They cannot, however, be used to buy or otherwise acquire budget or gadget points.

Each resource is explained in greater detail below.

BUDGET POINTS

Budget points come in two varieties — personal budget and mission budget. The first determines the gear your agent carries with him all the time. The second determines the gear he is assigned for each mission.

Personal Budget: During Step 10 of the agent creation process, multiply your Charisma modifier by 5, then add 40 + your class budget bonus. The result is your personal budget.

Example: Donovan's Charisma is 13, so his Charisma modifier is +1. He is a soldier, so his first-level class budget bonus is 2. His personal budget is 47 (5 × 1, plus 40 + 2).

You may spend your personal budget to requisition anything from the standard-issue section of this chapter. Once requisitioned, this gear remains with your agent and follows him from mission to mission. If lost, stolen, or destroyed, it is automatically replaced at the start of the next mission.

Every time you gain a level, your personal budget is recalculated and you may requisition new personal gear. This new personal gear replaces your old personal gear, and follows you from mission to mission until you gain another level and requisition another new set of items.

If lost or destroyed, gear requisitioned with your personal budget is replaced at the start of every mission.

Mission Budget: During the Gearing Up phase of every mission (usually after the mission briefing, per your GC), roll 2d4 and multiply the result by your Charisma modifier (positive or negative), then add your class budget bonus and an amount determined by the Agency's threat code for the mission *(see page 201):*

Threat Code	Mission Budget Bonus
Code: Yellow	15
Code: Red	25
Code: Black	35

Action dice may not be spent to increase this roll. The combined result is your mission budget for the current assignment.

Example 1: Donovan is a 3rd-level soldier with a Charisma of 13. During the Gearing Up phase of a Code: Red mission, he rolls a 7 (4 + 3), so he receives a mission budget of 38 (7 × 1 = 8, plus his class bonus of 6, plus the threat code bonus of 25).

Example 2: Harrigan, a uncharismatic new recruit (1st-level fixer with a Charisma of 6) receives his budget for a Code: Yellow mission. He rolls a 3 (2 + 1), so he receives a mission budget of 10 (–2 × 3 = –6, plus his class bonus of 1, plus the threat code bonus of 15).

Finally, any mission bonus result of 0 or less becomes 0. The agent simply receives no budget for that mission.

Like personal budget, your mission budget may be spent on anything in the standard-issue gear section, unless otherwise stated. All equipment not lost, stolen, or destroyed is returned at the end of each mission.

GADGET POINTS

Technologically advanced items ("gadgets") and expensive standard-issue gear (usually vehicles) cost gadget points instead of budget. Gadget points represent your 'pull' with Research and Development, and what lengths they'll go to in order to make sure you're properly equipped.

During the Gearing Up phase of every mission (usually after the mission briefing, per your GC), you receive the gadget point bonus listed on your class advancement table, plus an amount determined by the Agency's threat code for the mission *(see page 201)*:

Threat Code	Gadget Point Bonus
Code: Yellow	2
Code: Red	4
Code: Black	6

You may spend these gadget points to requisition items listed in the gadgets and vehicles section (page 131). A gadget is only permanent when its description says so. All other gadgets are returned at the end of the mission.

Note: The GC often hands out gadgets to the team that are necessary to the mission. He may require the team to spend some or all of their gadget points on these gadgets, but should only do so when the mission parameters or challenge level of the mission warrant it.

FIELD EXPENSES

Missions frequently require you to spend hard cash in the field, away from the Agency. Your budget (which only exists as a gauge of what gear the Agency can or will allot you) doesn't help in these situations. For that reason, the Agency routinely doles out field expenses to each agent. These field expenses can be either cash or anonymous credit cards (using an alias).

During the Gearing Up phase of every mission (usually after the mission briefing, per your GC), roll 2d4, add it to your class budget bonus, and multiply this total by $100. Action dice may not be spent to increase this roll. The result is your field expense account for this mission.

You may spend your expenses as cash on any items in the field, from clothing to weapons (legal or not, minding local restrictions and safeguarding your identity) to hotel suites to information. If you run low and need additional emergency expenses, you may voluntarily reduce your next XP reward by 1 for every $10 you require (to a maximum of your 500 times your level in XP exchanged during any single mission). Expenses gained in this manner are immediately available, as if you were assigned them at the start of the mission.

Example: Donovan is out of expenses but he has to throw an extra $500 at an informant. As a third-level agent, he may reduce his next XP reward by up to 1500 XP for additional expenses. He trades 50 XP for the $500, so his next XP reward is reduced by 50.

XP rewards may be reduced to 0 (though not below) with this option. Any deficit remaining carries on to your next XP reward, and so on, until you have paid for your emergency expenses.

All unused Field expenses are returned to the Agency at the end of each mission.

SHARED BUDGETS

Unless otherwise stated, mission budgets, gadget points, and field expenses may always be shared with other members of your team. Personal budgets, on the other hand, may not be shared with anyone — they are used to requisition your own gear, or forfeited. If gear requisitioned with personal budget consistently "goes missing," or is given away, the Agency (and GC) is within its rights to reduce the agent's permanent personal budget until the agent improves.

BUDGET VS. FIELD EXPENSES

Budget points are a representation of the Agency's available resources, as well as the agent's "pull" with his superiors. The most experienced he is, the more the Agency is likely to trust him with valuable or experimental gear. Budget points are also a way to balance the utility of pivotal gear, such as weapons and armor, against the challenge of the mission at hand. Agents with too much gear can find a mission boring, while agents with too little gear, or the wrong gear, may find an otherwise simple mission overwhelming.

For these reasons, the budget system is abstract and has absolutely nothing to do with real-world monetary conventions. Budget points have no dollar value, and budget point costs are based on utility, not the actual value of an item.

Field expenses, on the other hand, are money. Every mission you embark upon warrants an expense account to cover your day-to-day living expenses and any unexpected costs, from bribes to purchasing gear when you can't get in touch with the Agency.

Budget points and field expenses are mutually exclusive, and may not be exchanged under any circumstances. Even though each standard-issue item has both values, there is no comparison between them.

SPYCRAFT

The Agency provides standard packages to help agents dive into missions quickly. These packages offer a significant discount to the starting agent, but their contents are fixed and non-transferable. Each bundle costs 25 of the agent's budget points.

Bundle A
Large briefcase and clothes carrier (to store bundle)
1 set average clothes
1 set designer clothes
Personalized tuxedo liner
Cell-phone
Digital audio recorder
+ 1 commercial-grade memory chip
Evidence kit
Personal digital assistant

Bundle B
Large "hockey bag" (to store bundle)
1 set average clothes
1 set trendy clothes
Assorted street and topographical maps
Cell-phone
Crowbar
Professional grade digital camera
+ 2 professional-grade memory chips
Duct tape, super-glue and rubber bands
First aid kit
Lock picking kit
Multi-purpose tool / pocket knife
20 disposable plastic restraints
Pocket flashlight
Personal digital assistant
2 tactical radios

Bundle C
Military "sea-bag" (to store bundle)
1 set plainclothes
1 set camouflage fatigues
All-weather lighter
Cell-phone
10 chemical lightsticks
5-day supply of field rations
Digging / entrenching tool
GPS receiver (hand-held)
.357 revolver or 9×19mm service pistol
+ Laser sight (either) or silencer (pistol only)
+ 100 bullets
2 tactical radios

REQUISITIONING GEAR WHILE IN THE FIELD

You may requisition gear, gadgets, and vehicles while in the field, though the budget or gadget point cost is doubled unless you have the fixer's procure ability. Still, because so many missions go awry, or thrust agents toward unexpected challenges, it is often vitally necessary to acquire some piece of technical wizardry at the last second.

You must be able to contact the Agency to requisition gear in the field. If you are near a major city, the gear arrives in 1 hour per 5 BP or 1 GP spent (rounded up). Otherwise, it arrives in 1 hour per 3 BP or ½ GP spent (again, rounded up).

Note: Budget and expenses are usually spent to requisition gear that you use personally. Gear and services that other people use, or which happen away from you (such as wire taps and bribing government officials) usually involve a favor check, as described on page 217.

CARRYING CAPACITY

Agents learn quickly to travel light. Heavy armor or equipment can slow an agent down enough to get him captured or killed. Encumbrance rules represent this.

Armor Encumbrance: Your armor determines your speed, as shown on Table: 5.10: Protective Gear. Most likely, this is all the encumbrance you need to worry about. However, if your agent is particularly weak or carrying a lot of gear, you'll also need to check your gear encumbrance, below.

Gear Encumbrance: In order to see if your gear is heavy enough to slow you down, total the weight of all your agent's gear, armor, and weapons. Compare the total to his Strength on Table 5.1: Carrying Capacity on the opposite page. If you are carrying a medium or heavy load, it slows you further, as shown on Table 5.2: Carrying Loads.

If you are subject to both armor and gear encumbrance, use only the largest penalty from each category (Max Dex Bonus, Check Penalty, and Run). These penalties do not stack.

Lifting and Dragging: An agent can lift up to his maximum heavy load over his head. He can lift twice this amount to his waist, but he can then only move 5 ft. as a full action and loses his Dexterity bonus to Defense while doing so. Finally, an agent can push or drag up to five times his maximum heavy load. This amount is doubled under good conditions (waxed floor, or a round object) and halved for poor conditions (uphill, or an awkwardly shaped object).

TABLE 5.1: CARRYING CAPACITY

STR	Light Load	Medium Load	Heavy Load
1	up to 3 lbs.	4–6 lbs.	7–10 lbs.
2	up to 6 lbs.	7–13 lbs.	14–20 lbs.
3	up to 10 lbs.	11–20 lbs.	21–30 lbs.
4	up to 13 lbs.	14–26 lbs.	27–40 lbs.
5	up to 16 lbs.	17–33 lbs.	34–50 lbs.
6	up to 20 lbs.	21–40 lbs.	41–60 lbs.
7	up to 23 lbs.	24–46 lbs.	47–70 lbs.
8	up to 26 lbs.	27–53 lbs.	54–80 lbs.
9	up to 30 lbs.	31–60 lbs.	61–90 lbs.
10	up to 33 lbs.	34–66 lbs.	67–100 lbs.
11	up to 38 lbs.	39–76 lbs.	77–115 lbs.
12	up to 43 lbs.	44–86 lbs.	87–130 lbs.
13	up to 50 lbs.	51–100 lbs.	101–150 lbs.
14	up to 58 lbs.	59–116 lbs.	117–175 lbs.
15	up to 66 lbs.	67–133 lbs.	134–200 lbs.
16	up to 76 lbs.	77–153 lbs.	154–230 lbs.
17	up to 86 lbs.	87–173 lbs.	174–260 lbs.
18	up to 100 lbs.	101–200 lbs.	201–300 lbs.
19	up to 116 lbs.	117–233 lbs.	234–350 lbs.
20	up to 133 lbs.	134–266 lbs.	267–400 lbs.
21	up to 153 lbs.	154–306 lbs.	307–460 lbs.
22	up to 173 lbs.	174–346 lbs.	347–520 lbs.
23	up to 200 lbs.	201–400 lbs.	401–600 lbs.
24	up to 233 lbs.	234–466 lbs.	467–700 lbs.
25	up to 266 lbs.	267–533 lbs.	534–800 lbs.
26	up to 306 lbs.	307–613 lbs.	614–920 lbs.
27	up to 346 lbs.	347–693 lbs.	694–1,040 lbs.
28	up to 400 lbs.	401–800 lbs.	801–1,200 lbs.
29	up to 466 lbs.	467–933 lbs.	934–1,400 lbs.
+10	×4	×4	×4

TABLE 5.2: CARRYING LOADS

Load	Max Dex	Check Penalty	Speed (40 ft.)	(35 ft.)	(30 ft.)	(25 ft.)	(20 ft.)	(15 ft.)	Run
Medium	+3	–3	25 ft.	25 ft.	20 ft.	20 ft.	15 ft.	15 ft.	×4
Heavy	+1	–6	25 ft.	20 ft.	20 ft.	15 ft.	15 ft.	10 ft.	×3

Bigger and Smaller Targets: Table 5.1: Carrying Capacity shows how much weight Medium agents can carry. Larger or smaller agents can carry different amounts depending on their size category: Fine (×1/8), Diminutive (×1/4), Small (×1/2), Large (×2), Huge (×4), Gargantuan (×8), and Colossal (×16).

Tremendous Strength: For Strength scores over 29, find the score between 20 and 29 that has the same ones digit as the agent's Strength, then multiply the figures by 4 to add 1 to the Strength score's tens digit. Continue until you reach the Strength score you want to calculate.

Thus, to figure out the carrying capacity for an agent with a Strength of 46, you'd look up 26 on the table, and then multiple the figures by 4 to calculate the values for a Strength 36. Then you'd multiply those figures by 4 again (for a total multiplier of ×16) in order to calculate the carrying capacity of an agent with Strength 46.

VISION AND LIGHT

Agents occasionally find themselves operating in dark underground passages or assigned on a night mission. Smart agents prepare themselves for such contingencies by bringing along a source of light or a way to see in the dark. See the table on the next page for the radius and duration of a light source, and check the Other Gear section (*see page 125*) for details about light-enhancement equipment.

Agents using special night-vision or infrared sensing equipment can see in dark areas as though they were lit.

Object	Light	Duration
Candle	5 ft.	1 hour
Flashlight	60 ft. cone*	12 hours
Floodlight	120 ft. cone*	4 hours
Glowstick	10 ft.	4 hours
Lantern	30 ft.	6 hours
Lighter	5 ft.	2 hours
Match	5 ft.	1 round
Torch	20 ft.	1 hour

*A cone is 5 ft. wide at the agent's location and widens 5 ft. for every 30 ft. it travels.

WEAPON QUALITIES

Blast damage: Weapons which cause blast damage, such as explosives and grenades, damage all characters and objects within an area of effect *(see page 172)*.

Double: A double weapon has two or more damage values (e.g. "1d6/1d6"), each representing a separate attack. When using a double weapon, you may make two attacks during one half action attack, following the rules for two weapon fighting *(see page 165)*. The damage value to the left is used for the first attack and the value to the right is used for the second attack. You may only make a double attack once per round, even if you also attack with your second half action.

Grenade-like: Grenade-like weapons are hurled or propelled, and deviate from the target square when attacks with them are unsuccessful *(see page 173)*.

Light: Melee weapons are considered light for you if their size is smaller than yours (e.g. if you are Medium size and wielding a Small weapon).

One-Handed: Melee weapons are considered one-handed for you if their size is equal to yours (e.g. if you are Medium size and wielding a Medium weapon). Wielding a one-handed melee weapon with two hands allows you to add 1.5 times your Strength modifier to damage rolled using it.

Subdual: Some gear can cause subdual damage, which can knock a character out but can't kill him. *See Subdual Damage, page 173.*

Two-Handed: Melee weapons are considered two-handed for you if their size is one size larger than yours (e.g. if you are Medium size and wielding a Large weapon). You add 1.5 times your Strength modifier to damage rolled using two-handed weapons. You may not use weapons two or more sizes larger than you.

GEAR DESCRIPTIONS

The rest of this chapter contains descriptions of standard-issue gear, gadgets, and vehicles (in that order). Within each section, entries are presented in alphabetical order, with the exception of default weapon and gadget options, and ammunition, which are listed first.

Each standard-issue gear section has a master table with all the pertinent costs and values, accompanied by a section of descriptions which the table refers you to for specific gear details. Gadgets are listed by housing or theme (e.g. attaché cases, vehicular options, etc.), which are presented in alphabetical order, as are options for each of the housings or themes. Finally, vehicles are presented in several tables grouping vehicles together by category (air vehicles, balance-based vehicles, etc.).

WEAPONS

The weapon tables each contain the following data.

Budget Points: The BP cost of the weapon.

Damage: The amount of damage the weapon does.

Error: The natural rolls that are considered errors when using the weapon (e.g. an Error entry of 1-2 means that natural 1s and 2s are both errors with that weapon).

Threat: The natural rolls that are considered threats when using the weapon (e.g. a Threat entry of 18-20 means that natural 18s, 19s, and 20s are all threats with that weapon).

Range Increment: The distance the weapon may fire without penalty. Each increment after the first applies a –2 modifier to all attacks with the weapon. Thrown weapons, such as grenades, have a maximum range of five range increments. Projectile weapons, such as bows or guns, have a maximum range of ten range increments.

Weight: The weight of the weapon, in pounds.

Actual Cost: The actual cost of the weapon, in field expenses.

PROTECTIVE GEAR

The Protective Gear table contains the following data.

Budget Points: The BP cost of the protective gear.

Defense Modifier: Unless otherwise directed, this modifier is applied to your Defense when wearing this protective gear.

Damage Reduction: Normally, all damage you take while wearing this protective gear is reduced by this number. There are a few exceptions and additional effects, however, as described on page 178.

Maximum Dexterity Bonus: Unless otherwise directed, this number is the maximum Dexterity bonus you may apply to Defense while wearing this protective gear. If this limit is greater than your Dexterity modifier, it has no impact on your Defense total.

Armor Check Penalty: When you use armor you do not have the proficiency feat for *(see page 68)*, you suffer this penalty to your attack rolls and all skill rolls involving movement (including Handle Animal when riding). When you use armor you have the proficiency feat for, you suffer this penalty to the Balance, Climb, Escape Artist, Hide, Jump, Move Silently, Sleight of Hand, Swim, and Tumble skills.

Speed Penalty: Regardless of modern advancement, armor is still bulky and often difficult to maneuver in, applying a penalty to your speed. This is in addition to encumbrance penalties for armor, which are derived from its weight *(see below and under Gear Encumbrance on page 106)*. When you use armor you do not have the proficiency feat for, your speed is reduced by two times this amount. When you use armor you have the proficiency feat for, your speed is reduced by this amount. If this reduces your speed to 0 or less, you may only make one bonus 5-ft. step *(see page 160)* per round while wearing this armor.

Weight: The weight of the protective gear, in pounds. The weight of armor is added to the weight of all other gear an agent carries for the purposes of determining encumbrance *(see page 106)*.

Actual Cost: The actual cost of the protective gear, in field expenses.

OTHER GEAR

The Other Gear table contains the following data.

Budget Points: The BP cost of the gear.

Weight: The weight of the gear, in pounds.

Actual Cost: The actual cost of the gear, in field expenses.

VEHICLES

The vehicle tables contain the following data.

Gadget Points: The GP cost of the vehicle.

Size: Vehicles use the same size category scale that human combatants use *(see page 175)*. Larger vehicles have an easier time surviving crashes, and inflict more damage when ramming other vehicles.

Handling: This number is added to all maneuver checks a driver makes while using a vehicle. Some vehicles have handling penalties, which are subtracted from maneuver checks.

Speed: This is how many squares a vehicle may move in one half action on a standard combat grid. The miles per hour speed of a vehicle is listed in parentheses next to this value.

Defense: This is a vehicle's base chance to be hit before taking the driver's skill into account. A driver adds his Dexterity modifier to his vehicle's Defense value when he's behind the wheel.

Wound Points: This determines how much damage a vehicle can take. Vehicles don't have vitality points.

Hardness: Just like object hardness *(see page 168)*, a vehicle's hardness is subtracted from all damage it suffers before the damage is applied to the vehicle's wound points.

Actual Cost: The cost of the gear in field expenses.

MELEE WEAPONS

Melee weapons cover a broad range of hand weapons available. To properly use any of the weapons listed here you must have the Weapon Proficiency (Melee) feat. Otherwise you suffer a –4 penalty to your attack rolls.

BAYONET

A bayonet is similar to a knife except that it's designed to attach to the end of a rifle. A bayonet not attached to the end of a rifle uses the statistics for a knife.

BRASS KNUCKLES

Brass knuckles add +1 to your damage when you make an unarmed attack. Newer models of brass knuckles are also made from composite materials to help prevent detection from electronic devices; the cost of one of these is double that of a normal set of brass knuckles.

CATTLE PROD

When attacking with a cattle prod, make a melee touch attack. The victim must make a Fortitude save (DC 15) or be stunned for 1d4 rounds.

CHAINSAW

Starting a chainsaw takes a half action. The listed damage is for a running chainsaw; otherwise it deals 1d6 subdual damage.

TABLE 5.3: MELEE WEAPONS

Weapon Name	Budget Points	Damage	Error	Threat	Range Increment	Weight	Actual Cost
Unarmed attacks							
S/M/L combatant	–	1d2/1d3/1d4	–	–	–	–	–
Brass knuckles*	1	Special	1	–	–	½ lb.	$20
Small							
Bayonet*	4	1d6	1	20	–	1 lb.	$40
Broken bottle	–	1d4	1-3	20	–	½ lb.	–
Butt, pistol	–	1d3+1**	1	20	–	as weapon	as weapon
Butt, rifle	–	1d6†	1-2	19-20	–	as weapon	as weapon
Garrote*	2	Special	1-2	–	–	¹⁄₁₀ lb.	–
Hook	3	1d6	1-2	20	–	1 lb.	$20
Knife	3†‡	1d4	1	20	5 ft.	1 lb.	$20
Punch dagger	4	1d3+1	1-2	19-20	–	2 lb.	$20
Sap	2	1d3+2**	–	–	–	3 lb.	$10
Stiletto	3	1d6	1-2	20	–	1 lb.	$40
Survival knife*	4†‡	1d6	1	20	5 ft.	3 lb.	$60
Switchblade	5	1d4	1-3	18-20	–	1 lb.	$60
Taser*	12	1d8**	1	–	5 ft.	2 lb.	$100
Medium							
Axe, medium	5	1d8	1-3	19-20	–	7 lb.	$40
Baton/club	4†‡	1d6	1	20	10 ft.	3 lb.	$20
Cattle prod*	8	1d10**	1	–	–	5 lb.	$300
Chain	4	2d4	1-3	20	–	10 lb.	$10
Fencing foil	7	1d6+1	1-3	18-20	–	3 lb.	$200
Lead pipe	4†‡	1d6+1	1-2	20	10 ft.	6 lb.	–
Machete/sword	4	1d8	1-2	20	–	4 lb.	$150
Sword cane*	7	1d6	1-2	19-20	–	4 lb.	$250
Large							
Axe, large	7	1d12	1-3	19-20	–	20 lb.	$200
Baseball bat	6	1d10	1	20	–	9 lb.	$20
Chainsaw*	11	2d8	1-3	18-20	–	15 lb.	$120
Spear	6†‡	1d10	1	20	20 ft.	9 lb.	$20
Sword, large	6	1d12	1-2	20	–	15 lb.	$300

* See item description for special rules concerning this weapon.

** This is subdual damage. This weapon cannot inflict normal damage.

† Use the hurled proficiency and listed range increment when this weapon is thrown.

‡ Add your Strength modifier to damage when this weapon is thrown.

GARROTE

A garrote, when wielded in both hands, adds +4 to damage you inflict while grappling someone. This damage may be subdual or normal at your discretion.

SURVIVAL KNIFE

A survival knife has a hollow handle which stores a small amount of essential survival gear. The back side of the blade is also serrated edge so that the weapon can be used as an improvised saw. The survival knife gives you +2 to all Survival checks.

SWORD CANE

A sword cane appears to be an ordinary cane. It is actually a sheath holding a short sword. A spot check (DC 20) identifies it.

TASER

When attacking with a taser, make a melee touch attack. If successful, the victim suffers the weapon's damage and must make a Fortitude save (DC 18) or be stunned for 1d8 rounds. Tasers have enough power for 50 shots before they must be recharged (costing 2 BP).

FIREARMS

This section includes the available types of small arms available for use. It is intentionally generic, with examples of various calibers/types listed for reference. Greater detail in this and all other standard-issue gear categories is forthcoming in the *Modern Arms and Equipment Guide,* out soon for the *Spycraft* roleplaying game.

HANDGUNS

The term "handgun" describes any firearm intended for one-handed operation by the user. To properly use any of the weapons listed in this category you must have the Weapon Proficiency (Handgun) feat; otherwise you suffer a –6 penalty to all your attack rolls.

Handguns may use any sighting system enhancement designed for use with handguns. No pistols or revolvers are capable of the burst or strafe abilities, unless you have Speed Trigger or a like feat or ability.

PISTOLS

Pistols generally keep ammunition in a magazine rather than a cylinder, making them quick to reload. Pistols are more susceptible to malfunctions caused by questionable ammunition quality and projectile design than revolvers, though unlike revolvers they may use silencers.

Backup: Backups come in a variety of calibers and are similar to service pistols in design and function, though smaller and featuring reduced ammunition capacities. These weapons carry 8 shots. *Examples:* Beretta Model 80 Cheetah, Glock 26 & 27, Heckler & Koch USP 45 Compact, Walther PPK.

Pocket: Similar in concept to the "Saturday Night Special" revolver, pocket pistols are easily concealed (–4 to the DC to Spot them on your person) at the cost of poor reliability and low ammunition capacity. These weapons carry 6 shots. *Examples:* Beretta Model 21 Bobcat, Walther TPH.

Service: The duty weapon of the vast majority of law enforcement agencies around the world, these pistols carry 10 shots. High capacity magazines holding 15 shots of ammunition can be requisitioned for $50 or by adding 1 to the weapon's budget point cost. *Examples:* Browning Hi-Power, Glock 17, Ruger P89, Sig Sauer P220, Smith & Wesson 410.

Target: These are highly customized versions of the service pistol which are designed for increased accuracy. The agent receives a +1 enhancement bonus to all attacks with this weapon. These weapons carry 10 shots. *Examples:* Glock 17L, Heckler & Koch USP Expert.

REVOLVERS

Revolvers hold ammunition in a rotating cylinder. When you rotate this cylinder, either by pulling the trigger or cocking back the hammer, the next round of ammunition aligns with the firing mechanism and barrel. Revolvers can fire a wide range of ammunition types and are less susceptible than pistols to malfunctions caused by poor ammunition quality. Due to the open space between the firing mechanism and the rear surface of the cylinder, revolvers cannot use silencers. Revolvers come in a wide range of models, calibers, and levels of quality.

Hunting: Generally too heavy to carry as an every-day weapon, these pistols are loaded with the most powerful handgun ammunition available. Custom hand loaded ammunition is common, as are telescopic sights (both options which must be requisitioned separately). These weapons carry 6 shots. *Examples:* Ruger Super Redhawk.

Saturday Night Special: "Saturday Night Specials" are cheap and of very low quality, carrying 5 shots of small caliber ammunition.

Service: Service revolvers were the standard sidearm of most law enforcement agencies for over 100 years. Less prevalent now, they still retain some popularity and appeal. These weapons carry 6 shots. *Examples:* Colt Python, Ruger SP 101, Smith & Wesson Model 10.

OTHER HANDGUN-LIKE WEAPONS

These weapons are similar to handguns in use, and are therefore covered by the same weapon group proficiency.

Mace spray: This small canister sprays a toxic jet stream or cloud of atomized droplets. You must strike a target in the face for this weapon to work, so your target receives a +4 bonus to his Defense against mace attacks. With a successful hit, the target must make a Fortitude check with a –4 penalty or suffer blindness *(see page 177)* for 1d10 rounds. Each canister contains enough spray for 2 uses.

Dart gun: This weapon fires small darts which work like hypodermic needles, injecting a fluid of the user's choice into the target's bloodstream when they inflict damage. If none of the dart gun's 1d4 damage is taken by the target as vitality or wound damage, the toxin is not delivered into his system. Any fluid can be loaded into dart gun ammunition. Several examples are listed on page 238. This weapon must be reloaded (a half action) each time it is fired. Darts are free – the toxin within them is not, and must be requisitioned with budget points or mission expenses as normal.

TABLE 5.4: FIREARMS AMMUNITION

Ammunition Type	Budget Points	Actual Cost	Effect
Hurled Weapons			
Arrows	1/50	$10/50 shots	No modifiers.
Bolts	1/50	$10/50 shots	No modifiers.
Pistol			
Military Ball*	1/50 shots	$15/50 shots	No modifiers.
Jacketed Hollow Point (JHP)*	1/50 shots	$25/50 shots	+1 damage per hit (not per die), double target's damage reduction.
Safety Slugs (SS)*	1/20 shots	$20/20 shots	–2 to each damage die (min. 1), double target's damage reduction.
Teflon-Tipped (TEF)*	2/20 shots	$40/20 shots	Reduce damage reduction by 1 (minimum 1).
Rifle			
Full Metal Jacket (FMJ)*	1/20 shots	$15/20 shots	No modifiers.
Armor Piercing (AP)*	3/20 shots	$30/20 shots	Reduce damage reduction by 2 (minimum 0).
Soft Point (SP)*	4/20 shots	$25/20 shots	+1 damage per hit to unarmored targets, completely ineffective (no damage) to armored targets and cover.
Tracer (T)*	2/20 shots	$40/20 shots	Add +2 to attack your roll, may only be used with rifles and machine guns.
Shotgun			
Slug*	1/20 shots	$10/5 shots	No modifiers.
Beanbag*	1/20 shots	$30/5 shots	Damage done is considered subdual.
Flechette*	3/20 shots	$20/5 shots	Attacks two adjacent targets in adjacent squares. Roll for each. Reduce damage reduction by 1 (minimum 1). Lose 1d4 damage for each range increment the shot travels.
Gas*	2/20 shots	$40/5 shots	Special*
Shot Shell*	2/20 shots	$15/25 shots	Attacks two adjacent targets in adjacent squares. Roll for each. Lose 1d4 damage for each range increment the shot travels.

* See item description for information concerning this ammunition.

RIFLES

The term "rifle" describes any firearm intended to be shoulder-fired. In order to properly use a weapon listed in this category you must have the Weapon Proficiency (Rifle) feat; otherwise you suffer a –4 penalty to all your attack rolls.

Rifles are divided into several different categories based on the type of action they use to operate the firing mechanism.

Assault Rifle: The modern combat rifle in use by most nations around the world. These weapons carry 30 shots and have the burst and strafe abilities. High capacity magazines holding 50 shots can be requisitioned for $100 or by adding 4 to the weapon's budget point cost. *Examples:* Colt M-16A1 & A2, Enfield L85A1, Heckler & Koch G3, Kalashnikov AK-47.

Bolt-Action: Bolt-action rifles are manually operated, making them very reliable but also reducing their rate of fire. These rifles tend to have excellent accuracy and are very popular for hunting and target shooting. These weapons carry 5 shots and do not have the burst or strafe abilities. *Examples:* Browning A-Bolt series, Remington 700 series.

Lever Action: Lever action rifles are manually operated, making them very reliable. They also tend to have a marginally better rate of fire than bolt-action rifles. Lever-action rifles are very popular for hunting in

TABLE 5.5: PISTOLS AND SUBMACHINEGUNS

Weapon Name	Budget Points	Damage	Error	Threat	Range Increment	Weight	Actual Cost
Handguns* [All handguns are Small weapons.]							
*Revolvers, Saturday Night Special** [All Saturday Night Specials hold 5 shots.]							
.22 LR	8	1d6+1	1-2	20	10 ft.	1 lb.	$50
*Revolvers, Service** [All service revolvers hold 6 shots.]							
.38 Special	11	1d6+2	1	20	15 ft.	2 lb.	$300
.357 Magnum	14	2d4+1	1-2	19-20	20 ft.	3 lb.	$400
.44 Magnum	21	2d6+2	1	19-20	20 ft.	3 lb.	$450
*Revolvers, Hunting** [All hunting revolvers hold 6 shots.]							
.44 Magnum	21	2d6+2	1	19-20	25 ft.	5 lb.	$500
*Pistols, Pocket** [All pocket pistols hold 6 shots.]							
.22 LR	6	1d6+1	1-4	20	10 ft.	1 lb.	$60
*Pistols, Backup** [All backup pistols hold 8 shots.]							
.380 ACP	8	1d8	1-2	20	10 ft.	2 lb.	$250
7.65mm	7	1d6	1	20	10 ft.	2 lb.	$300
9×19mm	11	1d10	1	20	15 ft.	2 lb.	$300
.40 S&W	13	1d12	1	20	15 ft.	2 lb.	$325
.45 ACP	18	1d10+2	1	19-20	15 ft.	2 lb.	$350
*Pistols, Service** [All service pistols hold 10 shots.]							
9×19mm	13	1d10	1	20	20 ft.	3 lb.	$400
.40 S&W	15	1d12	1	20	20 ft.	3 lb.	$425
.45 ACP	22	1d10+2	1	19-20	20 ft.	3 lb.	$450
.50 Magnum	27	2d8	1-2	19-20	30 ft.	6 lb.	$1000
*Pistols, Target** [All target pistols hold 10 shots.]							
9×19mm	18	1d10	1	20	30 ft.	5 lb.	$500
.45 ACP	25	1d10+2	1	19-20	30 ft.	5 lb.	$600
Other handgun-like weapons							
Mace spray*	7 each	Special	1-2	—	2 ft.	2 lb.	$25
Dart Gun*	7 + toxin	1d4/Special	1-2	—	15 ft.	4 lb.	$200
Submachineguns* [All submachineguns are Medium-size weapons and hold 30 shots.]							
.380 ACP	14	1d8	1-2	19-20	20 ft.	5 lb.	$800
9×19mm	18	1d10	1	19-20	50 ft.	6 lb.	$1000
.45 ACP	21	1d10+2	1-2	19-20	50 ft.	7 lb.	$1200

* See item description for special rules concerning this weapon.

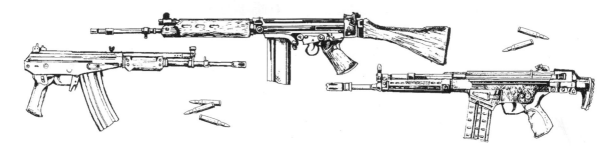

TABLE 5.6: RIFLES AND SHOTGUNS

Weapon Name	Budget Points	Damage	Error	Threat	Range Increment	Weight	Actual Cost
Rifles* [All rifles are Large weapons.]							
*Rifles, Single Shot** [All single shot rifles hold 1 shot.]							
.22 LR	7	1d6+1	1	20	20 ft.	4 lb.	$50
*Rifles, Bolt-Action** [All bolt-action rifles hold 5 shots.]							
.22 LR	9	2d4	1	20	20 ft.	2 lb.	$200
.30-06	27	2d10	1	19-20	80 ft.	8 lb.	$400
*Rifles, Lever-Action** [All lever-action rifles hold 8 shots.]							
.30-30	27	2d8+2	1	19-20	80 ft.	5 lb.	$400
*Rifles, Semi-Automatic** [All semi-automatic rifles hold 10 shots.]							
.22 LR	9	1d6+1	1-2	20	20 ft.	5 lb.	$200
5.56×45mm	26	2d8+1	1-2	19-20	100 ft.	6 lb.	$500
7.62×39mm	22	2d8	1	20	90 ft.	6 lb.	$400
7.62×51mm	26	2d10	1-2	20	120 ft.	8 lb.	$800
.30-06	30	2d10	1-2	19-20	150 ft.	10 lb.	$1000
*Rifles, Assault** [All assault rifles hold 30 shots.]							
5.56×45mm	31	2d8+2	1-2	19-20	100 ft.	6 lb.	$1500
7.62×39mm	25	2d8	1	20	90 ft.	6 lb.	$1000
7.62×51mm	32	2d10	1-2	19-20	120 ft.	8 lb.	$2000
*Rifles, Sniper** [All sniper rifles hold 5 shots.]							
5.56×45mm	29	2d8+2	1	18-20	150 ft.	8 lb.	$1000
7.62×51mm	31	2d10	1	18-20	200 ft.	10 lb.	$1200
7.62×54mm	33	5d4	1	18-20	175 ft.	10 lb.	$800
.50 BMG	45	2d10+4	1-2	17-20	300 ft.	20 lb.	$2000
Shotguns* [All shotguns are Large weapons.]							
*Shotguns, Single Shot** [All single shot shotguns hold 1 shot.]							
10 gauge	25	5d4	1	19-20	25 ft.	7 lb.	$200
12 gauge	21	4d4	1	19-20	25 ft.	7 lb.	$125
20 gauge	16	3d4	1	19-20	25 ft.	7 lb.	$100
*Shotguns, Pump Action** [All pump action shotguns hold 8 shots.]							
10 gauge	27	5d4	1-2	19-20	25 ft.	8 lb.	$400
12 gauge	22	4d4	1-2	19-20	25 ft.	8 lb.	$300
20 gauge	17	3d4	1-2	19-20	25 ft.	8 lb.	$300
*Shotguns, Close Assault Weapon System** [All CAWS hold 12 shots.]							
12 gauge	29	4d4	1-3	19-20	40 ft.	12 lb.	$1000

* See item description for special rules concerning this weapon.

rough, wooded terrain. These weapons carry 8 shots and do not have the burst or strafe abilities. *Examples:* Marlin Model 336C, Winchester Model 94.

Semi-Automatic: During the period between World War II and the Vietnam conflict most nations adopted semi-automatic rifles as their standard issue combat rifles. Most semi-automatics are now used by civilian sport shooters and hunters, and a few have found their way into the hands of particular snipers. These weapons carry 10 shots and have the burst but not the strafe ability. *Examples:* Bushmaster M17S, Colt AR-15, Henry US Survival, Marlin 795, Ruger 10/22.

Single Shot: Once very popular for big game hunting, these rifles are capable of firing the most powerful rounds available. They are still popular with enthusiasts and challenge-seekers. These weapons carry 1 shot and do not have the burst or strafe abilities. *Examples:* Marlin Model 15YN, Savage Mark I-G.

Sniper Rifle: Sniper rifles are customized, highly accurate versions of the bolt action rifle. They hold 5 shots and come standard with a telescopic sight and bipod (i.e. these items are factored into the cost of the weapon). Standard attack actions take one full round when using a sniper rifle (in order for the agent to take advantage of its added accuracy). If fired with a half action attack, their threat range is 20. Sniper rifles do not have the burst or strafe abilities. *Examples:* Chinese Type 79, Dragunov SVD, Galil 7.62 sniper.

SHOTGUNS

Shotguns are shoulder-fired weapons, originally intended for hunting, which fire a round comprised of multiple small projectiles. Shotguns are categorized by their "gauge," which is a measure of their bore size. The smaller the number, the larger the bore (i.e. a 10 gauge shotgun has a larger bore than a 20 gauge shotgun). The larger the bore, the larger the projectiles the shotgun fires.

Shotguns have a maximum range of 5 increments.

To properly use any of the weapons listed in this category you must have the Weapon Proficiency (Rifle) feat; otherwise you suffer a –4 penalty to all attack rolls.

Shotguns are divided into three different categories.

Close Assault Weapon System (CAWS): The CAWS is used exclusively as a military weapon. It has the burst and strafe abilities and comes only in a 12 gauge model. This weapon holds 12 shots.

Single Shot: Single shot shotguns are used almost exclusively for hunting. These weapons carry 1 shot and do not have the burst or strafe abilities. Double barrel shotguns can be requisitioned for 2× the cost of a single shot shotgun (or by adding 2 to the weapon's budget point cost), and carry 2 shots. *Examples:* Fabarm Monotrap, New England Firearms Camo Turkey.

Pump Action: Pump action shotguns are commonly referred to as "pumps," and are used for hunting, personal defense, and combat. These weapons hold 8 shots and do not have the burst or strafe abilities. *Examples:* Browning BPS, Ithaca 37, Mossberg M500, Remington 870, Winchester 1300 Defender.

SUBMACHINEGUNS

Submachineguns (SMGs) are small, light shoulder-fired firearms that use pistol ammunition. In order to properly use any of the weapons listed in this category you must have the Weapon Proficiency (Rifle) feat; otherwise you suffer a –4 penalty to all your attack rolls.

Submachineguns have the burst and strafe abilities. These weapons hold 30 shots. High capacity magazines holding 36 shots can be requisitioned for $50 or by adding 2 to the weapon's budget point cost. *Examples:* Beretta 93, Colt 635, Glock 13C, Heckler & Koch MP5, Ingram Mac-10 and Mac-11, Uzi.

AMMUNITION

Weapons that require ammunition are requisitioned empty. Unless otherwise stated, all ammunition – including the first load – must be requisitioned separately of the weapon. Magazines are free and come with ammunition requisitioned.

With the exception of some tactical weapon rounds *(see Table 5.7)*, ammunition has no practical weight for the purposes of calculating encumbrance.

Blanks may be requisitioned as pistol, rifle, or shotgun ammunition at a cost of 1 budget point per 20 shots.

REVOLVER AMMUNITION

Standard Bullets: This is the most common type of revolver ammunition. All revolver attacks are assumed to be using bullets unless otherwise stated. There are no modifiers for using standard revolver ammunition, which costs 1 BP or $15 for a box of 50 shots.

PISTOL AMMUNITION

Military Ball (MB): This is the most common type of pistol ammunition. All pistol attacks are assumed to be using MB ammo unless otherwise stated. There are no modifiers for using MB ammunition, which costs 1 BP or $15 for a box of 50 shots.

Jacketed Hollow Point (JHP): The jacketed hollow point is designed for maximum expansion when it hits an object. This substantially reduces the penetrating ability of the round but greatly increases its damage potential. Each successful hit with these rounds inflicts an additional +1 damage and doubles the target's damage reduction. When used in pistols and submachineguns, increase the error rating of the weapon by 1. JHP ammunition costs 1 BP or $25 for a box of 50 shots.

Safety Slugs (SS): Safety slugs are low powered rounds designed for special situations where penetration is of greater concern than taking opponents down. Sample sensitive areas include chemical laboratories, weapons facilities, and airplane interiors, where accidental damage to the wrong area can be disastrous. Safety slugs offer minimum penetration balanced by limited damage potential. Modify the damage done by –2 per die rolled (minimum 1) and double the target's damage reduction when using these rounds. When used in pistols and submachineguns, increase the error rating of the weapon by 2. Safety slug ammunition costs 1 BP or $20 for a box of 20 shots.

Teflon-tipped (TEF): These rounds have a special coating of teflon applied to the projectile's point to increase its penetration ability without compromising the round's expansion properties. This offers excellent penetration while maintaining reasonable damage potential. The target's damage reduction is reduced by 1 (minimum 1) when he is successfully hit with these rounds. Teflon-tipped ammunition costs 2 BP or $40 for a box of 20 shots.

RIFLE AMMUNITION

Armor Piercing (AP): Armor piercing ammunition has a hardened jacket made from an alloy of brass and bronze surrounding a steel core, designed to provide the projectile with maximum penetration. The target's damage reduction is reduced by 2 (minimum 0) when using these rounds. Armor piercing ammunition costs 3 BP or $30 for a box of 20 shots.

Full Metal Jacketed (FMJ): Full metal jacketed ammunition is the most common type of rifle ammunition. All rifle attacks are assumed to be using FMJ ammo unless otherwise stated. There are no modifiers for using Full Metal Jacketed ammunition, which costs 1 BP or $15 for a box of 20 shots.

Soft Point (SP): The tip of a soft point projectile expands when it hits an object. This substantially reduces the penetrating ability of the round but greatly increases its damage potential as it erupts into flesh and bone. Each successful hit with these rounds inflicts an additional +1 damage and doubles the target's damage reduction. When used in a semi-automatic rifle or assault rifle, increase the error rating of the weapon by 1. Soft point ammunition costs 2 BP or $25 for a box of 20 shots.

Tracer (T): Tracer ammunition has a phosphorus coating on the tip of the round that ignites when the round is fired, enabling the agent to view where the rounds are impacting and adjust his fire accordingly. Add +2 to your attack roll, in addition to the effects of either full metal jacket or armor piercing ammunition (tracer shots may not be used in conjunction with soft point ammunition). This ammunition may only be used with rifles and machine guns. Tracer ammunition costs 2 BP or $40 for a box of 20 shots.

SHOTGUN AMMUNITION

Slug: A slug is a round containing a single projectile. Commonly used for hunting, slugs are also good for use against barricades and for forced entry. When using a slug there are no modifiers to the attack or damage rolls. Slugs cost 1 BP or $10 for a box of 5 shots.

Beanbag: Beanbag rounds are non-lethal alternative ammo for riot and civil unrest situations where deadly force may not be authorized or desired. Beanbag rounds must be loaded one round at a time (requiring a half action each time unless you have the Quick Load feat). Damage done with a beanbag round is considered subdual. Beanbag rounds cost 2 BP or $30 for a box of 5 shots.

Flechette: Flechette rounds are loaded with several metal darts called flechettes. These rounds scatter many projectiles at a target, each similar to, though smaller than, regular shot shells *(see below)*. This provides increased armor defeating potential at the cost of range. When using flechette rounds you may attack two adjacent targets with each shot, rolling normally for each. Each successful that hit with these rounds reduces damage reduction by 1 (minimum 1). Additionally, your damage values are decreased by 1d4 for each range increment the shot travels. Flechette rounds cost 3 BP or $20 for a box of 5 shots.

Gas: Gas rounds are designed to dispense a small charge of riot control toxin at the point of impact (one 5-ft. square). This toxin disperses in 1d6 rounds. Anyone caught in the square filled with the toxin must make a Fortitude save (DC 15) or be blinded and stunned *(see page 177)* for 2d6 rounds. Anyone wearing a gas mask is unaffected by the attack. Gas rounds cost 2 BP or $40 for a box of 5 shots.

Shot: Shot shells are comprised of several small lead projectiles encased in one round, and are the most common ammunition used in shotguns. All shotgun attacks are assumed to be using shot shells unless otherwise stated. When using shot shells you may attack two adjacent targets with each shot, rolling normally for each. Additionally, your damage values are decreased by 1d4 for each range increment the shot travels. Shot shells cost 2 BP or $15 for a box of 25 shots.

TACTICAL WEAPONS

Tactical weapons cover a broad range of arms including explosives, grenade launchers, and fire support weapons. In order to properly use one of the weapons listed here you must have the Weapon Proficiency (Tactical) feat; otherwise you suffer a –4 penalty to all of your attack rolls.

EXPLOSIVES

These weapons cause blast damage (see page 172). All explosives come with enough detonators to use the explosives as described, at no cost to the agent.

C4: This explosive has a blast increment of 2 squares (10 ft.) You may create shaped charges from C4 using the Demolitions skill (see page 48).

Dynamite: This explosive has a blast increment of 1 square (5 feet), and can be thrown, using the hurled weapon proficiency. When hurled dynamite misses the target, use the rules for grenade-like weapons on page 173.

FLAMETHROWERS

When using a flamethrower, you gain +1 to your attack roll for each previous consecutive action you've used the flamethrower to attack the same target (e.g. if you've used your last three actions to attack your current target with the flamethrower, you receive a +3 bonus to your attack this round). Anyone hit by a flamethrower may catch fire, as described on page 230. A flamethrower holds enough fuel to make 10 attacks. Additional fuel tanks cost 2 BP or $40 for one full load (another 10 attacks' worth). This weapon can strafe (using one shot per square), but not autofire or burst (even if you have Speed Trigger or a like feat or ability).

GRENADE-LIKE WEAPONS

Attacks with these weapons deviate from the target square when you miss with them (see page 173). Also, some are explosive; any listed with a blast increment use the blast damage rules described on page 172.

Grenade Launcher: Grenade launchers must be reloaded after each shot (requiring a half action each time unless you have the Quick Load feat). They can be mounted on an assault rifle or fired independently using a detachable shoulder stock and sight. Grenade launchers do not have either the burst or strafe abilities.

When firing a grenade launcher, its damage value and threat and error ratings are replaced by those of the ammunition fired (see below). Grenade launchers can use the following types of ammunition:

- *Baton:* These low-lethality projectiles are designed to disperse crowds, similar in function to the beanbag round covered under shotgun ammunition. Baton rounds have a blast increment of 1 square (5 ft.) and inflict subdual damage (see page 173).

- *CS Gas:* CS gas is a riot control toxin designed to incapacitate the target by causing intense irritation of the eyes, nasal passages, and exposed skin. A CS gas round emits a vapor cloud covering a 1-square (5-ft.) area. This cloud disperses in 2d6 rounds in ventilated areas, or 1d6 rounds when used outdoors. Anyone caught in the radius of the toxin must make a Fortitude save (DC 15) or be blinded and stunned (see page 177) for 2d6 rounds. Anyone wearing a gas mask is unaffected by the attack.

- *Flash:* When a flash round goes off it emits an intense flash designed to temporarily blind and stun its target. Anyone looking in the direction of a flash round when it detonates must make a Fortitude save (DC 18) or be blinded (see page 177) for 2d6 rounds.

- *Flash/Bang:* Like the flash round, but the flash/bang also explodes with a deafening noise. Anyone looking in the round's direction when it goes off must make a Fortitude save (DC 18) or be blinded (see page 177) for 2d6 rounds. In addition, anyone within a 2-square (10-ft.) radius of the blast must make a Fortitude save (DC 15) or be deafened and stunned (see page 177) for 1d6 rounds.

- *Flechette:* This round is similar in design and function to the flechette round covered under shotgun ammunition. When using flechette rounds you may attack two adjacent targets with each shot, rolling normally for each. Any shots that hit reduce damage reduction by 1 (minimum 1). Additionally, the round's damage value is decreased by 2 points for each range increment the shot travels.

- *Fragmentation:* This basic anti-personnel round has a blast increment of 1 square (5 feet).

- *Illumination:* At the point of detonation the illumination round disperses a parachute flare that emits a bright light covering a 6-square (30-ft.) radius. Each round after the first, the area illuminated drops by 1 square (5 ft.) as the flare drops to earth (e.g. the first round the flare is fired it illuminates a 6-square radius, the next round it illuminates a 5-square radius, etc.)

- *Smoke:* Smoke grenades deal no damage, instead filling a 2-square (10-ft.) radius with thick smoke that blocks line of sight (including night sight) and provides concealment. Available in various colors, smoke grenades are also useful for signaling and marking areas. This smoke disperses in 2d6 rounds.

SPYCRAFT

TABLE 5.7: TACTICAL WEAPONS

Weapon Name	Budget Points	Damage	Error	Threat	Range Increment	Weight	Actual Cost
Small							
Explosives*							
C4*	20/¼ lb.	4d6/¼ lb.	1	—	—	¼ lb.	$100/¼ lb.
Dynamite*†	12/stick	2d6/stick	1–3	—	5 ft.	½ lb./stick	$10/stick
Large							
Flamethrower*	20	2d6 + fire	1–3	—	10 ft.	30 lb.	$1250
Grenade Launcher*	20	Per ammo	Per ammo	Per ammo	40 ft.	20 lb.	$1500
Baton*	12 each	5d4**	1–3	—	—	½ lb.	$50
CS gas*	10 each	Special	1–4	—	—	½ lb.	$50
Flash*	10 each	Special	1–4	—	—	½ lb.	$30
Flash/bang*	10 each	Special	1–4	—	—	½ lb.	$50
Flechette*	10 each	2d8+2	1–3	—	—	½ lb.	$60
Fragmentation*	12 each	2d10	1–4	—	—	½ lb.	$60
Illumination*	5 each	Special	1–3	—	—	½ lb.	$50
Smoke*	5 each	Special	1–4	—	—	½ lb.	$20
Mortar*	40	Per ammo	Per ammo	Per ammo	600 ft.	15 lb.	$1500
HE*	10 each	2d10	1–3	—	—	5 lb.	$150
Illumination*	5 each	Special	1–3	—	—	3 lb.	$100
Smoke*	5 each	Special	1–3	—	—	3 lb.	$75
Rocket Launcher*	30	Per ammo	Per ammo	Per ammo	300 ft.	15 lb.	$3000
HE*	15 each	3d10	1–3	—	—	3 lb.	$100
A/A*	15 each	3d10	1–2	—	+200 ft.	5 lb.	$1000
A/T*	15 each	3d10	1–3	—	–200 ft.	5 lb.	$500
ATGM*	18 each	3d12	1–2	—	—	10 lb.	$1000

Machine Guns*

*Squad Automatic Weapon (SAW)** [All SAW machine guns hold either 30 or 100 shots.]

5.56×45mm	31	2d8+2	1–3	19–20	100 ft.	8 lb.	$2000
7.62×39mm	27	4d4	1–2	20	90 ft.	8 lb.	$1500

*General Purpose Machine Gun (GPMG)** [All GPMG machine guns hold 100 shots.]

7.62×51mm	40	3d8	1–3	19–20	120 ft.	18 lb.	$3000
7.62×54mm	39	4d6	1–2	20	110 ft.	18 lb.	$2500
.30-06	39	3d8	1–4	19–20	150 ft.	25 lb.	$2500

*Heavy Machine Guns (HMG)** [All HMG machine guns hold 50 shots.]

.50 BMG	43	5d4+2	1–3	18–20	200 ft.	100 lb.	$10,000
14.5mm*	44	6d4	1–3	18–20	200 ft.	100 lb.	$9,000

* See item description for special rules concerning this weapon.

** This is subdual damage. This weapon cannot inflict normal damage.

† Use the hurled proficiency when this weapon is thrown.

Mortar: Mortars come in three sections: the tube assembly, the base plate, and the mount assembly. It requires 4 full rounds to assemble a mortar, but only 2 full rounds to disassemble one. Mortars use three primary types of ammunition, as follows.

Mortars must be reloaded after each shot (requiring a half action each time unless you have the Quick Load feat), and do not have either the burst or strafe abilities.

When firing a mortar, its damage value and threat and error ratings are replaced by those of the ammunition fired *(see below)*. Mortars can use the following types of ammunition:

- *High Explosive (HE):* High explosive rounds have a blast increment of 1 square (5 ft.). When a Reflex save is successfully made to halve this damage, the damage is rounded up, not down.

- *Illumination:* This round is similar to the illumination round fired by the grenade launcher, except that it covers a 10-square (50-ft.) radius on the first round (which then drops each following round in the same way as the shell described for the grenade launcher).

- *Smoke:* This round is similar in function to the smoke grenade previously described for the grenade launcher, except that it fills a 3-square (15-ft.) radius.

Rocket Launcher: Rocket launchers are man-portable, shoulder-fired weapons that can launch a variety of rockets at opponents. They have little recoil but their large backblast area can give away an otherwise well concealed position (anyone looking in your direction receives a +4 bonus to Spot checks to notice where a rocket was fired from).

Rocket launchers are unwieldy and inherently difficult to target with, and all attacks with them suffer a –2 penalty. Rocket launchers must be reloaded after each shot (requiring a half action each time unless you have the Quick Load feat), and do not have either the burst or strafe abilities.

Generally, rockets are of the fire-and-forget variety, meaning that once the rocket is launched you have no control over the flight of the rocket. When firing a rocket launcher, its damage value and threat and error ratings are replaced by those of the ammunition fired. Some types of ammunition affect the rocket launcher's range increment as well (see below). Rocket launchers can use the following types of ammunition:

- *High Explosive (HE):* A general purpose fire-and-forget rocket, with a 1-square (5-ft.) radius of effect. High explosive rockets have a blast increment of 2 squares (10 ft.). When a Reflex save is successfully made to halve this damage, the damage is rounded up, not down.

- *Anti-Aircraft (A/A):* The anti-aircraft rocket has a heat-sensing guidance system that homes in on the heat signature of an aircraft's engine exhaust and has a higher range increment (+200 ft.) to accommodate speeding air targets. Although it is possible to attack ground-based targets, the range increment is reduced to 100 ft. when doing so as the guidance system has difficulty acquiring targets surrounded by the ambient temperature at ground level. Anti-aircraft rockets have a blast increment of 2 squares (10 ft.).

- *Anti-Tank (A/T):* The anti-tank rocket is a fire-and-forget projectile that uses a shaped-charge projectile to defeat armor. A successful attack ignores 5 points of hardness, but the attacker has a –4 penalty to hit targets that are smaller than Large size. Anti-tank rockets have a lower range increment than other rocket launcher rounds (–200 ft.) with a blast increment of 2 squares (10 ft.).

- *Anti-Tank Guided Missile (ATGM):* The anti-tank guided missile is a wire-guided projectile that can take evasive action to remain on target so long as the agent holds the guidance reticle over the target while it is in flight. A common tactic used against this weapon involves finding the person with the controls and disabling him; when the targeting reticle drops off the target, the missile crashes into the ground.

Due to the weight of the projectile, the rocket launcher must be mounted on a bipod, tripod, or vehicle. The attacker receives a –2 penalty for attacking any target smaller than Large size. A successful attack ignores 10 points of hardness. ATGM rockets have a blast increment of 2 squares (10 ft.).

MACHINE GUNS

Machine guns are fully automatic weapons designed to provide massive amounts of firepower for a sustained period. All machineguns fall into one of four categories *(see below)*, and have the burst and strafe abilities. Unless otherwise noted, machineguns use the same ammunition listed for rifles on Table 5.4: Firearms Ammunition.

14.5mm Machine Gun: There is no equivalent rifle ammunition available for this weapon. It can fire either of the following ammunition types.

- *Full Metal Jacketed-Tracer (FMJ-T):* Unless otherwise noted, assume that a 14.5mm machine gun is firing this type of ammunition. When using this ammo, add +2 to your attack roll. FMJ-T ammunition costs 4 BP or $100 for a 50-shot belt of ammunition.

- *Armor Piercing-Tracer (AP-T):* This round is used when opponents are expected to be using armored vehicles.

When using AP-T ammunition, reduce damage reduction by 2 (minimum 0) and add +2 to your attack roll. AP-T ammunition costs 6 BP or $150 for a 50-shot belt of ammunition.

General Purpose Machine Gun (GPMG): Like SAWs *(see below),* GPMGs are used for direct fire support. Yet due to their size, they normally require a two-man crew — one person carrying the weapon and operating it and the other carrying the ammunition and spare barrels. GPMGs are equipped with a bipod and may also be mounted on a tripod mount (which offers a +2 bonus to your attack rolls). GPMGs use 100-shot belts of ammunition (multiply the cost of standard rifle clip by 5 to requisition these).

Heavy Machine Gun: These mammoth "vehicle-crackers" are not typically used as an anti-personnel weapons. Due to their size, a tripod or vehicle mount is required to fire them. Heavy machine guns use 50-shot belts of ammunition (multiply the cost of a standard rifle-clip by 2.5, rounding up, to requisition these).

Squad Automatic (SAW): These man-portable weapons come equipped with a bipod and use either a 100-shot belt of ammunition or a 30-shot detachable box magazine (assault rifle magazines of the same caliber are interchangeable). To requisition ammunition for these weapons, multiply the cost of standard rifle ammunition 1.5 (for 30) or by 5 (for 100).

HURLED WEAPONS

Hurled weapons includes anything that is physically thrown, including bows and grenades. In order to properly use one of the weapons listed here you must have the Weapon Proficiency (Hurled) feat; otherwise you suffer a –4 penalty to all of your attack rolls.

BOLA

The bola inflicts no damage but it can tangle opponents' feet up, causing them to fall to the ground. When using a bola, make a ranged touch attack *(see page 159).* With a hit, your opponent is tripped and must make a grapple check against your attack roll. If your opponent fails this roll, he is grappled. Your opponent may free himself with one full action. Bola cannot be used on targets greater than Large-size, and have a maximum range of three increments (30 feet).

GRENADES

Attacks with these weapons deviate from the target square when you miss with them *(see page 173).* Also, some are explosive; any listed with a blast increment use the blast damage rules described on page 172.

Weapon Name	Budget Points	Damage	Error	Threat	Range Increment	Weight	Actual Cost
Small							
Bola*	4	Special	1-2	20	10 ft.	5 lb.	$20
Grenades*							
Concussion	15 each	5d4**	1-4	—	10 ft.	½ lb.	$60
CS gas*	12 each	Special	1-4	—	10 ft.	½ lb.	$50
Flash*	12 each	Special	1-4	—	10 ft.	½ lb.	$30
Flash/bang*	15 each	Special	1-4	—	10 ft.	½ lb.	$50
Fragmentation	15 each	2d10	1-4	—	10 ft.	½ lb.	$60
Incendiary*	15 each	3d6 + fire	1-2	—	—	½ lb.	$100
Smoke*	6 each	Special	1-4	—	10 ft.	½ lb.	$20
Molotov cocktail*	1	1d4 + fire	1-4	—	5 ft.	2 lb.	$10
Throwing dart	1 for 3	1d3†	1	20	20 ft.	½ lb.	$5
Throwing knife	2 for 3	1d4†	1-2	20	20 ft.	1 lb.	$40
Medium							
Composite bow	10	1d6†	1	19-20	100 ft.	3 lb.	$500
Crossbow	8	1d8	1-2	20	80 ft.	6 lb.	$400
Netgun*	7	Special	1-2	20	10 ft.	10 lb.	$75
Speargun	9	1d6	1	20	10 ft.	5 lb.	$300
Throwing axe	1 each	1d6†	1-3	19-20	10 ft.	4 lb.	$80

* See item description for special rules concerning this weapon.

** This is subdual damage. This weapon cannot inflict normal damage.

† Add your Strength modifier to this weapon's damage.

- *Concussion:* These low-lethality grenades are designed to disperse crowds by stunning them into submission. Concussion grenades have a blast increment of 1 square (5 ft.) and inflict subdual damage *(see page 173).*

- *CS Gas:* CS gas is a riot control toxin designed to incapacitate the target by causing intense irritation of the eyes, nasal passages, and exposed skin. A CS gas grenade emits a vapor cloud covering a 1-square (5-ft.) radius. This cloud disperses in 2d6 rounds in ventilated areas, or 1d6 rounds when used outdoors. Anyone caught in the radius of the toxin must make a Fortitude save (DC 15) or be blinded and stunned *(see page 177)* for 2d6 rounds. Anyone wearing a gas mask is unaffected by the attack.

- *Flash:* When a flash grenade goes off it emits an intense flash designed to temporarily blind and stun its target. Anyone looking in the direction of a flash grenade when it detonates must make a Fortitude save (DC 18) or be blinded *(see page 177)* for 2d6 rounds.

- *Flash/Bang:* Like the flash grenade, but the flash/bang also explodes with a deafening noise. Anyone looking in the grenade's direction when it goes off must make a Fortitude save (DC 18) or be blinded *(see page 177)* for 2d6 rounds. In addition, anyone within a 2-square (10-ft.) radius of the blast must make a Fortitude save (DC 18) or be deafened and stunned *(see page 177)* for 1d6 rounds.

- *Fragmentation:* This basic anti-personnel grenade has a blast increment of 1 square (5 feet).

- *Incendiary:* Sometimes referred to as a 'thermite' grenade, this weapon is used to destroy enemy equipment. This weapon is not thrown, but placed on its intended target. When detonated it creates a tremendous amount of heat and can burn through almost any material if given enough time. A thermite grenade burns for 1 minute (10 rounds) or until extinguished, which requires that all oxygen be removed from the affected area. This is best accomplished by smothering the grenade with sand or a similar material. Unlike most grenades, there is no thermite grenade equivalent available for a grenade launcher.

- *Smoke:* Smoke grenades deal no damage, instead filling a 2-square (10-ft.) radius area with thick smoke that blocks line of sight (including night sight) and provides concealment. Available in various colors, smoke grenades are also useful for signaling and marking areas. This smoke disperses in 2d6 rounds.

MOLOTOV COCKTAIL

This weapon has a blast increment of less than 1 square (2 ft.) and can cause fires *(see page 230).*

NETGUN

When you use a netgun, make a ranged attack against your target. With a hit, your target is entangled. Entangled agents have –2 to attack rolls and –4 to Dexterity, and may only move up to half their speed within the 30-ft. range of the netgun unless they succeed with an opposed Strength check against you—the net is secured by a line attached to the gun, which they must rip free of your hands to move away. Entangled targets may not charge or run, though they may make a full-action Escape Artist check (DC 20) to slip free of the net. Alternately, they can break (DC 20) or destroy (5 wp) the net. Netguns may only be used on targets of Tiny to Large size, inclusive, and have a maximum range of three increments (30 feet).

EXOTIC WEAPONS

Exotic weapons cover a wide array of melee and ranged weapons not normally encountered. In order to properly use one of the weapons listed here you must have the Weapon Proficiency (Exotic) feat for the weapon group in question; otherwise you suffer a –4 penalty to all of your attack rolls.

The *Spycraft* core release features two exotic weapon groups—archaic weapons and martial arts weapons.

ARCHAIC WEAPONS

These weapons are rarely used today, but are commonly seen in the exotic locales featured in popular spy movies and books.

Blowgun: Blowguns can be made from a wide variety of materials ranging from bamboo to modern materials such as aluminum. To increase the damage inflicted, blowgun darts are often poisoned. *(For Poison rules, see page 238.)*

Boomerang: If you miss when throwing a boomerang, it returns to you and you may catch it with a Dexterity check (DC 13) as a free action.

Sling: Ammunition for this weapon is free.

Whip: Although a whip is used as a melee weapon, treat it as a projectile weapon with a maximum range of 1 increment (15 ft.) and no range penalties. You can make trip attacks with a whip. If you are tripped during your own trip attempt (as someone yanks the business end of the whip, hoping to bring you down), you can drop the whip to avoid being tripped. When using a

TABLE 5.9: EXOTIC WEAPONS

Weapon Name	Budget Points	Damage	Error	Threat	Range Increment	Weight	Actual Cost
Archaic Weapons							
Small							
Boomerang*	4	1d8†	1	20	20 ft.	2 lb.	$10
Sling*	2	1d4	1	–	20 ft.	–	$5
Whip	3	1d6**	1-2	–	15 ft.*	2 lb.	$10
Medium							
Blowgun*	10	1d3*	1	16-20	5 ft.	2 lb.	$10
Large							
Scimitar	8	1d12*	1	19-20	–	8 lb.	$500
Martial Arts Weapons							
Small							
Kama	5	1d8	1	20	–	2 lb.	$20
Nunchaku*	5	1d6	1-2	19-20	–	2 lb.	$20
Sai*	4	1d6	1	20	–	2 lb.	$150
Shuriken*	1 for 9	1 point	–	19-20	10 ft.	1/10 lb.	$10 each
Tiger claws*	1	Special	1	20	–	1/2 lb.	$60/pair
Medium							
Katana*	10	1d10	1	19-20	–	5 lb.	$500
Large							
Bo stick	7	1d6/1d6	1	19-20	–	4 lb.	$10

* See item description for special rules concerning this weapon.

** This is subdual damage. This weapon cannot inflict normal damage.

† Add your Strength modifier to damage when this weapon is thrown.

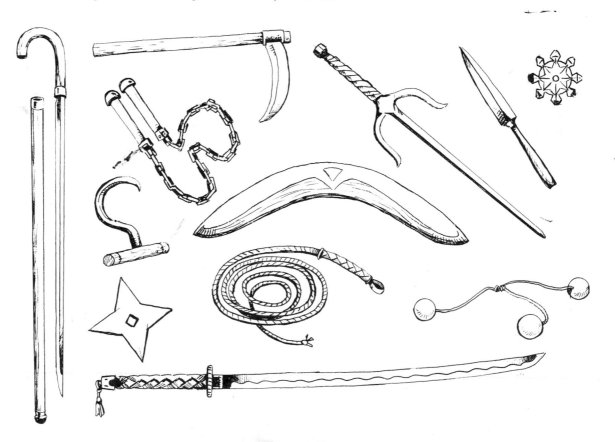

whip, you receive a +2 bonus to your opposed attack roll when attempting to disarm an opponent (including the roll to keep from being disarmed if you fail to disarm your opponent).

MARTIAL ARTS WEAPONS

These primarily eastern weapons are extraordinarily effective, even against well-armed ranged combat experts.

Katana: The agent receives a +1 enhancement bonus to all attacks with this finely crafted weapon.

Nunchaku: An attack with a nunchaku is considered an unarmed attack, but the damage, threat, and error ratings of the nunchaku replace your normal unarmed attack values.

Sai: When wielding a sai, your Defense is increased by +1 against melee and unarmed attacks. You lose this bonus if you lose the use of your Dexterity bonus for any reason.

Shuriken: You may hurl up to 3 shuriken at the same target with a single standard attack action, but you must roll to hit separately with each. Your Strength modifier is not applied to damage with this weapon.

Tiger Claws: Tiger Claws add +2 to your damage when you make an unarmed attack, and +2 to all Climb checks.

PROTECTIVE GEAR

See page 109 for protective gear effects. In addition, when you roll a threat attacking a target in medium or heavy armor, you must spend two action dice instead of one to activate the critical hit. Finally, getting into and out of protective gear takes one half action per point of BP the gear costs.

ASSAULT VEST

Due to its weight, the assault vest is typically reserved for special response and assault teams entering dangerous tactical environments. Special ceramic inserts are available to increase the vest's protection in critical areas. Inserts must be requisitioned independently of the vest.

BOMB SQUAD SUIT

This suit offers you +4 to all saves vs. explosions.

FLASH GOGGLES

These goggles offer you +4 to all saves vs. blinding lights.

GAS MASK

A gas mask offers you +4 to all saves vs. poisonous gases and other inhaled substances.

HELMET, SEALED

A sealed helmet offers you +2 to all saves vs. poisonous gas or sonic attacks. Its internal air supply lasts for one hour before it must be vented and recharged from surrounding air.

KEVLAR BATTLE DRESS UNIFORM (BDU)

The kevlar BDU incorporates extra layers of kevlar material covering critical areas of the body for maximum security against penetrating wounds.

KEVLAR VEST

This vest is worn by most law enforcement personnel. Special ceramic inserts are available which increase the vest's protection in critical areas. These inserts are used most often during riots and violent uprisings, and must be requisitioned independently of the vest. A kevlar vest's damage reduction is only useful against firearms damage.

SUITS

These suits protect you from inhospitable conditions.

Asbestos: This suit offers you a +4 bonus to all saves vs. heat and provides a damage reduction of 3 against fire.

Gore-Tex: This suit offers you a +4 bonus to all saves vs. cold and provides a damage reduction of 3 against cold.

Ghillie: So long as this sniper's camouflage matches the surrounding terrain and the wearer doesn't move, Spot and Surveillance checks to find him suffer a –4 penalty.

NBC: An NBC (Nuclear, Biological, and Chemical) suit allows you to operate in any environment contaminated with radioactive fallout, or chemical or biological agents. You are immune to the effects of all diseases, gases, and radiation while wearing this suit. If the suit takes 3 or more points of damage, it is rendered useless.

SCUBA: The SCUBA (Self Contained Underwater Breathing Apparatus) suit allows you to operate underwater for up to 1 hour before the oxygen tanks must be recharged.

Space: This suit allows you to operate in a vacuum (most commonly outer space). If it takes 3 or more points of damage, it is rendered useless. Space suits are not available to the public, though the Agency can acquire them through their specialists and political clout. Purchasing a space suit costs 1 gadget point *(see Gadgets, page 131)*.

HUNT 01

TABLE 5.10: PROTECTIVE GEAR

Armor Name	Budget Points	DB	DR	MDB	ACP	Speed	Weight	Actual Cost
Light Armor								
Kevlar vest*	30	+1	4/0*	+4	−1	Same	8 lb.	$600
Insert*	+10	+0	+1	+3	−1	Same	4 lb.	$200
Tuxedo liner*	20	+1	2	+4	0	Same	7 lb.	$500
Medium Armor								
Chain shirt	20	+0	5	+3	−3	Same	25 lb.	$250
Steelweave vest	25	+1	8	+2	−5	−10 ft.	20 lb.	$750
Kevlar BDU*	35	+1	5	+5	−2	−5 ft.	15 lb.	$1,000
Heavy Armor								
Assault vest*	40	+0	8	+1	−4	−10 ft.	25 lb.	$1,500
Insert*	+10	+0	+2	+1	−	−	7 lb.	$500
Bomb squad suit*	35	−1	11	+0	−6	−15 ft.	30 lb.	$2,000
Door-gunner vest	50	−2	14	+0	−7	−15 ft.	40 lb.	$3,000
Other Armor								
Helmets								
Motorcycle	5	+1	−	−	−1	Same	1 lb.	$100
Military	7	+2	−	−	−2	Same	1 lb.	$30
Sealed*	10	+2	−	−	−2	Same	2 lb.	$500
Shield								
Riot	5	+1	−	−	−1	Same	6 lb.	$100
Other Protective Gear								
Flash goggles*	5	−	−	−	−1	Same	1 lb.	$300
Gas mask*	5	−	−	−	−1	Same	2 lb.	$100
Suit								
Asbestos*	7	−	−	−	−2	−10 ft.	50 lb.	$400
Gore-tex*	7	−	−	−	−1	−5 ft.	15 lb.	$400
Ghillie*	5	−	−	−	−	Same	4 lb.	$100
NBC*	8	−	−	−	−2	−10 ft.	18 lb.	$500
SCUBA*	6	−	−	−	−1	−10 ft.	60 lb.	$400
Space*	−	−	−	−	−2	−10 ft.	75 lb.	Special

* See item description for special rules concerning this item.
Abbreviations: ACP = Armor Check Penalty; DB = Defense Bonus; DR = Damage Reduction;
MDB = Maximum Dexterity Bonus

TUXEDO LINER

This is a special kevlar liner woven into normal clothing to provide some ballistic protection without revealing the presence of body armor. A tuxedo liner must be sculpted for each wearer individually; if someone wears a tuxedo liner that was not sculpted for him, all of its beneficial values are cut in half (rounding down) and others gain a +10 bonus to Spot the liner beneath his clothes. Street sources require one full day to prepare clothing laced with this armor; the Agency can cut this time down to one hour.

OTHER GEAR

This gear is used in day-to-day operations.

COMMUNICATIONS

Cell phone: Digital phones work anywhere there is cellular service (most major cities and travel hubs, plus several corporate centers around the world). With the assistance of the Agency's dedicated satellite system, service is extended to all but the most remote environs. Internal batteries power the cell phone for up to 24 hours.

Headset, Radio: A radio headset allows its wearer to talk to anyone wearing a similar headset (tuned to the same frequency) at ranges up to 1 mile away. For each additional 1 mile of range, double the cost. Headset radios may be rigged to transmit and receive encrypted messages at the cost shown on the gear table. This option applies a –4 penalty to all Cryptography rolls to decode the messages sent through the headsets.

Satellite Communications Terminal: The SCT utilizes orbiting satellites for real-time voice communication with another SCT anywhere in the world. The SCT can also act as a computer modem to send and receive computer data (this requires both parties to have a power-rating 2+ computer connected to the SCT). Finally, the SCT can transmit and receive video feeds (this requires the sender to have a video camera and the recipient to have a video monitoring device).

SCT signals are susceptible to bad weather. During weather which has a Wind DC *(see page 232)*, you must make a Computers or Electronics skill check against this DC or lose the signal to the storm. You may try to reacquire a lost signal once each hour for as long as you like.

Tactical Radio: This hand-held radio has a range of 1 mile. For each additional 1 mile of range, double the cost. A tactical radio may be rigged to transmit and receive encrypted messages at the cost shown on the gear table. This option applies a –4 penalty to all Cryptography rolls to decode the messages sent using the radio.

COMPUTERS

Computers are priced according to their power rating. The price listed on the table is for a +1 computer. To upgrade your computer by +1 power rating, you must pay the cost listed for the upgrade option.

Desktop: Desktops are awkward to carry around and must be plugged into a wall to operate.

Laptop: Laptops can be carried around and used without an external power source. Typically, a laptop can operate 2-4 hours before needing a recharge.

PDA: A Personal Digital Assistant is a small, battery powered computer used to store limited data and perform simple programming tasks. PDAs are capable of sharing information with other PDAs, laptops, or desktops through the use of infrared ports or cable connections. PDAs can operate up to 12 hours before needing a recharge. PDAs cannot be upgraded.

DRUGS AND POISONS

Any of these can be prepared as a liquid or a gas, or to work on contact with skin. They can also be loaded into darts for the dart gun *(see page 111)*. All of these options cost the standard amount for the drug or poison in question. Actual costs listed are the black market rates—none of these items are commonly available on the open market.

HAZARDOUS TERRAIN GEAR

"Bomb sniffer": This hand-held device has a range increment of 5 ft. and grants a +2 bonus to Search and Gather Information skill checks to identify chemical explosives. A bomb sniffer is effective out to 4 range increments.

Chemical analyzer: This device has a range increment of 10 ft. and grants a +2 bonus to Search and Gather Information skill checks to find and identify toxins and suspicious gases. A chemical analyzer is effective out to 4 range increments.

Geiger counter: This device recognizes the presence of radiation in the area.

Global Positioning System (GPS) receiver: This device receives location data from a number of orbiting satellites, enabling the user to determine his position within 5 meters, anywhere on Earth.

Metal detector: This hand-held device has a range increment of 5 ft. and grants a +2 bonus to Search and Gather Information skill checks to identify metal and alloys. A metal detector is effective out to 4 range increments.

effects of exposure to radiation, or chemical or biological agents. An agent injected with this shot gains a +4 bonus to saves against radiation and chemical and biological agents, including poisons and disease, for a number of hours equal to his Constitution modifier.

Liquid Skin Patch: A liquid skin patch quickly heals wounds an agent has suffered. The first patch applied to an injured agent during a 24-hour period heals 1d8 wound points. The second heals 1d6 wound points, and each additional patch that day heals 1d4 wound points.

Stimulant Shot: You do not need to make a skill check to administer a stimulant shot to an agent. A stimulant shot injected into the heart of a dying agent stabilizes him.

OPTICS

Binoculars: When used to see something far away, binoculars grant a +2 to spot checks.

Night vision goggles: These binoculars amplify the existing ambient light in an area, allowing the agent to see at night without modifiers. A small amount of light (moonlight or better) must be present for these binoculars to operate properly.

Thermal imager: This hand-held device allows you to see people, animals, fires, and other sources of heat in total darkness, and through fog, smoke, and mist. Images are presented on a green CRT screen with heat signatures appearing as either white-hot or black-hot. The viewer module can be detached from the imaging body to allow remote viewing with the use of a 10-ft. fiber-optic cable. I/O ports can export images to data recorders, computers and monitoring devices, where they can be stored for later analysis.

POLICE GEAR

These items are commonly carried by law enforcement officials around the world. Many law enforcement officers also carry firearms, batons, mace spray, and tasers.

Handcuffs: These have a Bind DC of 30 *(see the Escape Artist skill, page 52, for more)*.

SURVEILLANCE

Third-party surveillance (such as phone taps) are usually handled by with favor checks *(see page 217)*.

Bugs: There are four basic bug options.

- *Audio, basic:* This is the most basic purpose-built audio bug. It's about the size of a nickel, and finding it requires a Search check against the Surveillance check total generated when planting the device. The basic bug has a transmission range of one mile through open air (half that in cities, and one-tenth that underground).

KITS

Kits are required to use certain skills. Without the proper kit, you are at a –4 penalty to skill checks.

Artisan: Used for the Craft skill.

Climbing: Used for the Climb skill.

Demolitions: Required to build a bomb as described on page 48. If built successfully, this bomb has the statistics for a shaped charge *(see page 118)*.

Disguise: Used for the Disguise skill.

Electronics: Used for the Electronics skill.

Evidence: Used for the Gather Information skill.

First Aid: Used for the First Aid skill.

Lockpicking: Used for the Open Lock skill.

Mechanics: Used for the Mechanic skill.

Survival: Used for the Survival skill.

Sweeper: Used for the Surveillance skill when attempting to detect electronic bugs, tracers, and the like.

MEDICAL

Antidote Shot: You do not need to make a skill check to inject an antidote into an agent. An antidote injection offers a patient temporary immunity from the

- *Video, basic:* Advances in digital photography and precision optics have reduced a fully functional camera to the size of a cuff link or shirt button. Such devices are easily hidden, and are often combined with audio bugs. Video bugs require line of sight and a carefully selected field of view, so they are somewhat easier to find through visual inspection compared to audio bugs (Spot and Search DC –4).

- *Digital memory:* This device records information gathered by basic audio and video bugs. It must be physically recovered at a later time to acquire its recordings, but it's very difficult to detect due to the lack of emissions, adding +6 to the DC of all attempts to find it.

- *Voice activated:* This randomly determines when it transmits, increasing the DC of detecting it with electronic Searches by +2.

Cameras: Unless otherwise noted, all cameras have 24 exposures. There are several basic camera options.

- *Standard:* These cameras can be reloaded and fitted with additional equipment to make them dramatically more useful. Standard cameras have a range increment of 30 ft.

- *Digital:* This camera stores images electronically (usually on removable memory chips), eliminating the normal time required for film to be developed. With the right equipment and cables, pictures taken with a digital camera can be uploaded into a computer, ready for email or printing. Digital cameras have a Spot check cap of 25 and a range increment of 40 ft.

- *Disposable:* The chief virtue of these cameras is they are cheap, light, and innocently common in the belonging of all travelers. They include a single internal roll of commercial grade film and cannot be reloaded. They also cannot be improved with additional lenses or support equipment. Disposable cameras have a range increment of 30 ft.

- *Miniature:* This camera can easily fit in the palm of your hand (in fact, it can be cradled within your palm so that when you flex your hand, a picture is taken). Miniature cameras cannot be improved with additional lenses or support equipment, have a range increment of 15 ft., and has 12 exposures.

- *Professional:* At this level the use of professional-grade film allows for dramatically higher quality images. For an additional $100, you can carry double the number of exposures in this camera. Professional cameras have a range increment of 50 ft.

AUDIO/VISUAL INTELLIGENCE

The photograph is one of an agent's most powerful tools. Pictures may be analyzed at your leisure, allowing you to take 20 with a Spot check, but the results are also limited by the medium. Most finished photographs are small (unless developed specifically for analysis), and suffer a Spot check penalty (–2 for 5 in. to 12 in. photos, –6 for "wallet size").

Cameras have range increments that work in the same fashion as firearms, and each type of film can only store so much information. Standard, commercial-grade film might only be sharp enough to reveal that a woman across the room is wearing a ring, but no amount of examination can tell you what's inscribed on the ring, because the film's resolution is too low. This means that even if enlarged, poor image quality creates a cap for Spot checks. Commercial-grade film generally has an upward limit of 20 (reduced by range penalties), meaning that even a professional agent (with a high Spot skill) often won't be able to determine more than a beginner using the same film. Fortunately, the use of special equipment (and gadgets) can improve this dramatically.

Photo-enhancement software increases the highest possible result of a Spot check by the computer's power rating (e.g. a +6 computer could be used to improve the quality of a normal photo (cap of 20) to allow Spot checks up to 26. No software can improve the results of a Spot check, though: the human mind is still the finest pattern recognition instrument known to man.

Recordings and transmissions — such as from bugs or wiretaps — work in much the same way, only they are interpreted with Listen checks. With time to repeatedly analyze a recording, you can take 20 to extract information from a recorded message. Like a small picture, an overly short snippet may not contain much to work with (applying a –2 penalty to the Listen check). Similarly, the quality of the recording device determines the initial cap for Listen checks made with it. Electronic enhancement and separation software is available, and like its video counterpart, adds the computer's rating to the Listen check cap.

Using cameras and recording devices in person uses the Spot or Listen skill, while installing remote audio and video bugs is a function of the Surveillance skill. Taking photos of moving targets is also a use of the Surveillance skill, and is subject to the same modifiers as making a ranged touch attack in combat. You may take 20 in either case if you have sufficient time to scout the location and position the device for optimal coverage.

TABLE 5.11: OTHER GEAR

Name	Budget Points	Weight	Actual Cost
Clothing			
Poor	–	5 lb.	$10
Average	1	4 lb.	$100
Fatigues	5	5 lb.	$100
Trendy	5	5 lb.	$750
Designer	10	3 lb.	$2,000
Sunglasses (mirrored)	1	–	$50
Communication gear			
Cell phone*	–	1/2 lb.	$40
Headset, radio*	2	1/2 lb.	$100
Encrypted	+3	–	+$100 ($200 total)
Satellite communications terminal*	20 for a pair	8 lb.	$5,000
Tactical radio*	5	1 lb.	$75
Encrypted	+3	–	+$100 ($175 total)
*Computers**			
Desktop*	5	25 lb.	$1,000
Upgrade	3	–	$500 per power rating (max. +3)
Laptop*	7	5 lb.	$2,000
Upgrade	4	–	$1,000 per power rating (max. +3)
PDA*	3	1/2 lb.	$500
*Drugs and Poisons (see page 238)**			
Contact poison	3 per use	–	$300 per use
Knockout drug	3 per use	–	$250 per use
Lethal poison I	7 per use	–	$500 per use
Lethal poison II	10 per use	–	$1000 per use
Nerve drug	5 per use	–	$400 per use
Paralytic poison	3 per use	–	$250 per use
Sodium pentothal (truth serum)	3 per use	–	$250 per use
Weakening poison	2 per use	–	$200 per use
Food and lodging			
Hotel room, 1 night			
One Star	–	–	$20
Two Star	–	–	$50
Three Star	2	–	$300
Four Star	5	–	$800
Five Star	10	–	$2,000
Martini (shaken)	–	1/10 lb.	$5
Meal			
Fast food	–	–	$5
Restaurant, dive	–	–	$10
MRE (military rations)	1 per day	–	$20
Restaurant, upscale	–	–	$50
Restaurant, gourmet	2	–	$200

TABLE 5.11: OTHER GEAR (CONTINUED)

Name	Budget Points	Weight	Actual Cost
Hazardous terrain gear			
"Bomb sniffer"*	3	1 lb.	$500
Chemical analyzer*	3	1 lb.	$250
Digging/entrenching tool	1	—	$10
Geiger counter	3	1 lb.	$250
GPS receiver*	5	1 lb.	$500
Magnetic compass	1	—	$20
Metal detector*	3	1 lb.	$500
Parachute	5	5 lb.	$500
*Kits**			
Artisan*	2	5 lb.	$100
Climbing*	3	10 lb.	$150
Demolitions*	10/1 lb. bomb	5 lb/1 lb. bomb	$1000/1 lb. bomb
Disguise*	4	5 lb.	$200
Electronics*	5	10 lb.	$400
Evidence*	2	5 lb.	$200
First aid*	3	5 lb.	$150
Lockpicking*	4	1 lb.	$250
Mechanics*	4	10 lb.	$300
Survival*	3	15 lb.	$250
Sweeper*	4	15 lb.	$250
Light Sources			
Flashlight	1	1 lb.	$10
Floodlight	2	75 lb.	$180
Glowstick	—	1/2 lb.	$10
Lantern	1	3 lb.	$40
Medical gear			
Antidote shot*	3	1/10 lb.	$100 each
Liquid skin patch*	5	1/10 lb.	$500 each
Stimulant shot*	3	1/10 lb.	$100 each
Optics			
Binoculars*	1	2 lb.	$100
Night vision goggles*	8	3 lb.	$1,000
Thermal imager	15	10 lb.	$5,000
Police gear			
Handcuffs*	1	1/2 lb.	$50
Surveillance gear			
Audio recorders			
Micro-tape recorder*	2	1/10 lb.	$50
Parabolic microphone*	5	5 lb.	$500
Personal tape recorder*	1	1/4 lb.	$25
Bugs			
Audio, basic*	3 each	1/10 lb.	$100
Video, basic*	3 each	1/10 lb.	$100
Digital memory*	3 each	1/10 lb.	$100
Voice activated*	3 each	1/10 lb.	$100

TABLE 5.11: OTHER GEAR (CONTINUED)

Name	Budget Points	Weight	Actual Cost
Cameras and accessories			
Standard*	2	1 lb.	$200
Digital*	6	1 lb.	$600
Disposable*	1	½ lb.	$15
Miniature*	4	–	$400
Professional*	8	3 lb.	$800
Video, standard*	10	5 lb.	$1000
Video, professional*	40	20 lb.	$4000
IR filter lens*	3	1 lb.	$300
Super-telephoto lens*	5	1 lb.	$200
Tripod*	2	5 lb.	$50
Film/tape			
Commercial grade*	1	–	$5
Professional grade*	2	–	$50
Intelligence grade*	5	–	$500
Snoop spray*	2	1 lb.	$150
Weapon accessories			
Bipod*	1	5 lb.	$50
Holster	–	1 lb.	$50
Flash suppressor*	1	⅒ lb.	$20
Laser sight*	2	1 lb.	$200
Silencer*	2	½ lb.	$100
Sling	–	1 lb.	$20
Telescopic sight*	2	1 lb.	$100
Tripod*	1	20 lb.	$100

* See item description for special rules concerning this gear.

- *Video:* Video-recording versions of the standard and professional camera are available. The cost is increased by a factor of five for video recording gear. Video cameras average 4 hours of recording time, which can be extended to 8 hours for an extra $250, and 12 hours for $500.

- *Infrared (IR) filter lens:* Increases the Spot check cap for detecting weapons or equipment on people by +5 and allows the insides of containers or even the far sides of standard walls to be examined for living beings or hot equipment.

- *Super-telephoto lens:* Multiplies a camera's range increment by 5.

- *Tripod:* Halves range penalties to both Spot checks and the Spot check cap. Tripods typically collapse into a cylinder about 5≤ in diameter and 18≤ long when not in use.

Film/tape: There are three basic types of film or tape.

- *Commercial grade:* Easily acquired; available for all cameras; no check required to use; maximum Spot/Listen check cap of 20; 30 exposures per roll, 1 hour per tape.

- *Professional grade:* Must be bought from specialty stores or ordered; matching conditions to equipment requires a Surveillance check (DC 12); maximum Spot/Listen check cap of 24; 30 exposures per roll; 1 hour per tape.

- *Intelligence grade:* Extremely rare — limited to militaries and intelligence agencies; must be matched to professional-grade cameras and recorders; usually loaded into fixed-position and vehicle-mounted surveillance units; capable of extreme enhancement; maximum Spot/Listen check cap of 30; 6 exposures per roll, 10 minutes of tape.

Micro-tape recorder: Using digital memory instead of tape, this device is no larger than a tube of lipstick. Sold mostly for commercial dictation, it may be pressed into service as an impromptu bug. The audio memory is good for 2 hours of commercial-grade recordings.

Parabolic microphone: This mike resembles a rifle in both appearance and function. Simply point it at an area and pull the "trigger." If there is much surrounding noise, picking out individual sounds requires a Listen check (DC 20). The parabolic mike has a range increment of 100 ft and can be hooked up to a computer or audio recorder to save sounds for later analysis.

Personal tape recorder: This standard small (1 in. × 2 in. × 5 in.) tape recorder is easily stashed in a handbag or fanny pack. It provides all the normal functions of a stereo tape player and a built-in or 5-ft. wire microphone produces acceptable sound quality with any commercial-grade tape.

Snoop Spray: This spray reveals any alarm beams in the area, laser or otherwise.

WEAPONS ACCESSORIES

Bipod/Tripod: When using a bipod (with a rifle) or tripod (with a machine gun), you are considered bracing.

Flash Suppressor: When you are using a flash-suppressed handgun or rifle, your opponents suffer a –4 penalty to their Spot checks to track you by muzzle fire.

Silencer: Silencers can only be used on weapons they are specifically designed for. Opponents receive a –4 penalty to Listen checks when trying to locate someone firing a weapon with a silencer attached.

Telescopic Sight: When attached to a rifle or pistol, a telescopic sight allows you to ignore the range penalties from the first and every other range increment (i.e. the 3rd, 5th, 7th, etc.), assuming you aim the weapon before firing it.

Laser Sight: Laser sights are generally only mounted on handguns and submachineguns, or on rifles used in close quarters. When using a weapon with a laser sight, you receive a +2 circumstance bonus to all ranged attack rolls. This bonus is effective up to 50 feet. Beyond 50 feet, or in strong weather conditions (anything worse than light rain or snow), the laser sight is useless.

GADGETS AND VEHICLES

All the items in this section are requisitioned with gadget points *(see page 105)*. Two or more agents may pool their gadget points to requisition costly gadgets.

GADGET HOUSINGS

Unless otherwise noted, gadgets look like extremely well-crafted versions of their original housings (if they have one), or an indecipherable item (if they don't). Most gadgets are listed with a Spot DC that is rolled against when someone inspects the gadget. With success, the person inspecting the gadget sees it for what it is (though he may not understand how it's possible). Those familiar with the concept of gadgets (such as enemy agents) receive a +5 bonus to the Spot check. R&D personnel receive a +10 bonus to the Spot check. Both must inspect the item to determine it's a gadget and glean its function. This Spot check is not made when someone is casually observing the agent or his gear, whether they're familiar with the concept of gadgets or not.

This Spot DC is also rolled against when people see the gadget in operation, unless one of the following traits supersedes this rule.

Spot DCs do not take efforts to hide gadgets into consideration. In this case, use the results of the Sleight of Hand skill check.

Automatic: The gadget's function is immediately visible. This is usually the case with advanced real-world weaponry and high-end technological gear.

No housing: Gadgets with this trait are not disguised as anything, and appear as pieces of indecipherable gear unless the observer makes his check against the item's Spot DC (in which case he understands the item's purpose but perhaps not how it works).

Obvious: Finally, some gadgets (flamethrower cigarettes, for example) are so blatant when used that everyone within line of sight notices them, regardless of their Spot DC. All gadgets with the obvious trait may be spotted by anyone – specialist or not – when they are being used.

Experts only: Only experts (R&D personnel, mechanics, designers, etc.) are allowed to make such a Spot check to see this gadget for what it is. Experts are people with 5 or more ranks in a skill relevant to the Spot check (such as Mechanics when inspecting a vehicle). Agents with a base attack bonus of +5 or more are considered experts with weapons they are proficient in. Those with 5 or more ranks in a skill relevant to their Spot check do not receive synergy bonuses unless such a bonus is mentioned in the skill description.

Super-science: Rarely do gadgets appear to use science beyond the limits of modern mechanics; when they do, they have this trait. A successful Spot check against this gadget's DC reveals that it is beyond the level of known science (posing a problem if the agent is attempting to keep a low profile).

SWAPPING HOUSINGS

Agents are likely to request gadgets in housings other than the ones listed. While often stunned that their first instinct wasn't the best possible choice, the R&D department often accommodates such requests – and the Game Control is encouraged to do the same (per his discretion).

If a gadget's new housing does not affect its utility or Spot DC, the gadget point cost is unchanged. New housings that affect the utility of a gadget (usually by augmenting or limiting its basic function) should increase or decrease the gadget point cost, to a recommended maximum adjustment of 5 points up or down (more than that means the agent should be requesting a different gadget). Housings that make the gadget more difficult to see add 2 gadget points per +5 to the Spot DC, and housings that make it easier to see likewise subtract 2 gadget points per −5 to the Spot DC.

Swapping a gadget's housing usually requires half an hour per point of cost adjustment.

ATTACHÉ CASES

Attaché cases may contain many options. You may take the standard attaché case option on its own, or take the standard option and then take more options from those below at the additional costs listed (e.g. taking a standard attaché case equipped with a booby-trap costs a total of 2 gadget points). You may have a maximum of three options (including the standard option) in any single attaché case. When more than one option offers the same benefit (such as increased hardness), only the highest benefit is applied.

Standard: This is the basic Agency briefcase.

Gadget Point Cost: 1 each   *Weight:* 5 lb.
Spot DC: 30

Mechanics: This briefcase has a hardness of 5 and 50 wound points. It can be used as a shield, adding +1 to the user's Defense. Search checks to find anything inside the case add +5 to their DC, and the DC of any Open Lock check to open the briefcase is 20.

This gadget (or another standard attaché case gadget) must be requisitioned as a housing first before you can add any of the options listed below.

Booby-trapped: Attaché cases, suitcases, and valises can all be wired to emit a powerful electric shock when the wrong combination is used.

Gadget Point Cost: +1   *Weight:* +½ lb.
Spot DC: +0

Mechanics: This gadget deals a severe electrical shock to anyone who attempts to open it without the combination. The victim must make a Fortitude save (DC 18) or be stunned for 1d8 rounds. A successful Open Locks check bypasses the trap, but the DC of the lock is increased by 5. For each additional gadget point spent on this option, the Fortitude save's DC is increased by 3.

Copycat unit: This briefcase computer can pick up and display what is shown on the screen of any computer, pager, PDA, or other electronic device within 25 ft.

Gadget Point Cost: +1   *Weight:* +1 lb.
Spot DC: −5

Mechanics: This gadget can display text, data, sounds, and video. The unit's storage capacity includes 48 hours of video and sound, or an effectively unlimited amount of text.

Counter-surveillance unit: An attaché case with this option allows agents to sweep rooms for bugs, intercept radio transmissions, or listen to tapped phones and rooms (by receiving a designated tap's signal).

Gadget Point Cost: +1   *Weight:* +1 lb.
Spot DC: +0

Mechanics: An agent using this case's equipment to sweep a room for bugs, taps, or other electronic surveillance equipment gains a +5 bonus to his roll.

"Magic box": This device gains its name by making documents disappear. Any documents placed within the case are incinerated by a tremendous burst of heat, confined to the interior of the case. As the papers are disintegrated, the heat simultaneously activates a powerful adhesive in the case lining, to which the powdered ashes stick. Anyone opening the case after the process sees a white textured interior, but no documents.

Gadget Point Cost: +1   *Weight:* +1 lb.
Spot DC: −5

Mechanics: This gadget can destroy any file no more than an inch thick. Agents may only use it three times before it must be returned to the home office (where the ashes are removed and new adhesive is applied).

Portable PC unit: This attractive business case contains a powerful personal computer, complete with a wireless modem, scanner, and printer.

Gadget Point Cost: +1   *Weight:* +3 lb.
Spot DC: +0

Mechanics: The computer has a power rating of +2. For each additional gadget point spent on it, the power rating increases by +1 (to a maximum of +5).

Safe passage unit: Secret compartments, lightweight 'safes,' and bulletproofing are all available with briefcases.

Gadget Point Cost: +1   *Weight:* +3 lb.
Spot DC: +0

Mechanics: This increases the hardness of the briefcase by 2, its wound points by 15, and the DC of its lock by +5. In addition, the DC of any Search checks to find anything inside the case are at an additional +5. This option can be bought up to three times for the same attaché case.

Submachinegun: This attaché-case hides a dedicated ceramic 9mm submachinegun and a 36-round magazine of ceramic bullets, rendering it invisible to metal detectors.

Gadget Point Cost: +1   *Weight:* +5 lb.
Spot DC: −5

Mechanics: When firing this 9×19 submachinegun, the agent suffers a −2 penalty to his attack roll. All weapon values are the same as the standard 9×19mm submachinegun *(see page 113)*. This submachinegun may be loaded with any type of pistol ammunition.

Setting the case's combination to a predetermined number unlocks the handle trigger; unfortunately, because the case is designed to appear seamless, agents cannot access the machine gun's internal components or clip without a mechanics kit *(see page 126)*. Agents cannot remove and fire the submachinegun independently. Search checks to find anything inside the case add +5 to their DC.

Surveillance unit: An attaché case with this option houses a high-end portable video surveillance suite. Images captured with it may either be recorded inside the durable case or piped through a dedicated H.U.D. displayed within tinted sunglasses and a hidden earpiece.

Gadget Point Cost: +1   *Weight:* +½ lb.
Spot DC: −5

Mechanics: This attaché case contains a micro-video camera with multi-spectral capabilities (i.e. it can record standard, thermal, and low-light images) and an auditory snoop device with a range of 1200 ft. It may record up to 48 hours of video and sound.

BACKPACKS

All of these normally look like high-tech gadgetry normally found in science-fiction movies, but can be concealed inside normal backpacks.

"Balloon-in-a-box": The outer shell of this unusual device "bursts" outward as its contents expand into a small, two-person, short-distance hot-air balloon, with handgrips for an agent to hold onto as he is lifted away.

Gadget Point Cost: 2   *Weight:* 10 lb.
Spot DC: 15 (obvious)

Mechanics: Works as a Large-sized hot-air balloon. It has a Defense of 12, 20 wound points, and a hardness of 0. For rules on hot air balloons, *see page 150.*

Collapsible glider wings: When needed, the contents of this unit unfold into a pair of glider wings.

Gadget Point Cost: 2   *Weight:* 5 lb.
Spot DC: 15 (obvious)

Mechanics: Works like a glider. *See page 150 for complete statistics.*

Jetpack: This classic gadget, first introduced in the late 1930s as a prototype for aerial reconnaissance, met with near-disastrous results when it was stolen by spies for the Nazi party and converted for combat use. The project was scrapped shortly thereafter, not to be revitalized until the mid-1960s when the Agency began testing a lightweight, more maneuverable version.

The latest incarnation of the jetpack is a simple, sleek metal design weighing only five pounds (ten when loaded with fuel), easily concealed within a standard high-school or camper's backpack. The standard issue jetpack is smoke grey in color so it can easily blend in with most clothes.

Gadget Point Cost: 4   *Weight:* 5 or 10 lb.
Spot DC: 5 (super-science, obvious)

Mechanics: This gadget allows the agent wearing it to fly at a speed of 500 ft. per round (50/100 mph). The handling modifier for this 'vehicle' is equal to 4 + the agent's Dexterity modifier. While in flight, the agent uses his standard Defense, modified by the speed he is currently moving relative to the attacker. The jetpack applies no armor modifiers or penalties to the agent.

The jetpack itself has a Defense of 18, a hardness of 1, and only 15 wound points.

Statistics for this gadget are also listed on the Air Vehicles table on page 150.

White noise generator: When used, this device emits a high-pitched sound, deafening anyone within 100 ft.

Gadget Point Cost: 3   *Weight:* 3 lb.
Spot DC: 20

Mechanics: Those within the area of effect must make Will saves (DC 16) or be stunned for 1d4 rounds. This unit comes with enough earplug filters for the agent's whole team. The unit uses a great deal of power and must be recharged at headquarters after each use.

BELTS

A number of useful gadgets are concealed within belts, which are rarely lost by an agent unless he is captured and strip-searched. You may take the standard belt option on its own, or take the standard option and then take more options from those below at the additional costs listed (e.g. taking a standard belt equipped with a lockpick set costs a total of 2 gadget points). You may only have a maximum of three options (including the standard option) in any single belt.

Standard: The standard Agency belt contains a powerful grappling hook.

Gadget Point Cost: 1 each   *Weight:* ½ lb.
Spot DC: 30

Mechanics: By depressing a hidden button on the this belt, a piton attached to a 100 ft. line can be fired into a surface and used as a grappling hook. The stylish buckle contains a high-tension motor capable of dragging up to 500 lbs., even straight up in the air. Finally, the belt has a "slow-fall" feature, allowing the agent to anchor the piton in a handy wall and descend up to 100 ft. The agent pushes the braking button when he's halfway down and the belt automatically slows him down in time for a safe landing.

This gadget (or another standard belt gadget) must be requisitioned as a housing first before you can add any of the options listed below.

Lockpick set: The belt contains a set of flexible non-metal lockpicks. The lockpicks cannot be felt, even if the belt is closely examined by hand, and they don't show up on metal detectors or x-rays. In order to use them, the agent simply wets the lockpick, causing it to harden long enough to get the job done.

Gadget Point Cost: +1   *Weight:* +½ lb.
Spot DC: +0

Mechanics: These finely crafted lockpicks add +2 to all Open Lock checks made when using them.

Razor's edge: When pulled tight three times in rapid succession, a micro-thin cable-blade is pushed to the belt's outer edges and it extends to 15 ft., making it a lethal whip-like weapon.

Gadget Point Cost: +1   *Weight:* +½ lb.
Spot DC: +0

Mechanics: With its blade extended, the belt serves as a whip that deals normal damage instead of subdual damage. The blade may be "resheathed" by pulling the belt tight a second time, requiring a half action.

BUG DETECTORS

These devices work very much like voice disguise units in that they are offered in both external and surgically implanted forms. Designed to pick up minute changes in the background sounds of an environment which is being monitored by surveillance gear, bug detectors effectively render an area safe — so long as an agent who has been alerted remains silent or does nothing unusual on camera.

External unit: This hand-held unit is roughly the size of a quarter and can be built into practically any housing (cuff-links and hair clasps are favorites). It merely registers the presence of a bug (usually by silently vibrating), not its location.

Gadget Point Cost: 1 each   *Weight:* —
Spot DC: 25 (sometimes no housing)

Mechanics: This device can sense any actively transmitting bug up to 25 ft. away. Some bugs can avoid this type of detection — either by only transmitting in bursts up to 45 minutes apart (by which time the agent may have already incriminated himself), or by sending information through a telephone line or other type of dedicated line.

The GC may also rule that a small number of cutting edge bugs can also escape this device, but unleashing such a dastardly device upon a team of agents requires him to spend an action die first.

Acoustic unit: This unit surgically enhances the agent's own ability to hear, and is invisible, even to doctors examining his ear canal. It works exactly like an external unit, but is virtually impossible to find during a search.

Gadget Point Cost: 4 each   *Weight:* —
Spot DC: 30 (experts only, super-science)

Mechanics: As above, except the device is implanted in the agent's head. A failed save against a sonic attack burns it out for 1 day, leaving the agent deaf until then.

The agent keeps this gadget after the end of the current mission, but it must be replaced once a year (at the full cost) as its power cells wear out. This implant cannot be detected through normal medical examinations — a medical professional must look for it.

BUSINESS CARDS

Business cards are often the easiest and most innocuous way of sneaking something onto another person.

Contact poison: Business cards are an easy delivery system for poisons.

Gadget Point Cost: 1 per 2   *Weight:* —
Spot DC: 30

Mechanics: This card's ink is a slow-acting poison that takes effect within 2d8 minutes after initial contact. This card can be laced with any poison listed on the Other Gear table (*see pages 128-130*), though poisons costing more than 5 BP per use increase the cost of this gadget by an additional +1 GP per 5 BP per use (rounded down). Regardless of the type of poison applied to the card, the delivery type (i.e. contact, inhaled, ingested, or injury) is now contact. The poison's drawback, however, is that the target must touch the card with his bare skin. Additionally, anyone handling the card must take the antidote beforehand or suffer from its effects. The ink has three applications, not counting anyone wearing gloves.

Frame-job cards: Often, the best way to frame someone is with their own help.

Gadget Point Cost: 1 per 5   *Weight:* —
Spot DC: 30

Mechanics: This business card has a coating of narcotics that does not affect the target, but is enough to alert drug-sniffing dogs and devices to its presence (adding +6 to their Wisdom checks).

Razor's edge: This card is well-balanced for throwing and its edge is lined with a micro-thin razor filament, making it a lethal thrown weapon.

Gadget Point Cost: 1 per 6   *Weight:* 1 lb. per 10
Spot DC: 20

Mechanics: Treat these cards as shuriken when thrown.

Tracking device: Business cards offer the perfect housing for a tracking device – and a reasonable excuse for giving it away.

Gadget Point Cost: 1 each   *Weight:* –

Spot DC: 25 (super-science)

Mechanics: This card's ink is actually a mesh of micro-circuitry protected beneath a plastic coating that allows the agent to track his target with a dedicated scanner. The tracer's range is limited to one mile due to the micro-transmitter's weak signal. Once activated, the tracer only has enough power to transmit for 2 hours.

CIGARETTES

The image of the smooth operating agent in a custom-tailored suit with a thin European cigarette has long fascinated spy enthusiasts. Gadget-makers have now exploited this image, making it a lethal underestimation of the modern superspy. All cigarette gadgets are disposable, and work in much the same way – light them, aim at a target, and wait for the fireworks.

Dartgun: Quiet and potentially lethal, this model is favored by subtle agents.

Gadget Point Cost: 1 per 2   *Weight:* –

Spot DC: 20

Mechanics: Acts as a one-use blowgun. The dart is pre-treated with either knockout drops or lethal poison I (*see page 238*), at the agent's option.

Flamethrower: More destructive agents prefer this model, which suddenly erupts in a gout of flame.

Gadget Point Cost: 3 each   *Weight:* –

Spot DC: 20 (super-science, obvious)

Mechanics: Acts as a flamethrower, but only contains enough fuel for one attack.

Grenade: Only the most suicidal agents dare to smoke a live grenade and then flick it at their enemies.

Gadget Point Cost: 2 each   *Weight:* –

Mechanics: Acts as a fragmentation grenade.

Pistol: One shot, one kill – an ethic agents should take to heart when using this one-shot pistol.

Gadget Point Cost: 1 each   *Weight:* –

Spot DC: 15

Mechanics: Acts as a one-use .22 LR pocket pistol.

Spray: Smoking kills, or at the very least blinds and incapacitates.

Gadget Point Cost: 1 per 2   *Weight:* –

Spot DC: 20

Mechanics: By blowing into this cigarette (or allowing the opponent to inhale one), a short-lived but noxious plume is ejected. This spray may be either pepper spray *(see aerosol mace page 111)* or knockout gas *(page 238)*. This item only affects the 5-ft. square immediately in front of the agent (unless smoked, in which case it only affects the person inhaling).

Welder: The only cigarettes that light themselves.

Gadget Point Cost: 1 each   *Weight:* –

Spot DC: 20 (obvious)

Mechanics: These cigarettes contain a unique, super-hot element that can burn through steel bars or metal plates. Once broken open, a chemical reaction in the cigarette burns intensely for 30 seconds (five rounds). This normally inflicts 1d4 damage if used in combat (requiring a touch attack). If applied against a surface continuously (or a person with a successful pin), the cigarette ignores up to 15 points of damage reduction/hardness and inflicts 2d8 damage.

CLOTHING

These options are most often incorporated into common street clothes or lycra bodysuits, but can be built into practically any clothing. You may take one of the standard clothing options on its own, or take a standard option and then take more options from those below at the additional costs listed (e.g. you could take standard liner clothing upgraded to armor for a cost of 2 gadget points). You may only have a maximum of two options (including the standard option) in any single set of clothing. When more than one option offers the same benefit (such as increased armor), only the highest benefit is applied.

Standard, cold suit: The is a full body suit specifically designed to mask the agent's heat signature, rendering him invisible to heat sensors, and various methods of thermal imaging.

Gadget Point Cost: 5 each   *Weight:* per clothing

Spot DC: 20

Mechanics: The agent may automatically evade unmanned security devices using heat sensors. In addition, any time someone attempts a Spot check to see the agent, he doesn't gain any benefit from thermal vision enhancement, instead receiving a –2 penalty.

This gadget (or another standard clothing gadget) must be requisitioned as a housing first before you can add any of the options listed below.

Standard, liner: All outfits requisitioned from the Agency have this feature.

Gadget Point Cost: 1 each   *Weight:* per clothing

Spot DC: 20

Mechanics: This gadget offers the wearer the benefits of wearing a tuxedo liner *(see pg. 125),* disguised as an ordinary suit of clothing.

This gadget (or another standard clothing gadget) must be requisitioned as a housing first before you can add any of the options listed below.

Standard, multi-environmental suit: This fashionable motorcycle ensemble converts into scuba gear.

Gadget Point Cost: 6 each   *Weight:* per clothing
Spot DC: 15 (obvious)

Mechanics: Out of water, the body suit and helmet are virtually indistinguishable from normal riding gear. In water the body suit's interstitial coating of neoprene keeps the diver warm, while the airtight helmet contains hidden micro tanks beneath the padding and serves as a mask and breathing regulator. Agents can remain submerged for one hour at a maximum depth of 100 ft.

This gadget (or another standard clothing gadget) must be requisitioned as a housing first before you can add any of the options listed below.

Armor: This suit is well armored.

Gadget Point Cost: +2   *Weight:* per clothing
Spot DC: –5

Mechanics: The Defense bonus of this suit is increased by +1. This does not affect the suit's armor check penalty or maximum Dexterity bonus.

Bungee suspenders: These stylish suspenders can stretch out to over 80 yards in length without losing their elasticity. The clasps can be converted into grappling attachments to allow for jumping nearly anywhere.

Gadget Point Cost: +1   *Weight:* per clothing
Spot DC: +0

Mechanics: The grappling attachments must be latched around a sturdy anchor (such as a railing or zeppelin strut) and can suspend up to 400 pounds. The suspenders can support the same weight, and stretch out to 250 ft.

Chameleon suit: Using advanced light-refraction technology, this suit renders its wearer invisible. Because agents can't be expected to repair such a complicated piece of technology, the suit repairs itself over time.

Gadget Point Cost: +5   *Weight:* per clothing
Spot DC: +0

Mechanics: As a free action, the wearer of this suit can become invisible, giving him total concealment *(see pages 170-171).* He may take any actions he desires, including attacking, without revealing himself. Environmental conditions such as snow, rain, or a spilled bucket of paint may reveal his position, however (reducing his concealment to three-quarters or one-half, at the GC's discretion). This ability may be used for up to a total of 10 minutes (60 rounds) a day.

Finally, if the wearer suffers more than 10 points of damage from a single hit, the suit's camouflage ability shorts out for the rest of the day while its self-repair circuits fix the damage.

Panic button: Sewn into the seams of clothing or disguised as jewelry, this gadget is a powerful transponder beacon that alerts the Agency of emergencies.

Gadget Point Cost: +1 each   *Weight:* per clothing
Spot DC: +0

Mechanics: Activating this device sends out a brief prerecorded message to every Agency listening post within 100 miles, alerting it to an emergency. The device then acts as a homing beacon for anyone within 20 miles of the agent's location for six hours.

Tie camera: This tie enables the agent to take color pictures without drawing attention to himself. The agent must simply "straighten his tie" to take a picture.

Gadget Point Cost: 1   *Weight:* —
Spot DC: 20

Mechanics: A miniature camera is built into this tie.

Trauma suit: Usually woven into undergarments or the lining of a business suit, jump suit, or tuxedo, this fine weave contains advanced bio-engineered dermal adhesives, stimulants, and antibiotics, capable of radically increasing the natural healing process. The trauma suit automatically recognizes when the agent wearing it is badly injured and responds by releasing regular doses of these chemicals into this system. This agent may also release the chemical on his own.

Gadget Point Cost: +8   *Weight:* +0
Spot DC: +0

Mechanics: At the start of the agent's next action after he sustains 20 or more points of damage, this suit heals 1d12 vitality, not to exceed the agent's maximum vitality. The agent may also elect to heal himself at any time by activating the suit (a half action for each 1d12 vitality healed). The trauma suit may only be activated 5 times, after which it must be returned to the home office to be recharged (at the suit's full GP cost).

COSMETICS AND JEWELRY

Only the most stylish fashion statements can house these useful spy toys.

Endless prism earrings: One of these earrings can be hung in front of a laser, causing it to endlessly bounce around inside, effectively circumventing a laser-based security sensor.

Gadget Point Cost: 1 per pair   *Weight:* —
Spot DC: 25

Mechanics: This earring allows its user to automatically succeed with one Electronics check made to bypass a laser-based security sensor. The earring must be left with the sensor in order to continue to work. As soon as the earring is removed from the beam, the sensor is triggered.

Micro-grenade earrings: Also commonly disguised as a necklace of explosive baubles, this device is attractive and understated right up until the moment the explosions start.

Gadget Point Cost: 1 each (2 per pair) *Weight:* –
Spot DC: 20

Mechanics: These earrings may be of any standard-issue grenade type *(see page 120)*, but have only half the damage value or duration (rounded down), as dictated by the grenade's description. Further, this device has an error rating one higher than a standard grenade (usually 1-5).

Poison lipstick: One kiss from a woman wearing this lipstick and the target is exposed to a debilitating, rapid-action contact poison. Of course, this is just one of the many contact toxins that can be used this way.

Gadget Point Cost: 2 per 3 uses *Weight:* –
Spot DC: 25

Mechanics: The agent applies an undercoat before putting on the lipstick that protects her from its poisonous effects. When requisitioning this gadget, the agent must specify whether the lipstick is treated as knockout drops or contact poison *(see page 238)*. In either case, there is enough for 3 applications.

Taser cufflinks: Disguised as ordinary cufflinks, these dress accessories generate a powerful electrical charge.

Gadget Point Cost: +1 per pair *Weight:* per clothing type
Spot DC: +0

Mechanics: Two seconds after these cufflinks are touched together, electricity flares between them. Anything caught in the middle is subject to a single attack with the same effect as a taser *(see page 110)*. This is a one-shot device; after use, the cufflinks must be recharged.

Woman's compact: This small makeup case includes all the necessary ingredients for both acid powder and a two-part explosive putty.

Gadget Point Cost: 3 per compact *Weight:* –
Spot DC: 25

Mechanics: Treat the powder as normal acid. Anyone inhaling or exposed to it follows the rules for acid on page 233. There is enough acid for one use. The putty is the equivalent of 1 lb. of C4. Only by touching the acidic powder does anyone realize that the compact is anything other than mundane.

DOCUMENT GADGETS

Even with the advent of the Internet and all the semi-reliable methods of fast information transfer out there, it is still often the best option to write something down. These gadgets assist agents forced into this position.

Document scanner: This item can scan folded documents while they are still sealed in an envelope.

Gadget Point Cost: 1 each *Weight:* 2 lb.
Spot DC: 15 (no housing, super-science)

Mechanics: A thin lead lining on the inside of the envelope can defeat this device, but such measures draw attention to the envelope's contents.

"ENIGMA Plus": Jokingly named by its creators, this item looks very much like a miniature laptop computer, with a small keyboard and screen, but it is much more. By typing a message into it and plugging any printer directly into the back of it, the agent can generate a message that appears as some indistinct foreign language but is in reality a coded transmission, decipherable only with a 20-digit alphanumeric code typed into a similar machine, or a computer with the equivalent software.

Gadget Point Cost: 4 each *Weight:* 5 lb.
Spot DC: 15

Mechanics: The ENIGMA Plus is considered a power rating +10 computer for purposes of Cryptography checks. It cannot be used for ordinary computer work.

Memory paper: Sheets of this paper can make near-perfect replicas of documents they are pressed against. This is often handy for quickly copying someone's signature or official documents.

Gadget Point Cost: 1 for 2 pages *Weight:* –
Spot DC: 30

Mechanics: Treat a document copied with memory paper as though it had been created with a Forgery skill of +10. Memory paper is extremely sensitive to liquids, and the copy is instantly ruined if it gets wet.

Microfiche reader: This ballpoint pen not only contains a secured compartment to hide microfiche, but it can also display the microfiche's contents as well.

Gadget Point Cost: 2 *Weight:* –
Spot DC: 25

Mechanics: The microfiche is kept safe within the pen's reinforced casing (1 hardness, 10 wound points). The miniature projector has a one-hour power source and can project the fiche from 3 inches square to 3 ft. square on any surface, as desired.

EVIDENCE ANALYSIS

These devices were conceived to assist agents when searching incident sites *(see page 214)*.

DNA analyzer: This device works like a tiny hand vacuum. It gathers skin flakes and hairs and performs DNA analysis. Then, if it finds a matching sample later on, it alerts the user and lists the site where the other sample was found.

Gadget Point Cost: 3   *Weight:* 3 lb.

Spot DC: 20 (no housing)

Mechanics: It takes 10 minutes to sweep a 10-ft. square room with the analyzer. Agents using this device when gathering and comparing evidence receive a +5 bonus to their Gather Information and related skill checks. The DNA analyzer can store 50 patterns and has a one-month battery.

Fingerprint camera: This device looks like a normal instant-print camera, but its filter recognizes and highlights fingerprints, digitally enhancing and separating them. The backgrounds appear hazy in pictures taken by this camera, while fingerprints appear clear and distinct, 'popping' out of the shot.

Gadget Point Cost: 1 each   *Weight:* ½ lb.

Spot DC: 25

Mechanics: All Search checks made to find fingerprints using this gadget receive a +5 bonus.

Fingerprint film: This translucent film is used to uncover code sequences. Simply lay it over a keyboard or keypad and it reveals the buttons pressed most recently, as well as the order in which they were pressed.

Gadget Point Cost: 1 per sheet   *Weight:* −

Spot DC: 15 (no housing)

Mechanics: This film must be stored in an airtight container (such as a sealed chewing gum wrapper), and is virtually invisible until used. Information is recorded with a limited invisible ink that can only be used once, after which the keys pressed are permanently visible on the film (the darkest keys are the ones most recently pressed, thus revealing the code's order). Fingerprint film dries out and is useless if left exposed to air for more then 10 seconds, and may be destroyed − leaving no trace, not even ash − by any open flame (such as a match).

Toiletry kit portable chem lab: This unisex toiletry kit contains everything a traveling agent needs in the field − toothpaste, soap, etc. Each of these items is actually a chemical compound or catalyst, harmless if used for its apparent purpose. The entire set, however, can be used as a field chemistry and forensics kit, allowing the agent to identify chemical compounds, check for blood and other fluid traces, and conduct ballistics tests.

Gadget Point Cost: 2   *Weight:* 4 lb.

Spot DC: 20

Mechanics: This kit adds +4 to all Knowledge (Chemistry), Profession (Forensics), and related checks made using it.

EXPLOSIVES

The strength and particular uses of explosives in spy operations varies widely. The following are three of the most common uses for gadgets.

Explosive pen: Identical to an ordinary pen in appearance, this pen can be used like a flash grenade.

Gadget Point Cost: 1 each   *Weight:* −

Spot DC: 25

Mechanics: Acts like a flash grenade *(see page 120)*.

Magnetic flask: Disguised as a slender metallic drinking flask, this item instantly becomes magnetic when its base is twisted halfway counter-clockwise. This also activates the internal timer attached to a flash charge, which ignites a generous supply of plastique.

Gadget Point Cost: 2 each   *Weight:* ¼ lb.

Spot DC: 25

Mechanics: When detonated, this flask explodes like 1/2 lb. of C4 *(see page 118)*.

Micro-burst gel: This small and unremarkable tube can be disguised as anything from toothpaste to foot cream, but it contains a powerful, clear explosive gel, set off by a bright flash of white light. The gel is like a concentrated version of napalm, burning fast and hot through practically anything. It makes little sound, and leaves behind only traces of common household cleaners.

Gadget Point Cost: 4 per 5 uses *Weight:* 1 lb.

Spot DC: 25

Mechanics: There is enough gel in one tube for 5 applications, along with 5 fuses. When ignited, each application inflicts 1d10 damage, ignoring hardness, to the object (or person) it is applied to, and it has a chance of setting the object on fire *(see Fire, page 230)*. More than one application can be used at once on the same object. The gel doesn't need oxygen to burn, and cannot be put out by immersion in water.

EYEWEAR AND EYE DROPS

Contact lenses have opened up an entire new realm of gadget design, including the items below (which also include Otherman Drops and some glasses as they are of roughly the same family). Contact lenses are limited to one gadget option per set of lenses. Agents must carry two or more sets of lenses and swap between them to gain more eyewear options.

Glasses, on the other hand, can include up to three eyewear options in one pair. The agent must pay 1 gadget point for the housing, and then the standard gadget point cost for each option, as normal. Glasses cannot duplicate the effects of eye drop gadgets.

Faceprint lenses: These lenses are specially designed to penetrate disguises, by recording and comparing facial structures. They can help to identify a specific individual, whose facial 'points' may be downloaded before the agent enters the field or recorded once the agent encounters him.

Gadget Point Cost: 3   *Weight:* —

Spot DC: 20 (super-science)

Mechanics: These lenses have two uses. First, if the agent downloads the facial structure of a specific individual when he requisitions the lenses (the target must be in the Agency's database), the agent automatically recognizes the individual whenever he encounters him, unless the target has scored a critical success with a Disguise check. The faceprint lenses can hold up to five such facial "maps."

Second, the agent can map someone's face with the lenses while in the field, though the total number of faces stored in the lenses still cannot exceed five. If the agent subsequently encounters the same individual, the agent automatically recognizes him (though again, a critical success with a Disguise check protects the target's identity, even from the faceprint lenses).

When searching for someone in a crowd, the agent gains a +5 bonus to Spot him using these lenses.

Hypnosis lenses: These lenses are designed to hypnotize anyone who looks at them directly by subtly repatterning the agent's irises.

Gadget Point Cost: 2   *Weight:* —

Spot DC: 20 (super-science)

Mechanics: If the agent is able to look directly into his target's eyes, these lenses grant him a +2 bonus to all Bluff, Diplomacy, and Intimidate skill checks.

Iris lenses: These lenses are designed to protect the agent's retina against overload. An artificial iris is built into the lens, which narrows when struck by extremely bright lights.

Gadget Point Cost: 2   *Weight:* —

Spot DC: 25 (super-science)

Mechanics: While wearing these lenses, the agent receives a +5 bonus to saves against being blinded by bright lights, flash/bang grenades, and the like. The lenses do not protect the agent against other methods of blinding such as salt, dirt, and eye gouges.

LCD lenses: LCD lenses display a semi-transparent video feed in the agent's field of view. The agent's depth perception allows him to focus past the display or concentrate on the information, as he chooses. The lenses include a microscopic receiver which allows them to display information transmitted by another gadget.

Gadget Point Cost: 1   *Weight:* —

Spot DC: 20 (super-science)

Mechanics: The LCD lenses are useless on their own, as the video feed requires a source designed to interface with them. When the agent selects this gadget, he must choose a piece of equipment (such as a laptop computer), or another gadget (such as copycat unit or Heads Up Display), which provides the lenses with a video feed. Thereafter, the agent may monitor the activity of these items without actually looking at them. This is particularly useful with a copycat unit, for example, as it allows the agent to view the pilfered information without even opening the attaché case.

Magnet-eyes: These lenses detect variances in the electromagnetic fields of others, alerting the agent to items secreted on their person, such as firearms and electronics.

Gadget Point Cost: 2   *Weight:* —

Spot DC: 25

Mechanics: Whenever the agent searches an NPC for weapons, gadgets, or electronic devices, he gains a +5 bonus to his Search skill check. With success, the presence of metals (like hidden guns) and electrical devices are revealed. These lenses do not reveal the specifics of the device, but the agent may make a Mechanics check (DC 15) to formulate a guess based on the electromagnetic flux.

Otherman drops: These eye drops are 'programmed' with a given eye color and pattern, which 'overlaps' the agent's when he uses them. These drops are even effective against electronic recognition systems, such as retina scanners. The effect only lasts one hour, after which the drops must be reapplied.

Gadget Point Cost: 1 per 3 uses   *Weight:* —

Spot DC: 25 (super-science)

Mechanics: Headquarters requires a DNA sample to create drops based on a specific individual, but once programmed, these lenses automatically fool a retina scanner into thinking the agent is the person in question. These drops add +2 to any Disguise check made using them. Finally, as a precaution, the agent's eyes begin to sting a little precisely one minute before the drops wear off.

Other-directional glasses: This option may not be chosen as contacts. These glasses are a great boon to agents on surveillance missions. They have two functions. First, they allow an agent to look in a direction other than where he appears to be looking, by channeling the correct field of view into the agent's pupil. Second, they provide the agent with "eyes in the back of his head." The outer edges of the lenses are mirrored, giving the agent a virtually unlimited field of view.

Gadget Point Cost: 1   *Weight:* —

Spot DC: 20

Mechanics: When an NPC makes a Sense Motive or Spot check in order to detect an agent using these glasses to watch him, he suffers a –4 penalty. Additionally, the agent receives a +4 bonus when using the Innuendo skill with his eyes. Finally, these glasses grant the agent a +2 bonus to all Spot skill checks to detect activity behind him, such as when an enemy agent is following him or sneaking up behind him.

Sealed lenses: These lenses are designed to protect the agent's eye against foreign substances. They are slightly larger than normal contact lenses, and create a seal between the contact lens and the eyelid. This prevents foreign substances from coming in contact with the eye.

Gadget Point Cost: 2   *Weight:* —

Spot DC: 20 (super-science)

Mechanics: The agent's eyes are protected from dirt, ashes, smoke, gas attacks, and the like. The agent may not be blinded by a foreign substance coming in contact with his eye (unless the object is large or sharp enough to physically damage his eyes). Additionally, these lenses also allow the agent to see clearly underwater, functioning as goggles.

Starlight lenses: These contact lenses are designed to gather and focus ambient light sources, enhancing the agent's night vision. If the agent needs to disable the lenses for any reason (just before a sudden flash of light, for example), he simply blinks twice in rapid succession. The lenses may be reactivated in the same fashion.

Gadget Point Cost: 1   *Weight:* —

Spot DC: 25

Mechanics: The agent suffers no penalties due to darkness. If the agent is exposed to a bright light source (such as a flashlight being shined in his face), he must make a Reflex save (DC 15) or be blinded for 1d4 rounds.

Telescopic lenses: These lenses are slightly thicker than normal. Contained within the lenses is a series of microscopic mirrors and additional lenses, designed to magnify the agent's field of vision – though not his field of view. The magnification feature must be activated by the agent, who may zoom in by squinting.

Gadget Point Cost: 2   *Weight:* —

Spot DC: 25

Mechanics: These lenses offer 20× magnification to the agent's vision. When the agent uses a ranged weapon, such as a pistol or bow, its range increment increases by 50%. Unfortunately, the magnification feature limits the agent's peripheral vision, and he suffers a –2 penalty to all Spot checks that depend on it.

Thermographic lenses: The coated glasses of these glasses allow the agent to see heat signatures.

Gadget Point Cost: 2   *Weight:* —

Spot DC: 25

Mechanics: Special filters in these lenses grant the agent a +5 bonus to Spot checks when tracking opponents by body heat within line of sight.

Translator lenses: These lenses allow the agent to read one designated language as if it were his own native tongue.

Gadget Point Cost: 3   *Weight:* —

Spot DC: 25 (super-science)

Mechanics: Each lens is programmed to translate text from one specific language into another (such as French into English). A lens can make one additional translation for each extra gadget point spent on it.

Transmitter lenses: These lenses are designed to transmit an agent's field of view to a remote display, such as a monitor, or another agent's LCD lenses.

Gadget Point Cost: 2   *Weight:* —

Spot DC: 20 (super-science)

Mechanics: The transmitter lenses allow anyone receiving the data to make Spot, Search, and similar skill checks as if he were seeing through the agent's eyes. In addition, if the observer has some way to communicate with the agent, the agent may benefit from the cooperation rules for skill checks in which he may watch what he's doing (such as Open Lock, or Sense Motive when speaking to someone face to face). The agent wearing the lenses must be the lead agent when using the cooperation rules.

X-ray lenses: These lenses allow an agent to see through objects, walls, clothes, and the like. Skin is transparent to these lenses—the agent only sees a target's bones, clothes, and anything he is carrying when looking at him.

Gadget Point Cost: 2   *Weight:* —

Spot DC: 25

Mechanics: These lenses allow the agent to see through up to 1 foot of solid material of hardness 5 or less at a visual range of 60 ft. Materials that deflect x-rays (such as lead) block the effects of these lenses.

SHOES

Most gadget-shoes have a 1in. × 1in. × 1in. secret compartment built into their heel. Some are a little more sophisticated...

Shoes may contain many gadget options. You may take the standard shoe option on its own, or take the standard option and then take more options from those below at the additional costs listed (e.g. taking a standard shoe equipped with a blade costs a total of 2 gadget points). You may only have a maximum of three options (including the standard option) in any single pair of shoes. When more than one option offers the same benefit (such as movement bonuses), only the highest benefit is applied.

Standard: Standard Agency shoes contain various sensors built into their soles to pick up gunpowder residue, blood stains (even after bleach has been used to wash visible signs away), and to magnify minute vibrations caused by nearby opponents. An inner layer of the shoe vibrates or pulses when the trigger goes off.

Gadget Point Cost: 1 per pair   *Weight:* 2 lb.

Spot DC: 30

Mechanics: This gadget only senses blood or gunpowder residue when the agent steps directly on the substance. The agent receives +1 to Spot checks made to avoid being surprised.

This gadget must be requisitioned as a housing first before you can add any of the options listed below.

Blade: Any small, thin blade can be concealed in the heel of a shoe, hidden until a trigger is depressed by the agent's big toe. Such blades are often coated with poisons or irritants.

Gadget Point Cost: +1   *Weight:* —

Spot DC: -5

Mechanics: Acts as a stiletto knife *(see page 110).* The cost of any poison applied to this blade must be paid separately.

Gun: This shoe hides all the working parts of a dedicated ceramic .22 LR pocket pistol with a 1-round chamber. The entire device is invisible to metal detectors if loaded with a ceramic bullet.

Gadget Point Cost: +1   *Weight:* +1 lb.

Spot DC: +0

Mechanics: When firing this weapon, the agent suffers a –2 penalty to his attack roll. This weapon holds only one round, and can be loaded with any type of ammunition. The first round is included in the cost of the gadget.

Homing beacon: These shoes contain an electronic homing beacon, just in case the agent gets into trouble.

Gadget Point Cost: +1   *Weight:* —

Spot DC: +0

Mechanics: The homing beacon has a range of 25 miles.

Phone: Cell phones and encrypted lines were once built into shoes. Today, these are less popular.

Gadget Point Cost: +1   *Weight:* —

Spot DC: –5

Mechanics: Acts as a cell phone *(see page 125).*

Roller/ice blades: Wheels or ice-skating blades pop out of the bottom of these augmented shoes.

Gadget Point Cost: +1 per type   *Weight:* —

Spot DC: –5

Mechanics: The movement of an agent wearing these shoes is doubled when he uses the roller or ice blades on smooth ground or ice, respectively.

Shock-tip shoes: A kick with that extra punch.

Gadget Point Cost: +2   *Weight:* —

Spot DC: +0

Mechanics: By flexing his toes, the agent can reveal a contact point at the tip of these shoes which works like a taser *(see page 110).* This effect does not include the damage from a kick, if such an attack is made. Insulated to protect the user, these shoes can also electrify puddles of water in which the agent is standing, delivering the effect to everyone in contact with the pool (all receive Fortitude saves). This gadget may be used twice before it must be recharged.

Suction shoes: These shoes adhere to nearly any surface with incredible strength, allowing the wearer to cling to or even climb sheer vertical walls with little trouble.

Gadget Point Cost: +1   *Weight:* —

Spot DC: +0

Mechanics: The wearer of these shoes gains a +3 bonus to Climbing checks. In addition, he may attempt to climb any relatively clean and dry surface, even those normally impossible for him.

Treads: The bottom of these shoes can be altered to leave different footprints than the agent's own.

Gadget Point Cost: +1   *Weight:* —

Spot DC: +0

Mechanics: The treads can be peeled away to reveal various imprints — everything from a smaller shoe size to bare foot tracks. Specific shoe prints can be included if a sample is provided (a photograph of half the shoe is enough to reconstruct the entire print, as is a cast of half or more of an original footprint). Only a critical success with the Track feat can distinguish tracks left by these shoes as false.

SONIC DEVICES

These devices utilize sound as a sixth sense, and to suppress electronic signals.

Sonic sensor: This headset uses sonar to allow the agent to sense his surroundings in dimly lit or unlit areas.

Gadget Point Cost: 2 each   *Weight:* —
Spot DC: 25

Mechanics: The agent ignores concealment bonuses from darkness while wearing the device.

Danger sensor: This headset allows the agent to sense subtle adjustments in his environment, allowing him to notice when danger looms near.

Gadget Point Cost: 2 each   *Weight:* —
Spot DC: 25

Mechanics: The agent receives a +2 bonus to all checks to avoid surprise while wearing the device.

White cone generator: This device is the size of a soda-can and emits a combination of low-level white noise emissions and broad spectrum jamming to temporarily disable any nearby bugs or remote listening technologies.

Gadget Point Cost: 4 each   *Weight:* —
Spot DC: 20 (no housing)

Mechanics: This gadget effectively blocks any audio bugging equipment within a 10-ft. radius circle around the unit. Only gadget-bugs can defeat this protection.

The GC may also rule that a small number of cutting edge bugs can also escape this device, but unleashing such a dastardly device upon a team of agents requires him to spend an action die first.

VOICE MODULATORS

These devices disguise the agent's voice by filtering its pitch, volume, and tenor.

External unit: This flesh-colored device is attached to the throat just over the larynx and modulates the sounds made when the agent is speaking. Unfortunately, while this model is easy to take off and throw away, it is also rather limited in its application (it may only be 'programmed' to mimic one voice), and lacks the range of a surgical implant (see below).

Gadget Point Cost: 1 each   *Weight:* —
Spot DC: 20

Mechanics: If used to impersonate a specific person's voice, this gadget adds +2 to Disguise checks.

Larynx implant: This implant surgically replaces the agent's larynx, permanently providing him with up to ten voices and accents or sound effects (total).

Gadget Point Cost: 4 each   *Weight:* —
Spot DC: 25 (experts only, super-science)
Mechanics: As above.

The agent keeps this gadget after the end of the current mission, but it must be replaced once a year (at the full cost) as its power cells wear out. This implant cannot be detected through normal medical examinations — a medical professional must look for it.

SURVEILLANCE GADGETS

These are enhanced bugs and video surveillance devices.

Non-sinusoidal transmission: Bugs can be altered to use exotic radiation for their broadcasts, thus preventing the signal from being jammed or noticed with counter-measures.

Gadget Point Cost: 2 per bug   *Weight:* —
Spot DC: 25 (experts only)

Mechanics: This option enhances any standard-issue or gadget-based bug, tap, or video surveillance equipment *(see page 126)* requisitioned during the Gearing Up phase of a mission. Apply the following effects. Traditional jamming is completely ineffective against this bug and the standard range of transmission is doubled. Further, the DC to detect the bug by electronic means is increased by +4.

If added to any bug gadget, this feature adds +1 gadget point to the device's cost.

Piezo-bug: This short-range (100-ft. range) bug is literally the size of a grain of sand.

Gadget Point Cost: 2 per bug   *Weight:* —
Spot DC: 30 (experts only)

Mechanics: This option enhances any standard-issue or gadget-based bug, tap, or video surveillance equipment *(see page 126)* requisitioned during the Gearing Up phase of a mission. Apply the following effects. This bug can only be detected by a search with an electronic bug finder (visual inspection always fails), and even then the DC to find the bug is increased by +5. Piezo-bugs are not reusable after being planted.

If added to any bug gadget, this feature adds +1 gadget point to the device's cost.

Tri-ference photography: A recent innovation of the R&D department, "triple interference photography" harnesses radical new chaos-based algorithms to extract data from minute variations between virtually identical photographs. The camera side of this technology includes a special high-speed film and shutter rate.

Gadget Point Cost: 1 per camera   *Weight:* —
Spot DC: 20 (experts only)

Mechanics: This option enhances any standard-issue or gadget-based camera requisitioned during the Gearing Up phase of a mission. Apply the following effects. The modified camera consumes film at triple the normal rate (using three exposures per image). Photographs taken with the camera may be enhanced beyond normal limits using tri-ference analysis software *(see below)*.

If added to any camera gadget, this feature adds +1 gadget point to the device's cost.

Tri-ference analysis: Using images captured by a tri-ference modified camera *(see above)*, this software package can refine the image with dozens of times the resolution of the original film.

Gadget Point Cost: 1 per camera   *Weight:* —
Spot DC: 20 (experts only)

Mechanics: This software triples the bonus from computer enhancement, but one full hour is required to process each image.

Video gyro-pack: This small (1 in. × 1in. × 3in.) and lightweight pod can mount onto any standard or professional camera, offering tripod stability without the weight.

Gadget Point Cost: 1 each   *Weight:* —
Spot DC: 20 (experts only)

Mechanics: This device provides tripod-quality stabilization without the cumbersome hardware (normally 20 lbs. — *see page 130)*.

Voice trigger: Cameras, firearms, and other simple devices may be fitted with an electronic trigger that allows the agent to activate the item with a simple voice command.

Gadget Point Cost: 1 per item   *Weight:* —
Spot DC: 25

Mechanics: The agent may use the item by voice command. If the item is a weapon, the attack uses the agent's base attack bonus or half their Surveillance skill (rounding down), whichever is lower.

TOOTH IMPLANTS

Tooth-implanted gadgets are highly valued by spy agencies, as they are easy to conceal and overlook. Also, they go everywhere with the agents they are built into, and can only be removed by surgery (or mutilation).

Hollow tooth: An agent's tooth can be hollowed out and fitted with a flip-top opening. Agents with hollow teeth usually practice opening and closing them with only their tongues, and contents are often clandestinely transferred with a kiss.

Gadget Point Cost: 2 each   *Weight:* —
Spot DC: 30

Mechanics: The center of a hollow tooth can only hold objects of fine size *(see page 175)*. The agent keeps this gadget after the end of the current mission.

Radio tooth: Various frequencies can be received through this tooth implant by twisting its crown (usually done with the agent's tongue). Sounds are transferred through the tooth's base and into the agent's inner ear.

Gadget Point Cost: 2 each   *Weight:* —
Spot DC: 25

Mechanics: The radio tooth can pick up signals from as far as 100 miles away, but it cannot transmit. The agent keeps this gadget after the end of the current mission, but it must be replaced once a year as its power cells wear out. When replaced, the agent must pay an additional 1 gadget point.

Suicide pill: Biting down hard on this tooth releases a poisonous gas or gel which is absorbed into the bloodstream through the agent's gums. Chemicals which simulate death (slowing the agent's heart rate and breathing) are also available.

Gadget Point Cost: 1 each   *Weight:* —
Spot DC: 30

Mechanics: When requisitioning this gadget, the agent should be careful to specify whether he wants the death version (lethal poison II, *see page 238*), or the feign death version (the agent falls comatose for 4 hours, during which time only a First Aid check of 30 or higher can tell that he's still alive.) The agent keeps this gadget after the end of the current mission.

TRACERS

Marking someone and following them back to their lair is one of the oldest spy moves in the book, and has inspired an entire subclass of inventions for just such an occasion.

Bullet tracers: These low-power projectiles are fired with a special pistol-like weapon, and cling to fabric with a hundred tiny 'legs.' Only 1mm across and usually gray or brown, they are very hard to spot.

Gadget Point Cost: 1 per package   *Weight:* —
Spot DC: 30

Mechanics: The tracer gun is fired like a pistol, but it ignores Defense bonuses from armor. Once in place, the tracer's signal can be tracked from up to 5 miles away. When requisitioned, this gadget comes with the gun, 2 tracer bullets, and a receiver tuned to the bullets' frequencies.

Echo tracers: These tracers do nothing but 'echo' a signal sent to them, tracking like sonar.

Gadget Point Cost: 1 per package   *Weight:* —
Spot DC: 30

Mechanics: These tracers have a range of 100 miles, but a bug detector used nearby automatically detects them when they send out an 'echo.' When requisitioning this gadget, the agent receives 3 tracers and a receiver tuned to the tracers' frequencies.

WATCHES

A long-time favorite of agents and gadget-makers alike, watches house many incredible inventions…

Watches may contain many gadget options. You may take the standard watch option on its own, or take the standard option and then take more options

from those below at the additional costs listed (e.g. taking a standard watch equipped with an explosive costs a total of 2 gadget points). You may only have a maximum of three options (including the standard option) in any single watch.

Standard: A tiny lens built into the side of this watch emits a powerful laser beam.

Gadget Point Cost: 1 each
Weight: –
Spot DC: 30 (super-science)

Mechanics: The laser inflicts 10d10 damage (ignoring hardness) of cutting damage to any object it is targeted at. This process takes 1 minute. Because it takes so long to use, it is generally useless against living or mobile targets. The watch contains enough energy to fire the laser beam for 5 minutes before it needs a recharge.

Explosive: Usually built with a quick-release latch, this gadget can be set to explode anywhere from 3 seconds to 5 minutes after it is activated.

Gadget Point Cost: +1
Weight: –
Spot DC: –5 (super-sciencc)

Mechanics: The explosion works like 1 lb. of C4 and destroys the watch (along with all options installed in it).

Garrote: Pulling the time-set button of this watch reveals a 3-ft. length of super-strong wire, useful for sliding along suspension wires or strangling enemies.

Gadget Point Cost: +1
Weight: –
Spot DC: +0
Mechanics: The watch has a built-in garrote.

GPS watch: This watch enables the agent to determine his position on the globe with a GPS (Global Positioning System) device. Coordinates are displayed on the digital watch face.

Gadget Point Cost: +1
Weight: –
Spot DC: –5

Mechanics: While the agent's coordinates are displayed on the watch face, the agent must still make an Education check (DC 15) to determine his exact location. With success, he knows which city or major landmark he is nearest, and how to get there by the quickest route.

Memory cache watch: The watch hides a miniature computer capable of accessing computer files remotely.

Gadget Point Cost: +4
Wcight: –
Spot DC: +0 (super-science)

Mechanics: This gadget contains a powerful microprocessor and remote-entry data compression system. By pressing the watch against an active terminal, the watch can download and store 1 gigabyte worth of information per minute with a maximum storage capacity of 3 gigabytes. The agent can then transfer that information to another computer for processing. Agents can also program the watch with specific keyword searches.

Poison spike watch: This device is innocuous, discreet, and good for surreptitious hits.

Gadget Point Cost: +3
Weight: –
Spot DC: +0

Mechanics: The watch contains a hidden, retractable needle coated with poison. This needle may be laced with any poison listed on the Other Gear table (*see pages 128-130*), though poisons costing more than 5 BP per use increase the cost of this gadget by an additional +1 GP per 5 BP per use (rounded down). The needle breaks off once used, inflicting one point of subdual damage. Three needles are contained in the watch, allowing the agent to use this touch attack three times before the watch must be refilled at headquarters. *See Poisons and Disease on page 238 for a list of potential toxins.*

Rotary saw: This gadget is highly useful for cutting through fences, rope, and even handcuffs.

Gadget Point Cost: +1

Weight: —

Spot DC: –5 (super-science)

Mechanics: The agent wearing this watch receives +6 to all Escape Artist checks (if the Escape Artist check is successful, the binding is cut). When used as a weapon, this device inflicts 1d2 damage.

weapons

AF Hush Puppy: The AF Hush Puppy is a .45 ACP pistol that uses sub-sonic caseless ammunition, allowing the action to be fully enclosed. It also has a sound suppressor running the length of the barrel that is integrated into the design, creating an almost silent firearm.

Gadget Point Cost: 3 each

Weight: 3 lb.

Spot DC: Automatic

Mechanics: Has the same statistics as the .45 ACP Pistol listed in the weapons section. Listen checks to hear an agent using this weapon suffer a –5 penalty.

Quick mine: This tiny explosive surprise is designed to harry unwanted pursuers.

Gadget Point Cost: 2 each

Weight: —

Spot DC: 20

Mechanics: This quarter sized device contains a high explosive charge, an adhesive coating, and wire spool. Once slapped on a wall, it activates after five seconds, shooting a tiny hook and wire out to 7 ft. If the wire hits nothing, the gadget detonates, inflicting 1d10 damage in a 1-square (5-ft.) radius. If the hook hits a wall, the wire tightens, and anyone tripping it detonates the explosive. This weapon is perfect for stringing across doorways or destroying locks and control pads.

Umbrella gun: The long barrel and natural handgrip of the ordinary umbrella makes for a perfect trigger and the umbrella's stock can conceal a powerful gun.

Gadget Point Cost: 2 each

Weight: per pistol

Spot DC: 25

Mechanics: Any pistol listed on page 113 may be built into an umbrella, with a three-shot cylinder concealed in the grip. It also works perfectly for keeping dry during a rainstorm.

weapon enhancements

Unless otherwise noted, these enhancements can be added to any existing weapon.

All-in-one revolver: This revolver comes with an assortment of barrels and cylinders enabling it to be configured to fire any available pistol ammunition.

Gadget Point Cost: 2

Weight: 5 lb. (barrels)

Spot DC: Automatic

Mechanics: A revolver fitted for these barrels may use any available pistol ammunition *(see page 132)*.

Breakdown gun: Any standard holdout pistol may be broken down into four to five innocent pieces.

Gadget Point Cost: 3 each

Weight: —

Spot DC: 30 (to recognize parts for what they are)

Mechanics: Each weapon is a custom job with a unique set of disguised parts. Building and breaking down the weapon requires 4 half actions.

CQB modification: The CQB modification offers an existing firearm enhanced close quarters fighting capabilities.

Gadget Point Cost: 1

Weight: —

Spot DC: 10 (experts only)

Mechanics: The range increment of the weapon is reduced to 10 ft. The agent receives a +1 bonus to attacks performed in the modified 1st and 2nd range increments when using this weapon. This modification may be performed on any submachinegun, assault rifle, or shotgun.

Cloaking device: This accessory makes weapons invisible to sensors.

Gadget Point Cost: 2 each

Weight: —

Spot DC: 10 (experts only, super-science)

Mechanics: The weapon is not detected by metal detectors, x-rays, or any other electronic sensor. This accessory does not conceal the weapon from visual or personal inspections (i.e. 'patting you down').

Dummy line: When an agent with this holster has lost his weapon, he can 'reel it in,' back to his hand. The model's internal motor is quite powerful.

Gadget Point Cost: 1 each

Weight: —

Spot DC: 15

Mechanics: The motor's effective Strength is 24 for purposes of retrieving a weapon. If an enemy agent is holding on to the weapon attached to the dummy line, make a contested Strength check. If the holster wins, the weapon is jerked out of the enemy's hand. The line extends up to 15 ft, and can be cut by dealing it 4 points of damage.

Hush Puppy CQB modification: This is an upgrade of the CQB modification listed above. It incorporates an integrated sound suppressor.

Gadget Point Cost: +1

Weight: —

Spot DC: 10 (experts only)

Mechanics: Listen checks to hear an agent using the CQB-enhanced weapon suffer a –5 penalty. This enhancement may only be made on a submachinegun with the CQB modification.

Knife launcher: A throwing knife may be launched from this holster at high speed with only moderate loss in accuracy. This attack often catches enemy agents completely off guard due to its unexpected nature.

Gadget Point Cost: 3 each

Weight: —

Spot DC: 10

Mechanics: This gadget may only be loaded with throwing knives, which must be purchased separately. Due to the suddenness of an attack with this gadget, the agent is allowed to make a Feint attempt on his target as a free action. This benefit is only gained once per combat. The agent suffers a –2 penalty to his attack roll due to the awkwardness of the device, and doesn't add his Strength bonus to damage.

Machine pistol modification: If you absolutely need a fully automatic handgun...

Gadget Point Cost: +1

Weight: —

Spot DC: 5

Mechanics: The agent must requisition the pistol separately. The pistol gains the burst ability, but its error range is increased by 2 (e.g. from 1 to 1-3, 1-2 to 1-4, etc.) Only a pistol may be modified with this option.

Match grade weapon: By choosing component parts that meet rigid tolerance standards the accuracy of standard firearms can be greatly improved.

Gadget Point Cost: +2

Weight: —

Spot DC: 10 (experts only)

Mechanics: All attack rolls using the modified weapon are increased by +1. This enhancement may be applied to any firearm purchased with mission budget or gadget points at the GP cost listed above. If applied to a firearm that is part of an agent's personal gear, the GP cost is tripled and the modification is kept after the end of the current mission.

Personalized fighting knife: This is a custom built fighting knife designed specifically for the intended user.

Gadget Point Cost: 1

Weight: —

Spot DC: 10 (experts only)

Mechanics: All attack and damage rolls the specified agent makes when using his personalized fighting knife are increased by +1 each.

Remote-operated gun mount: This unit comes complete with a remote-operated tripod mount, imaging system with transmitter, and a video receiver. This unit allows for the user to mount a firearm on the tripod mount and target and fire the weapon from a remote location.

Gadget Point Cost: 3

Weight: 15 lb.

Spot DC: Automatic

Mechanics: Any firearm up to GPMG size may be mounted on this tripod. The remote signal has a range of 500 ft.

Silenced revolver: This modification reduces the tolerance of an existing revolver, enabling it to use a silencer.

Gadget Point Cost: 1

Weight: —

Spot DC: 10

Mechanics: The agent must requisition the revolver separately.

Spring-loaded weapon holsters: The 'old classic,' this holster is strapped around the agent's wrist and loaded with a small, sleek pistol or melee weapon which can leap into his hand when needed.

Gadget Point Cost: 1

Weight: —

Spot DC: 25

Mechanics: This holster works like the Quick Draw feat, allowing the agent to draw the Small weapon loaded in the holster as a free action instead of a half action.

Weapon accurizing: This enhancement further increases the performance of a match grade weapon by custom fitting it to meet your exact measurements, along with some additional fine-tuning.

Gadget Point Cost: 2

Weight: —

Spot DC: 10 (experts only)

Mechanics: All attack rolls using the modified weapon are increased by +1. This enhancement may only be applied to a match grade firearm, and its effects stack with the match grade enhancement. This enhancement may be applied to any firearm purchased with mission budget at the GP cost listed above. If applied to a firearm that is part of an agent's personal gear, the GP cost is tripled and the modification is kept after the end of the current mission.

GEAR

TABLE 5.12: PERSONAL VEHICLES AND MOUNTS								
Vehicle Name	GP	Size	Hnd	Speed*	MPH**	Def†	WP	Hrd	Skill Used
Vehicles									
ATC (3-wheeler)	2	Medium	+5	150 ft.	15/30	15	20	2	Driver
Bicycle	($100)	Medium	+6	50 ft.	5/10	16	30	1	Driver
Chopper	3	Large	+6	400 ft.	40/80	15	50	2	Driver
Dirt Bike	1	Medium	+6	200 ft.	20/40	16	30	2	Driver
Jet Ski	1	Medium	+4	150 ft.	15/30	14	30	1	Boating
Motorcycle	2	Medium	+8	500 ft.	50/100	18	35	1	Driver
Quad (4-wheeler)	2	Medium	+6	200 ft.	20/40	16	50	2	Driver
Racing cycle	4	Large	+7	750 ft.	70/140	17	25	2	Driver
Snowmobile	2	Medium	+6	250 ft.	25/50	16	50	2	Driver
Mounts ‡									
Camel	2	Large	−1	30 ft.	3/6	13	15	0	Handle Animal
Horse	2	Large	+0	40 ft.	4/8	13	12	0	Handle Animal
Mule	1	Large	−3	30 ft.	3/6	13	14	0	Handle Animal

* Speed is listed in feet per standard combat round.

** The number before the slash is the vehicle's cruising speed. The number after the slash is the vehicle's maximum speed.

† The vehicle's size is already factored into this value.

‡ Gadgets cannot be installed on mounts.

Abbreviations: GP = gadget points; Hnd = handling; MPH = miles per hour; Def = Defense; WP = wound points; Hrd = hardness.

TABLE 5.13: CARS AND TRUCKS

Vehicle Name	GP	Size	Hnd	Speed*	MPH**	Def†	WP	Hrd
Cars								
Classic	3	Large	−4	500 ft.	50/100	5	100	6
Compact	3	Large	+2	500 ft.	50/100	11	80	4
Economy	2	Large	+0	500 ft.	50/100	9	80	4
Limo	5	Huge	−5	350 ft.	35/70	4	140	7
Luxury	4	Large	−2	550 ft.	55/110	7	110	7
Mid-Size	3	Large	+0	550 ft.	55/110	9	90	5
Muscle	3	Large	−1	650 ft.	65/130	8	110	7
Police	4	Large	+4	700 ft.	70/140	13	110	7
Sedan	3	Large	+1	600 ft.	60/120	10	100	6
Sports	4	Large	+5	800 ft.	80/160	14	70	3
Station Wagon	2	Large	−3	500 ft.	50/100	6	100	6
Sub-compact	1	Medium	+3	450 ft.	45/90	13	70	3
Trucks								
Ambulance	4	Large	−3	550 ft.	55/110	6	120	6
Box Truck	5	Huge	−6	500 ft.	50/100	3	140	8
Bus	6	Garg.	−7	450 ft.	45/90	2	150	9
Humvee	8	Large	−5	500 ft.	50/100	4	170	10
Jeep	2	Large	+1	600 ft.	60/120	10	100	5
Mini-van	3	Large	−1	600 ft.	60/120	8	110	5
Off-road	2	Large	+0	600 ft	60/120	9	110	5
Pick-up	3	Large	−2	550 ft.	55/110	7	120	6
Semi (empty)	7	Garg.	−8	450 ft.	45/90	2	150	9
Semi (loaded)	−	Garg.	−9	450 ft.	45/90	2	150	9
SUV	4	Large	−4	500 ft.	50/100	5	140	7
Van	4	Large	−4	550 ft.	55/110	5	130	7

* Speed is listed in feet per standard combat round.

** The number before the slash is the vehicle's cruising speed. The number after the slash is the vehicle's maximum speed.

† The vehicle's size is already factored into this value.

All vehicles on this table use the Driver skill.

Abbreviations: GP = gadget points; Hnd = handling;
MPH = miles per hour; Def = Defense;
WP = wound points; Hrd = hardness.

TABLE 5.14: WATER VEHICLES

Vehicle Name	GP	Size	Hnd	Speed*	MPH**	Def†	WP	Hrd
Aircraft Carrier	20	Colossal	−15	200 ft.	20/40	2	1,000	15
Canoe	($100)	Medium	−2	40 ft.	4/8	8	10	1
Diving Bell	2	Large	N/A	20 ft.	2/4	4	50	5
Diving Drone	3	Small	+2	10 ft.	1/2	13	40	3
Fishing Boat	3	Huge	+0	80 ft.	8/16	8	75	3
Luxury Liner	12	Colossal	−10	100 ft.	10/20	3	500	7
Mini-Sub	5	Large	+1	150 ft.	15/30	10	75	4
Oil Tanker	15	Colossal	−13	80 ft.	8/16	2	700	10
Rowboat	($150)	Medium	−3	30 ft.	3/6	7	15	2
Speedboat	3	Large	+5	400 ft.	40/80	14	60	3
Submarine	9	Colossal	−6	150 ft.	15/30	3	100	8
Submersible Car	7	Large	+4	100 ft.	10/20	13	85	5
Swamp Boat	4	Large	+4	200 ft.	20/40	13	40	3
Zodiac	3	Large	+3	120 ft.	12/24	12	20	1

* Speed is listed in feet per standard combat round.

** The number before the slash is the vehicle's cruising speed. The number after the slash is the vehicle's maximum speed.

† The vehicle's size is already factored into this value.

All vehicles on this table use the Boating skill.

Abbreviations: GP = gadget points; Hnd = handling; MPH = miles per hour; Def = Defense; WP = wound points; Hrd = hardness.

TABLE 5.15: AIR VEHICLES

Vehicle Name	GP	Size	Hnd	Speed*	MPH**	Def†	WP	Hrd
Autogyro	7	Large	+6	200 ft.	20/40	15	30	3
Fighter jet	18	Huge	+12	4,000 ft.	400/800	20	100	8
Gunship	16	Huge	+8	1,200 ft.	120/240	16	100	7
Hang glider	2	Large	+1	50 ft.	50/100	10	15	2
Helicopter	9	Large	+5	1,000 ft.	100/200	14	75	5
Hot air balloon‡	1	Garg.	—	—	5/10	2	10	0
Jetpack	4	Small	+7	500 ft.	50/100	18	25	1
Jumbo jet	12	Colossal	−1	3,100 ft.	310/620	3	120	6
Parasail	2	Large	+0	100 ft.	10/20	9	15	1
Space shuttle	40	Colossal	−5	10,000 ft.	1000/2000	2	600	10
Ultralight	3	Large	+3	250 ft.	25/50	12	40	4
VTOL	15	Huge	+2	650 ft.	65/130	10	100	7
Zeppelin	8	Colossal	−6	350 ft.	35/70	2	60	1

* Speed is listed in feet per standard combat round.

** The number before the slash is the vehicle's cruising speed. The number after the slash is the vehicle's maximum speed.

† The vehicle's size is already factored into this value.

‡ The hot air balloon drifts on the wind, and pilots of such vehicles cannot choose maneuvers. Hot air balloons automatically lose any round of a chase.

All vehicles on this table use the Pilot skill.

Abbreviations: GP = gadget points; Hnd = handling; MPH = miles per hour; Def = Defense; WP = wound points; Hrd = hardness.

TABLE 5.16: ARMORED AND HEAVY VEHICLES

Vehicle Name	GP	Size	Hnd	Speed*	MPH†	Def‡	WP	Hrd
2 1/2-ton Truck	8	Huge	–7	400 ft.	40/80	2	220	11
AAV	11	Huge	–6	300 ft.	30/60	2	260	13
APC	8	Huge	–8	400 ft.	40/80	2	240	12
Armored Car	7	Large	–4	400 ft.	40/80	5	220	11
Bullet Train§	14	Colossal	–	900 ft.	90/180	2	300	12
Half-track	9	Huge	–9	350 ft.	35/70	2	240	12
Hovercraft	10	Garg.	–5	300 ft.	30/60	2	200	10
Tank	13	Huge	–10	450 ft.	45/90	2	280	14
Train§	12	Colossal	–	350 ft.	35/70	2	300	13

* Speed is listed in feet per standard combat round.

† The number before the slash is the vehicle's cruising speed. The number after the slash is the vehicle's maximum speed.

‡ The vehicle's size is already factored into this value.

§ See pages 195-196 for more about using trains in chases. If a train hits something, it inflicts 3d6 damage for every 5 mph it is traveling at the time. If the vehicle is Huge or larger, the train has a chance of derailing (Huge: 20% chance, Gargantuan 50%, Colossal 80% chance). If the train derails, everyone inside suffers damage as normal for a crash (see page 193).

All vehicles on this table use the Driver skill.

Abbreviations: AAV = Amphibious Assault Vehicle; APC = Armored Personnel Carrier; GP = gadget points; Hnd = handling; MPH = miles per hour; Def = Defense; WP = wound points; Hrd = hardness.

"THE USUAL REFINEMENTS"

The usual refinements are a collection of universal gadget modifications made to vehicles before they are assigned for use in the field. They are broken into package upgrades of several vehicular gadgets, applied as a whole to greatly improve the performance of a single vehicle.

USUAL REFINEMENTS MECHANICS

Requisitioning 5 or more refinements for a single vehicle reduces the cost of all the package refinements by half (rounded up). Vehicular gadgets must be requisitioned together for their cost to be reduced in this way. Vehicular gadgets may also be requisitioned individually at their full cost.

You may install a maximum number of options in any single vehicle equal to its wound points divided by ten (rounded up). When more than one option offers the same benefit (such as handling bonuses), only the highest benefit is applied. Usual refinements add no weight to vehicles (which are not weighed to begin with).

Example: A sports car has 70 wounds, so up to 7 vehicular gadgets may be installed on one. If you chose to install auto-tint (1 GP), improved handling (1 GP), a pop-up shield (1 GP), and a nitrous oxide system (2 GP), the cost of all four gadgets would be 3 GP (5/2).

Note: Due to the great variety of possible vehicle-gadget combinations, some make no sense. For instance, auto-inflating tires have no place on a tracked snowmobile. Further, no vehicular gadgets can be installed on an animal. Obviously impossible combinations should be ignored.

VEHICULAR GADGETS

Autopilot: The vehicle may be set to drive itself — either along a pre-programmed path or just to keep itself on the road.

Gadget Point Cost: 1   *Spot DC:* 20 (experts only)

Mechanics: Maneuver checks are made as if the vehicle had a +5 Driver skill.

Auto-tint: The degree of tint over the vehicle's windows can be adjusted from the dashboard, darkening from crystal clear to pitch black. Even at its darkest shade, this tinting doesn't hinder the ability of those within to see outside.

Gadget Point Cost: 1   *Spot DC:* 25 (experts only)

Mechanics: Darkening the windows is a free action so long as the agent can reach the dashboard. While active, no one can see inside the vehicle and flash and laser attacks cannot affect those within.

Black headlights: Not actually headlights, this gadget modifies a vehicle's windshield (or appropriate window) so the agent can drive at night without using headlights to reveal his position. Specially polarized glass makes this possible — at the expense of some of the driver's depth perception.

Gadget Point Cost: 1

Spot DC: 20 (super-science)

Mechanics: The DC of any Spot check to notice this vehicle is increased by +6 at night. However, all Driver checks involving depth perception (such as crash checks involving approaching terrain) suffer a –2 penalty. When being used this refinement is obvious to anyone inside the vehicle.

Concealed machine gun: This machine gun is set into the front of the vehicle. It is concealed when not in use.

Gadget Point Cost: 3

Spot DC: 25 (super-science, obvious)

Mechanics: This machine gun works like a 7.62×51mm GPMG *(see page 118)* and holds 125 rounds of ammo. Using it applies a –4 penalty to hit, and restricts the driver to targets in front of the vehicle. This refinement is obvious to everyone in the area when the machine gun is being fired.

Optionally, the machine gun may be mounted on the roof of the vehicle, reducing the Spot DC by 10 (to 15), at the cost of 1 additional gadget point. This option offers the machine gun a 180-degree horizontal firing arc and the ability to fire upon air targets anywhere but immediately above the vehicle.

Ejection seats: The vehicle's seats are fitted with a number of small rockets which propel them up and away from the vehicle, allowing them to descend at a safe distance by means of a parachute. These seats can be activated automatically after a certain amount of damage is dealt to the vehicle, by the use of a concealed ripcord on each individual seat, or with a hidden control near the driver of the vehicle. A variant version of this device – called the "escape pod" – can be installed for vehicles that travel in hostile environments, such as underwater or in orbit.

Gadget Point Cost: 1

Spot DC: 20 (super-science, obvious)

Mechanics: The ejection seat activates when 80% of the vehicle's total wound points have been exhausted. This setting may be adjusted or overridden by the agent driving the vehicle.

Electrified frame: The vehicle's body can become a capacitor, sending thousands of volts across anyone touching it.

Gadget Point Cost: 1

Spot DC: 25 (experts only, super-science)

Mechanics: This device is set into the frame of the vehicle, and delivers 2d6 points of subdual damage to anyone clinging to the outside of it when activated. Victims who take damage after hardness is applied must make a Will save (DC 15) or lose his grip and fall off.

Extra armor: This modification places armor plates under the vehicle's natural shell.

Gadget Point Cost: 1

Spot DC: 20 *(see description)*

Mechanics: The entire vehicle (including its windows) gains 5 points of hardness. This refinement is obvious once any damage has made it through the plating (i.e. the vehicle has taken damage beyond its hardness); only experts may notice it until then.

Heads Up Display (H.U.D.): Outside the Agency, this refinement is commonly seen in aircraft, however Agency engineers have modified it for use in other vehicles. The H.U.D. presents a wide array of information, superimposed as a transparent image over the driver's field of view using either a liquid crystal display or a holographic projection. Information includes nearby vehicles' speeds and distances (as well as their projected movement in coming seconds), integrated targeting reticles for on-board weapons, and the status of the vehicle's armor, engine, and other components.

Gadget Point Cost: 1

Spot DC: 15 (super-science)

Mechanics: When driving a vehicle with a H.U.D., agents may substitute their Wisdom modifier for their Dexterity modifier for any Driver skill checks.

Hidden compartment: Part of the vehicle's body (specified by the agent, per GC approval) is hollow, allowing the agent to hide one objects (or people) within.

Gadget Point Cost: 1

Spot DC: 30

Mechanics: Once this option is installed, the number of refinements that may be installed on the vehicle *(see opposite)* is increased by 25% (rounded up). Gadgets installed in these extra slots receive the benefits of the compartment's Spot DC (30), unless they are obvious. Alternately, a compartment may be set aside where one Medium-sized person or an equivalent size and weight of objects may be stored. This compartment is sealed, in case the vehicle dives underwater or into orbit, and air must be siphoned from the vehicle's main cabin.

Improved handling: The stock control systems are removed from the vehicle and replaced with a drive-by-wire system, which uses a computer and a set of hydraulics to pilot the vehicle.

Gadget Point Cost: 1

Spot DC: 15 (expert only)

Mechanics: The vehicle's handling is increased by 2.

Laser mount: Still experimental, the chief difficulty with this small vehicular laser remains the enormous power required to energize the beam. To date, R&D has not been able to build a power cell for this weapon with more than 3 shots in its energy reserve. R&D has very few prototypes of this weapon, and Controls are rarely known to authorize their use without a global threat demanding it.

Special Note: GC approval required (may only be released with Control's permission)

Gadget Point Cost: 3 per shot (maximum 3)

Spot DC: 20 (obvious, super-science)

Mechanics: Limited power cells must be requisitioned for this vehicular weapon — the laser may not be powered by a vehicle's battery. For each 3 gadget points the agent spends on this device (up to a maximum of 6), one shot may be fired before it must be recharged at the home office.

Damage	Error	Threat	Range	Weight
3d10	1-4	18-20	200 ft.	7 lbs.*

Nitrous oxide system: With some minor engine modifications and the addition of this little bottle, any vehicles acceleration can be greatly increased.

Gadget Point Cost: 2

Spot DC: 15 (obvious)

Mechanics: NO_2 is sprayed into the fuel mixture in six stages. For every stage applied, increase the vehicle's cruising and top speeds, and MPH, by 25% of their original value. For every stage applied, also decrease the handling rating of the vehicle by 1. The effects of each stage last for 2 rounds and up to 4 stages can be applied in a single round. NO_2 is highly volatile — for each stage applied, roll 1d6; a roll of 1 indicates that the NO_2 has ignited and the vehicle is on fire. Apply damage each round according to the rules on page 230.

Oil slick: The vehicle can eject a stream of super-slick oil onto the road behind it to foil pursuers.

Gadget Point Cost: 1

Spot DC: 20

Mechanics: When activated, pursuers suffer a –5 penalty to their next maneuver check. This effect may be combined with a smoke screen. This gadget may be used once before it must be refilled back at headquarters or by an agent with one or more ranks in the Mechanics skill. Refill canisters cost 1 additional gadget point per use and are stored near the oil slick mechanism.

Pop-up shield: This device raises a steel plate in the rear of the vehicle.

Gadget Point Cost: 1

Spot DC: 20 (obvious)

Mechanics: The shield provides a hardness 10, 60 wound point protective wall against any critical hit scored on one of the vehicle's windows.

Proteus package: With extensive re-engineering of a vehicle, the Proteus Package enables it to function as another type of vehicle altogether. For example, a car might be modified to become submersible, hover, or fly.

Gadget Point Cost: 4

Spot DC: 15 (super-science, obvious)

Mechanics: The agent chooses the original vehicle, then chooses another that it can assume the functions of (paying the gadget point cost for the more expensive vehicle of the two). This cost is in addition to the 4 points paid for this conversion refinement.

When the Proteus Package is activated, the vehicle assumes the form of the second vehicle (or as close an approximation as possible), and gains all the statistics of that vehicle as well. No vehicle may have more than two sets of statistics. Size, wound points, and hardness all remain the same as the original vehicle, even in its second form.

Example: Donovan has a sports car and wants the Proteus Package. He chooses a submersible car *(see page 149)* as his vehicle's second form. In addition to the cost of the more expensive vehicle (the submersible car — 7 gadget points), he must pay 4 additional gadget points (for the Proteus Package), for a total of 11 gadget points. When he activates the Proteus Package, his car's handling drops from +4 to +3, its speed drops from 800 ft. (on land) to 100 ft. (underwater), its MPH drops from 80/160 to 10/20, and its Defense drops from 14 to 13. The vehicle's size (Large), wound points (70), and hardness (3) all remain the same. But now he can dive into the ocean whenever he wants!

Should this transformation be triggered while the vehicle is in operation, the agent behind the wheel must make a skill check (DC 20) for whichever vehicle he has the lower skill value with (for instance, Donovan has Driver at +6 and Boating at +3; if he were to suddenly activate his Proteus Package while leaping the vehicle off a pier, he'd make the skill check using his Boating skill). Failure results in an immediate crash check *(see page 193)*.

This refinement is obvious to anyone watching when the vehicle shifts function, or if the vehicle's two forms are wildly different (such as a boat converting into a helicopter).

Reinforced tires: These automatically are durable and reinflate when burst. Shredded, melted, or otherwise destroyed tires cannot reinflate.

Gadget Point Cost: 1

Spot DC: 25

Mechanics: Each tire may only be burst three times before it must be replaced back at HQ, or with a non-gadget spare. Additionally, these tires are tougher than normal, requiring 10 points of damage to burst.

Remote control: The vehicle can be steered remotely by means of a key chain from up to 2 miles away.

Gadget Point Cost: 1

Spot DC: 30 (expert only, super-science)

Mechanics: All maneuver checks suffer a –5 penalty when a vehicle is being piloted remotely.

Revolving license plate: Though first invented nearly forty years ago, this vehicular refinement has never gone out of style.

Gadget Point Cost: 1

Spot DC: 20

Mechanics: The vehicle may have up to four license plates, which it can cycle through with the flick of a switch. Swapping license plates is a free action so long as the agent can reach the dashboard.

Rocket launcher: This refinement is usually installed in the front or flank of a vehicle, though it can be mounted on the roof by special order.

This option may be taken as "torpedoes" for submersible cars and other water vehicles.

Gadget Point Cost: 4

Spot DC: 25 (super-science, obvious)

Mechanics: This rocket launcher holds 4 rockets of any type (which must be requisitioned separately). Using it applies a –4 penalty to hit, and restricts the driver to targets in front of the vehicle. This refinement is obvious to everyone in the area when the rocket launcher is being fired.

Optionally, the rocket launcher may be mounted on the roof of the vehicle, reducing the Spot DC by 10 (to 15), at the cost of 1 additional gadget point. This option offers the rocket launcher a 180-degree horizontal firing arc and the ability to fire upon air targets anywhere but immediately above the vehicle.

Smoke screen: Twin hidden pipes at the back of the vehicle spew chemical mixes (commonly non-toxic) into the path of pursuers.

Gadget Point Cost: 1

Spot DC: 20 (obvious)

Mechanics: The smoke screen requires a half action to activate, and applies a –5 modifier to the next maneuver check of all pursuing vehicles within a number of feet equal to twice the current speed of the agent's vehicle (after the range between the vehicles has been calculated for this round). This effect may be combined with an oil slick.

As with the oil slick, the smoke screen may only be used once before it must be refilled back at headquaters or by an agent with one or more ranks in the Mechanics skill. Refill canisters cost 1 additional gadget point per use and are stored near the smoke screen mechanism.

Spike dropper: A small compartment beneath the rear license plate can flip open, dropping dozens of razor-sharp caltrops onto the road behind the vehicle.

Gadget Point Cost: 1

Spot DC: 20

Mechanics: Any wheeled vehicles chasing the refined vehicle must make a Driver check (DC 15) or suffer 1d8 damage to each tire.

Tire slasher: The hub cap of this car (or an appropriate part on another vehicle) opens to reveal a rotating spike that can rip into enemy vehicles.

Gadget Point Cost: 1

Spot DC: 25 (obvious)

Mechanics: With a successful Driver check (DC 15), this vehicle deals 1d6 damage to one tire or the body of another adjacent vehicle (or a vehicle within 1 length during a chase). If the damage is done to the target vehicle's body, the slasher is destroyed and must be replaced.

Voice Activated Command System (V.A.C.S.): At one time of another, every wheelman has wished for another set of hands. This is the next best thing. The V.A.C.S. allows the driver to give verbal commands (such as "Left turn: ninety degrees" and "Shift Gear: 3rd"), freeing his hands up to perform other actions.

Gadget Point Cost: 2

Spot DC: 30 (expert only, super-science)

Mechanics: When using the V.A.C.S., the driver may perform an extra half action as if he were not driving, though he must remain within the vehicle, where speakers can pick up his commands. All the driver's skill checks with the vehicle suffer a –2 penalty while using this device.

Tubular space frame: This major modification creates a completely new custom-built enclosed tubular chassis, greatly increasing the handling and performance of the vehicle along with making it much safer.

Gadget Point Cost: 4

Spot DC: 20 (expert only)

Mechanics: Increase the handling and hardness ratings of the vehicle by +1 each and increase its top speed and wound points by 10% of the original value (rounded up) each.

Wind resistance reduction: This major modification takes an existing vehicle and runs it through wind tunnel testing. Using this information, a new body is designed for the vehicle making compromises to ensure the vehicle retains a stock appearance even as its speed and handling are increased dramatically.

Gadget Point Cost: 2

Spot DC: 20 (expert only, *see below*)

Mechanics: Increase the handling rating of the vehicle by +1 and increase its top speed by 10% of the original value (rounded up). If you're not really concerned about the modifications being noticeable (Spot DC 10), you can increase the handling rating by +2 and top speed by 25% of the original value (rounded up), but the modifications are noticeable to all (though not overly alarming – the vehicle just looks streamlined, built for speed.)

"You don't just go around punching people.
You have to say something cool first."

– Joe Hallenbeck,
The Last Boy Scout

COMBAT

THE BASICS

This section describes the key terms that are used to describe combat. You should become familiar with them before reading the rest of this chapter.

THE ATTACK ROLL

To make an attack roll, roll 1d20 and add your attack bonus. If the total is equal to or greater than your target's Defense, you hit and deal damage based on the weapon or feat you used to attack. Everything from range to special equipment can modify your attack roll.

ATTACK BONUS

Your attack bonus with a melee weapon or unarmed attack is:

Base attack bonus + Strength modifier + size modifier

With a ranged weapon, your attack bonus is:

Base attack bonus + Dexterity modifier + size modifier + range modifier

STRENGTH MODIFIER

A high Strength allows you to make unarmed or melee strikes with more speed and control, so your Strength modifier is added to all unarmed and melee attacks.

DEXTERITY MODIFIER

A high Dexterity gives you finer hand-eye coordination and aim, so your Dexterity modifier is added to ranged attacks.

SIZE MODIFIER

It's easier to hit a large target than it is to hit a small target. Since most agents are Medium-sized, the size modifier is usually 0. Larger targets decrease your DC to hit a target, while smaller targets increase your attack roll DC. Modifiers range from –8 (for Colossal-sized targets) to +8 (for Fine-sized targets). To determine the size modifier for a target larger or smaller than Medium, *see Table 6.7: Face and Reach, on page 175.*

RANGE MODIFIER

All ranged weapons have a range increment, such as 15 ft. for a 9mm backup pistol. Any attack from a distance of less than one range increment has a range modifier of 0. Each full range increment beyond that distance adds a –2 penalty to the attack roll.

Example: Firing a 9mm backup pistol, which has a range increment of 15 ft., at a target 80 ft. away would apply a penalty of –8 (five full range increments, or 75 ft.; the extra 5 ft. fall short of another full range increment, and therefore don't apply another –2 modifier).

Example 2: Firing a grenade launcher—which has a range increment of 40 ft. – at a target 120 ft. away would apply a penalty of –4 (for three full range increments).

Hurled weapons, such as grenades, have a maximum range of five range increments, as do shotguns. Projectile weapons, such as bows or guns, have a maximum range of ten range increments.

DAMAGE

When you strike an opponent with a weapon, you inflict damage according to the weapon used. Aside from damage reduction, penalties cannot reduce your damage below 1.

Damage with a ranged or melee weapon is typically:

(Weapon damage + Strength modifier + other damage modifiers) × damage multiplier + bonus damage dice – damage reduction

WEAPON DAMAGE

Different weapons deal different amounts of damage *(see Chapter 5: Gear)*. Unarmed attacks normally inflict 1d3 points of damage, unless martial arts are used.

STRENGTH MODIFIER

You add your Strength modifier to damage rolls when making an unarmed attack, grappling, or using a melee weapon, hurled weapon, bow, or sling. Off-hand attacks receive only half the Strength modifier, while two-handed attacks receive one and a half times the Strength modifier. The damage for explosives, such as grenades, is never modified by Strength, whether hurled or not.

OTHER DAMAGE MODIFIERS

Equipment, Game Control fiat, and other situations can also modify damage. As long as such modifiers don't take the form of additional damage dice (such as from a sneak attack), they are counted when multiplying damage (see next).

DAMAGE MULTIPLIER

Sometimes specific weapons, ammunition, and rules multiply damage. In this case, you roll the damage a number of times equal to the multiplier (i.e. two times in the case of a ×2 multiplier) applying modifiers each

COMBAT REFERENCE SHEET

ROUNDS

Combat occurs in 6-second rounds. Each round, an agent may take one full action or two half actions. In addition, an agent may also take as many free actions per round as the GC allows.

ACTIONS

A table showing the various actions you can take and their type is found on page 161.

INITIATIVE CHECK

At the start of combat, everyone makes an initiative check (the GC makes these checks for NPCs). Agents then act in order from highest to lowest initiative. Once all agents have gone, a new round begins and the process repeats.

Initiative Check: 1d20 + base initiative bonus + Dexterity modifier.

ATTACKS

A standard attack is a half action. A table showing common attack modifiers is found on page 170.

ATTACK ROLL

Your attack roll is based on the type of attack you are making — unarmed, melee, or ranged. In either case, your attack roll must equal or exceed your target's Defense in order to hit.

Melee Attacks: 1d20 + base attack bonus + Strength modifier + size modifier.

Ranged Attacks: 1d20 + base attack bonus + Dexterity modifier + size modifier + range modifier.

DEFENSE

10 + class (or equipment) bonus + Dexterity modifier + size modifier.

INFLICTING DAMAGE

When an attack hits, roll damage and deduct it from the target's vitality points (with any leftover damage being deducted from the target's wound points). Critical hits *(see page 164)* are deducted directly from the target's wounds.

For common damage modifiers, *see page opposite.*

MOVEMENT

Your agent has a speed value (usually 30, less if you're wearing armor). As a half action, you may move your speed in feet.

If you move next to an opponent, you must stop moving. While adjacent to an opponent, you can't move more than one 5-ft. step unless you have the Mobility feat or you are withdrawing.

DAMAGE AND HEALING

0 Vitality Points: While at 0 vitality points, you are fatigued (you have a –2 penalty to your Strength and Dexterity, and must make a Fortitude saving throw at DC 10 or be stunned for 2d6 rounds). All damage you suffer is now applied to wound points.

0 Wound Points: While at 0 wound points, you are unconscious and cannot take any actions.

–1 to –9 Wound Points: As at 0 wound points, plus you must roll d% every round. If you roll over your Constitution, you lose 1 wound point; otherwise you stabilize.

–10 Wound Points: Agent dies.

Healing: You can be stabilized with a First Aid check (DC 15), or with at least 1 point of healing (any kind). Once your wounds are above 0, you can resume acting as normal.

SAVING THROWS

Base Save: 1d20 + base save bonus + ability modifier.

Fortitude Save: Use to resist physical hardship. Add your Constitution modifier to Fortitude saves.

Reflex Save: Use to react quickly. Add your Dexterity modifier to Reflex saves.

Will save: Use to resist mental stress. Add your Wisdom modifier to Will saves.

ACTION DICE

You may spend an action die after any die roll to add to it. You can also gain temporary Defense, activate critical hits, or heal when not engaged in combat. Full rules for action dice are found on page 179.

USING MINIATURES

When using miniatures to keep track of where agents and NPCs are, use a scale of 1 inch = 5 feet.

time. Thus, if your normal damage was 1d8+3, a ×3 multiplier would modify that to 3d8+9.

If two or more multipliers are combined, add them together, subtracting 1 for each multiplier beyond the first (i.e. ×2 + ×3 + ×2 = ×5).

BONUS DAMAGE DICE

Bonus damage dice (+1d6 from a sneak attack, for example) are added to the attack roll after all multipliers have been applied. So, if an attack that dealt 1d8+4+1d6 had a ×2 multiplier applied to it, the final damage would be 2d8+8+1d6.

DAMAGE REDUCTION

Certain equipment and abilities allow a target to absorb some or all damage when it is taken. Unless otherwise directed, you subtract the value of any damage reduction you have from each damage total you suffer, including wound damage from critical hits. Damage reduction is subtracted from damage after all other modifiers have been applied.

Example: Donovan wears a tuxedo liner which grants him 2 points of damage reduction. When he is shot for 7 points of damage, he only suffers 5.

SUBDUAL DAMAGE

Subdual damage is caused by typically non-lethal attacks (e.g. unarmed attacks, tasers, and the like), and is used to incapacitate enemies without killing them. When you suffer subdual damage, you keep track of it separately in the subdual damage box on your agent sheet. *Subdual damage is not deducted from your vitality or wounds.*

Unlike normal damage – which reduces your vitality and wound points – subdual damage is tracked separately. If your subdual damage ever equals your current vitality points, you are staggered *(see page 177)*. If your subdual damage ever exceeds the sum of your current vitality and wound points, you fall unconscious and are helpless.

Example: Donovan inflicts 29 points of subdual damage on a minion. The henchman's vitality is 25 and he has 12 wounds, so he is staggered but not unconscious. The henchman's current vitality and wounds remain at 25 and 12, respectively and the GC jots 29 down in the subdual damage box of the henchman's record sheet. If the henchman suffers 8 more points of subdual damage, he will fall unconscious.

Damage reduction is twice as effective as usual against subdual damage (e.g. 2 points of damage reduction prevents 4 points of subdual damage).

DEFENSE

Your Defense makes it harder for opponents to hit you. It is used as the DC for your opponents' attack rolls. The Defense for an average person is 10. Your Defense is:

10 + either *class* or *equipment bonus + Dexterity modifier + size modifier + dodge bonus + natural armor*

CLASS AND EQUIPMENT BONUS

Your class level gives you an innate bonus to your Defense that always applies, even when you're flat-footed. If you choose to wear armor, your class bonus is replaced by your equipment bonus – the two are *not* cumulative, and you may *not* choose to apply your class bonus when wearing armor.

DEXTERITY MODIFIER

Your Dexterity affects your ability to dodge incoming blows. However, wearing armor can restrict your mobility, and limits your Dexterity bonus *(see page 109)*. Also, if you can't react to an incoming attack, you can't use your Dexterity bonus to Defense. (If you don't have a Dexterity bonus, nothing happens.) For instance, you couldn't use your Dexterity bonus while rock climbing, or when struck by a sneak attack.

SIZE MODIFIER

As described under The Attack Roll on the previous page, a big target is easier to hit than a small one. Most targets are Medium-sized, so your DC modifier is 0. Targets larger or smaller than Medium size, however, are respectively easier and more difficult to hit. Modifiers range from –8 (for Colossal-sized targets) to +8 (for fine-sized targets). To determine the size modifier for a target larger or smaller than Medium, *see Table 6.7: Face and Reach, on page 175.*

DODGE BONUS

The Sidestep feat grants you either a +1 dodge bonus to your Defense against all opponents, or a +2 dodge bonus against one opponent. Several other abilities and feats also offer dodge bonuses. However, any situation that prevents you from using your Dexterity modifier also negates dodge bonuses. Happily, dodge bonuses are not limited by armor (unlike your Dexterity modifier), and as described in the Stacking Bonuses box on page 38, all dodge bonuses stack (i.e. they're added together) unless otherwise stated.

NATURAL ARMOR

Some combatants also have natural armor, such as scales or fur, that improves their Defense, and works like normal armor without replacing their class bonus or placing limitations on their Dexterity modifier.

COMBAT

TOUCH ATTACKS

Some attacks, such as a taser or a missile lock, ignore armor (both artificial and natural). In these cases, your attacker makes a touch attack roll. The attack roll is made as normal, but your Defense does not include any armor or natural armor bonus. Your size modifier, Dexterity modifier, and class bonus (if you aren't wearing armor) all still apply, and the attacker must still worry about range modifiers if using a ranged attack.

INITIATIVE CHECK

When you enter combat, you make an initiative check to determine when during the round you get to act. Initiative checks work like attack rolls, with a d20 roll plus a bonus from your class level and your Dexterity modifier. Your initiative check bonus is:

Base initiative bonus + Dexterity modifier

Combatants may act in order of highest initiative total to lowest initiative total. Once you have made your initiative check for a particular combat, you keep the total for the rest of the combat *(unless you regroup — see page 163)*.

ROUNDS

Time in combat is divided into 6-second intervals called 'rounds.' Anything a person could reasonably accomplish in 6 seconds can be done by your agent in 1 round.

SAVING THROWS

When your agent is subjected to an unusual attack, such as brainwashing or explosives, he is allowed a saving throw to reduce or avoid the effect. Saving throws work like attack rolls, with a d20 roll plus a bonus from your agent's class level and an ability score. Your agent's saving throw bonus is:

Base save bonus + ability modifier

There are three types of saving throws, each with a different use and applicable ability. They are:

Fortitude: Used when your agent suffers tremendous physical damage, or an attack against his health, such as poison, diseases, or paralysis. Your agent's Constitution modifier is added to his Fortitude saving throws.

Reflex: Used when your agent is trying to dodge massive attacks such as explosives, or reacting quickly to a deadly situation, such as dodging out of the path of an oncoming bus. Your agent's Dexterity modifier is added to his Reflex saving throws.

Will: Used to resist mental influencing or coercion such as seduction or brainwashing. Your agent's Wisdom modifier is added to his Will saving throws.

The DC for a save is determined by the attack itself. For instance, arsenic poisoning might call for a Fortitude save against DC 15, while a seduction attempt might call for a Will save against DC 24.

SPEED

Your agent's speed tells you how far he can move in a single half action. Most agents move 30 ft., often less when wearing armor. Your agent can take two standard move actions in order to move up to twice his speed in a round, or he can run, moving up to four times his speed in a round.

VITALITY VS. WOUNDS

Players may envision their agents shrugging off countless bullet wounds, broken bones, and other injuries in *Spycraft*. After all, every one of those vitality hits must indicate some physical damage, right? Not exactly.

The vitality/wound system is intended to simulate the flow of most big-budget action features. Heroes in those movies dive through endless showers of lead before they take a single serious hit in the final reel.

Your vitality points represent all the near misses and combat fatigue you can wade through before you start to suffer real injuries. When you lose wound points, that's when the blood starts flowing.

VITALITY POINTS

Your agent's vitality points determine how long he can go in a fight before he starts becoming wounded. Your agent's vitality points are based on his class (usually 1d8, 1d10, or 1d12 per level) and Constitution modifier.

When your agent's vitality points are reduced to 0, he become **fatigued** (he is unable to run or charge, and his Strength and Dexterity are each reduced by 2). Also, he must make a Fortitude saving throw (DC 10) or be stunned (unable to do anything) for 2d6 rounds. *See also the Injury and Death section, page 177).*

WOUND POINTS

Your agent's wound points determine the amount of damage he can take before falling unconscious or dying. Your agent's wound points are equal to his Constitution.

When your agent reaches 0 wound points, he falls unconscious. If his wound points fall to –1, he's dying, and you must roll d% each round. If you roll equal to or less than his Constitution, he stabilizes; otherwise he loses 1 wound point. If your agent's wound points ever reach –10, he's dead *(see page 178)*.

COMBAT SEQUENCE

During combat you have a number of options available to you, the most common of which is some form of attack or movement. This section explains how much you are allowed to do during a round of combat and when everyone's actions happen (initiative). The specifics of various actions (including attacks and movement) can be found in later sections.

ROUNDS AND DURATION

When considering how long an effect lasts, a full round is defined as a span of time from an initiative number (initiative count) during one round to the same initiative number in the next round unless otherwise stated. Effects that last one or more full rounds end just before the initiative count that they began on. For instance, a soldier lays down cover fire for a friend at initiative count 12 that lasts for one full round. The benefits of the cover fire expire immediately before initiative count 12 in the next round.

ACTION TYPES

To help you determine what you can and can't do in a single 6-second round, actions are grouped into three action types: full, half, and free. When an agent's turn comes up in the initiative order *(see Initiative, opposite)*, he performs his entire round's worth of actions, as described below.

FULL AND HALF ACTIONS

You may take either one full action or two half actions during a round. Full actions are more involved, and use up all your concentration for the round. Half actions are simpler, and you can — under most circumstances — perform two of them per round.

See Table 6.1 on the facing page for a list of example actions, and what type they are (full, half, free).

FREE ACTIONS

Free actions take up little or no time. You may perform as many free actions in a round as you like in addition to your usual full or half actions. Your GC may place limits on the number of free actions you can accomplish during any given round.

Sometimes you will receive a **single attack.** All single attacks are free actions granted by a feat or circumstances. Unlike half actions used to make an attack, single attacks never become multiple attacks, even if you have a feat or ability that allows you to make multiple attacks with a single half action.

BONUS STEP

In addition to all other actions you take during the round, you may take one free 5-ft. step before or after one of your actions during the round. However, if you take (or plan to take) a movement action such as a run or charge during the round, then you cannot use your bonus step. Once you have taken your bonus step, you may not then take a movement action.

COMBAT

INITIATIVE

Initiative determines who goes first during combat. Often, getting the jump on your opponent is important, but sometimes seeing what they're up to before you act is even more important.

THE SEQUENCE OF COMBAT

Combat is carried out in the following order of events. Don't worry if this doesn't make sense yet. Everything will be explained by the time you finish reading this section. You may wish to refer back to this section at the beginning of each combat until you are familiar with it:

1. Each combatant starts the battle flat-footed. Once a combatant acts, or is successfully attacked, he is no longer flat-footed.

2. Combatants roll for initiative.

3. If the Game Control decides that some but not all of the combatants were aware of their opponents before combat begins, then a surprise round occurs. During the surprise round, in initiative order (starting from the combatant with the highest initiative and ending with the combatant with the lowest initiative),

each combatant who is aware of their opponents before the combat receives one half action. Unaware combatants receive no opportunity to act during the surprise round, and thus remain flat-footed unless successfully attacked.

4. The first normal round begins. In initiative order, all combatants receive their choice of one full action, or two half actions. In addition, any combatant who does not otherwise move during the round may take one 5-ft. step during their turn.

5. After all combatants have performed actions, a new round begins. Repeat steps 4 and 5 until the combat ends.

RULES FOR INITIATIVE

There are several rules to keep in mind when determining who goes first during combat.

ROLLING FOR INITIATIVE

At the start of combat, each combatant makes an initiative check. The Game Control then counts down from highest result to lowest, with each combatant acting in turn. Unless an agent takes an action that changes it (such as regroup), their initiative result remains the same for the rest of the combat.

TABLE 6.1: COMBAT ACTIONS

Action	Type	Action	Type
Initiative Actions		*Other Common Actions*	
Delay	Free	Activate an item	Free
Ready	Full	Drop an item	Free
Regroup	Half	Drop to the ground	Free
		Speak	Free
Attack Actions		Aim a ranged weapon	Half
Standard attack	Half	Brace a firearm	Half
Autofire	Full	Draw or holster a weapon	Half
Burst attack	Half	Load a weapon	Half
Disarm	Half	Move a heavy object	Half
Feint (uses Bluff skill)	Half	Open a door	Half
Grapple	Half	Pick up an item	Half
Strike an object	Half	Retrieve a stored item	Half
Taunt (uses Bluff skill)	Half	Stand up from being prone	Half
Trip	Half	Stabilize a dying person	Half
Coup de grace	Full	Move an extremely heavy or awkward object	Full
Cover fire	Full		
Strafe attack	Full	Refresh	Full
Suppressive fire	Full	Use a skill or feat	See entry
		Other actions	Per the GC
Movement Actions			
Standard move	Half		
Charge	Full		
Run	Full		
Total defense	Full		
Withdraw	Full		

The Game Control may find it easiest to write down each agent's name in initiative order to speed up combat. If two or more combatants are tied for initiative, the agent with the highest Dexterity goes first. If their Dexterity is the same, roll dice to determine who goes first (highest roll goes first).

Joining a Battle

If an agent enters a combat after it has already begun, he makes an initiative check immediately and acts whenever his turn comes up in the existing order. If a battle overtakes an agent, he is flat-footed *(see below)*; if he takes action to enter the combat, he is not flat-footed.

Opponent Initiative

The Game Control can either make a single initiative check for all opponents, or separate the opponents into several groups and make an initiative check for each. The first option makes combat go faster, but it is sometimes more appropriate for a mastermind or henchman to get his own initiative check rather than getting lumped in with his minions.

Flat-Footed

Until your turn to act has come up at least once in the initiative order during combat or you've been successfully attacked at least once, you are flat-footed. This means that you cannot add your Dexterity or dodge bonuses to your Defense, and certain opponents may be able to perform a sneak attack on you.

RULES FOR SURPRISE

When combat starts, if your opponents are aware of you, but you are unaware of them, you are surprised.

The Surprise Round

If some, but not all, of the combatants involved in a combat are aware of each other, a surprise round takes place. In initiative order, combatants who are aware of their opponents receive one half action. If all or none of the participants in the battle are aware of each other, no surprise round takes place.

Determining Awareness

The GC determines who is aware of opponents at the start of a combat. Skill checks are often appropriate to determine whether or not an agent is surprised. Some of these skills and the situations in which they might apply are:

Listen: When an agent is being stalked with Move Silently.

Sense Motive: When a trusted friend suddenly draws a weapon.

Spot: When an agent is being ambushed with Hide.

It's not practical to list all the possible situations in which an agent might be surprised, so your Game Control must be the final arbiter of who is surprised and who is not.

Unaware Combatants

Unaware combatants do not act during the surprise round, and therefore remain flat-footed until their first action during the first normal round, or until they've been successfully attacked.

INITIATIVE ACTIONS

Initiative actions generally allow you to modify your initiative result in some manner with the hope of gaining a tactical advantage. These are advanced actions, and you may wish to wait until you've become familiar with combat before trying them out.

Delay (Free Action)

By delaying your action, you can wait to see what other combatants do before committing yourself to a course of action. When it's your turn to act in a round, you may voluntarily reduce your initiative total by 1. At the start of the next initiative count, you may act before all other combatants or delay again, reducing your initiative count by 1 more. If more than one character has delayed, they may act in order of their original (total) initiative counts for the round, or delay until the following initiative count.

You may perform a number of delay actions each round equal to your initiative bonus +10. Once you have performed this many delay actions, or the round ends, you must act or lose your action for the round.

When a new round begins, all combatants' initiative totals return to normal, and they may once again delay their actions, if they wish.

Example: Donovan's initiative result is 22 and his initiative bonus is 5. He may take 15 delay actions, reducing his initiative total to 7, before he must act or lose his turn.

Ready (Full Action)

Readying allows you to take an action later in the round in response to a predetermined trigger that you choose when you take this action. This is sometimes referred to as 'going on overwatch.'

When you take this action, you must decide upon two things: a half action that you will take later in the round, and a trigger that will cause you to begin the action. For example, you could decide to fire your gun (standard attack action) at the first person to come around a corner.

Because you are watching and waiting for the right moment to act, your action may come either just before or just after the action that triggers it, at your discretion. Your Game Control may impose restrictions on when you can react to the trigger actions, however. In the example above, you'd obviously have to wait until after the person comes around the corner before shooting them, so the Game Control would likely determine that you could only follow, not precede, that action.

Should you decide that you want to cancel your action when the trigger occurs (in the event that one of your teammates is the first person to come around the corner, for instance), you must make a Reflex save (DC 15) in order to do so. If you fail this save, you must go through with your action, regardless of the consequences.

Finally, if the trigger you've decided upon doesn't actually occur during the round, you lose your action. Thus, if no one comes around the corner in the example above, you just sit there watching the corner for the entire round.

REGROUP (HALF ACTION)

Sometimes it is advantageous to take stock of your situation, calm your thoughts, and carefully decide on your next course of action. By taking this action, your initiative result is increased by 5 for the rest of the combat. This action can be taken as often as you like.

ATTACKING

Ultimately, your goal in combat is to stop your opponents from hurting you, by any means necessary. This typically involves putting them out of commission before they can do the same to you.

RULES FOR ATTACKING

Before you make an attack action, you should be aware of the requirements and special rules attached to attacks.

MELEE ATTACKS

With a normal melee weapon or unarmed attack, you can strike any opponent adjacent to you (i.e. within 5 feet of you).

RANGED ATTACKS

With a ranged weapon, you can attack any opponent who is within the weapon's maximum range (five range increments for hurled weapons; ten range increments for projectile weapons) and in line of sight. A target is in line of sight if there are no obstacles completely obscuring it from your view. *See the diagram below for an example.*

LINE OF SIGHT

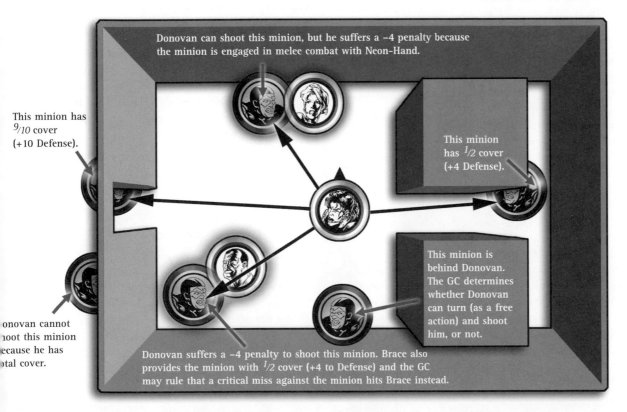

Donovan can shoot this minion, but he suffers a –4 penalty because the minion is engaged in melee combat with Neon-Hand.

This minion has 9/10 cover (+10 Defense).

This minion has 1/2 cover (+4 Defense).

Donovan cannot shoot this minion because he has total cover.

This minion is behind Donovan. The GC determines whether Donovan can turn (as a free action) and shoot him, or not.

Donovan suffers a –4 penalty to shoot this minion. Brace also provides the minion with 1/2 cover (+4 to Defense) and the GC may rule that a critical miss against the minion hits Brace instead.

ATTACK ROLLS

An attack roll can represent one attack, or multiple attacks in the same amount of time. Your attack roll is 1d20 + your attack bonus *(see page 156)* with the weapon you're using. If the result is equal to or greater than your target's Defense, you hit and deal damage.

AUTOMATIC MISSES AND HITS

A natural 1 (an actual roll of 1 on a d20) is always a miss, while a natural 20 (an actual roll of 20 on a d20) is always a hit. A natural 20 might also be a critical hit, while a natural 1 might be a critical miss *(see below and opposite)*.

DAMAGE ROLLS

If an attack hits, roll your weapon's damage and subtract that number from your target's vitality points, if the target has any. If he has no vitality points, or if there's additional damage left over after the target's vitality points have been reduced to 0, then the remaining damage is subtracted from the target's wound points. If the target's wound points drop to 0 or less, then he's out of the fight *(see Injury and Death, page 177)*.

CRITICAL HITS

Whenever you roll a natural 20 (the d20 is actually showing a 20) for an attack roll, you automatically hit your opponent, and you've scored a threat – a potential critical hit. In order to turn a threat into a critical hit, you must spend one action die. If you choose not to do so, then your attack is just a normal hit.

Sometimes you can score a threat with a natural roll lower than 20 (usually because you're wielding a particularly deadly weapon). The natural rolls required for a threat are collectively called your threat range – see Chapter 5: Gear for a list of common threat ranges. Any natural roll lower than a 20 is not an automatic hit, and if the attack misses, it doesn't count as a threat, either.

A critical hit instantly reduces a minion (one of the faceless hordes the GC uses) or Standard NPC *(see page 265)* to 0 wound points. When an agent scores a critical hit against a minion or Standard NPC, he may voluntarily treat the target as a Special NPC *(see below)* when rolling damage, in the hopes of reducing his wounds low enough to kill him.

Against a more important opponent, such as a mastermind, henchman, foil, or Special NPC *(see page 265)*,

a critical hit means that you apply the damage directly to the victim's wound points without first reducing his vitality points.

Example 1: Donovan is using a weapon which has a threat range of 18-20. He rolls a natural 20, which is both an automatic hit and a threat. He may spend an action die to turn the threat into a critical hit.

Example 2: Still using the same shotgun, Donovan rolls a natural 18. This is a threat (his threat range is 18-20) but not an automatic hit. Even adding his attack bonus (+6), his total attack roll (24) is not enough to defeat his target's Defense (25). Since the attack did not hit, the threat is canceled, as if it had not been rolled.

Masterminds, henchmen, foils, and Special NPCs are capable of critical hits, but minions and Standard NPCs are not *(see page 265)*.

CRITICAL MISSES

Whenever you roll a natural 1 (the d20 is actually showing a 1) for an attack roll, you automatically miss your opponent, and you've scored an error—a potential critical miss. In order to turn an error into a critical miss, your Game Control must spend one or more action dice depending on the result he wants.

You can sometimes score an error on a roll higher than 1 (usually because you're wielding a particularly shoddy or experimental weapon). The natural rolls required for an error are collectively called your error range – *see Chapter 5: Gear* for a list of common error ranges. Any roll higher than a 1 is not an automatic miss, and if the attack hits, it doesn't count as an error.

Critical misses are bad because they usually cost you precious seconds – to clear a jammed gun, or to pick up a dropped weapon. Depending on how many action dice your Game Control spends, even worse things can happen, particularly if you're firing into a melee involving your teammates. Your Game Control has complete rules on critical misses and can inform you of your options when one occurs.

Example: Donovan attacks an opponent using a pistol that has an error range of 1-2. He rolls a 1, which is an error. His GC decides that this is a good time for a bit of tension and spends 2 action dice, causing the gun to jam. Donovan must spend a full action clearing it before he can fire again.

MULTIPLE ATTACKS

Multiple attacks are usually gained through the use of feats. Each feat that offers this ability describes what you have to do in order to gain the extra attacks.

UNARMED ATTACKS

Typically, unarmed attacks from a Medium-sized agent inflict 1d3 points of damage (plus Strength modifiers, as usual). This damage is subdual *(see Subdual Damage, page 173),* and cannot cause a critical hit. However, there are a variety of unarmed combat feats that can modify your unarmed attacks, increasing damage, offering the ability to inflict criticals, and even increasing your threat range.

Unarmed attacks count as light weapons for purposes of off-hand penalties and other effects.

ATTACKING WITH TWO WEAPONS

If you wield a second weapon, then once per round, you can make an extra attack during one of your actions (using that weapon). This style of fighting is difficult, however: you suffer a –6 penalty to all attack rolls with the weapon in your primary hand and a –10 penalty to all attack rolls with the weapon in your off-hand. There are several ways to reduce these penalties, and you may benefit from more than one of them at once.

If your off-hand weapon is smaller by one size category or more than your primary weapon, it is considered a light weapon, and your primary and off-hand penalties are each reduced by 2.

If you have the Ambidexterity feat, your off-hand penalty is reduced by 4.

Finally, if you have the Two-Weapon Fighting feat, your primary and off-hand penalties are each reduced by 2.

DOUBLE WEAPONS

Some weapons have two damage values (e.g. "2d6/1d4"). These are called double weapons because they grant you an extra attack once per round. The penalties for using a double weapon are equal to those for using a light weapon (see above), reduced by 2 each.

Example: The bo stick has a damage value of 1d6/1d6. When using a bo stick, an agent may make two attacks, each with a 1d6 damage value. Assuming the agent has no feats or abilities which affect his attack modifiers for double weapons, his first attack suffers a –2 penalty (–6, reduced by 2 by the light weapon modifier and reduced by 2 more by the double weapon modifier), while his second suffers a –6 penalty (–10, reduced by 2 by the light weapon modifier and reduced by 2 more by the double weapon modifier). Damage is applied for the attacks which hit.

ATTACK ACTIONS

Attack actions generally allow you to hurt your opponents in some way. In keeping with the fast-paced action movies of today, even 1st-level agents can make two half-action attacks in a round. Additional attacks can be gained through the use of feats or certain types of equipment.

The following is a list of standard attack options.

STANDARD ATTACK (HALF ACTION)

When you take this action, you make a single attack on the target of your choice, following the guidelines under Making Attacks, *above.* Certain feats or equipment may allow you to make more than one attack during a standard attack — their descriptions explain how the extra attacks work. If you are using a weapon with ammunition, a standard attack (or each attack, if feats allow more than one) uses up 1 shot.

AUTOFIRE (FULL ACTION)

You may only take the autofire action if you are firing a weapon with the strafe ability *(see Chapter 5: Gear).* This action allows you to focus an automatic weapon on a single target in an attempt to bring him down. After selecting a number of three-shot volleys up to one-third the remaining ammunition in your weapon (rounded down), make a single attack roll with a –1 penalty for each volley fired (applying all normal modifiers as well). For every 4 full points by which your attack roll beats the target's Defense, you score an additional hit, applying the weapon's normal damage plus applicable modifiers. You may only score a number of hits up to the number for volleys fired. If a critical hit is scored, only the damage from the first hit is applied directly to the target's wounds.

Example 1: Donovan is firing a 7.62x39mm assault rifle with 15 shots left. He uses the autofire action to attack one target with five three-shot volleys (using up all 15 shots remaining in his weapon). He makes an attack roll of 25, reduced to 20 by the autofire penalty (–1 × 5 volleys fired). This exceeds his target's Defense of 12 by 8, so he scores three hits (one for beating the target's Defense, plus two more for beating the target's Defense by 8). Donovan rolls 6d8 damage (three hits at 2d8 damage each).

Example 2: Donovan is firing an assault rifle with 13 shots left. He may fire four volleys of autofire, but not five.

Autofire uses up 3 shots per volley fired. If your weapon has less than 6 shots left, you may not perform an autofire action.

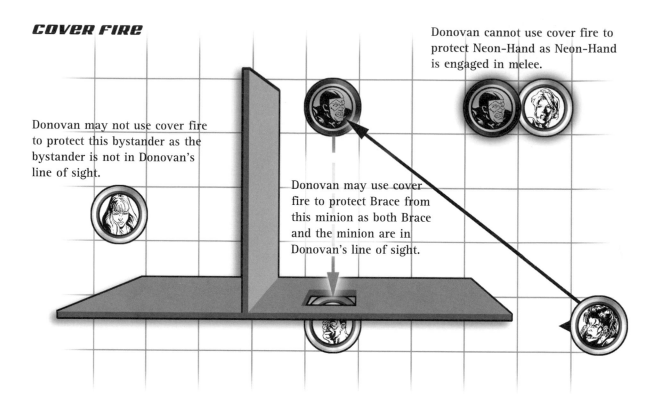

COVER FIRE

Donovan may not use cover fire to protect this bystander as the bystander is not in Donovan's line of sight.

Donovan cannot use cover fire to protect Neon-Hand as Neon-Hand is engaged in melee.

Donovan may use cover fire to protect Brace from this minion as both Brace and the minion are in Donovan's line of sight.

BURST ATTACK (HALF ACTION)

You may only take the burst action when firing a weapon with the burst ability (see Chapter 5: Gear). This action allows you to fire a short burst of ammunition in a controlled manner, increasing your chances to hit and damage a single target. When taking a burst action, you choose the degree of control you want (narrow or wide burst), and the following effects:

Narrow burst: You receive a –3 circumstance modifier to your attack roll and a +2 circumstance modifier to your damage roll.

Wide burst: You receive a +1 circumstance modifier to your attack roll.

A burst attack uses up 3 shots.

COUP DE GRACE (FULL ACTION)

By taking this action, you attempt to kill a helpless foe *(see page 177)* who is adjacent to you. You automatically score a critical hit (and agents with sneak attack bonuses get to use those as well). Even if the foe survives the damage, he must make a Fortitude save (DC 10 + damage dealt) or die from the shock of the blow. You cannot use this action against a target who is immune to critical hits. Coup de grace may be used with any attack, including ranged and unarmed attacks.

COVER FIRE (FULL ACTION)

By laying down cover fire with a firearm, you can protect your teammates when they are forced into a situation where an enemy has a good shot at them. When you take this action, you choose a single ally in your line of sight who receives a +4 dodge bonus to his Defense for 1 round against enemies who are also in your line of sight. (You have to be able to shoot at them to force them to keep their heads down, or this action won't work.) You cannot lay down cover fire for an ally who is involved in a melee. Each agent beyond the first who lays down cover fire for the same individual grants only an additional +1 dodge bonus, and then only against foes within their line of sight. Laying down cover fire uses up 5 shots.

DISARM (HALF ACTION)

This action replaces an attack, and allows you to attempt to take away your opponent's weapon. If attempted with an unarmed or melee attack (physically seizing the target's weapon), the target must be within one square of you. Disarm actions with ranged strikes (shooting the weapon out of your target's hands) may only be attempted within three range increments. Disarm actions never cause any damage to the target.

When attempting a disarm action, you and your target each make an attack roll with your respective weapons, with ties going to the agent with the higher

Strength. If you and the target are wielding different-sized melee weapons, then the agent with the larger weapon receives a +4 bonus to his attack roll per size category difference. If your target is holding his weapon in both hands, he gets a +4 bonus.

If you win, your target is disarmed. If you attempted the disarm action with an unarmed or melee attack and were unarmed when you made the disarm attempt, then you now have the weapon; otherwise it's on the ground at the target's feet.

If you lose a disarm check when using a melee weapon, your target may make a free attempt to disarm you in return, using the same method.

FEINT (HALF ACTION)

You can use the Bluff skill to mislead an opponent so that he can't dodge your next attack. A feint is opposed by the target's Sense Motive skill. If your check succeeds, your target may not add his Dexterity bonus to Defense against your next attack. This effect lasts until you attack the target or the end of your next action, whichever comes first.

Circumstance	Modifier*
Opponent has INT of 6 or less	–4
Opponent has INT of 2 or less	–8
Opponent is non-intelligent	Impossible

* These modifiers are not cumulative.

GRAPPLE (HALF ACTION)

This action replaces a melee attack, and lets you attempt to wrestle with your target. It's useful when you want to immobilize foes instead of killing them. Grappling is more complicated than most actions and is completely described under Special Attacks and Damage *(see page 172)*.

STRAFE ATTACK (FULL ACTION)

The strafe action may only be taken if you are firing a weapon with the strafe ability *(see Chapter 5: Gear)*. This action allows you to fire a long burst of ammo in an attempt to take down several opponents at once with a hail of fire. A strafe attack can affect multiple adjacent 5-ft. squares at once, as long as none are directly in front of the others *(see the diagram below)*. You must also have a line of sight to each square you are targeting.

After selecting a number of adjacent 5-ft. squares equal to up to half the remaining ammunition in your weapon (rounded down), make a single attack roll with a –2 penalty for each square beyond the first (applying all normal modifiers as well). Compare this attack roll with the Defense of each target in the target squares separately, hitting or missing each as usual. If one or more hits are scored, make a single damage roll and apply it to each target who was hit. A strafe attack uses up 2 shots per targeted square.

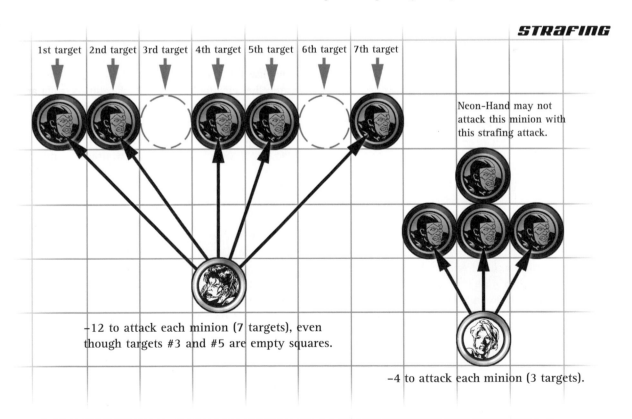

STRAFING

1st target 2nd target 3rd target 4th target 5th target 6th target 7th target

Neon-Hand may not attack this minion with this strafing attack.

–12 to attack each minion (7 targets), even though targets #3 and #5 are empty squares.

–4 to attack each minion (3 targets).

A strafe attack may not be used to target the same square more than once, nor can it be used to alternately target two adjacent squares.

Targets Larger Than One Square: If a big target occupies more than one square you are strafing, you receive +2 to your damage roll for every square of the target beyond the first that you strafe.

Optional Rule: Your GC might decide to make separate attack and damage rolls for each target affected by a strafe attack. This adds realism at the expense of speedy game play.

Example: Donovan is faced with three opponents all standing next to each other—a henchman (Defense 19) and two minions (Defense 12). He decides to strafe all three of them as a full action. He expends 6 shots from his submachinegun and makes a single attack roll with a –4 penalty. Rolling a 14, he hits the two minions, but not the henchman. He rolls damage only once, applying it to both minions.

STRIKE AN OBJECT (HALF ACTION)

Sometimes you need to hit something inanimate. You might have to tag a button with a hurled knife, split a rope with a bullet, or break a remote control in the villain's hand. When that happens, you take this action. The difficulty of hitting an object depends on its size and whether or not it's moving or being held.

Immobile objects have a Defense of 5 + their size modifier. If you are attacking an immobile object with a melee weapon, you receive a +4 to your attack roll. If you take a full-round action to line up your shot, then you score an automatic hit if using a melee weapon, or receive a +5 to your attack roll if using a ranged weapon.

Objects carried or worn by an agent have a Defense of 10 + their size modifier + the agent's Dexterity modifier and class bonus to Defense.

Held objects are easily moved out of the path of an incoming attack. They have a Defense of 15 + their size modifier + the agent's Dexterity modifier and class bonus to Defense.

Damaging Objects: Weapon damage is rolled normally against objects, which are immune to critical hits. An object typically has wound points and hardness. Object wound points work similar to agent wound points — an object with 0 wound points remaining is ruined. Hardness is similar to damage reduction — hardness is subtracted from the damage each attack inflicts, so a hardness of 2 would reduce 8 points of damage to 6.

Your Game Control may determine that certain objects are immune to or particularly vulnerable to certain types of damage. For example, while it's easy to shoot through asbestos, it's almost impossible to burn it.

Saving Throws: Objects that are immobile (i.e. objects that are not being touched, held, or worn) never receive saving throws — they are always considered to have failed their saving throws when the need comes up. Otherwise, the object gets the same saving throw as the agent in contact with it.

Breaking Objects: Finally, if you try to break an object using force, make a Strength check to see if you succeed. To calculate the DC to break an object, look up its construction quality on Table 6.2: Base Breaking DCs. This table is only a general guideline, and the Game Control may impose modifiers for large, tough, fragile, or awkward to grip objects. If the object loses more than half its wound points, the DC to break it is reduced by 2.

TABLE 6.2: BASE BREAKING DCS

Construction Quality	DC to Break
Shoddy	5
Standard	10
Good	15
Excellent	20
Formidable	25
Military Grade	30
Cutting Edge	35–40

SUPPRESSIVE FIRE (FULL ACTION)

You can use a firearm to pin down an opponent with suppressive fire, forcing him to seek cover and making it difficult for him to fire back. To do this, choose a single opponent in your line of sight who receives a –4 penalty to his attack rolls and skill checks for 1 round while he remains in your line of sight. In addition, the opponent must either leave your line of sight or take at least one-quarter cover by the start of your next action (provided the opponent has had at least one action in the meantime) or you get a single attack against him as a free action.

You cannot lay down suppressive fire on an opponent who is involved in a melee.

Each agent who coordinates suppressive fire on a single target beyond the first imposes an additional –1 penalty to the target's attack and skill rolls, for as long as the target remains in both attackers' lines of sight. All suppressing agents receive a free attack if the target fails to take cover.

Laying down suppressive fire uses up 5 shots.

TAUNT (HALF ACTION)

You can use the Bluff skill to goad an opponent into attacking you. A taunt is opposed by the target's Sense Motive skill. If you succeed with your check, your target must attack you with his very next action.

Circumstance	Modifier
Opponent is an adversary*	+6
You appear to be helpless	+4
Opponent is hostile*	+3
Opponent is angry with you	+2
You appear to be unarmed	+2
Opponent is unfriendly*	+1
Opponent has another target	–2
Opponent is fleeing	–6
Opponent has INT of 2 or less	–8
Opponent is non-intelligent	Impossible

See the Disposition system, page 269.

TRIP (HALF ACTION)

This action replaces a melee attack, and lets you attempt to trip an opponent who is up to one size category larger or smaller than you. First, you must make a successful melee touch attack to begin the trip attempt. Then, you make a Strength check, which is opposed by either your opponent's Strength or Dexterity, whichever is higher. If your target is larger than you, he receives a +4 bonus to his roll. If you are larger than your target, you receive a +4 bonus to your roll. In addition, your target gets a +2 bonus to his roll if he is braced or otherwise more stable than you.

If you win the opposed check, your target becomes prone. A prone target suffers a –4 penalty on melee attack rolls, and melee attacks against him receive a +4 bonus. Ranged attacks upon a prone agent, however, receive a –4 penalty unless the attacker is adjacent to the target. Standing up requires a half action unless you have the Jump Up feat.

If you lose the opposed check, your target may make a free attempt to trip you in return, using the same method.

TABLE 6.3: SUBSTANCE HARDNESS AND WOUND POINTS

Substance	Hardness	Wound Points
Paper	0	2/inch of thickness
Cloth	0	2/inch of thickness
Rope	0	2/inch of thickness
Ice	0	3/inch of thickness
Glass	1	1/inch of thickness
Pottery	1	1/inch of thickness
Leather	2	1/inch of thickness
Drywall	3	6/inch of thickness
Hard Plastic	4	8/inch of thickness
Wood	5	10/inch of thickness
Bone or Ivory	6	12/inch of thickness
Concrete	7	14/inch of thickness
Stone	8	15/inch of thickness
Reinforced Concrete	9	20/inch of thickness
Metal (Iron, etc.)	10	30/inch of thickness
Strong Metal (Steel, etc.)	15	35/inch of thickness
Super Strong Material	20	40/inch of thickness

TABLE 6.4: SAMPLE OBJECTS

Object	Hardness	Wound Points	DC to Break
Drywall (1 inch thick)	3	6	10
Sandbags (12 inches thick)	5	120	13
Wooden door (1 inch thick)	5	10	13
Computer	5	15	14
Cue ball	6	36	21
Rope (1 inch diameter)	0	2	23
Chain	10	5	26
Handcuffs	10	10	26
Metal bars	10	15	30
Metal door (5 inches thick)	10	150	35
Concrete wall (24 inches thick)	7	336	40
Blast door (24 inches thick)	15	840	45

ATTACK MODIFIERS

Agents have a knack for getting into fights in the most unusual places – atop skyscrapers, dangling from helicopters, or even skydiving from a plane. This section describes the bonuses and penalties such unusual circumstances can impose on combat.

FAVORABLE AND UNFAVORABLE CONDITIONS

Your Game Control may impose any or all of the following bonuses or penalties when you attack, depending on the circumstances. In addition, he may impose blanket modifiers for conditions not listed here. These modifiers are usually applied in 2-point increments (i.e. –4, –2, +2, +4, etc.).

COVER

When you find yourself under enemy fire, the best thing you can do is take cover. Crouching behind a car, a wall, or a door frame provides a bonus to your Defense. The more complete your cover is, the better the bonus you receive *(see Table 6.6: Cover and Concealment)*.

Cover provides two bonuses. The first bonus (the Cover Defense Bonus) is added to your Defense when you are attacked. Your GC may rule that this cover bonus doesn't stack with other modifiers, such as the bonus for kneeling (since this bonus is already factored into your cover).

The second type of bonus (the Cover Reflex Save Bonus) is added to your Reflex saving throws against any area effects that originate or spread from the other side of the cover.

If the Cover Defense Bonus is all that keeps an attack roll from hitting a target, the cover is hit instead. Roll damage and apply it to the cover *(see the Strike an Object attack option, page 168)*. If there is more than enough damage to destroy the cover, a hole develops and excess damage is applied to the target hiding behind the cover. So, while hiding behind some drywall is better than nothing, smart agents seek out better cover when possible.

Using Hostages as Cover: If you use someone else as cover, then anytime the cover is hit (as described above) and the attack roll equals or exceeds the hostage's Defense, then the hostage is hit and suffers the damage. Make sure to control your hostage, however: if the hostage can use his Dexterity or dodge bonuses, and this bonus is the only thing that causes the attack roll to miss him, then the hostage has dodged out of the way of the attack, which hits you after all.

CONCEALMENT

If you can't take cover, then the next best thing you can do is hide yourself from sight, such as behind some bushes or in some dense smoke. Conditions such as these – where nothing physically stops attacks aimed at you, but something interferes with your attacker's accuracy – are referred to as concealment.

TABLE 6.5: ATTACK MODIFIERS

Circumstance	Melee	Loses Ranged	Dex Bonus?
Attacker aiming	–	+1	No
Attacker bracing	–	+2	No
Attacker flanking defender	+2	–	No
Attacker on higher ground	+1	+0	No
Attacker prone	–4	–4	No
Attacker running	+0	–2†	No
Defender sitting or kneeling	+2	–2	No
Defender stunned, cowering, or off balance	+2	+2	Yes
Defender climbing (cannot use shield)	+2	+2	Yes
Defender surprised or flat-footed	+0	+0	Yes
Defender running	+0	–2†	No
Defender grappling (attacker not)	+0	+0‡	No
Defender pinned	+4	–4	Yes
Defender prone	+4	–4	No
Defender has cover	See rules for Cover *(above)*		
Defender concealed or unseen	See rules for Concealment *(above)*		
Defender helpless	See rules for Helpless Defenders *(opposite)*		

† If both the attacker and defender are running, each suffers a –4 penalty to attack the other.

‡ Roll randomly to see which grappling combatant you strike. That defender loses any Dexterity bonus to Defense.

The effectiveness of concealment is dependent upon your attacker. If the attacker can see your body heat (e.g. if he's using a thermal sight), hiding in the darkness or behind some light foliage provides no benefit.

Concealment provides a Concealment Defense Bonus, which is similar to the Cover Defense Bonus. However, you don't have to worry about whether or not an attacker's shot hits your concealment (as there's nothing to hit). This bonus can be used in combination with a Cover Defense Bonus (e.g. hiding behind a brick wall on a foggy night), but if there are multiple concealment conditions that apply to an attack, only use the highest one (e.g. if you are hiding behind light foliage in total darkness, only the total darkness bonus applies).

DEGREE OF COVER OR CONCEALMENT

Your GC subjectively assesses cover and concealment, using Table 6.6 as a guideline. Ultimately, the situation determines how effective your cover or concealment is. After all, standing behind a low wall is much more effective against a short or prone opponent than it is against a sniper on a nearby roof.

HELPLESS DEFENDERS

A melee attack against a helpless opponent (an opponent who is bound, sleeping, unconscious, or otherwise unable to defend himself) receives a +4 bonus to the attack roll. Ranged attacks do not receive this bonus. In addition, the defender's Dexterity bonus is considered to be –5 (as though they had a Dexterity of 0). You can take a Coup de Grace (see page 177) action to target a helpless defender if you so desire.

FIGHTING DEFENSIVELY

You can choose to fight defensively just before you take an action, taking a –4 penalty to all of your attacks and skill checks that round to gain a +2 dodge bonus to Defense for that same round.

FLANKING

When you and an ally attack an opponent directly between you, you are each considered to be flanking that opponent. You and your ally each gain a +2 flanking bonus to your attack rolls, and you can perform sneak attacks if you have that ability.

SHOOTING OR THROWING INTO A MELEE

If you shoot or throw a ranged weapon at an opponent who is adjacent to one of your allies, you suffer a –4 penalty to your attack roll. If your ally is unconscious or immobilized, you don't suffer this penalty unless the ally is being attacked.

TABLE 6.6: COVER AND CONCEALMENT

Degree	Examples	Cover Defense Bonus	Cover Reflex Bonus	Concealment Defense Bonus
One-quarter	Standing behind a short wall; light fog or foliage*; moderate darkness*	+2	+1	+1
One-half	Fighting from around a corner; standing at an open window; behind an agent of the same size; dense fog at 10 ft.*; precipitation*	+4	+2	+2
Three-quarters	Peering around a corner; dense foliage*	+7	+3	+3
Nine-tenths	Standing at a narrow opening; behind a slightly open door; near darkness*	+10	+4**	+4
Total	Entirely behind a solid wall; total darkness; attacker blind*; dense fog at 20 ft.*	–	–	+6

* Concealment examples. ** No damage if your save is successful, half damage if you fail.

SPECIAL ATTACKS AND DAMAGE

This section describes several unusual types of attacks and damage that deserve special attention.

BLAST DAMAGE

Some weapons affect every character and object within an area. These are called blast weapons, and they inflict blast damage. Blast damage has a base radius of effect, called a blast increment, which is measured in squares (*see the diagram below*). Everyone and everything within this blast increment from the target takes takes the full blast damage rolled. This damage is reduced by half (rounding down) within each blast increment out from the center of the blast. Blast damage below 1 point has no effect.

Example: Donovan is inside the third blast increment of an explosion with a blast damage value of 24. He takes 6 points of damage (24 halved for the second increment, then halved again for the third).

When you suffer blast damage, you may make a Reflex save (DC 15 +1 per die of damage) in order to dive for cover, halving the damage you suffer from the explosion (rounding down). When you succeed with such a Reflex save, you have moved to the nearest square in next ring outward from the center of the blast.

Example: The original blast damage value of the explosion in the example above was 4d6, so Donovan's Reflex save DC is 19 (15 + 4). He rolls a 21, which reduces the damage he suffers from 6 to 3.

GRAPPLING ATTACKS

When you're wrestling with an enemy, you are said to be grappling. You usually do this in order to pin an opponent. There are several steps to a grappling attack.

1. **Enter your opponent's square:** You must move into your target's square to start a grappling action. This is an exception to square occupancy (*see Moving, page 174*).

2. **Grab your opponent:** When you attempt to start a grapple, make a melee touch attack. Instcad of applying the usual size modifier to this roll, you receive a +4 bonus for every size category you are above Medium, or a –4 penalty for each size category below Medium. This roll is called a grab check. If your grab check misses, you fail to start a grapple. If your target is already grappling someone else, then your grab check automatically succeeds.

3. **Hold your opponent:** Once you have grabbed your opponent, you must make another grapple check — this one opposed by the target — in order to start the grapple and deal damage as an unarmed attack. If you lose,

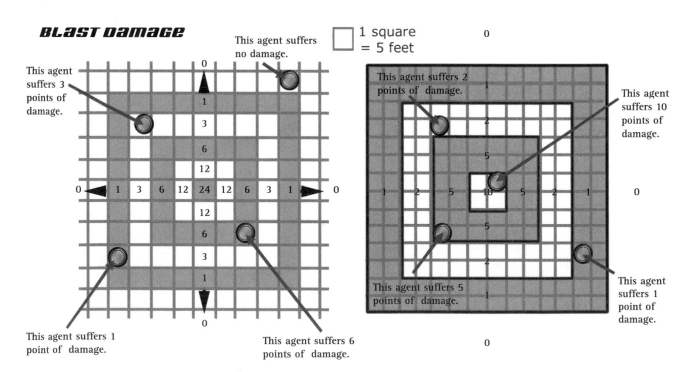

BLAST DAMAGE

This agent suffers no damage.

This agent suffers 3 points of damage.

1 square = 5 feet

This agent suffers 1 point of damage.

This agent suffers 6 points of damage.

24 points of blast damage with a blast increment of 1 square.

This agent suffers 2 points of damage.

This agent suffers 10 points of damage.

This agent suffers 5 points of damage.

This agent suffers 1 point of damage.

10 points of blast damage with a blast increment of 2 squares.

or your target is two size categories or more larger than you are, you fail to start the grapple.

Once you have completed these steps successfully, you and your target are grappling. Once you are grappling, you can attempt an opposed grapple check as one of your attacks to perform any of the following grappling moves:

1. **Inflict Damage:** You inflict damage as though making an unarmed attack.

2. **Pin:** Hold your opponent immobile for 1 round. While you have someone pinned, your allies receive +4 to their melee attack rolls against him. While pinning someone, you can still use your actions to perform grappling moves.

3. **Break a Pin:** Break free of an opponent's pin or free an ally from a pin. Make an Escape Artist check opposed by your opponent's grapple check to perform this move.

4. **Escape:** If your opposed grapple check beats all your grappling opponents' check results, you can leave the grapple and take a standard move action. You may make an Escape Artist check opposed by your opponents' grapple checks to perform this move.

5. **Attack with a Light Weapon:** You may make one attack using a light weapon against a grappled opponent.

While grappling, you lose your Dexterity and dodge bonuses to Defense.

While pinned, you are held immobile (but not helpless) for 1 full round. The only grappling move you can take while pinned is to attempt to break the pin you're held in.

Multiple combatants can grapple a single opponent, though the number of attackers is limited by the victim's size. Up to four combatants can grapple a target of their size category, while as many as eight can grapple an opponent of a larger size category. Up to two combatants may grapple a target that is one size category smaller than they are, and only one combatant may grapple a target two or more size categories smaller.

When multiple people grapple a single target, consult the skill coordination rules on page 39 to resolve the attack.

Grenade-like Weapon Attacks

Weapons that are hurled or propelled (like knives, grenades, and rockets) may deviate from the target when attacks with them are unsuccessful. These weapons are referred to grenade-like weapons.

When an attack with a grenade-like weapon misses, the weapon or ammunition deviates from its intended

target. Roll 1d3 and add +1 to the total for every range increment the weapon traveled to see how many squares away from the intended square the weapon lands. To determine which direction the weapon deviates, roll 1d8 and consult the grenade-like weapon deviation diagram below.

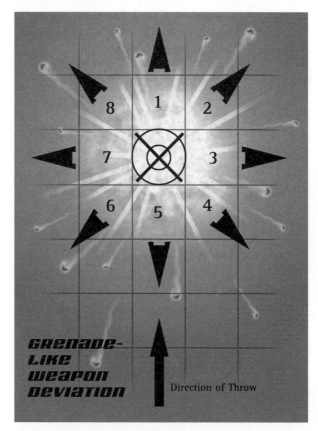

GRENADE-LIKE WEAPON DEVIATION — Direction of Throw

Subdual Damage

Subdual damage is caused by typically non-lethal attacks (e.g. unarmed attacks, tasers, and the like), and is used to incapacitate enemies without killing them. When you suffer subdual damage, you track it separately in the subdual damage box on your agent sheet. *Subdual damage is not deducted from your vitality or wounds.*

Unlike normal damage — which reduces your vitality and wound points — subdual damage rises as a separate number. If your subdual damage ever equals your current vitality points, you are staggered *(see page 177).* If your subdual damage ever exceeds the sum of your current vitality and wound points, you fall unconscious and are helpless.

Example: Donovan inflicts 29 points of subdual damage on a minion. The henchman's vitality is 25 and he has 12 wounds, so he is staggered but not unconscious. The henchman's current vitality and wounds remain at 25 and 12, respectively and the GC jots 29 down in the subdual damage box of the henchman's record sheet. If the henchman suffers 8 more points of subdual damage, he falls unconscious.

When you score a threat with an attack that causes subdual damage, you may spend an action die to compare the damage to your target's wound points. If the damage exceeds the target's wound points, the target immediately falls unconscious. Whether the subdual damage exceeds the target's wounds or not, it is still added to the target's running subdual damage total.

Example: In the example above, if Donovan had scored a critical hit, he could have spent an action die to compare the 29 points of subdual damage to the minion's 12 wounds, causing him to fall unconscious.

Action dice may be spent to increase subdual damage in the same way that they are spent to increase normal damage (i.e. roll the action die and add the total to the damage dealt).

Damage reduction is twice as effective as usual against subdual damage (e.g. 2 points of damage reduction prevents 4 points of subdual damage).

At any time and with any attack that causes normal damage, you can accept a –4 penalty to your attack roll to deal subdual damage instead. Likewise, if a weapon usually deals subdual damage *(see Chapter 5: Gear),* you may accept a –4 penalty to your attack roll to deal normal damage. Damage converted in this fashion is cut in half before it is applied to the target (e.g. 22 points of subdual damage becomes 11 points of normal damage, and vice versa).

Subdual damage heals independently of normal damage (i.e. they heal at the same time). Every time you heal vitality damage *(see Injury and Death, page 177),* you also heal the same amount of subdual damage. If your vitality is at maximum, any subdual damage heals at the rate of 1 point per hour of rest. Medical facilities, trained professionals, and healing aids can increase this rate, as described on page 179.

Since you may take an unlimited amount of subdual damage, and cannot die from taking it (though the coup de grace attack option may be used to kill you once you're unconscious), it is possible for you to be laid up for extended periods of time to bring your subdual damage back down to 0.

Example: Donovan has taken a shocking 60 points of subdual damage. Since subdual damage heals at the same rate as vitality damage (1 point per hour with rest), Donovan will be sleeping for a little over two days before he's ready for some pay-back.

UNARMED ATTACKS

Kicks, punches, and martial arts moves are all unarmed attacks. Normally, unarmed attacks from a Medium-sized agent deal 1d3 points of subdual damage. However, you can take a –4 penalty to your attack roll to deal normal damage instead of subdual damage.

In addition, there are several feats you can take to increase the effectiveness of your unarmed attacks. These might let you deal extra damage, take extra attacks, or use other special abilities.

Moving

Aside from attacking your opponents, most of your time in combat is spent moving around — either to get into position for a better shot, or to take cover from your opponents' fire. This section explains when and how far you can move.

RULES FOR MOVING

In modern combat, cover, position, and movement are key to success. If you let your opponents surround you, it's over.

To accurately represent movement and position, it's easiest to use miniature figures to represent the agents and their opponents. By placing them on a grid of 1-inch squares, you can easily eliminate arguments about cover and range. The standard scale used in this book is 5 feet for every 1-inch square. Distances of less than 5 feet should be ignored.

HOW FAR CAN YOU MOVE?

A Medium-sized agent has a speed of 30 ft. per round. Wearing armor reduces this by the armor's speed penalty in feet per round (twice the penalty if the agent doesn't have the proper armor proficiency). A medium or heavy load *(see Carrying Capacity, page 106)* reduces an agent in light or no armor by 10 ft. per round.

SQUARE OCCUPANCY

Only one combatant of Medium or greater size may occupy any single square at one time. (Two combatants of small or lesser size may occupy a single square at the same time if they are allies.)

PASSING THROUGH

You may move through an occupied square if any of these conditions apply:

1. The occupant of the square is an ally.

2. The occupant of the square is dead or helpless.

3. You successfully use the Tumble skill to pass through the square.

4. The occupant of the square is three or more size categories smaller than you.

FACE AND REACH

Combatants who are larger or smaller than a normal human present special concerns in combat. Larger opponents, for instance, can be attacked by more people at once, but their reach enables them to attack targets who are further away. As for smaller opponents, more of them can gang up on a single target, but they can only attack those in their own square. When fighting such opponents, you may attack into your own square.

A combatant's face determines how big it is when represented in the standard scale. Note that larger combatants have more squares that are adjacent to them, and therefore can be attacked by more opponents at once.

A combatant's reach determines how far away the combatant can perform a melee attack on an opponent.

See Table 6.7: Face and Reach for more about both these statistics.

MOVEMENT ACTIONS

These actions generally allow you to move during combat, often in an effort to find cover, close with the enemy, or flee. If you take a movement action during the round, then you cannot make use of your 5-ft. bonus step *(see page 160)*.

STANDARD MOVE (HALF ACTION)

This action normally allows you to move your agent's speed in feet. However, many nonstandard forms of movement also fall under this action, such as climbing or swimming (move up to ¼ your speed with a skill check). Using some other forms of transportation, such as skis and motorcycles, is also considered a standard move. *(For more information about vehicles and other methods of transport, see Chapter 5).*

If you are adjacent to an opponent, you can't move more than a 5-ft. step without the Mobility feat, unless you're taking a withdraw action, or your opponent is prone.

CHARGE (FULL ACTION)

Charging allows you to move up to twice your speed in a straight line, stopping to take a standard attack action against your target as soon as you are within striking distance. Your charge ends as soon as you move adjacent to an opponent — you cannot run past one opponent to charge another. When charging an opponent, your standard attack roll receives a +2 bonus. However, you suffer a penalty of –2 to your Defense for one round (until your next action) because of the reckless behavior inherent in a charge.

RUN (FULL ACTION)

When you run, you move up to four times your speed in a straight line (three times your speed if you are wearing heavy armor). You lose your Dexterity bonus to Defense, since you can't avoid attacks while running.

TABLE 6.7: FACE AND REACH				
Opponent Size	Example of Size	Size Modifier	Reach	Face
Fine	Fly	+8	Same square	100/square
Diminutive	Gecko	+4	Same square	25/square
Tiny	Opossum	+2	Same square	4/square
Small	Child	+1	1 square	1 square
Medium	Adult human	0	1 square	1 square
Large (tall)	Gorilla	–1	2 squares	1 square
Large (long)	Polar bear	–1	1 square	1 × 2 squares
Huge (tall)	Giraffe	–2	3 squares	2 × 2 squares
Huge (long)	Elephant	–2	2 squares	2 × 4 squares
Gargantuan (tall)	Office building	–4	4 squares	4 × 4 squares
Gargantuan (long)	Humpback whale	–4	2 squares	4 × 8 squares
Colossal (tall)	Skyscraper	–8	5 squares	8 × 8 squares
Colossal (long)	Blue whale	–8	3 squares	8 × 16 squares

You may run for a number of rounds equal to your Constitution score without a roll, but after that you must succeed with a Constitution check (DC 10) to continue. You have to check again each round you continue running, and your DC increases by 1 with each additional check. Once you fail a check, you must stop running and rest for 1 minute (10 rounds) before you can start running again. While you are resting, you may move no further than your speed in feet each round, unless you use a vehicle or someone is carrying you.

If you are adjacent to an opponent, you can't move more than a 5-ft. step without the Mobility feat, unless you're taking a withdraw action, or your opponent is prone.

TOTAL DEFENSE (FULL ACTION)

This action allows you to focus exclusively on defending yourself from harm. You receive a +4 dodge bonus to your Defense for 1 round, and you may move up to your speed in feet, when taking this movement action.

If you are adjacent to an opponent, you can't move more than a 5-ft. step without the Mobility feat, unless you're taking a withdraw action, or your opponent is prone.

WITHDRAW (FULL ACTION)

You can break away from your opponents by taking this action. You may move up to twice your speed, provided that you move away from all opponents, and that your first 5-ft. step does not leave you adjacent to an opponent (unless you have the Mobility feat, in which case you can continue to withdraw regardless).

Other Common Actions

Other types of actions, including guidelines for categorizing unlisted actions, are described in this section.

CATEGORIZING ACTIONS

If you decide to do something during combat that isn't mentioned in this chapter, then your Game Control determines what category of action it falls into.

Free actions typically require little or no time or attention to accomplish. If you can do it in an instant, such as dropping an item, then it's a free action.

Only the most demanding tasks are full actions. Disarming a bomb, rappelling down the side of a building – anything that would take up more than a few seconds in an action movie qualifies.

If an action doesn't fit either of the above descriptions, classify it as a half action.

MISCELLANEOUS ACTIONS

This section details actions that don't fit easily into any of the earlier sections.

FREE MISCELLANEOUS ACTIONS

Simple, nearly instant actions are free actions. This includes things like activating an item, dropping an item, dropping prone, or saying something quickly. Your Game Control may rule that certain lengthy actions you take, such as reciting the St. Crispin's Day speech, are not actually free actions.

AIM A WEAPON (HALF ACTION)

By taking this action, you aim a ranged weapon at a specific target. As long as your target doesn't move more than 5 ft. before your next attack on it, and you do nothing to disturb the weapon's aim, you receive a +1 circumstance bonus to your next attack roll against that target. You may both aim and brace a ranged weapon, stacking the bonuses from each (for a total bonus of +3).

BRACE A WEAPON (HALF ACTION)

In order to take this action, you must have a stable surface or corner to level your ranged weapon against, and you must choose a target to aim it at. As long as your target doesn't move before your next attack on it, and you do nothing to disturb the weapon's aim, you receive a +2 circumstance bonus to your next attack roll against that target. You may both aim and brace a ranged weapon, stacking the bonuses from each (for a total bonus of +3).

DRAW OR HOLSTER A WEAPON (HALF ACTION)

You may draw or holster a weapon by taking this action. You can draw or holster two weapons at once if they are both light weapons. Taking the Quick Draw feat makes this a free action (that you can use twice per round).

LOAD A WEAPON (HALF ACTION)

This action allows you to replenish the ammo in your weapon. It allows you to load one clip (or cylinder), or three bullets if the weapon doesn't use clips. This can also be used to feed a belt into a weapon, or change out a power pack. Taking the Quick Reload feat makes this a free action (that you can use once per round).

MANIPULATE AN OBJECT (HALF ACTION)

This action allows you to move a heavy object, open a door, pick up an item, retrieve a stored item, or perform a similar task. Your Game Control may rule that your activity takes a full action if it is particularly difficult, such as moving an extremely heavy or awkward item.

REFRESH (FULL ACTION)

You may attempt to rest for a moment, get your bearings, and otherwise refresh yourself. At the end of the round in which you perform this action, you may spend one action die and add the result to your vitality, or recover 2 wounds (with no roll). However, if you are the target of any attacks this round (whether successful or not), you may not spend this action die, and you lose your action this round.

STABILIZE A DYING AGENT (HALF ACTION)

If you make a successful First Aid check (DC 15), you can stabilize an adjacent, dying combatant. The agent regains no vitality or wound points, but stops losing them. This skill check may not be attempted by untrained agents.

STAND UP (HALF ACTION)

You can take this action to rise from a prone position. Taking the Jump Up feat makes this a free action.

USE A SKILL OR FEAT (SEE SKILL OR FEAT)

Using a skill or feat is often a half or full action. See the skill and feat descriptions in Chapters 2 and 3 for more information.

INJURY AND DEATH

This section describes conditions that your agent or your enemies may acquire and the many ways to gain and lose vitality and wound points.

COMBAT CONDITIONS

The effects of these conditions stack unless otherwise noted. Additional effects are caused by vitality and wound point loss (see Damage and Dying, page 178).

Ability Damaged (see also page 16): The agent has lost 1 or more ability points, temporarily or not, which return at a rate of 1 point per day per ability (unless otherwise specified by the effect which caused the damage). If an agent's Strength or Dexterity drops to 0, he falls to the ground and is helpless. If an agent's Constitution drops to 0, he dies. If an agent's Intelligence, Wisdom, or Charisma drops to 0, he falls unconscious (see page 178).

Blinded: An agent who is blinded is unable to see anything, and so everything has full concealment to him. He misses in combat 50% of the time (roll a d20 after a successful attack — on a 1-10, he in fact missed), loses any positive bonus to Dexterity, and his enemies gain a +2 bonus to attack him. He may not move faster than half his speed in any round, and suffers a –4 penalty with any Strength or Dexterity-based skill requiring eye-hand coordination. Finally, he may not make any Spot, Search, or other visual skill checks.

Deafened: The agent cannot hear, and suffers a –4 penalty with all initiative checks and any skill check requiring audio feedback (such as using the Sense Motive skill based on the tone of someone's voice). Further, he may not make any Listen checks.

Entangled: Entangled agents suffer a –2 penalty to attack rolls and –4 with all Dexterity-based checks. If their bonds are anchored, they can't move. Otherwise, they move at half speed, and can't run or charge.

Flat-footed (see also page 162): Flat-footed agents lose their Dexterity bonus to Defense, if any. Everyone is flat-footed during combat until they act for the first time, or until they are successfully attacked.

Grappled (see also page 172): While grappled, an agent cannot move and loses his Dexterity bonus to Defense against anyone not involved in the grapple. He may attack with a small weapon or attempt to break free of his opponent. Others may pass by agents who are involved in a grapple without stopping (see page 174).

Helpless (see also page 171): Agents are helpless when they are bound, sleeping or unconscious. Melee attacks against helpless agents receive a +4 bonus. Ranged attacks receive no bonus. Finally, adjacent opponents may use the coup de grace option (see page 166) against helpless defenders.

Prone: The agent is lying on the ground and must spend a half action to rise to his feet (unless he has the Jump Up feat). While prone, an agent makes melee attacks with a –4 penalty. Ranged attacks against him suffer a –4 penalty unless the attacker is adjacent. Melee attacks against him receive a +4 bonus.

Staggered: Agents who are staggered lose their Dexterity modifier to Defense and can take only one half action each turn. Additionally, they must make a Fortitude check each round (DC 15 + number of rounds they've been staggered) or fall unconscious. Opponents receive a +2 bonus to attack a staggered agent.

Stunned: A stunned agent loses his Dexterity bonus to Defense and can take no actions.

Damage Reduction

Certain equipment and abilities allow a target to absorb some or all damage when it is taken. Unless otherwise directed, you subtract the value of any damage reduction you have from each damage total you suffer — including wound damage from critical hits. Damage reduction is subtracted from damage after all other modifiers have been applied.

Example: Donovan wears a tuxedo liner which grants him 2 points of damage reduction. When he is shot for 7 points of damage, he only suffers 5.

Certain types of damage ignore damage reduction, including (but not limited to) damage taken from touch attacks (such as tasers), falling, poison, and anything inhaled or ingested. When other types of damage ignore damage reduction, it is mentioned in their descriptions.

Unless otherwise stated, whenever damage reduction reduces damage to 0, it also negates any special effects that accompany the damage, such as poison delivered by a normal attack. Further, each time the agent's damage reduction reduces the damage from any single source (attack, feat, etc.) to 0 or less, the agent takes 2 points of subdual damage *(see page 173),* cumulative with all other subdual damage the agent has taken (including subdual damage caused by previously absorbed damage). It is obvious to agents when their damage reduction has completely absorbed damage (reduced it to 0 points or less).

Occasionally, damage reduction is listed as a number followed by a slash and a term (e.g. "DR 2/explosives"). When this is the case, the term refers to types of damage which can bypass the damage reduction, and which are applied without modifier to the agent.

Damage and Dying

Usually, when you get hurt, you lose vitality or wound points. When this happens, you subtract that damage from your total vitality or wound points to arrive at your current vitality or wound points.

WHAT ARE VITALITY POINTS?

Vitality points are your capacity to keep going when the going gets tough. They represent a mixture of endurance, luck, and experience. Losing vitality points is less a representation of actual physical damage than it is combat fatigue; it gradually becomes more difficult to avoid being physically injured. As your vitality points drop, you're edging closer to exhaustion and the possibility of a nasty wound.

WHAT ARE WOUND POINTS?

Wound points are your capacity to absorb physical trauma. When your wound points drop, you've been physically injured in some fashion.

EFFECTS OF DAMAGE

You suffer no ill effects from damage unless either your vitality or wound points drop to 0, or you suffer 50 points of vitality or wound damage in a single hit. At 0 vitality points, you're fatigued *(see below)*; at 0 wound points, you're unconscious *(see below)*; and if you suffer 50 points of damage in a single hit, you must make a Fortitude saving throw (DC 15) or you die (your wound points drop to –10 immediately).

Fatigued (0 Vitality Points)

At 0 vitality points, you agent becomes fatigued. A fatigued agent is unable to run or charge, and suffers a –2 penalty to Strength and Dexterity. In addition, any damage that you suffer while your vitality points are at 0 is applied directly to your wound points. Finally, you must make a Fortitude saving throw (DC 10) or be stunned for 1d6 rounds. Once your vitality points rise above 0, you return to normal.

Vitality points may not drop below 0.

Unconscious (0 Wound Points)

If your wound points drop to 0, you fall unconscious. You are helpless and can't take any actions until your wound points rise above 0, when you are awake once more.

Dying (–1 to –9 Wound Points)

When your wound points drop to between –1 and –9 inclusive, you fall unconscious (if you aren't already) and can take no actions. At the end of the round in which you dropped below 0 wound points and every round thereafter until you are stabilized, roll d%. If you roll equal to or less than your Constitution, you stabilize; otherwise you lose 1 wound point.

Another agent can stabilize you with a First Aid check (DC 15). You likewise stabilize if you are healed of even 1 wound point (though you cannot spend an action die to do so unless the combat has ended). If your wound points are raised above 0, you return to normal.

Dead (–10 Wound Points or less)

Once an agent reaches –10 wound points, he's dead— that's it. Unless your GC has arranged a special way to bring him back from the grave, death is a one-way trip.

SUBDUAL DAMAGE

Subdual damage has its own set of rules, described on page 173. Subdual damage heals like vitality damage.

EXTREMELY DEADLY SITUATIONS

Your agent may find himself in any number of extremely perilous situations, such as taking a gunshot to his back or falling from a skyscraper. Just as in real life, these situations are not to be taken lightly. The GC may spend an action die and rule that an attack that occurs in such an obviously lethal situation is an automatic critical hit. Of course, this can work to your benefit if the situation is reversed. When you have someone in such a situation, you may spend an action die to make one of your attacks a critical hit, pending GC approval.

STABILIZING INJURIES

Dying agents sometimes stabilize on their own (see Dying, above), but more likely another agent must stabilize them, either by making a First Aid check (DC 15) or through some other means, such as special equipment.

Once stabilized, an agent no longer needs to make d% rolls to avoid losing wound points, and he regains them at the rate of 1 per full day of rest. Should a stabilized agent suffer additional damage before he reaches 1 wound point (or drop below 1 wound point thereafter), he is no longer stable and must begin rolling to avoid wound point loss once more.

HEALING

There are several ways to regain lost vitality or wound points – natural healing, hospital care, and special equipment among them. However, no form of healing can raise your vitality or wound points past their normal maximum.

NATURAL HEALING

You regain 1 vitality point per agent level per hour of rest, and 1 wound point per day of rest, as long as you restrict yourself to light activities (i.e. no combat) during that time. For instance, while resting, a 2nd-level soldier recovers 2 vitality points every hour and 1 wound point every day. The reason higher-level agents recover vitality points faster isn't because they actually heal faster – it's because each vitality point is proportionally less of their total vitality.

ASSISTED HEALING AND HOSPITALIZATION

If an agent uses the long-term care option under the First Aid skill to care for a wounded ally, the ally regains lost vitality and wound points at double the normal rate. Hospital facilities can increase this to triple the normal recovery rate.

EQUIPMENT

Certain equipment can quickly restore lost vitality or wound points. A stimulant shot can stabilize a dying agent, for instance, and a liquid skin patch can quickly restore a few wound points. *See Chapter 5 for more information.*

USING ACTION DICE FOR HEALING

When not engaged in combat, you may spend any number of action dice to regain some vitality or wound points. For each action die you spend, you either roll a die *(see below for the die type)* and regain that many vitality points, or regain 1 wound point.

LIMITATIONS ON HEALING

You may never regain more vitality or wound points than you've lost. You cannot raise your current vitality or wound points higher than your maximum total through healing or any other method.

ACTION DICE IN COMBAT

You may call upon your reserves of luck and skill in the form of action dice. Sometimes, spending an action die at the proper moment can mean the difference between success and failure, or life and death.

You may spend action dice during or after combat for the following effects.

1. ADDING TO ROLLS

You may spend an action die after any die roll you make during combat, including attack rolls, damage rolls, and saving throws. Roll an additional die (type determined as shown below) and add it to the result of your previous die roll. You may continue spending action dice to add to a roll as long as you still have action dice to spend.

Level	Die Type
1st-5th	d4
6th-10th	d6
11th-15th	d8
16th-20th	d10

When rolling an action die, if you roll the highest number possible on the die (such as a 6 on a d6), it "explodes," meaning that you re-roll the die, adding the number you roll to the previous total. So, if you roll a 6 on a d6, and then re-roll it, getting a 4, the total value of the action die is 10. An action die can keep exploding as long as you keep rolling its maximum value.

Example 1: A 1st-level pointman rolls a 17 for an attack roll, just shy of the 19 he needs. He decides to spend an action die, then rolls a d4, getting a 3. Adding that to his previous total of 17, he now has a total of 20, more than enough to hit.

Example 2: A 6th-level soldier rolls a 12 for a Move Silently check and needs a 20. Spending an action die, he rolls a d6 and gets a 6. The die explodes, so he re-rolls it, this time getting a 3. When added to the previous 6, this gives a total of 9, enough to increase the 12 to a 21, a success.

2. TEMPORARY DEFENSE

At the start of any round, you may spend one action die to gain a luck bonus to your Defense for one round equal to the action die's roll. You may not use this ability again while your Defense is affected by a previous action die bonus.

3. ACTIVATING CRITICAL HITS AND MISSES

When you roll a threat, you may spend an action die in order to score a critical hit. Likewise, you may spend an action die when the GC scores an error to activate his critical miss.

4. HEALING (AFTER COMBAT)

As usual, after combat, you may spend any number of action dice to regain some vitality or wound points. For each action die you spend, you either roll a die (type determined as shown above) and regain that many vitality points, or regain 2 wound points.

COMBAT EXAMPLE

FADE IN...

Donovan's team infiltrates an Omegadyne facility to download Kholera's secret project files directly from the central computer. Everything goes smoothly until they find a henchman and a squad of minions guarding the master terminal. Donovan orders a surprise assault — the team must take the master terminal at all costs!

Donovan Godding (Codename: Sideshock) is a 5th level D-4 Soldier (Str 13, Dex 16, Con 17, w/vp 17/53). His class abilities include 1 point of damage reduction, Armor Use +1, and the Lay Down Fire, Point Blank Shot, and Precise Shot feats. He is wearing an assault vest (DR 8, MDB +1, ACP −4, and Speed −10 ft.) and a military helmet (Def +2 and ACP −2), and carrying a 7.62x39 assault rifle (2d8 damage) with an extended magazine

(50 shots). His total Defense is 13, his total Armor Check penalty is −5, and he has a total attack bonus of +8 with his rifle (+9 if inside one range increment).

Jonathan Grail (Codename: Brace) is a 5th level D-0 Pointman (Str 12, Dex 16, Con 13, Cha 16, w/vp 13/40). He is armed with a .44 Magnum (2d6+2). His class abilities include Assistance, Lead 2/session, and Tactics, and he has the Expertise feat. His total Defense is 15. His total attack bonus with the Magnum is +6.

Hitomi Sakamori (Codename: Neon-hand) is a 5th level D-1 snoop (Str 10, Dex 14, Con 14, w/vp 14/36). She has the Jury Rig and Backdoor class abilities and the Combat Instincts and Mark feats. She has a total Defense of 16 and a total attack bonus of +4 with her 9×19mm service pistol (1d10).

In the vault is Cedric Holts (Codename: Onyx), a henchman of Dr. von Nueman. He is a 4th level pointman/2nd level soldier (Str 11, Dex 14, Con 14, Wis 13, w/vp 12/52). He has the Lead and Tactics abilities, and 1 point of damage reduction from his soldier class, as well as the Confident Charge, Improved Initiative, Mobility, Point Blank Shot, and Quick Draw feats. He is wearing a kevlar vest (Def +1, DR 4/0, MDB +4, ACP −1) and is armed with two .45 ACP submachineguns (1d10+2) and a taser. He has a total Defense of 11, a +7 to hit with his gun, and a +5 bonus with melee attacks.

There are also seven Omegadyne security guards (2nd level soldiers w/vp 10/12) guarding the terminal, also armed with .45 ACP submachineguns (1d10+2). Each has the Point Blank Shot feat, and a total Def of 11 plus 1 point of DR, with a +2 bonus to hit with his weapon (+3 inside the first increment).

Omegadyne's secure computer vault is a 40-ft. × 40-ft. cube with many terminals and security cameras. The walls are both sound- and bulletproof. Neon-hand spoofs the cameras, ensuring the team won't be discovered — so as long as the fight is quick, of course.

ROUND 0: SURPRISE ROUND

All combatants begin the fight flat-footed.

The players roll a d20 for initiative, adding their class and Dexterity modifiers. Brace rolls a total of 17, Sideshock 13, and Neon-hand a 7. The GC rolls for Onyx and the guards (opting to roll once for all the guards to speed things along) and receives a 20 for Onyx (including the +4 from his Improved initiative feat) and 10 for the guards.

The GC declares that the agents receive a surprise round due to their flawless entry into the building.

Brace delays his action, waiting for Sideshock to start the show. He can delay his action up to 17 times (10 + his initiative bonus) without losing his action during this round. Sideshock takes a 5-ft. bonus step to place himself squarely in front of the vault's glass doors.

He fires a burst from his rifle to shatter to doors (the GC lets him do so without a roll, as it's a trivially easy task, though it does use up three shots from his assault rifle). Now Brace takes his action, crouching at the side of the 10-ft. wide doorway and firing at the nearest guard. His total is 14 — a hit — and he rolls 8 points of damage. The guard loses 7 vitality (he has 1 point of damage reduction) and is no longer flat-footed. Disappointed with her initiative roll, Neon-hand takes two regroup actions, raising her initiative count to 17.

A shower of glass and lead is the first sign that something is wrong. Two figures, one standing brazenly in the midst of the shattered doorway, approach from the hallway!

ROUND 1

All enemies except the guard who was attacked last round are still flat-footed.

Onyx uses his Quick Draw feat to ready his SMG as a free action. As another free action he instructs one of the guards to sound the alarm. Finally he takes two shots at the most prominent figure in the doorway, Sideshock. With totals of 16 and 23, Onyx hits and rolls 8 and 5 points damage — both hits are totally absorbed by the assault vest (and each does 2 points of subdual damage instead).

Brace uses his Expertise feat to subtract 3 from his attack rolls this round and add +3 to his Defense (the maximum number he can shift with a base attack bonus of +3). He takes two more shots at the guard he attacked previously and then uses his bonus step to enter the vault. He rolls over 11 both times, even with the –3 penalty. The guard suffers 4 and then 7 points of damage (after subtracting damage reduction), which reduces the guard's remaining vitality from 3 to 0. The remaining 8 points of damage are taken off his wounds, which drop to 4. The guard becomes fatigued and must make a Fort save (DC 10) or be stunned. The GC's roll succeeds and the guard is not stunned.

Neon-hand goes for the heart of the matter by taking a bonus step to reach the doorway (gaining ½ cover), spending a half action to aim (granting her a +1 bonus to her attack roll) and using her last action to fire at the one man in the room who isn't in a security uniform. She rolls a total of 22, a hit, then rolls 9 points of damage (inflicting 4 vitality upon Onyx after his vest and DR are considered).

Sideshock does what he does best, laying down cover fire for Brace (a full round action), bringing his rifle down to 42 shots remaining. Normally, Sideshock's cover fire action would grant Brace a +4 dodge bonus for a round, but with Sideshock's Lay Down Fire feat this is increased to +6.

The guards finally swing into action. One moves to a large wall-mounted alarm button and presses it — but nothing happens. Three guards draw their weapons and open up on Sideshock with narrow bursts (–3/+2). All of them hit, and with three separate 1d10+3 rolls for damage (+2 for the burst, +1 for Point Blank Shot), they inflict 5, 10, and 12 points of damage on the agent. Sideshock's armor and DR absorbs the first hit (resulting in another 2 subdual damage in the process, for a total of 6 taken so far), but the last two hits reduce his vitality by 4.

The other guards draw their weapons and fire wide bursts at Brace before using their 5-ft. bonus steps to take 1/4 cover behind the desks that litter the room. Even with their Point Blank Shot and burst bonuses, the guards can't touch Brace's Defense of 24 without rolling a natural 20. They miss.

As the rattle of SMGs joins the heavy chugging of Sideshock's assault rifle, Neon-hand flinches at the destruction taking place in the vault. "Watch out for the terminal!" she warns the team, then focuses her attention on the large henchman barring their path.

ROUND 2

Onyx changes tactics: he drops his SMG as a free action, makes a standard move to become adjacent to Brace, draws a taser as a free action (using his Quick Draw feat again), and attacks the agent with it. Brace is now engaged in melee combat and losses the benefit of Sideshock's cover fire. Using the taser is a melee touch attack which would ignore armor — if Brace were wearing any. Onyx adds his melee attack bonus (+5) to his roll, coming up with a 17. This hits Brace despite his Expertise feat. Brace takes 1d8 subdual damage (Onyx rolls a 6) and has to make a Fortitude save with a DC of 18 or be stunned for 1d8 rounds. He rolls a 13, but spends an action die to increase his total. The natural 4 he scores with the action die explodes, giving him another roll and a total of +9 with his department bonus. Added to his initial roll of 13, he makes his save!

Brace takes a 5-ft. step away from Onyx before firing two shots at him (still using his Expertise feat, mindful of so many enemies nearby). He hits both times doing 9 more points of damage (which is subtracted from Onyx's remaining vitality), plus 4 subdual.

Neon-hand takes two more shots at Onyx. One misses, but the other deals out maximum damage (she rolls a 10), subtracting another 7 vitality from Onyx and adding 2 to the henchman's subdual total.

Sideshock takes a half action to brace against the doorway and fires a narrow burst at one of the guards. The brace grants him a +2 bonus while the burst applies a penalty of –3. He hits, doing 9 damage to the guard.

The agents face a withering hail of fire from the guards as they all take two wide bursts this round, with four firing at Neon-hand, six at Sideshock, and four at Brace. Neon-hand's Defense of 20 (including cover) saves her from all four attacks (though one does strike the doorway right next to her — having been blocked only by the cover bonus). All but one hit Sideshock, dishing out 2 vitality and 10 subdual. Two beat Brace's Defense of 18 and he loses 13 vitality.

Sideshock's shout of warning goes unheard as the whine of bullets ricochets off the hardened steel walls...

ROUND 3

Onyx still has one more trick up his sleeve — he draws another gun, turns as a free action, and takes two half actions to strike an object: the master terminal! He makes the attacks easily (the DC is only 7), rolling 9 and 7 points of damage (a total of 6 wounds after applying the computer's hardness of 5), severely damaging the computer's delicate machinery.

Brace knows he's got to discourage any more attacks on the computer and makes two attacks on the henchman, still using his Expertise feat to the fullest. He rolls an 11 (just barely hitting) and a 17. His damage is 7 and 15 points, inflicting total of 12 vitality and 4 subdual after damage reduction.

Neon-hand takes two more shots at Onyx. One misses, but the other does 3 more points of damage after the henchman's DR is subtracted (reducing his vitality by 3), plus 2 subdual.

Sideshock opts to mow down the guards before they can further harass the team. He makes a strafe attack on 8 squares (he must fire on two empty squares to reach the guard who went for the button last round), resulting in a whopping −14 modifier to his attack! He rolls a 14, +1 for Point Blank Shot, +2 for being braced, and +7 for class and Dexterity. This brings his total attack roll up to 24. At −14 for the strafe he is one short to hit the guards without cover, and 3 short of hitting the ones behind the desks. Sadly Sideshock is out of action dice (having spent them during the break-in). But Brace still has action dice left and uses his Generous ability to roll one for his teammate, adding 5 to Sideshock's roll for a final total of 15. Sideshock hits them all, and rolls 11 points of damage! Brace spends his last action die to increase Sideshock's damage total by 4. This kills the first injured guard and knocks the second out of the fight. The others are reduced to 0 vitality points and take 3 wounds each. Two of them fail their saves and are stunned for 1d6 rounds (the GC rolls a 2 and a 5 in this case).

All three conscious guards dive for cover and go prone behind the desks, gaining 9/10 cover, rather than attacking this turn.

Onyx screams, watching his minions fall to enemy fire or dive for cover, and vows that those who live will pay dearly for their betrayal...

ROUND 4

Onyx has lost 35 vitality and has taken 14 points of subdual damage. He is only 3 points of damage away from being staggered, and can't afford to take another hit. The GC spends one of his action dice to increase Onyx's Defense (rolling an 8, which brings Onyx's total Defense to 19). Onyx decides to flee and return with minions he can lead from the rear. As a free action he uses his Tactics ability to order the remaining guards to "hold them 'til I get back!" He then makes a Total Defense action (adding 4 more to his Defense, for a total of 23), and uses his Mobility feat to run rapidly out of the vault, sliding past all three agents.

Brace delays his action.

Sideshock (knowing he only has one bullet left before he must reload) waves his weapon and threatens, "Drop 'em and live." The GC calls this an Intimidation check, and grants the guards the +1 Tactics bonus against it. Sideshock beats the DC of 12 easily, and the GC decides that the three remaining (and overpowered) guards surrender. After all, their leader just abandoned them. The guards throw down their arms and Brace and Neon-hand use their actions to bind and gag them.

"He's getting away!" Sideshock screams to the rest of the team.

"He's already gone," Brace responds, "and we have bigger problems."

Both agents gaze over to the sparking master terminal, its screen burst and its housing battered...

ROUND 5

Brace secures the three guards while Neon-hand begins an Electronics skill check augmented by her Jury-Rig ability to repair the computer. Sideshock reloads before moving a desk towards the door, preparing some cover. The guards are now considered prone and helpless, and are also gagged. Sideshock has taken only 6 points of vitality damage thanks to his armor, but has 20 points of subdual damage to show for it! Brace has taken 13 vitality and 6 subdual, while the cautious Neon-hand somehow managed not to get hit at all.

Sideshock leaps into action. "We're pressed for time here, Neon. Give me good news."

The snoop is already clipping wires from the back of her armored-laptop to the master terminal's exposed circuits. "Shouldn't be too difficult. They haven't busted a computer I can't fix!"

Brace takes up a nervous watch at the doorway, waiting for the next wave of minions to arrive...

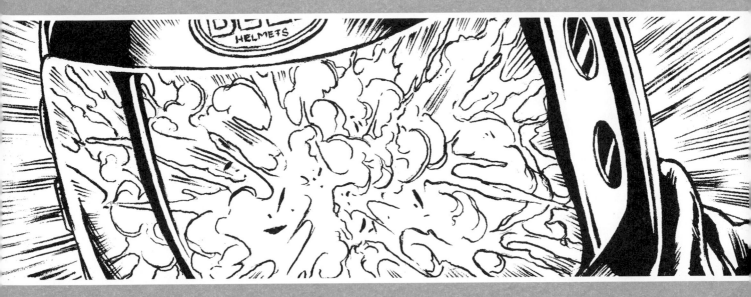

"I feel the need. The need for speed."
– Maverick,
Top Gun

CHASES

THE BASICS

One of the most prominent features of the spy serial is the chase sequence. Whether streaking across the Florida Keys in military transports, racing through alleyways of downtown London in sports cars, cutting through the narrow canals of Venice in high power speedboats, or weaving through the buttes and crevasses of the Grand Canyon in jet fighters, chases are the ultimate expression of raw speed and pure, unadulterated adrenaline.

No two chases are the same. Between hundreds of possible vehicles, thousands of possible locations, and the unexpected occurrences that plague movie chases, it is nearly impossible for a rules system to include all that might happen. *Spycraft* keeps the action abstract and fast moving, leaving the agents and the GC plenty of room to generate specifics along the way.

Special Note: The chase rules cover landbound vehicular chases in great detail. Other types of chases employ similar principles and are easily mastered once the basic system is understood. Different types of chases and ways of combining them with ground chases are described at the end of this chapter.

THE GOAL OF A CHASE

The obvious goals of any chase are, respectively, pursuit and flight. But there is more to conducting a movie chase than just motion. Especially in spy epics, chases are filled with extraordinary scenery, incredible and brazen feats of skill, and non-stop entertainment. Chases should never be dull — not for a moment. The Game Control should endeavor to present interesting backdrops and obstacles at every turn, and the agents should work individually and as a team to tackle them with exuberance and flair.

Heroism and diligence should be part of every chase. Not only is it important to pursue your prey (or attempt to escape the henchmen and minions of your enemies), it's essential that you remember the point of the game: to have fun. Chases are an excellent opportunity to take those amazing risks that the spies of myth so frequently indulge in, and to impress and entertain the other players with your sense of adventure.

Chases demand quick thinking and great ingenuity from all players. Game Controls are especially encouraged to read these rules thoroughly before running a chase sequence, so they can smoothly present the action at a breakneck pace.

VEHICLE STATISTICS

As shown on pages 147-151, vehicles have a short, simple set of statistics that define everything from how well they handle to how tough they are.

DEFENSE

This is a vehicle's base chance to be hit before taking the driver's skill into account. In practice, a driver adds his Dexterity modifier to his vehicle's Defense value when he's behind the wheel. Size is already factored into this value.

HANDLING

This number is added to all maneuver checks a driver makes while using a vehicle. Some vehicles have handling penalties, which are subtracted from maneuver checks.

HARDNESS

Just like object hardness *(see page 168),* a vehicle's hardness is subtracted from all damage it suffers before the damage is applied to the vehicle's wound points. Certain types of damage ignore hardness, including damage taken from excessive speed. When damage ignores hardness, it is mentioned in its description.

SIZE CATEGORY

Vehicles use the same size category scale as everything else *(see page 175).*

SPEED

This is how feet a vehicle may move in one full action on a standard combat grid. A vehicle's cruising and maximum speeds in miles per hour are listed under "MPH". Chase speed is determined by the MPH of one of the vehicles involved in the chase, as described under Terrain.

WOUND POINTS

This determines how much damage a vehicle can take. Vehicles don't have vitality points.

GETTING STARTED

Chases in *Spycraft* are intentionally abstract, leaving tremendous room for the GC and agents to elaborate on their maneuvers, successes, and failures. As a result, this chase system may be inserted whenever needed, allowing chases to erupt suddenly and unexpectedly, in any locale.

During a chase, one vehicle — the "predator"— is assumed to be trying to catch the other — the "prey."

TERRAIN

The Game Control and the agents should have an idea of the terrain a chase is taking place in before getting started. Terrain establishes the general conditions of a chase, as well as obstacles that drivers must avoid. Terrain falls into three basic categories: open, close, and tight.

OPEN TERRAIN

Open terrain is easy to traverse, with only slight changes in elevation and few imposing obstacles. Open terrain is defined differently for each type of chase. A few examples follow.

- **Ground chases:** Empty highways, salt flats, racetracks.

- **Water chases:** Lakes, empty marinas, open seas with fair to excellent weather.

- **Air chases:** Clear skies at 1,000 feet or higher.

- **Foot chases:** Wide, flat plains and large paved areas with few structures, fences, or obstructions.

In open terrain, the speed of a chase begins at ¾ of the maximum MPH of the fastest vehicle involved (rounded down). Open terrain chases in which one vehicle's maximum MPH is less than ¾ that of the opponent vehicle are usually over before they start.

A vehicle's maximum MPH is critical in open terrain, and the vehicle with the highest maximum MPH receives a +2 speed modifier to all maneuver checks *(see page 190)*. If only one vehicle in a chase is considered to be in open terrain (either due to two or more types of local terrain, feats, or mixed vehicle types) then that vehicle automatically receives the +2 speed bonus.

By its very nature open terrain contains few large, hard obstacles. GCs should roll a d10 each chase round which occurs in open terrain – a natural 1 indicates an obstacle has cropped up. The average DC for obstacles in open terrain is 12.

Even if a crash occurs in open terrain, vehicles usually overrun whatever they hit with little or no damage. Critical failures in open terrain are particularly bad, however, as the vehicles involved are typically moving as fast as possible.

CLOSE TERRAIN

Close terrain is generally narrow and filled with plenty of stuff to run into, clip, and burst through. Close terrain is defined differently for each type of chase. A few examples follow.

- **Ground chases:** City streets, winding dirt roads.

- **Water chases:** Narrow rivers with many rocks, busy docks, choppy seas.

- **Air chases:** Cloudy mountaintops, fields with occasional power lines, light to medium rain.

- **Foot chases:** Narrow alleys and open areas with many obstructions (such as stairways, and hospital corridors.)

Because of the difficult driving conditions, the speed of a chase in close terrain begins at ½ of the fastest vehicle's maximum MPH (rounded down).

Most obstacles in close terrain are simply overrun by vehicles going fast enough. The Game Control should roll a d6 each chase round which occurs in open terrain – a natural 1 indicates an obstacle has cropped up. Typical DCs for obstacles in close terrain is 18.

TIGHT TERRAIN

This is the most dangerous of all terrain, filled with sharp drops and large, dense obstacles. Tight terrain is defined differently for each type of chase. A few examples follow.

- **Ground chases:** Congested highways, steep downhill inclines, battlegrounds, debris-riddled areas.

- **Water chases:** Whitewater rapids, crowded marinas.

- **Air chases:** Ground level (under obstacles!), bad weather.

- **Foot chases:** Staircases, corridors, indoor parking garages, hedge mazes.

In tight terrain, the speed of a chase begins at ¼ of the fastest vehicle's maximum MPH (rounded down). Such close quarters favor nimble drivers, so if both predator and prey are in tight terrain the driver whose vehicle has the highest handling gains an additional +1 speed bonus to all maneuver checks.

Tight terrain is unstable, and drivers in these areas should be prepared for anything. GCs should roll a d4 each chase round which occurs in open terrain — a natural 1 indicates an obstacle has cropped up with a DC of 24.

INITIAL LEAD

The distance between vehicles during a chase is called the "lead," and is measured in "lengths." Lengths are an adjustable unit determined by the vehicles being used in the chase. Unless otherwise noted, one length equals 10 ft. Lengths are particularly important when the drivers shoot at each other.

At no time can the lead be less than 0 or greater than 30. If any effect reduces the lead to less than 0, the lead becomes 0. Similarly, if any result increases the lead above 30, the lead becomes 30.

Chases can start in a number of ways, but most boil down into one of two categories: predator-initiated and prey-initiated. This determines how much of a lead the prey has at the start of the chase. When the predator begins a chase, the initial lead is equal to 2d6+3 lengths (or 50-150 ft. in most cases). When a chase begins with the prey fleeing, the initial lead is 2d6+8 (or 100-200 feet). If there is no clear initiator in a chase, both sides roll initiative and the highest result is considered to have started the chase.

CHASE SPEED

Chase speed is measured in miles per hour (MPH), and is determined by terrain at the start of a chase *(see pages 185-186)*. Chase speed changes throughout the chase according to the maneuvers chosen by the both drivers each round *(see Step 1, page 187)*.

Whenever the chase speed exceeds the maximum speed of one or more involved vehicles at the end of a chase round, the vehicles in question each take 4 points of damage (reduced to 2 if the driver has the Daredevil ability). This damage is not reduced by the vehicle's hardness, and is applied in addition to all damage caused by maneuvers, crash checks (and crashes), and other effects.

CHASES: STEP BY STEP

There are seven steps to chases, which are explained in broad strokes here and then in detail in the following sections. These seven steps continue in cycles until the chase ends — either with the crash or escape of one of the vehicles.

Step 1: Choose Maneuvers

Each vehicle (or group of vehicles) secretly chooses a maneuver from the list offered. Each maneuver has strengths and weaknesses, and is usually geared toward a specific goal.

Step 2: Maneuver Checks

The drivers make an opposed maneuver check with their respective vehicle skills, applying their vehicles' handling ratings as modifiers to their rolls.

Step 3: Spend Action Dice

Each driver may spend action dice to increase his maneuver check, or activate critical successes or failures.

Step 4: Resolve Maneuvers and Adjust Lead

The effects of the maneuver which succeeds is applied and the number of lengths between the vehicles is adjusted.

Step 5: Lead & Obstacles

The lead determines which maneuvers both drivers may take in the next round of the chase. The GC rolls for obstacles.

Step 6: Other Actions

Assuming the chase continues, each passenger of each vehicle in the chase may perform one full action or two half actions. A driver may perform one half action, but receives a –4 penalty to his next maneuver check if he does so.

Step 7: Crash Rolls (if any)

If warranted, drivers check to see if they have collided with anything.

STEP 1: CHOOSE MANEUVERS

The first step during each round of a chase is choosing maneuvers. We have broken maneuvers into two basic categories: predator and prey (after the vehicles which may choose from each category).

Due to the abstract nature of chases, the distance covered and the specific locations of each vehicle are left up to the imaginations of the GC and the agents. What's important is the distance between them at any given time. The initial lead is determined as part of getting started, but should be rechecked at the start of each round. Many maneuvers may only be chosen by drivers with a certain minimum or maximum lead.

Ultimately, the goal of the predator is to decrease the lead enough that he can perform one of the finishing maneuvers (see the next step) and catch the prey, while the prey is trying to do the inverse. Chases continue until either the predator or the prey successfully performs a finishing maneuver, someone crashes, or one of the vehicles is disabled *(see Step 7)*.

MANEUVER DESCRIPTIONS

Several elements go into the description of each maneuver. Following the maneuver name is a general statement of intent for the predator or prey. The Game Control may need to modify these basic concepts slightly to fit the particulars of each chase. This is followed by several entries for most maneuvers.

Lead: This describes the minimum or maximum distance between predator and prey required to perform the maneuver. Both predator and prey tend to have more options as the two vehicles become more closely entangled.

Speed: Succeed or fail, both predator and prey's maneuvers may temporary modify the current chase speed. In the case that both predator and prey choose maneuvers that alter the chase's speed, only the highest modifier (positive or negative) applies.

Success: This describes the effects of the maneuver, which applies when a driver who chose it wins the opposed maneuver roll for the chase round.

Special: Any additional information the GC or players should be aware of about the maneuver.

Maneuvers marked "Daredevil" stress a vehicle to the limit. Agents with the Daredevil ability are able to use these maneuvers more reliably and with less damage to their vehicles. Those marked "Daredevil Only" are so extreme that only agents with the Daredevil ability may attempt them. The last maneuver in each category — "That's Impossible!" — may only be performed by an agent with the "That's Impossible!" wheelman ability.

Finishing maneuvers end the chase if performed successfully and have prerequisites that must be fulfilled before they can be attempted.

PREDATOR MANEUVERS

Each round the predator should write his maneuver down on a piece of paper and keep it secret.

All predator maneuvers are geared toward slowing down or catching the prey.

Box In (Daredevil Only, Finishing)

It takes skill to trap an opponent with minimal damage, but sometimes it's essential to use the kid gloves and take the prey intact. This requires a level of skill and panache most drivers simply do not possess, and is restricted to agents with the Daredevil class ability.

Lead: 5 lengths or less.

Success: The predator wins the chase, forcing the prey into a corner from which there is nowhere to run.

Crowd (Finishing)

Crowding, or "tailgating," is getting right up into the prey's backside and trying to force him into a collision with the environment. Generally, this option is safer for the predator than ramming, but is less likely to work.

Lead: 2 lengths or less.

Success: The predator wins the chase. If the predator's maneuver check exceeds the prey's by at least 5, the prey collides with an obstacle (a tree, storefront, or debris). The prey is assumed to have failed a crash check as described under Step 7, and the predator comes to a safe stop.

Cut Off (Daredevil, Finishing)

Generally without warning, the predator speeds up and pulls out in front of the prey, cutting him off. The predator's own vehicle becomes a barrier to stop the prey from escaping. Like most predator maneuvers, cutting someone off is invariably destructive.

Lead: 0 lengths.

Speed: The chase speed is reduced by 25 MPH this round.

Success: The predator wins the chase, pulling in front of the prey and cutting him off. If the prey fails his maneuver check, he automatically collides with the predator's vehicle; no crash check is required. Damage is applied to both vehicles per the directions under Step 7. The predator may make a Jump check (leaping from a stationary vehicle) to avoid taking damage in the collision.

Gun It

Gun it is the basic predator maneuver, in which the predator attempts to catch up with the prey in a straightforward manner, without frills or significant chance of a mishap.

Lead: Any distance.

Speed: Increase the chase speed by 10 MPH this round.

Success: The lead is reduced by a number of lengths equal to the difference between maneuver checks.

Herd

Forcing the prey to make bad choices can be as effective as chasing him down. By keeping the pressure on and cutting off the prey's options, the predator uses strategy and brute force to drive the prey into dangerous situations.

Lead: 10 lengths or less.

Success: The lead is reduced by 1 length and the prey is required to make a crash check with a DC increased by the difference between the maneuver checks. The predator is also required to make a crash check this round (but without the additional penalty).

Special: With a critical success or by beating the prey's maneuver check by 5 or more, the predator may choose to reduce both the predator and prey's crash check DCs by 5 to shift the terrain by one step at the end of the round (open or tight becomes close, and vice versa). Alternately, the predator may ignore the crash check and terrain shift entirely.

Jockey

By carefully matching the prey's movements, the predator can force the relative speeds of the two vehicles down to almost zero, stabilizing the chase so that others in the vehicle can attack.

Lead: 10 lengths or less.

Success: The lead is reduced by 1 length and the driver and all passengers in the predator vehicle gain half the difference between the maneuver checks (rounded down) as a cooperation bonus to all their attack and skill rolls targeting the prey.

Ram (Finishing)

Ram is pretty straightforward: the predator speeds up and slams into the prey, forcing him off the road, into the ground, or onto the shore. It's dirty, but generally gets the job done a lot faster than Crowd.

Lead: 5 lengths or less.

Success: The predator wins the chase, colliding with the prey. Both are assumed to have failed a crash check as described under Step 7. After the collision, both vehicles come to a halt.

Redline (Daredevil)

Redline is an advanced version of gun it, during which the predator suddenly accelerates to and remains at the vehicle's top speed. This causes incredible wear and tear on the vehicle as the engine literally burns up.

Lead: Any distance.

Speed: Increase the chase speed by 20 MPH this round.

Success: The prey's lead is reduced by a number of lengths equal to twice the difference between maneuver checks. The predator's engine suffers 4 points of damage (see Step 6). Daredevil drivers are skilled at feathering the throttle, and their engines take only 2 points of damage from redline.

Shortcut

Shortcuts can be incredibly helpful in catching up with the prey, especially in close quarters, where the prey cannot see what the predator is doing. Unfortunately, this generally means that the predator has reduced his line of sight as well, which can result in a nasty spill.

TABLE 7.1: CHASE MANEUVERS									
	Box In	Crowd	Cut Off	Gun It	Herd	Jockey	Ram	Redline	Shortcut	"That's Impossible!"
Barnstorm	–	–	–	–6/0	–	–	–	–8/0	0/–6	0/0
Bootleg Reverse	0/–6	0/–4	–8/0	0/–6	0/0	0/–2	–4/0	–4/0	–6/0	0/0
Hairpin Turn	–	–	–	0/–4	–	–	–	–2/0	0/–4	0/0
Lure	0/–4	–4/0	0/–4	–2/0	–2/0	0/0	0/–2	0/–2	0/–6	0/0
Pull Ahead	–6/0	0/–4	–2/0	0/0	–6/0	–2/0	–2/0	0/–4	0/–4	0/0
Set Up	–2/0	–4/0	0/–4	0/–4	0/–2	–2/0	0/–4	0/0	–4/0	0/0
Stunt	–	–	–	–2/0	–	–	–	–4/0	0/–2	0/0
Vanish	–	–	–	0/–4	–	–	–	0/–6	–4/0	0/0
Zig-zag	–2/0	0/–6	–2/0	–6/0	0/–6	0/–2	–4/0	–2/0	0/0	0/0
"That's Impossible!"	0/0	0/0	0/0	0/0	0/0	0/0	0/0	0/0	0/0	0/0

How to Use This Table: Find the predator maneuver across the top and the prey maneuver along the side. Cross reference to find the modifier for each vehicle this round. The modifier before the slash is applied to the predator's maneuver check this round, while the number after the slash is applied to the prey's maneuver check this round.

Lead: Any distance.

Speed: The chase speed is reduced by 15 MPH this round.

Success: The lead is reduced by a number of lengths equal to the twice the difference between maneuver checks. The predator must make a crash check during Step 7.

"That's Impossible!" (Daredevil Only, may be Finishing)

"That's Impossible!" allows you to choose any other predator maneuver and benefit from its effects without applying the modifiers from Table 7.1: Chase Maneuvers. This is generally beneficial for the higher-level driver in the chase.

Lead: Per maneuver.

Success: Per maneuver.

PREY MANEUVERS

Each round the prey should write his maneuver down on a piece of paper and keep it secret for now.

All prey maneuvers are geared toward escaping the predator.

Barnstorm (Daredevil, Finishing)

"Barnstorming" is commonly associated with planes, but any vehicle may attempt it. A car, for instance, can storm a shopping mall, while a boat may storm the wreckage of a burning oil tanker.

Lead: 25 lengths or more.

Success: The prey wins the chase, barreling through a cluttered area. The prey's vehicle automatically takes 10 points of damage. Daredevil drivers make this sort of thing look easy, and their vehicles only suffer damage equal to 10 minus the difference between the maneuver checks. Both drivers must make crash checks during Step 7.

Bootleg Reverse (Daredevil)

In this cinema staple, the prey brakes and turns hard to one side, so that he is suddenly pointing in the opposite direction. This is incredibly useful to suddenly increase the prey's lead. Unfortunately this only works when the predator is a little too close for comfort.

Lead: 10 lengths or less.

Speed: The chase speed is reduced by 15 MPH this round.

Success: The lead is increased by a number of lengths equal to twice the difference between maneuver checks. The prey's tires suffer 4 points of damage *(see Step 6)*. Daredevil drivers are highly practiced at controlled spins, and their tires take only 2 points of damage from pulling a bootleg reverse.

Hairpin Turn (Finishing)

Just like zig-zag, hairpin turn forces the predator down an erratic path as both cars speed around tight bends and whip around blind curves until one falls out of the race. Hairpin turns tend to be longer and far sharper than those taken with zig-zag, resulting in a much greater chance of crashing.

Lead: 20 lengths or more.

Speed: The chase speed is reduced by 25 MPH this round.

Success: The prey wins the chase, taking one or more turns the predator can't manage. Both the predator and prey must make crash checks during Step 7.

Lure

In many ways the prey controls the direction of the chase, and can lead the predator into all kinds of foolish situations.

Lead: Any distance.

Success: The lead is increased by 1 and the predator is required to make a crash check with a DC increased by the difference between the maneuver checks. The prey is also required to make a crash check this round (without the additional penalty).

Special: With a critical success or by beating the predator's maneuver check by 5 or more, the prey may choose to reduce both the predator and prey's crash check DCs by 5 to shift the terrain by one step at the end of the round (open or tight becomes close and visa versa). Alternately, the prey may ignore the crash check and terrain shift entirely.

Additionally, if the prey beats the predator's maneuver roll by 4 or more using this maneuver, he may reverse the vehicles' positions, becoming the predator until the end of the current chase round. This allows the prey to attack with any forward-mounted vehicular weapons during Step 6.

Pull Ahead

This is the fundamental prey maneuver, attempting to get as far ahead of the pursuit as possible.

Lead: Any distance.

Speed: Increase the chase speed by 10 MPH this round.

Success: The prey's lead is increased by a number of lengths equal to the difference between maneuver checks.

Set Up

Instead of running, the prey leads the predator on a merry chase — usually to the tune of gunfire.

Lead: 10 lengths or less.

Success: The lead is increased by 1 and the driver and all passengers in the prey vehicle gain half the difference between the maneuver checks (rounded down) as a cooperation bonus to all their attack and skill rolls targeting the predator.

Additionally, if the prey beats the predator's maneuver roll by 4 or more using this maneuver, he may reverse the vehicles' positions, becoming the predator until the end of the current chase round. This allows the prey to attack with any forward-mounted vehicular weapons during Step 6.

Stunt (Daredevil Only, Finishing)

Stunts are incredible feats of skill, such as leaping a car across a rising toll bridge or skipping a boat across a pier, setting off an explosion among a line of conveniently-placed gasoline cans. This sort of maneuver is just this side of suicidal, and only the most talented or foolhardy drivers can attempt to setup this 'perfect' escape.

Lead: 20 lengths or more.

Success: The prey wins the chase, performing a stunt the predator just can't manage. If the prey's maneuver check exceeds the predator's by at least 5, the predator must make a crash check in Step 7.

"That's Impossible!" (Daredevil Only, May be Finishing)

"That's Impossible!" allows you to choose any other prey maneuver and benefit from its effects without applying the modifiers from Table 7.1: Chase Maneuvers. This is generally beneficial for the higher-level driver in the chase.

Lead: Per maneuver.

Success: Per maneuver.

Vanish (Finishing)

In a display of driving virtuosity and pure velocity, the prey leaves all pursuit behind, choking on his dust.

Lead: 30 lengths.

Speed: Increase the chase speed by 20 MPH this round.

Success: The prey wins the chase.

Zig-Zag

Zig-zag involves purposefully clipping neighboring obstacles, terrain, and even other vehicles in an attempt to direct them into the predator's path, slowing him down. Unfortunately, this increases the chance that one of the prey's "clips" may become a collision.

Lead: Any distance.

Success: The lead is increased by a number of lengths equal to twice to the difference between maneuver checks. The prey must make a crash check during Step 7.

STEP 2: MANEUVER CHECKS

The drivers reveal their maneuvers. Determine any changes to the chase speed this round as a result of maneuvers. Each driver makes an opposed check with his respective vehicle skill, possibly applying modifiers from the following sources:

- Their vehicles' handling modifiers.
- Any speed bonuses they may gain from the terrain.
- Modifiers from Table 7.1: Chase Maneuvers.
- Any chase feats the drivers may have.
- Any damage their vehicles have suffered *(see Step 7)*.

If one driver succeeds, the effects of his maneuver are applied during Step 4. If neither driver succeeds or the opposed roll results are a tie, the effects of neither maneuver are applied, and the chase continues without any maneuver effect (except for speed, which is always applied). If both drivers succeed, the effects of the maneuver taken by the driver with the highest check are applied during Step 4.

If a driver scores a critical success with a maneuver check, then he may only lose the opposed check to another critical success with a higher total, and receives a +4 bonus to his maneuver check the following round. If a driver scores a critical failure with a maneuver check, he must make a crash check during Step 7.

STEP 3: SPEND ACTION DICE

After making their maneuver checks, drivers may spend action dice to increase their rolls and activate critical successes or failures. Remember that some class abilities may allow the driver to roll two dice for every action die spent.

STEP 4: RESOLUTION

The effects of the winning driver's maneuver are applied to the chase. Once again, the lead cannot at any time be less than 0. If any effect reduces the lead to less than 0, the lead becomes 0. If the winning driver chose a finishing maneuver, then the chase ends after the remainder of this round's steps are completed. If not, the chase will continue with a new round following Step 7, unless obstacles, crash checks, or combat end the chase.

STEP 5: OBSTACLES

The Game Control may wish to throw in some obstacles to add to the action. These can range from an overturned gas tanker and sections of heavy road construction (for ground chases) to a blimp or a fireworks display (for air chases) to a low bridge or a whale (for water chases) to a locked door (for foot chases). An obstacle requires either a Reflex save or vehicle skill roll against the obstacle's DC. If the roll fails, the driver must make a crash check during step 7.

The prey makes his obstacle check before the predator does. The base DC for avoiding an obstacle is determined by the terrain *(see page 185)*, and the GC may increase or decrease the DC by up to +/- 2 depending on the size or complexity of the challenge.

Obstacles are intended as spice, not the main focus of chases, and can be ignored completely by the GC. If the predator and prey get in a rut, GCs should use obstacles to shake things up. If the drivers are keeping things dynamic, the GC should reserve obstacles for a more effective time. The frequency that obstacles crop up is based on the local terrain *(see page 185)*.

Optional Rule: The GC may either only introduce an obstacle by spending an action die, or use the recommended random die rolls to determine when obstacles show up and spend an action die for each extra obstacle he includes.

STEP 6: OTHER ACTIONS

Whether the chase has ended due to a finishing maneuver or not, all passengers of all vehicles are allowed one full action or two half actions. In addition, any driver may take one half action at the cost of a –4 penalty to his next maneuver check. In most ways, chase combat follows the rules presented for standard combat, with a few significant differences.

ACTIONS DURING CHASES

During chases, agents act in initiative order as usual, but many actions are restricted or illogical. The driver of a vehicle is limited to a single half action (at most) and thus is restricted from taking any full actions.

Initiative Actions During Chases
Initiative actions work normally during chases.

Attack Actions During Chases
A passenger in a moving vehicle suffers a –2 penalty to his attack rolls. This penalty is increased to –6 for the driver of the vehicle. Further, the driver and all passengers suffer an additional –2 penalty to their attack rolls for every 50 mph the vehicle is traveling (rounded down).

Melee attacks may only be made if the prey's lead is 0 and/or the attacker is in or on the same vehicle as his target.

Movement Actions During Chases
Movement actions may be taken, but a Balance check is needed in most cases. A Jump check is required to leap between two moving vehicles. Finally, if an agent falls from a moving vehicle, he suffers normal falling damage *(see page 236)* using the speed of the vehicle (in MPH) as the distance of the fall. Thus, an agent who falls off a car traveling at 75 MPH takes damage as though he has fallen 75 ft.

Other Actions During Chases
Other actions may or may not be possible, and are subject to the Game Control's discretion. In general, only skills and feats that don't require movement remain unaffected.

ATTACKING VEHICLES

During a chase, vehicles are attacked more often than agents. Consequently, chase attacks are assumed to hit an opposing vehicle unless a critical hit is made or the driver is attempting to ram bystanders *(see page 192)*. The difficulty of striking a vehicle is determined by its Defense *(see below)*.

Agents in vehicles may fire hand weapons (from pistols to portable rocket launchers) in any direction. This may require them to shoot out one of their own windows or hang out the side of the vehicle to take a shot, but when the heat is on few agents flinch at such behavior.

Because most vehicle weapons (particularly those mounted on aircraft) can only be fired in a forward arc, the predator has a distinct advantage when it comes to tactical weapons (tank turrets and rear mounted weapons being clear exceptions). However, if the prey beats the predator's maneuver roll by 4 or more using the Lure or Set Up maneuvers, he may reverse the vehicles' positions, becoming the predator until the end of the current chase round. This allows the prey to attack with any forward-mounted vehicular weapons during this step. Also, if the predator ever breaks off the chase, the prey may choose to become the predator, maintaining the current lead (and allowing him to attack with forward-mounted weapons).

Vehicle Defense
A vehicle's Defense is equal to its base Defense plus the driver's Dexterity modifier. A vehicle's base Defense already takes its size into account.

Critical Hits Against Vehicles
When you score a critical hit against an auto, truck, or other enclosed ground vehicle, roll on the following table.

d10 Roll	Group/Location
1	Engine
2-3	Steering
4-7	Tires
8-9	Weapon
0	Window

When attacking a motorcycle or open-topped (convertible) vehicle it becomes much easier to hit the occupants. Use the following table.

d10	Group/Location
1	Engine
2-3	Steering
4-6	Tires
7	Weapon
8-0	Window

After you have rolled a hit location, consult the appropriate entry to determine the critical hit's effect.

Engine: The vehicle's hardness is not subtracted from the damage done by the critical hit. On the second and each subsequent engine critical, the vehicle loses 10% of its top speed. This loss is cumulative with previous speed losses. Thus, if a vehicle suffers three critical hits to its engine, it loses 30% of its top speed.

Steering: In addition to suffering the normal damage from the attack, the vehicle's handling is reduced by 1 for every 10% of its maximum wound points the attack inflicts (rounded down). Thus, a vehicle with 45 wound points would lose 1 point from its handling modifier for every 4 points of damage a critical hit inflicts to its steering.

Tires: Instead of dealing damage to the vehicle, one of its tires is attacked. Normal tires can suffer 5 wound points before bursting. When a tire bursts, the driver must make a crash check (applying all handing penalties for burst tires). In addition, the driver suffers a –2 handling penalty for each tire that bursts (if the vehicle has 9 or fewer tires), or for each 2 tires that burst (if the vehicle has 10 or more tires). The maximum penalty burst tires can apply is –10, no matter how many tires the vehicle has. If all if the vehicle's tires have already burst (or if it has no tires!) when this critical result comes up, this critical hit instead targets the vehicle's steering.

Weapon: The damage done by the attack is applied to one of the vehicle's mounted weapons (see Damaging Objects, page 168). At the GC's discretion, this critical hit may strike one of the vehicle's communications or sensor items (e.g. a scanner, radio, or radar antenna) instead. If the target has no mounted weapons or equipment, this critical hit instead targets the vehicle's tires.

Window: When this result comes up, it means that the attack has smashed through a window or "soft spot" in the vehicle and is likely to hit an occupant. Select one of the occupants at random (or rely on the GC to determine who is in the line of fire) and compare the attack roll to his Defense (ignoring Dexterity modifiers) to see if he is hit. If not, and there is someone sitting behind him in the line of fire, check to see if that person is hit. If the attack doesn't hit either occupant, then it is considered to have harmlessly passed through the passenger compartment.

BYSTANDERS

Sometimes, the GC may determine that the chase terrain contains bystanders who can attack and be attacked by vehicles involved in the chase. This usually happens in close and tight terrain, where chases can take place in populated areas like warehouses and parking garages.

When attacking bystanders with a vehicle, the driver uses his Driver skill to make the attack, applying all attack modifiers that normally apply in chases. If he

hits, he does 1d6 damage for every 10 MPH of his vehicle speed. Critical hits are applied to wounds as normal.

Bystanders can target vehicles and their occupants as well, using the rules under Attacking Vehicles, above.

STEP 7: DAMAGE & CRASHES

The last step in every chase round is to apply damage (if any) to each vehicle, and see if they have collided with the environment (or each other).

VEHICLE DAMAGE

When a vehicle has been hit by an attack, damage is rolled normally and any applicable cover is subtracted *(see page 170)*. Then the vehicle's hardness (if any) reduces the number again *(see page 184)*. Any damage remaining must be absorbed by the vehicle itself.

VEHICLE WOUND CHECKS

There are four conditions a vehicle can be in after suffering damage.

Vehicle Okay: A vehicle which has not yet been reduced by half its maximum wound points has no modifiers.

Vehicle Crippled: A vehicle which has been reduced to fewer than half its maximum wound points is crippled. Its handling is reduced by 5. The driver must make an immediate crash check with a +5 modifier to the DC.

Vehicle Disabled: A vehicle which has been reduced to 0 wound points or less stalls and comes to a halt. The chase ends. The driver must make an immediate crash check with a +10 penalty to the DC.

Vehicle Destroyed: A vehicle which has suffered more than twice its maximum wound points is destroyed. The vehicle rolls, skids, or plummets to a halt and then explodes. This deals damage like a failed crash check without the extra damage from the driver's failed check *(see opposite)*. Occupants of the vehicle make Jump or Tumble checks (DC 20, +2 for every 25 MPH the vehicle was traveling when the crash occurred) to jump free of the crash, reducing their damage from the crash by half.

CRASH CHECKS

Crash checks should be made in four instances.

- When the vehicle's tire bursts.
- When the driver scores a critical failure with his maneuver check.
- When a successful maneuver calls for a crash check.
- When damage to a vehicle calls for a crash check.

A crash check works like a maneuver check, but a driver makes only one crash check per round. The base DC for a crash check is 15. If a driver is required to make multiple crash checks in a round he instead makes a single check, adding 5 to the DC for every additional crash check the driver has been asked to make this round.

In addition, the following modifiers apply:

Circumstance	DC Modifier
Open terrain	–5
Close terrain	+0
Tight terrain	+5
Every full 25 MPH of speed	+2

Whenever a driver fails a crash check, his vehicle collides with the environment (or the other vehicle, if the successful maneuver calls for it). Damage to each vehicle (and occupant) equals 1d6 for every 10 MPH of vehicle speed, +1 for every point by which the driver failed his crash check.

Each occupant of the vehicle may make a Jump or Tumble check (DC equal to the failed crash check) to jump free of the vehicle, reducing the damage by half.

After the wreck, roll d%. If you roll over the speed (in MPH) the vehicle was traveling at the time of the wreck, then it is upright after the crash. If the vehicle survives the wreck with at least 1 wound point, then it still runs.

REPAIRING DAMAGE TO VEHICLES

An agent with the Mechanics skill may attempt to repair a damaged vehicle if he has the proper parts and tools. At the end of every day of repair, the agent makes a Mechanics check and consults the table below to see how many wound points are restored to the vehicle. Repairs cost 1/50 the original value of the vehicle per day if you perform them – a professional demands 1/25 the original value of the vehicle per day to repair the damage.

A critical success with the Mechanic check means that you automatically repair the maximum number of wound points possible according to the table rather than rolling for it (e.g. if you score a critical success with a Mechanics check of 27, you repair 30 wound points instead of 5d6).

A critical failure with a Mechanics check not only fails to repair damage, it lowers the vehicle's maximum wound points by 1d6. If this reduces a vehicle to less than 1 wound point, the vehicle is irreparably destroyed.

Mechanics Check	Damage Fixed
Up to 9	2d4 (1)*
10-14	2d6 (2)
15-19	3d6 (3)
20-24	4d6 (4)
25-29	5d6 (5)
30-34	6d6 (6)
Every +5	+1d6 (+1)

* The numbers in parentheses are the number of handling points repaired that day (if any have been lost to damage).

GETTING OFF THE GROUND

The *Spycraft* chase system is designed to accommodate all types of chases, though it primarily simulates action between ground vehicles. Few alterations are needed to handle air, foot, or water chases, though. Simply adjust the name and feel of the various maneuvers to make them more appropriate to the type of chase at hand. For instance, you might fly through cloud cover when performing a zig-zag maneuver during an air chase.

The only real game effect you need to worry about during such hybrid chases is the effect of the chase's environment on the maneuvers and crashes. After all, a jet crashing into the side of a mountain is far likelier to result in fatalities than an ocean liner that runs ashore. To represent this, your GC may wish to double or halve the damage caused by crashes, or apply bonuses or penalties to maneuver checks, as he deems appropriate.

AIR CHASES

Aircraft chases come in two general categories: fast and really, really fast! Some terminology is swapped out ("drivers" become "pilots") and naturally the maneuver rolls are based on the Pilot skill. Because aircraft have more room to maneuver in most cases, and any sort of collision between them can easily be fatal for both parties, most chases end with one or the other vehicles being forced down by damage. To give a better feel for the action, switch the maneuver names as follows:

Predator Maneuver	Air Equivalent
Crowd	Force Down
Shortcut	Intercept
Cut Off	Collision!

Prey Maneuver	Air Equivalent
Bootleg Reverse	Roll Out
Hairpin Turn	Veer Off!
Pull Ahead	Afterburn
Zig-Zag	Break Right! / Left!

Civilian prop-planes, helicopters, hang-gliders, and ultralights can all become involved in fast air chases. Like ground vehicles, the basic length for such chases is 10'. Small aircraft tend to use low altitude and ground features for cover, so chases can quickly shift into close and even tight terrain. Obstacles include power-lines, radio antennas and even flocks of birds.

High-speed air chases involve jet aircraft and exotic gadget-based vehicles. Altitudes tend to be higher but speeds are increased to such a degree that cloud banks and whole mountain ranges start to crowd the sky a bit. Lengths are increased to 100 ft., but vehicles (and range increments) tend to be much larger when fighting in the open sky.

Also, agents can often parachute out of high-speed aircraft (either in ejection seats or with strap-on chutes). When this happens, the pilot makes a single vehicle skill check (DC equal to the vehicle's crash check) to evacuate all the vehicle's occupants. If successful, all agents in ejection seats or chutes are able to escape with only minor (1d6–1) injuries.

CRASHES

Air chases are conducted in the same fashion as ground vehicle chases, but crashing is both less frequent and much more severe. The base DC for crash checks is reduced to 10. If there is no hard terrain or other aircraft logically available to collide with, the aircraft stalls out. The pilot may make a single Mechanics check (DC equal to the full DC for the crash check, without the –10 modifier for air chases) to restart the aircraft. If he fails, he must either eject or face impact.

The increased speeds of air combat make crash damage potentially very high, but most aircraft have superior safety equipment to mitigate a good deal of it. Aerial crash damage is only 1d10 for every 50 MPH the aircraft is going. This is considered a "rough landing" rather than a truly cataclysmic collision. If a pilot ever rolls a critical failure with a crash roll he comes in for a "hard crash," computing damage using the more deadly 1d6 per 10 MPH ratio.

CRITICALS

Aircraft are far more vulnerable to strikes against their engines than ground vehicles. Any two criticals against an aircraft's engines force the vehicle to break off the chase and make a crash check or suffer a rough landing, as described above. A third critical to the

engines results in an automatic hard crash. Flaps replace wheels, and mirror them in all respects, including taking damage from a bootleg reverse/roll out maneuver.

d10	Group/Location
1-3	Engine
4-6	Steering
7	Flaps
8-9	Weapon
0	Window

WATER CHASES

High speed ski-boats and powerful racing are almost as much a staple of spy action as the muscle car. The Driver skill is replaced by the Boating skill for all rolls. Terrain depends on the weather and the room the boats have to maneuver. Innocent fishing boats or slow tugs provide convenient obstacles for the GC, and narrow waterways can channel the action as easily as a road. Lengths remain at 10 ft. and all driving maneuvers parallel with similar techniques on the water.

CRASHES

Speeds, safety equipment, and damage are comparable to ground chases, with one exception: jumping into water hurts less. If an agent is able to jump out of the vehicle he takes one fewer point of damage per die (to a minimum of one point of damage per die).

CRITICALS

Boats risk the possibility of being damaged below the waterline and taking on water. This possibility replaces "steering" criticals, and mirrors the effects of that critical hit in all respects.

d10	Group/Location
1-2	Engine
3-5	Holed
6-7	Weapon
8-0	Window

FOOT CHASES

The last major variation well suited for the chase system is the foot chase. This variation also includes scuba chases and the use of aids like horses or diver-draggers. If an agent is on foot he uses the Balance skill to make maneuver checks. While swimming or in scuba gear he uses the Swim skill. Agents on horseback use the Handle Animal skill. Lengths are standard 5-ft. squares during foot chases. Agents on foot are considered to have a handling equal to their Dexterity modifier (which is effectively doubled as their Dexterity modifier is normally added to handling to determine the maneuver check bonus).

Obstacles for foot chases range from fences and stacks of boxes to milling crowds of people and parked or moving cars.

CRASHES

A crash on foot is a "spill" as the agent falls down, collides with a wall, or tears his wet suit on sharp coral. The damage is 1d6, with a +1d6 penalty to the agent's next maneuver roll as he regains his feet or rights himself in the water. Agents on a mount or riding a bicycle double this (2d6 damage and a +2d6 maneuver penalty as they re-mount).

CRITICALS

Without a vehicle, criticals for foot chases are handled per the normal combat rules in Chapter 6.

OTHER CHASE VARIATIONS

This section details all the miscellaneous rules which don't fit well anywhere else in the chapter.

VEHICLE TEAMS

Sometimes the predator or prey has the advantage of a whole fleet of vehicles with which to chase or distract their opponents in a chase. When this happens, use the coordination rules on page 39 to make all vehicle skill rolls.

Optional Rule: If you prefer to make a single roll for all the vehicles on a team, designate one driver and his vehicle as the leader; he makes all the vehicle rolls during the chase, adding a +2 bonus for each additional vehicle on the team (to a maximum of +10 to his roll).

MASSIVE PREY

Agents often find themselves forced to pursue massive vehicles that cannot be stopped by ordinary means. Trains, heavily armored buses, experimental aircraft carriers, jetliners, and even rogue intercontinental ballistic missiles could fall into this category.

While such vehicles often have virtually non-existent handling ratings, they can quickly reach formidable speeds and simply plow through most obstacles. Massive prey are always considered to be in open terrain (though vehicles chasing after them are not always so fortunate — especially if debris is left behind after a massive vehicle shatters an obstacle).

Massive vehicles may not be herded, boxed in, or crowded by the predator (eliminating those options from the predator's maneuver choices). Ram or cut off may be options, but the predator must carefully consider whether doing so will cause enough damage to the prey to slow it down or disable it (and how much damage it will cause to the predator vehicle as well).

Similarly, the prey may only choose between pull ahead and set-up, and has no finishing maneuvers except vanish. If the prey vehicle does not know it is being chased, is uncontrolled, or is on autopilot, it may only choose pull ahead until it reaches a lead of 30 lengths, at which point it attempts to vanish (switching back to pull ahead if the lead drops below 30 lengths).

While most instances require one side to disable or destroy their opponent to bring the chase to a close, chases with massive vehicles may end with the predator boarding the massive prey. Any time the predator succeeds with a crash check, he may make a Jump check (DC equal to the crash check DC) to board the massive prey vehicle. Failure results in the chase continuing as normal. A critical failure indicates that the agent attempting to board the massive prey vehicle has fallen away from both vehicles, taking damage according to the relative speeds of the vehicles (if on the ground or in the water), or the distance fallen (if in the air).

Because the predator usually has to parallel the course of the massive prey, add one length to the lead when determining the distance for any weapons fire exchanged between the vehicles.

HYBRID CHASES

Cars chasing robbers fleeing on foot, helicopters barreling after speedboats, even old-style horse riders racing alongside a slow-moving train – the options are limitless. Hybrid chases mix elements from almost any type of chase. There are a few things to consider when creating such innovative scenarios. Most important is whether the prey can easily elude the predator. A car chase after a man on foot (usually) ends the moment he ducks into a building. A truck chasing a boat along a dock only works as long as the boat can't turn away and leave the hunter at the pier's edge. While the chase system can handle such hybrid chases, they are likely to end within one or two rounds, with the obvious result (unless the GC has arranged for the terrain to limit the prey's options). In such cases, the chase system becomes a distraction from the action rather than the focus of it, and you're usually better off with a blanket description of the brief chase before getting on with the rest of the mission.

Another feature of hybrid chases is that obstacles don't have to be symmetrical. The driver of a sports car streaking into a tunnel may not have to deal with any obstacles, but the pilot of the helicopter chasing him is likely to have a very serious problem on his hands! Common-sense use of the terrain and maneuver rules should allow for an endless variety of chases to match the most inventive movie scenes – use them as a guide to apply conditional modifiers and interpret the maneuver results with as much zeal as you can muster!

TIME LIMIT

The presence of a bomb, the arrival of reinforcements, or the approach of a steep cliff can place a time limit on a chase. Such elements can add an extra dimension of tension and excitement to the process. It's important, however, to allow enough time for a reasonable outcome before the time limit expires. The GC is encouraged to permit at least 5 rounds for agents to escape or overtake the opposition before unleashing the special consequences. Further tension can be introduced if the GC doesn't tell the agents how much time is left...

CHAIN REACTION

A chase may call for the prey to elude several pursuers in a row, as newcomers take over for failed predators. This is particularly common when eluding the police, who may route a variety of hunters to the scene as early efforts are thwarted. This is also a good time to utilize hybrid chases: after escaping from a group of patrol cars, an agent might have to shake a helicopter or two before making it home free.

CHASE EXAMPLE

FADE IN...

Agents Donovan Godding (codename: Sideshock) and Helen Walker (Codename: Feather) are tailing a known terrorist-courier. Sideshock is a 5th-level soldier (Dex 16), as is Feather, who's also an excellent shot with her .30-06 rifle. Sideshock is driving their Agency-issued Lancer-Sport sedan (Wnds 100, Def 10, Max MPH 110, Hnd +3, Hrd 4) with a Driver skill of 8 and the Speed Demon feat.

Eiji Nakamuro (Codename: Skybreaker) has been hired to transport a canister containing a dangerous toxin. Skybreaker is a 6th-level wheelman (Dex 17) who prefers airborne operations. Still, he has a Driver skill of 6 and, more importantly, the Daredevil ability, Baby It and One Hand on the Wheel feats. He is driving Saito-Industrial's Race/Arrow 2000 racing motorcycle (Wnds 25, Def 17, Max 140, Hnd +7, Hrd 2). The canister is hidden in a nondescript ice-chest strapped to the back of his bike.

The chase starts on an empty freeway (open terrain), so the average speed is a blazing 105 mph (3/4 the Arrow's top speed). The GC decides that the bio-weapon counts as the motorcycle's "weapon" on the critical hits table. With the predator initiating the chase, Sideshock is able to close to 9 lengths (2d6+3, rolling a 6) before Skybreaker realizes he's been made. Rolling initiative as normal gives Skybreaker a 16, Feather a 13, and Sideshock a 9.

ROUND 1

(Lead: 9 lengths; Terrain: Open; Speed: 105 mph)

Step 1: Sideshock opts to redline as his first maneuver, hoping to close quickly. Skybreaker opts to set up so he can shoot at the car with his machine pistol.

Step 2: The redline maneuver punches the chase speed up to 125 mph! This is greater than the Lancer's maximum speed so the car takes 4 points of damage. Sideshock adds his Driver skill, Dex mod, skill feat bonus, handling, and bonus from the table (8 + 3 + 2 + 3 + 0) for a bonus of +16 to his maneuver roll. Skybreaker adds his Driver skill, Dexterity modifier, handling, speed bonus (he has the faster vehicle and is in open terrain), and table bonus (6 + 3 + 7 + 2 + 0) for a total of +18 to his roll. Sideshock rolls a 6 for a total of 22. Skybreaker rolls a commanding 17, for a total of 35.

Step 3: Sideshock knows that an action die isn't going to change the outcome this turn, so he decides not to spend any. Skybreaker's got all the edge he needs, so he saves his dice for later.

Step 4: Skybreaker's set up increases the lead by 1 to 10, and gives him a +6 ((35−22 = 13) / 2) bonus to attack rolls targeting the predator this turn. He opts not to turn his vehicle on Sideshock's Lancer-S (an option since he beat Sideshock's maneuver total by 4 or more).

Step 5: The GC rolls a d10 for obstacles — 6, none yet.

Step 6: Skybreaker acts first, taking a half-round action to fire a burst at the car following him. He receives a −6 penalty for shooting while driving and another −4 for going over 100 MPH, but that is partially offset by the +6 bonus he racked up from his maneuver. The distance between the vehicles is 100 ft. (10 lengths at 10 ft. each). As a 6th level wheelman with a 17 Dex using burst fire, his total ranged attack bonus is +6. He rolls a 10, easily hitting the Lancer-S (Def 10 + Sideshock's Dexterity modifier of +3, for total of 13). He rolls 8 points of damage, doing 4 wounds to the Lancer after its hardness (4) reduces the damage. Feather, not wanting to hit the toxin, opts to take the regroup action to improve her initiative (raising it to 18). Sideshock decides to keep both hands on the wheel.

Step 7: Neither vehicle is at risk of crashing this round.

Sideshock and Feather look on in horror as their prey not only pulls forward, but opens up on them with a machine pistol! Bullets rattle off the car like hail and a spider web of broken glass appears across the windshield. "He's too fast!" Sideshock yells. "We have to force him off this freeway!"

ROUND 2

(Lead: 10 lengths, Terrain: Open, Speed: 125 mph)

Step 1: Skybreaker tries to build an unbeatable lead with pull ahead. Sideshock chooses herd.

Step 2: Skybreaker pulling ahead raises the chase speed even higher, to 135 mph, which inflicts another 4 wounds on his vehicle (reducing its total wounds to 17). Skybreaker suffers a −2 penalty to his maneuver check for the half action he took last round (normally −4, reduced by One Hand on the Wheel...) so he adds +16 to his roll. Sideshock receives a terrible −6 penalty from the table, leaving him at only +10. Skybreaker rolls a 16, but Sideshock rolls 19 – a threat with his Speed Demon feat!

Step 3: Sideshock activates his critical success, which assures him of victory — as well as the result he most needs this round. Skybreaker knows that he can't win the maneuver check without a critical, so he spends no action dice.

Step 4: The successful herd maneuver drops the lead by one to 9, and both drivers must make a crash check. Since he scored a critical success, Sideshock may drop the crash check DCs by 5 to shift the terrain one category. He does so, opting for the terrain to change to close at the end of the round.

Step 5: The GC rolls a 3 — still no obstacles.

Step 6: Feather has the first action now and aims before firing. The range is still 90 ft. (less than 1 range increment for her rifle). But shooting from a vehicle as a passenger applies a −2 penalty, and going over 50 MPH applies another −2. Hitting the cycle requires a 20 (17 Defense, plus Skybreaker's +3 Dex mod). Feather rolls a total of 20, just enough! She rolls a 4 for damage, reduced to 2 by the bike's hardness. Sideshock also takes a shot (he knows he's got the bonus from his critical coming next round), but he suffers a −6 for being a driver and another −2 for the current chase speed. He rolls a 5, missing.

Skybreaker devotes himself fully to the chase this round and does not take a half action.

Step 7: Both drivers make a crash check, reduced by 5 in Step 4. The 135 mph speed adds a +10 modifier to the DC, bringing it to 20 (15 + 10 − 5). Sideshock rolls a 15 and Skybreaker rolls an 18 – both succeed, and neither vehicle crashes.

In a freakishly effective play, Sideshock's Lancer suddenly swerves towards the Arrow, forcing it down a nearby off ramp. A shot rings out and Skybreaker feels his ride jerk under him as the high-power slug glances off the rear wheelguard.

ROUND 3

(Lead: 9 lengths; Terrain: Close, Speed: 70 mph)

Step 1: The terrain is now close, so the average speed of the chase resets to 70 mph (half the Arrow's top speed). This turn, Skybreaker's once again chooses the pull ahead maneuver. Sideshock, sensing the cycle's next move, redlines again.

Step 2: Redlining has the largest speed modifier, and raises the chase speed to 90 mph. Sideshock gets a +4 modifier for his critical last turn, but that is balanced by the –4 he suffers from having taken a half action. He rolls a 15 (+16), for a total of 31. Skybreaker lost his +2 speed bonus when he was forced out of open terrain, and receives a –4 from the maneuver table. He rolls a 9 (+12, after the maneuver table result is applied), for a total of 21.

Step 3: Skybreaker spends an action die. Because of his core ability, he rolls two dice (both d6s, for a total of +11, bringing his total to 32). Sideshock smells the chance for victory and spends an action die as well (it explodes, for a result of +5, and a total of 36).

Step 4: Sideshock's Lancer-S automatically takes 4 points of damage from redline and the lead is cut by twice the difference between the maneuver rolls (from 9 to 1).

Step 5: The GC rolls a d6 for obstacles – 2, none this round.

Step 6: Feather takes another half action to aim, then fires again, rolling a natural 20 – bullseye! She activates the critical and rolls on the critical table for motorcycles and other open vehicles. Hoping not to hit the ice chest, she rolls the die and gets a 3 (the steering). After rolling damage and subtracting hardness, 8 wounds go into the steering of the bike. This is more than 30% of the Arrow's original wounds, so Skybreaker receives a –3 penalty to the vehicle's handling. Skybreaker has the Baby It feat, though, and can ignore the first critical to his vehicle. The Baby It feat does not, however, negate the effects of the bike's damage (currently 18 wounds, reducing its condition to "crippled"). Skybreaker's handling bonus is reduced by –5 (to +2) and he must make an immediate crash check.

Step 7: Skybreaker rolls an 18 for his crash check, for a total result of 27, just enough to beat the crash check DC of 24.

With a smell of sizzling rubber Sideshock closes within feet of the fleeing courier. Feather pumps another round square into his forks, shredding one of the pistons supporting the front of the bike. She lets out a low whistle as the helmeted racer manages to hold a nearly straight line even as the front wheel begins to wobble like a punch-drunk boxer. "Why isn't that guy working for us?!?" she screams over the engine.

ROUND 4

(Lead: 1 length; Terrain: Close; Speed: 70 mph)

Step 1: Sideshock is wishing he had the Daredevil ability so he could box in the cyclist, but he has to settle for crowding. Skybreaker takes advantage of the close range with a bootleg reverse.

Step 2: The bootleg reverse drops the speed by 15 to 55 mph. Sideshock's maneuver roll is 23. With the –4 modifier from the maneuver table, Skybreaker's roll is 21. If nothing changes, Sideshock will force the cycle to crash, ending the chase!

Step 3: Both drivers spend action dice. Sideshock spends his last die (+3, total of 26), but Skybreaker's two rolls add a crushing +10, bringing him to 31!

Step 4: The successful bootleg reverse inflicts two points of damage to Skybreaker's tires, leaving the cycle with 5 wp – five more points of damage and the cycle is disabled. His amazing roll reverses the situation as he gains 10 lengths on his pursuer (double the 5-point difference between their maneuver totals).

Step 5: The GC rolls a 1, triggering an obstacle (crowds of people are milling across the intersection the vehicles are now speeding across). Both drivers must make Driver checks (DC 18 for close terrain). Skybreaker easily manages the roll, but Sideshock misses the DC by 1. He must make a crash check at the end of the round during Step 7.

Step 6: Feather takes two shots. They are still doing over 50 MPH, so she suffers a –2 penalty for speed. Her first roll (7) goes wide, but the second (17) finds the mark. Feather spends an action die to increase the damage from 12 to 17 – even after subtracting the Arrow's hardness, this is more than enough to disable the fleeing motorcycle! Skybreaker is out of the chase and must make a crash check with a +10 modifier to the DC.

Step 7: The current chase speed (55 mph) confers a +4 modifier to crash checks. Sideshock breezes through his DC of 19 (15 + 4). Skybreaker fails his DC of 29 (15 +10 + 4) by 7. He fails the subsequent Jump check (DC 29, same as the crash check) and takes 6d6+7 points of damage. Ouch. He's out of it. The GC rules that the ice chest is destroyed, but the armored canister is fine.

"We're losing him!" Sideshock shouts to Feather as they swerve through a handful of pedestrians. Leaning out the window, Feather pumps two quick shots out of her rifle. In moments the cycle goes down. Sideshock fights for control of the Lancer, narrowly missing a tourist couple in the street, and the damaged car slid to a halt beside the wrecked motorcycle.

Feather retrieves the gleaming silver cylinder out of the field of ice spilled from the shattered ice chest. "We got it," she announces with a grin, observing the unconscious courier, "and we got him."

"Come Watson. The game is afoot!"
– Sherlock Holmes,
The Adventure of Abbey Grange

TRADECRAFT

Espionage

In the last century, the espionage genre has become one of the most widespread and romantic domains of popular entertainment. Books, movies, and television programs have all delved into the world of espionage, the escapades of real-life spies like Mata Hari and fictional agents like James Bond thrilling audiences again and again.

Like many of these entertainments, this game concerns itself with over-the-top, larger-than-life action and adventure. Agents are heroes in the traditional sense of the word, a cut above the masses they are sworn to protect. No matter how fantastic or impossible their exploits, however, the game's premise is still firmly rooted in the real world of espionage.

AGENCY ORGANIZATION

The organization your agents work for in *Spycraft* is left purposefully vague to allow you to superimpose your own ideas over the model. In your games, the Agency might be the CIA, or the Cold War-era KGB, or a group of your own creation. We have taken the liberty of adding some generic layers to the Agency, however, so that you have something to work with.

Spycraft's Agency is broken into departments *(see page 17),* where agents are trained; and sections — field offices in every major city where missions are assigned and agents are briefed. Operatives of outside organizations (such as espionage and law enforcement agencies) are often called in to assist your agents, and are called "neutrals." Finally, private sector support personnel, and civilians with knowledge or training required by Agency teams (such as forensics experts, lawyers, and the like), are called "specialists."

As always, we encourage you to reorganize your Agency and its supporting offices.

WHAT IS ESPIONAGE?

Generally speaking, true espionage is about collecting information that can be helpful to a government or organization, and can aid the decisions and actions it makes. This information and the process of acquiring it is known as intelligence, or intelligence gathering. The act of detecting and thwarting intelligence gathering is called counterintelligence.

WHAT IS A SPY?

A spy is an operative employed by a government or organization to meet its intelligence collecting needs. Spies are the footsoldiers in the espionage war, carrying out their duties through both open (overt) and secret (covert or clandestine) methods. More often than not, spies indulge in the latter, living among the shadows of the world we know.

Spies are certainly not a recent phenomenon. Throughout history, their services have been utilized by chieftains, kings, and governments, leading some to joke that the craft of a spy is "the world's second oldest profession."

Regardless of their history, though, it's safe to say that the tools of a spy have advanced with civilization, while their purpose remains the same.

WHAT DOES IT MEAN TO BE A SPY?

A spy faces many trials and tribulations throughout his career, some of which are seemingly contradictory. For instance, a spy must be disciplined and able to follow precise orders, yet remain independent and resourceful enough to get the job done under the most unexpected circumstances.

Ultimately, there are two traits that every successful spy must develop: loyalty and discretion (though a great many villainous spies ignore both these standards with wild success). A spy's loyalty to the government or organization he works for is paramount. His are the unseen hands of his employers, and his actions define their ulterior motives. Without loyalty, the spy is merely a loose cannon — and a potentially disastrous one at that. He is soon to become a liability, and then a target of the people he once worked for. Loyalty, therefore, is a spy's best defense.

Discretion is the key word for anyone engaged in acts of espionage. Intelligence and counterintelligence are both about discovering secrets and using them to tactical advantage. To be successful in his work, the spy must keep the truth a secret from everyone, parceling it out in small doses when he feels that it is of the most benefit to him and his mission. Families, friends, colleagues — everyone is a danger when told the truth, unless that truth somehow ensures their loyalty, support, or silence. Even when captured, spies must hold the truth close, taking it to the grave if necessary.

To be a spy, you have to accept that information is both a precious commodity and a lethal weapon.

TYPES OF SPIES

By definition, spies engage in espionage. What makes the mission and method of each spy unique is the type of intelligence they are trying to collect or prevent from being collected. As such, most information can be broken down into one of five different categories: central, diplomatic, economic, industrial, or military.

Spies working with central intelligence are dealing in matters of security, whether for a single organization or an entire nation. Once gathered, central intelligence is used primarily for defensive purposes, though counter-intelligence is infamous for pre-emptive measures that eliminate threats altogether (i.e. counter-attacks geared to destroy an enemy before he can destroy you).

Diplomatic intelligence requires a spy to collect information for implementation in the policy-making decisions and actions of his employer. There is a lot of diversity in this category, but the main focus is on understanding the motives and methods of a given target.

A spy collecting economic intelligence is concerned with the fiscal resources of a government or organization. Like diplomatic intelligence, this offers a better understanding of a target's capabilities.

Industrial intelligence is closely linked to economic intelligence, but details the methods and products of manufacturing enterprises. Spies here are expected to uncover "trade secrets" so that the target cannot acquire a technological advantage.

Lastly, spies working with military intelligence are concerned about tactical information that can be of use in warfare. Troop movements, their level of training, their commanders, their munitions, and even the terrain they are fighting on are all important components in a secret war governed by the actions of spies.

THE NEW WORLD

Now that the Cold War has ended, the world's intelligence agencies are reorganizing their agendas. Contending ideological differences and arsenals of nuclear weapons are considered less important now than dealing with international and domestic terrorism and violence. In an age of electronic currency and global communications, new security risks are emerging that would have been impossible to consider in years past.

It is a new millennium filled with new concerns, and the stakes have risen to meet the times. The war of words has become a war of action — which is where the heroes of *Spycraft* come in. They are the footsoldiers on a new field of battle, where information has lethal import.

Missions

This section covers mission types, methods, and protocols. It is required reading for new recruits.

HOW DO MISSIONS HAPPEN?

Most of the time, *Spycraft* gameplay involves your agents being assigned missions by Control, their superior at the Agency. Missions have many variations, ranging from the agents prompting the action to happenstance events during the agents' downtime, but the classic cinematic model occurs most often.

This model sometimes begins with a quick and fun **opening sequence**, in which the agents tackle a minor threat or challenge, often starting *in media res* (already in the midst of the action) to kick-start the adventure with little preamble. Opening sequences sometimes foreshadow elements of the coming mission, others don't.

Whether an open sequence is included or not, nearly all missions continue with the **mission briefing**, during which the GC spells out the problem at hand, assigns it a **threat code** *(see page 203),* and tasks the agents with resolving it. Relevant world events are described and short dossiers of all involved characters are offered. Special restrictions (such as time limits and gear restrictions) are also mentioned. Finally, Control sometimes offers special equipment to the agents — often gadgets — that he suspects will be useful in the field. (Any equipment given to the agents in this way is not counted toward their budget point and gadget point allotment).

The next portion of most missions is the **Gearing Up phase,** during which the agents come up with a plan for completing their mission and requisition gear they need. Equipment requisitioned during the Gearing Up phase is counted toward the agents' budget point and gadget point allotments.

The agents then set out on their mission, usually (but not always) following an initial lead pointed out by Control. Nearly always, missions are more complex than they appear at the outset, and the initial and subsequent leads take the agents to locations and encounters they don't expect. Each such location or encounter is called a **scene,** and agents sometimes requisition additional gear (also counted toward their budget point or gadget point allotments) or use field expenses in-between. The difficulty of each scene is generally higher than the last, leading toward an inevitable slam-bang confrontation with the actual threat of the mission.

This formula is sound, and has worked for countless espionage movies and books. We recommend you use it for early games, branching out with new and unusual mission structures as you gain experience with the *Spycraft* game system and desire a fresh challenge.

TYPES OF MISSIONS

So just what is it that secret agents do? Sure they save the world from demented madmen, but how do they find these guys in the first place? A mission rarely starts out with "Count Sinister has acquired a satellite death ray. Go stop him from slagging Hong Kong." Instead, agents begin one mission, and, over the course of their investigation, discover what Count Sinister is really up to in his high-tech underwater base. Listed below is an overview of some of the most common mission types your agent might be assigned to carry out at the start of a game session.

ASSASSINATION AND REVENGE

Assassination is a dirty business, but spy agencies sometimes find it necessary. The agent must kill someone the Agency considers a threat. Assassination methods vary. In some cases, the agent simply takes the target out, but this is an extremely volatile way to accomplish the mission. Often the agent must find a way not only to kill the subject but also to make it look like someone else did it. The idea is not to destabilize a region with a high-profile murder but instead make it look like a coup or accidental death. This is a complex mission and has great risk of failure. Many of the episodes of the original *Mission: Impossible* series involved this sort of mission: get rid of someone, but make sure it looks like the U.S. had nothing to do with it.

Revenge missions are similar to assassination, but they often have a different motivation. In this case, the agent's organization wants to 'send a message' to the world. The target of such a mission has hurt the Agency or its government, warranting its elimination with extreme prejudice. This type of mission is designed to warn other villains of the Agency's stance. Sometimes, these missions are designed to embarrass the subject in addition to killing him. This type of mission is often employed against successful agents who thwarted villainous organizations; S.P.E.C.T.R.E. hatches such a plan against James Bond in *From Russia with Love*.

DEFECTION

An enemy agent has decided to switch sides and needs help escaping from his employers. The defector generally offers some piece of equipment or information as incentive for the Agency to assist his defection, making this type of mission a variation on theft *(opposite)*. *The Living Daylights* and *The Hunt for Red October* feature defection story lines.

INFILTRATION

This is a very common mission type, but it is likely to be only one part of an agent team's adventure. Infiltration involves posing as a member of another organization, or sneaking into one of their locations. The agent enters the organization to learn more about it, effectively operating as a double agent. Infiltrators may be performing simple reconnaissance to learn more about the target group, or seeking to betray or kill someone in the group. Infiltrators sometimes offer false information to their targets, causing them to make mistakes.

Agents use infiltration in two ways. First, they often work with NPC agents who have penetrated a foe's organization to get the information they need to carry out their missions. Second, they may infiltrate the organization themselves, hoping to get close to the bad guy and discover the nature of his plans.

SALVAGE AND RECOVERY

One of the agency's operatives or ships has been destroyed. A key piece of equipment was lost in the event. The agent is asked to recover this equipment, or at the very least make sure it doesn't fall into enemy hands. The mission often begins with the agent investigating the site of the original incident and then tracing it back to the thief. Many of the James Bond films use this type of mission, with *Thunderball* and *For Your Eyes Only* being two excellent examples.

SEARCH AND RESCUE

These missions generally fall into one of two categories: find someone who has gone missing, or rescue someone who has been kidnapped. In the first, the agent is usually assigned to track down someone the Agency has lost. This person can be a spy from another agency, a potential defector, an important scientist, a key political figure, or even the son or daughter of a high-ranking official in the Agency's government. Often, the subject of the mission was under observation or has access to key information that can't fall into the wrong hands. He was last seen recently and has now disappeared without a trace. The agent is given a dossier on the person including their known habits, acquaintances, and frequented locations, and told to bring them home.

Search and rescue missions usually have one of three results. First, the subject is killed (usually for political reasons or because he "knew too much"), in which case the job generally becomes a mission of revenge. Second, the person has actually been kidnapped, making this a rescue mission. Third, the subject is part of the villainous organization that the spy must stop (once he discovers it). This last variation is particularly dreadful — the target vanishes to complete his assignment, often betraying the agents before he leaves. Sometimes the target is actually the mastermind at the center of the new mission.

Rescue missions are more straightforward. The subjects of the mission have been captured or taken hostage by a hostile force, and the agent must find where they are being held and liberate them. Sometimes these characters are held for political reasons. Other times they have some key information that the enemy hopes to exploit before disposing of them.

THEFT

This mission type is similar to salvage and recovery but here, the agent's job is to steal the equipment in question, which might represent a serious edge for the enemy, or give the agent's own government a leg up on its foes.

The agent is briefed on the nature of the gear and where it can be acquired. There is often a double agent, defector, or dupe in the enemy organization who can help the agent acquire the device. Once the theft is made, the agent must escape the authorities and get it back to headquarters without being caught. *From Russia with Love* and *Firefox* are both good examples.

THREAT CODES

Control assigns the mission a threat code, which relates the Agency's level of concern and the resources allocated to the assigned agents. **Code: Yellow** threats are the least important dangers the Agency contends with, and usually involve few expected casualties and little chance of exposure. Code: Yellow threats range from stolen document recovery to diplomat protection and recruitment. Code: Yellow missions often take place over long periods of time, and weeks or months pass with no progress. Active Code: Yellow missions are often investigative, with little clear direction from the home office.

Code: Red threats are more serious, and usually involve a direct threat of some kind — low-level criminal masterminds, upstart dictators with personal armies, and incidents which can spark an international crisis all fall into this category. Agents are always dispatched to deal with Code: Red threats immediately. Code: Red mission parameters always include precise mission goals, and very frequently include sharp deadlines.

The Agency's last threat level is **Code: Black.** If a situation is labeled Code: Black, all hell has generally broken loose. These situations involve serious threats to global peace, including tensions that could touch off open war, stolen documents or technology being used to bring the world to its knees, defections of top world officials, and concrete proof that the Agency exists.

ASSIGNING MISSION LEVELS

Game Controls who have difficulty determining the level their missions should be rated can refer to the following examples below.

Code: Yellow

Agent Daniella Bianchi, a Level 2 Canberra Programmer, has gone missing. She was last seen three days ago and hasn't been home. Find out what happened to her and if the Agency has been compromised. Bring her back if at all possible, but make certain she can't damage the Agency.

Code: Red

Agent Daniella Bianchi, a Level 2 Programmer on the Top Secret Defense Satellite System project, has gone missing. She was last seen on holiday in Gibraltar with a known enemy agent. Preliminary investigations indicate she was severely in debt and may be be the subject of blackmail. Find Agent Bianchi, determine if she sold secrets to the enemy, and make certain that no one makes use of any information she may have passed on.

Code: Black

We have determined that Agent Daniella Bianchi was a double agent working for the enemy. We were about to arrest her when she disappeared. She resurfaced two days later in Gibraltar where she met with other enemy agents before going to ground again. Bianchi has sensitive information on the Top Secret Defense Satellite System project that we believe she has passed to her controllers. Find Bianchi and her controllers and make certain that the enemy can't use the stolen information to complete a weapons satellite capable of destroying whole cities.

Few missions start out with a rating of Code: Black. More often, they are Code: Yellow or Code: Red missions that get upgraded when the full extent of the villain's plot becomes known.

The Agency responds to these threats by dispatching a team of agents to solve the problem as quickly as possible, using any means necessary — up to and including lethal force.

METHODS AND MEANS

Although many modern espionage agencies have evolved into quasi-autonomous entities with little or no accountability, virtually all of them have roots in government. And like any government organizations, they have procedures to follow in almost any situation. The Agency and its sections (home offices around the world) are no different.

Agents are expected to be familiar with the Agency's standards and follow them at all times. Maverick operatives who consistently ignore the established codes of conduct can expect to find themselves severely reprimanded or even removed from active duty (unless their methods achieve considerable success, in which disciplinary action is up to Control).

The following sections detail some of the Agency's procedures – and for the industrious, a few ways around them.

MISSION ASSIGNMENTS

Agents are given considerable leeway when choosing how to tackle a given assignment, but they are expected to execute their operations within certain parameters. The most inflexible procedure followed by espionage agencies is the briefing and debriefing process, during which these parameters are handed out.

A briefing is more than simply telling the agents what they must do. It presents all the facts they need to complete their assignment (all those facts, that is, they are cleared to receive). Every known variable is accounted for, and every probable complication addressed. During this ritual process, the agents clear their minds and commit everything presented to memory. Their briefing is the framework from which they conceive and implement every stage of their mission.

Similarly, debriefing is an absolute necessity. This is the means by which the Agency determines what unfinished business remains and what further action, if any, is required to close the file. Control exhaustively questions agents about the status of every variable introduced during the briefing, as well as any new information gained in the field. The debriefing determines whether additional operations are warranted. It also serves as catharsis for the agents involved, mentally 'cleansing' them before they return to the field.

The Agency places enormous importance upon briefing and debriefing its agents, particularly those of outside organizations. Given the exotic locales their operatives visit and their agents' independent (and often eccentric) natures, this is commonly the only time that Control hears about events in the field; either the agents make it home safely with word of success, or they turn up dead.

COMMUNICATIONS

When in the field, it is not uncommon for agents to contact one another for information or assistance. This is risky, as agents are often under surveillance. Any non-secure communication which can be used to pinpoint an agent in the field as an intelligence operative is a possible death sentence. With this in mind, there are many ways to safely send encoded, seemingly innocuous messages from the field.

Digital: Electronic communication is a double-edged sword. While it is the most accessible form of communication, it is also one of the easiest for third parties to monitor. Fortunately, most modern countries have such an enormous glut of electronic communication that a skilled agent can "lose their message in the crowd," so to speak.

Intelligence agencies maintain email accounts on public forums and websites with encrypted news groups that agents can access. Because of the accessibility of these mediums, however, it is essential that the agents use a code or cipher of some sort. One common method is the use of metaphors known only to the agents and recipient to convey simple, broad topics.

Pen & Paper: Sometimes it's best to call on the classics. Messages written in code, blind mail drops, anonymous couriers, and even courier pigeons and disappearing ink still see use in modern espionage. On the plus side, a lone physical letter adrift in a sea of mail can be very difficult for the enemy to track down (if they know about it to begin with). Ultimately, however, the "Old Boys' way" is rarely used unless alternate communication lines prove unreliable.

Telephone Lines: The telephone has the distinction of being the easiest means of communication to monitor. Governments can tap phones with a minimum of fuss and often little or no legal preamble. The only safe means to communicate openly via telephone is through an encrypted and scrambled cell unit. Unfortunately, these units are quite expensive to develop and use, and are rarely issued to field agents unless they are absolutely necessary to the mission at hand—and even then, the encryption on these devices can be bypassed, given enough time and the proper technical resources.

TRANSPORTATION

Occasionally agents find themselves in possession of sensitive information that requires a discreet means of transport. One such method employs the system of tractor-trailers that move cargo across most countries. The men and women working in this system call themselves "truckers," come from all strata of society, and have minimal supervision. This makes it very simple for intelligence agencies to plant deep cover operatives within the industry, creating a network of contacts who can

---

In a typical spy campaign, the Game Control creates adventures ("missions"), and then the players receive their orders, reacting to what is set before them. But there may be times when the players wish to be the ones to start the action. This requires a bit more work on the GC's part, but the end result can be quite satisfying.

The active approach requires the GC to think quickly on his feet. The players do some of the work for him, letting him know the mission they want to pursue ("Let's track down the assassin who escaped us two sessions ago"). But then the GC must come up with some answers: Where is the protagonist? What level is he now? What obstacles has he set up since they last met?

The players usually take the next step, offering their plan. Faces and snoops are critical at this early stage, as such plans begin with tracking the target down. In general, they should have to work for this information, as with any other mission.

The agents often won't have support from their home office. Worse, their superiors might take active steps against them. Their reaction shouldn't be so extreme that the agents are ultimately fired, but should help the GC set up challenges.

The final decision for the GC to make is what the target is doing. If she's just sitting around the hacienda, it's going to be a boring mission. This is the last place to add complexity. For example, the agents are trying to catch an assassin who is trying to kill someone, and that someone has no idea where the agents stand. The team must try to save someone who has no idea who they are, or even if their intentions are benign. For excellent examples of active missions, watch the James Bond movies *The Living Daylights* or *License to Kill*.

---

transport items or information across the nation with virtually no chance of detection or interception.

Furthermore, the average trucker has no agency affiliation and can be contracted easily, making him perfect for transporting items and information at a moment's notice — for a small fee, of course. Civilians on America's highways, for example, drive by these men and women every day, oblivious to the true importance of their cargoes.

Transporting extremely sensitive or actively sought items requires a more secure — and usually more expensive — solution. Fortunately for agents, the criminal element has just such a system — the so-called "black market." Most underworld channels are extremely adept at handling sensitive items or information, utilizing

CONTACTING THE HOME OFFICE

There are times when a mission goes badly, or when totally unforeseeable situations arise, and the agents must immediately contact the Agency. This is discouraged in all but the most extreme cases, as it can reveal the section if the communiqué is intercepted. Nevertheless, the stakes sometimes demand "contacting the home office."

The vast majority of modern espionage agencies (the Agency included) have dozens of legitimate businesses that serve as a front for their operations, and which exist for just such a situation. By contacting any of perhaps a hundred 1-800 numbers, an agent can recite an ambiguous code phrase that sends up a warning flag, requesting immediate aid. Usually, such a call is immediately followed by a "dead drop," in which the agent or his handler leaves a message or item in an innocuous location (such as a garbage can, tree knot, or inside a designated item in a mall lost and found), which is later picked up by the other. The same dead drop is sometimes used to relay a return message or item, but is rarely used for another exchange until weeks or months have passed. Otherwise, it becomes too obvious a part of the operatives' routines.

There are similar methods for contacting agencies online via email, which is monitored around the clock.

code words, cover identities, double blinds, and other espionage tactics to cover their tracks. But there is one significant drawback to calling upon them: they generally require tremendous compensation, in cash — usually in quantities larger than agents carry. Still, black marketeers can be found in virtually every major metropolitan area in the world, and their system is uniquely equipped to handle clandestine enterprises. The Agency, of course, warns against the use of felons during sensitive missions, and officially frowns upon their use, but sometimes they are an agent team's best option.

AGENT RESOURCES

Intelligence agents are by their very nature inventive and independent. They adapt and improvise, making the most of what they have to overcome the challenges they face. But sometimes agents require something extra to complete their missions. The Agency realizes this, and has developed a support structure for agents to call upon.

The Archive: Although data concerning covert operations, field agents, specialists, criminal activity, and sociopolitical shifts are possessed by most intelligence agencies, none can rival the Agency's collection, called the "Archive." Virtually every mission undertaken by the Agency's sections since its inception (and quite a few handled by other groups) is meticulously recorded here, noting individuals, places, times and ramifications.

Additionally, computer clusters across the world constantly search for relevant media information to add to the file entries, updating the status of both open and closed case files. While the Agency does not allow outside agencies access to the Archive, it is generally available for field agents during briefing and debriefing and by request.

Control: When an agent team is unable to complete a mission on its own, its first stop might be Control (their section commander, who is usually the person who briefed them in the first place). In such a case, Control determines if the request is justified. Requesting underwater gear to infiltrate the opposition's island facility is quite reasonable, for example. Asking for anti-tank weaponry to assault a public location, on the other hand, is unacceptable (and likely to incur a severe reprimand when the agents return home).

Ultimately, the Agency prefers that its agents — who are all recruited at least partially for their ability to contend with unforeseen situations — avoid contacting the home office until their mission is successfully completed, but it also understands that some situations require the direct intervention of Section Controls. Rarely are Agency personnel directly involved in such requests (unless they are among the field agents requesting it in the first place); if the Agency's answering the call, the threat is probably global.

Research & Development: Most agents are regularly briefed about R&D's latest gadgets, and new items are often designed for specific missions. Agents can usually requisition gadgets in the field using their gadget points *(see page 105)*.

Training: Training is perhaps the most invaluable tool at an agent's disposal. While external resources are an unknown and often variable factor in an assignment, an agent's training is constant. Modern espionage agencies train their operatives in the basics of a wide range of skills including computer operation, unarmed combat, marksmanship, deception, melee combat, disguise, and stealth. Each discipline also offers advanced skill courses for agents who wish to pursue them. Some operatives choose to specialize in one area, while others prefer to be trained in a wider variety. Still others eschew training as an ineffective means of honing one's skills, believing instead that true prowess can only be developed with experience. Such agents are usually destined to become either legends in the espionage arena, or fodder for the enemy.

Tactical Concerns

In a world of international espionage and global threats, there are times when just looking and being cool doesn't get the job done, and you and your team must start thinking about tactics — the strategy of getting in and out of a location or situation alive.

Briefing the Team

Before agents engage in any mission, they are briefed on the potential dangers inherent to the assignment: number and type of enemy (often estimated if the actual information isn't known), what weapons they generally carry, security systems and methods used, and, of course, a breakdown of the expected plan they are executing.

The briefing also informs the team of any codewords, standard operating procedures, and special objectives that the team's organization requires of them, particularly if a new member has just joined the team.

Finally, each member of the team is assigned a specific task and special protocols are offered to each. One of the team's first functions is to determine any common formations they intend to use, along with emergency plans and ways of signalling for them.

Common Team Formations

There are many ways to put a team together. Some of the most common ones are listed below, covering many of the archetypical missions your team may find itself assigned to.

The formations below can be used for any type of mission. Generally, it's up to the GC, or whomever is in charge, to decide who does what and how the mission is approached.

Standard: This formation was used in *Mission: Impossible* and *MI2*: a team leader, a coordinator (who doesn't actually enter the field unless absolutely necessary), a computer specialist (if required), and a number of agents to assist in the field, each with one or two functions. The size of the group depends on the type of mission.

Lone Operative: This is the James Bond 'formation': one man in the field with occasional back-up from headquarters and only his wits and instincts to help him through most of the time.

One-Man Team: This refers to any formation in which one agent takes full responsibility for how the mission is run, with no back-up or contact with the home office. Such teams always take along a computer specialist (snoop), a wheelman, and someone to carry each of the other facets of the mission: a demolitions expert, for example, or a cryptographer.

Police Entry Technique

This is standard operating procedure for getting into a location that is both heavily guarded and (usually) watching for trouble. Generally it involves a group at the main entrance, where the team leader commands one to three small, possibly one-man, teams that converge on other exits. These smaller teams provide assistance, watch the others' backs, or engage in the forced entry run. Police always make detailed observations of a location's surroundings and build simple, efficient plans to get in and obtain their objective with a minimum of violence. They also usually have detailed secondary and tertiary plans as well. This process should become familiar to agent teams, as they are likely to require plans of their own during missions.

When the Bullets Start Flying

No matter how careful the team, there are times when you come into direct conflict with the enemy. When entering a gunfight, your primary concern should be disabling the enemy as quickly as possible. Evaluate the situation, decide what (or who) the greatest threat is, where your escape routes are, and what you have to work with, and act accordingly.

How do I acquire equipment in the field?

Sometimes agents require certain tools to get the job done. Unfortunately, they often don't know this in advance and find themselves out in the field without the proper gear. This begs the question: when faced with an unexpected situation during a mission, how does an agent team get the tools it needs?

Protocol is to contact the agent team's section, from which Control dispenses equipment as necessary. This is the easiest route for agents in need, as the Agency handles all of the transportation itself. This option is covered by budget and gadget points — *see page 104.*

However, if Control proves unable (or unwilling) to produce the equipment, agents may have to consult local contacts or purchase the gear in the field (assuming it can be found, of course). This option is covered by field expenses — *see page 105.*

When all else fails, some agents resort to the less honorable and far riskier option: theft. Stealing is quick and relatively easy for trained intelligence operatives, but has its own obvious drawbacks and consequences as well. Control tends to frown upon the theft of particularly unusual equipment, as it leaves a trail that can lead back to the home office. This option is, obviously, covered by the agent's skills.

Try to communicate in code when possible; use established hand signals and innocuous voice commands rather than speaking aloud and giving the enemy an insight about your tactics. Small "whisper-based" communicators are helpful here.

DEALING WITH AUTHORITIES

In espionage, the first rule when dealing with public authorities is: don't.

Secret agencies maintain their covert status by avoiding the attention of the authorities. Government and local authorities are not secure. They are invariably perforated with leaks, monitored by reporters, and supervised by politicians.

Mission teams avoid the attention of the authorities as well, usually by direct order. Either a team is to get in and out with the locals none the wiser, or they're to be long gone by the time that the results of their mission are noticeable.

Unfortunately, no mission plan ever survives contact with the the enemy. In this age of heightened awareness and international terrorism, random security sweeps may uncover agent teams as they move to and from mission sites. Some governments also maintain their own counter-intelligence branches and conduct 'spy wars,' often using the local authorities for 'advance warning' and to enforce their ends.

This section should offer agents a few tips for protecting their interests (and their lives) in the field, where anyone can be an enemy, and accidentally drawing attention is a death sentence.

FALSE IDENTITIES

Agents traveling publicly require at least one, and typically two or more, false identities. The first is their cover identity. This identity is a false biographical history. Secret agencies maintain thousands of such identities.

The primary element of a cover is employment. The Agency maintains a variety of businesses. Many of the employees of these businesses have no idea they are working for a spy organization. Often these businesses even turn a small profit, which goes to finance the Agency. Some businesses also "launder" resources for the Agency. They can function as safe houses and provide inter-city transportation resources.

These businesses provide covers for agents. Agents are issued passports, business cards, and other necessary evidence of working for such a business, and the company maintains suitable employee records. Calls to the business verify that the agent is dutifully employed.

More substantial deep-cover identities are provided to operatives who function in one area for long periods

of time. Agents operating as part of a mobile mission team rarely need this degree of "history."

A second type of identity is an escape ID. These "use-and-lose" IDs can withstand only casual scrutiny. They are intended to be shown when the agent needs something to pass a quick inspection, but can't offer his cover ID. The companies they refer to usually have complicated bureaucracies, poor phone service, and other ways to prevent authentication. Escape identities have two benefits: they preserve a cover ID, so it can be used later, and they require less effort to create.

Whenever possible, an agent's organization tries to match the agent's areas of expertise to a business the organization maintains. Typical businesses include finance, trade, journalism, computers, law, engineering, security, fine arts, and antiquities.

GETTING AROUND

Travel is typically arranged in one of three ways. First, if the Agency has a cover business in the mission area, it can provide vehicles for nearby agents. (The agents must still usually requisition the vehicles, using their gadget points. *See page 105 for more.)*

If the Agency has no businesses in the vicinity, or it has overcommitted its transportation resources, the cover businesses of one or more of the participating agents can often arrange a rental, or ship special vehicles directly to the mission team. Agents may also rent civilian vehicles. Expenses are commonly reimbursed. (In both these cases, the agents must still pay for the rental with field expenses, as described on page 105.)

Casual destruction of vehicles is frowned upon. If you must trash a vehicle, try to make it one the Agency owns. Destructive agents often find themselves without support in the future.

WHEN YOUR COVER IS BLOWN

Casual combat is discouraged. Moral principles aside, such acts draw undesirable attention to the Agency. Flight rather than fight is recommended during confrontations. Judicious use of bribes is a desirable alternative.

Whether this is possible depends on the level of threat the authorities pose. In democratic societies, non-violent means are more desirable. In most hostile regimes, however, flight and bribery may not be feasible. The authorities may take a "shoot first" approach, and capture may be a non-option. In this case, violence is often sanctioned.

Safe house information is provided to all agents during mission briefings. Safe houses are provided by the Agency in charge of the mission area. Typically, there are two types of safe houses.

Cover businesses are the most secure, since the Agency can use existing security precautions to protect against enemy agents. Agents should not visit safe houses unless they are positive they have avoided pursuit. Otherwise, they risk compromising the safe house's security.

The Agency also maintains more casual safe houses within its areas of control. These are typically rented apartments and hotel rooms, warehouses, suburban homes, and the like. They are far less secure, since they cannot have enhanced security without compromising their anonymity. They are stocked only with the common supplies and foodstuffs normally found in such places.

If agents are arrested, standard procedure is for their cover business to claim they have false papers and have never heard of them. An operative working undercover in law enforcement may then arrive and identify the agents as criminals and arrange for them to be extradited. Whether they actually do so depends on how serious the agents' crime is, and the type of local government. This is another reason why shootouts with authorities are discouraged: the agent team's chance of being extradited decreases if they are caught.

The organization won't approve additional resources to break an imprisoned agent team out of jail. Any remaining members of the team may, at their discretion, take steps to rescue their allies, but they must also be wary of compromising Agency protocols, lest they wind up in jail also.

If the procedure above (or a similar one) is not feasible due to security concerns, the agents are on their own. They are at the mercy of the authorities' legal system. Suicide is preferable if their case draws too much attention and threatens their home organization, or if there is a risk that they are to be interrogated as spies.

TRANSPORTING WEAPONS

The Agency rarely allows agents to carry licensed weapons. Having a permit for a gun as part of a security-related cover tends to draw more attention than the weapon is worth. It's preferred that authorities never discover the agents' weapons at all, concealed or otherwise.

Research and development uses gadget technology to create a method for smuggling weapons. Their creation: a modified carrying device (briefcase, purse, luggage) with inserts simulating commonplace items. This insert shows up on x-rays as the chosen item(s). Micromesh screening protects against metal detectors. Finally, hidden compartments foil all but the most determined searches.

EMERGENCY PROTOCOLS

On any given mission, something is bound to go wrong, and though agents are trained to fall back on their superiors when things spiral out of their control, that luxury isn't always available in the field. Consequently, the Agency trains its agents to expect (and handle) the unexpected. Here are some of their methods.

THE AGENCY'S LAST WISHES

Operative: As you sit in your jail cell, awaiting trial, imprisonment, or execution, know that you die for a noble cause. As you well know, we can only exist in an environment of absolute secrecy. Your punishment, at the hands of some of those we strive to protect, is the ultimate price we all pay.

A suicide capsule has been provided for you. If it is unavailable to you, or you cannot find other means of ending your life to maintain Conspiracy protocols, one of our undercover operatives will close your contract.

Your sacrifice will not be forgotten.

– The Agency

AUTHORIZED USE OF FORCE

The Agency recognizes that it simply can't oversee every aspect of every mission, particularly if teams are working undercover. Therefore, the Agency field teams are always authorized to use necessary force to deal with problems. Operatives are instructed to carry out their assignments as quietly as possible, but they are also given discretion to react to the situation at hand. This often means killing.

Agency teams are assured by their superiors that killing – if necessary to complete the mission, or in self-defense – is sanctioned. It is partly Control's responsibility to make sure that agents are not 'brought to justice' for killing enemy agents in the field. Captured spies can expect the Agency to attempt to free them or, at the very least, prevent them from being placed on trial.

Despite this policy, killing remains a risky business. The Agency cannot be everywhere at once, and if a team of agents is captured and charged with murder, they are obliged to attempt escape on their own. Sometimes, the Agency's best efforts to free a captive team are not enough, and operatives who are involved in spectacular or high profile killings may even find themselves cut loose. This is called "burning" the agents, and it is only done to protect the Conspiracy as a whole. All field agents understand that if Control feels they cannot be saved, or they are a risk, they will be burned.

Agents who frequently engage in unnecessary and gratuitous murder are not tolerated. Killing, while sometimes necessary, is a filthy business. Agents with a ravenous bloodlust are burned or killed.

CLEANERS

A cleaner is an individual whose job it is to fix major screw-ups in the field, to make whatever happened look like something else — something *mundane*. Field agents are instructed to call for a cleaner whenever their operations have left behind collateral damage that cannot be easily explained away. As many cleaners are ruthless killers with no compunction about eliminating those they see as a threat to security — including agents — most teams are careful not to warrant calling them in.

RETIREMENT

A retiring agent represents a potential security risk. Agency operatives are thoroughly debriefed before they quit the service and instructed never to discuss anything related to their spy careers. They are then given new identities and placed far away from any former mission site to prevent them from being recognized. Plastic surgery is often employed to help with the ruse. Retired agents who break their oath of silence, or who are observed making contact with former colleagues or known enemy agents, are liquidated quickly and ruthlessly.

INVESTIGATION

One of the most important things that secret agents do is conduct investigations. Like the gumshoes of old pulps and globe-trotting reporters of today, secret agents are responsible for detecting and interpreting all the little clues that lead to their opponents, deciphering what is critical in every scene and determining how to use it to their advantage.

This section describes many methods and devices used in standard espionage missions, along with some advice for inexperienced espionage roleplayers. New *Spycraft* players should read this section before their first session of play.

PREREQUISITES FOR SPIES

When roleplaying a superspy — particularly during a game run by a fastidious or detail-oriented Game Control — players should strive to take part in the mystery of each mission. There are several traits that all successful players share which help games run more smoothly.

BE ATTENTIVE

Players should take special care to listen to what the Game Control says, as well as how he says it. Follow leads that appear important, and let go of ones that don't. Exhaustive research into the situation at hand is the first step toward tackling the mission without getting lost in the details.

Remain mindful of the tools at your disposal. Don't forget that you can ask for inspiration, education, and favor checks, as well as spend action dice, when you need help.

DON'T GIVE UP

One of the most destructive decisions you can make is to throw your hands in the air and give up. The game grinds to a halt and everyone — yourself included — becomes irritable and disillusioned. Remember that it is part of the GC's job to make sure you find the pieces of the puzzle and have all the information you need to put them together. Trust that he has your best interests in mind, and is trying to make the game fun — even when he seems to be harassing you. He is running the villains, after all, and the other half of his job is making sure they don't seem like push-overs, and that the challenges you face en route to them are formidable enough for you to feel proud of your success after they are vanquished.

DON'T LET FRUSTRATION RULE YOUR DECISIONS

When you find yourself stumped as to what to do next, take care not to become frustrated with the mission, or with your Game Control. It is the GC's job to bring everything you need to your attention. You just have to look for it. Sometimes this requires special actions on your part (many of which are covered in this section). Other times, it simply requires persistence and attention to detail. Allowing frustration to dictate your agent's actions runs the risk of angry roleplaying, which is nearly as destructive as giving up. Taking aggressions out on NPCs is even less productive, and often leads to the death of innocent bystanders or, worse, those with the information you needed in the first place. Instead, focus on the facts at hand, the clues you have, and the GC's hints and guidance.

REMAIN SELF RELIANT

Espionage roleplayers must strike a balance between using their authority and abusing it. Being part of a multinational conspiracy with connections in every world government offers players a great deal of power, which they can bring to bear in the form of favor checks *(see page 217)* to acquire information, money, technology, specialist support, and access to lab equipment and other exclusive tools. There are, however, two potential pitfalls to look out for. First, the in-game concern is that your actions might bring the Agency to light, disrupting their activities. Second, there is the very real possibility that such widely defined authority can derail the GC's scripted mission, bringing the entire game to a halt.

Players should watch out for both these problems, and strive to recognize when their efforts are being counter-productive. It's better to roll with the punches than prematurely end a game through overzealous dependence upon third parties. And there's plenty of justification for not using this authority: superspies are typically expected to tackle missions with only minimal assistance (mainly what is offered during the mission briefing). Also, they are usually the last line against global threats, and by the time they come in, the Agency and its host organizations have often spent many of their resources, without success.

TAKE THE INITIATIVE

Ultimately, superspies are adventurers of the highest caliber. They rarely sit around waiting for the action to come to them. Missions generally require active participation from the players, or their agents wind up sitting by the sidelines while the mastermind and his cronies take over the world.

Be bold. Be daring. Take chances that you might not consider in real life. Remember that *Spycraft* is a game about roleplaying the best spies in the world, the men and women nations call upon to save their bacon. You have the right to expect the GC to give you a fair chance when you attempt the impossible. Of course, you should also understand when he refuses you, or rules that you are unsuccessful. Winning, after all, is hollow if there are no losses.

THINK ON YOUR FEET

Perhaps the most important lesson about investigative and espionage roleplaying: you are responsible for putting the clues together and driving the mission forward. Some missions are combat-oriented and require little more than a quick trigger finger. Others require you to look beyond the evidence that you discover, to question the reasons for that evidence, and to make leaps of logic to bring the mastermind's plan to light. This is not always easy, and often requires you to look beyond the obvious.

Your best bet in such situations is often to take a step back and look at every clue you have uncovered so far, with an eye toward how it connects to the puzzle as a whole. Ask yourself five basic investigative questions — "Why is this happening?", "Who is behind it?", "What is causing this to happen?", "How is this happening?", and "Where can I find out more about what is happening?". An objective outlook can often reveal information you can't see "in the thick of things."

Clues doled out during a mission often relate to others given much earlier (perhaps even in previous missions), so that the entire picture only becomes clear when they are considered together. Other clue chains are presented with intentionally missing pieces that can only be discovered if you consider the villains' personalities, known motives, or other information not handed out as an obvious lead. Piecing such clue chains together is one of the most difficult challenges facing espionage roleplayers, but it is also one of the most rewarding when successfully accomplished.

WORKING WITH THE TEAM

Finally, it is vital that you work with the other players, relying on their strengths and filling in for their weaknesses, just as they must do for you. In the violent, unpredictable world of espionage, an agent's teammates often become his surrogate family, the only ones he can trust to support him, to safeguard his interests, and to cover his back when the chips are down. Many missions are specifically geared for teams, featuring challenges that require the attention of more than one type of sleuthing, combat ability, or finesse. To overcome these challenges, you must learn when to let others take the lead, and when your talents are required, but most importantly, you must learn to work with the team to make these decisions.

SOURCES OF INFORMATION

The following sections detail many standard methods and tools at every agent team's disposal, and offer advice for how to use them to your advantage. Players should familiarize themselves with these tools, and employ them during play. Likewise, Game Controls should factor them into their mission scripts, expecting players to call upon them, and preparing for it.

COMPUTER INTELLIGENCE

Computers have revolutionized the act of intelligence gathering. Between masterminds' headquarters featuring computerized security, data storage, and sometimes even life support, and the wealth of information available about practically anything on the Internet, computers are one of a superspy's greatest tools. *Rules for using the Computers skill can be found on page 44,* but some players may wonder what it can do for them.

First of all, players with the Computers skill should learn to think in terms of information sources (i.e. government, private, etc.). By hacking into the Department of Motor Vehicles, for instance, agents can call up records of traffic tickets, state of residence, and — by extension — tax records and social security information (which, as experienced hackers know, is the Rosetta

security-conscious people don't always realize how easy it is to access secrets stored on a computer. Deleted information can be recovered by a talented or determined programmer, and viruses can be engineered to either destroy information or to copy it. Getting access to an enemy's computer system can provide invaluable information about his operations.

The Internet: The Internet is one of the single greatest sources of information in the world. A good search engine can provide mounds of information about anything that isn't classified. Hackers *(see below)* can go further. A person's residence (or at least his billing address) can be learned by checking with his ISP, and someone who is online can be traced to a location – assuming he is using a dial-up connection and the authorities (or a hacker) grant access to the line. Finally, Internet service providers (ISPs) can be hacked for credit card numbers, personal information, and patterns of computer use, not to mention a list of recently visited websites.

Cracking: Cracking involves breaking into secure databases and computer systems. It's a difficult and dangerous business, but it can yield great results. Crackers, or "hackers," employ programs which access and decrypt information so that unauthorized personnel can read it. While cracking is illegal, virtually every intelligence organization calls upon it to discover information about their enemies.

GOVERNMENT INTELLIGENCE

Governments routinely collect enormous volumes of data on their citizens, their enemies, and the plans and resources of both. As an example, two parallel systems called CARNIVORE and ECHELON monitor central Internet hubs in the U.S. and Europe, respectively, copying any email containing suspect words or key phrases and sending it to a human processor for review. Though both systems are reputed to be secure and non-invasive, these messages (and the recommendations made from them) are a possible source of clues for agents. The FBI and local law enforcement organizations also keep files on suspected criminals, terrorists, subversive groups, and their activities. Then there are the myriad secrets governments keep about their own affairs, which are often the focus of agent operations.

Much of this information is available to agents with the proper connections. Through personal contacts (usually developed during play – Game Controls are not likely to allow them at the start of a game without feats to support them) and specialists assigned by the Agency *(see page 266),* agents can access practically anything in the ally's or specialist's grasp – for the right price. Rarely do government contacts risk their employment or lives for nothing.

Stone of electronic sleuthing). Credit histories (available through several central electronic hubs for such information) can paint a picture of people's private lives, their travels, their personalities, and even their secrets. Criminal records are available on secured federal and state systems (and in parallel locations in other countries), and provide tremendous information about anyone who has been arrested, as well as whether they were convicted, incarcerated, or acquitted.

When using computers to gain information that is not covered under the Computers skill, players should simply identify a system they wish to hack into and a question they are looking for an answer to. With a die roll, this offers the Game Control all the information he needs to determine if the attempt is successful.

The Computers skill assumes that users are attempting to cover their tracks at all times, usually by bouncing their connection off of as many "routers" (satellites, servers, etc.) as possible, using aliases, and the like. Agents should also take care to remain connected for as little time as possible to avoid being traced.

PCs: Personal computers are perhaps the single greatest boon for an intelligence-gathering agent. They store information almost indefinitely, and even

Public Record: You'd be surprised what you can learn through publicly available records. For example, the Registrar of Deeds keeps a public record of who owns every piece of property in its principality. Thus, you can find out that the villainous Dr. Dread, under an alias, owns that mountain hideaway where people are said to disappear. Likewise, corporations must register ownership with the local government. An enterprising snoop can discover what their holdings are and who is on the Board of Directors. Need to track an FBI agent? Their cases are not openly accessible, but their expense reports are a matter of public record. By scrutinizing these, you can ascertain where they have been and cross-reference that information with local news agencies to get an idea of what they might have been working on.

The Trade: Many intelligence agencies cooperate with each other. An agent working for MI6 can usually expect cooperation from other NATO agencies as well as the Mossad, Interpol, and others. Further, there are a great many informants who can provide information. Payment is usually "tit for tat" in these cases. Other agencies and informants barter information — make sure to bring something to the table that the other party might be interested in.

HUMAN INTELLIGENCE

The primary questions you should ask yourself when dealing with NPCs is whose side they are on (if any), and whether you can risk contacting them directly. The first question may require you to psychologically evaluate, or "profile" them. This is handled during play with the Sense Motive skill, using the guidelines offered on page 63. Be sure to ask the GC pointed questions about the NPC to receive useful information, and allow time for results. *For more information, see Conducting Interviews on page 215.*

Handling: Remember also that, as an intelligence operative, you are trained to "handle" or "run" operatives of your own. This means you know how to recruit and supervise specialists, middle men, and others who can be used to gain information about your enemies and missions. These NPCs can come from any walk of life, and need not have anything to do with the intelligence world. The only requirement is that you are able to offer them something they want in exchange for their assistance (money, power, satisfaction, etc.). The emotionally unstable, unhappy, destitute, and those who are fleeing from the law are all prime candidates for such service. Generally, you should use these operatives to perform risky tasks or enter situations you aren't comfortable with yourself, such as theft, sabotage, assassination, communication and hand-offs with dangerous people, and the like. Be careful, however, not to become reliant upon them, however; the more people you recruit into your service (whether they realize they are helping you or not), the more chance there is the Agency's involvement may be revealed. Also, running numerous agents increases the possibility that one will turn out to be a double-agent.

PHOTOGRAPHIC INTELLIGENCE

Always ask if there is a security camera on site when you are investigating a scene. Video and photographic footage is usually the most direct method of determining what has happened, and determining the next course of action.

Also, check every site for cameras, photos, and other imaging devices which might assist your investigation.

PHYSICAL INTELLIGENCE

Learn everything you can from a location, body, item, or other physical clues before moving on. This requires you to be attentive when the GC offers a description, and inquisitive when following up with it. Again, pose pointed questions to the GC to receive useful information, ask yourself the five basic investigative questions, and learn to catalog evidence and notes during your missions. There is one all-important caveat, however — when the GC makes it clear you have ventured down a blind path or reached a dead end, trust and accept his counsel. No matter how much you would like a mission to switch gears and move in a new direction, it is often impossible for the GC to accommodate you, and few GCs want to make up the entire mission as they go along. They'll indulge your search to a point, after which they must be able to bring the mission back on track.

Incident Sites: Approaching and dissecting event locations deserves special attention, and is covered in its own section *(see page 214)*.

SIGNALS INTELLIGENCE

Never forget that you work for an organization which devises and builds some of the most sophisticated surveillance devices on Earth. If you can read about it in Popular Mechanics, you can potentially requisition it from the Agency with some of your mission budget — assuming you have the funds, of course. If you can get into someone's house or office, you can wiretap their phones through the receiver of the phone box (if there is one). You can set the wiretap to record automatically when the phone is used, to transmit calls to a portable or mobile station you set up (inside a van or nearby location), or even redirect calls to a switchboard set up by your team. You can also requisition portable parabolic "gun-mikes" which, when pointed at a location, can pick up sounds several hundred feet away.

INCIDENT SITES

As a government operative, you are frequently responsible for the investigation of an incident site. In the world of law enforcement, these sites are commonly referred to as "crime scenes." In the world of espionage, "incident site" refers to a much broader range of locations, from murder crime scenes to kidnapping sites to dead drop locations. In all cases, it's your agent's responsibility to both secure the location and perform the initial investigation.

Unlike most law enforcement agencies, the clandestine nature of your operations often demands that you handle the site alone, without a crime scene investigation unit. This section offers a few guidelines to remember when doing so.

COLLECTING EVIDENCE

Here we get to the crux of the matter — where to look for all the clues you need to move the mission along, and what to do with them (see Using Evidence and Evidence Analysis on page 216). The primary thing to be concerned with during any scene is the clue trail or the challenge at hand. The former requires close attention to the details provided by the GC, and the ability to logically rebuild what happened. The specifics of each scene vary with each mission, but several of the most common things to look for follow.

First and foremost, secure the scene. Make sure that you or other members of your team haven't contaminated any chemical evidence (such as blood stains, powder burns, and the like). Make sure any witnesses are taken aside where they can't do the same (and where they can be quietly questioned). Then do your best to stop newcomers from wandering into the scene unexpectedly (usually by assigning someone to watch the perimeter or by preventing others from coming into the scene). Finally, scan the scene for anything that looks important (see below for several possibilities) and make sure it won't be disturbed before you get to it.

As soon as the site is secured, interview anyone who was present when you arrived, or who might have been a witness. If you are working with a team, assign this task to someone else and move on to the particulars of the site. Time is nearly always of the essence during your investigations.

Even if you're not sure they'll be needed, take pictures or make physical sketches of the scene for reference later in the mission. Once you've recorded the site, proceed to the items you considered important upon arriving. Take notes about each, along with any theories they provide which can later be used to support or disprove eyewitness accounts, or build new ideas concerning the mission.

Look for ways that the villains entered or exited the site, and anything they left behind. Either of these can lead to further understanding of their abilities, or where they are now. Try to discern the general "action" that took place at the location. Was there a fight? If so, how many people were involved? Who won or lost? Look for fingerprints on doors, windows, objects obviously out of place (fallen lamps, overturned tables and chairs, etc.) and new or unusual stains or fibers. Take samples of everything you find that seems remotely out of the ordinary and — if possible — analyze it at a professional crime lab or with a portable forensic gadget. Fingerprints transferred to transparent tape can be compared to Department of Justice or INTERPOL felon lists if you have access to them. Spent casings and bullets can determine the type of weapons used, and where they were fired from, painting a more complete picture of the combat.

Even if the important events occurred months or years ago, you can discern important clues. Bloodstained surfaces — even after they have been bleached — can be discovered by spraying a chemical called fluorescein onto them. DNA can be recovered in hair and blood samples (even after they've dried), and human remains offer an enormous amount of information, including method of death and the weapon used.

APPROACHING THE SITE

The first and arguably most important step agents must take is to secure the location. Contaminated sites are of little use to anyone, least of all investigating agents. Ordinarily, the best course of action is to summon the local law enforcement and request that they cordon off the area. In the world of espionage, however, such attention is not always beneficial.

The trick, in this case, is to secure the area without exposing yourself or your activities. How this is achieved largely depends on the time and resources at your team's disposal. Given the time and wherewithal, an excellent course of action is to disguise yourselves as a city utilities crew and fake a gas main leak or other public health hazard near the site to keep people away. At least in large cities, such occurrences are hardly out of the ordinary, and can give your team plenty of time to investigate the site. It's doubtful that even the police would bother to wonder what's going on.

Of course, such an elaborate deception is not always possible. If your team is in a hurry, or the site is already crowded, less subtle means may be necessary. Never forget that the best way to clear a building is to shout "Fire!" Never forget, also, that in such conditions, your investigation time is limited — the fire department is likely on the way.

THE TREES

The second step is to catalog the site. The devil, as they say, is in the details. Take note of everything, and take as many photographs as you can. Record whether the lights are on or off, the position of furniture and doors, even the weather. Every piece of information is potentially an important clue.

Search desks and other places that people spend a lot of time — these are the most likely places to find clues. Take evidence with you. You are not the police, and are not beholden to their procedure. Besides, leaving important clues behind for someone else to follow up on is to invite others (potentially those whom you are opposed to) to join the party.

Don't dawdle. Some evidence is time sensitive, and must be collected quickly. Gunshot residue is an excellent example, as are shoe prints — especially during inclement weather.

It's important to remember that a great deal of potential evidence is not visible to the naked eye. Again, gunshot residue is an example, as is DNA. Take samples of anything that might be useful (blood, errant fibers, unidentified dust) for later analysis in a forensics lab or with a portable kit.

THE FOREST

At times, the sheer amount of available data can be overwhelming; when this happens, focus on the leads, not the evidence. Sometimes, as with a dead drop location, simply performing proper surveillance of the incident site is enough. Sooner or later, the culprit may return.

More often, careful attention must be paid to the details: Was an obvious exit used (showing you where the culprit went)? Did he leave anything behind (a weapon, an article of clothing, fingerprints, or bodily fluids such as blood or saliva)? Most importantly, did anyone see anything?

Careful attention to detail is required in every step of the process, but never lose sight of your investigation or your mission goal.

CONDUCTING INTERVIEWS

Information can come from numerous sources: civilians involved near the crime wanting to help uphold the law, miscreants looking to decrease their jail time, or if you're really lucky (or extremely persuasive) important enemies willing to turn.

Of course, there's always the possibility that someone ostensibly 'helping' you is actually trying to send you down the wrong path. It's a good idea to find corroborating witnesses and confirm stories with supporting evidence.

There is an art to knowing a witness' motivation, just as there is an art to knowing how to question them. As described earlier, the Sense Motive skill concerns the former. Here we deal with the latter.

PREPARING FOR THE INTERVIEW

Before you start to question or interrogate someone, it's important to establish what you need to know, and what tools you have to help convince the witness or suspect to offer it. Ask yourself: Do you have any supporting information? Do you know what the witness' fears and hatreds are?

INCENTIVE

One method of convincing people to talk is to offer them incentive: money, protection from potential assassins, safe housing, or in the case of villains reduced prison time or even immunity from prosecution. It must be emphasized that this last incentive is used very rarely, as most villains that agents come across pose global threats, and the Agency prefers not to become involved in legal matters unless it must.

One other incentive you can offer is asylum — either within your organization for a short time, or under a country's supervision. This is often useful with international witnesses, especially if you can offer them a better lifestyle than they enjoy in their home country.

APPLYING PRESSURE

Not everyone you come across during an investigation is forthcoming, especially if they distrust the government. Many villains have trained or brainwashed their troops to resist interviews, making a Q&A session with them very much like a test of wills. In these cases, the best option is sometimes the very careful 'application of pressure.'

This does not mean torture. First and foremost, you're agents of an organization whose mission statement it is to *protect* the world, not injure or exploit it. Torture would make you as base and vile as the criminal organizations you strive to bring down.

Psychology is often your best option when pressuring witnesses, particularly those you are sure are involved in your enemies' schemes. Between playing your own strengths (as a "good cop" or "bad cop") off the rest of your team and fabricating evidence to panic the witness into offering testimony, a great deal of quality information can be gleaned. Should you have the time and resources, you can run complex scams to convince witnesses that their best option is to confide in you.

Of course, lying is dangerous, as it risks your relationship with the witness. This is particularly perilous if the witness is a long-term source of information to you.

Even more dangerous than lying is extortion — forcing the assistance of a suspect or witness by threatening him with compromising information, photos, etc. These tactics should only be adopted when the need for the person's help outweighs his long-term usefulness.

USING EVIDENCE

First and foremost, the all-important lesson about evidence in *Spycraft:* superspies aren't interested in building a case against the culprit of a crime, only stopping him. Their goal is laid out for them during their mission briefing. They never have to prosecute in a court of law (though they may be assigned to secure information for others who do). Ultimately, they're only interested in tracking down the threat at hand and defusing it.

With this in mind, how do you benefit from the evidence you've collected? You can use the photographs and sketches that you've taken to build computer composites of the scene, allowing you to recreate the events and (hopefully) trace them back to their source. You can use DNA analysis to identify people involved in the events — especially if samples of their DNA are available from earlier encounters or Agency records, or the records of a supporting government or agency. You can determine the weapon preferences of your enemies (and therefore how to counter them) by performing ballistics tests. Vehicles can be identified by comparing tire tread photos to vehicle profiles, and distinctive cracks, uneven wear and tear, and the like can even identify specific vehicles. Fingerprints (or anything else that identifies someone who was at the scene) can be used to acquire an address and place of employment, and open the door for other investigations such as those described earlier in this section.

In all cases, this requires careful deduction. Strive to consider not only what you have just found, but what came before that might be relevant to the mission at hand. Bringing it all together is one of a secret agent's most valuable talents — one which players should always seek to develop.

EVIDENCE ANALYSIS

The life of a spy isn't all about fast cars, beautiful women, and high-octane action. Sometimes it's about taking a step back from the chaos and looking at what you've got, to decide where you're going next. Collecting evidence is a major part of your life as a spy: it provides leads, gives clues as to which organizations may be involved and what weapons were used, and may even give others the evidence to put people in jail.

TYPES OF EVIDENCE

There is a wide variety of information that can be gathered during an investigation: detailed photographs, video footage, fingerprints, blood, dust, and hair samples, weapons, documents, bullets, ballistics information (tracking the action that happened by the wreckage left behind), and many other elements.

The most important things to consider when analyzing evidence are what exactly happened, and where you should go next to learn more about your mission. The following sections might help you in these two endeavors.

Analysis: Many of the Agency's analysis techniques require that the evidence be taken back to a central lab or base, but occasionally it's necessary to analyze the evidence while in the field. If it's known ahead of time that 'on the fly' analysis is needed, then you may benefit from requesting a specialist ahead of time (which has its own inherent problems), or from asking for special equipment or training before embarking on your mission.

DNA Analysis: This is the testing of blood, hair, or any other organic substance at a scene, to determine its DNA composition. Many agencies keep DNA profiles for the major criminals they face, and you can sometimes gain access to the national health files of a country to identify possible civilian involvement. It is essential when collecting DNA to keep it as pure as possible; contaminated samples can lead to inaccurate results. Toward this end most teams carry kits with them that include syringes, test tubes, jars, and gloves.

Cryptography: There are two common types of cryptographic evidence.

- *Physical Coding:* Documents and verbal code phrases can be decoded using a number of cryptography basics. By determining which parts of a message are extraneous and filtering them out, for instance, the remainder can be compared to existing word lengths.

- *Computer Coding:* If computers on the scene you are investigating have been infiltrated or sabotaged, your computer specialist, or snoop (if you have one), may come into play — especially if the action was perpetrated by a professional. Otherwise, specialists may need to be called in, or a remote hack (from the home office) may be necessary.

Photo Analysis: Using state-of-the-art computer imagery to focus and magnify photos, you can pick out the tiniest pieces of evidence from a photo. Faces in the background can be enhanced and compared to existing "mug shots," often through criminal databases like those at INTERPOL. If enough photos have been taken of the scene it may even be possible to generate a 3D model of the scene and surrounding area, and then to build a realistic simulation of the area and recreate what transpired there.

Weapons and Bullets: If you're lucky, you may find weapons and bullets on site that can offer clues about the action that occurred there and the people involved. Some weapons are signature sidearms of specific individuals (like James Bond's Walther PPK) or of organizations. Also, bullets are "scored" when they travel down the barrel of a gun, identifying the type of weapon used and allowing a bullet to be matched to the weapon that fired it.

Agent Tools

As experienced operatives of a multinational espionage organization, you have a wide variety of tools at your disposal. Chief among these are the support of the Agency, the incredible wealth of information you have acquired over the years, and your ability to think outside the box. These perks are handled mechanically with favor checks, education checks, and inspiration checks, respectively.

Note: These checks are often prompted by the mission briefing, and therefore made before the agents even leave the home office. This sort of planning is common to *Spycraft,* and should be encouraged.

FAVOR CHECKS

Though a team of operatives is expected to operate independently, and agents are assigned budgets and field expenses to acquire gear in the field, it's still common for them to request aid from the home office. When they do, it's referred to as a "favor check."

An agent may request a favor check by spending an action die, then contacting headquarters and rolling 1d20, adding the agent's level, then comparing that against the DC of the aid the team is requesting (as shown on Table 8.1: Favor Checks). As usual, a 1 automatically fails, a 20 automatically succeeds, and action dice may be spent to improve the roll. A request may only be made once every 24 hours, as the requests take time to filter through the proper channels.

The action die spent to request a favor check is not added to the roll, though you may spend additional action dice to improve your roll as you wish.

In some cases (such as requesting false passports and supporting credentials before they have left the home office), the GC may rule that a favor does not need to be rolled for. In these cases, the favor is simply granted and no action die must be spent to request the favor.

Example: Donovan has been captured by German authorities and is languishing in a holding cell as the sensitive files he was carrying make their way across the continent in the hands of his arch-nemesis. He spends an action die and asks the GC for government intervention to free him. The GC rules that this favor has a DC of 10. Donovan rolls a 2 and adds his level (6); not enough. He spends a second action die to improve his roll and gets a 3, which brings his total to 11. Donovan is freed in the morning.

ACCESSING AGENCY ASSETS

The Agency has a variety of assets around the world that agents may want to use during a mission. This includes sending encoded messages back to base to be decoded by the Agency's supercomputers and top-notch translators, arranging for false credentials, and meeting with an Agency employee to pick up equipment requisitioned in the field.

There are no bonuses when requesting aid form the home office.

GOVERNMENT INTERVENTION

Often, agents must deal with problems so large that they involve multiple governments, such as a villain with legal immunity or the need to quarantine a large area exposed to a deadly virus. In these cases, the agents must tread softly or risk exposing the Agency.

Pointmen receive a +2 bonus to their roll when requesting governmental intervention, since they have friends working in the governmental liaison department.

INFORMATION SEARCHES

The Agency can perform extensive data searches for operatives in a hurry. They can conduct automated Internet searches, call up spy satellite photographs – even compile financial and personal records down to someone's SAT scores or last year's credit card bills. Secure topics – such as military operations and top secret research projects – must first be approved with a security clearance request, below.

Snoops receive a +2 to their roll when requesting information searches, since they have friends working in the information retrieval department of the Agency.

LEGAL ASSISTANCE

Some of the world's most powerful lawyers owe favors to the Agency. This is handy when agents make a bit too much noise and get themselves in trouble with the local authorities, or need to circumvent pesky constitutional amendments.

Facemen receive a +2 bonus to their roll when requesting legal assistance, since they have friends working in the legal department of the Agency.

TABLE 8.1: FAVOR CHECKS

Asset Type	Examples	DC
Very common	find safe house, forgery without supporting credentials	5
Common	decrypt message, translate document	10
Uncommon	medical evacuation, vehicle repair in the field, forgery with supporting credentials	15
Very uncommon	exotic substance analysis, call bomb squad	20
Rare	requisition prototype gadget, recharge used gadget	25

Intervention Type	Examples	DC
Very common	bypass customs, initiate minor manhunt	5
Common	release criminal, initiate major manhunt	10
Uncommon	revoke legal immunity, extradite citizen	15
Very uncommon	revoke citizenship, extradite politico	20
Rare	quarantine major city, extradite government leader	25

Information Type	Examples	DC
Very common	Internet search, credit history	5
Common	DMV records, criminal records	10
Uncommon	psychiatric or legal records, private email	15
Very uncommon	spy satellite data, corporate finance records	20
Rare	military secrets, major corporate email archives	25

Assistance Type	Examples	DC
Very common	legal advice, pay bail	5
Common	attorney services, call off law enforcement	10
Uncommon	erase/alter legal documents, bypass jurisdiction	15
Very uncommon	illegal wiretaps, governor's pardon	20
Rare	presidential pardon, violate Constitution	25

Clearance/Check Type	Examples	DC
Very common	access to low priority base, check civilian	5
Common	access to mid-priority base, check politico	10
Uncommon	access to top-priority base, access for politico	15
Very uncommon	access to nuclear facility, access for civilian	20
Rare	access to experimental facility, access for criminal	25

Specialist Type	Examples	DC
Very common	Skill/ability bonus of +3	5
Common	Skill/ability bonus of +6	10
Uncommon	Skill/ability bonus of +9	15
Very uncommon	Skill/ability bonus of +12	20
Rare	Skill/ability bonus of +15	25

Transportation Type	Examples	DC
Very common	covert pick-up, rental car	5
Common	bus, train, passenger plane	10
Uncommon	hovercraft, spy plane or military aircraft	15
Very uncommon	Concorde, bomber, submarine	20
Rare	space shuttle, aircraft carrier	25

SECURITY CLEARANCE AND CHECKS

The Agency can help operatives get into military and top secret research installations, but they are accompanied by an armed escort at all times while on the premises — the military takes its secrets very seriously. Additionally, the Agency can access the security records of any law enforcement agency in the world and check out known aliases, past criminal records, and similar information.

Soldiers add +2 to their roll when requesting security clearances or checks, as they have friends working in the security department of the Agency.

SPECIALIST SUPPORT

The Agency has much support in the civilian and private sectors, and can call in specialists to tackle problems the agents aren't equipped for. Specialists range from scientists (forensics specialists, hackers, and the like) to military personnel (demolitions experts, tacticians, etc.) to linguists, forgers, and many more.

Fixers add +2 bonus to their roll when requesting specialists, as they have friends working in the outside personnel department of the Agency.

TRAVEL ARRANGEMENTS

The Agency is capable of making even the most unusual travel arrangements, though they draw the line at joy rides through the outer atmosphere.

Wheelmen add +2 bonus to their roll when requesting travel arrangements, as they have friends working in the transportation and mechanics department of the Agency.

EDUCATION CHECKS

Your agent knows things that you (as a player) don't — things he learned over the course of his espionage training. When you want to call upon information that you feel your agent should know based on his background, make an education check.

First, your Game Control assigns a DC to the information you are asking for. Typically, simple information has a DC of 10-15, while more complex information might range up to a DC of 30. Once this has been decided upon, roll 1d20 and add your agent's overall agent level plus his Intelligence modifier. Thus, a 3rd-level fixer/2nd-level wheelman with a +2 Intelligence modifier would add +7 to the roll. If the check succeeds, then your Game Control gives you the information you asked for; if the check fails, you don't know it.

Education checks are free actions, though you may only make one per round and may not ever retry a roll you have failed. If you miss an education check, you simply don't know the information (though you can research it in-game by asking the right questions to NPCs and following the right leads).

There is no action die cost to make an education check, but you may spend action dice to improve your roll.

The GC may refuse you an education check at any time by saying, "You don't know this information."

Example: While casing a Monaco casino, Donovan spots a dangerously beautiful woman at the bar. He suspects that she is someone important, and asks to make an education roll to see if he has encountered her before. The GC sets the DC at 20 and Donovan makes his roll (12). Adding his level (6) and his Intelligence modifier (+3), his education total is 21, just enough. The GC informs Donovan that the woman is an agent of Russia's Chief Intelligence Directorate (GRU). Donovan has read the Agency's file on her. He may now ask general questions about her background or make additional education checks to learn more sensitive information about her (within the bounds of the first check's results).

On occasion, your GC may prompt an education check — usually when he needs to help the game along.

INSPIRATION CHECKS

Sometimes a sudden flash of insight strikes you. When you are stumped as to what to do next, you can spend an action die and make an inspiration check.

First, your GC assigns a DC to the check — the higher the DC, the less likely you are to have a flash of inspiration. Typically, the more stuck you are, the lower your GC sets the DC. Once this has been decided upon, roll 1d20 and add your agent's overall agent level plus his Wisdom modifier. Thus, a 3rd-level fixer/2nd-level wheelman with a +2 Wisdom modifier would add +7 to the roll. If the check succeeds, your GC gives you a hint to the correct course of action to take at this time; if the check fails, you don't get a hint.

Inspiration checks are free actions, though you may only make one per round. You may retry inspiration checks as often as you like, provided you have the action dice to fund them (see below) and the GC permits them.

Making an inspiration check (whether successful or not) costs one action die. You may spend additional action dice to improve your roll if you wish.

Inspiration checks are the "great equalizer" and can help a GC to bring a serial back on track after the players have diverged from the plot. They should not become a crutch, however, and so the GC may refuse them at any time.

Example: Donovan is tracking his latest quarry through Buenos Aires and has hit a dead end, seemingly out of leads. He spends an action die and requests an inspiration check. The Game Control sets the DC at 15, wanting a reasonable chance for Donovan to figure it out. Donovan rolls a 16, more than the DC without his level and Wisdom modifiers. The GC reminds Donovan about a local contact mentioned in his mission briefing, bringing the serial back on track.

On occasion, your GC may prompt an inspiration check — usually when he is aware that your agent might know something important to the mission at hand that you (as a player) aren't likely to ask about. When this happens, the education check has no action die cost.

TRAVEL

There are three movement scales the Game Control may wish to use during play, as follows.

TACTICAL MOVEMENT

This movement scale is used during combat. It is measured in feet per round and is described in more detail under Moving in Chapter 6: Combat *(see page 174)*.

To determine your tactical movement at any time, consult Table 8.3: Movement and Distance on Foot on the opposite page.

LOCAL MOVEMENT

This movement scale is used when agents are exploring an area. It is measured in feet per minute. A running agent must follow the rules on page 175.

To determine your local movement at any time, consult Table 8.3: Movement and Distance on Foot on the opposite page.

OVERLAND MOVEMENT

This movement scale is used when agents are traveling long distances (such as from city to city or country to country). It is measured in miles per hour or per day. Normally, a day of travel represents 8 hours, but this can vary depending on your method of transportation. When traveling on foot using the hustle option *(see opposite)* for more than 1 hour in any day, you suffer 1 point of subdual damage for the second hour hustling. After that, the subdual damage doubles for each additional hour hustled. You cannot run over such long periods of time.

Terrain: Different types of terrain affect your travel distance, as illustrated on Table 8.5: Terrain and (Overland) Movement (on the opposite page).

Forced March: You may push yourself to travel more than 8 hours a day by performing a forced march. However, for each extra hour you travel, you must make a Fortitude save (DC 10 + 1 per extra hour traveled) or suffer 1d6 points of subdual damage. You can't recover any of this damage normally until you've rested for at least 4 hours.

Common Air Travel Times: We have provided you with the average air travel times between common cities *(see page 223)*, as well as a number of things to remember when making your way around the world. The latter is found throughout the rest of this section.

TRAVEL CONSIDERATIONS

Espionage organizations pride themselves on maneuverability and quick response time. In the fast-paced world of international espionage, arriving an hour late results in a failed mission. Thus, determining how the team arrives in a mission area is the first step during most operations.

This section is concerned with large-scale movement: getting from mission area to mission area. Traveling within a city is a matter of agent preference, local resources, and the availability of special equipment.

There are four standard ways to travel.

PLANES...

Airplanes are the quickest method of getting around the world, and thus the most desirable. They are also the only form of transportation that offers rapid transport from continent to continent.

The sheer volume of passengers using commercial airlines provides excellent cover for covert operatives, and the first test of their cover identities *(see page 208)*. Gadgets often allow small equipment to be smuggled with little fuss. And as most criminal organizations cannot risk open action any more than the Agency can, commercial airplane travel substantially reduces the risk of hostile encounters en route.

Agents traveling by plane are at the mercy of the airline and weather conditions, which can lead to unforeseen delays that can imperil a mission. The Agency typically books agents on reliable flights, but weather is completely out of the hands of even the most dependable airlines.

The final condition which airplane passengers must contend with is the lack of privacy. Agents can't openly discuss their mission en route, nor can they view sensitive documents or data.

The advantages and disadvantages above apply to commercial airlines. Private jets are the ideal means of transport for agents on the go — they're fast, versatile, private, and secure. Unfortunately, they're expensive.

TABLE 8.2: SPEED CONVERSIONS

Speed	Per Hour	Per Day	Speed	Per Hour	Per Day
10 ft.	1 mile	8 miles	450 ft.	45 miles	360 miles
15 ft.	1.5 miles	12 miles	500 ft.	50 miles	400 miles
20 ft.	2 miles	16 miles	550 ft.	55 miles	440 miles
30 ft.	3 miles	24 miles	600 ft.	60 miles	480 miles
40 ft.	4 miles	32 miles	650 ft.	65 miles	520 miles
50 ft.	5 miles	40 miles	700 ft.	70 miles	560 miles
60 ft.	6 miles	48 miles	750 ft.	75 miles	600 miles
70 ft.	7 miles	56 miles	800 ft.	80 miles	640 miles
80 ft.	8 miles	64 miles	850 ft.	85 miles	680 miles
90 ft.	9 miles	72 miles	900 ft.	90 miles	720 miles
100 ft.	10 miles	80 miles	950 ft.	95 miles	760 miles
150 ft.	15 miles	120 miles	1,000 ft.	100 miles	800 miles
200 ft.	20 miles	160 miles	+1,000 ft.	+100 miles	+800 miles
250 ft.	25 miles	200 miles			
300 ft.	30 miles	240 miles			
350 ft.	35 miles	280 miles			
400 ft.	40 miles	320 miles			

Notes: Riding vehicles are not blocked by non-road terrain. Because sea vessels can sail through the night, double their per-day travel distance.

TABLE 8.3: MOVEMENT AND DISTANCE ON FOOT

	Speed				
	15 ft.	20 ft.	25 ft.	30 ft.	40 ft.
One Round (Tactical)					
Walk	15 ft.	20 ft.	25 ft.	30 ft.	40 ft
Hustle	30 ft.	40 ft.	50 ft.	60 ft.	80 ft.
Run (×3)	45 ft.	60 ft.	75 ft.	90 ft.	120 ft.
Run (×4)	60 ft.	80 ft.	100 ft.	120 ft.	160 ft.
One Minute (Local)					
Walk	150 ft.	200 ft.	250 ft.	300 ft.	400 ft.
Hustle	300 ft.	400 ft.	500 ft.	600 ft.	800 ft.
Run (×3)	450 ft.	600 ft.	750 ft.	900 ft.	1,200 ft.
Run (×4)	600 ft.	800 ft.	1,000 ft.	1,200 ft.	1,600 ft.
One Hour (Overland)					
Walk	1½ miles	2 miles	2½ miles	3 miles	4 miles
Hustle	3 miles	4 miles	5 miles	6 miles	8 miles
Run	—	—	—	—	—
One Day (Overland)					
Walk	12 miles	16 miles	20 miles	24 miles	32 miles
Hustle	—	—	—	—	—
Run	—	—	—	—	—

TABLE 8.4: HAMPERED MOVEMENT

Condition	Example	Movement Penalty
Obstruction		
Moderate	Undergrowth	× 3/4
Heavy	Thick undergrowth	× 1/2
Surface		
Bad	Steep slope or mud	× 1/2
Very bad	Deep snow	× 1/4
Poor visibility	Darkness or fog	× 1/2

TABLE 8.5: TERRAIN AND MOVEMENT

Terrain	Paved Road	Dirt Road/Trail	Wilderness
Plains	×1	× 1	×1
Scrub, rough	× 1	× 1	× 3/4
Forest	× 1	× 1	× 1/2*
Jungle	× 1	× 3/4	× 1/2*
Swamp	× 1	× 3/4	× 1/2*
Hills	× 1	× 3/4	× 1/2
Mountains	× 3/4	× 1/2	× 1/4*
Desert	× 1	× 1	× 1/2
Tundra	× 1	× 1/2	× 1/2

* Vehicles cannot pass through this terrain.

Very expensive. The Agency has only few private jets at its disposal, which are saved for emergency situations. But if a mission warrants it, and the consequences are dire enough should the agent team not arrive as soon as is humanly possible, one may be made available. Agents trying to convince their superiors to loan them a plane without a clear and present global emergency are likely to be ignored.

A compromise on the issue of privacy is first-class travel. This tends to attract more attention than most spy organizations prefer, but enterprising agents, particularly those with a taste for the good life, have been known to convince their superiors to overlook the expense. Some agents – particularly those operating in Europe – gladly pay for first-class tickets out of their own pockets.

Of course, particularly wealthy agents may have their own private jets.

Trains...

There are many disadvantages to rail travel. Trains rarely travel from one continent to another, and they are considerably slower than planes. Many countries lack a reliable train service.

That is not to say that trains completely lack advantages, however. In cases where speed is not the greatest concern, trains are an incredibly relaxing mode of transport. They also offer perhaps the greatest degree of privacy and concealability of any commercial travel. And you can leave a train (albeit with a degree of effort and risk) at any time while it is in transit.

The primary time to use trains for mission transport, though, is when the destination area lacks any other method of travel. This is particularly true in less-affluent countries, where poor air service and neglected roads leave trains as the only viable option. Trains also arouse very little suspicion, allowing teams to potentially get the drop on enemies.

Trains are often a favorite of criminal organizations, which use them to transport troops, supplies, and victims from one clandestine location to another. Villain groups sometimes even use train cars as mobile HQs.

Automobiles...

Many agents have a fondness for fast cars, and some even use their own private vehicles on missions. Cars are the most flexible form of vehicle transport, as they can go anywhere that a road exists (and a few places where they don't). They can be modified for a wide range of mission objectives, and can also provide transport within the mission area. And the chance of witnesses realizing that an agent is doing something suspicious while using a car is greatly reduced.

Unfortunately, cars are relatively slow, and are difficult to transport between continents. Also, drivers are unable to concentrate on anything but driving, leaving them little time to review mission briefings or discuss team stratagems in transit.

The use of cars is also affected by the number of agents involved. Traveling to a mission area in multiple automobiles can be complicated, but then so is cramming eight operatives into the back of a Volkswagen.

Most often, cars are not used until the agents arrive in the mission area, and then they are rented by their organization. Typically, Control provides one or more cars for a team when they arrive in a mission area via other means of transport, as mentioned in Dealing With the Authorities *(see page 206)*. If a mission team has arrived by car (usually because their home office is in the same area), they are generally expected to use the same vehicles through the mission.

Automobiles, like trains, are typically used as transport only when time is not of the essence. If Control suspects that the agents may have to travel to multiple sites within a relatively small area (such as Europe or Japan), autos generally become the mission team's primary means of transport.

...And Everything Else

Water travel is the slowest form of transport available. In other ways it is similar to train travel. The areas that commercial ocean liners serve are strictly limited and no variation from the scheduled destination is possible. It is even harder to leave a ship in the middle of the trip without drawing attention to oneself (and access to a powerboat or submarine).

Ocean liners are used primarily when the means of transport is the mission: if something or someone of a non-time-sensitive nature is being transported, or there is information on board that the team requires. A ship is larger than a train, providing more areas for concealment and covert battle. It's also easier to dispose of any evidence.

The Agency tends to have even few yachts available. Heavily equipped private ships are often available, but these are reserved either for missions that require a direct military strike or a floating base of operations.

Smaller sportsman-sized cruisers or fishing boats may sometimes be provided as mission transport if the destination area is one or more islands, such as Hawaii, Cuba, or the Bahamas. A native Wheelman with boating skills and extensive local knowledge comes with the boat if necessary, leaving the agents free to devote their attention to the mission at hand rather than driving the boat.

TABLE 8.6: APPROXIMATE DIRECT FLIGHT TRAVEL TIMES (IN HOURS)

	BAN	BER	BUE	CAI	CAS	DEL	FRA	HK	IST	LON	LA	MAD	MEX	MON	MOS	NY	PAR	RIO	ROM	SIN	SYD	TOK	WAS
Bangkok	—	9.5	19	8	12	3.5	10	2	8.5	11	15	11.5	17.5	10.5	8	15.5	10.5	18	10	1.5	8.5	5	16
Berlin	9.5	—	13.5	13.5	3	6.5	0.5	10	2	1	10.5	2	11	1	2	7	1	11.5	1.5	11	18	10	7.5
Buenos Aires	19	13.5	—	13.5	10.5	18	13	21	14	12.5	11	11.5	8.5	12.5	15	9.5	12.5	2	12.5	18	13.5	20.5	9.5
Cairo	8	13.5	13.5	—	4	5	3.5	9	1.5	4	14	4	14	3	3.5	10	3.5	11	2.5	9.5	16.5	11	10.5
Casablanca	12	3	10.5	4	—	9	2.5	12.5	3.5	2.5	11	1	10	2	5	6.5	2	8.5	2.5	13.5	20.5	13	7
Delhi	3.5	6.5	18	5	9	—	7	4.5	5	7.5	14.5	8	16.5	7	5	13.5	7.5	16	6.5	4.5	12	6.5	27
Frankfurt	10	0.5	13	3.5	2.5	7	—	10.5	2	0.5	10.5	1.5	11	1	2.5	7	0.5	11	1	11.5	18.5	10.5	7.5
Hong Kong	2	10	21	9	12.5	4.5	10.5	—	9	11	13	12	16	11	8	14.5	11	20	10.5	3	8.5	3.5	15
Istanbul	8.5	2	14	1.5	3.5	5	2	9	—	3	12.5	3	13	2	2	9	2.5	11.5	1.5	10	17	10	9.5
London	11	1	12.5	4	2.5	7.5	0.5	11	3	—	10	1.5	10	1	3	6.5	0.5	10.5	1.5	12.5	19.5	11	6.5
Los Angeles	15	10.5	11	14	11	14.5	10.5	13	12.5	10	—	10.5	3	11	11	4.5	10.5	11.5	11.5	16	13.5	10	4
Madrid	11.5	2	11.5	4	1	8	1.5	12	3	1.5	10.5	—	10	1	4	6.5	1	9	1.5	13	20	12	7
Mexico City	17.5	11	8.5	14	10	16.5	11	16	13	10	3	10	—	11	12	4	10.5	8.5	11.5	18.5	14.5	13	3.5
Monte Carlo	10.5	1	12.5	3	2	7	1	11	2	1	11	1	11	—	3	7	1	10	0.5	12	19	11	7.5
Moscow	8	2	15	3.5	5	5	2.5	8	2	3	11	4	12	3	—	8.5	3	13	2.5	9.5	16.5	8.5	9
New York	15.5	7	9.5	10	6.5	13.5	7	14.5	9	6.5	4.5	6.5	4	7	8.5	—	6.5	8.5	8	17.5	18	12.5	0.5
Paris	10.5	1	12.5	3.5	2	7.5	0.5	11	2.5	0.5	10.5	1	10.5	1	3	6.5	—	10.5	1	12	19	11	7
Rio	18	11.5	2	11	8.5	16	11	20	11.5	10.5	11.5	9	8.5	10	13	8.5	10.5	—	10.5	18	15.5	21	8.5
Rome	10	1.5	12.5	2.5	2.5	6.5	1	10.5	1.5	1.5	11.5	1.5	11.5	0.5	2.5	8	1	10.5	—	11.5	18.5	11	8
Singapore	1.5	11	18	9.5	13.5	4.5	11.5	3	10	12.5	16	13	18.5	12	9.5	17.5	12	18	11.5	—	7	6	17.5
Sydney	8.5	18	13.5	16.5	20.5	12	18.5	8.5	17	19.5	13.5	20	14.5	19	16.5	18	19	15.5	18.5	7	—	9	17.5
Tokyo	5	10	20.5	11	13	6.5	10.5	3.5	10	11	10	12	13	11	8.5	12.5	11	21	11	6	9	—	12.5
Washington D.C.	16	7.5	9.5	10.5	7	27	7.5	15	9.5	6.5	4	7	3.5	7.5	9	0.5	7	8.5	8	17.5	17.5	12.5	—

How to use this Table: Find the city from which you are departing in the left column and cross-reference it with the city to which you are traveling. The resulting number is the approximate travel time between the cities by plane, in hours. These numbers represent standard 747 airline travel (at an average of 550 mph) and are rounded to the nearest half-hour. For more accurate travel times, we recommend checking with online travel services and airline homepages, or recalculating using the distance between locations and the speed of any private transportation being used.

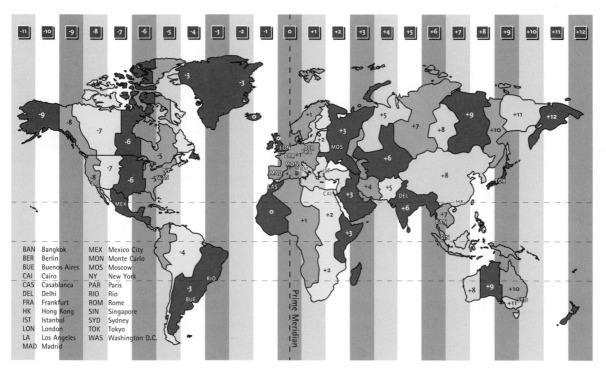

BAN	Bangkok	MEX	Mexico City
BER	Berlin	MON	Monte Carlo
BUE	Buenos Aires	MOS	Moscow
CAI	Cairo	NY	New York
CAS	Casablanca	PAR	Paris
DEL	Delhi	RIO	Rio
FRA	Frankfurt	ROM	Rome
HK	Hong Kong	SIN	Singapore
IST	Istanbul	SYD	Sydney
LON	London	TOK	Tokyo
LA	Los Angeles	WAS	Washington D.C.
MAD	Madrid		

How to use this Diagram: Cities listed on the travel time matrix above are shown on this world map, along with time zones and regions which vary from the GMT standard. The numbers on the map and along the top of this graphic represent the number of hours a region is ahead or behind GMT (add or subtract this number from GMT to find the region's local time).

Greenwich Mean Time (GMT): Also known as Zulu Time (to aviators and military personnel), Greenwich Mean Time is derived from the Prime Meridian in Greenwich, England. World Time Zones are established every 15 degrees East and West of the Prime Meridian, as illustrated above.

TRAVEL CONCERNS

The primary concern of agents traveling abroad is interception, which can arrive from two sources — authorities and enemy opposition. Dealing With the Authorities *(see page 206)* provides some Agency guidelines for the former. Cover papers provided by Control should pass all but the most detailed inspection. The chance that they may fail increases dramatically, however, if enemies have tipped the authorities off, or if the mission area is controlled by a hostile government.

If a team's cover is blown, flight or bribery are the recommended options. Combat is a distant third, as it risks revealing the home office and increases the chance of punishment if the authorities catch the agent team.

Should an enemy attempt to intercept the team, the agents are commonly authorized to use whatever defensive measures they deem necessary. Maintaining Agency security should be considered, but the home office can reimpose secrecy after the fact: it can't resurrect dead agents.

The trickiest situation comes when the opposition either infiltrates the authorities, or uses the authorities as unwitting pawns. In this case, the authorities should be treated as threats. If an enemy operative is confirmed to be among the authorities, the agents should attempt to remove him if possible. Casual killing is, as always, frowned upon.

When leaving a mission area, particularly in a hazardous situation, the use of escape identity papers *(see page 208)* is recommended. Agent teams should guard against the possibility of authorities tipping off law enforcement at the agents' next destination, if it is known. Agents should always strive to dupe the authorities if this is suspected, or take steps upon arrival to avoid capture, using flight, bribery, or flight. The nearest allied section usually provides a safe house for the team until alternate transport can be arranged.

A second concern for traveling agent teams is how to bring their equipment with them. Certain gadgets are designed to smuggle small weapons and equipment, of course, but secondary plans should also be considered.

Larger equipment is often shipped via Agency cover businesses, usually along a different route than the agents to avoid possible connections between the two. Other operatives at the receiving end take possession and arrange for delivery to the agents.

Shipping cargo out of a mission area can be a bit trickier. When possible, Control provides agents with a contact — possibly an agent of an allied organization native to the area. This contact not only handles the incoming equipment, but also ships out any large equipment, usually through his organization's local businesses. The agents are commonly left out of the details, simply handing their cargo over to the contact (approved through codewords or other official means) and meeting someone at the other end to pick it up.

Cargo shipments out of a mission area may include not only any large equipment the agents brought with them, but also any mission objectives recovered in the field: computers, volatile chemicals, nuclear warheads, and other sensitive items. The team should try to remove such items by themselves only if no other alternatives are available, and then should strive to use third parties (such as unaligned transport firms) whenever possible. As usual, expenses for such emergencies are typically reimbursed after the team returns to the home office.

CROSSING BORDERS

In this day and age, transportation across borders is fairly simple. The main difficulty, whether you are traveling between nations or within a nation, is the type of government that controls the area.

Democracies generally have fairly loose restrictions on travel within their borders, and against outsiders crossing their borders. With proper papers (or papers that look proper), agents should have little trouble entering and leaving such nations, and traveling within them.

More dictatorial nations place much heavier sanctions upon travel by both natives and foreigners (though the latter are commonly questioned more thoroughly before they are allowed to travel). Cover identities still offer the team's first, and often best, chance to make it across the border undetected. Fortunately, such countries often seek outside business investors, and cover IDs in this vein offer excellent protection.

Countries completely isolated from tourist and business interests are rare. In such areas, Control often arranges for non-commercial transport (e.g. midnight arrival by boat, parachute drop, or hiding inside large crates). This tactic is avoided when possible, as there is no acceptable explanation for someone caught in such a compromising position.

Control may also employ non-commercial transport when a full-blown strike team is sent along (or when the agent team is the full-blown strike team), especially if the mission occurs within secured borders. Control may also do so when the mission at hand requires large equipment (such as specialized all-terrain ground vehicles) that cannot be safely imported past border inspectors.

*"The truth? The truth... There is no truth.
These men just make it up as they go along."*
*– Alex Krychek,
The X-Files*

CONTROL

GAME CONTROL TOOLS

This section introduces a number of rules specific to the Game Control. It contains many ways to exploit the *Spycraft* system and add depth to your games.

SETTING DCS

Players often want to perform actions that aren't explicitly listed anywhere in these rules. In these instances, you must set a DC for the action. See table 9.1 for a few samples.

POSITIVE AND NEGATIVE MODIFIERS

If you are unsure how a given factor should affect an agent's odds of success, use this rule of thumb. If a factor makes it more likely for the agent to succeed (such as high quality gear) lower the DC by 2. If a factor makes it less likely for an agent to succeed (such as an oily road) increase the DC by 2.

CALCULATING ODDS OF SUCCESS

In order to calculate an agent's odds of success on a given roll, subtract the bonus he receives to the roll from the DC he's trying to hit and consult Table 9.2: Odds of Success.

ACTION DICE

Your agents aren't the only ones who can call upon freak occurrences to help them out. Sometimes the dice don't go your way, and one of your villains is in imminent danger of dying prematurely. When that happens, you have your own storehouse of action dice to spend. This section covers how you can use them to slow the agents down and keep things interesting.

THE GAME CONTROL'S ACTION DICE

At the start of each game session, you receive a number of d12 action dice equal to the highest number of action dice any of your players begins with (see Table 1.3: Action Dice for how many action dice each player starts with).

In addition, you receive one extra action die for every agent on the team. Thus, if one of the agents on your team gets 4 starting action dice and there are 5 agents on the team total, you receive 9 action dice at the start of the game session.

You gain one additional action die every time you award one to one of your players. Thus it is important to keep awarding your players for keen intuition and hearty laughter; otherwise, you will run out yourself.

SPENDING YOUR ACTION DICE

You may spend your action dice at any time you want, for any of the following Game Control purposes.

1. ADDING TO NPC ROLLS

You may add the total roll of an action die to any die roll you make for an NPC, unless the ability, feat, or rule prompting the roll says otherwise.

You may add the total of one or more action dice to an NPC roll at any time, *even after the roll*. However, you may not use action dice after you have described the outcome of an action or roll.

When spending an action die to increase an NPC's roll, you roll one of your action dice and add the result to the NPC's attack roll, damage roll, skill check, saving throw, etc. You may keep spending action dice to increase an NPC's die roll as long as you have action dice left to spend, up to the point when you describe the outcome.

When rolling an action die, if you roll a 12 on the die, it "explodes," meaning that you re-roll the die, adding the number you roll to the previous total.

TABLE 9.1: DIFFICULTY CLASS EXAMPLES

DC	Sample Action	Skill Used
5	Climb a knotted rope	Climb
8	Climb a muddy hill	Climb
10	Tie a good knot	Use Rope
15	Stabilize a dying person	First Aid
18	Break down an average wooden door	None (Strength)
20	Notice a hidden compartment	Search
20	Pick a simple lock	Open Lock
20	Bypass a simple electronic eye	Electronics
25	Notice that another agent has been brainwashed	Sense Motive
28	Bypass a triply-redundant alarm system	Electronics
30	Open a wall safe	Open Lock
35	Hack into NORAD	Computers

So, if you roll a 12, and then re-roll it, getting a 4, the total value of the action die is 16. An action die can keep exploding as long as you keep rolling 12s.

Example 1: You roll a 17 for an NPC's Driver check, just shy of the 20 he needs to succeed. You decide to spend an action die, then roll a d12, getting a 3. Adding that to the NPC's previous total of 17, he now has a total of 20, enough to succeed.

Example 2: You roll a 5 for an NPC's attack roll and he needs a 20. Spending an action die, you roll a d12 and get a 12. The die explodes, so you re-roll it, this time getting a 3. When added to the previous 12, this gives the NPC a total of 15, which increases his 5 to a 20, a hit.

2. TEMPORARY DEFENSE FOR NPCs

At the start of any round, you may spend one action die to increase an NPC's Defense total by the total you roll. This luck bonus remains in effect until the end of the round. You may not use this ability again on the same NPC while the first luck bonus is active.

Example: One of your NPCs is close to unconsciousness, and needs to avoid being hit this round. You spend an action die, rolling an 12 and a 2 (for a total of 14). His Defense is increased by 14 until the end of the round.

3. ACTIVATING THREATS AND AGENT ERRORS

When you roll a threat for one of your NPCs during an attack roll or skill check, you may spend an action die in order to score a critical success or critical hit. In addition, when one of your players scores an error with an attack roll or skill check, you may spend an action die to turn it into a critical failure or miss. You decide upon the exact effects of the critical, though each skill has several suggestions listed in its description and we have provided a list of potential critical miss effects based on the number of dice you spend *(see Table 9.3: Sample Critical Miss Effects on page 228)*.

Example 1: One of your NPCs rolls a natural 20 when using his Jump skill. You spend an action die to turn the threat into a critical success, which indicates that he has leapt the maximum distance possible *(see page 57)*.

Example 2: Donovan rolls a 1 when firing at one of your henchmen. You spend one action die and Donovan drops his weapon. He must pick it up again.

Example 3: Using example 2, above, you spend two action dice. Donovan's gun jams and must be cleared.

TABLE 9.2: ODDS OF SUCCESS

DC minus Bonus	Chance of Success	Chance of Failure	Difficulty
1 or less	95%	5%	Very Easy
2	90%	10%	
3	85%	15%	
4	80%	20%	
5	75%	25%	Easy
6	70%	30%	
7	65%	35%	
8	60%	40%	
9	55%	45%	
10	50%	50%	Average
11	45%	55%	
12	40%	60%	
13	35%	65%	
14	30%	70%	
15	25%	75%	Hard
16	20%	80%	
17	15%	85%	
18	10%	90%	
19+	5%	95%	Very Hard

4. HEALING NPCs

When an NPC is not engaged in combat, you may spend any number of action dice to regain some of the NPC's vitality or wound points. For each action die you spend, you either roll 1d12 and regain that many of the NPC's vitality points, or regain 2 of the NPC's wound points.

Example: After an NPC has narrowly survived a combat with Donovan, you spend an action die to heal him. You roll 1d12, getting a 7. The NPC regains 7 vitality points. You could have chosen to heal two of the NPC's wound points instead.

AWARDING ACTION DICE

You should award an action die to any player who does something particularly clever or amuses the group. On average, try to hand out at least one action die every 20 to 30 minutes to keep things interesting. Also, try to spread the action dice you award among the players — if one player is shy or not as witty as the rest, it's all the more important to reward him when he does something noteworthy. In the end, the most important thing is to reward behavior that you want repeated, and ignore behavior you'd rather not see again.

GAINING MORE ACTION DICE

You gain an action die every time one of you award an action die to one of your players. Remember to keep handing out action dice, or you might run out yourself.

TABLE 9.3: SAMPLE CRITICAL MISS EFFECTS

Action Dice Spent	Effect
Agent is unarmed...	
1	Agent trips and falls prone.
2	Agent stuns himself for 1 round.
3	Agent hurts himself for 1d6 damage.
4+	Agent hurts himself for 2d6 damage.
Agent is wielding a melee weapon...	
1	Weapon dropped, half action to pick it up.
2	Weapon stuck, full action to free it.
3	Weapon breaks.*
4+	Weapon breaks, hurts agent for 1d6 damage.*
Agent is wielding a gun...	
1	Weapon dropped, half action to pick it up.
2	Gun jams, full action to clear it.
3	Gun misfires and is ruined.*
4+	Gun explodes, agent takes 1d6 damage.*

* Signature gear and gadgets are immune to this critical miss effect.

YOU CONTROL THE VERTICAL...

Action dice are a tool meant to make the game more enjoyable for everyone. They can enable the players to succeed when it's really important, and can help you get a mission back on track if the dice fail you. They also serve as a tangible reward for creative players.

However, their effectiveness depends upon how you use them. If you spoil a player's big moment of glory, or constantly pick on a single player, it ruins everyone's fun. You can make situations more dramatic with a critical failure that leads to a subplot, or make the players work a bit harder for their victory, and they'll thank you for it.

ENCOUNTERS

When starting an encounter, the first thing you need to do is determine the distance between the groups coming upon each other. This helps determine the range of any missile attacks that occur during the encounter.

ENCOUNTER DISTANCE

Encounter distance is determined by visibility and the two groups' state of alertness. Outside, the terrain and time of day are most important. Inside, distances rely on lighting conditions and line of sight. To determine the distance at which an encounter starts, follow these steps:

1. Choose terrain and visibility conditions from Table 9.4: Spotting Distance.

2. If line of sight is listed next to the condition you've chosen, start the encounter just at the edge of the agents' vision (considering any surrounding walls or other visual obstructions). Otherwise, roll for distance according to the condition you've chosen.

3. All members of both groups make Spot checks to see if they notice each other. Table 9.5: Spotting Difficulty determines the Spot check's DC. Anyone who succeeds has spotted the other group. If all members of both groups fail the check, start the encounter at half the rolled range.

SPOTTING HIDDEN GROUPS

If one of the groups is hiding, that group moves at half its normal overland speed and suffers a −2 penalty to its Spot checks to notice other groups (since they're trying to stay hidden). However, the base DC to spot a group that's hiding is equal to 25 + the lowest Hide skill modifier in the group. Normal modifiers apply except for size (which is already taken into account in the group's Hide skill) and contrast (which may be replaced by bonuses received from natural camouflage, special coloring, etc.).

Finally, a group attempting to hide isn't automatically spotted at half the encounter distance. Instead, the other group must make a normal opposed Spot check against the hiding group's Hide check.

THE ENVIRONMENT

Missions can take agents to the most exotic — and inhospitable — places on earth. These rules cover the rigors and dangers of the natural world. In some cases, these rules mention statistics for dangerous thresholds the human body can withstand. These thresholds should not be consulted for any activity in the real world (such as diving). In such cases, you should always consult a reputable resource — such the official Navy tables for decompression in the case of diving — for accurate real-world information.

COLD DANGERS

Hypothermia and frostbite are constant dangers to unprepared agents who find themselves in frigid climates.

Extreme Cold: Agents in very cold weather (30° F or less) without the proper protective gear must make a Fortitude save every hour (DC 15 + 1 for each previous check) or take 1d6 damage from hypothermia. Once unconscious, an agent automatically fails his save every hour. Heavy clothing grants a +4 bonus to these saves, and an agent with Survival can make a skill check to gain a further bonus *(see page 65)*.

At 0° F or less, an agent must makes a save every 10 minutes instead of every hour.

At –40° F or less, an agent automatically suffers 1d6 damage every minute if breathing the freezing air, and he must make a save every 5 minutes as above.

An agent that has taken damage from extreme cold is fatigued. He cannot run or charge, and he has an effective –2 penalty to both his Strength and Dexterity. Neither this fatigue nor the damage suffered can be healed until the agent is warmed up, and has a full day of rest to recuperate.

Cold or Freezing Liquids: An agent takes 1d6 points of damage per minute from hypothermia when swimming or standing in very cold water or other liquids.

TABLE 9.4: SPOTTING DISTANCE

Terrain	Distance (Average)
Smoke or heavy fog	2d4 × 5 ft. (25 ft.)
Jungle or dense forest	2d4 × 10 ft. (50 ft.)
Light forest	3d6 × 10 ft. (105 ft.)
Scrub, brush, or bush	6d6 × 10 ft. (210 ft.)
Grassland, little cover	6d6 × 20 ft. (420 ft.)
Indoors (lit)	Line of sight
Total darkness	Line of sight / Range of illumination

TABLE 9.5: SPOTTING DIFFICULTY

Circumstances	DC
Base	20
Size (other than Medium)	+/–4 per size category smaller/larger
Contrast	+/–5 or more
Other group not engaged in distracting activity (such as moving through rugged terrain)	+5
6+ members in other group	–2
Moonlight *	+5
Starlight †	+10
Total darkness ‡	Impossible

* +5 bonus to Spot check if spotter has low-light, night, or infrared sight.

† +5 bonus to Spot check if spotter has low-light sight, +10 if spotter has infrared or night sight.

‡ Only possible with infrared or night sight, in which case spotter gets +10 bonus to Spot check.

Size: Add +4 to the DC for every size category the opposing group is smaller than Medium. Subtract –4 from the DC for every size category the opposing group is larger than Medium.

Contrast: This is how visible the opposing group is against the terrain they are in. Camouflage generally adds to the opposing group's DC, while bright or contrasting colors generally subtract from the opposing group's DC. This modifier is halved against colorblind beings and agents.

Other Group Not Moving: If a group is sitting still, this modifier is added to the DC of the other group.

6+ Members in Other Group: If a group has 6 or more individuals in it, this modifier is subtracted from the DC of the other group.

Moonlight: If it is nighttime with a bright moon (or similar level of lighting) this modifier is added to the DC of both groups.

Starlight: If it is nighttime with a dim or new moon (or similar level of lighting) this modifier is added to the DC of both groups.

Total Darkness: In darkness, a group using illumination cannot see beyond the range of their illumination, while other groups can see their illumination from far away.

Immersion in extremely cold liquids (such as liquid oxygen) cause 1d6 points of damage per round from freezing unless the agent is fully immersed, in which case the damage is 10d6 points per round of exposure.

Ice: An agent walking on ice makes a Balance check each minute (DC 15) to avoid slipping and falling. Agents in contact with ice for prolonged periods must also check for extreme cold damage, as above.

HEAT DANGERS

Heat and fire are not only natural hazards, but the focus of many weapons, such as the thermite grenade and rudimentary molotov cocktail.

Extreme Heat: An agent active (i.e. hard labor or combat) in very hot weather (90° F or above) must make a Fortitude save every hour (DC 15 + 1 for each previous check) or take 1d4 damage from heat exhaustion. Once unconscious, an agent automatically fails his save every hour. Heavy clothing or armor of any sort imposes a –4 penalty to these saves, but an agent with Survival can make a skill check to gain a bonus to them.

In extreme heat (110° F or above), an agent makes a save every 10 minutes instead.

In incredible heat (140° F or higher), an agent automatically suffers 1d6 damage every minute if breathing the scalding air, and he must make a save every 5 minutes as above.

An agent who has taken damage from extreme heat is fatigued. He cannot run or charge, and he has an effective –2 penalty to both his Strength and Dexterity scores. Neither this fatigue nor the damage suffered by extreme heat can be healed until the agent is cooled down, and has a day of rest to recuperate.

Boiling Liquids: Boiling water or other boiling liquid causes 1d6 points of damage from scalding unless the agent is fully immersed, in which case the damage is 10d6 points per round of exposure.

Fire: An agent at risk of catching on fire (exposed to burning oil or gasoline, a bonfire, etc.) must make a Reflex save (DC 15) or catch fire, suffering 1d6 damage. Each round thereafter, the agent makes another Reflex save (still DC 15), with failure meaning the fire continues to burn, doing another 1d6 damage. Once the agent succeeds at a save, the fire is out and he takes no further damage. An agent may automatically put himself out by jumping into a large enough body of water. Failing that, rolling on the ground or smothering the fire with blankets or the like gives the agent another save with a +4 bonus.

An agent carrying flammable items on his person when he catches fire must make an additional Reflex save (DC 15) for each item, with failure meaning the item catches fire as well.

An agent immersed in fire (in the middle of a bonfire, etc.) automatically fails his Reflex save each round.

Smoke Inhalation: A hazard commonly associated with fire is smoke inhalation. An agent breathing heavy smoke must make a Fortitude save each round (DC 15 +1 for each previous check) or spend the round coughing and choking. An agent that coughs for two consecutive rounds suffers 1d6 damage.

Heavy smoke also gives one-half concealment to those obscured by it.

Lava: Lava causes 2d6 points of damage from scalding unless the agent is fully immersed, in which case the damage is 20d6 points per round of exposure. Damage from lava persists for 1d4 rounds after exposure, but only inflicts half damage (1d6 or 10d6 damage, as appropriate).

LANDSLIDES AND AVALANCHES

Landslides and avalanches offer two danger zones: the bury zone (directly in the path of the falling debris), and the slide zone (the area the debris spreads out across).

Agents in the bury zone take 8d6 damage (half that if they make a successful Reflex save at DC 15). They are also pinned (see below).

Agents in the slide zone take 3d6 damage (or no damage if they make a successful Reflex save at DC 15). If they fail the saving throw, they're pinned and take the damage.

Pinned agents suffer 1d6 points of subdual damage every minute. If a pinned agent falls unconscious, he must make a Fortitude save at DC 15 every minute, with failure inflicting 1d6 points of normal damage. This continues until the agent is either freed or dies. A pinned agent may buy himself one hour with no required saving throws by spending an action die.

STARVATION AND THIRST

Active agents require a gallon of fluids and 2000 calories (for females) to 3000 calories (for males) every day in order to avoid starvation and dehydration. This number of calories is equal to about a pound of fresh food, though some preserved foods – such as military meal packets (MREs) and trail mix – contain the appropriate caloric intake with far less weight. In very hot climates, the liquid requirement is increased to two gallons of fluids.

After an agent has been without food for 3 days, he must begin making Fortitude saves every day (DC 10 + 1 for each previous check), suffering 1d6 damage from starvation for each failed save.

After an agent has been without fluids for 1 day plus a number of hours equal to his Constitution, he must begin making Fortitude saves every hour (DC 10 + 1 for

each previous check), suffering 1d6 damage from dehydration for each failed save.

An agent who has taken damage from dehydration or starvation is fatigued *(see page 178)*. He cannot run or charge, and he has an effective –2 penalty to both his Strength and Dexterity. Neither this fatigue nor the damage suffered can be healed until the agent gets food or water as needed, and has a day of rest to recuperate.

WATER DANGERS

Water is a relentless foe, with thousands drowning or lost at sea every year.

The Bends: A scuba diver who remains underwater for more than 1 hour and dives below 100 ft. must surface slowly, a process that takes 5 minutes for every 50 ft. the diver submerged. Failure to do so causes the bends, which causes extreme pain as nitrogen in the blood begins to bubble. This leaves him unable to take any actions and inflicts 1d6 points of normal damage to him every minute until he is placed in a pressure tank and slowly decompressed. Even after being decompressed, the diver requires a full day of rest to get back on his feet.

Calm and Rough Waters: Any agent may wade in calm water that isn't over his head without a skill check. Swimming in calm water requires Swim checks against DC 10, and although trained swimmers can take 10, armor or heavy gear can make swimming difficult (a –1 penalty is applied to the check for every 5 lbs. of gear the agent is carrying).

Rough or fast water is very dangerous, requiring Swim checks against DC 15. If the agent succeeds, he still suffers 1d4 points of damage (1d6 if the agent is going through rocky rapids). On a failed check, the agent suffers damage as before, but must succeed at a second Swim check (DC 15) or begin to drown.

Drowning: An agent can hold his breath for a number of rounds equal to twice his Constitution. After that, he must make a Constitution check every round (DC 10 + 1 for every previous consecutive check) in order to keep holding his breath. Failure indicates that the agent has begun to drown. In the first round, his vitality points drop to 0. The second round, his wound points drop to 0. Thereafter, he suffers 1 point of damage every round until reaching –10, at which point he is dead. An agent can be stabilized as normal if pulled out of the water before reaching –10 wound points.

Euphoria (Nitrogen Narcosis): A scuba diver that remains underwater for more than 1 hour and dives below 50 ft. is susceptible to euphoria caused by the way nitrogen acts in the blood at that depth. The diver receives a –4 to all Wisdom- and Intelligence-based checks until he has surfaced and rested for 10 minutes or succeeds with a Fortitude save (DC 25), each hour.

Pressure Damage: When 60 or more ft. underwater, an agent must make a Fortitude check every minute (DC 15 + 1 for each previous check) or suffer 1d6 points of subdual damage, plus another 1d6 for every full 30 ft. he is below the 60-ft. threshold.

Example: Donovan is 120 ft. below the surface. He makes his first Fortitude check at 15 and succeeds. A minute later, however, he fails his second check (at DC 16). Still at 120 ft. below the surface, he immediately suffers 3d6 subdual damage (1d6 for the first 60 ft. and 2d6 for the next 60 feet). He must make another check in a minute's time.

Pressurized diving suits or underwater vehicles prevent this damage, but they can collapse if they go too deep, causing 1d6 points of normal damage for every 100 ft. the suit or vehicle is below the surface when pressure causes it to collapse.

Underwater Combat: Anyone without 5 ranks in the Swim skill suffers a –4 penalty to all Reflex saves, initiative, and attack rolls made while more than 50% submerged. Combatants native to water are immune to this modifier.

Agents without masks or other eye protection suffer an additional –1 penalty to all attack rolls, as well as kill checks requiring visual cues. Additionally, poor visibility is commonplace underwater, and the GC is encouraged to apply appropriate concealment penalties at his discretion.

All weapons except melee and exotic arms, and explosives, are useless underwater. Further, the damage of melee weapons that add the agent's Strength modifier is reduced by half (rounding down). Finally, the error range of all melee weapons is increased by 2 when underwater. Weapons that are designed for underwater use ignore these penalties.

Weapons that cause blast damage are actually more effective when submerged–blast increments are doubled underwater. Unfortunately, the error range of explosives not designed for use underwater is increased by 2.

WEATHER HAZARDS

The following weather conditions range from merely annoying to highly lethal.

Fog: Fog obscures all sight, except infrared, beyond 5 feet. Agents within 5 feet get one-half concealment.

Flash Floods: Agents in the path of a flash flood must make a Fortitude save against DC 15. Large or smaller characters who fail the save are swept away, suffering 1d6 damage per round (1d3 on a successful Swim check). Huge items and vehicles are knocked down and may be submerged. Gargantuan and Colossal items and vehicles are checked, but remain in place as the water washes over them.

Powerful Storms: Some of the worst that inclement weather has to offer, these storms greatly impair the actions of agents in their wake. Visibility is reduced to zero. Ranged attacks and Spot, Search, and Listen checks are all impossible. Protected flames have a 75% chance of being extinguished (unprotected flames are automatically doused).

- *Blizzard:* Blizzards consist of a combination of strong (75% chance) or severe (25% chance) winds, heavy snow (1d4 feet), and temperatures under 30° F.

- *Hurricane:* Hurricanes consist of hurricane winds and heavy rain, and may (25% chance) be accompanied by flash floods. See also Wind (opposite).

Precipitation: Usually, this is rain, but in freezing temperatures, it can be snow, sleet, or hail. Precipitation that is followed by freezing temperatures can produce ice (see Cold Dangers, page 229).

- *Rain:* Rain acts like severe wind, opposite. It also reduces visibility by half and imposes a –4 penalty to Spot and Search checks.

- *Snow:* Snow acts like moderate wind, opposite. It also reduces visibility and penalizes Spot and Search checks

TABLE 9.6: OTHER EFFECTS FROM WIND			
Wind Force	Creature Size	Wind Effect	Wind DC
Light	Any	None	–
Moderate	Any	None	–
Strong	Tiny or smaller	Knocked Down	10
	Small or larger	None	
Severe	Tiny	Blown Away	15
	Small	Knocked Down	
	Medium	Checked	
	Large or larger	None	
Windstorm	Small or smaller	Blown Away	18
	Medium	Knocked Down	
	Large or Huge	Checked	
	Gargantuan or larger	None	
Hurricane	Medium or smaller	Blown Away	20
	Large	Knocked Down	
	Huge	Checked	
	Gargantuan or larger	None	
Tornado	Large or smaller	Blown Away	30
	Huge	Knocked Down	
	Gargantuan or larger	Checked	

Checked: People who are checked must make a Fortitude save against the wind's DC or be unable to move that round. Those in flight without protection from the elements (e.g. those using hang gliders, jetpacks, or the like) are instead blown back 1d6x5 ft.

Knocked Down: Anyone knocked down must make a Fortitude save against the wind's DC or they become prone. Those flying without protection from the elements are instead blown back 1d6x10 ft.

Blown Away: Those blown away are knocked prone and rolled 1d4x10 ft., suffering 1d4 points of damage per 10 ft. Those flying without protection from the elements are instead blown back 2d6x10 ft. and suffer 2d6 damage from battering.

like rain while falling. Finally, once on the ground, it reduces movement by half.

- *Sleet:* Sleet has the same effect as rain when falling (except that it has a 75% chance to extinguish flames instead of a 50% chance), and as snow once it's on the ground.

- *Hail:* Hail imposes a –4 penalty to Listen checks and there is a 5% chance that it is big enough to inflict 1d4 points of damage (per storm) to anything in the open. Once on the ground, it acts like snow.

Storms: Storms reduce visibility by three-quarters, and impose a –8 penalty to Spot, Search, and Listen checks. Non-gun ranged attacks are impossible, and guns have a –4 penalty to attacks. Protected flames have a 50% chance of being extinguished (unprotected flames are automatically doused).

- *Dust storm:* A lesser dust storm (90% chance) consists of severe winds and leaves behind 1d6 inches of sand. A greater dust storm (10% chance) consists of a windstorm, inflicts 1d3 damage per minute on anyone caught out in the open, and presents a choking hazard (use the drowning rule.) Anyone with a scarf or similar facial protection may 'hold their breath' for a number of rounds equal to ten times their Constitution.) Greater dust storms leave 2d6–1 inches of sand.

- *Snowstorm:* A snowstorm leaves 1d6 inches of snow on the ground.

- *Thunderstorm:* Once per hour, roll d% three times. If you get 00 all three times, lightning strikes someone out in the open, inflicting damage equal to 1d10 8-sided dice. One in ten thunderstorms is accompanied by a tornado.

Wind: Winds cause damage according to their power and confer a number of effects, as described here and on Table 9.6: Other Effects From Wind.

- *Light (0-10 mph):* No game effect.

- *Moderate (11-20 mph):* 50% chance of extinguishing small open flames, like candles.

- *Strong (21-30 mph):* Automatically extinguishes small open flames. Imposes a –2 penalty to hurled attacks and Listen checks.

- *Severe (31-50 mph):* As strong, with 50% chance of extinguishing protected flames. Penalty to hurled attacks and Listen checks increases to –4.

- *Windstorm (51-74 mph):* As severe, with 75% chance of extinguishing protected flames. Hurled attacks are impossible; all other ranged attacks are made at –4. Listen checks are made at –8.

- *Hurricane (75-174 mph):* All flames are put out. All non-hurled ranged attacks at –8, and Listen checks are impossible. Trees may be felled by the wind. See also Storms *(page the opposite column).*

- *Tornado (175-300 mph):* As hurricane, but all ranged attacks are impossible. Agents in close proximity to a tornado must make a Fortitude save (DC 30) or get sucked towards the tornado, where they are picked up and whirled around for 1d6 rounds, suffering 1d10 damage each round, until expelled (falling damage may also apply). Tornadoes uproot trees, destroy buildings, etc.

OTHER HAZARDS

The section covers a few more hazards agents could face.

Acid: An agent exposed to corrosive acid suffers 1d6 damage per round of exposure, unless the agent is fully immersed, in which case the damage is 10d6 points per round of exposure.

In addition, acidic fumes are poisonous, and those who breathe them must make a Fortitude save every minute (DC 10 +1 for each previous check) or take 1d4 points of temporary Constitution damage.

Falling Objects: For each 200 lbs. that a falling object weighs, it deals 1d6 damage if it has fallen at least 10 ft. The object deals a further 1d6 damage for every additional 10 ft. it has fallen, up to 20d6.

Objects smaller than 200 lbs. must fall further to deal damage. The objects deal 1d6 damage for every falling increment *(see Table 9.7: Damage from Falling Objects, below)* they have fallen, provided they have fallen at least one increment.

TABLE 9.7: DAMAGE FROM FALLING OBJECTS	
Object Weight	Falling Increment
200-101 lbs.	20 ft.
100-51 lbs.	30 ft.
50-31 lbs.	40 ft.
30-11 lbs.	50 ft.
10-6 lbs.	60 ft.
5-1 lbs.	70 ft.
Less than 1 lb.	1d4 normal damage*

*No matter how far the object falls

High Altitude/Low Oxygen: Agents exerting themselves in low oxygen conditions (such as on top of a mountain) must make a Fortitude save every hour (DC 15 + 1 for each previous check) or take 1d4 subdual damage from exhaustion. Once unconscious, an agent automatically succeeds at his save every hour, and eventually recovers due to natural healing. Low oxygen cannot kill an agent.

An agent that has taken damage from low oxygen is fatigued. He cannot run or charge, and he has an effective –2 penalty to both his Strength and Dexterity. Neither this fatigue nor the damage suffered can be healed until the agent receives normal levels of oxygen and has an hour of rest to recuperate.

Space and Vacuum: An agent exposed to vacuum must make a drowning check each half action (twice per round) and takes 1d6 normal damage per round from skin blistering.

Suffocation: An agent with no air (buried in sand, etc.) uses the drowning rules *(page 231).*

An enclosed space contains enough air for 1 Medium-sized character to breathe for 6 hours for every 1,000 cubic ft. (i.e. 10 ft. × 10 ft. × 10 ft. cube) of space. This is reduced proportionally for multiple characters. A character takes twice as much air for each size category it is larger than Medium and half as much air for each size category it is smaller than Medium. A sleeping or unconscious character consumes air at half this rate. A torch or similar-sized fire is counted as a Medium-sized character, with larger or smaller fires counting as larger or smaller characters accordingly.

After the space's air runs low, each character takes 1d6 damage every 15 minutes until dead or given fresh air to breathe.

SCENERY

Construction in the modern world has become very standardized. Often, a wall in one part of the world looks just like a wall in another part of the world. This is good news for you since it allows you to work with a much smaller set of 'standardized scenery' than you would otherwise need.

DOORS

Doors are perhaps the most common obstacle agents face, and they come in varying levels of difficulty to bypass.

Wooden Doors: Most modern wooden doors are made of plywood or particleboard, which looks solid enough but in reality breaks fairly easily. Sturdier doors are made of solid oak, and sometimes reinforced with metal around the edges.

Metal Doors: Metal doors are designed to keep people out of restricted areas. If agents are confronted with a sturdy enough metal door, they'll need to either find a key or blow it up.

Special Doors: Some of the more unusual doors are listed below.

- *Blast Doors:* Remnants of the Cold War, blast doors were designed to survive a nuclear war. Nothing short of a full-scale assault is liable to even scratch them.

- *Elevator Doors:* Although elevator doors are tough enough to stop the occasional bullet, they're designed to be easy to open.

- *Glass Doors:* More for show than any practical use, glass doors are transparent and typically offer little protection against someone determined to get past.

FLOORS

Floors also come in many types.

Concrete Floors: These floors are simply a poured concrete slab with no carpeting or other flooring put in place.

Carpeted Floors: Thick carpeting is more comfortable to walk on than a hard floor, and gives a +2 to any Move Silently checks.

Hardwood Floors: Although wooden floors are attractive and easy to maintain, loose boards have a tendency to creak, imposing a –2 penalty to any Move Silently checks.

Tile Floors: Attractive and usually pretty durable, tile floors are easily scratched, possibly resulting in a clue for observant agents.

				Break DC	
TABLE 9.8: DOORS					
Door Type	Typical Thickness	Hardness	Wound Points	Stuck	Locked
Blast	2 ft.	15	840	45	45
Elevator	2 in.	10	60	15	15
Glass	1 in.	1	1	12	12
Iron	2 in.	10	60	28	28
Steel	2 in.	15	70	30	30
Stone	4 in.	8	60	28	28
Wooden, simple	1 in.	5	10	13	15
Wooden, good	1½ in.	5	15	16	18
Wooden, strong	2 in.	5	20	23	25
Lock	—	15	30		
Hinge	—	15	30		

Special Floors: Sometimes you'll want to use a more unusual floor, such as one of the following.

- *Grates:* Grates cover pits or other lowered areas. Most grates are made from iron or steel, and some can be locked in place, while others are part of the structure they're built into. A typical 1-inch grate has 35 wound points, a hardness of 15, and a DC of 30 to break or tear away.

- *Ledges and Bridges:* Ledges usually circle around pits, serve as balconies, or provide a raised area for gunmen to stand on, while bridges typically connect two raised areas. Narrow ledges or bridges may require the use of the Balance skill.

- *Transparent Floors:* Sometimes villains use glass or bulletproof glass to create a viewing window looking into important areas such as arenas or jail cells.

- *Sliding Floors:* These floors are often in areas where they can slowly slide back, tipping agents into dangerous traps, such as acid vats or shark tanks.

- *Electrified Floors:* These floors have electrical current running through them at regular intervals. Anyone standing on the floor when this happens suffers 1d6 damage.

- *Weight-sensitive Floors:* These floors are rigged to trigger some kind of trap or alarm when weight is added or subtracted from them. Typically, they are turned off during normal business or high-traffic hours.

Furnishings and Such

Buildings are typically filled with a variety of decorations, furnishings, and other features.

Stairs and Escalators: Running or maintaining balance on an escalator that suddenly stops or starts requires a Balance check (DC 10). When fighting on an incline, such as a staircase, characters receive a +2 terrain bonus when attacking targets below them.

Laundry chutes: A desperate agent can jump down a laundry chute, but if there's nothing soft to land on below, he suffers normal falling damage.

Pillars: These stone supports can provide good cover during a firefight.

Vaults: Typical vault walls are solid metal and often contain sensors that sound an alarm if the integrity of the walls is compromised.

Elevators: Elevators have emergency braking systems designed to keep them from falling in the event of an emergency, and a hatch leads into the elevator shaft, where a ladder allows maintenance access to its workings.

Secret Doors: Modern secret doors are typically built into wall panels and open with a twist of a nearby decoration or furnishing or the push of a hidden button somewhere in the room. Sometimes a certain book must be pulled in a bookshelf, other times part of a statue must be twisted to open the door.

Walls

Most buildings nowadays are built from brick, drywall, concrete, or wood. However, there's still the occasional carved stone or masonry structure, not to mention the adobe mud and straw huts found in many places in the third world.

Brick Walls: These are the typical red brick walls you often see, complete with handy grout lines that a skilled climber can use to his advantage.

Concrete Walls: Often used in military installations (particularly those designed to survive a nuclear war) concrete walls are usually thick and reasonably smooth.

Drywall Walls: Today's cheap construction material of choice, particularly in apartment buildings, drywall is smooth and typically about an inch thick. A good punch often goes right through it.

Wooden Walls: Primarily used in upper class modern houses, wooden walls often use pressure-treated material that doesn't rot easily and is resistant to insects.

Special Walls: Sometimes you'll want to use a less common type of wall, such as the following.

- *Adobe Walls:* These mud and straw walls are lumpy and brown, and buildings with adobe walls often have a sod roof. Sturdier than drywall, adobe is still far inferior to a nice stone or concrete wall.

- *Paper Walls:* These walls are used as screens to block sight, but offer no real cover.

- *Rebar/Concrete Walls:* Rebar is short for "reinforcing bars", half-inch bars of iron that are inset into a concrete wall to give it added strength and durability.

Traps, Hazards, and Alarms

Especially when sneaking into an enemy installation or criminal mastermind's stronghold, agents face a wide variety of traps, security systems, and other lethal devices.

Cave-ins and Collapses

An underground cave-in works the same way as a landslide or avalanche does *(see Environment, on page 228).*

In one minute, using only his hands, an agent may clear rocks and debris equal to five times his heavy load rating *(see Carrying Capacity, page 106).* The amount of loose debris that fills one 5-ft. square is 1 ton (2,000 lbs.). An agent armed with digging utensils may work twice as fast.

FALLING

An agent takes 1d6 damage for every 10 ft. he falls, up to 20d6. Damage reduction does not reduce this damage. If an agent deliberately jumps down and makes a successful Jump check, the falling damage is reduced by 1d6. In addition, if the agent falls onto a soft, yielding surface, the damage is reduced by 1d6 (cumulative with the reduction from the Jump check).

If an agent falls into water, he takes no damage from a fall of 20 ft. or less as long as the water is at least 10 ft. deep. The next 20 feet do subdual damage (1d4 points per 10 feet), and after that, falling damage is normal.

If an agent dives into water, as long as it's at least 10 ft. deep for every 30 ft. he falls, he can make a Swim or Tumble check (DC 15 + 5 for every 50 ft. of the dive) to suffer no damage.

SPIKES

Spikes or other sharp objects at the bottom of a fall may impale anyone who falls on them. Such spikes deal damage as knives with a +10 attack bonus and a +1 damage bonus for every 10 ft. of the fall (up to +5). If there are multiple spikes, the agent is 'attacked' by 1d4 of them. This damage is in addition to any normal falling damage the agent may suffer.

TRAPS, ELECTRONIC

Electronic traps are largely constructed from electronic parts such as transistors, circuits, and sensors. They are detected using a Search check, and they are disarmed using a Electronics check.

Sample Electronic Traps, Sensors, and Alarms: The following are common electronic traps. Each trap has a challenge rating *(CR, see page 263)* for a trap's attack bonus or method of sensing (where applicable), damage value, and DCs for saving throws or skill checks to find, disable, and/or avoid it.

The most common electronic traps are various types of sensors hooked up to alarm systems which alert their owners if triggered.

- *Electric eye:* CR 1; opposed Spot check (+4) against Hide to sense; Search (DC 20); Electronics (DC 20). Note: Sounds alarm or activates other device (such as a trap).

- *Noise sensor:* CR 1; opposed Listen check (+4) against Move Silently to sense; Search (DC 20); Electronics (DC 20). Note: Sounds alarm or activates other device (such as a trap).

- *Motion sensor:* CR 2; Balance check against DC 20 to avoid being sensed; Search (DC 22); Electronics (DC 22). Note: Sounds alarm or activates other device (such as a trap).

- *Heat sensor:* CR 3; any detectable body heat within 20 ft. is sensed; Search (DC 23); Electronics (DC 23). Note: Sounds alarm or activates other device (such as a trap).

- *Vibration sensor:* CR 4; anyone within 20 ft. is sensed; Search (DC 24); Electronics (DC 25). Note: Sounds alarm or activates other device (such as a trap).

- *Improved electric eye:* CR 5; opposed Spot check (+12) against Hide to sense; Search (DC 25); Electronics (DC 25). Note: Sounds alarm or activates other device (such as a trap).

- *Improved noise sensor:* CR 5; opposed Listen check (+12) against Move Silently to sense; Search (DC 25); Electronics (DC 25). Note: Sounds alarm or activates other device (such as a trap).

- *Improved motion sensor:* CR 6; Balance check against DC 28 to avoid being sensed; Search (DC 26); Electronics (DC 26). Note: Sounds alarm or activates other device (such as a trap).

- *Improved heat sensor:* CR 7; any detectable body heat within 60 ft. is sensed; Search (DC 27); Electronics (DC 27). Note: Sounds alarm or activates other device (such as a trap).

- *Improved vibration sensor:* CR 8; anyone within 60 ft. is sensed; Search (DC 28); Electronics (DC 28). Note: Sounds alarm or activates other device (such as a trap).

- *Electrified floor:* CR 4; section of floor (3d10); Reflex save (DC 14) for half damage; Search (DC 23); Electronic (DC 23).

- *Ultrasonic siren:* CR 5; no attack roll (10d6 subdual damage); Fortitude save (DC 22) for half damage; Search (DC 23); Electronics (DC 25).

- *Laser beam:* CR 8; +16 missile attack (8d6); Reflex save (DC 24) for half damage; Search (DC 25); Electronics (DC 28).

TRAPS, MECHANICAL

Mechanical traps are largely constructed from mechanical parts such as springs, gears, and motors. They are detected using a Search check, and they are disarmed using a Mechanics check.

Sample Mechanical Traps: The following are common mechanical traps. Each trap has a challenge rating (CR, *see page 263)*, attack bonus (where applicable), damage value, and a DC for saving throws or skill checks to find, disable, and/or avoid it.

- *Pit (20 ft):* CR 1; no attack roll needed (2d6); Reflex save (DC 20) avoids; Search (DC 20); Mechanics (DC 20).

- *Spiked pit (20 ft):* CR 2; no attack roll needed (2d6); +10 melee (1d4 spikes for 1d4+2 points of damage per successful hit); Reflex save (DC 20) avoids; Search (DC 20); Mechanics (DC 20).

- *Pit (40 ft):* CR 2; no attack roll needed (4d6); Reflex save (DC 20) avoids; Search (DC 20); Mechanics (DC 20).

- *Spiked pit (40 ft):* CR 3; no attack roll needed (4d6); +10 melee (1d4 spikes for 1d4+4 points of damage per successful hit); Reflex save (DC 20) avoids; Search (DC 20); Mechanics (DC 20).

- *Pit (60 ft):* CR 3; no attack roll needed (6d6); Reflex save (DC 20) avoids; Search (DC 20); Mechanics (DC 20).

- *Spiked pit (60 ft):* CR 4; no attack roll (6d6); +10 melee (1d4 spikes for 1d4+5 points of damage per successful hit); Reflex save (DC 20) avoids; Search (DC 20); Mechanics (DC 20).

- *Pit (80 ft):* CR 4; no attack roll needed (8d6); Reflex save (DC 20) avoids; Search (DC 20); Mechanics (DC 20).

- *Spiked pit (80 ft):* CR 5; no attack roll (8d6); +10 melee (1d4 spikes for 1d4+5 points of damage per successful hit); Reflex save (DC 20) avoids; Search (DC 20); Mechanics (DC 20).

- *Pit (100 ft):* CR 5; no attack roll needed (10d6); Reflex save (DC 20) avoids; Search (DC 20); Mechanics (DC 20).

- *Spiked pit (100 ft):* CR 6; no attack roll needed (10d6); +10 melee (1d4 spikes for 1d4+5 points of damage per successful hit); Reflex save (DC 20) avoids; Search (DC 20); Mechanics (DC 20).

- *Acid pit (20 ft):* CR 8; no attack roll needed (2d6 plus acid immersion); Reflex save (DC 20) avoids; Search (DC 20); Mechanics (DC 20).

- *Spring-loaded blade:* CR 1; +8 melee (1d8); Search (DC 21); Mechanics (DC 20).

- *Steam vent:* CR 2; section of corridor (2d8); Reflex save (DC 18) for half damage; Search (DC 22); Mechanics (DC 24).

- *Knockout gas vents:* CR 2; no attack roll needed *(see note below);* Search (DC 21); Mechanics (DC 25). Note: Trap releases knockout gas *(see Poison, page 238).*

- *Poison needle:* CR 3; +8 ranged (1, plus deadly poison); Search (DC 22); Mechanics (DC 20). Note: *See page 238 for a description of deadly poison and its effects.*

- *Flooding chamber:* CR 5; no attack roll needed (see note, below); Search (DC 20); Mechanics (DC 25). Note: Room floods in 4 rounds *(see Drowning, page 231).*

- *Crushing walls:* CR 10; no attack roll needed (20d6); Search (DC 20); Mechanics (DC 25).

POISON AND DISEASE

Few tactics are as heinous as the use of poison, and few situations hit as close to home as becoming infected with a virulent disease. But both of these are distinct possibilities in a secret agent's line of work.

The rules for poisons and disease simulate the danger inherent with them by striking directly at an agent's abilities.

Note: Regardless of the examples below, any of the poisons and diseases on Tables 9.9 or 9.10 can be used as a contact toxin, a gas, or a liquid with no changes to their effects.

POISON

An agent that consumes a poison, suffers wound point damage from a poisoned weapon, or inhales a poisonous gas must make a Fortitude save against the poison's DC or suffer the poison's initial damage. If this save fails, the agent must then make a second save at some later point (usually 1 minute later) or suffer the poison's secondary damage.

All ability damage from poisons is temporary and heals as usual unless otherwise stated. Other effects last for 3 hours.

The following information is found on Table 9.9: Poisons for several types of poison.

Type: Method of delivery and the poison's DC.

Initial Damage: Damage suffered upon failing the first saving throw for the poison.

Secondary Damage: Damage suffered upon failing the second saving throw for the poison.

The Perils of Using Poison: An agent applying poison to a weapon has a 5% chance of poisoning himself. In addition, a critical miss with a poisoned weapon can be disastrous *(see Activating Agent Errors, page 226).*

DISEASES

An agent who comes in contact with a disease (through tainted food, an infectious carrier, or by suffering wound damage from a disease attack) makes a Fort save against the disease's DC. If successful, his immune system fights off the disease. If he fails, then after the listed incubation time, he suffers the disease's initial damage *(see below)*. Once per day afterwards, he makes another saving throw to avoid the disease's secondary damage. If the agent makes two successful saving throws in a row, he fights off the disease.

Table 9.10: Diseases has the following info.

Type: Method of delivery and the disease's DC.

Incubation: The amount of time before the initial damage of a disease is inflicted.

Initial Damage: Damage suffered upon failing the first saving throw for a disease. Ability damage is temporary unless marked with an asterisk (*), in which case it's permanent.

Secondary Damage: Damage suffered upon failing the second and successive saving throws for a disease. Ability damage is temporary unless marked with an asterisk (*), in which case it's permanent.

TABLE 9.9: POISONS			
Poison	Type	Initial Damage	Secondary Damage
Contact poison	Injury DC 18	1d4 Con	2d4 Con
Knockout drops	Ingested DC 12	1d6 Dex	Unconscious (stable)
Knockout gas	Inhaled DC 18	1d6 Dex	Unconscious (stable)
Lethal poison I	Ingested DC 15	1d6 Con	2d6 Con
Lethal poison II	Ingested DC 18	2d6 Con	2d6 Con
Nerve gas	Inhaled DC 18	Paralyzation	1d4 Con
Paralytic poison	Injury DC 15	1d6 Dex	Paralyzation
Truth serum (sodium pentothal)	Inhaled DC 12	1d6 Wis	2d6 Wis
Weakening poison gas	Inhaled DC 12	1d6 Str	2d6 Str

TABLE 9.10: DISEASES				
Disease	Type	Incubation Period	Initial Damage	Secondary Damage
Flesh-eating virus	Ingested DC 13	1d6 days	1 Con	1d2 Con/1d2 Str*
Tetanus	Injury DC 15	1d4 days	1 Con/1 Str	1d4 Con/1d4 Str
Yellow fever	All DC 14	2d4 days	1 Con/1 Dex	1d2 Con*/1d2 Dex*
Tuberculosis	Inhaled DC 13	1d8 days	1 Str	1d2 Con*/1d4 Str
Malaria	All DC 12	1d6 days	1 Con	1d3 Con†

† Malaria is incredibly persistent. Even after recovering from the disease, the next time the victim suffers 1 or more points of Con damage (temporary or permanent) there is a 50% he contracts malaria again while weakened. Only after avoiding reinfection three times in a row does the victim finally fully recover.

Healing Diseases: Use of the First Aid skill can halt a disease's advance for up to 10 days, but after that, only hospital care can aid in the patient's recovery. Hospital care provides a bonus to the patient's saving throws ranging between +1 and +8, depending on how effective the Game Control rules the hospital to be. His decision is based on the nation where the hospital is, the conditions of the surrounding city, and the knowledge of its doctors.

REWARDS

You should always reward your players for a job well done. Not only do rewards keep them interested in the game, a well-chosen reward can greatly enhance a player's enjoyment and level of participation. Normally, experience points (XP) are handed out at the end of a session, but you might decide to give out other rewards as well.

EXPERIENCE AWARDS

Agents can receive XP for a number of reasons during a mission including mission awards, action awards, encounter awards, and action die bonuses.

Mission Awards: These awards are handed out at the end of a successful mission. Generally, the magnitude of these awards is based upon the length of the mission and how many of the mission objectives the agents accomplished.

Some sample mission objectives might include: "rescue a hostage," "don't kill anyone," or even "bug the villain, but let him escape." Such mission parameters are handed out during a mission briefing. Game Controls and players should both be mindful of making them clear at the outset of any serial.

Action Awards: These awards are handed out to the team when they perform a task during the course of a mission that you wish to reward them for.

TABLE 9.11: SAMPLE MISSION AWARDS

Achievement	Award
Completed short/simple mission	500 XP times average agent level
Completed medium/average mission	1,000 XP times average agent level
Completed long/hard mission	2,000 XP times average agent level
For each mission objective completed	+10%
For each mission objective failed	−10%

TABLE 9.12: SAMPLE ACTION AWARDS

Task	Award
Convinced a henchman to go straight	100 XP times average agent level
Pulled a clever scam on a villain	100 XP times average agent level
Did something else unexpected but awesome	100 XP times average agent level
Avoided a fight through their wits	50 XP times average agent level
Formulated ingenious plan to enter base	50 XP times average agent level
Did something else unexpected and cool	50 XP times average agent level
Disabled enemy vehicles before fleeing	25 XP times average agent level
Took careful precautions against surveillance	25 XP times average agent level
Did something else clever	25 XP times average agent level
Encounter* (EL >2 levels lower than the team's avg. level)	75 XP times average agent level
Encounter* (EL 1-2 levels lower than the team's avg. level)	150 XP times average agent level
Encounter* (EL equal to the team's avg. level)	300 XP times average agent level
Encounter* (EL 1-2 levels higher than the team's avg. level)	450 XP times average agent level
Encounter* (EL >2 levels higher than the team's avg. level)	600 XP times average agent level

* For more about encounter levels (ELs) and balancing XP rewards for them, *see page 263.*

TABLE 9.13: SAMPLE ENCOUNTER AWARDS

Clue Chain Was...	Award
Simple and straightforward	10 XP times average agent level
Moderately difficult	25 XP times average agent level
Long and complicated	50 XP times average agent level

Average agent level: To find average agent level, add all the agent levels in a team together and divide by the number of agents in the team (rounding off).

TABLE 9.14: BASE GADGET POINT COST			
Gadget Points	Reusability	Damage / Skill Bonus	Examples
1	1 / 5 days (1 use)	None / +2	explosive pen, standard shoes, grafter
2	1 / 2 days (3 uses)	1d4 / +4	armored suit, balloon-in-a-box
3	1 / day (5 uses)	1d6 / +6	spring-loaded weapon holster
4	2 / day (10 uses)	1d8 / +8	acoustic unit ear implant
5	Unlimited	1d10 / +10	chameleon suit, jetpack backpack

TABLE 9.15: COMMON COST MODIFIERS	
Modifier	Gadget Point Cost
Bonus to DC of Search checks to find gadget (between +10 and +25, depending on size)	+½
Implanted device (kept by the agent for 1 year)	+4
(kept by the agent permanently)	+10
Simulates a feat	+2
(for every prerequisite feat the simulated feat has)	+1 extra
Extra die of damage	+1 each
Stun damage	−1

Encounter Awards: Some encounters are reached by following a trail of clues. If the agents successfully make it to such an encounter, you may wish to award them some XP for following the clues correctly.

Action Die Bonuses: In addition, whenever you award an action die to a player for entertaining the group or otherwise contributing positively to the game, they receive an extra 50 XP times their agent's overall agent level.

OTHER REWARDS

Besides XP, you may wish to hand out the following kinds of rewards.

Money: Although most agents have their needs provided for by the Agency, a significant cash reward, such as the bounty on the head of a villain they've brought down, might allow them to indulge in a sports car or similar luxury. Although not necessarily of any benefit during play, such rewards can be fun for the players.

Gear: You might allow the players to keep a gadget they found particularly useful or became otherwise attached to. Just make sure you don't give them a gadget that you don't want in your campaign on a long-term basis.

Reputation: While the agents work under a veil of secrecy, their peers within the world's intelligence agencies still hear about them and their exploits. Agents with illustrious reputations can expect increased attention and respect from their peers. Of course, this could backfire on the agents at some point when a villain that has heard of them takes elaborate precautions to hold them prisoner.

Ranks, Titles, or Honors: One of the agents might be put in charge of the team, if an NPC previously held the position. Agents could quietly receive a title from world leaders in private ceremonies, and the agency itself might bestow some hard-won honor on a deserving team of agents, even if it's just their superior taking them out for drinks at an out-of-the-way bar.

DESIGNING NEW GADGETS

While we have provided a number of gadgets for your agents to purchase while gearing up for use during missions, you'll want to create your own at some point. To help you out, we've provided some guidelines that can help you determine the gadget point cost of almost anything you might want to create.

BASE GADGET POINT COST

The initial cost of a gadget should be determined by its reusability and the amount of damage per use or skill bonus it grants (if any). Simply consult table   and average the gadget point costs for each column (add them together and divide by 2). This gives you a good baseline for the gadget's cost.

Reusability: This column refers either to how often a gadget can be used, or the total number of uses it was designed for, your choice.

Damage / Skill Bonus: This column refers either to the damage inflicted by the gadget per use, or the skill bonus granted by it while in use, your choice.

COMMON COST MODIFIERS

Table 9.14 lists modifications commonly made to gadgets that you may wish to use. Simply apply this cost to the base cost of the gadget.

OTHER FUNCTIONS AND GC ADJUDICATION

Finally, since the possibilities for gadgets are endless, you'll have to adjudicate other functions yourself using the existing gadgets as guidelines. Gadgets of less use should be reduced in cost, while highly prized gadgets should be increased in cost.

GAMBLING

A few rounds of roulette or baccarat before retiring to the balcony to take in the view of the Mediterranean with a beautiful femme fatale. A high-stakes game of poker or mah-jongg with a quarter million dollars in the pot and the fate of the free world as table talk. Such situations are par for the course for an experienced agent. Gambling is an essential part of the spy genre, and agents who make their way through their social graces need to know a few of the rules.

Gambling can be divided into two broad groups — house games and competitive games. House games, fittingly enough, pit one or more players against the house. In these games, the odds always favor the house. Slot machines, blackjack and roulette all fall into this category.

Competitive games pit one or more players against each other. Here the element of luck is equally divided on all sides. Aficionados of both types of games swear that skill is a factor for either (particularly for their favorite), but skill usually plays a larger role in competitive games.

HOUSE GAMES

Playing a house game is very simple. The agent places a bet (determining the stakes), chooses his odds (establishing a DC), and rolls a d20. The house (usually represented by the GC) rolls a single d20 also, and subtracts it from the agent's roll. If the result beats the DC the agent set, he wins, recovering his bet and more depending on the odds. A simple "2 for 1" bet only requires the agent to score a 1 or higher.

Suggested rules for specific house games follow.

Blackjack: This is a simple card game in which the player tries to accumulate cards with a value as close to 21 as possible without going over, or "busting." He is dealt two cards, one face up, and may "hit," accepting another card, as many times as he likes, until he hits 21, busts, or "stays" (i.e. accepts his total). The house then goes through a similar process, except that the dealer must stay on anything over a 16 and must hit on anything 16 or lower.

In blackjack, the house wins all ties. While the house's rules for drawing additional cards are simple, they are also statistically very strong.

Because the player has the opportunity to see all of his cards and one of the house's initial two cards, he has the option of raising his bet after rolling his die, but before the house rolls. This makes the game a favorite with professional gamblers, many of whom swear that while the house wins more rounds, it is possible for a smart gambler to beat the house in earnings.

Most casinos use variations with multiple decks to prevent players from "card counting" (i.e. keeping track of all the cards that have appeared), gaining a significant advantage over the house's fixed strategy.

Roulette: A popular game in American and European casinos, roulette uses a spinning wheel with 38 slots and a metal ball to randomly determine a number (and a color). The slots are numbered from 1 to 36 plus 0 and 00. Half of the numbers are red and half are black, except for the 0 and 00, which are green.

Bets are placed on a large field with marked areas for the various numbers, colors, and combinations. All bets are final when the ball is thrown into the wheel.

Because the odds are figured without counting the green slots, they always favor the house. Typical 2 to 1 bets include "red," "black," "low" (numbers 1-18), and "high" (numbers 19-36) and pay if the agent makes a DC of 1 or higher. 3 to 1 (DC 4) and 6 to 1 (DC 8) bets are also common. Betting on any pair (including the infamous 0/00) pays 18 to 1 with a DC of 14. Betting a single number pays 36 to 1 with a DC of 16, and is considered the ultimate expression of pure luck.

It is possible with roulette to construct elaborate betting schemes that pay a mixture of odds through overlapping risks (placing some chips in different parts of the field), but agents can generally get by using the simpler betting structure outlined above.

COMPETITIVE GAMES

Gamblers tend to be fiercely competitive, confident in their skills and willing to put it all on the line to prove it. Agents often play for more than just money, including promises of information, stolen technology, or even their own lives or the lives of innocents.

Competitive games are perfect for both these situations, as they rely heavily on strategy, knowledge of the rules, and the ability to read your opponents' intentions. Most competitive games are played in a series of "rounds" (often called "hands" when playing with cards or tiles).

In competitive games' simplest form, each competitor places money (often called their "ante") into the common pool (often called the "pot" or the "stakes"), and then rolls a d20, adding both their Bluff and Sense

Motive skill ranks to the total. The highest number wins the round and claims the pot.

Additional rules to reflect the intricacies of common competitive gambling games follow.

Poker: One of the most popular of all western games, poker uses a standard pack of cards (sometimes with the jokers, sometimes without). Several cards are dealt to each player, who hopes to forms a "hand" of certain combinations of cards. Each combination is rated for strength, from one pair of the same suit or value to the famous "royal flush," a 10 through Ace of the same suit. The best hand wins the pot.

Betting takes place in rounds and each player has an opportunity to exchange cards for new ones or reveal more cards as each hand progresses. Combined with the ability to concede a hand rather than face rising stakes, this game is as much or more a function of acting, bravado, and discernment as it is a game of chance.

The volume of major rules variations is staggering, and even experienced players can find themselves playing with rules new to their experience. Fortunately, the essential skills – bluffing, and judging your opponent's actual situation – extend to most of them, so the basic rules for competitive games are unchanged. Optionally, the GC may impose a –4 penalty to players who are unfamiliar with the "house rules" of a casino, but such a penalty drops to –2 for the agent's second roll, and is ignored entirely thereafter (once he has gotten the hang of the local system).

Mah jongg: One of the East's most popular games, mah jongg is played with a set of thick (preferably ivory) tiles in much the same way cards are used in other games. An elaborate system of suits (houses, bamboo, and beads), winds (from the four directions), dragons (of different colors), and seasons and flowers (four of each) creates an environment far more complex and daunting than most Western card games.

During each hand, the players attempt to gather favorable combinations of tiles by drawing and discarding, or seizing the discards of other players. Certain combinations can be accomplished only by drawing or seizing a single key tile. Other players may seek to build up points by playing and seizing multiple smaller combinations, ensuring that play is both fast and dramatic.

All tiles are concealed until the end of a round, when they are all revealed at once.

Ritual surrounds the game, from the seating of the players to the placement of the tiles in "walls," from which they are drawn. Combined with a scoring system that changes from year to year, this game has infinite variety and savage difficulty. Playing mah-jongg without a deep understanding of the rules is an invitation to disaster. While it only takes about an hour to learn the

essentials, any player entering a game without previous experience faces a –6 penalty to their rolls. This penalty decreases by 1 each hand until they are able to play on a (mostly) even footing.

MORE THAN LUCK

Two factors can influence any type of game. First, agents are lucky people; sometimes absurdly so. Agents (and the GC) may spend action dice to improve their rolls. This can heavily tilt the field in their favor, at least when it counts. Second, people sometimes cheat. Cheating is quite difficult, and is frowned upon (to put it mildly). Most cheating involves switching cards or game pieces, and requires a Sleight of Hand Check with a DC 25 (or 30 in a casino). Success allows the cheater to roll twice for his gambling attempt that round, keeping the result he prefers.

MASTERMIND DESIGN

As GC, you have a complex and consuming journey ahead of you. It is your responsibility to define the world the agents operate within, and populate it with interesting characters doing interesting things. This is no simple task. Players are unknown quantities and second-guessing them is difficult even in the best of times. But fear not. This book provides many tools to help you decide what you want your personalized *Spycraft* game to look and feel like, not the least of which is this simple system for designing your very own criminal mastermind, organization, and lieutenants to pit against your players in an ever-escalating series of adventures leading to a blow-out climax.

Here's how it works: You, the Game Control, play the role of the campaign's central mastermind, the man (or woman) pulling the strings behind the scenes, guiding the actions of each of the villains the agents face. Consider the classic example: S.P.E.C.T.R.E., headed by the sinister Ernst Stavro Blofeld. Using the first five Bond films as an example, Blofeld (the criminal mastermind) wasn't even seen during the first (*Dr. No*), only felt. Dr. Julius No was foiled alone, and only vague intimations of the larger threat were posed during the film. Then, S.P.E.C.T.R.E. came to the fore (and Blofeld was 'seen' for the first time) during the second film, *From Russia With Love*, when the organization struck out at Bond directly. Bond faced a number of Blofeld's lieutenants during Russia, notably Rosa Klebb and Donald "Red" Grant. The series took a break from the organization during the third installment, *Goldfinger*, pitting 007 against an independent villain, Auric Goldfinger, then

returned to S.P.E.C.T.R.E. with *Thunderball,* as the group stole a NATO Vulcan bomber carrying a number of full-yield nukes. During *Thunderball,* Bond defeated S.P.E.C.T.R.E.'s Number Two, Emilio Largo, the man closest to Blofeld. Never had the action been closer to the true threat, Blofeld, who was defeated (for a time) in the fifth film, *You Only Live Twice.*

So the mastermind you design here becomes the defining villain of the backstory, the head of your very own criminal organization. His lieutenants face off with the players' agents during missions, along a roughly predetermined path you create ahead of time. Then, preferably during the final scenes of the campaign, the agents face your mastermind and bring the storyline to a close.

TERMS YOU NEED TO KNOW

In keeping with the serialized nature of the *Spycraft* game, we have broken the classic adventure/campaign structure into **Scenes, Serials,** and **Seasons.**

A scene is an encounter or combat sequence. Scenes are brief, usually revolving around a single goal, plot point, or revelation. Examples of scenes include the snow-chase from *The World is Not Enough* and the tower sequence from the *Charlie's Angels* feature film.

Serials (otherwise known as adventures, or missions) are groups of scenes which span one or more plotlines. Typically, serials are two to six scenes in length, though this is only a rough standard. A movie can be roughly equated to a serial.

Finally, serials are grouped into seasons (or campaigns), which focus on larger, multi-story plot-arcs. One serial introduces the campaign theme, several more continue it, and eventually, a final serial closes the season, commonly also setting the stage for future plotlines.

THE PILLARS OF VILLAINY

There are four core types of villains. Become familiar with them before designing your first mastermind and his organization. *(For additional information about these villain types, see the NPC section on page 265.)*

MASTERMINDS

These characters are at the top of the villain food chain. They are the ones who concoct nefarious schemes that threaten the fragile balance of world peace. Most missions involve thwarting the plans of a mastermind. Masterminds should be carefully defined, as their goals, personality, and other quirks affect the organization and its operation throughout the season. Masterminds are the focus of a season.

HENCHMEN

These guys are the principal thugs in a mastermind's organization. They are generally lieutenants whose job it is to execute key orders, and they are often dispatched to deal with delicate problems like nosy agents. They are the right-hand men of the masterminds they serve, and are usually fanatically loyal to their employers. Henchmen should also be well-defined, tailored for the particular serial they are the focus of.

MINIONS

In the criminal world, minions are a dime a dozen. They are the faceless hordes and bit characters that agents overcome to get to the henchmen or mastermind of the serial. Usually, minions appear in crowds, which share similar traits, a common shtick, and identical statistics.

FOILS

Finally, foils are the wild cards of any serial. Often referred to as a femme fatales, the motives of foils are rarely simple, and their loyalty is usually suspect. They are the romantic yet dangerous element in any serial that agents must wonder about, sometimes until the bitter end.

STEP 1: SEASON LENGTH

First, you have to decide how long a season (campaign) you want to run. If this is your first time running a season, we recommend a short one to greatly reduce the work on your part. There's plenty of time for longer seasons once you've gotten the hang of running the game.

The length of the season grants you mastermind points (MP) to cover the costs of your various options, as follows:

- **Base (all season lengths):** 75 + (5 per average agent level) for first serial.

- **Short Season (3-5 serials):** Add 70 + (5 per average agent level) for each additional serial.

- **Medium Season (6-9 serials):** Add 80 + (5 per average agent level) for each additional serial.

- **Long Season (10-12 serials):** Add 90 + (5 per average agent level) for each additional serial.

Example: If the average level of your agents is 2 and you want to run a 4-serial season, you receive 325 MP ((75 + 10 for first serial) + ((70 + 10) × 3 for serials 2-4) to spend on your central villain, his organization, henchmen, etc.

STEP 2: MASTERMIND DESIGN

Start at the center of your organization, with your mastermind. There are three things to consider here (though you may decide to personalize your mastermind even further).

MASTERMIND HOOK

This is the core mastermind concept, and costs no points. Examples include "industrialist czar," "deranged scientist," and "rogue Control."

MASTERMIND QUIRKS

These include all the little physical, mental, and personality quirks that make your mastermind memorable. Quirks help you decide on your mastermind's statistics, but offer no mechanical benefit of their own. Again, being purely flavor, quirks have no point cost. Examples include "obsessed with gold," "bloated ego," and "overconfident."

MASTERMIND LEVEL (4–20; 5 MP PER LEVEL)

Finally, decide the level of your mastermind, which can range from 4 to 20, just like agents. Each level costs 5 MP to purchase. Be careful not to spend all your points here, or your organization and henchmen will be underpowered. Masterminds should always be of higher level than the agents, as the agents will gain levels during the missions leading up to the confrontation with your mastermind (while he remains largely static). Plan ahead, using the following guideline:

- **Short Season:** The mastermind should be 3-4 levels higher than the average starting agent.

- **Medium Season:** The mastermind should be 5-6 levels higher than the average starting agent.

- **Long Season:** The mastermind should be 7-8 levels higher than the average starting agent.

DESIGN YOUR MASTERMIND

Finally, design your mastermind using the standard rules for agent design (see Chapters 1-4 and the Player's Handbook™). We recommend you perform this step last, after the rest of the steps here, and that you use diceless ability score generation (see the DMG) to ensure that your mastermind is everything you want him to be.

Masterminds are Special NPCs – see NPC Types, page 265.

Special Note: Masterminds gain BPs, GPs, and other bonuses from their classes and feats as well, which may further modify elements of a season. GCs who want to crunch the numbers can milk much more out of their threats by carefully choosing and applying such effects.

MINIONS (MULTIPLE OPTIONS — SEE DESCRIPTION)

At least one minion type is purchased for each serial, though more than one may be purchased using the rules under Multiple Villain Options per Serial (page 247).

Each minion type has a level (just like an agent), squad size (the number of that type commonly encountered together), vitality die, ability scores, saving throws, skills, and very occasionally feats. The gear of all minion types purchased for a season is determined by the organization's Resources Level *(see opposite).*

Minions are Standard NPCs – see NPC Type, page 265.

Minion Level (1–18; 1 MP per Level): Minions must be at least two levels lower than the mastermind or henchman they serve. Minions should generally be of the same level as the agents they encounter. One or two challenges with minions of a higher level is acceptable; more than that will overwhelm the team. Minions should never be more than two levels higher than the agent team, as they would devastate the team.

Minion Squad Size (no cost): The number of minions encountered together is determined by their level compared to that of the mastermind or henchman they serve. Like the rest of this system, squad sizes are carefully balanced to present a suitable challenge for the agent team. Vary them at your own risk.

- **2 levels below leader:** Squad size of 3-4 (per GC)

- **3 levels below leader:** Squad size of 5-6 (per GC)

- **4 levels below leader:** Squad size of 7-8 (per GC)

- **5 levels below leader:** Squad size of 9-10 (per GC)

- **6 levels below leader:** Squad size of 11-12 (per GC)

- **7 levels below leader:** Squad size of 13-14 (per GC)

THREAT CHALLENGE RATINGS

Like NPCs *(see page 269),* threats have a challenge rating that is used to gauge their strength against the ability of an agent team, and determine how many XP they are worth once they are defeated. The challenge rating of an encounter is based on the challenge ratings of all masterminds, henchmen, minions, and foils working against the agents in a given encounter *(see page 263).* For more about using challenge ratings to determine XP awards, see page 239.

Under nearly all circumstances, masterminds, henchmen, and foils have a challenge rating equal to their agent level (i.e. the sum of their class levels). Minions, on the other hand, have a challenge rating equal to their agent level, minus 1 (minimum 1).

Minions should never be 8 or more levels lower than the mastermind or henchman they serve. The Game Control sets the size of these minion squads within the recommended range. Minion squads are fielded as needed for the serial.

Minion Vitality Dice (1–3; 5 MP per Level): Each level bought here grants a higher minion vitality die: d4, d6, and d8, in order of ascending cost. These determine minion vitality points, as described on page 14.

Minion Ability Scores (0–15; 4 MP per Level): When assigning ability scores to a minion type, you have 60 points + 5 per level purchased here. Ability scores from 1 to 13 cost their level (i.e. you spend 12 points for an ability score of 12). Higher scores have the following costs.

Score	Cost	Score	Cost
14	15	17	22
15	17	18	25
16	19	19	29

Each ability score above 19 costs an additional 4 MP (cumulative). Thus, a score of 21 costs 37 MP.

Example: Designing a minion type with the Str 17, Dex 12, Con 14, Int 8, Wis 9, Cha 4 would cost a total of 70 points, or 2 levels of minion ability scores.

Minion Saving Throws (no cost): Minions make saves as soldiers *(see page 30)*.

Minion Skills (no cost): Minions gain skills as soldiers.

Minion Feats (0–3; 3 MP per feat): Minions do not have to buy armor and weapon proficiency feats. Minions buy feats one at a time. No minion type may have more than three feats. Minions must meet the prerequisites of a feat to purchase it.

A Note on Minions

Masterminds and henchmen are individuals, with their own personalities and styles. Minions, on the other hand, are a *type* of villain, and share carbon-copy statistic packages for easy use during play. Still, you should strive to create minion types that are memorable. Examples of well-conceived minion types include the circus from Octopussy and the legions of COBRA from the *G.I. Joe* cartoon series. An extreme example of a very cool fringe minion type are the "thumb-thumbs" from the movie *Spy Kids*.

Of course, minions may also be designed as pairs or groups of individuals (as seen in some of the threats in this book and the *Shadowforce Archer Worldbook*). This is merely cosmetic, and has no mechanical effect. The choice is up to the GC.

STEP 3: ORGANIZATION DESIGN

Next, choose the power level and scope of your mastermind's organization. Each part of this process gives bonuses or adds limits to henchmen, minions, gear, and other elements. These effects are intended to represent the "combat readiness" of the NPCs in question, not the overall scope or physical trappings of the organization itself. Every criminal organization is assumed to have all the servants, mansions, non-combat vehicles, private islands, underwater bases, satellite relays, and the like that it needs to function. The following modifiers are in addition to whatever standard you set for your private criminal empire.

RESOURCES (1–5; 15 MP PER LEVEL)

This is a measure of the money and equipment at your organization's disposal.

Effects: You must purchase at least one resource level. Each resource level offers budget points to purchase gear for the minions, henchmen, and foils of your organization, as well as the personal gear for your mastermind. Each NPC begins with a fixed number of budget points, according to his role in the organization:

Role	Starting Budget Points
Mastermind	50
Henchman or Foil	40
Minion	25

The budget points allocated to each NPC are increased by a number determined by their organization's resources rank and the average starting level of the agent team, as follows.

- **Level 1 (Poor):** Each NPC gains a bonus number of BP equal to ¼ times the average starting agent level (rounded up). This yields a bonus ranging from +1 to +5 BP.

- **Level 2 (Underfunded):** Each NPC gains a bonus number of BP equal to ½ times the average starting agent level (rounded up). This yields a bonus ranging from +1 to +10 BP.

- **Level 3 (Average):** Each NPC gains a bonus number of BP equal to the average starting agent level (rounded up). This yields a bonus ranging from +1 to +20 BP.

- **Level 4 (Wealthy):** Each NPC gains a bonus number of BP equal to 2 times the average starting agent level (rounded up). This yields a bonus ranging from +2 to +40 BP.

- **Level 5 (Independently Wealthy):** Each NPC gains a bonus number of BP equal to 4 times the average starting agent level (rounded up). This yields a bonus ranging from +4 to +80 BP.

Average starting agent level: To find the average starting agent level of a team, add the agent levels of all the team members together and divide by the number of agents on the team (rounding down).

These budget points are used when the organization is created to purchase one set of gear for each mastermind, henchman, and minion (minions usually have one set of gear for every member of each squad). This gear is carried with the NPC throughout the entire season. BPs may not be shared or traded, and any BPs not used to buy gear for an NPC are lost.

GCs should generally assume that threat NPCs have all the mundane necessities (clothes, non-tactical ammunition, etc.) that they need, in addition to their organization's resource level.

Example: If you chose Level 3 (Average) resources and your players have agents whose average level is 8, the mastermind has 58 BP (50+8), each henchman has 48 BP (40+8), and each minion has 33 (25+8) to spend on personal gear.

GADGETS (0-20; 4 MP PER LEVEL)

This is a measure of your group's technological superiority (above the standard for the setting). Low gadget levels indicate little super-science; high levels offer gadgets of increasing power.

Effects: You cannot field gadgets or vehicles without purchasing at least one gadget level. For every gadget level, your organization gains one gadget point per serial, which may be distributed to the villains (or kept by the henchman or mastermind) as you wish. Each gadget purchased with this option is unique; once lost or destroyed, it cannot be replaced during this season. Multiple copies of a gadget may be purchased, as desired.

Further, if the mastermind or henchman of a serial is a wheelman, each of his minions receives a number of gadget points equal to half the wheelman's custom ride bonus, rounded up. These gadget points may be used to purchase a vehicle for each minion, or pooled to buy larger vehicles. Any such gadget points not spent on minion vehicles are lost.

LOYALTY (0-10; 4 MP PER LEVEL)

This is a measure of your minions' devotion to your mastermind's cause.

Effects: Every loyalty level adds +1 to minion ability and skill checks involving loyalty, or the DC of such checks made against them.

CENTRAL HEADQUARTERS (MULTIPLE OPTIONS — SEE DESCRIPTION)

Now choose the features of your mastermind's central headquarters, or the location where he confronts the agents in the season's final serial. There are two options for you to consider here.

- **Personnel (0-10; 2 MP per Level):** This is a measure of the number of personnel on site. When agents enter a new room, and for every 20 minutes they are inside, roll a d20; if the roll is under this level + 5, the agents encounter a squad of minions.

- **Security (0-10; 3 MP per Level):** This is a measure of the difficulty of breaking into the final location. This level is added as a modifier to the DC of all traps and security devices on site.

STEP 4: SERIAL DESIGN

Here you outline and design the details of each serial leading up to the season's climax. Start with a henchman—the central villain of the serial—his minions, and their headquarters, then add any extra options that you desire. You should have at least one henchman for each serial you intend to run leading up to the final mission, though you can gain more using the rules under Multiple Villain Options per Serial on the opposite page. These rules also allow you to buy extra minions and foils for each serial, and add extra henchmen, minions, and headquarters for the final serial (alongside the mastermind), if you wish.

HENCHMAN HOOK AND QUIRKS

These steps are identical to mastermind design.

HENCHMAN LEVEL (3-20; 2 MP PER LEVEL)

Also the same, save for the henchman's level, which should be higher than the average starting agent depending on which serial they appear in.

- **Serials 1 and 2:** 1-2 levels higher

- **Serials 3 and 4:** 2-3 levels higher

- **Serials 5 and 6:** 3-4 levels higher

- **Serials 7 and 8:** 4-5 levels higher

- **Serials 9 and 10:** 5-6 levels higher

- **Serial 11:** 6-7 levels higher

CONTROL

Sometimes, it may better fit your vision to include more than one henchman in a single serial, or give a single henchman multiple minion types, or even provide a combat-weak mastermind with a burly henchman bodyguard. The mastermind system is balanced for the mastermind to have his own serial (without a henchman, but with his own single minion type), and for each serial to feature one henchman, plus his minions, and perhaps a foil.

Special Note: Adjusting the numbers in this way can unbalance encounters unless special care is taken.

For each serial you wish to adjust in this way, modify the number of mastermind points you spend as shown on the table below, then adjust the agents' XP bonus for completing that serial by the corresponding amount.

Change	MP	XP
Add a henchman	+ ((Serial number+2) + 6 per average agent level)	+10%*
Add a minion type	+ ((Serial number/2) + 3 per average agent level)	+5%*
Add a headquarters	+1 per mastermind or henchman level†	+50 per average agent level
Add a foil	+ (Serial number + average agent level)	+50 per average agent level (+100 per average agent level if she allies with the villains)

Round all divisions down when calculating bonus MP.

Bonus MP may only be spent on the option they are gained for (e.g. you cannot spend MP you get for a bonus minion type to beef up a henchman, whether he's in the same serial or not).

* Cumulative (two +10% XP bonuses and one +5% bonus become one +25% bonus for the serial in question).

† If more than one villain is featured in the serial, the bonus MP gained for the additional headquarters is based on the villain with the highest level.

Example: Adding a henchman to the third serial of a season that you intend to run for a team with an average agent level of 4 yields a total of 29 MP ((3+2) + 6×4). Adding a minion to the same serial yields another 14 MP ((3/2) + 3×4).

DESIGN YOUR HENCHMAN

As with masterminds, design your henchman using the standard rules for agent design (Chapters 1-4). Again, we recommend you perform this step last, after going through the rest of the steps here.

Special Note: Henchmen gain BPs, GPs, and other bonuses from their classes and feats as well, which may further modify elements of a season. GCs who want to crunch the numbers can milk much more out of their threats by carefully choosing and applying such effects.

Henchmen are Standard NPCs – *see NPC Types, page 265.*

HEADQUARTERS (SEE MASTERMIND DESIGN)

You must have at least one headquarters per serial, though you may add more *(see Multiple Villain Options per Serial, above)*. Designing these headquarters is identical to doing so for the mastermind *(see page 245)*.

MINIONS (MULTIPLE OPTIONS— SEE MASTERMIND DESIGN)

This is identical to mastermind design.

STEP 5: FOILS

Finally, the Game Control determines the number of foils he would like to feature in his season, and the chance that they ally with the villains of the season. In all ways, foils are designed like masterminds or henchmen. Multiple foils can be included using the rules under Multiple Villain Options per Serial, above

FOIL HOOK AND QUIRKS

This part is identical to mastermind design.

FOIL LEVEL (1–20; 1 MP PER LEVEL)

Also the same, save that the number of levels each foil should be above the average agent is determined by the serial they appear in.

- **Serials 1 and 2:** 1 level higher
- **Serials 3 and 4:** 1-2 levels higher
- **Serials 5 and 6:** 2-3 levels higher
- **Serials 7 and 8:** 3-4 levels higher
- **Serials 9 and 10:** 4-5 levels higher
- **Serial 11:** 5-6 levels higher

A foil's level also determines the extent of any organization he may run and any followers he has, as follows:

- **Levels 1–3:** No organization or minions.

- **Levels 4–7:** Six times the foil's level in points to spend on organization and minions.

- **Levels 8–10:** Eight times the foil's level in points to spend on organization and minions.

- **Levels 11–15:** Ten times the foil's level in points to spend on organization and minions.

- **Levels 16–20:** Twelve times the foil's level in points to spend on organization and minions.

The cost of a foil's organization and minions are the same as for a Mastermind *(see page 245)*.

These points are in addition to the MP the Game Control is given for the rest of the season, and may not be spent on other items (such as additional henchmen and minion types). The GC may also choose to ignore the foil's organization points and rule that any foil has no organization of her own.

Foils are Standard NPCs — *see NPC Types, page 265*.

FOIL LOYALTY (0–10; 1 MP PER LEVEL)

A foil may be of either gender. He or she begins the game as an unknown quantity, his or her allegiance initially undetermined. Either when the foil is encountered or at any point during the serial they appear in, the GC rolls a d20. If the result is lower than the foil's loyalty level + 5, they are loyal to the agents' enemies. If equal, they are undecided or a rogue agent, as the GC desires. If higher, they are loyal to the agents or an allied group.

Regardless of their loyalty, foils may be swayed by the agents or other parties, per skill rolls and the Game Control's discretion.

SAMPLE THREATS

What's a spy to do without an egomaniacal madman threatening world peace to take down? The following pages present several original criminal organizations (called "threats" in the *Spycraft* system), each of which is ready to run as the central villain of a season or to be dropped into an existing game.

As introduced under Mastermind Design, each threat is broken down into a mastermind and one or more henchmen, all with one or more minion packages. Some threats feature foils as well. Additional detail about each of these NPC types is described further under Serial Design, on page 265.

Finally, one or two plot hooks are included at the end of each threat description, offering a few ways for the GC to introduce the threat into his game.

JULIAN BOSQUE

This short-season (3-serial) threat is appropriate for a team of 1st level agents.

The enemies of superspies are not always over-the-top global criminal organizations, or even extreme left-wing terrorist radicals. Sometimes, superspies must contend with the basest of villains, whose weapons are nothing more complicated than political power, information, and cold-hard cash and whose motives are rooted in the eldest character flaws. The following is an example of one such threat.

MP Cost: 230
Resources: 4 (27 BPs for minions; 42 BPs for henchmen and foils, 52 BPs for masterminds)
Gadgets: 2 (2 gadget points per serial)
Loyalty: 4 (+4 to loyalty checks)
HQ Personnel: 3   **HQ Security:** 7

SERIAL THREE: JULIAN BOSQUE

A wealthy French entrepreneur who made his first fortune in space aeronautics before branching out into computer technology, Julian Bosque controls a multi-national conglomerate of corporations that have made him a billionaire, as well as one of the most respected and influential businessmen in Europe. His reputation in the nations comprising the European Union is unquestioned.

Unfortunately, Bosque is a slave to his greed. He has been steadily investing in satellite communications for over a decade, and believes that he can elevate the status of Bosque Industries by eliminating his two chief competitors — Rice-Fielding Future Technologies and Global Reach Communications. To accomplish this, Bosque plans to frame his competitors for using their dedicated satellite systems to spy on democratic and UN-supported countries around the world, and selling the information they gain to the highest bidder. Further, Bosque intends to promote his role in bringing his rivals to justice, in the hope that the public's increased opinion of him will be reflected in the value of his corporate stock.

Bosque intends to contact the affected governments with news of the Rice-Fielding/Global Reach treachery (which he has fabricated using corporate moles and industrial sabotage). He expects the UN to conduct a formal investigation and (eventually) shut his rivals down. Even if Rice-Fielding and Global Reach are exonerated, he expects that the negative publicity and disruption of the companies' operations will ensure Bosque's role as the industry leader.

Unfortunately for the corporate magnate, the Agency takes a keen interest in matters of global security, and dispatches a team of agents to investigate the activities of Rice-Fielding and Global Reach. If they're successful in ferreting out the true threat in this scenario, the agents might bring him to justice, or — if they're not careful — create a new criminal mastermind with a grudge against the Agency.

Julian Bosque, 4th-level pointman (mastermind);
CR 4. SZ M; v/wp: 28/11; Init +3 (+2 class, +1 Dex); Spd 30 ft.; Def 13 (+2 class, +1 Dex); Atk: 9x19mm target pistol +4 (1d10); Face 1 square; Reach 1 square; SA None; SQ None; SV Fort +2, Ref +3, Will +3; Str 14, Dex 13, Con 11, Int 16, Wis 9, Cha 10; Skills: Appraise +6, Bluff +7, Bureaucracy +7, Computers +8, Cryptography +6, Diplomacy +7, Driver +6, Knowledge (Big Business) +10, Languages +5, Profession (Entrepreneur) +6, Sense Motive +5. Feats: Sidestep, Surge of Speed. Gear: Weapons, 46 BPs; Gadgets and Vehicles: Cigarette pistol, jetpack.

Corporate Enforcers: Julian Bosque employs these smartly dressed thugs to guard his holdings and secure enemies for 'private meetings.'

Corporate Enforcers, 2nd-level minions (squads of 4). CR 1. SZ M; v/wp: 2d6+4 (14)/14; Init +4 (+2 class, +2 Dex); Spd 30 ft.; Def 12 (+2 Dex); Atk: 9x19mm submachinegun +4 (1d10); Face 1 square; Reach 1 square; SA None; SQ None; SV Fort +5, Ref +4, Will +2; Str 14, Dex 14, Con 14, Int 10, Wis 10, Cha 10; Skills: Craft (Gun Cleaning) +4, Driver +6, Intimidate +5, Jump +4, Spot +3. Feats: None. Gear: Weapons, 7 BPs.

SERIAL TWO: SIMON HAGUE

Ex-fighter pilot and NASA explorer Simon Hague is Bosque's intrusion expert, tasked with obtaining industrial intelligence from Bosque's competitors.

Simon Hague, 3rd-level wheelman (henchman);
CR 3. SZ M; v/wp: 36/14; Init +6 (+2 class, +4 Dex); Spd 30 ft.; Def 16 (+2 Class, +4 Dex); Atk: .45 ACP submachinegun +7 (1d10+2); Face 1 square; Reach 1 square; SA None; SQ None; SV Fort +3, Ref +7, Will +2; Str 12, Dex 18, Con 14, Int 11, Wis 12, Cha 12; Skills: Driver +10, Electronics +3, Mechanics +6, Pilot +10, Spot +7, Surveillance +7. Feats: Controlled Burst, Point Blank Shot, Rapid Shot. Gear: Weapons, 27 BPs; Gadgets and Vehicles: Autogyro, 3 ultralights (for minions), LCD lenses, 2 (1) GPs.

HQ Personnel: 3   **HQ Security:** 3

JULIAN BOSQUE

Aeronauts: Once part of Hague's air command, these paratroopers now specialize in the use of ultra-light gliders designed by Skyways, one of Bosque's subsidiary companies and a military hardware supplier. They are Hague's surprise assault force, used to conduct covert operations and (when needed) physical assaults.

Aeronauts, 1st-level minions (squads of 3). CR 1. SZ M; v/wp: 1d6 (6)/10; Init +3 (+1 class, +2 Dex); Spd 30 ft.; Def 13 (+1 armor, +2 Dex); Atk: 9x19mm service pistol +3 (1d10); Face 1 square; Reach 1 square; SA None; SQ None; SV Fort +2, Ref +3, Will +0; Str 11, Dex 14, Con 11, Int 11, Wis 11, Cha 11; Skills: Balance +6, Jump +2, Pilot +4, Survival +3, Swim +3. Feats: None. Gear: Weapons, motorcycle helmet, 9 BPs. Gadgets and Vehicles: Ultralight.

SERIAL ONE: MERCY DAMIEN

Mercy Damien is a low-profile fence working out of New York City, where she 'redistributes' valuable objects of questionable ownership. Her network is small but growing with her reputation along the eastern seaboard. Mercy is currently wanted in three states (New York not being one of them) for possession of stolen property, fraud, and connections to organized crime. Mercy specializes in the use of poisons, particularly those that can be administered through amorous contact, such as a kiss. Simon Hague hired Mercy as part of Bosque's North American smuggling operations.

In exchange, she keeps some items she transports, including the high-end bike parts she uses to ensure her minions' loyalty *(see next)*.

> **Mercy Damien, 3rd-level fixer (henchman);** CR 3.
> SZ M; v/wp: 19/10; Init +4 (+1 class, +3 Dex); Spd 30
> ft.; Def 16 (+3 class, +3 Dex); Atk: knife +4 (1d4+2
> w/3 uses of lethal poison I); Face 1 square;
> Reach 1 square; SA None; SQ None; SV Fort +2,
> Ref +6, Will +1; Str 14, Dex 16, Con 10, Int 12,
> Wis 10, Cha 17; Skills: Appraise +9, Bluff +9,
> Driver +7, Forgery +9, Gather Information +7,
> Hide +8, Innuendo +6, Jump +6, Knowledge
> (underworld) +7, Listen +5, Move Silently +7,
> Profession (Fence) +6. Feats: Master Fence, Quick Use
> (Appraise). Gear: Weapons, 19 BPs; Gadgets and
> Vehicles: poison lipstick (3 uses), woman's compact.
> **HQ Personnel:** 3   **HQ Security:** 4

The Scarlet Halo Racers: These dregs of society are members of the illegal racing circuit cropping up along the eastern seaboard. When the authorities jailed the racers' leader, Mercy came to his rescue. Now the racers work as Mercy's personal hit squad in exchange for specialty parts for their 'crotch rockets,' parts they would otherwise never have the resources to acquire. Julian Bosque is unaware of Mercy's minions (they are another of her "dirty little secrets"), and she goes to great lengths to claim their successes as her own.

FRANZ LIEBER

> **The Scarlet Halo Racers,** 1st-level minions (squads
> of 4). CR 1. SZ M; v/wp: 1d6+1 (7)/12; Init +1 (class);
> Spd 30 ft.; Def 10; Atk: 5.56x45mm semi-automatic
> rifle +1 (2d8+1); Face 1 square; Reach 1 square;
> SA None; SQ None; SV Fort +3, Ref +1, Will +0; Str 12,
> Dex 10, Con 12, Int 9, Wis 8, Cha 9; Skills: Climb +3,
> Driver +3, Intimidate +3; Jump +3, Tumble +3.
> Feats: None. Gear: Weapons, 1 BP

PLOT HOOK #1

A gala is being held in Los Angeles to celebrate the opening of the new U.S. office of Global Reach Communications, which will house the control center for its latest satellite network, launched one week ago. News of Global Reach's allegedly illicit activities has not yet been released to the public, and the Agency dispatches the agents to the event in the hope that they can learn more before the UN makes a move.

Mercy Damien is on hand at the event, posing as a new executive at the office (Megan Winters), and Rice-Fielding has sent a team of corporate scouts to investigate the site as well. Otherwise, no one on hand is aware of the drama brewing between the Agency, Bosque Industries, and Rice-Fielding. They will be, however — quite soon...

POSSIBILITIES

1. Unable to obtain the encryption codes for Global Reach's new satellite system through other avenues, Bosque dispatches Mercy Damien and Simon Hague to secure the codes from the control center at the gala site. Hague and the Aeronauts attack once the event is in full swing, arranging for Mercy to slip away unnoticed in the chaos. She meets the Scarlet Halos elsewhere in the building and they use a stolen military-issue laser weapon to breach the control center's security and steal the code (if the GC desires, this stolen laser weapon can act as another hook to include this threat in the game). If the agents stop one henchman but not the other, they are tasked with tracking down the one who escaped, a mission that eventually leads back to Bosque and his master plan. If both henchmen are stopped, the Agency orders that the agents track down and determine the involvement of "the new player" — the henchmen's superior, Bosque.

2. Through one of his government spies, Bosque discovers the Agency's investigation and intends to make sure their findings support his accusations. He arranges for Simon Hague and the Aeronauts to attack the event, targeting the agents and making it appear that Mercy Damien (posing as a Global Reach executive) is responsible. The Aeronauts are also ordered to make sure Damien is killed in the crossfire before she can reveal

the truth (cutting off the Agency's only source of information, and ensuring that they assume the attack to originate with Global Reach). Unexpectedly, one of the Aeronauts (Killian Lake) is in love with Damien, and attempts to save her during the chaos. Whether he succeeds or not, Lake comes to the agents seeking asylum (or retribution if he is severely wounded), offering them Hague's location and a rundown of the henchman's defenses. Through Hague, the agents discover Bosque's master plan.

3. Bosque discovers that Mercy is stealing from his shipments, and that she has recruited a personal army outside his organization, and decides to cut her loose. He sets her up to steal the codes as described in possibility #1, and orders Hague and the Aeronauts to eliminate her as described in possibility #2. The GC can then include Killian Lake to further complicate matters, if he likes.

Plot Hook #2

Wendell Olaus, an engineer working on Global Reach's latest satellite network, vanishes in the dead of night from his home on the grounds of a joint military installation in the South Pacific. Wendell Olaus occasionally works as a specialist for the Agency, and is currently reporting to them about the satellite system. His communications have never contained anything to warrant Agency interest, but his disappearance worries the organization. The agents are sent to investigate.

Possibilities

1. Simon Hague and the aeronauts have seized control of the military installation, killing and replacing the soldiers stationed there. Olaus was a victim of circumstance, still on site a day after he was scheduled to return to the United States (he remained to complete another infiltration of the base's computer system for the Agency). The agents, unaware that the base is held by an enemy force, are entering the proverbial lion's den, though if they survive they'll be able to prevent Bosque from taking control of Global Reach's new satellite system and should have leads back to the fledgling mastermind as well.

2. Olaus is a Bosque Industries plant, and assisted Hague and the Aeronauts in taking over the installation. When the agents arrive, Olaus is used as bait to lure them into a trap. Captured agents are taken to Bosque's world HQ in Geneva and interrogated about their affiliation.

3. The agents arrive to find the installation a smoking ruin and are able to piece together that the jet fuel on site was ignited during a firefight. After careful inspection, the bodies of all installation personnel except Olaus are

accounted for. The truth is that Hague's plan to assume control of the installation went awry when Olaus discovered the Aeronaut's presence and warned the station commander. Hague ordered the Aeronauts to contain the site (by killing everyone), but Olaus escaped in a small reconnaissance plane. Evidence points the agents to the missing plane and encrypted email sent by Olaus during his final minutes on the island leads them to a friend's home in Morocco. But the agents also find evidence that their mysterious opponent (Hague) has also discovered Olaus' destination. Now the race is on to find the one man who can identify the culprits and lead the agents back to Julian Bosque.

FRANZ LIEBER

This short-season (3-serial) threat is appropriate for a team of 3rd level agents.

In an age of rampant global terrorism, superspies are frequently called upon to counter the nefarious plots of third-world dictators looking to increase the power or influence of their nations, religious or political zealots seeking to make a statement with violence, and similar villains. Such missions are typically plagued by media interference, as world news services compete for the best exclusive or a fresh angle to the story. The following drama is a twisted example of what such conditions can produce.

MP Cost: 260
Resources: 2 (27 BPs for minions; 42 BPs for henchmen and foils; 52 BPs for mastermind)
Gadgets: 0 (0 gadget points per serial)
Loyalty: 3 (+3 to loyalty checks)
HQ Personnel: 3   **HQ Security:** 4

Serial Three: Gracio Demane

The nephew and sole heir of a reclusive Italian billionaire, Gracio is the product of decades of twisted indulgence. He has been offered every deranged entertainment he's ever expressed an interest in and committed countless crimes (all of which have been overlooked by subverted authorities). Now he seeks to play what he considers the ultimate game — terrorism — against a worthy foe. To do this, he has created a villain for the world to hate — Franz Lieber — and a force to hunt him down with ruthless dedication: the Millennium Militia, led by ex-GIGN counter-terrorist Paulo Targeno. Demane has ordered both sides to inflict as much destruction as possible, hoping to attract one or more outside agencies into the fray.

Demane is rarely found outside his mountain villa, where he chisels life-size statues of his perceived enemies, and blasts them to smithereens with highly illegal firepower.

Gracio Demane, 7th-level fixer (mastermind); CR 7.
SZ M; v/wp: 30/9; Init +3 (class); Spd 30 ft.; Def 16 (class); Atk: fencing foil +4 (1d6+1) / grenade launcher w/2 fragmentation grenades +5 (2d10); Face 1 square; Reach 1 square; SA None; SQ None; SV Fort +3, Ref +5, Will +3; Str 9, Dex 10, Con 9, Int 16, Wis 12, Cha 12; Skills: Appraise +10, Bluff +9, Boating +8, Escape Artist +7, Forgery +12, Hide +10, Hobby (Fencing) +10, Hobby (Sculpting) +10, Innuendo +6, Knowledge (Idle Gossip) +10, Listen +10, Move Silently +8, Open Lock +7, Search +10. Feats: Extreme Range, Far Shot, Point Blank Shot, Weapon Finesse. Gear: Weapons, 8 BPs. Gadgets and Vehicles: Jeep, w/rocket launcher, 1 GP.

Regional Police: Demane owns his local constabulary, with whom the agents must also contend once they know the true villain.

Regional Police, 5th-level minions (squads of 4).
CR 4. SZ M; v/wp: 5d8+10 (33)/14; Init +10 (+4 class, +2 Dex, +4 Improved Initiative); Spd 30 ft.; Def 14 (+2 class, +2 Dex); Atk: .380 ACP backup pistol +7 (1d8) / taser +7 (1d8 + special); Face 1 square; Reach 1 square; SA None; SQ None; SV Fort +6, Ref +5, Will +3; Str 14, Dex 15, Con 14, Int 12, Wis 10, Cha 11; Skills: Balance +10, Climb +10, Driver +10, Profession (Police) +6, Spot +8, Tumble +4. Feats: Improved Initiative, Quick Draw. Gear: Weapons, 7 BPs.

SERIAL TWO: FRANZ LIEBER

Franz is formerly of the HVA (*Hauptverwaltung Aufklarung*, the East German Foreign Intelligence Agency), and a SMERSH killer. Since "the Great Thaw," he went to ground, resurfacing a few years ago as a mercenary hit man.

Franz Lieber, 5th-level soldier (henchman); CR 5.
SZ M; v/wp: 79/16; Init +7 (+4 class, +3 Dex); Spd 30 ft.; Def 15 (+3 class, +2 Dex); Atk: punch dagger +8 (1d3+4) / survival knife +8 (1d6+3) / 6 throwing knives +8 (1d4+3); Face 1 square; Reach 1 square; SA None; SQ None; SV Fort +7, Ref +6, Will +4; Str 16, Dex 16, Con 16, Int 12, Wis 12, Cha 10; Skills: Balance +11, Climb +10, Intimidate +6, Profession (Assassin) +8, Spot +8, Survival +6. Feats: Weapon Focus (Survival Knife, Punch Dagger), Improved Weapon Focus (Survival Knife, Punch Dagger), Weapon Master (Survival Knife). Gear: Weapons, C4 (¼ lb), 20 BPs.
HQ Personnel: 3   **HQ Security:** 2

New Liberation Army (NLA): Members of Lieber's faux terrorist group are fond of saying they are with "Never Lie Again," after the group's goal of drawing European secret services into the open.

New Liberation Army, 3rd-level minions (squads of 4).
CR 2. SZ M; v/wp: 3d8+6 (22)/14; Init +5 (+3 class, +2 Dex); Spd 30 ft.; Def 13 (+1 class, +2 Dex); Atk: .380 ACP submachinegun (1d8); Face 1 square; Reach 1 square; SA None; SQ None; SV Fort +5, Ref +4, Will +2; Str 12, Dex 14, Con 14, Int 11, Wis 11, Cha 11; Skills: Climb +7, Demolitions +6, Profession (Terrorist) +6, Spot +6. Feats: Quick Use (Demolitions), Track. Gear: Weapons, 13 BPs.

SERIAL ONE: PAULO TARGENO

The 'hero' of Demane's media drama is Paulo Targeno, who recently changed his name (and his face) when a British counter-terrorism team got a little too close for comfort. His thirst for blood lives on through the Millennium Militia.

Paulo Targeno, 5th-level pointman (henchman); CR 5. SZ M; v/wp: 58/18; Init +3 (+2 class +1 Dex); Spd 30 ft.; Def 13 (+2 class, +1 Dex); Atk: .45 ACP service pistol +4 (1d10+2); Face 1 square; Reach 1 square; SA None; SQ None; SV Fort +6, Ref +4, Will +6; Str 18, Dex 12, Con 16, Int 14, Wis 14, Cha 10; Skills: Bluff +8, Cultures +7, Disguise +5, Diplomacy +9, Driver +8, First Aid +10, Knowledge (Underworld) +9, Languages +7, Profession (Terrorist) +8, Sleight of Hand +5. Feats: Quick Healer, Toughness. Gear: Weapons, 45 BPs. Gadgets and Vehicles: Standard clothing liner, 2 GPs.
HQ Personnel: 3   **HQ Security:** 2

The Millennium Militia: This grass-roots paramilitary unit hunts Franz Lieber with near-fanatic dedication, using a hodge-podge of hardware bought from European militaries.

The Millennium Militia, 2nd-level minions (squads of 5). CR 1. SZ M; v/wp: 2d8+2 (14)/12; Init +3 (+2 class, +1 Dex); Spd 30 ft.; Def 11 (+1 Dex); Atk: 7.62x39mm semi-automatic rifle +3 (2d8); Face 1 square; Reach 1 square; SA None; SQ None; SV Fort +4, Ref +3, Will +3; Str 12, Dex 12, Con 12, Int 10, Wis 12 Cha 12; Skills: Driver +5, First Aid +6, Gather Information +2, Spot +6, Search +3. Feats: Increased Speed, Track. Gear: Weapons, 5 BPs.

FOIL (ANY SERIAL): SUSAN FRANKS

This U.S. news correspondent is reporting on the apparent "terrorist feud" in Eastern Europe. She considers this her big break, and suspects that

things are not as they seem, but she has little field experience. She makes an excellent foil for the agents, or a possible love interest for one of them, one of the villains, or both.

Susan Franks, 5th-level snoop (foil);
loyalty 7: CR 5. SZ M; v/wp: 40/12; Init +5 (+3 class, +2 Dex); Spd 30 ft.; Def 16 (+4 class, +2 Dex); Atk: punch +2 (1d3); Face 1 square; Reach 1 square; SA None; SQ None; SV Fort +2, Ref +5, Will +6; Str 11, Dex 14, Con 12, Int 14, Wis 16, Cha 16; Skills: Bureaucracy +11, Computers +9, Cultures +11, Cryptography +9, Driver +8, Diplomacy +11, Gather Information +11, Hide +9, Languages +6, Move Silently +8, Profession (News Reporter) +9, Search +10. Feats: Expertise, World Traveler. Gear: Professional video camera and micro-tape recorder, 10 BPs. Gadgets and Vehicles: Helicopter.

Global News Interests

Susan works for Global News Interests, an up-and-coming cable channel. Their resources are spread thin at the moment, and they have only allotted her a team of two assistants and a helicopter to cover the Lieber story. In her short career, she has already acquired a reputation as a loose cannon, so her producer, Samuel Stevens, sometimes accompanies her in the field.

Resources: 1 (+1 BP for Susan, 1 BP for minions)
Gadgets: 4 (4 gadget points per serial)
Loyalty: 0 (+0 to loyalty checks)
HQ Personnel: 0
HQ Security: 0

GNI News Crew: Allie Haines, a pilot, and Hector Gomez, a cameraman, have been assigned to Susan's story about Franz Lieber. They will not risk their lives for anything short of a Pulitzer. In an effort to protect GNI's investment, and prevent Franks from taking too many unnecessary risks, Stevens has decided to accompany the trio.

GNI News Crew, 3rd-level minions (squads of 3). CR 2. SZ M; v/wp: 3d4 (8)/10; Init +3 (+3 class); Spd 30 ft.; Def 11 (+1 class); Atk: taser +3 (1d8 + special); Face 1 square; Reach 1 square; SA None; SQ None; SV Fort +3, Ref +2, Will +3; Str 9, Dex 10, Con 10, Int 12, Wis 14 Cha 9; Skills: Bluff +0, Driver/Pilot* +5, Gather Information +2, Profession (TV News Producer)* +7, Spot +7, Surveillance +5. Feats: None. Gear: Weapons, camera equipment and satellite feed (which allows them to transmit live to the studio).

* The helicopter pilot has the Pilot skill. The cameraman has the Driver skill. The producer has the Profession (TV News Producer) skill.

Plot Hook #1

One of the agents meets Susan Franks, through business, pleasure or possibly both. During one of the battles between the New Liberation Army and the Millennium Militia, Susan and her team get a little too close to the action. She is captured and the agents must intervene.

Possibilities

1. Franks is an innocent and must be rescued. She and her crew are taken to Demane's hidden mountain villa in the Italian Alps. The agents must wade through the layers of Demane's organization in order to rescue them. Even after Franks is rescued, the serial is not over – she refuses to leave the villa until the true story behind the terrorist feud is documented on film.

2. As above, but Demane paid Susan's cameraman (Hector Gomez) to set her up when he wasn't pleased with the way she was covering "his" story. Now the cameraman is enjoying the hospitality of Demane's villa until things cool down. If found there by the agents, he tries to hide any involvement he had in Susan's capture, and set the team up to be caught by the regional police.

3. Susan is a decoy who is being used to suck the agents into Gracio Demane's game. Once he has his hands on her, Demane takes her to his villa and leaves an obvious trail for the agents to follow. When they arrive, a deadly game of cat and mouse in the mountains of Italy begins – with the agents as the prey.

Plot Hook #2

The agents are ordered to bring the terrorist feud to an end by whatever means necessary. They are assisted, it seems, by Paulo Targeno, who has recently contacted the Agency with an offer to turn over "the man behind this bloody conflict." The agents are sent to meet with Paulo Targeno, assess the situation, and resolve the fighting. Unfortunately, Targeno turns up dead before the agents arrive, and they are left with a volatile situation and no apparent allies.

Possibilities

1. Lieber killed Targeno, and swears to Demane that it was an accident. The mastermind is certain that Targeno's death was intentional, however, and orders the Millennium Militia to destroy their opponents once and for all, sparking even bloodier conflict throughout Eastern Europe. The reality of Targeno's death is that Lieber was growing more and more nervous about deliberately drawing outside agencies into the picture, particularly since he would be their prime target.

His attempt to quell hostilities has now backfired, however, and he finds himself fighting a defensive war against his former benefactor. Perhaps the agents can strike a deal with him?

2. Demane discovered Targeno's betrayal and had the Millennium Militia kill him. When the agents arrive, the Militia tells them that Lieber is at fault and offers to assist them in bringing him down. Secretly, Demane informs GNI about the agents' involvement (whether they agree to the Militia's offer or not), compromising their cover and embroiling them in his drama as the new 'heroes' come to take down the vicious NLA and their leader.

3. Paulo is alive, and trying to bring Demane down from the inside. He faked his own death when it became clear that Demane had learned of his communication with the Agency, and the Militia's orders to eliminate him. With the help of a few of the Militia who are loyal to him, Paulo is now in hiding, waiting for an opportunity to aid any agents who come after Lieber, and consequently, Demane.

KHOLERA

This short-season (3-serial) threat is appropriate for a team of 5th level agents.

The archetypical foe of the superspy is the criminal mastermind, often brilliant and nearly always deranged. The schemes of criminal masterminds are varied and convoluted, and frequently involve the fate of the entire human race. The following threat is an example of all these things.

MP Cost: 290
Resources: 3 (30 BPs for minions; 45 BP for henchmen and foils; 55 BPs for mastermind)
Gadgets: 5 (5 gadget points per serial)
Loyalty: 5 (+5 to loyalty checks)
HQ Personnel: 4   **HQ Security:** 4

SERIAL THREE: DR. FRIEDRICH KHOLERA

This evil genius was once a mild-mannered political theorist who worked for the U.S. government, CNN, and the Vatican. Disgusted with society, he has dedicated his life — and the life of his wife, Janet — to developing a constantly mutating virus with a 99% yield (i.e. it will kill 99 out of every hundred people contaminated with it). He hopes to use the virus to wipe out the bulk of mankind and start fresh, with himself and his antidote-protected elite as the ruling class.

Dr. Friedrich Kholera, 9th-level snoop (mastermind): CR 9. SZ M; v/wp: 63/15; Init +5; Spd 30 ft.; Def 17 (+7 class); Atk: sword cane +4

(1d6); Face 1 square; Reach 1 square; SA None; SQ None; SV Fort +5, Ref +4, Will +6; Str 11, Dex 10, Con 15, Int 17, Wis 15, Cha 14; Skills: Balance +5, Bluff +8, Computers +15, Concentration +16, Cultures +14, Diplomacy +11, Electronics +14, Hide +6, Hobby (Bonsai Trees) +12, Knowledge (Biology) +16, Knowledge (Chemistry) +16, Knowledge (Occult) +5, Profession (Political Theorist) +14, Sense Motive +4. Feats: Scholarly, Advanced Skill Mastery (Scholarly), Unlocked Potential (Knowledge: Biology), Training. Gear: Weapons, 66 BPs; Gadgets and Vehicles: Helicopter, external bug detector unit, safe passage attaché case (where he stores the virus), 2 GPs.

The Zero Sum: Kholera indulges in a special torture for his most hated enemies — a flesh-eating pathogen that he uses to ensure their loyalty as his personal guard. Only he knows the formula for the injection they must receive each day to survive, which he has never written down.

The Zero Sum, 6th-level minions (squads of 5). CR 5. SZ M; v/wp: 6d6+6 (27)/12; Init +8 (+5 class, +3 Dex); Spd 30 ft.; Def 15 (+3 Dex, +2 armor); Atk: .45 ACP submachinegun +9 (1d10+2); Face 1 square; Reach 1 square; SA None; SQ None; SV Fort +6, Ref +6, Will +5; Str 12, Dex 16, Con 12, Int 14, Wis 14, Cha 12; Skills: Climb +8, Driver +10, First Aid +9, Jump +8, Profession (Spy) +9, Spot +9, Tumble +10, Use Rope +8. Feats: Sidestep. Gear: Weapons, 9 BPs.

SERIAL TWO: IMELDA NUF

Imelda is a beautiful Indian woman with a mean streak. She was abused as a girl and has grown to hate and distrust men. At the age of 19, she's already seen a fair amount of violence and perpetrated a great deal of it herself. Now she is a seductress, luring in Kholera's enemies and killing them. Her favored technique is to seduce her victims and stab them with a stiletto blade before or as their lust is consummated. Imelda and her minions are Kholera's most trusted couriers.

Imelda Nuf, 7th-level faceman (henchman): CR 7. SZ M; v/wp: 60/12; Init +7 (+6 class, +1 Dex); Spd 30 ft.; Def 15 (+4 class, +1 Dex); Atk: stiletto dagger +7 (1d6+2), Kick +7 (1d3+2); Face 1 square; Reach 1 square; SA None; SQ None; SV Fort +5, Ref +3, Will +3; Str 14, Dex 13, Con 12, Int 15, Wis 8, Cha 16; Skills: Bluff +12, Diplomacy +6, Disguise +12, Driver +7, Escape Artist +6, Innuendo +9, Jump +7, Languages +6, Open Lock +8, Search +11. Feats: Quick Draw, Weapon Focus (Stiletto Dagger), Improved Weapon Focus (Stiletto Dagger). Gear: Weapons,

63 BPs; Gadgets and Vehicles: Sports car, suicide pill tooth (given to her by Kholera — no known antidote), belt w/ razor's edge (for Sascha), 2 dartgun cigarettes (for Suede).

HQ Personnel: 4   **HQ Security:** 3

Suede, Shade, and Sascha: These vivacious vixens are fanatically loyal to their mistress, Imelda, and lethal with throwing knives and darts of all kinds.

Suede, Shade, and Sascha, 5th-level minions (squads of 3). CR 4. SZ M; v/wp: 5d6 (18)/10; Init +5 (+4 class, +1 Dex); Spd 30 ft.; Def 13 (+2 class, +1 Dex); Atk: throwing knife (6 each) +6 (1d4+2), throwing dart (3 each) +6 (1d3+2); Face 1 square; Reach 1 square; SA None; SQ None; SV Fort +4, Ref +4, Will +3; Str 14, Dex 12, Con 10, Int 10, Wis 10, Cha 13; Skills: Intimidate +7, Jump +9, Spot +6, Swim +9, Tumble +7. Feats: None. Gear: Weapons, 25 BPs.

SERIAL ONE: JASON HELLMAN

The lowest rung of the ladder in Kholera's criminal empire is Jason Hellman, an unstable dilettante who launders money and weapons for the organization.

Jason Hellman, 6th-level pointman (henchman); CR 6. SZ M; v/wp: 29/9; Init +6 (+2 class, +4 Improved Initiative); Spd 30 ft.; Def 12 (class); Atk: .40 S&W service pistol +4 (1d12), knife +3 (1d4-1); Face 1 square; Reach 1 square; SA None; SQ None; SV Fort +2, Ref +3, Will +8; Str 9, Dex 11, Con 9, Int 16, Wis 16, Cha 10; Skills: Bluff +9, Boating +8, Bureaucracy +7, Craft (Woodworking) +11, Driver +4, Forgery +11, Hobby (Boat Repair) +11, Knowledge (Finance) +12, Sleight of Hand +8, Surveillance +11, Swim +3. Feats: Darting Weapon, Expertise, Improved Initiative. Gear: Weapons, 45 BPs; Gadgets and Vehicles: Jeep (for himself), pick-up trucks (two — for the Whitlows), suicide pill tooth (given to him by Kholera — no known antidote).

HQ Personnel: 3   **HQ Security:** 2

The Whitlows: This deranged family of hired killers and social deviants has been hired on by Hellman to defend his schemes and eliminate the inevitable retaliation from the world's spies.

The Whitlows, 3rd-level minions (squads of 5). CR 2. SZ M; v/wp: 3d6+6 (18)/14; Init +4 (+3 class, +1 Dex); Spd 30 ft.; Def 12 (+1 class, +1 Dex); Atk: 12 gauge pump-action shotgun +4 (4d4); Face 1 square; Reach 1 square; SA None; SQ None; SV Fort +5, Ref +3, Will +1; Str 13, Dex 12, Con 14, Int 6, Wis 8, Cha 4; Skills: Demolitions +0, Intimidate +4, Spot +3, Use Rope +4. Feats: None. Gear: Weapons, 8 BPs.

KHOLERA

FOIL (ANY SERIAL): JANET KHOLERA

Janet Kholera is as yet unaware of the horror her husband plans to unleash upon the world. She is remarkably loyal to her seemingly devoted husband, who courted her through her first troubled marriage. What she doesn't realize is that Kholera, who was her doctor before they became romantically involved, only married her out of shame. Kholera used his patients as test subjects for his viral experiments, infecting and curing them of more and more potent viral solutions in an effort to achieve his goal of a 99% yield. Unfortunately, one such experiment resulted in the miscarriage of Janet's only child, after which she was diagnosed as barren. Unable to conceive any other way to atone for his "mistake," Kholera arranged for Janet's first husband to fall victim to a sudden and violent case of pneumonia and then pursued her until she agreed to marry him.

Janet, like the rest of Kholera's inner circle, is now immune to his virus, but she is haunted by the tragedy of her first marriage, and is subconsciously wracked with guilt over the death of her child. Her life is hollow, and she fills it with her consuming loyalty to the one man who has shown her any kindness. If presented with the truth about her husband, however, and a reasonable way to capture her husband alive, she might assist an operation against him.

MARTIN ST. JAMES

Janet Kholera, 8th-level snoop (foil); loyalty 6: CR 8. SZ M; v/wp: 34/11; Init +6 (+5 class, +1 Dex); Spd 30 ft.; Def 11 (Dex); Atk: 9x19mm backup pistol +5 (1d10); Face 1 square; Reach 1 square; SA None; SQ None; SV Fort +2, Ref +5, Will +6; Str 10, Dex 13, Con 11, Int 20, Wis 14, Cha 16; Skills: Bluff +5, Bureaucracy +11, Climb +5, Computers +13, Concentration +10, Diplomacy +10, Disguise +8, First Aid +12, Gather Information +10, Handle Animal +8, Jump +5, Listen +8, Move Silently +9, Read Lips +12, Ride +6, Search +10, Sport +3, Spot +13. Feats: Animal Affinity, Point Blank Shot, Precise Shot. Gear: Weapons, 34 BPs.

Janet has no organization or minions of her own.

PLOT HOOK #1

Every inhabitant of Green Vale, a small Nebraska town, is found dead. Investigation by the Agency or the CDC (or both) reveals that one person who was known to be staying in the town is unaccounted for – Janet Kholera. The agents are dispatched to find her and bring her in, likely with the help of one or more chemical warfare specialists and the proper protective gear.

POSSIBILITIES

1. Kholera has adjusted the viral loads in each of his henchmen and their minions and sent them to locations around the world to perform meaningless tasks, spreading the virus along the way. Janet learned

of his plan when they moved into his self-contained biosphere, which triggered her loyalty check (the GC should make the roll or determine her loyalty before the start of the serial). If she is loyal to her husband, she is now spreading the virus voluntarily. In this case, she may be captured and interrogated for information about her husband and his henchmen. Otherwise, she was held against her will at the biosphere (which in this case is in a secret location in Green Vale), escaped, and is spreading the virus as she searches for help. Either way, the agents are likely to be infected when they catch up with her, further increasing the need to find and stop Kholera.

2. Janet found records proving that her husband's death was not incidental and is delving into her history (and that of her husband). Kholera has sent Imelda Nuf and her vixens to reclaim her and charged Jason Hellman and the Whitlows with eliminating those Janet has spoken with during her investigation. Unfortunately, the Whitlows are using the real virus to eliminate these witnesses, rather than the diluted (and non-contagious) version Kholera told them to use. Now the virus has been released, and is spreading, and the agents must find a way to stop it – and its mad creator.

3. The virus in Janet has mutated once again, and when she visits her parents in Green Vale she accidentally infects the entire town. The terror of watching all her family and friends causes her to snap, and forces a loyalty roll. If loyal to Kholera, she decides that his way is best and sets about spreading the newly mutated virus as far and wide as possible. If loyal to the agents, she returns to the biosphere, steals the antidote, and flees for help. Kholera sets his henchmen after her. If loyal to neither, she goes into hiding, withdrawing into her own private hell. Regardless, the agents must find her before she spreads the virus any further.

PLOT HOOK #2

While in transit during another mission (on a boat, plane, train, or other mode of transportation), the agents – and everyone else on board – are infected with Kholera's virus. Once the first victims fall to the virus (hours after the voyage is over), the agents must strive to contain the outbreak and seek out the source – before they succumb to its effects.

POSSIBILITIES

1. The only passengers on board who aren't affected are Imelda Nuf and her beautiful minions, posing as an up-and-coming fashion designer and her assistants. Imelda's next stop is a fashion show in Milan, where the virus will be released through aerosol perfume samples.

2. One of the passengers on board is Stewart Whitlow, who reveals Kholera's plot to the agents before he dies of the virus (Hellman gave him a placebo instead of the real antidote). Stewart offers the agents Hellman's name, as well as the hotel where he passed the virus and placebo on to Stewart (in the city the transport left from). The agents must track Hellman down and link him to Kholera, which is easier said than done as he is protected by Imela Nuf and/or the Zero Sum. If the GC desires, the rest of the Whitlow brood may intervene to help the agents, seeking retribution for their cousin.

3. The virus was released by Greg Reynolds (Janet's son). Greg was not stillborn, as Kholera claimed, but was instead raised by Jason Hellman's corrupt clan. Now that Greg has discovered the truth about his mother's new husband, he infects the agents and then offers them the antidote if they agree to kill Kholera and return his mother.

MARTIN ST. JAMES

This short-season (3-serial) threat is appropriate for a team of 10th level agents.

Spy organizations regularly contend with foreign governments and their operatives, their classic enemies. As they also often operate without the approval of their own governments, allied departments can become obstacles or even villains for them. Worse, there is always the threat of rogue agents and ex-friendlies who have turned to a life of crime. The following is an example of this last possibility.

MP Cost: 365
Resources: 3 (35 BPs for minions; 50 BPs for henchmen and foils; 60 BPs for mastermind)
Gadgets: 2 (2 gadget points per serial)
Loyalty: 4 (+4 to loyalty checks)
HQ Personnel: 1   **HQ Security:** 3

SERIAL THREE: MARTIN ST. JAMES

Martin St. James is a British secret agent gone bad. Infuriated by his country's waning power, St. James dreams of the day when Britain will once again be on top of the world. His current scheme is to reacquire Hong Kong as a British colony. Toward that end, he has used Triad connections both in Hong Kong and on the Asian mainland to stage a coup. He plans to assassinate key figures in the Chinese government, replacing them with pawns of his Triad connections, simultaneously starting a major conflict in Hong Kong over Chinese control. As tensions rise, his friends in the House of Lords will push for British intervention, and his Chinese patsies will ask for British help in restoring order.

Martin St. James, 13th-level pointman (mastermind); CR 13. SZ M; v/wp: 106/18; Init +9 (+5 class, +4 Dex); Spd 30 ft.; Def 19 (+5 class, +4 Dex); Atk: 5.56x45mm assault rifle +13 (2d8+2); Face 1 square; Reach 1 square; SA None; SQ None; SV Fort +10, Ref +10, Will +10; Str 16, Dex 19, Con 18, Int 17, Wis 14, Cha 16; Skills: Bluff +17, Bureaucracy +14, Computers +15, Cryptography +15, Diplomacy +13, Disguise +16, Driver +18, First Aid +12, Gather Information +15, Knowledge (Spy Agencies) +14, Languages +14, Profession (Spy) +16. Feats: Point Blank Shot, Marksman, Precise Shot, Rapid Shot, Sharp-Shooting. Gear: Weapons, 68 BPs; Gadgets and Vehicles: Humvee (with the usual refinements), laser watch, telescopic contact lenses.

Rogue Agents: These former MI6 agents have joined St. James' crusade to bring their nation back to power. They are career spies, with all the associated training and contacts.

Rogue Agents, 10th-level minions (squads of 5). CR 9. SZ M; v/wp: 10d6+30 (69)/16; Init +12 (+8 class, +4 Dex); Spd 30 ft.; Def 18 (+4 class, +4 Dex); Atk: 7.62x39mm assault rifle +14 (2d8); Face 1 square; Reach 1 square; SA None; SQ None; SV Fort +10, Ref +9, Will +8; Str 16, Dex 18, Con 16, Int 16, Wis 16, Cha 16; Skills: Climb +14, Cryptography +8, Disguise +8, Driver +13, First Aid +12, Intimidate +12, Profession (Spy) +12, Spot +12, Survival +12, Swim +14, Tumble +13. Feats: Athletic, Sidestep. Gear: Weapons, basic audio bug (1 each), basic video bug (1 each), disguise kit, 3 BPs.

SERIAL TWO: ERIN "LADY" LOVELOCK

This unerring businesswoman, known as the "Terror of Tokyo," is a formidable power in the Asian world of commerce, with a long string of failed relationships (and broken lovers) behind her. Lovelock has agreed to work with St. James on the condition that her company, Eclipse Capital Ventures, is offered the first commercial options when the British move in to take over the area.

Erin Lovelock, 12th-level fixer (henchman); CR 12. SZ M; v/wp: 84/14; Init +11 (+5 class, +2 Dex, +4 Improved Initiative); Spd 30 ft.; Def 22 (+10 class, +2 Dex); Atk: .40 S&W backup pistol +11 (1d12); Face 1 square; Reach 1 square; SA None; SQ None; SV Fort +8, Ref +10, Will +8; Str 12, Dex 14, Con 14, Int 15, Wis 18, Cha 18; Skills: Appraise +15, Bluff +19, Boating +12, Concentration +11, Driver +10, Forgery +10, Hide +12, Hobby (Chinese Finger Painting) +16, Innuendo +16, Knowledge (Big Business) +15, Listen +16, Profession (CEO) +16,

Search +13. Feats: Confident Charge, Expertise, Improved Disarm, Improved Initiative, Sidestep. Gear: Weapons, 49 BPs; Gadgets and Vehicles: Helicopter, portable PC attaché case, translator lenses, 1 GP.

HQ Personnel: 2   **HQ Security: 2**

Bodyguards: Given her dangerous links to the underbelly of the espionage world and her cutthroat business practices, Lovelock is wise to keep these men close.

Bodyguards, 9th-level minions (squads of 6). CR 8. SZ M; v/wp: 9d6+36 (70)/18; Init +9 (+7 class, +2 Dex); Spd 30 ft.; Def 16 (+4 class, +2 Dex); Atk: .45 ACP backup pistol +11 (1d10+2); Face 1 square; Reach 1 square; SA None; SQ None; SV Fort +10, Ref +6, Will +6; Str 18, Dex 14, Con 18, Int 14, Wis 14, Cha 12; Skills: Bureaucracy +5, Computers +6, Concentration +6, Driver +12, Intimidate +11, Profession (Bodyguard) +12, Spot +12, Tumble +10. Feats: Great Fortitude, Unlocked Potential (Intimidate). Gear: Weapons, earpiece two-way radio (encrypted), 12 BPs.

SERIAL ONE:
MASTER EDWARD STILES

This gentleman secret agent of the early Cold War has come out of retirement for one last lark with St. James, whose philosophy supports his own mad obsession with Queen and Country. Stiles is determined to show the others that he is not the "crusty old buzzard" they say he is.

Sir Edward Stiles, 11th-level snoop (henchman); CR 11. SZ M; v/wp: 50/12; Init +9 (+7 class, +2 Dex); Spd 30 ft.; Def 21 (+9 class, +2 Dex); Atk: 7.62x45mm semi-automatic rifle +7 (2d8+1) / bayonet +7 (1d6+2); Face 1 square; Reach 1 square; SA None; SQ None; SV Fort +4, Ref +7, Will +8; Str 15, Dex 14, Con 12, Int 16, Wis 16, Cha 16; Skills: Appraise +13, Bureaucracy +13, Computers +13, Concentration +13, Craft (Painting) +13, Cryptography +13, Cultures +10, Diplomacy +13, Gather Information +13, Hide +10, Hobby (Art Collection) +13, Knowledge (Spy Agencies) +13, Languages +12, Listen +13, Move Silently +13, Profession (Spy) +10, Surveillance +13. Feats: Cleave, Power Attack, Stealthy, Surge of Speed, World Traveler. Gear: Weapons, 30 BPs; Gadgets and Vehicles: Classic car, 2 bullet tracer packages, shoe blade, 6 GPs.

HQ Personnel: 1   **HQ Security: 2**

The Royal Colonials: Modeled after the British foreign military occupational forces of the late nineteenth century (though with a decidedly updated style), these men enforce Master Stiles' plans, attending to all the 'dirty details' he won't contend with himself.

The Royal Colonials, 7th-level minions (squads of 7). CR 6. SZ M; v/wp: 7d8–7 (32)/9; Init +7 (+6 class, +1 Dex); Spd 30 ft.; Def 14 (+1 Dex, +3 armor); Atk: .30-06 bolt-action rifle (made to look like a musket) +8 (2d10); Face 1 square; Reach 1 square; SA None; SQ None; SV Fort +4, Ref +5, Will +3; Str 9, Dex 12, Con 9, Int 9, Wis 9, Cha 12; Skills: Spot +9, Survival +9, Use Rope +11. Feats: Zen Focus. Gear: Weapons, 8 BPs.

PLOT HOOK #1

One of the agents studied under Stiles, and is contacted by his daughter. She informs the team that she has discovered her father's involvement in a plot against the Chinese government, and requests their help.

POSSIBILITIES

1. The young lady is telling the truth – except for one detail. Her father has trained her as an agent and she wants to prove herself by bringing him in. The agents discover this when some overanxious members of the Royal Colonials attack them. Stiles' daughter assists the agents in combating the Colonials, and aids the agents in their attempts to bring her father to justice. In the process, the agents are drawn into St. James' plot.

2. As above, but Stiles' daughter has inherited his obsession with Queen and Country. She plans to prove herself to him, and earn a place at his side in the plot to overtake Hong Kong.

3. Unbeknownst to his daughter, Stiles works for the Agency and is running a sting operation against St. James' organization. His motives are flawed, however. He's trying to prove that he still has the stuff to be on the front lines, a goal that could lead to poor judgment during the mission.

PLOT HOOK #2

Over the course of the last several months a disturbing picture has been put together at the Agency. Everything points to a Triad war in Hong Kong. The agents are assigned to find out what is causing the tension on the street, and defuse the powder keg before it blows.

POSSIBILITIES

1. The Triads are aware of St. James' plan to push for British intervention, but they are going along with it in name only. The criminals are looking for a way to eventually double-cross him. They want control of their city for themselves. The twist? Erin Lovelock is in fact a Triad boss, and is playing everyone for the fool.

2. Erin Lovelock and St. James are romantically involved, but she actually controls a large percentage of the Triads. The Agency's information about the situation is based on the fact that the two factions are starting to come into conflict on the streets. Neither Lovelock nor St. James are ready to make their final move, but it is inevitable the two lovers will become rivals.

3. As #1 or #2, but the Triad war is a set-up to lure the agents in. St. James wants to exact revenge on the Agency. He ultimately doesn't care what happens to the Triads — or any of his minions, for that matter. He simply wants to get his hands on some of the Agency's "best and brightest," and beat them in a staged game of spy vs. spy. He'll sacrifice anyone — including Lovelock — to prove that he's better than the youngsters who have replaced him.

ANTONIO GUADALUPE

This short-season (2-serial) threat is appropriate for a team of 15th level agents.

World military forces pose a significant threat to the world order, whether operating under the flag of an established nation or as the private army of a criminal mastermind. The following is an example of the second case, a Russian career soldier whose lust for power has outweighed his sense of duty.

MP Cost: 295
Resources: 1 (29 BPs for minions; 44 BPs for henchmen and foils; 54 BPs for mastermind)
Gadgets: 2 (2 gadget points per serial)
Loyalty: 2 (+2 to loyalty checks)
HQ Personnel: 3   **HQ Security:** 2

SERIAL TWO:
ADMIRAL IVAN ILYCH ROSTOV

Admiral Rostov commanded the Soviet Arctic fleet at the height of the Cold War. With the fall of the Soviet Union and the downsizing of the fleet, he found most of his ships slated for mothballs or the scrapyard. Feeling betrayed, he stole several state-of-the-art nuclear submarines (including his flagship, a Typhoon-class sub named "Leviathan") and made his way to South America, where he has established a puppet regime under the name "Antonio Guadalupe." No one ever sees the merciless dictator, whose enemies mysteriously vanish in the dead of night.

In truth, Guadalupe's Amazon forest stronghold is merely a distraction, a death-trap for those who would try to track the warlord down. Rostov commands this operation from the *Leviathan*, usually off the cost of Cuba, where he trains a private army of disenchanted Russian soldiers who have forsaken their nation.

Rostov's most recent development is a drug called "Flashback," which allows its users to relive their happiest moments over and over again. The drug has no apparent side effects or addictive properties. In truth, however, the drug brainwashes its users to give up their lives and travel to join Rostov's army.

Admiral Ivan Rostov, 17th-level soldier (mastermind); CR 17. SZ M; v/wp: 240/22; Init +18 (+14 class, +4 Dex); Spd 30 ft.; Def 21 (+7 class, +4 Dex); Atk: .40 S&W backup pistol +21 (1d12). 5.56x45mm sniper rifle with telescopic sight +21 (2d8+2); Face 1 square; Reach 1 square; SA None; SQ None; SV Fort +16, Ref +12, Will +15; Str 19, Dex 18, Con 22, Int 16, Wis 20, Cha 12; Skills: Boating +11, Climb +16, Demolitions +13, First Aid +19, Mechanics +7, Profession (Military) +25, Spot +17, Swim +20, Survival +19, Tumble +15, Use Rope +19. Feats: Diving Shot, Extreme Range, Far Shot, Increased Precision, Iron Will, Marksman, Master Sniper, Mobility, Outdoorsman, Point Blank Shot, Precise Shot, Sharp-Shooting, Shot on the Run, Sniper, Toughness. Gear: Weapons, 44 BPs; Gadgets and Vehicles: Stolen submarine, 1 GP.

Frogman Assassins: Most of these ex-Russian soldiers joined Rostov before his voyage. All are responsible for eliminating Rostov's enemies — using Special Forces tactics to sneak into their homes and kidnap or kill them. Rostov's frogman assassins are the scourge of the South American coast.

Frogman Assassins, 15th-level minions (squads of 4). CR 14. SZ M; v/wp: 15d6 (52)/11; Init +13 (+12 class, +1 Dex); Spd 30 ft.; Def 17 (+6 class, +1 Dex); Atk: survival knife +16 (1d6) / composite bow +16 (1d6) / silenced 9x19mm service pistol +16 (1d10); Face 1 square; Reach 1 square; SA None; SQ None; SV Fort +9, Ref +8, Will +7; Str 12, Dex 12, Con 11, Int 14, Wis 10, Cha 10; Skills: Balance +13, Boating +6, Climb +13, Demolitions +10, Hide +6, Intimidate +10, Move Silently +7, Spot +10, Survival +12, Swim +16. Feats: Point Blank Shot, Stealthy, Track. Gear: Weapons.

SERIAL ONE: PYTHON

This native warrior was raised to defend his Amazon tribe, which was destroyed by local drug lords several years ago. Rostov offered him the chance for retribution if he joined the Admiral's ranks, and he has acted as an assassin and commander of the Russian's troops ever since.

ANTONIO
GUADALUPE

Python, 15th-level fixer (henchman); CR 15. SZ M; v/wp: 95/15; Init +11 (+6 class, +5 Dex); Spd 30 ft.; Def 27 (+12 class, +5 Dex); Atk: punch/kick +15 (1d3+4); Face 1 square; Reach 1 square; SA None; SQ None; SV Fort +9, Ref +14, Will +7; Str 18, Dex 20, Con 15, Int 15, Wis 15, Cha 10; Skills: Appraise +17, Bluff +14, Boating +21, Climb +21, Escape Artist +20, Forgery +17, Hide +22, Innuendo +15, Jump +20, Knowledge (Underworld) +17, Listen +16, Move Silently +22. Feats: Kicking Arts, Kicking Mastery, Martial Artist, Stealthy, Throwing Arts, Throwing Mastery. Gear: 59 BPs; Gadgets and Vehicles: 17 GPs.
HQ Personnel: 3   **HQ Security: 2**

Cuban Drug Smugglers: Only the strongest and most efficient of the local cartel were allowed to live through the massacre that took their former employers. They made up a force nearly military in its strength and precision, further bolstered by training from the frogmen. These men and women now operate Rostov's inland enterprises and man his collection camp for flashback devotees / deathtrap for would-be heroes and liberators. They comprise the force which agents meet when they approach the jungle base.

Cuban Drug Smugglers, 10th-level minions (squads of 9). CR 9. SZ M; v/wp: 10d8+30 (85)/16; Init +11 (+8 class, +3 Dex); Spd 30 ft.; Def 17 (+4 class, +3 Dex); Atk: 12-gauge single-shot shotgun +13 (4d4); Face 1 square; Reach 1 square; SA None;

SQ None; SV Fort +10, Ref +8, Will +7; Str 18, Dex 16, Con 16, Int 16, Wis 15, Cha 14; Skills: Boating +7, Climb +12, Driver +14, Innuendo +6, Intimidate +8, Jump +11, Knowledge (Underworld) +7, Spot +14, Swim +11, Tumble +11, Use Rope +11. Feats: Increased Speed, Quick Reload. Gear: Weapons, 8 BPs.

PLOT HOOK #1

Several influential people associated with various governments have vanished. The Agency has only been able to turn up one connection: they all attended an exclusive party in Washington DC. Unknown to them (or the agents sent to determine what's happened), the mind-altering drug Flashback was distributed at the party, and all the dignitaries are prisoners of Python and his minions (or en route to the collection camp).

POSSIBILITIES

1. One dignitary hasn't vanished yet, and the agents are assigned to secretly safeguard him while seeking the truth about the disappearance of the others. The official in question is cantankerous, stubborn, and independent. He also happens to have a great deal of influence over budgets — and he's not a big fan of the Agency. The agents are ordered to tread with extreme care.

2. As above, but the political figure is already missing and must be found. The trail is set up to lead the agents to the Amazon stronghold, where they face Python and discover the true threat, Rostov. All of the delicacy in handling the politico is still requested by their superiors.

3. Clues lead the agents to the Amazon. The twist, however, is that Python can be convinced to switch sides again – if the agents agree to fund and supply his war on the drug lords. If they refuse, Python fights them to the death on his own deadly turf. As above, leads to Rostov may be found in Python's stronghold.

PLOT HOOK #2

A CIA station north of Ahmadabad, India has been silent through its last two routine radio bursts. With the station so close to the Pakistani border, and the rise in local turmoil, the Agency assigns the team the task of determining what has happened.

POSSIBILITIES

1. The station is ransacked and the operatives are dead. Evidence on site points to the Pakistanis as those responsible, but the truth of the matter is that Rostov's assassins have staged the massacre to incite the U.S. to

expand their military operations in Central Asia. Rostov has already stuck a deal with Pakistani extremists to support their struggle from the sea – a position from which he will be able to lead one last great battle against a superpower.

2. As possibility #1, above, except that the CIA operatives intercepted radio traffic between Rostov's assassins and his sub, and were therefore warned of the attack. They have escaped and are waging a guerrilla war against the assassins as they flee to nearby allies.

3. Two operatives are dead at the station house. A third, Daniel Hemming, is missing. Daniel's father, Captain Douglas Hemming, is a United States nuclear submarine captain who clashed repeatedly with Rostov during the Cold War, and who is now on his way to San Diego, California, to decommission his submarine and retire. Rostov refuses to let him retire without one last great battle, and intends to use Daniel as leverage to force the Captain's hand.

SERIAL DESIGN

This section covers the design of serials (adventures), including the various genres of espionage, balancing encounters, and designing and using NPCs.

THE GENRES OF ESPIONAGE

The focus of this book has been to present a set of rules which allows you to play a game capturing the feel of your favorite action-adventure movie or book series. Up until now, we've focused on the exploits of larger-than-life spies that work behind the scenes to maintain global security, but the action-adventure genre is diverse, and there are many different ways to present it.

For the sake of convenience, we have divided these possible presentations into categories. Think of them as filters to run a series or single mission through, and keep in mind that they can and usually do overlap.

THE HISTORICAL SERIAL

The last century was a hotbed of action and intrigue all across the globe. There is no reason why the Game Control cannot set back the calendar and explore these events with his players, portraying the stories that went on behind the scenes. The *Shadowforce Archer* and *Spycraft* product lines will include regular releases to support this approach.

The official *Shadowforce Archer* timeline *(see the Shadowforce Archer Worldbook)* can be used as a road map for those looking for a place to start, but we also encourage players and the GC to branch out and recreate their own historical seasons.

Effects: Much of the gear available in the superspy serial is still experimental or hasn't been invented yet. You may wish to change some items from standard gear to gadget status depending on the time period you've selected.

THE MERCENARY SERIAL

The mercenary serial is a close cousin to the super-spy serial *(see page 263)*. Again, agents are expected to be highly trained specialists whose talents raise them above and beyond the norm. The difference is that they are not motivated by loyalty to a particular government, organization, or cause. They are freelancers, selling their skills for profit.

The *A-Team* and Martin Bishop's close-knit crew of security analysts from the movie *Sneakers* are great examples of fictional mercenary units, but those who would like to learn about real mercenaries throughout history should read *Mercs: True Stories of Mercenaries in Action* by Bill Fawcett.

A mercenary serial can be as realistic or as far-fetched as the GC and the players are comfortable playing. Like the superspy serial, though, a pitfall is that it can easily become nothing but a series of reactive assignments. There are creative ways around this, ranging from roleplaying the agents' search for employment or even having them orchestrate situations where their skills are needed (the films *Yojimbo* and *A Fistful of Dollars* are excellent examples of how this dynamic can enrich a storyline).

Effects: Gadgets are difficult or impossible to get in a mercenary serial. Reduce or eliminate gadget points appropriately.

THE PARANORMAL SERIAL

The 1990s brought with them a resurgence of interest in the paranormal, this time with an espionage twist. A new genre was born in which agents working for private organizations and governments investigated cases no one else considered worthwhile — alien abductions, hauntings, the dead returning to life (or a shambling semblance thereof), and cults dedicated to otherworldly gods.

The paranormal serial offers GCs the chance to ignore the standard conventions of espionage roleplaying, focusing a little more on elements of horror and the supernatural. Likewise, players can let loose and indulge in a little monster hunting, pitting their skills against a puzzle (and perhaps a foe) that is both unexpected and unpredictable.

One of the most effective ways to utilize this serial is by surprise. Begin a game as a normal serial of another type listed here and spring the weird elements on the players slowly over time (building suspense as the players try to apply mundane techniques and theories to the problem), or all at once, as a shocking divergence.

Alternately, a paranormal serial can be played in reverse, with the Agency aware of the supernatural and using it to their advantage. Agents might even be paranormal in nature (ghosts make perfect spies). In such games, the GC and players must determine whether they are playing a standard espionage game with monsters, or something entirely new.

Effects: The Knowledge (Occult Science) skill plays a much heavier role in the paranormal serial, and the Basement *(see page 19)* may expand from investigating fringe cases to handling all things supernatural. Finally, gadgets are likely to become more focused on the paranormal (like the accelerators and containment equipment in *Ghostbusters*).

THE POLITICAL THRILLER SERIAL

Often coupled with aspects of the techno-thriller (see below), a political thriller serial is rooted in today's headlines. Terrorist activities, government scandals, and deadly conspiracies all find a place in this category. *Clear and Present Danger, The Day of the Jackal,* and *The Russia House* are best-selling novels in this genre, and the films *Enemy of the State, The Odessa File,* and *The Manchurian Candidate* are notable movies to draw inspiration from.

The mass appeal of the genre is that it is grounded in realism, playing out some of the deepest fears we have about the world around us. Paranoia is a strong element that the GC should invoke, and agents should rarely (if ever) have a clear view of "the big picture." Action is constant, but violence is sporadic — just enough to keep players on their toes. When events do take a violent turn, they are never pleasant or glamorized. Agents in this genre are just as often regular citizens as government agents.

To make the political serial as effective as possible, the Game Control should have serviceable, factual knowledge of the real-world political environment, economics, and history of the area where the serial unfolds. The more facts that are available, the more authentic the serial appears.

Mechanics: To simulate the realism and danger of a political thriller, reduce or eliminate vitality points. In such a serial, death is common and fire fights are short and brutal.

THE PSYCHOLOGICAL SUSPENSE SERIAL

Even for players who like to portray every aspect of their agents, the psychological suspense serial can be a real challenge. In this genre, the mental state and motivations of agents and important NPCs are peeled back, piece by piece, until their deepest, darkest secrets come to light.

Strong characterization is omnipresent with this genre, even superseding plot complexity as a primary thrust of missions and backstory. Through the filter of the psychological suspense drama, a simple hostage negotiation may become an intense battle of wills, both sides launching emotionally charged assaults even though the physical situation is stalemated. Picture Clarice Starling and Hannibal Lecter from *The Silence of the Lambs* on opposite sides of a terrorist stand-off and you get an idea of the potential with this style of action-adventure storytelling.

The movie *Se7en* is a great example of a psychological suspense mission and can easily be converted to feature spy or espionage characters. The killer, John Doe, is clearly a devious criminal mastermind. Imagine if he had decided to carry out his scheme on a global scale...

Effects: To simulate the shock and horror of the unnerving situations that agents in a psychological suspense serial often face, use Will saves frequently, stunning agents that fail a roll, and possibly leaving them open for a brutal sneak attack.

THE SPOOF SERIAL

As a testament to the popularity of action-adventure serials, they are routinely lampooned. The above example with *The Simpsons* is really just the tip of the iceberg, with other notables including the *Austin Powers* films, *Spy Hard!, The Man From U.N.C.L.E., Our Man Flint, Get Smart,* and *Hudson Hawk.*

So why let Hollywood have all the fun?

The secret to a successful spoof serial is to revere the genre but not take it seriously. The level of humor can span from dry, sophisticated wit to cartoonish acts that would make the Three Stooges proud. Ultimately, the Game Control must set the standard that the players follow.

Like double-fudge brownies, the spoof serial is best served as a special treat rather than a regular meal. What is funny once or twice becomes wearisome with repetition. However, as long as what you are doing is fun, you are doing it right.

Effects: To encourage the proper lack of respect, only award action dice to players that make the entire group laugh out loud.

THE SUPERSPY SERIAL

The superspy serial is *Spycraft's* default *modus operandi*. It draws inspiration from the James Bond novels and movies, along with the *Mission: Impossible* franchise and sundry other popular sources.

In the superspy serial, players assume the roles of the world's foremost secret agents, dedicated to serving a government, organization, or cause in whatever capacity is necessary. In essence, they are troubleshooters, taking on situations only they have the skills and experience to resolve.

The action in this category is over-the-top, with heroes (and villains) capable of performing incredible physical and mental feats. Everything happens on an epic scale, and there is usually a clear delineation between good and evil.

A common dilemma that a superspy serial succumbs to is that it is inherently reactive. In other words, time and again, agents are sent out to respond to a mastermind's scheme already in progress. While this is certainly the standard for the genre, it isn't the only way to do things. GCs should read the box entitled Active Missions on page 205 for information about avoiding this pitfall.

Mechanics: Use the *Spycraft* rules 'out of the box' for this type of serial.

THE TECHNO-THRILLER SERIAL

Thanks to the works of Tom Clancy and other authors, techno-thrillers have become one of the most successful action-adventure genres of all time. The key to running a techno-thriller serial is understanding that technology is the foundation and emphasis of every plot, with the action resulting from its use (and, more often than not, misuse). A agent's physical abilities regularly take a back seat to nifty gadgets and devices, and heroes are commonly average people with just the right tool or knowledge at the right time.

The GC must do a lot of research to give a techno-thriller serial the rich (and very technical) detail generally found in the sources that inspire it, and there is a fine line to be walked. Technology that is only theoretically possible is a genre standard, but abuses quickly turn a techno-thriller into a work of science fiction or even science fantasy.

Books like *The Hunt for Red October* and *The Tin Man* are excellent examples of this category, as are movies like *The Net* and (pushing theoretical technology to the limit) *Strange Days*.

Effects: If you wish to simulate an agency with access to more technology, increase or double the number of gadget points agents receive.

THE VILLAIN SERIAL

The villain serial embraces the fact that there are two sides to every story. Instead of players assuming the roles of heroic agents out to foil the schemes of crafty masterminds, they get to be the bad guys.

All levels of action and realism are appropriate here, but the most important thing to remember is the agents' motivation. Most likely, they do not see their actions as wrong or even questionable. They believe that their cause is just and that their methods are excusable. Of course, there also exist sadists and deviants that revel in the harm and chaos they cause.

A factor that must be considered in a villain serial is the status of the agents. There are really only three options to choose from. First, all the agents are the minions of a mastermind NPC. Second, one agent plays the mastermind and the others are his subordinates. Third, all the agents are masterminds, united in one cause. Each choice includes its own obvious benefits and drawbacks.

Films that approach this idea in a serious manner include the *Godfather* Trilogy, *Reservoir Dogs,* and *A Clockwork Orange.* The ultimate comedic take on the idea is "You Only Move Twice," an episode of *The Simpsons* in which Homer goes to work for the charismatic Hank Scorpio and his mysterious Globex Corporation.

Effects: To allow the players to play minions or masterminds, simply turn the tables, allowing them the opportunity to use the Mastermind system *(see page 242)* while you sit back and throw problems at them.

ENCOUNTERS

Note: Encounters are generally scenes of a serial, though it is possible that a single scene can contain more than one encounter (e.g. a scene in which there is a combat followed by a chase).

The relative difficulty of a scene is gauged by its encounter level (EL), which is determined by the combined challenge ratings (CRs) of all threats facing the team (NPCs they are fighting, security systems they are facing, etc.), as shown on Table 9.16 (see page 264). Most of the time, you want to pit a team of four agents against an encounter with a level equal to their own average level.

Example: Your players have a team of four agents whose average level is 3. You should generally throw encounters of level 3 at them. Referencing Table 9.16: Encounter Levels, we see that this means you can safely design encounters with one threat of CR 3 or 4, two threats of CR 1 or 2, three threats of CR 1, four threats of CR ½ or 1, five or six threats of CR ½, seven to nine threats of CR ⅓, ten to twelve threats of CR ¼, or a mixed pair of CRs 2 and 1.

Teams larger than four agents can usually handle encounters of slightly higher level. As a general rule, increase the ELs a team may face by 1 for every two agents they have beyond the standard size of 4.

Example: If the team mentioned in the example above were composed of six agents with an average level of 3, they could generally face the threats described for EL 4.

Assuming a team of four facing an encounter of equal level, you can roughly assume a 20% loss of resources (wp, gadgets, etc.). Four such scenes is about all such a team can handle; a fifth would overwhelm them.

A team can roughly face twice as many scenes with an encounter level two lower than their own average level, twice that many again if the scene's encounter levels drop by two more, and so on. Discrepancies like this drastically affect the amount of XP such scenes are worth *(see page 239).*

Commonly, you should design serials to include a variety of ELs, both to vary the challenge and spice up the game. Here's a good rule of thumb when composing the various encounters in your serials.

% of Serial	Encounter	Description
10%	Easy	EL lower than team level
20%	Easy if handled	Special *(see below)*
50%	Challenging	EL equal to team level
15%	Very difficult	EL 1-4 higher than team level
0-5%	Overpowering	EL 5+ higher than team level

You should not include overpowering encounters unless the agents have gotten in over their heads or you are using the encounter as a dramatic device.

Example: If you were designing a ten-encounter serial for a team of agents with an average level of 3, you should consider having five challenging encounters (EL 3), two encounters which are easy if handled properly (EL below 3 with elements that make it more difficult), two very difficult encounters (EL 4-8), and one easy encounter (EL below 3).

TABLE 9.16: ENCOUNTER LEVELS (BY COMBINED CHALLENGE RATING)

EL	One	Two	Three	Four	Five or Six	Seven to Nine	Ten to Twelve	Same Pair	Mixed Pair
1	1 or 2	1/2	1/3	1/4	1/6	1/8	1/8	1/2	1/2 + 1/3
2	2 or 3	1	1/2 or 1	1/2	1/3	1/4	1/6	1	1 + 1/2
3	3 or 4	1 or 2	1	1/2 or 1	1/2	1/3	1/4	1	2 + 1
4	3, 4, 5	2	1 or 2	1	1/2 or 1	1/2	1/3	2	3 + 1
5	4, 5, 6	3	2	1 or 2	1	1/2	1/2	3	4 + 2
6	5, 6, 7	4	3	2	1 or 2	1	1/2	4	5 + 3
7	6, 7, 8	5	4	3	2	1	1/2	5	6 + 4
8	7, 8, 9	6	5	4	3	2	1	6	7 + 5
9	8, 9, 10	7	6	5	4	3	2	7	8 + 6
10	9, 10, 11	8	7	6	5	4	3	8	9 + 7
11	10, 11, 12	9	8	7	6	5	4	9	10 + 8
12	11, 12, 13	10	9	8	7	6	5	10	11 + 9
13	12, 13, 14	11	10	9	8	7	6	11	12 + 10
14	13, 14, 15	12	11	10	9	8	7	12	13 + 11
15	14, 15, 16	13	12	11	10	9	8	13	14 + 12
16	15, 16, 17	14	13	12	11	10	9	14	15 + 13
17	16, 17, 18	15	14	13	12	11	10	15	16 + 14
18	17, 18, 19	16	15	14	13	12	11	16	17 + 15
19	18, 19, 20	17	16	15	14	13	12	17	18 + 16
20	19+	18	17	16	15	14	13	18	19 + 17

Same pair: Generally, two threats of the same CR constitute an encounter level 2 points higher. For instance, two enemy agents with CRs of 4 actually have an EL of 6. Every time you double the number of same-pair threats, the EL of the combined threat rises by 2. For example, four enemy agents with CRs of 4 have a combined EL of 8, eight such agents have a combined EL of 10, and so on.

Mixed pair: This column shows which combinations of CRs constitute higher ELs. For instance, combining a threat with a CR of 6 and a threat with a CR of 4 garners a combined EL of 7.

You should also be mindful of factors which can affect a scene's encounter level, such as bad terrain or weather, enemy tactics, large numbers of lesser enemies, enemy abilities, security considerations, fixed chase obstacles, and the like, and adjust scenes to ensure that the circumstances do not make them too powerful for the agents to face.

Finally, you should watch the development of your team, both the progression of the agents and the players' ability with designing agents and using (and abusing) the system. If it becomes clear that the players have refined their agents and play styles to a point where they can easily overcome encounters equal to their level, you may want to consider designing future encounters as if the agents were a level or two above their actual agent levels. If you do this, make sure to award XP as if they were this higher level as well (i.e. the agents shouldn't be gaining more XP for defeating the more challenging encounters that you are forced to pitch at them).

Experience points are determined by the EL of an encounter in comparison to the agents' average level, as shown on table 9.12: Sample Action Rewards.

NPCS

This section is dedicated to populating your world and creating foes you can use to challenge your players. It covers the core non-player character (NPC) archetypes that the agents might meet. We have broken NPCs into three rough categories, according to the side each particular type normally is on during a serial. Of course, the GC may choose to design a minion — normally part of a mastermind's organization and blindly loyal to the evil genius — who finds his life despicable and tries to get out. Or he can design a Control who has sold out to the enemy. These categories are merely for organization.

NPC STATISTICS

When generating NPC (not threat) statistics, you should generally follow these guidelines. (For threat statistics, see page 242.) As always with serial design, feel free to lift any restrictions when you feel it enhances the game without unbalancing it.

NPC Type: All *Spycraft* NPCs are one of two types — standard or special. Standard NPCs are reduced to 0 wound points when they suffer a critical hit, and cannot inflict critical hits themselves. This NPC type usually includes minions and everyday individuals. Special NPCs operate in all ways like agents, and can both score and suffer critical hits normally. This NPC type includes masterminds, henchmen, foils, and other NPCs deemed important by the GC. The Game Control determines the types of all NPCs.

Ability Scores: Roll 3d6 for each ability score, rerolling if you are unsatisfied with the results, and apply any modifier listed on Table 9.17: NPC Statistic Ranges. Alternately, you can simply assign NPC ability scores.

Department: Unless from the Agency, NPCs have no department or department bonuses.

Classes: Choose an agent class from Chapter 2 or another *Spycraft* supplement.

Skills: Guidelines for skills levels are listed on Table 9.17: NPC Statistic Ranges, as either equal to the NPC's level ("L"), equal to the NPC's level plus a modifier ("L+X," where X is the modifier), or equal to the NPC's level minus a modifier ("L–X," where X is the modifier). If a listed skill is a cross-class skill for the NPC, it should be reduced by half (after any modifiers have been applied). Finally, if a skill is not listed, it is not a common skill for the NPC — if a score is needed, generate it randomly or assign a value (up to the maximum allowed by the NPC's class and level).

Feats: Feats should generally only be assigned to combat-oriented NPCs, such as adversaries. Assign any feats you desire, so long as the NPC meets the feats' requirements and has enough free slots.

Action dice: The GC spends his action dice on NPCs, just as he does on villains. Dice spent on NPCs come from the same pool as those spent on villains.

Gear: NPCs have 1 BP per level or whatever their class allots them, as appropriate, to spend on standard-issue gear.

Vitality/Wound Points: Roll your NPC's vitality points according to his class and Constitution score. His wound points are equal to his Constitution score.

ALLIES

The first NPC category consists of all those who normally support the agents. This support generally comes in one of two ways — as support (the NPC works away from the team), or as assistance (the NPC works with the team in the field). The first type of ally — Control — is usually the former.

MULTI-CLASS ABBREVIATIONS

A multiclassed agent does not gain several first-level benefits of his second or later classes (maximum vitality points, quadruple skill points, personal budget, and core abilities). For this reason, it is important to keep track of an agent's first class (the one that does offer him all these benefits). This is especially important with NPCs, whose statistics are often presented in abbreviated form. For this reason, all published *Spycraft* and *Shadowforce Archer* material assumes that the class listed first under any NPC (regardless of level) is the class in which he started his career.

Controls: Control NPCs are the agents' primary contacts with their home office. A Control gives the mission team its orders, provides the initial briefing, and is typically the team's contact with their agency during an assignment.

Control typically remains in one area, usually one which belongs to their agency or one of its protectorates. For instance, MI6 Controls generally work in Britain, a British-controlled area, or an area where Britain has political or economic interest.

During the mission briefing, Control assembles a team at a place of his convenience, and provides the team with what he thinks they need to know about their assignment: no more and no less. Controls very rarely become "friendly" with their charges, as this compromises their objectivity. They also handle many different mission teams within their designated area, and have little time for personal attachments.

Control is the mission team's main contact once the mission is under way. The team is usually given a "blind" contact number and is expected to use public telephones if necessary (since cell phone signals are easily intercepted). Mission teams are expected to operate with a great deal of autonomy, so casual calls to Control are frowned upon. In general, teams should only contact Control if they suffer casualties or get in over their heads, or to provide an update if the mission status has changed significantly.

If a mission requires teams to travel out of the initial mission area on short notice, they should notify Control as soon as possible (assuming they have a secure method of communication). He can provide overseas contacts, but is unlikely to travel with the team to the new mission area. In the very rare instance when Control travels to the new mission area, he never travels with the mission team, instead arranging separate, unconnected (and inconspicuous) transportation of his own.

When Control feels that a team requires supervision in its new mission area, he may turn the team's management over to a local Control at their destination. The new Control generally contacts the team through an intermediary in the new area, or another "blind" phone number.

The original Control has responsibility for the team, but it's not unusual for two Controls — particularly from two different agencies or sections — to provide contradictory orders or information. Completing the assigned mission is always the highest priority; mission teams are trained to ignore inter-department rivalries. A team that accomplishes its mission is usually forgiven for disregarding orders from Control that may have hindered their mission.

To their credit, few Controls are so egotistical as to substitute their judgment for that of their mission teams. Most Controls prefer a hands-off approach once a mission has begun. Autonomy cuts both ways: a Control who doesn't interfere with a team's operations is much less likely to be blamed if the mission fails.

Agents: The game of spy vs. spy is an everyday indulgence for the international super-operative. Enemy agents vie for important information and neutrals carefully observe missions in their territory for violations of inter-department treaties and protocols. Even friendly agents are a source of potential worry. Mission teams must always be mindful of those who are close to them — regardless of their perceived allegiance.

Agents come in far too many flavors to be easily pigeon-holed with blanket descriptions. When undefined, they are skulking, watchful men and women in dark suits with earpieces and suspicious bulges beneath their armpits.

Specialists: Specialists are knowledgeable in a given field, or skilled with a particular craft. They are assigned to teams who request support personnel in the field. A team needing to get across a tightly-secured border might request a forger, while a team needing to destroy an enemy stronghold might request a demolitions expert.

Specialists are assigned through Control after a mission team comes up against a situation it can't handle on its own. As always, Control frowns upon agents relying on specialists to do their jobs for them; if there is another way to get past the problem without calling a specialist in, the agents are expected to follow it. Also, specialists are not always available when they are needed.

ADVERSARIES

One of the most important elements of a good *Spycraft* game is a host of interesting villains for your agents to foil. Stopping the nefarious schemes of these fiends is what agents do, and you'll want to keep your players happy and interested by presenting them with engaging foes.

As discussed on page 243, espionage villains usually fall into three primary categories: masterminds, henchmen, and minions. Each is discussed further here.

Masterminds: Masterminds come in many varieties. They could be rogue generals trying to spark a revolution, rich dilettantes seeking to impose their vision of social order on the world, mercenaries looking to profit from a war or other political upheaval, or just madmen trying to destroy or conquer the world. Each has his own motivations for devising the schemes that the agents must stop.

TABLE 9.17: NPC STATISTIC RANGES

NPC Type	Ability Scores						Classes (d20)					
	Str	Dex	Con	Int	Wis	Cha	Fac	Fix	Ptm	Sol	Snp	Whl
Allies												
Control	+0	+0	+0	+3	+2	+1	1-3	4-6	7-10	11-14	15-17	18-20

Common Skills: Bluff (L), Bureaucracy (L+1d3), Diplomacy (L), Gather Information (L+1d3), Knowledge (area he controls, L+1d3), Language (L), Sense Motive (L).

NPC Type	Str	Dex	Con	Int	Wis	Cha	Fac	Fix	Ptm	Sol	Snp	Whl
Agent	+1	+1	+1	+1	+1	+1	1-3	4-6	7-10	11-14	15-17	18-20

Common Skills: Balance (L), Climb (L), Computers (L+1d3), Disguise (L), Driver (L+1d3), Escape Artist (L−1d3), First Aid (L), Gather Information (L), Hide (L+1d3), Innuendo (L), Jump (L), Listen (L+1d3), Move Silently (L+1d3), Open Lock (L+1d3), Search (L+1d3), Spot (L), Surveillance (L).

NPC Type	Str	Dex	Con	Int	Wis	Cha	Fac	Fix	Ptm	Sol	Snp	Whl
Specialist†	+0	+1	+0	+3	+2	+0	1-4	5-8	9-10	11-12	13-16	17-20

Common Skills: Computers (L), Craft (L), Cryptography (L), Demolitions (L), Electronics (L), Forgery (L), Handle Animal (L), Hobby (L), Knowledge (any, L), Languages (L), Mechanics (L), Profession (any, L), Survival (L).

Adversaries

NPC Type	Str	Dex	Con	Int	Wis	Cha	Fac	Fix	Ptm	Sol	Snp	Whl
Mastermind	+2	+2	+2	+3	+3	+0	1-4	5-6	7-10	11-14	15-18	19-20

Common Skills: Appraise (L), Bluff (L+1d3), Concentration (L), Cultures (L), Disguise (L), Escape Artist (L+1d3), Gather Information (L), Innuendo (L), Intimidate (L+1d3), Knowledge (any, L), Listen (L), Sense Motive (L).

NPC Type	Str	Dex	Con	Int	Wis	Cha	Fac	Fix	Ptm	Sol	Snp	Whl
Henchman	+3	+3	+3	+1	+1	+1	1-3	4-6	7-10	11-14	15-17	18-20

Common Skills: Balance (L), Climb (L), Demolitions (L), Driver (L¹, Intimidate (L), Search (L), Spot (L), Survival (L).

NPC Type	Str	Dex	Con	Int	Wis	Cha	Fac	Fix	Ptm	Sol	Snp	Whl
Minion	+0	+0	+0	+0	+0	+0	1-2	3-6	7-9	10-13	14-16	17-20

Common Skills: Climb (L−1d3), Craft (L−1d3), Driver (L−1d3), Hide (L−1d3), Jump (L−1d3), Mechanics (L−1d3), Use Rope (L).

Others

NPC Type	Str	Dex	Con	Int	Wis	Cha	Fac	Fix	Ptm	Sol	Snp	Whl
Foil	+0	+1	+0	+0	+2	+3	1-5	6-8	9-11	12-14	15-17	18-20

Common Skills: Bluff (L+3), Cultures (L), Diplomacy (L+1d3), Disguise (L), Driver (L), Escape Artist (L), Gather Information (L), Innuendo (L+1d3), Languages (L), Listen (L), Perform (L+1d3), Read Lips (L), Sense Motive (L+1d3), Sleight of Hand (L), Spot (L).

NPC Type	Str	Dex	Con	Int	Wis	Cha	Fac	Fix	Ptm	Sol	Snp	Whl
Criminal*	+0	+0	+0	+0	+0	+0	1-2	3-4	5-6	7-8	9-10	10-10

Common Skills: Appraise (L+1d3), Bluff (L), Climb (L), Craft (any criminal, L), Disguise (L), Driver (L), Electronics (L), Forgery (L), Hide (L+1d3), Jump (L), Knowledge (any criminal. L), Move Silently (L+1d3), Open Lock (L+1d3), Search (L), Survival (L).

NPC Type	Str	Dex	Con	Int	Wis	Cha	Fac	Fix	Ptm	Sol	Snp	Whl
Govt. Figure	+1	+1	+1	+1	+1	+1	1-3	4-6	7-9	10-13	14-17	18-20

Common Skills: Bureaucracy (L+1d3), Computers (L), Cryptography (L), Diplomacy (L+1d3), Gather Information (L), Intimidate (L), Knowledge (conspiracies and cover-ups, L), Profession (any government, L), Search (L).

NPC Type	Str	Dex	Con	Int	Wis	Cha	Fac	Fix	Ptm	Sol	Snp	Whl
Military Man	+2	+2	+2	+0	+0	+0	1-3	4-6	7-9	10-14	15-17	18-20

Common Skills: Bureaucracy (L), Climb (L), Computers (L−1d3), Cryptography (L), Demolitions (L+1d3), Driver (L), Electronics (L), First Aid (L), Hide (L), Intimidate (L), Jump (L), Mechanics (L), Profession (any military, L), Survival (L+1d3), Swim (L), Tumble (L).

* Apply a +2 bonus to the criminal's three lowest abilities.

† The specialist automatically has the highest possible skill ranking (his level +3, or half that if it's a cross-class skill) in any skill he has been called in to use.

This supersedes any value listed under his Common Skills, above.

As the motivation for an entire season, you should spend the most time designing your masterminds to ensure that they are exciting enemies. Oftentimes, it's best to start not with the character itself but rather with his plan. What is the mastermind attempting to accomplish? Is he building the ultimate weapon? Selling nuclear secrets? Does he want to wipe out humanity and institute a master race in its place?

Knowing the mastermind's plan helps to determines his personality and resources. For instance, if he wants to wipe out the human race, you have to ask yourself: why? This is a suicidal plan on the surface, and it behooves you to know why the mastermind thinks it's necessary, and what he plans to do after the event. He might believe that humanity is ultimately corrupt and must be purged from the Earth to make room for his own followers (who are, of course, forthright and pure). He may be a cult leader with a twisted vision of perfection. More importantly for your purposes, however, a mastermind with a genocidal cause must have the resources to somehow engineer the destruction of humanity while at the same preserving his own people—no small feat under any circumstances.

In general, masterminds should be powerful characters. They don't have to be incredibly tough in a fight (though some of them certainly are), but they should command great resources. They are generals, heads of industry, political leaders, or commanders of large villainous organizations. Whatever plan the mastermind hatches, he must have the resources necessary to enact it. Masterminds don't have to be rich, but if they're not, they should have personnel, gadgets, or other significant resources at their disposal — preferably resources geared toward their goal.

Every mastermind should have a unique personality. While some masterminds are clearly insane, you should avoid the "gibbering madman" stereotype, and instead attempt to provide each with greater depth. Is your mastermind a fire-and-brimstone religious type? Does he seek physical perfection (which fuels his need to instill the same in the rest of humanity)? The answer to these questions partially dictates how the mastermind behaves. For instance, he might feel that killing in cold blood is wrong and therefore give all of his captives a chance to fight for their lives (typically in some strange ceremonial fashion). Such a character trait provides you with a unique villain (and also sets you up with a thrilling death-trap to spring on the agents late in the season).

Finally, don't feel that every villain must be bent on world domination. A mastermind who wants to "rule the world" is a valid foe, but if all of your masterminds have this motivation, the game quickly grows boring. There are countless plot possibilities; use as many of them as you can in your game. One villain may want to conquer the world, while another may want to spark a war between two world powers so that he can profit from arms sales to both sides. Still another might strictly be interested in toppling an enemy organization, with the agents scrambling to pick up the pieces. Just make sure that the small-scale plots are as interesting as the big ones. A serial wherein Top Secret U.S. military documents are being sold to the enemy isn't very interesting, but one in which those documents contain the agents' personal data is.

Henchmen: Henchmen are the principal thugs a mastermind employs to help pull off his plan. These characters are tough, unquestionably loyal, and generally must be defeated before the agent can thwart the mastermind. Henchmen are usually the focus of a serial; their defeat leads the agents closer to the leader of their organization, the mastermind.

Like masterminds, henchmen come in a variety of types. While Jaws from *The Spy Who Loved Me* is perhaps the best-known archetype for this NPC type, not every henchman has to be a behemoth that stretches the agents' fighting skills to the limit. A psychotic killer like Xenia Onatopp from *Goldeneye* makes an equally interesting villain, and a henchman might also be an expert sniper, hacker, or the head of a vicious spy network. The common traits that henchmen all share is that they are both lethal and obsessed with accomplishing their masters' goals.

You can put a little less effort into these characters since they are essentially high-powered thugs. The trick to having successful and memorable henchmen is making them unique. One of the easiest ways to do this is to give each henchman a signature method of killing. For instance, you could have two henchmen who are simply assassins. But if one of them always leaves an orchid on his victims while the other uses a special gun that fires razor-sharp mini-discs, you have two unique NPCs. Henchmen often have unique codenames as well. In the above example you might name the characters Orchid and Razor. This can help solidify them in the players' minds.

Minions: Finally, there are minions, the rank and file of criminal organizations, who perform most of the work — especially the hands-on or "grunt" work — for their hidden masters. Minions are also the most commonly encountered adversary. Like agents, minions operate in teams, though the strength of minions is usually in numbers rather than skill.

Minions can be summed up quickly as they spend far less time "on screen" (as it were), and are really only in the game as impediments before the agents reach henchmen or the mastermind. One identifying trait, such as a tattoo, emblem, or consistent physical charac-

teristic, is enough for a minion type. Armies of minions (as seen in many of our published organizations) are often fleshed out much more thoroughly.

EVERYONE ELSE

Finally, we come to all the NPCs whose motives and allegiances are most often unknown.

Foils: While many foils are femme fatales, these NPCs can be of either gender. The role of these NPCs is usually to seduce or distract the agents (thereby drawing them away from the action), to steal something from the agents, or to kill them. Foils may be henchmen, and are sometimes even the mastermind of a season (per *The World is Not Enough*). They can also be minions, at your discretion.

These characters are gorgeous obstacles that the agents must overcome, or potential plot hooks for you to build upon. You should put about as much effort into them as you do henchmen, with one caveat: the goals of foils are rarely known at the start of a mission. You should design them with enough room to side with the mastermind, the agents, or themselves if the situations warrants it.

Foils are *Spycraft's* 'wild cards.' Each has a loyalty rank *(see page 248),* which is rolled against, or 'tested,' during the serial. The outcome of this roll determines whom they side with – the agents, the mastermind, or themselves. In keeping with this mechanic, you should strive to present foils as complete NPCs, with backgrounds, lifestyles, careers, and the like, but withhold their true motivations until the last possible moment. Of course, more this condition more often than not leads foils to a bad end, but such is their unfortunate lot.

Because they typically deal with just one of the agents (and may turn against him), a foil should generally not have statistics that exceed those of an average agent on the team.

Criminals: The seedy underbelly of society has an ability and skill package devoted to greed and survival.

Government figures: Politicians, statesmen, intelligence analysts, and retired military figures all fall into this type.

Military Men: When agents unexpectedly run afoul of the military, you can start with this simple package, and develop the soldiers from there.

CHALLENGE RATINGS FOR NPCS

In general, NPCs have challenge ratings equal to their level, and doubling the number of NPCs encountered increases the challenge rating of that encounter by 2 (assuming that the NPCs are hindering and not helping the agents, of course).

Example: A henchman with a level of 4 has a CR of 4. Two such henchmen have a CR of 6, four a CR of 8, and so on.

THE DISPOSITION SYSTEM

This is a quick and easy way of determining how NPCs react to agents and their actions. All NPCs are categorized into one of seven dispositions ranging from bitter adversaries to staunch allies. Each category includes some basic concepts on how the an NPC with that disposition acts towards the agents and creates situational modifiers for certain skills in social settings.

Ally: The NPC is strongly committed to the agent's cause and well-being, and risks combat and even potentially life-threatening situations to aid him. Such characters expect to be treated fairly, but tolerate bargains and exchanges that clearly favor the agents with the understanding that the agents will 'make good' at a later time. Allies speak on behalf of the agent (without being asked to) and generally relay the best possible impression of the agent and his activities to others. If present during a fight, allies leap to the agent's defense and sort out the whys and wherefores afterwards. Other agents from the agents' organization who have worked closely with them in the past, close family members, and long time friends may fall into this category.

Helpful: These NPCs favor the agent and his goals, and risk injury (but not death) to aid them. They accept bargains and deals that slightly favor the agent, believing it contributes to the greater good. They usually volunteer a good opinion of the agent. If involved in the vicinity of a fight involving the agents, helpful NPCs try to offer indirect aid (shouted advice, information about the enemy's location), and may join the fighting if certain of the agent's cause. Co-workers, allies from other organizations, distant family members, and good friends are all likely to fall into this category.

Friendly: The NPC is mildly disposed in the agent's favor, and provides minor aid if it does not otherwise impair his own efforts. He is unwilling to risk injury unless it's clear that his own circumstances will worsen if he doesn't. Friendly NPCs are open to negotiation and accept most bargains of equivalent value to both parties. If asked they cheerfully offer up knowledge they have of the agent (if appropriate to do so) and emphasize the good, while not necessarily concealing the bad. If nearby when combat breaks out, friendly NPCs often remain nearby to help out afterwards, and may become involved in the final rounds if it is clear the agent is going to win. Members of related branches of the Agency, staff of loosely allied groups, estranged family, and casual acquaintances often fall into this category.

Neutral: Most NPCs have no stake in the agent's activities. They take direction from the agent only if it's clearly in their best interests, or is supported by offers of reward or threats. If willing to negotiate at all, they seek to gain at least a slight advantage in the deal or decline the offer. If questioned they offer a disinterested recounting of the agents, and otherwise tend to ignore them. Neutral parties rarely become involved in the fights of others, and either actively remove themselves from the area (often alerting the authorities) or return after the fighting ends to survey the scene (and perhaps loot the fallen if less scrupulous).

Unfriendly: This NPC has a mild dislike for the agent. This may be impersonal, an aversion to the agent's nationality or ethnicity or to a group or agency the agent appears to be affiliated with. If personal, the NPC has some bad history with the agent. Either way the NPC goes out of his way to not assist the agent in any way. He is unwilling to negotiate unless given highly favorable terms, and even then may try to twist the bargain or renege if he believes he can get away with doing so. If questioned he presents a poor impression of the agent and may even volunteer (or fabricate) negative commentary. If the agent is in combat nearby the NPC most likely withdraws, and may even provide token assistance to the agent's enemies or summon the authorities (if doing do increases his own safety or troubles the agent). Still, most abuse this NPC heaps on the agent is petty in nature rather than dangerous. Poorly paid or unmotivated minions may fall into this category, as do agents of rival organizations, along with people with great troubles of their own or those whom the agent deliberately antagonizes.

Hostile: This NPC considers himself the agent's enemy, but most highly regards his own advantage and well being. He may initiate combat if he believes he will win quickly or escape punishment. Otherwise he limits himself to abusive behavior, attempting to ruin the agent's reputation. Hostile NPCs are unwilling to negotiate unless forced or promised exactly what they want at little or no cost. Even then they are likely to bend or discard the terms of the agreement if they're able. Hostile NPCs join any on-going combat against the agents, even at the risk of personal injury. If the fight appears to be life threatening, they may instead try to offer assistance to the agent's opponents. Hostile NPCs include well-paid or highly motivated minions, professional combatants committed to fighting against the agent or his superiors, all henchmen who are not blindly loyal, agents of other organizations who are actively at war with the agent's group, violently adversarial family members, and most long-time 'professional' rivals.

Adversary: This NPC is a fervent enemy of the agent. He uses any opportunity to bring the agent harm, and risks criminal behavior and injury to do so. Adversaries only bargain if forced, and attempt to offer as little (and gain as much) as possible in the exchange. Adversaries cheat the agent unless their own sense of honor prevents them from doing so (and even then may be able to rationalize it). They seize all opportunities to smear the agent's reputation. Adversaries are completely untrusting of the agent's motives and goals, and cheerfully join into combat against them. Only individuals with strong, abiding, and long-term reasons for despising the agents (or what they represent) fall into this category, which includes fanatical zealots, obsessed rivals, and true sociopaths. Even masterminds are likely to retain a more detached (hostile) viewpoint unless repeatedly thwarted by the agent.

DISPOSITION EFFECTS

An NPC's disposition toward an agent dramatically influences the effectiveness of many of the agent's skills when they are used on the NPC. Disposition works both ways — NPCs apply the same modifiers when dealing with agents.

Disposition	Effect on Agent
Ally	+1 to Sense Motive, +2 to Diplomacy, +4 to Gather Information
Helpful	+1 to Diplomacy and Sense Motive, +2 to Gather Information
Friendly	+1 to Gather Information and Intimidate
Neutral	+2 to Intimidate
Unfriendly	+1 to Intimidate, −1 to Diplomacy and Gather Information
Hostile	−1 to Bluff and Diplomacy, −2 to Gather Information
Adversary	−1 to Bluff, −2 to Diplomacy, −4 to Gather Information

INFLUENCING DISPOSITION

From the above descriptions the GC should be able to determine the most likely level of reaction for most NPCs the agents interact with. However it is possible for an agent to improve (or sometimes worsen) an NPC's disposition with his behavior and manner. When an agent first interacts with an NPC outside of combat, that agent should roll a single d20, adding his Charisma modifier, and compare the results to Table 9.18: Influencing Disposition. In most cases it is only possible to shift an NPC's disposition one grade in either direction, but a critical success or failure shifts an NPC's disposition one additional grade.

In most cases it is harder to antagonize an NPC who is already favorable towards you, while those who think they already have cause to dislike you are watching for any justification of their dislike. Speaking a language the NPC doesn't understand offers a –2 modifier to the roll. Having 8 or more ranks in Cultures adds a +2 modifier to the roll. A natural 20 is always a threat, and a 1 is always an error.

THE GREAT SEDUCTION

One of an agent's greatest accomplishments is often turning a key member of the opposition to his side. This is done through sheer personal magnetism (one of Mr. Bond's deadliest weapons), supported by a cunning combination of flattery, and promises of wealth, power, position, or pleasure. While attempts at seduction are generally aimed at members of the opposite sex, powerful appeals to an agent's greed, patriotism, ideals, or dreams can have the same effect, at least for a time. An example of such a non-sexual seduction is the relationship between the two central characters in the movie Training Day.

The goal of a seduction attempt is to turn an agent with an unfriendly (or worse) disposition into a helpful figure or sometimes even an ally (if they really buy into your line). Agents and masterminds cannot be targeted with a seduction attempt. Players always control their own actions (although a clever GC may be able to tempt them anyway), and masterminds are far too focused to be turned, though they may play along with agents who are unaware that they are dealing with a mastermind. The details of a seduction depend upon the ploy being used, but generally involve three steps.

1. An Innuendo check to make the offer in a subtle fashion, planting the seeds of the seduction.

2. A Sense Motive check to read the target's reaction and work out how best to proceed.

3. A Bluff check to make an irresistible offer to the target.

The DC for each of these checks is based on the NPC's disposition towards the agent (DC 15 for neutral, 20 for unfriendly, 25 for hostile, and 30 for adversary). The target adds his Intelligence modifier to the DC of the Innuendo DC, his Charisma modifier to the Sense Motive DC, and his Wisdom modifier to the Bluff DC.

The rolls do not have to be made during a single encounter. Indeed it is quite common to let the target mull over an offer for a time. If all three checks are successful, the target secretly becomes helpful to the agent. If one or more of the rolls produce a critical success the target becomes an ally (at least temporarily). If any of the rolls fail, the attempt is a failure and the target's disposition is permanently worsened by one step. If any of the rolls results in a critical failure the target feels betrayed and immediately becomes an adversary.

Characters who have been seduced actively try to help the agent, so long as they continue to believe in the agent's sincerity. Each time the agent seeks aid or assistance from a seduced character he must make another Bluff check with a DC of 15 plus the target's Wisdom modifier. If the roll fails the consequences are the same as during the main seduction (the target drops to one lower than they started or becomes an adversary if the roll was a critical failure).

RUNNING SERIALS

This section covers how to run serials (adventures).

GETTING STARTED

How a serial begins sets the tone for the entire mission. As GC, it's one of your responsibilities to devise intriguing openings that set the tone and style for the rest of the mission.

TABLE 9.18: INFLUENCING DISPOSITION

Initial Disposition	Modified Disposition						
	Adversary	Hostile	Unfriendly	Neutral	Friendly	Helpful	Ally
Adversary	1-20	21+	*	—	—	—	—
Hostile	1-9	10-23	24+	*	—	—	—
Unfriendly	†	1-7	8-22	23+	*	—	—
Neutral	—	†	1-5	6-21	22+	*	—
Friendly	—	—	†	1-3	4-20	21+	*
Helpful	—	—	—	†	1	2-19	20+

* This result is only possible if the agent rolls high enough to improve the target's disposition and scores a critical with the attempt.

† This result is only possible if the agent suffers a critical failure with the attempt to influence the target's disposition.

BUSINESS AS USUAL

More often than not, the agents begin with a mission briefing or resume an operation already in progress. This is a perfectly legitimate approach, and one that captures the feel of classic espionage quite well. If your group is comfortable with the established routine, and enjoys roleplaying the everyday lives of intelligence operatives (whatever they consider 'everyday'), then this is the approach you're likely to settle into. Remember, however, that variety is the spice of life. Just because a serial begins in a relatively 'ordinary' fashion doesn't mean that it must continue that way.

GRIM REALITY

Beginning a game with a tragedy that strikes close to home can shift the tone from heroic action to grim vengeance or angry determination. Doses of grim reality can considerably heighten the opportunities for roleplaying in your game, so long as they aren't overused. Loss and revenge are powerful forces which can create powerful stories, but repeated use of them deadens players' reactions to them.

Serials beginning with grim events should be constructed to support the tone throughout, never letting up for comedy or other elements which might blunt their impact. Such missions should be reserved for important turning points in the careers of the agents, their organization, or the setting.

PLAYER'S CHOICE

Allowing the players to decide how a mission starts is a wonderful creative exercise. Simply allow them to describe their activities in the field *in medias res,* as if each agent is currently wrapping up another mission or enjoying some downtime. Encourage the players to make up situations which suit their agents well and develop their backgrounds and lifestyles, and reward interesting and funny results. Then, once everyone's into the groove, move on to the briefing.

STARTING WITH A BANG!

Thrusting the agents into an explosive situation is very effective with groups whose attention tends to wander. It does raise the bar for action during the serial, however, and you should keep a high level of excitement throughout or the players are likely to become distracted. Explosive gunfights and deadly car chases are usually the order of the day after this opening.

WORKING WITH THE PLAYERS

One of the most important things you must do as the GC is work with the players. Ultimately, this boils down to entertaining them, keeping their trust, and treating them with respect. Don't speak down to them, or treat them like they are dense for not figuring out your puzzles. Never make them feel like your job at the table is more important than theirs. In fact, do just the opposite: make the players feel like they are the all-important center of the action at all times.

This is not as difficult or selfless as it sounds. Ultimately, a roleplaying game revolves around the players. It's a simple step to assume the mindset that everything you do — every decision you make, every challenge you create, and every fun twist you include in the plot — is there to entertain them.

Release the reins to a degree. Let the players take charge when they want to. Give them the responsibility for part of your game world, the part they create and use the most — the supporting cast of NPCs that they hang around with, their friends and family, their day-to-day lives. You'll find that a lot of the work involved in running the game is suddenly in the players' hands, and they're happy to do it. Seasons are a team effort; look at the players the same way you would a sports team or a friendly group of coworkers.

Now, one of your jobs is interpreting the rules. Your call must be the last word when a rules question comes up, but disputes should remain friendly. Avoid becoming a dictator, and prevent rules disputes from turning into open debates at the table. It's often best to give a little in such a situation — to rule in the agents' favor if you can't find a reason not to — and let the players know that you'll discuss the final ruling at a later time, after the session is over. That way, you avoid harsh feelings, and diffuse any possible resentment.

Of course, you should stand firm when you feel your interpretation of a rule is right, or in situations where you desire a certain feel for the game. Don't allow the players to bully you into rulings that make the game less fun.

The best way to keep your players' trust is to take their input. Constantly. Never assume you're doing what they want. The fact that they show up and roll dice isn't insurance that they're happy. Ask for feedback regularly. What they enjoyed a month ago might not be what they enjoy now. Maybe they just saw a new spy movie and have a few new ideas they'd like to share, or maybe they've grown to dislike a part of the game over time. Maybe they just feel like experimenting. It's always best to ask.

Ask the players what they like to see their agents doing. Does the team's wheelman like the idea of cars, or planes, or boats? Does he have a particular 'feel' in mind for chases? Does the soldier prefer tactical situations or blow-'em-up action? Does he crave a certain type of enemy?

The best way to make sure the players feel important is to reward them for what they do. For example, an agent who has been designed to sneak around is lurking through a minor encounter and rolls a threat while climbing an ordinary fence. You *could* spend an action die and trip him up in the barbed wire along the fence just as the building's guards are passing by. But doing so would be penalizing the player for doing just what he is supposed to do, and having a bit of bad luck.

If you're a stickler for honoring the random foibles of agents (which is not always a bad thing, especially as foreshadowing of greater mistakes), you can simply offer a moment of tension as the agent tumbles over the fence and the guards sweep flashlights toward him. Make him sweat for a moment (maybe give him a simple stealth roll – if he fails it *again*, then there might be trouble!), then have the guards move on.

Oftentimes this problem can be circumvented simply by ignoring the roll. If the agent is doing something he's supposed to be great (or at least professional) at – and it's not a critical part of the scene – tell the player to put away his dice and describe his success. It's a bit radical, sure, and you must be mindful of the players who just want to roll their dice and watch their agents sail across the fence flawlessly, but it is a powerful tool the rest of the time.

Feel free to do this more often if the group works as a team to help each other. Making things difficult for teams which have spent time and effort considering their options and building what they consider the best plan for a situation is a great way to convince them never to bother doing so again.

There are of course exceptions to this guideline. One of the most significant is dealing with problem players who undercut their teammates. *Spycraft* is about mission *teams;* loners who threaten the enjoyment of others at the table are threats to the trust that you've built with the others, and need to be carefully reminded that they are not playing nice. Should they persist in making the game less fun for others, then a more heavy-handed approach is required. Treat the agent in question a little more firmly. Make him roll for everything, and be less forgiving when he fails. If he continues to be a problem, a few words outside the game may be needed, or you may have to focus less on him for a while.

This is one of two instances where a firm hand is warranted. The other is during those critical moments of the game that simulate the last reel of the action movie, when the bomb is counting down and the bullets are flying fast and furious. It is important to know when players want you to be strict in your interpretation of the rules, when they are excited to see where the chips fall, and to accommodate them. Most players won't respect a GC who wimps out in the last moments of the game any more than they will a tyrant who refuses to let them have fun getting there.

Know your moments, and respect the players', and you'll be well on your way to running the best game on the block.

KEEPING THINGS ON TRACK

Inevitably, players devise plans that can shatter your well-constructed, extensively-planned serial. If your mission depends on them parachuting onto a jungle island, they'll naturally want to go in via sea. They don't mean to make your life difficult; it's just in their nature. But you do have options to salvage your plans for the evening.

Redirect. Gently guide the players back to your prepared material. Using the example above, the waters around the island might be mined or shark-infested, or maybe both. Don't push the players too hard, however, or they'll feel forced.

Improvise. Why not go with the flow? Whip up a few sharks and a terrorist jet ski or two and let the players have their way. It may take a little work on your part adapting your planned obstacles to a new environment, but the rewards of players who feel they are in charge of their own destiny cannot be matched.

DISSEMINATING CLUES AND PROPS

As the person most in tune with your group, you're the best judge of what they can (and want to) handle. If your players like intense problem-solving, give them complicated puzzles to mull over. If they obsess over the villains' plans, give them clues to piece together and counter the serial's plot. And if they quickly tire of the game when you put a prop in front of them *(see page 276)*, focus more on the action.

CHALLENGE, DON'T CONDEMN

The best way to maintain your players' interest in the game is to challenge their agents in interesting and meaningful ways. Make sure to script your serials so that each agent has some role at each point in the mission. Keep the players interested by keeping them active and challenged. Condemning the wheelman to sit in the car until the chase at the very end of the session bores that player, and boredom leads to distraction. By giving everyone something worthwhile to do, you invest them in your story.

SAYING "NO"

Sometimes the simplest way to keep players on track is to prevent them from wandering off the plot-path in the first place. If they decide to strike off on a wild tangent and request the necessary equipment to make it happen, offer a reasonable explanation for the gear not being available. Or simply have Control veto the plan. This can be a very clear signal to the players that another avenue might be more productive.

On occasion players become frustrated and discouraged when they can't decipher the clues you've given them, and each proposed course of action deviates farther and farther from your intended adventure. Finally one player blurts out "I don't think we're on the right track." It might be best to respond simply, "No, you're not. Maybe you should reconsider the clues you've been given." It may be out of character, but if it gets everyone back on the same page and back into enjoying the game, then it's well worth the momentary lapse.

PLAYER GRATIFICATION

Players need to feel a sense of accomplishment. They need to feel that they have achieved the goals they have set for their agents in order to develop a sense of own-ership in the game. By including opportunities for agents to achieve their goals during the course of a mission, you offer them something to attend to consistently throughout the session. This may require some extra work on your part, but it can provide for an extremely satisfying and enjoyable experience for everyone.

HANDLING ACTION

Regardless of the spy genre you play, there's always a place for action: high-speed car chases, rooftop gun battles, and desperate showdowns with the season's criminal genius. Action is integral to espionage — not to mention roleplaying — and developing your own style when presenting action scenes at the table can greatly enhance your experience. The players get to know when they should reach for their pistols, and perhaps more importantly, when they shouldn't.

SPY PHYSICS

One of the first things to consider when deciding on the action in the game is what the agents and their enemies are capable of. Is the game rooted in the familiar world, making super-heroic actions unlikely or even impossible, or is your world populated by agents who regularly defy the laws of physics? Is there a happy medium? Determining how closely you adhere to real world physics gives the agents boundaries, and lets them know what they can get away with.

Take a look at the opening sequence of *Goldeneye*: James Bond speeds a motorcycle over a cliff after the getaway plane, freefalls to the plane's door, scrambles in, and pulls it out of a nose dive. At the very least, this is an astounding bit of luck and daring. It could also be considered a flagrant violation of the laws of nature. But ultimately, it's fun to watch.

On the other hand, no character in *Three Days of the Condor* or *The Spy Who Came In From the Cold,* or even *Sneakers,* would consider such a stunt. They inherently know that such an action would only get them killed.

Players need to have the same automatic understanding of their environment. If your world features over-the-top action, encourage the players to attempt wild stunts. If not, be sure to offer stiff warnings about the potential consequences of actions that go too far, usually through the agents' senses ("You're pretty sure that would get you killed.").

This is not a decision that must follow you for the duration of your GC career, but merely for a season. To illustrate, consider the two *Mission: Impossible* feature films. The action in the first is only a shade more unlikely than anything seen in the real world, while the action in the second utilizes less-realistic Hong Kong action physics.

OTHER CONSIDERATIONS

Beyond the physical limitations that affect action in the game, you should decide the frequency and intensity of such action. Are you looking for a frantic, slam-bang free-for-all every time you and your players gather at the table, or do you want the action to be unpredictable and explosively violent? Subdued? Chaotic?

GETTING IT ACROSS

Once you have determined the nature of the action in the game, you need to relate it to the players. Of course, the best way to do the former is to simply include them in the decision to begin with. Listen to their requests and try to build a happy medium that suits everyone who is playing (including you). Should they have been excluded from the decision, or want you to define the world for them, one of the easiest ways to get the nature of the action across to them is to name a movie or book that illustrates it. This can help solidify the action style in their minds, and foster some ideas for agents as well.

Just as important as letting the players know what you expect of them, however, is to *show them* what you expect. If you are running a game in which the incredible is rare, avoid including lots of exaggerated villain action and keep the world around the agents on a level keel. If, however, the action of Saturday morning cartoon fare is the name of the day, NPCs should regularly engage in crazy stunts and players should be given the impression that they can follow suit, with bonuses or support from you when they do.

SEGUES AND SCENE STYLES

As you become comfortable as the GC, you may want to attempt more complex storytelling techniques. Several follow.

DREAM SEQUENCES

Before we discuss how dreams can be used, let's touch on how they should *not* be used. Never tell your players, "You wake up. It was all a dream," after a campaign has strayed from your plans. This undermines the players' trust in the game, and destroys their suspension of disbelief.

On the other hand, dreams can be used to reiterate clues, or foreshadow plot twists. The key is to couch the dream in symbols, and remember that dreams can be confusing. The significance of a dream is often apparent only after the fact. Try to throw the team a bone occasionally. If they don't feel the dream is useful, they won't be as keen to figure it out.

FLASHBACKS

Flashbacks are an excellent opportunity to add a sense of depth and history to your campaign. Typically, flashbacks should be brief: the villain's tale of how he escaped death last time he encountered the team, or an agent recalling the first time he met a contact. Often, these can be related out of character as well.

Flashbacks can be greater in scale. If a season centers on the rise of a new Nazi Reich, you might devote an entire session to an adventure set in the final days of World War II, establishing the mood and importance of present-day events.

The most important thing to remember about flashbacks is to remain consistent with the future. If a character is alive today, he obviously can't have died 20 years ago. This doesn't mean you can't throw the team a curve ball. Perhaps a character in the game dies in a flashback. Later, the team discovers that the modern-day character is actually the flashback character's son.

"MEANWHILE..."

Important events sometimes occur away from the team, and it often helps to fill them in. This provides the players with a better sense of the ongoing story, and also offers proof they don't exist in a vacuum.

The greatest danger with this type of scene is boredom, since the agents can't interact with anything. There are ways around this, however. First, keep it short and snappy. Second, mention the team often; the more your players' characters are mentioned, the more interested they'll be. Third, you might want to describe the scene through a TV or radio, allowing the agents to react in character while they observe the events.

PARALLEL SCENES

When something interesting is happening in two places at once, you can often deal with them one at a time, but sometimes it's best to interweave them. If, for example, the team is being interrogated separately, you might cut from one agent to another between questions. It keeps all of the players involved, and gives them the sense that their captors are testing the consistency of their stories. It's important not to get in over your head, though. Fight scenes in two places often overwhelm and frustrate the players.

ENDING THINGS

All good things must come to an end, even missions. This offers a sense of closure and 'resets' the players for their next adventure. Ending things on a sour note, however, can bring an otherwise successful season to a screeching halt. As the GC, it's your responsibility to bring missions to a satisfactory close, regardless of the agents' success.

STAYING TRUE TO THE MISSION

A mission's conclusion should mirror the serial's theme whenever possible. A mission which began with the death of a loved one or another agent shouldn't close with a parade any more than a mission to save the world should end with a funeral. But swapping these closing scenes offers each serial a lasting image for agents to remember, and gives the players a chance to deal with any baggage they have acquired.

It's best to have at least two different endings in mind for any mission – one for agents who are successful and one for agents who are not. Also, give the players time to contend with their emotions about the serial before diving into something new. Like any experience, an adventure requires closure (be it cheering in the living room or the quiet ride home) before the participants can move on.

CONSEQUENCES

Roleplaying games are a form of escapism, and they include many fantastic elements that depart from reality. But the agents don't exist in a vacuum. People, places, and things they encounter shouldn't cease to exist simply because the agents have moved on. There should always be consequences for the choices and actions the agents take during a mission.

The events of a serial can have permanent effects on the agents and the setting. While the players are responsible for roleplaying these changes, you have to determine them, and remain true to those changes during future sessions. If the agents have defied Control and created a rift within the command structure of the Agency, that rift should be included, when appropriate, in future serials.

Also, consider what mechanical changes are required after a mission. Ability score adjustments, the loss of equipment, and the loss or gain of backgrounds, should be discussed with the players and modified as appropriate to the serial's close.

AGENT DEATH

Agents die. It can be an integral part of the story or it can be the random result of a dice roll, but it can and does happen. When should it happen, and how does it affect the group? This is up to you, the players, and the needs of the season.

Intentional Death: The scripted death of a hero can be a powerful storytelling tool, but it is not to be included lightly. Discuss the possibility with the agent's player beforehand, and make certain they agree with the intent of the agent's death (and have another waiting in the wings).

Random Roll of the Dice: Death can come at the most unexpected times. Players recognize this possibility, but not everyone is ready for it. As the GC, you should be watchful for situations where agents are likely to die, and handle them carefully. You must strike a careful balance between keeping the agents from dying needlessly and sending your players the message that they are immortal. Try to place agents in mortal jeopardy only as part of critical, climactic scenes and turning points in the story. Strive to give them ways out of situations in which they might die from bad die rolls – if they refuse, they should be ready to face the possible consequences. Ultimately, agent death should be a matter of calculated risk on the part of the players. If their agent dies, they should feel it was worth the risk.

SETTING THE STAGE

An important element in any campaign is atmosphere. During great spy movies, your pulse pounds and your hands sweat; you're involved. This is only partly due to your investment in the characters. The rest is movie magic—music, lighting, camera angles, and direction. These elements can be simulated at the table with a little preparation, as follows.

PROPS

Let's say your team has intercepted a dead drop message intended for an enemy agent. There are two ways you might handle this. First, you could tell them, "The note is a jumble of letters and digits, arranged at random," and let them make the appropriate skill checks. Alternately, you could hand them a facsimile of the note which they can read for themselves. Such physical handouts are called props, after the movie-making term for bits of scenery the characters cart around.

Props instantly draw your players into the action and offer a unique approach to puzzles posed in the game. In the former case in which the agents intercept an enemy message written in code, an industrious GC might actually devise a code for the players to decipher, perhaps making it part of the clue chain in the serial — each piece of the communication they decipher offers them another location to visit.

LIGHTING

Lighting can have a subtle effect on the mood of a game. In fact, it probably already does. Usually, we play games in well-lit rooms with very few shadows. We're comfortable that way. Besides, we need to be able to read our dice. But lowering the lights (or even playing by candlelight) during critical or moody moments can increase the drama and tension, and send a clear message to the players that they've entered an important location.

SOUND

Sound is perhaps the most difficult prop to use effectively, but handled well, it can be the most versatile weapon in your arsenal. The most important rule here is not to overwhelm the narration. If the players can't hear you, nor you them, the music's obviously too loud. Just as easily, however, the music can be too soft. If your players are straining to hear the tune, they aren't paying attention to the game.

The best use of a soundtrack in most games is to enhance the pace or mood of a scene. If your players are involved in a running gunfight or wild martial arts melee, a faster tempo of music is required than if they're trying to shadow a dangerous enemy agent.

In general, lyrics should be avoided. They are distracting, not to mention confusing.

If you look hard enough, you can also find sound effect collections. Want to spring an ambush on your players? Cue the "machine gun fire" track before the session starts, jack the volume, and watch them jump when you hit "play."

A FINAL WORD

The most important considerations in all of this are safety and comfort. First, never bring weapons to the table. Second, if any of the players become uncomfortable, back off. Don't make them give you a reason, don't make them explain. If someone asks you to put away the photo, or turn the music off, do it. You're playing the game to have fun, after all.

SERIAL ADVENTURING

Classic "serials" are stories told in episodes, usually with cliffhangers at the tail end of each one, and sometimes before each commercial break. They also tend to have "a surprise behind every curtain," so to speak, and keep a lively, engaging pace. The *Spycraft* and especially *Shadowforce Archer* games are built to easily accommodate this type of storytelling.

Serialized roleplaying can be an exciting and rewarding experience, and may be similar (or even identical) to the way you already play games. The players not only benefit from watching their agents grow week to week, but — with the successful use of cliffhangers and foreshadowing — they go home from each session chomping at the bit for more.

CLIFFHANGERS

The first step in developing a serialized gaming experience is to end sessions with a cliffhanger. While it's helpful to end missions with cliffhangers as well, the purpose is very different. Ending a session with a cliffhanger leaves the players wanting more, and keeps the excitement level for the game high when the group is away from the table. Session cliffhangers usually involve a new threat, or an immediate risk to the agents, or a development that adds new dimensions to the story. Mission (serial) cliffhangers, on the other hand, usually offer something new about the setting, or develop the backstory or "mythology" of the game. Serial cliffhangers rarely leave anything for the agents to do other than come back for another mission next week — and wonder about the cliffhanger's ultimate meaning. Classic session cliffhangers often introduce a mastermind, especially if he has been spoken of only in hushed whispers before.

Particularly effective cliffhangers also leave the players with options to consider. Giving the players choices to think about during the time between sessions is the best way to keep them interested. When using this approach, always describe the crux of the cliffhanger thoroughly before breaking for the evening, so that the players can formulate plans before they come back to the table. They'll take pride in their plan and you can take pride in the success of your story.

FORESHADOWING

A well-planned serial allows plenty of room for foreshadowing. A sly GC often scatters hints throughout each episode that may not come to fruition until later in the current season, or even later. Such hints should be subtle and, when revealed, give the player a feeling that his agent's actions are part of vibrant, living, developing world.

For instance, suppose the agents hack into an enemy organization's database to retrieve information about a psychotic criminal in its employ. During their investigation, they find many bits of information that seem arbitrary, such as the code of an upcoming video game being produced by one of the organization's front companies. Next season, when the video game is blamed for causing violence and anti-social behavior in school children, the agents already have a good idea who's responsible, and can take appropriate action.

Of course, when using foreshadowing, you should be careful the players' don't get the impression that the world is predetermined, that they cannot affect the course of events. For instance, agents who decide to scramble or erase the aforementioned video game's coding might become frustrated if the game still showed up on the shelves, right on schedule and without a hitch. If the plot were instead elevated to a virtual reality system after "hackers destroyed the game's original beta version," the players would feel their actions had done something — and the villains would have a new toy. Everyone wins.

Spy Jargon

The authors also recommend the "Spooktalk" section of the phenomenal *GURPS Espionage,* an invaluable resource for spy jargon.

Abort: to terminate a mission before it is completed, usually abruptly

Access: an agent's ability to obtain sensitive information through government channels

Agency: slang for the CIA; also the term used to describe the organization most agents work for in *Spycraft* (which may or may not be the CIA, per the GC's discretion)

Agent: an operative; a spy

Agent of influence: an agent with political power in a nation of interest to his agency

Agent provocateur: a spy who generates social and political turmoil

Alimony: compensation paid to a long-term undercover agent when his assignment is complete

Angel: slang for a spy of an opposing agency

Apparatus: a spy ring; also called a "cell"

Asset: any resource – human, information, technical, etc .– that an intelligence organ can use to its benefit

Attaché: a military officer assigned to a foreign capital as a liaison and to gather data

Babysitter: spy slang for a bodyguard

Bag job: breaking and entering to steal or photograph intelligence material

Bigot list: the names of people who know of a certain clandestine activity, and who must therefore be safeguarded, or prevented from speaking about the projects to outsiders

Bird watcher: British slang for a spy

Black: term used in specific phrases to signify something is covert or illegal in nature

Blind Date: meeting someone at their choice of place and time, with all the associate risks

Blowback: false rumors spread in enemy territory that are reported by their news agencies as the truth

Bodywash: a mundane explanation for an agent's death, to prevent outside suspicion

Bogie: an unidentified agent or organization

Broken: a term applied to an agent who has become a liability; also known as "going bad"

Burn: to publically uncover an agent's true identity; also used by agencies, meaning to cut off from Control an agent who has become a liability

Clandestine: unseen and unheard

Classified: sensitive material shown only on a need-to-know basis. Classifications include confidential, secret, and top secret, in ascending order of security

Clearance: approval to read or handle classified material

Clean: to make secure; also known as "pacify"

Clear (or plain) text: a decoded message

Cobbler: Russian slang for a forger; also called a "shoe-maker"; Russians call fake passports "shoes"

Cold: the mental state of a spy working in hostile territory, often for months or years at a time; to get out is called "coming in from the cold"

Consumer: the final user of intelligence data

Control: the person in charge of an agent, operation, or organization; also known as a "case officer" or "handler"

Cooking the books: slang for skewing intelligence to support political aims

Counterespionage: the protection of domestic or allied personnel, installations, and intelligence from hostile foreign agencies

Cousins: British spy slang for the CIA

Cover: a false ID; also called a "cryptonym"

Covert: seen but not noticed

Cryptanalysis: the study of ciphers and codes with the intent of decoding them without the original keys

Cryptography: the use of codes and ciphers to render intelligence secure

Customer: an agency receiving intelligence

Cutout: middleman between agent and agency

Dead drop: a location where an agent can safely leave intelligence data or reserves; also known as a "dead letter box"

Decode: interpreting a coded message into comprehensible form

Deep cover: long-term insertion into hostile territory under an assumed identity

Defector: someone who voluntarily shifts his allegiance from one nation or organization to another; defectors are said to have "turned"

Dirty: treacherous

Disposable: a term applied to anything that can be sacrificed to ensure a mission's success

Doctor: Russian term for police; agents arrested are said to have an "illness"; agents in jail are said to be at the "hospital"

Double agent: someone openly working for one intelligence agency and secretly working for another; also called a "double"

Ears only: data that is too sensitive to be committed to paper

ECM: electronic countermeasures; the use of electronic devices to secure information

Encode: the process of coding a message

Eyes only: data that should not be discussed without explicit permission

False drop: a place where an agent pretends to leave messages, or where messages are left in spoof code

Fence: Russian slang for a national border

Firm, The: British spy slang for MI6

Flaps and Seals: spy term for mail tampering

Floater: someone used for a one-time or occasional operation, often unwittingly

Fumigate: to sweep for bugs

The (Great) Game: the intelligence and counterintelligence profession

Go over: to shift loyalty between agencies

Go private: to retire from the Game

Go to ground: to hide; to run

Handler: a spy who trains and directs other spies

Headquarters: the place where an agent, agent team, or spy cell operates from; usually also where Control is located. Also known as "the home office"

Home office: see headquarters

HUMINT: human intelligence; data gathered by agents, rather than satellites or computers

Illegal: a spy working in enemy territory with no diplomatic protection, usually with a legend

IMINT: imagery intelligence; data gathered by aerial and satellite photography

Institute: Israeli slang for the Mossad

Key: the means to decipher a coded message

Lamplighters: British support operatives

Legal: an agent protected by diplomatic immunity

Legend: an artificial identity and history, usually employed by deep cover operatives

Letter box: a cutout serving in the same capacity as a dead drop (a third party who passes innocuous-looking messages between spies).

Liquidate: used by agencies, meaning to eliminate wayward agents in their employ

Load: to leave something at a dead drop

Make: to recognize someone

MICE (Money, Ideology, Compromise, and Ego): the four most common motivations exploited by agent recruiters

Mischief, Incorporated: derogatory slang for the British spy agencies (MI5 and MI6)

Mobile agent: a spy not restricted to a single zone of operation

Mole: an agent working in another country's intelligence agency; also known as a "plant"

Mule: a covert courier

Noise: slang for collateral attention agents draw to themselves or their mission while in the field. Noise is nearly always discouraged

Operational climate: a description of a locale and the chance of a mission succeeding there

Overt: both seen and heard

Padding: extra characters added to the beginning and end of encrypted data to help prevent it from being deciphered

Peeps: photographs used for blackmail

Plausible deniability: the valuable ability to effectively refute involvement with an operation

Plumbing: plugging leaks within an agency

Poacher: British slang for a spy in the field

Proprietary company: a business owned by an intelligence agency to assist its operations

Puzzle palace: slang for the NSA

Safe house: location that involves low risk of discovery; also a well-known contact point in Milwaukee, Wisconsin

Salesman: slang term for an agent

Sanitize: to eliminate all evidence of an agency's involvement

Scalp hunter: British slang for agent specializing in recruiting defectors and doubles

Shopped: British slang for someone who has been assassinated

SIGINT: signals intelligence; data gathered through eavesdropping on electronic signals

Sleeper: an agent established in a target area who does nothing beyond his cover until activated

Smudger: spy slang for a photographer

Sponsor: slang for an agency that finances, controls, or carries out an operation

Spoof code: letters jumbled up to look like a real code to fool enemy spies

Spook: slang for an intelligence operative, with both positive and negative connotations

Stringer: a freelance agent

Target: the purpose of a mission

Task: to give an order (i.e. "to task with")

Tradecraft: the tools and practices of spies

Walk-in: someone who approaches an intelligence agency without being prompted

Wetwork: assassination (also known as "closing a contract," "neutralizing," "sanctioning," "terminating with extreme prejudice," or "demoting maximally")

White: slang for a known covert operation

BIBLIOGRAPHY

Many years of spy novels and passion for the non-fictional experiences of the world's intelligence agencies went into this and the *Shadowforce Archer Worldbook*, but the following were on our reference shelf through active writing and design. The authors of each deserve many special thanks.

Bamford, James. *The Puzzle Palace*. Houghton Mifflin Company, 1982.

Benson, Raymond. *Zero Minus Ten to Doubleshot* (6 novels and several short stories). Various publishers, 1997-2000.

Broughton, Richard S. *Parapsychology: The Controversial Science*. Random House, 1991.

Bunson, Matthew E. *Encyclopedia Sherlockiana*. Macmillan Publishing Company, 1994.

Conrad, Joseph. *The Secret Agent*. Penguin Books, 1907.

Copeland, Miles. *Without Cloak or Dagger*. Simon and Schuster, 1974.

Cotterell, Arthur. *Encyclopedia of World Mythology*. Parragon Books, 2000.

Courtenay-Thompson, Fiona and Phelps, Kate. *The 20th Century Year by Year*. Barnes and Noble Books, 1999.

Crowe, John H. III. *The Weapons Compendium*. Pagan Publishing, 1995.

Deacon, Richard. *Spyclopedia*. William Morrow and Co., 1987.

Dulles, Allen. *Great Spy Stories*. Book Sales, Inc., 1969.

Dunnigan, James F. and Bay, Austin. *A Quick & Dirty Guide to War: Third Edition*. William Morrow and Company, Inc., 1996.

Evans, Bergen. *Dictionary of Mythology*. Dell Publishing, 1970.

Evans, Ivor H. *The Wordsworth Dictionary of Phrase and Fable*. Wordsworth Editions, Limited, 1993.

Fido, Martin. *The World of Sherlock Holmes*. Adams Media Corporation, 1998.

Fleming, Ian. *Casino Royale* through *The Living Daylights* (14 novels). Various publishers, 1953-1966.

Forsyth, Frederick. *The Day of the Jackal*. Viking Penguin, Inc., 1971.

Franklin, Fay. *History's Timeline*. Barnes and Noble Books, 1996.

Gardner, John. *License Renewed* through *Cold Fall* (17 novels). Various publishers, 1981-1996.

Garner, Joe. *We Interrupt This Broadcast*. Sourcebooks, 1998.

Glennon, Lorraine. *The 20th Century: An Illustrated History of Our Lives and Times*. JG Press, Inc., 2000.

Gorden, Greg. *Torg: Roleplaying the Possibility Wars*. West End Games, 1990. (Special thanks also to Douglas Kaufman, Christopher Kubasik, Paul Murphy, Bill Slavicsek, Ray Winninger, and many others for this amazing game, which served as a guiding light through our own design.)

Grady, James. *Six Days of the Condor*. W.W. Norton and Company, 1974.

Hunt, E. Howard. *The Hargrave Deception*. Stein and Day Publishing, 1980.

Hurst, Michael. *GURPS High-Tech: Third Edition*. Steve Jackson Games, 1998.

Kane, Thomas M. *GURPS Espionage*. Steve Jackson Games, 1992.

Klug, Gerard Christopher. *James Bond 007 RPG*. Victory Games, 1983.

Koehler, John O. *Stasi: The Untold Story of the East German Secret Police*. Westview Press, 1999.

Ludlum, Robert. The Bourne Trilogy (3 novels). Bantam Books, 1984-1986.

Martini, Teri. *The Secret is Out: True Spy Stories*. Little, Brown and Company, 1990.

Melton, H. Keith. *The Ultimate Spy Book*. Houghton Mifflin Company, 1996.

Newman, Joseph. *Famous Soviet Spies: The Kremlin's Secret Weapon*. U.S. News and World Report, 1973.

Polmar, Norman and Allen, Thomas B. *The Encyclopedia of Espionage*. Random House, 1997.

Price, Dr. Alfred. War in the Fourth Dimension: *U.S. Electronic Warfare, from the Vietnam War to the Present*. Greenhill Books, 2001.

Richelson, Jeffrey T. *A Century of Spies*. Oxford University Press, 1995.

Rose, Greg. *GURPS Special Ops, Second Edition*. Steve Jackson Games, 2000.

Sawyer, Ralph D. *The Tao of Spycraft*. Westview Press, 1998.

Singh, Simon. *The Code Book*. Random House, 1999.

Stephenson, Neal. *Cryptonomicon*. Avon Books, 1999.

Suvorov, Viktor. *Inside Soviet Military Intelligence*. Macmillan Publishing Company, 1984.

Thompson, Leroy. *Hostage Rescue Manual: Tactics of the Counter-Terrorist Professionals*. Greenhill Books, 2001.

Index

THE OPEN GAME LICENSE

The following text is the property of Wizards of the Coast, Inc. and is Copyright 2000 Wizards of the Coast, Inc ("Wizards"). All Rights Reserved.

1. **Definitions:** (a) "Contributors" means the copyright and/or trademark owners who have contributed Open Game Content; (b) "Derivative Material" means copyrighted material including derivative works and translations (including into other computer languages), potation, modification, correction, addition, extension, upgrade, improvement, compilation, abridgment or other form in which an existing work may be recast, transformed or adapted; (c) "Distribute" means to reproduce, license, rent, lease, sell, broadcast, publicly display, transmit or otherwise distribute; (d) "Open Game Content" means the game mechanic and includes the methods, procedures, processes and routines to the extent such content does not embody the Product Identity and is an enhancement over the prior art and any additional content clearly identified as Open Game Content by the Contributor, and means any work covered by this License, including translations and derivative works under copyright law, but specifically excludes Product Identity. (e) "Product Identity" means product and product line names, logos and identifying marks including trade dress; artifacts; creatures, characters; stories, storylines, plots, thematic elements, dialogue, incidents, language, artwork, symbols, designs, depictions, likenesses, formats, poses, concepts, themes and graphic, photographic and other visual or audio representations; names and descriptions of characters, spells, enchantments, personalities, teams, personas, likenesses and special abilities; places, locations, environments, creatures, equipment, magical or supernatural abilities or effects, logos, symbols, or graphic designs; and any other trademark or registered trademark clearly identified as Product identity by the owner of the Product Identity, and which specifically excludes the Open Game Content; (f) "Trademark" means the logos, names, mark, sign, motto, designs that are used by a Contributor to identify itself or its products or the associated products contributed to the Open Game License by the Contributor (g) "Use", "Used" or "Using" means to use, Distribute, copy, edit, format, modify, translate and otherwise create Derivative Material of Open Game Content. (h) "You" or "Your" means the licensee in terms of this agreement.

2. **The License:** This License applies to any Open Game Content that contains a notice indicating that the Open Game Content may only be Used under and in terms of this License. You must affix such a notice to any Open Game Content that you Use. No terms may be added to or subtracted from this License except as described by the License itself. No other terms or conditions may be applied to any Open Game Content distributed using this License.

3. **Offer and Acceptance:** By Using the Open Game Content You indicate Your acceptance of the terms of this License.

4. **Grant and Consideration:** In consideration for agreeing to use this License, the Contributors grant You a perpetual, worldwide, royalty-free, non-exclusive license with the exact terms of this License to Use, the Open Game Content.

5. **Representation of Authority to Contribute:** If You are contributing original material as Open Game Content, You represent that Your Contributions are Your original creation and/or You have sufficient rights to grant the rights conveyed by this License.

6. **Notice of License Copyright:** You must update the COPYRIGHT NOTICE portion of this License to include the exact text of the COPYRIGHT NOTICE of any Open Game Content You are copying, modifying or distributing, and You must add the title, the copyright date, and the copyright holder's name to the COPYRIGHT NOTICE of any original Open Game Content you Distribute.

7. **Use of Product Identity:** You agree not to Use any Product Identity, including as an indication as to compatibility, except as expressly licensed in another, independent Agreement with the owner of each element of that Product Identity. You agree not to indicate compatibility or co-adaptability with any Trademark in conjunction with a work containing Open Game Content except as expressly licensed in another, independent Agreement with the owner of such Trademark. The use of any Product Identity in Open Game Content does not constitute a challenge to the ownership of that Product Identity. The owner of any Product Identity used in Open Game Content shall retain all rights, title and interest in and to that Product Identity.

8. **Identification:** If you distribute Open Game Content You must clearly indicate which portions of the work that you are distributing are Open Game Content.

9. **Updating the License:** Wizards or its designated Agents may publish updated versions of this License. You may use any authorized version of this License to copy, modify and distribute any Open Game Content originally distributed under any version of this License.

10. **Copy of this License:** You MUST include a copy of this License with every copy of the Open Game Content You Distribute.

11. **Use of Contributor Credits:** You may not market or advertise the Open Game Content using the name of any Contributor unless You have written permission from the Contributor to do so.

12. **Inability to Comply:** If it is impossible for You to comply with any of the terms of this License with respect to some or all of the Open Game Content due to statute, judicial order, or governmental regulation then You may not Use any Open Game Material so affected.

13. **Termination:** This License will terminate automatically if You fail to comply with all terms herein and fail to cure such breach within 30 days of becoming aware of the breach. All sublicenses shall survive the termination of this License.

14. **Reformation:** If any provision of this License is held to be unenforceable, such provision shall be reformed only to the extent necessary to make it enforceable.

15. **COPYRIGHT NOTICE:** Open Game License v1.0 Copyright 2000, Wizards of the Coast, Inc.

THE OPEN GAME CONTENT

This printing of the Spycraft™ Espionage Handbook is done under version 1.0 of the Open Game License and the draft version of the d20 System Trademark License, d20 System Trademark Logo Guide and System Reference Document by permission of Wizards of the Coast. Subsequent printings of this book will incorporate final versions of the license, guide and document.

AEG's intention is to open up as much of the Spycraft Espionage Handbook as possible to be used as Open Game Content (OGC), while maintaining Product Identity (PI) to all aspects of the Spycraft intellectual property. Publishers who wish to use the OGC materials from this book are encouraged to contact AEGJohnZ@aol.com if they have any questions or concerns about reproducing material from the Spycraft Espionage Handbook in other OGL works. AEG would appreciate anyone using OGC material from Spycraft in other OGL works to kindly reference Spycraft as the source of that material within the text of their work. Open Game Content may only be used under and in accordance with the terms of the OGL as fully set forth in the opposite column.

DESIGNATION OF PRODUCT IDENTITY: The following items are hereby designated as Product Identity in accordance with section 1(e) of the Open Game License, version 1.0: Any and all Spycraft logos and identifying marks and trade dress, including all Spycraft product and product line names including but not limited to The Spycraft Espionage Handbook, Control Screen, Faceman/Snoop Class Guide, Fixer/Pointman Class Guide, Soldier/Wheelman Class Guide, Season Book #1 and subsequent Season books, and all Spycraft logos; any elements of the Spycraft setting, including but not limited to capitalized names, department names, section names, threat names, characters, gadgets (including but not limited to the usual refinements and other gadgets), historic events, and organizations; any and all stories, storylines, plots, thematic elements, documents within the game world, quotes from characters or documents, and dialogue; and all artwork, symbols, designs, depictions, illustrations, maps and cartography, likenesses, poses, Agency or department logos, symbols, or graphic designs, except such elements that already appear in the d20 System Reference Document and are already OGC by virtue of appearing there. The above Product Identity is not Open Game Content.

DESIGNATION OF OPEN CONTENT: Subject to the Product Identity designation above, the following portions of the Spycraft Espionage Handbook are designated as Open Game Content. Chapter One: all agent statistics and new classes. Chapter Two: new skills. Chapter Three: new feats. Chapter Four: all agent statistics and the rules for action dice and backgrounds. Chapter Five: the rules for acquiring equipment, weapons, and vehicles (except for the description of threat codes), and the rules for gadgets and individual gadget mechanics. Chapter Six: the entire chapter. Chapter Seven: the entire chapter. Chapter Eight: the rules for favor checks, education checks, and inspiration checks, and the rules for travel. Chapter Nine: the statistics blocks for described NPCs and threats, the rules for gambling, encounters, and designing NPCs (except the descriptions of Spycraft-specific NPC types, such as masterminds, henchmen, minions, and foils), the Mastermind system, and the Disposition system.

USE OF MATERIAL AS OPEN GAME CONTENT: It is the clear and expressed intent of Alderac Entertainment Group to add all classes, skills, feats, equipment, prestige classes, and threat and NPC statistics contained in this volume to the canon of Open Game Content for free use pursuant to the Open Game License by future Open Game publishers.

Some of the portions of this book which are delineated OGC originate from the System Reference Document and are © 1999, 2000 Wizards of the Coast, Inc. The remainder of these OGC portions of this book are hereby added to Open Game Content and if so used, should bear the COPYRIGHT NOTICE: "Spycraft Copyright 2002, Alderac Entertainment Group."

The mention of or reference to any company or product in these pages is not a challenge to the trademark or copyright concerned.

'd20 System' and the 'd20 System' logo are Trademarks owned by Wizards of the Coast and are used according to the terms of the d20 System License version 1.0. A copy of this License can be found at www.wizards.com.

Dungeons & Dragons® and Wizards of the Coast® are registered trademarks of Wizards of the Coast, and are used with permission.

All contents of this book, regardless of designation, are copyrighted year 2002 by Alderac Entertainment Group. All rights reserved. Reproduction or use without the written permission of the publisher is expressly forbidden, except for the purposes of review or use consistent with the limited license above.

SPYCRAFT™

AGENT RECORD SHEET

CHARACTER NAME

CODE NAME

PLAYER

CLASS   LEVEL   AGENT LEVEL

SECOND CLASS   LEVEL   DEPARTMENT

THIRD CLASS   LEVEL   NATIONALITY

AGE   GENDER   HEIGHT   WEIGHT   EYES   HAIR

Abilities

ABILITY NAME	ABILITY SCORE	ABILITY MODIFIER	TEMP SCORE	TEMP MODIFIER
STR STRENGTH				
DEX DEXTERITY				
CON CONSTITUTION				
INT INTELLIGENCE				
WIS WISDOM				
CHA CHARISMA				

VITALITY   TOTAL   CURRENT   DIE TYPE

WOUNDS   SUBDUAL DAMAGE

DEFENSE = 10 + ___ / ___ + ___ + ___
TOTAL   CLASS / ARMOR   DEX   SIZE   MISC

INITIATIVE TOTAL = CLASS + DEX + MISC

ACTION DICE TOTAL   DIE TYPE   SPENT

BASE SPEED TOTAL

INSPIRATION = WIS MOD + MISC

EDUCATION = INT MOD + MISC
TOTAL

SAVES

	TOTAL BONUS	BASE SAVE	ABILITY MODIFIER	MISC MODIFIER
FORTITUDE CONSTITUTION	=	+	+	
REFLEX DEXTERITY	=	+	+	
WILL WISDOM	=	+	+	

ATTACKS

	TOTAL BONUS	BASE ATTACK	ABILITY MODIFIER	MISC MODIFIER
UNARMED	=	+	+	
MELEE	=	+	+	
RANGED	=	+	+	

WEAPON

	ATK BONUS	DAMAGE	ERROR	THREAT

RANGE	WEIGHT	TYPE	SIZE	SPECIAL PROPERTIES

AMMO TYPE	SPECIAL PROPERTIES	AMMO COUNT

AMMO TYPE	SPECIAL PROPERTIES	AMMO COUNT

WEAPON

	ATK BONUS	DAMAGE	ERROR	THREAT

RANGE	WEIGHT	TYPE	SIZE	SPECIAL PROPERTIES

AMMO TYPE	SPECIAL PROPERTIES	AMMO COUNT

AMMO TYPE	SPECIAL PROPERTIES	AMMO COUNT

ARMOR

	DEF BONUS	DAM RESISTANCE	ARMOR CHECK

TYPE	MAX DEX MOD	SPEED	WEIGHT	SPECIAL PROPERTIES

ARMOR

	DEF BONUS	DAM RESISTANCE	ARMOR CHECK

TYPE	MAX DEX MOD	SPEED	WEIGHT	SPECIAL PROPERTIES

SKILLS

MAX RANKS ___ / ___

CLASS SKILL	SKILL NAME	KEY ABILITY	SKILL BONUS		RANKS	ABILITY MODIFIER	MISC MODIFIER	ERROR RANGE	THREAT RANGE
☐	APPRAISE ■	INT		=	+	+			
☐	BALANCE ■	DEX*		=	+	+			
☐	BLUFF ■	CHA		=	+	+			
☐	BOATING ■	DEX		=	+	+			
☐	BUREAUCRACY ■	CHA		=	+	+			
☐	CLIMB ■	STR*		=	+	+			
☐	COMPUTERS ■	INT		=	+	+			
☐	CONCENTRATION ■	WIS		=	+	+			
☐	CRAFT (___)	INT		=	+	+			
☐	CRYPTOGRAPHY	INT		=	+	+			
☐	CULTURES	WIS		=	+	+			
☐	DEMOLITIONS	INT		=	+	+			
☐	DIPLOMACY ■	CHA		=	+	+			
☐	DISGUISE ■	CHA		=	+	+			
☐	DRIVER ■	DEX		=	+	+			
☐	ELECTRONICS	INT		=	+	+			
☐	ESCAPE ARTIST ■	DEX*		=	+	+			
☐	FIRST AID ■	WIS		=	+	+			
☐	FORGERY ■	INT		=	+	+			
☐	GATHER INFORMATION ■	CHA		=	+	+			
☐	HANDLE ANIMAL	CHA		=	+	+			
☐	HIDE ■	DEX*		=	+	+			
☐	HOBBY (___)	WIS		=	+	+			
☐	INNUENDO ■	WIS		=	+	+			
☐	INTIMIDATE ■	STR / CHA		=	+	+			
☐	JUMP ■	STR*		=	+	+			
☐	KNOWLEDGE (___)	INT		=	+	+			
☐	LANGUAGES ■	WIS		=	+	+			
☐	LISTEN ■	WIS		=	+	+			
☐	MECHANICS	INT		=	+	+			
☐	MOVE SILENTLY ■	DEX*		=	+	+			
☐	OPEN LOCK	DEX		=	+	+			
☐	PERFORM ■	CHA		=	+	+			
☐	PILOT	DEX		=	+	+			
☐	PROFESSION (___)	WIS		=	+	+			
☐	READ LIPS	INT		=	+	+			
☐	SEARCH ■	INT		=	+	+			
☐	SENSE MOTIVE ■	WIS		=	+	+			
☐	SLEIGHT OF HAND	DEX*		=	+	+			
☐	SPORT ■ (___)	STR / DEX*		=	+	+			
☐	SPOT ■	WIS		=	+	+			
☐	SURVEILLANCE	WIS		=	+	+			
☐	SURVIVAL	WIS		=	+	+			
☐	SWIM ■	STR		=	+	+			
☐	TUMBLE	DEX*		=	+	+			
☐	USE ROPE ■	DEX*		=	+	+			
☐	___			=	+	+			
☐	___			=	+	+			
☐	___			=	+	+			

Skills marked with ■ can be used normally even if the character has zero (0) skill ranks.

Mark class skills with ☒. *armor check penalty, if any, applies.

©2002 Alderac Entertainment Group, Inc. Permission granted to photocopy for personal use only.

AEG™

CAMPAIGN _____

EXPERIENCE POINTS _____

FIELD EXPENSES _____ FIELD EXPENSES REMAINING _____

STANDARD ISSUE GEAR

ITEM	WT.	ITEM	WT.
		TOTAL WEIGHT CARRIED	

LIFT OVER HEAD	LIFT OFF GROUND	PUSH OR DRAG
Equals max heavy load	Equals 2x max heavy load	Equals 5x max heavy load

GADGETS

GADGET	EFFECT	SPOT DC

VEHICLE

	SIZE	HANDLING
		Blown tires: ☐ ☐ ☐ ☐ −2 per tire.

CRUISING SPEED	TOP SPEED	MPH	CURRENT MPH

DEFENSE	HARDNESS	TOTAL WOUND POINTS	CURRENT WOUND POINTS
			☐ Crippled (½ WP) −5 to Handling and crash check (DC +5).
			☐ Disabled (0 WP) Can't run and crash check (DC +10).
			☐ Destroyed (2x WP) Damage as failed crash check.

GADGETS	WEAPONS

BUDGETS

PERSONAL BUDGET	MISSION BUDGET	GADGET POINTS

Permission granted to photocopy for personal use only.

COMBAT ACTIONS

INITIATIVE ACTIONS	TYPE	EFFECT
Delay	Free	You may voluntarily reduce your initiative by up to 10 + your initiative bonus, at which time you must act or lose your turn.
Ready	Full	Choose an action and a trigger that will prompt it; if it doesn't happen, you lose your turn.
Regroup	Half	+5 to your initiative total.

ATTACK ACTIONS	TYPE	EFFECT
Standard attack	Half	None; uses 1 shot.
Autofire	Full	Fire a number of 3-shot volleys up to one-third the ammo in your firearm and make an attack with a −1 penalty per volley; if you hit, one volley hits the target; for every 4 over the target's Defense, another volley hits; uses 3 shots per volley.
Burst (narrow)	Half	−3 attack; +2 damage; uses 3 shots.
Burst (wide)	Half	+1 attack; uses 3 shots.
Coup de grace	Full	Helpless target must make a Fortitude save (DC 10 + damage done) or die.
Cover fire	Full	Offer +4 dodge bonus to Defense of a single ally against enemies within your line of sight for one round; uses 5 shots.
Disarm	Half	Make an opposed attack roll; if you win, your target is disarmed.
Feint	Half	Make a Bluff check opposed by your target's Sense Motive; if you succeed, your target may not add his Dexterity modifier to Defense when you attack him next.
Grapple	Half	Special (see *Spycraft Espionage Handbook*, page 172).
Refresh	Full	If you are the target of no attacks this round, you may spend one action die at the end of the round to recover the result in vitality points, or 2 wounds.
Strafe attack	Full	Target a number of adjacent squares up to half the ammo in your firearm and make an attack with a −2 penalty per square beyond the first; all targets hit suffers the same damage; uses 2 shots per targeted square.
Strike object	Half	Special (see *Spycraft Espionage Handbook*, page 168).
Suppressive fire	Full	One target within your line of sight suffers a −4 penalty to attack and skill rolls for 1 round; uses 5 shots.
Taunt	Half	Make a Bluff check opposed by your target's Sense Motive; if you succeed, your target must attack you with his next action.
Trip	Half	Make a melee touch attack; if you hit, make a Strength check opposed by Strength or Dexterity; if you succeed, your target is prone.

MOVEMENT ACTIONS	TYPE	EFFECT
Standard move	Half	Move your Speed in feet.
Charge	Full	+2 attack, −2 Defense for 1 round.
Run	Full	Move 4x your Speed in feet.
Total defense	Full	+4 dodge bonus to Defense for 1 round.
Withdraw	Full	Move 2x your Speed in feet away from combat.

OTHER ACTIONS	TYPE	EFFECT
Aim ranged weapon	Half	+1 bonus to next attack.
Brace firearm	Half	+2 bonus to next attack.

FEATS & SPECIAL ABILITIES

FEAT	EFFECT

LANGUAGES

LANGUAGE	NATIVE	LANGUAGE	NATIVE
	☐		☐
	☐		☐
	☐		☐
	☐		☐
	☐		☐